CW00401285

Critical Theorists and Inte Relations

A wide range of critical theorists is used in the study of international politics, and until now there has been no text that gives concise and accessible introductions to these figures. *Critical Theorists and International Relations* provides a wide-ranging introduction to thirty-two important theorists whose work has been influential in thinking about global politics.

Each chapter is written by an expert with a detailed knowledge of the theorist concerned, representing a range of approaches under the rubric 'critical', including Marxism and post-Marxism, the Frankfurt School, hermeneutics, phenomenology, postcolonialism, feminism, queer theory, poststructuralism, pragmatism, scientific realism, deconstruction and psychoanalysis.

Key features of each chapter include:

- a clear and concise biography of the relevant thinker
- an introduction to their key writings and ideas
- a summary of the ways in which these ideas have influenced and are being used in international relations scholarship
- a list of suggestions for further reading.

Written in engaging and accessible prose, *Critical Theorists and International Relations* is a unique and invaluable resource for undergraduates, postgraduates and scholars of international relations.

Jenny Edkins is Professor of International Politics at Aberystwyth University. Her books include *Global Politics: A New Introduction*, with Maja Zehfuss (Routledge, 2008).

Nick Vaughan-Williams is Lecturer in International Relations at the University of Exeter. He is co-editor of *Terrorism and the Politics of Response* (Routledge 2008).

Contributors: Claudia Aradau; James Brassett; Angharad Closs Stephens; Martin Coward; Neta Crawford; Elizabeth Dauphinee; François Debrix; James Der Derian; Robin Durie; Kimberly Hutchings; Vivienne Jabri; Peter Jackson; Catarina Kinnvall; Milja Kurki; Cristina Masters; Rens van Munster; Himadeep Muppidi; Andrew Neal; Louiza Odysseos; Patricia Owens; Columba Peoples; Fabio Petito; Vanessa Pupavac; Diane Rubenstein; Mark Rupert; Latha Varadarajan; Nick Vaughan-Williams; Ritu Vij; Maja Zehfuss

Interventions

Edited by:
Jenny Edkins, Aberystwyth University and Nick Vaughan-Williams, University of Exeter

'*As Michel Foucault has famously stated, "knowledge is not made for understanding; it is made for cutting." In this spirit the Edkins – Vaughan-Williams Interventions series solicits cutting edge, critical works that challenge mainstream understandings in international relations. It is the best place to contribute post disciplinary works that think rather than merely recognize and affirm the world recycled in IR's traditional geopolitical imaginary.*'

Michael J. Shapiro, University of Hawai'i at Mānoa, USA

The series aims to advance understanding of the key areas in which scholars working within broad critical post-structural and post-colonial traditions have chosen to make their interventions, and to present innovative analyses of important topics.

Titles in the series engage with critical thinkers in philosophy, sociology, politics and other disciplines and provide situated historical, empirical and textual studies in international politics.

1. Critical Theorists and International Relations
Edited by Jenny Edkins and Nick Vaughan-Williams

Critical Theorists and International Relations

Edited by
Jenny Edkins and Nick Vaughan-Williams

Routledge
Taylor & Francis Group

LONDON AND NEW YORK

First published 2009
by Routledge
2 Park Square, Milton Park, Abingdon, Oxon, OX14 4RN

Simultaneously published in the USA and Canada
by Routledge
711 Third Avenue, New York, NY 10017

Routledge is an imprint of the Taylor & Francis Group, an informa business

Typeset in Times New Roman by
Taylor & Francis Books

British Library Cataloguing in Publication Data
A catalogue record for this book is available from the British Library

Library of Congress Cataloging in Publication Data
Critical theorists and international relations / edited by Jenny Edkins and Nick Vaughan-Williams.
   p. cm. – (Interventions ; 1)
Includes bibliographical references and index.
   1. International relations. 2. Critical theory. 3. International relations–Philosophy. I. Edkins, Jenny. II. Vaughan-Williams, Nick.
   JZ1242.C76 2009
   327.101–dc22
                    2008036410

ISBN 10: 0-415-47465-5 (hbk)
ISBN 10: 0-415-47466-3 (pbk)
ISBN 10: 0-203-88184-2 (ebk)

ISBN 13: 978-0-415-47465-8 (hbk)
ISBN 13: 978-0-415-47466-5 (pbk)
ISBN 13: 978-0-203-88184-2 (ebk)

Contents

Notes on contributors   viii

Introduction   *1*
JENNY EDKINS AND NICK VAUGHAN-WILLIAMS

1   Theodor Adorno   7
COLUMBA PEOPLES

2   Giorgio Agamben   19
NICK VAUGHAN-WILLIAMS

3   Hannah Arendt   31
PATRICIA OWENS

4   Alain Badiou   42
CLAUDIA ARADAU

5   Jean Baudrillard   54
FRANÇOIS DEBRIX

6   Simone de Beauvoir   66
KIMBERLY HUTCHINGS

7   Walter Benjamin   77
ANGHARAD CLOSS STEPHENS

8   Roy Bhaskar   89
MILJA KURKI

9   Pierre Bourdieu   102
PETER JACKSON

10   Judith Butler   114
CRISTINA MASTERS

11 Gilles Deleuze   125
ROBIN DURIE

12 Jacques Derrida   137
MAJA ZEHFUSS

13 Frantz Fanon   150
HIMADEEP MUPPIDI

14 Michel Foucault   161
ANDREW NEAL

15 Sigmund Freud   171
VANESSA PUPAVAC

16 Antonio Gramsci   176
MARK RUPERT

17 Jürgen Habermas   187
NETA C. CRAWFORD

18 G.W.F. Hegel   199
RITU VIJ

19 Martin Heidegger   205
LOUIZA ODYSSEOS

20 Immanuel Kant   217
KIMBERLY HUTCHINGS

21 Julia Kristeva   221
VIVIENNE JABRI

22 Emmanuel Levinas   235
ELIZABETH DAUPHINEE

23 Karl Marx   246
MILJA KURKI

24 Jean-Luc Nancy   251
MARTIN COWARD

25 Friedrich Nietzsche   263
ROBIN DURIE

26 Jacques Rancière 266
RENS VAN MUNSTER

27 Richard Rorty 278
JAMES BRASSETT

28 Edward Said 292
LATHA VARADARAJAN

29 Carl Schmitt 305
LOUIZA ODYSSEOS AND FABIO PETITO

30 Gayatri Chakravorty Spivak 317
CATARINA KINNVALL

31 Paul Virilo 330
JAMES DER DERIAN

32 Slavoj Žižek 341
DIANE RUBENSTEIN

Bibliography   354
Index   389

Notes on Contributors

Claudia Aradau is Lecturer in International Studies in the Department of Politics and International Studies, The Open University (UK). Her research interrogates the effects of politics deployed at the horizon of security and of catastrophe. She has worked on the securitisation of human trafficking and migration, governing terrorism and exceptionalism. Her current research focus lies in the exploration of the political and historical relations between security, freedom and equality. She is the author of *Rethinking Trafficking in Women: Politics out of Security* (Palgrave, 2008). She is currently co-writing a book on the politics of catastrophe together with Rens van Munster.

James Brassett is RCUK Fellow and Assistant Professor, Department of Politics and International Studies, University of Warwick. His work on the politics of global ethics has been published in journals such as *Ethics and International Affairs* and *Millennium*.

Angharad Closs Stephens is Lecturer in Human Geography at the University of Durham and studied for her PhD in International Relations at Keele University. Her research work focuses on contemporary attempts to imagine political community without unity, drawing on ideas of time, and inspired by postcolonial and feminist theories in particular. She has recently published in *Alternatives: Global, Local, Political* and with Nick Vaughan-Williams, is co-editor of *Terrorism and the Politics of Response* (Routledge). She is co-convenor of the BISA Poststructural Politics Working Group.

Martin Coward is Lecturer in International Relations at the University of Sussex, UK. His research focuses on post-structuralist theory and political violence. He is author of *Urbicide: The Politics of Urban Destruction* (Routledge, 2008). He edited a Special Issue of the *Journal for Cultural Research* on Jean-Luc Nancy (Volume 9, Number 4, 2005).

Neta C. Crawford is Professor of Political Science and African American Studies at Boston University. She is the author of *Argument and Change in World Politics: Ethics, Decolonization and Humanitarian Intervention* (Cambridge

University Press, 2002) and the co-editor with Audie Klotz of *How Sanctions Work: Lessons From South Africa* (Macmillan, 1999). She has written about argument, ethics, war, and peace in *Ethics & International Affairs; International Organization; International Security; Perspectives on Politics; Naval War College Review; Orbis*; and the *Journal of Political Philosophy*.

James Der Derian is Watson Institute Research Professor of International Studies and Director of the Institute's Global Security Program at Brown University. Der Derian also founded and directs the Global Media Project <http://www.watsoninstitute.org/globalmedia> and the Information Technology, War, and Peace Project <http://www.infopeace.org> at the Watson Institute. He has also made three documentaries with Amedia Productions, *VY2K, After 911*, and *Culture War*. His most recent book is *Virtuous War: Mapping the Military-Industrial-Media-Entertainment Network*.

Elizabeth Dauphinee is Assistant Professor in the Department of Political Science at York University. She is the author of *The Ethics of Researching War: Looking for Bosnia* (Manchester University Press, 2007) and has published articles in *Millennium: Journal of International Studies, Security Dialogue*, and *Dialectical Anthropology*.

François Debrix is Associate Professor of International Relations at Florida International University in Miami. He is the author of *Re-Envisioning Peacekeeping* (1999) and *Tabloid Terror: War, Culture, and Geopolitics* (2007). He is currently editing a book (with Mark Lacy) titled *The Geopolitics of American Insecurity*. His work has appeared in journals such as *Millennium, Alternatives, Philosophy and Social Criticism*, and *Geopolitics*. Over the years, he has translated several of Jean Baudrillard's texts for the journal *C-Theory*.

Robin Durie is Senior Lecturer in Politics at the University of Exeter. He has published on the philosophy of time, and on theories of difference and immanence, as well as on complexity theory. Committed to trans-disciplinary practice, he has collaborated with artists, architects, physicists and biologists in the past, and is currently working on two major transdisciplinary projects studying the evolution of culture in human and non-human societies, and sustainability. He has also collaborated widely with non-academic partners in health-care and community regeneration work.

Jenny Edkins is Professor of International Politics at Aberystwyth University. She has published widely, including most recently, *Sovereign Lives: Power in Global Politics* (edited with Véronique Pin-Fat and Michael J. Shapiro. Routledge 2004), *Trauma and the Memory of Politics* (Cambridge University Press 2003) and *Whose Hunger? Concepts of Famine, Practices of Aid* (University of Minnesota Press 2000, 2008) and *Poststructuralism and International Politics: Bringing the Political Back In* (Lynne Reinner, 1999). She is co-editor with Maja Zehfuss of a major new Routledge textbook *Global Politics: A New Introduction* (2008) and with Nick Vaughan-Williams of a book series with Routledge called 'Interventions'.

Kimberly Hutchings is Professor of International Relations at the LSE. She is the author of *Kant, Critique and Politics* (Routledge, 1996); *International Political Theory: re-thinking ethics in a global era* (Sage, 1999); *Hegel and Feminist Philosophy* (Polity, 2003) and *Time and World Politics: thinking the present* (Manchester University Press, 2008). Her research interests include the philosophies of Kant and Hegel, feminist thought, international political theory and ethics. She is currently working on an introductory book on global ethics and (with Elizabeth Frazer) on the relation between politics and violence in canonic western political thought.

Vivienne Jabri is Professor of International Politics in the Department of War Studies, King's College London. Her research and writing focus on critical and poststructural thought, with a particular interest in the implications for politics and political subjectivity of war, conflict and practices of security. Her most recent book is *War and the Transformation of Global Politics* (Palgrave, 2007).

Peter Jackson is Reader in International Politics in the Department of International Politics, Aberystwyth University and Editor of *Intelligence and National Security*. His books include *France and the Nazi Menace: Intelligence and Policy-Making* (Oxford, 2000) and (with Jennifer Siegel) *Intelligence and Statecraft: The Uses and Limits of Intelligence in International Society* (Praeger, 2005). He is now finishing a book entitled *Political Cultures of National Security in France, 1914–1932*.

Catarina Kinnvall is Associate Professor at the Department of Political Science, Lund University, Sweden. She is the author of a number of books and articles. Her most recent publications include: *On Behalf of Others: The Ethics of Care in a Global World* (ed. with S. Scuzzarello and K. Monroe, Oxford University Press, 2008); *Globalization and Religious Nationalism in India: The Search for Ontological Security* (Routledge 2006); *Globalization and Democratization in Asia: The Construction of Identity* (ed. with K. Jönsson, Routledge 2002). She is currently finalizing a book entitled: *The Political Psychology of Globalization: Muslims in the West*, together with Paul Nesbitt-Larking. She is also former Vice-President of the International Society of Political Psychology (ISPP).

Milja Kurki is Lecturer in International Relations Theory at Aberystwyth University. Her research investigates matters at the intersection of international relations theory and philosophy of social science, especially the issue of causation. She is the author *of Causation in International Relations: Reclaiming Causal Analysis* (Cambridge University Press, 2008) and co-editor (with Tim Dunne and Steve Smith) of *International Relations Theories: Discipline and Diversity* (Oxford University Press, 2007).

She has published articles in the *Review of International Studies* and the *Millennium.*

Cristina Masters is Lecturer at the University of Manchester and the co-editor of *The Logics of Biopower and the War on Terror: Living, Dying, Surviving (Palgrave 2007).* She is the author of a chapter, 'Bodies of Technology and the Politics of the Flesh', in *Rethinking the Man Question: Sex, Gender and Violence in International Relations* (Zed Books. 2008), edited by Jane L. Parpart and Marysia Zalewski, and a founding member of the Research Network on Love at the University of Manchester.

Himadeep Muppidi is Associate Professor, Department of Political Science, Vassar College. He is the author of *The Politics of the Global* (University of Minnesota Press, 2004) and is currently completing his second book titled *The Colonial Signs of International Relations.*

Andrew W. Neal is Lecturer in International Relations at the University of Edinburgh. He is the author of *Exceptionalism and the Politics of Counter-Terrorism: Liberty, Security and the War on Terror* (Routledge, 2009), co-editor (with Michael Dillon) of *Foucault on Politics, Security and War* (Palgrave, 2008), and he has published journals articles as sole and joint author on Foucault, exceptionalism and critical approches to security.

Louiza Odysseos is Senior Lecturer in International Relations at the University of Sussex. Her research interests are in international theory, ethics, and post-structuralist philosophy. She is the author of *The Subject of Coexistence: Otherness in International Relations* (University of Minnesota Press, 2007), a critical book-length treatment of the work of Martin Heidegger in IR, as well as coeditor, with Fabio Petito, of *The International Political Thought of Carl Schmitt: Terror, Liberal War and the Crisis of Global Order* (Routledge, 2007) and, with Hakan Seckinelgin, of *Gendering the International* (Palgrave Macmillan, 2002). She has also guest-edited special issues on the themes of gender and international relations in *Millennium: Journal of International Studies* (27 (4), 1998) and on the international theory of Carl Schmitt for *Leiden Journal of International Law* (19 (1), 2006).

Patricia Owens is Senior Lecturer in Politics at Queen Mary University of London. She is the author of *Between War and Politics: International Relations and the Thought of Hannah Arendt* (Oxford, 2007), *War and Security: an Introduction* (Polity, forthcoming) and co-editor of *The Globalization of World Politics* (4th edition) (Oxford, 2008). Articles have been published in *Review of International Studies, International Affairs, Millennium, International Politics,* and *Alternatives.* She has held research positions at Princeton, Berkeley, University of Southern California and Oxford.

Columba Peoples is Lecturer in Politics and International Relations at the Department of Politics, University of Bristol. He has primary research interests in Critical Security Studies, Critical Theory, and critical approaches to technology within the study of International Relations with a particular focus on the issues of nuclear security, ballistic missile defence and space security. He has published articles on these and other related topics in *Cambridge Review of International Affairs, Global Change, Peace and Security, Cold War History* and *Social Semiotics*.

Fabio Petito is Lecturer in International Relations at the University of Sussex. His research interests lie in International Political Theory and the International Politics of the Mediterranean. He is co-editor (with Louiza Odysseos) of *The International Political Thought of Carl Schmitt: Terror, Liberal War, and the Crisis of Global Order* (Routledge, 2007) and (with Pavlos Hatzopoulos) *Religion in International Relations: The Return From Exile* (Palgrave, 2003).

Vanessa Pupavac is Lecturer in International Relations at the University of Nottingham. Her research encompasses international human rights, children's rights, linguistic rights, humanitarian and development politics. She has published in journals such as *Development in Practice, International Journal of Human Rights, Third World Quarterly,* and *International Peacekeeping*.

Diane S. Rubenstein is Professor of Government and American Studies at Cornell University. Her research and teaching addresses the critical interaction between continental theory (primarily French, German, and Italian) and contemporary manifestations of ideology in Franco-American political culture. She is author of *What's Left? The Ecole Normale Supérieure and the Right* (Wisconsin, 1990) and *This is not a President: Sense, Nonsense, and the American Political Imaginary* (New York, 2008). Her essays on Lacan, Baudrillard, and Foucault have appeared in *Political Theory, Theory and Event, Philosophy and Social Criticism, Modern Fiction Studies, UMBR(a), Journal of Politics, Journal of European Studies, New Centennial Review*.

Mark Rupert is Professor of Political Science at Syracuse University's Maxwell School of Citizenship and Public Affairs, and teaches in the areas of international relations, political economy, and the political theories of Karl Marx and Antonio Gramsci. His research focuses on the intersection of the US political economy with global structures and processes. He is the author of *Producing Hegemony: the politics of mass production and American global power* (Cambridge, 1995); and *Ideologies of Globalization: Contending Visions of a New World Order* (Routledge, 2000); and co-author (with Scott Solomon) of *Globalization and International Political Economy* (Rowman and Littlefield, 2006). His home page can be found at: http://faculty.maxwell.syr.edu/merupert/merindex.htm.

Rens van Munster is Lecturer in International Politics at the Department of Political Science, University of Southern Denmark. His main research interests concern the political consequences of security politics within the contexts of immigration and terrorism. He is the co-editor of a special volume of *Security Dialogue* on 'Security, Technologies of Risk and the Political'. His work has been published in edited volumes and international journals, including *Alternatives, European Journal of International Relations, International Journal for the Semiotics of Law* and *International Relations*.

Latha Varadarajan is Assistant Professor of Political Science at San Diego State University. Her research interests include the issues surrounding the contemporary manifestations of imperialism, globalization, transnationalism, and diasporas politics. Her articles on these themes have been published in journals like *Review of International Studies; Millennium: Journal of International Studies; Diaspora: A journal of transnational studies*; and *New Political Science.*

Nick Vaughan-Williams is Lecturer in International Relations at the University of Exeter. His research analyses borders and bordering practices and their implications for International Theory and Security and he has recently received funding from The British Academy on this theme. He is author of *Border Politics: The Limits of Sovereign Power* (Edinburgh University Press, 2009) and co-editor, with Angharad Closs Stephens, of *Terrorism and the Politics of Response* (Routledge, 2008). Recent articles have been published or accepted for publication in *Alternatives, International Political Sociology, Millennium*, and the *Review of International Studies*. He is co-convenor of the BISA Poststructural Politics Working Group and co-editor of the Routledge book series 'Interventions'.

Ritu Vij joined the Department of Politics and International Relations, University of Aberdeen, in 2006, after completing a two-year fellowship at Keio Univerity (Tokyo) as the recipient of a Fellowship awarded jointly by the Social Science Research Council (USA) and the Japan Society for the Promotion of Science (JSPS). Her research interests include social theory and comparative political economy, globalization and social policy, civil society and subjectivity. She is author of *Japanese Modernity and Welfare: Self, State and Civil Society in Contemporary Japan* (Palgrave, 2007) and editor of *Globalization and Welfare: A Critical Reader* (Palgrave, 2006).

Maja Zehfuss is Professor of International Politics at The University of Manchester. She is the author of *Constructivism and International Relations: The Politics of Reality* (Cambridge University Press, 2002) and *Wounds of Memory: The Politics of War in Germany* (Cambridge University Press, 2007) and the co-editor, with Jenny Edkins, of *Global Politics: A New Introduction* (Routledge, 2008). She is currently writing a book on war and the politics of ethics, in which she examines how the problematic of ethics is produced, enacted and negotiated in war.

Introduction

Jenny Edkins and Nick Vaughan-Williams

A number of things have proved striking as we have edited this book. First, we have very much enjoyed reading these introductions to a range of thinkers, some of whom we were totally unfamiliar with before, others with whom we had a passing acquaintance, and yet others who have inspired our own work directly. In each case the chapters provide captivating insights into the thinkers discussed, throwing light on their background, their key contributions and intellectual trajectories, and their relation to the field of study and scholarship we call international relations. And all of the chapters lead enticingly on to further reading and engagement. In addition, the chapters illuminate the thinking and research—and, in some instances, the personal location—of the chapter contributors themselves. Each of the authors has a close relationship with the thinker they elucidate and writes from an enviable grasp of, and a deep involvement with, the thought concerned.

One of the most striking things about the process of reading through the chapters, and one which we think readers of the book will find as captivating as we have, is the way in which this compilation of chapters provokes unexpected— and unscripted—interconnections. When we set out on this project, we imagined that we were putting together a collection of rather disparate thinkers, from a series of distinct traditions and sub-traditions, who might sit rather uncomfortably together. What we have found, by contrast, is a web of common concerns and an interweaving of approaches to tackling them. This explodes the caricatures of distinct and irreconcilable strains of thought— and hence painful choices—that scholars in politics and international politics sometimes feel they are faced with. Instead, we find in the critical theorists we cover a rich tapestry—or palimpsest—of thought and struggle, both conceptual and political, where the close connections between intellectual life and the life of the world become apparent.

A struggle each of our authors has faced has been that prompted by the title of the book: *Critical Theorists and International Relations*. Surprisingly for us, some chapter authors have taken the field of international relations to comprise, in a very traditional, not to say 'mainstream', sense, questions to do with relations between states. This had led them to focus, in discussions of identity or subjectivity for example, on the state as subject or actor—or on other 'collective actors'. It has led to a concern with topics that slot neatly into ideas of the international arena: wars and conflicts, refugees and asylum seekers, terrorism and the like. In introducing the work of critical thinkers whose work spans a wide range of topics it is necessary to be selective, and as editors we encouraged detailed engagement with particular texts rather than broad-brush overviews. However, we did not predict that a number of people would make their choices based on some fairly standard ideas of what the field in which the book was to be situated was, essentially. It is interesting to reflect on how these constructions of 'the discipline of international relations' survive and reproduce themselves, even in critical theorising. Now clearly the editors and publishers are in a large extent responsible for this: publishing and marketing still takes place within defined disciplinary fields and, quite understandably, this text is specifically designed for scholars and students who see themselves as having an interest in international politics. However, an engagement with theorists such as those included in this book seems to demand, prompt, and follow from, a re-examination of some of the assumptions upon which the traditional constitution of the field is based.

A fundamental way in which current critical theory re-opens assumptions that have grounded our political thought has been by questioning the starting point of thinking politically. One of the traditional questions of politics has been how we can live together, or in other words, how individuals with a range of backgrounds, beliefs and interests can or do co-exist, peacefully or otherwise. What forms of organisation, institutional or social, promote what forms of co-existence? How do we think through the possibilities of political organisation? What constraints are imposed on these possibilities, for example, by our nature as human beings or by our rights as individuals? When translated to the international sphere – traditionally regarded as distinct from the domestic, and hence the rationale for a distinct field of study – these become the familiar issues of inter-state relations, configured as relations between distinct, bounded and sovereign domestic spheres. How can sovereign states co-exist in an international society or anarchic system?

A variety of critical theorists have challenged this starting point. Rather than thinking about how discrete entities, whether individuals or states, can live together, the question they want to pose is a different one. The challenge is one that is posed at the level of ontology. Instead of thinking of the world as made up of objects or entities that relate to each other in various ways, a number of thinkers want to attempt to put forward an ontology based on a world of interconnectedness or being-with, a world in which there are no distinct objects—whether states, individuals or anything else. To think in this way is taxing, and has led several of those examined in the book to work with mathematical approaches, sometimes based on set theory, which enable the thinking of relationality and being in a way not permitted by language – a way that does not start with the 'one'. This clearly leads to a very different figuration of the international, and to adopt this approach demands broadening the scope of concern, away from states and relationships between states to an interest in what might be meant by inter-relations in the first place, at whatever 'level' of social organisation.

The book can be approached from different angles according to the purpose the reader has in mind. It is essentially a collection of thinkers who have impacted upon analyses of contemporary political life in a global context. This could be thought of as a playlist. Tracks are often put together on playlists for a particular purpose or occasion: for someone's birthday; to make an apology; or perhaps to ease a long-distance journey. In the same way, our purpose is to bring together different social and political theorists so that scholars and students of international politics can better appreciate the inspiration behind recent work in the discipline. On the one hand, like any playlist, our compilation of writers is necessarily selective: it is not comprehensive and could include many other thinkers. On the other hand, thinking of the book in terms of a playlist allows for a different way of reading than that textbooks usually encourage. Rather than working through each chapter in turn the idea of a 'shuffle' is instructive here: readers might want to dip in randomly to allow for chance encounters with the thinkers we have chosen to include. And indeed one of the aims of the book is to encourage such chance encounters.

In 1969 Edward Packard wrote *Sugarcane Island*, which came to inspire a generation of children's books published in the 'Choose Your Own Adventure' series. Readers determine what course of action each character takes along the way thus allowing for the possibility of a multiplicity of plots and endings. In one adventure book, *UFO 54–40*, the reader is offered the promise of reaching paradise, but none of the formal choices actually lead there. Only by abandoning the set structure and going through the text at random can paradise be found. Whilst this book is unlikely to lead to paradise, it does offer an opportunity for readers to determine for themselves where to start and where to end up.

What happens if there is no pre-set structure? Perhaps the most interesting way to approach this book would be to take the idea of *UFO 54–40* seriously. This can be associated with the notion of a rhizomatic reading. In *A Thousand Plateaus: Capitalism and Schizophrenia* (1980) Gilles Deleuze and Félix Guattari discuss the figure of the rhizome. A rhizome has no beginning or end. Rather, it is always in the middle of things and establishes connections. Rhizomes do not involve points or positions: a rhizome is distinct from an arborescent structure like a tree, which has roots, fixed foundations and a set order. As such, a rhizomatic reading involves the invention of different connections, and these spread beyond the 'covers' of a text. In this way, those reading the book might not only seek links within and between different chapters but with other thinkers, or even with novels, films and everyday experiences.

Although each of the chapters is devoted to a particular theorist, the focus running throughout is on specific texts. We are not concerned to give a comprehensive overview of *all* of a person's work or writings. This would be an impossible enterprise in any case within the limits we have here. Rather, the aim is to bring out ways in which a theorist's thought might be – or indeed has been—useful in the context of global politics through a focus on *selected* texts or writings. This approach serves three functions.

First, it guards against the urge to make generalised claims about an individual thinker. Often, for example, people refer to 'the early Foucault' or 'the later Derrida'. Distinctions are drawn between a writer's work at different 'stages' of what is seen as their intellectual development. However, these categorisations can be misleading and distract attention from detailed engagement with particular writings. Moreover, merely pointing out contradictions or incoherence within the work of a theorist can be equally distracting. To some extent we are all incoherent: there are always polyphonic voices as meaning is less stable than is sometimes assumed. What matters is a willingness for close engagement with the text in order to appreciate its complexity and subtlety.

Second, a focus on specific texts will hopefully encourage readers to follow up by looking at original works for themselves. In this way our hope is that the book will not be treated as a substitute for actually reading the thinkers it attempts to cover. Rather, it is designed to provide a way in to a direct reading of the texts discussed, and others. For this reason, as well as offering detailed readings of selected texts, each chapter provides a further reading list in order to steer you in the right direction. In particular, we suggest good places to start reading particular thinkers. Other commentaries and examples of uses of a particular author to think through questions of international politics will also be suggested.

Third, by examining texts rather than authors of texts per se it is possible to move away from the tendency to group or box people into specific 'schools of thought'. Such a tendency involves a divisive way of reading that is at best problematic given the overlapping nature of the questions or issues that many of the authors seek to address. At worst, it can lead to a focus on critique – and even dismissal or caricature – at the expense of the attempt at understanding and engagement. Rather, to reiterate, a rhizomatic approach privileges the invention of different connections between diverse writers. Moreover, such an approach reflects a certain hospitality and openness to texts, which we believe is potentially more productive than adopting a fixed and/or dogmatic position.

Each chapter of the book is written by someone whose own research draws upon the respective theorist and contemporary illustrations are given in this context. Chapter contributors have been encouraged to think in terms of four elements:

- A short intellectual biography of the theorist setting their work in context.
- A summary of some key aspects of their ideas and writings.
- An overview of some of the ways in which these ideas and writings have influenced or might be useful for thinking about international politics.
- A list of suggestions for further reading, briefly annotated.

Contributors interpret and combine the various elements in different ways, so there is no uniform structure to the chapters as such.

In our selection of writers for the playlist, we have first and foremost chosen theorists who have been influential in the field of international politics. There are other books that deal with thinkers who have influenced developments in politics or political science; in this book we have focused explicitly on those we consider most important in contemporary thinking about *international* politics. So, the selection reflects both our idea of what constitutes international politics, and our assessment of the most influential theorists in that field. Others would think differently, and make different judgements of importance. Our idea of 'international politics' is very broad and expansive, and it is not one that relies upon an easy distinction between 'domestic' politics and 'international' politics. Our selection has also been governed by the recognition that scholarship in international relations is not as narrow as it once used to be. We regard this as a crucially important development. Most noticeably, there is a growing body of scholarship in two areas: feminist work, and work that could broadly be labelled as post-colonial. In both these areas, exciting and ground-breaking work is being produced. This work draws on critical theorists often otherwise invisible; we have included a number of these thinkers in this book.

Finally, although it is necessary to stop somewhere, we did not feel that a book on critical theorists and international relations would be complete without some introduction to earlier thinkers on whom the theorists we include draw. Of course it has not been possible to be comprehensive here, or to include as substantial an introduction to each of the people we include as they undoubtedly warrant. Nevertheless, the reader will find brief chapters on Freud, Hegel, Kant, Marx and Nietzsche, which are intended to inform and complement readings of other writers. These thinkers were selected because of the way in which their work in particular has impacted upon critical thinking in the twentieth century. This impact, and the interrelations between other writers we discuss, can be traced throughout the book and readers are encouraged to follow connections between different chapters.

As well as selecting writers for the playlist, we have also made some decisions about the order in which we present them. The chapters are arranged alphabetically by the name of the writer concerned. Other ways of organising the book, such as a historical periodisation of different eras of thought, or a 'schools of thought' approach are highly problematic. There is a sense in which *any* attempt to categorise such a diverse range of thinkers on whatever basis is always going to be unsatisfactory. Indeed, many of the thinkers in this volume are sceptical of notions of categorisation or even reject them completely. In a general sense, the act of categorisation tries to foist a shapeliness or coherence where matters are often far messier. It is for this reason that many categorisations will often be seen to break down. In this way, the act of categorising reveals more about the priorities and assumptions of those in a position to categorise than anything else. Thinking in terms of a playlist makes the initial ordering less important, of course, and we expect readers to trace their own paths through the book.

Indeed, we hope that you will enjoy reading and exploring this book as much as we have enjoyed putting it together. In the process we have learned a great deal about the range and scope of critical thinking that is currently informing research in international relations and global politics. This area of scholarship has undoubtedly been rejuvenated through such engagements, and the range of questions and problems now being explored is exciting and impressive. We very much look forward to further critical thinking informed by the theorists covered in this book, and others as yet uncharted, whose work will no doubt continue to challenge and inspire future generations of scholars working on international politics.

1   Theodor Adorno

Columba Peoples

Theodor Wiesengrund Adorno's work leaves a legacy of wide ranging analysis (on topics as diverse as anti-Semitism, psychoanalysis and jazz), an equally broad and sophisticated conceptual vocabulary (instrumental reason; negative dialectic; damaged life) and a range of reflections at once poignant and provocative: 'Life has become the ideology of its own absence' (Adorno 2005a: 190); 'Enlightenment is totalitarian' (Adorno and Horkheimer 1997: 6).

This chapter briefly illustrates the key themes of Adorno's thinking and its potential relation to international relations. To do so it outlines how Adorno's key ideas evolved and their relation to critical theory, the extent to which international relations figures in the writings of Adorno and, conversely, the extent to which Adorno has informed and might still inform the study of international relations.

Adorno and Critical Theory

In many ways it could be argued that Adorno's intellectual development and his life story are inseparable. Adorno's 'damaged life' (to paraphrase the subtitle of his 1951 work *Minima Moralia*) was marked by the events of war, catastrophic social change and exile, the effects of which can be traced even in some of his most abstract philosophical work. But it is also marked by rigorous intellectual engagement and debate with a variety of other key thinkers now conventionally associated with the Critical Theory tradition (see Jay 1996a).

Born Theodor Wiesengrund in Frankfurt am Main in 1903 (Adorno was his wife's maiden name, adopted in the 1930s due to the Jewish origins of Wiesengrund (Jarvis 1998: 3)), Adorno had by the 1920s already established himself as a precociously gifted thinker. Under the influence of his mentor Siegfried Kracauer, the German sociologist and cultural critic, the young Adorno was already well versed in both Western philosophy – Hegel, Marx and, in particular, Kant – and in the work of contemporary theorists such as Georg Lukács, Ernst Bloch and Max Weber (Wiggershaus 1986: 66–69). Adorno was thus immersed both in the tradition of German idealist thinking and contemporaneous debates in Marxist theory, exemplified at the time in the work of thinkers like Lukács and Bloch. This intellectual depth pervades all of Adorno's work, which is rich in its allusions to both classical and modern philosophy, and his writings frequently presume a knowledge of both.

Adorno was not, however, directly concerned with philosophy during the 1920s, instead pouring himself into his first (and lasting) concern, music criticism and musicology (Wiggershaus 1986: 70; Adorno 2007). It was not until the 1930s, during the period that he came into contact with the group of thinkers that has since come to be known collectively as the Frankfurt School, that Adorno became known more for his engagement with philosophy and debates in social theory.

The term Frankfurt School, along with its defining characteristics and membership, is itself a source of much contention (Jay 1996b: 39). Often used interchangeably with the term Critical Theory (in the upper case), it is usually taken to refer to a brand of Western Marxist or Late Marxist thinking emanating from the Institut für Sozialforschung (Institute of Social Research, or IfS) first established in Frankfurt in 1923. Key thinkers usually listed under the Frankfurt School rubric include Adorno and his frequent intellectual collaborator Max Horkheimer as well as Herbert Marcuse, Leo Lowenthal and Freidrich Pollock. Other more loosely affiliated thinkers include Walter Benjamin, Franz Neumann, Otto Kircheimer and Eric Fromm (Held 2004: 14–15).

Although debates persist about the unity or otherwise of the Frankfurt School (Held 2004: 14; Jay 1996b: 39), broadly speaking this early or first generation Frankfurt School thinking, of which Adorno was an important part, is marked by a number of recurring concerns and features. These are worth sketching briefly in order to get a better sense of the evolution of Adorno's own thinking. One is its self-consciously inter-disciplinary nature, as is illustrated by the fact that Adorno and his colleagues were in turn embedded within different intellectual backgrounds (Adorno in musicology, Horkheimer in sociology, Marcuse in philosophy, Benjamin in literary criticism, Fromm in psychoanalysis, and so on). Another is the shared grounding of its different constituent thinkers (albeit to varying extents) in a tradition of German idealist, and specifically, Marxist thought. The different intellectual and philosophical concerns of these thinkers, however, took them into terrain – art, mass culture, psychoanalysis, the family – that was generally unfamiliar in the orthodox Marxism of the time (Held 2004: 13–14). Indeed one of the overarching concerns that did bind the early Frankfurt School into a fluid whole was a shared sense of disillusionment not only with capitalist society but also with the Marxist orthodoxy of the time. Initially at least, the group that formed around the Institute for Social Research were concerned with accounting for what they perceived to be the abortive form of socialism manifest in Stalinist Russia and with explaining the conditions (such as the rise of fascism and authoritarianism) that seemed, against the predictions of orthodox Marxists, to have inhibited the onset of socialism in Germany and industrialised Western Europe more broadly.

Since the problematique of radical change was more complex than it was portrayed in orthodox Marxism, the goal of the IfS was to develop a more sophisticated form of analysis that, whilst upholding the Marxist commitment to radical social change and Marx's analytic categories (Antonio 1981: 330–31), was also open to other philosophical strands (including Hegel, Kant, Schopenhauer and Nietzsche) and contemporary theorists (such as Weber, Lukács and Freud). Theorising social change required a deeper understanding of society, and this in turn required a more varied theoretical palette. Hence the deliberately interdisciplinary character of the IfS, and, in part, the intellectual reason for Adorno's association with the institute.

The driving intellectual force behind the institute during Adorno's initial association was not, however, Adorno himself but Max Horkheimer. Horkheimer, who assumed the directorship of the IfS in 1930, established a programme of research that Adorno in part contributed to and which he in turn helped to shape and, arguably, later push in a different direction. In keeping with the themes outlined above, Horkheimer set out a programme for the institute which was aimed at a radical reinterpretation of the relationship between philosophy and practice, the social and natural sciences, and human beings and nature, which he hoped would combine into a programme of social research highlighting the possibilities for a radical transformation of society (Wiggershaus 1994: 36–40).

The task of Critical Theory, in Horkheimer's view, was in large part to uncover and encourage those potentialities latent in society that could further this end (Horkheimer 1972). Horkheimer illustrated this task through a critique of what he termed Traditional Theory, a form of theory which he associated particularly with scientific positivism and those forms of social science that tried to imitate the objectivity of the natural sciences. For Horkheimer, such pretensions to objectivity were always based on an illusory assumption of the theorist's detachment from the social world (or what Horkheimer terms as science's 'imaginary self-sufficiency') (Horkheimer 1972: 242). Yet, Horkheimer argues, scientific activity is itself part of the social fabric and the system of capitalism as is manifest in, in particular, the relationship between science, technology and production.

Critical Theory, by contrast, challenges both the foundations of Traditional Theory and, in doing so, the social fabric with which it is inherently bound up. By challenging 'bourgeois scientific thought', critical thinking is therefore, for Horkheimer, a form of 'transformative activity' (Horkheimer 1972: 232). Initially Horkheimer believed that the work of the Institute in this direction could contribute to developing a degree of critical social consciousness latent in the masses (Held 2004: 38) and, in so doing, help to turn the means of production and technological development towards emancipatory rather than exploitative ends. 'The future of humanity', Horkheimer declared in his 1937 essay on 'Traditional and Critical Theory', 'depends on the existence today of the critical attitude' (Horkheimer 1972: 242).

The entrenchment of Nazism in Germany in the late 1930s not only fractured Horkheimer's optimism regarding the diffusion of the 'critical attitude' among the proletariat irreparably, it also fragmented the Institute. Its members were forced into exile due to their socialist leanings and, in the case of many members, their Jewish background (Adorno included, as his father was an assimilated Jew). Whilst many members of the IfS sought sanctuary in the US, Adorno initially found refuge in Oxford at Merton College in 1933. From there he continued to contribute to the journal of the exiled IfS (by now re-established at Columbia University, New York), primarily in the form of essays on music criticism (Jarvis 1998: 12). In one sense this seems distinctly distanced, not only geographically but also theoretically, from Horkheimer's vision of Critical Theory. Yet Adorno, in his reflections on art and music, was already incorporating and honing a conceptual vocabulary integral both to his own thinking and Critical Theory more generally. Prime among these is the concept of immanent critique. Originally espoused by Horkheimer, who in turn drew on Hegel and Marx in this regard (Antonio 1981), the concept of immanent critique refers to the method of critiquing a concept, theory or situation by critically evaluating it on its own terms, highlighting the contradictions inherent *within* it. Rather than appealing to an external measure or Archimedean point therefore, the method of immanent critique is, by its very definition, immanent rather than transcendent: the critique comes from within, rather than without.

Though essentially faithful to this understanding, Adorno's interpretation and application of immanent critique in his music criticism is less indebted to Hegel than is Horkheimer's interpretation and 'owes as much to Kant's notion of "antinomies"' – the idea that the use of reason can lead ultimately to the uncovering of contradictions, (Brunkhorst 1999: 36). However, Adorno does not simply follow Kant either, and engages in a critique of the Kantian notion of aesthetics (Adorno 1984). In opposition to Kantian idealism, which assumes beauty is experienced subjectively, Adorno maintains a qualified materialist account of aesthetic experience in which works of art hold a 'truth content' (a key term in Adorno's thinking). For Adorno beauty, the experience of the truth content of an object, is neither simply experienced by the individual subject, nor is it simply an 'objective' truth: 'Works of art, for Adorno, are not merely inert objects, valued or known by the subject; rather they have themselves a subjective moment because they are themselves cognitive, attempts to know' (Jarvis 1998: 96). Thus there is a dialectical tension between subject and object that Adorno believes to be inherent to artwork itself (Held 2004: 202), and a degree of truth content that can be adduced via critical reflection. The same could be said, in Adorno's view, of different philosophical perspectives, which would also be characterised by internal antagonisms and should be similarly subject to critical analysis, particularly in terms of the relation between material context and apparently abstract philosophies.

Thus whereas Horkheimer attempted the development of a critical perspective through an examination of the social functions of systems of thought, such as positivism, Adorno concentrated on '*the way philosophy expresses the structure of society*' (Held 2004: 201, emphasis added). Though this led Adorno to concentrate more on detailed and dense technical analyses of particular philosophies, his metacritique of philosophy is broadly in keeping with the wider effort within Critical Theory to develop a 'critical social consciousness' (Adorno 1973: 323) parallel to Horkheimer's efforts (Held 2004: 201).

On enlightenment as totalitarianism: Dialectic of enlightenment

The late 1930s also saw Adorno and Horkheimer moving closer together, both geographically and intellectually, when Adorno was invited to join the IfS in New York in 1937. Horkheimer's earlier optimism regarding the prospects for radical social change had dissipated rapidly with the rise of Hitler and the events of World War II, as was exemplified by the more pessimistic tone of his 1947 work *Eclipse of Reason* (Horkheimer 2004). Adorno, it is fair to say, had never fully shared Horkheimer's belief in the revolutionary potential of the working class. In 1939 he remarked to his close friend Walter Benjamin on Franco's victory in Spain that 'the same masses cheered the fascist conqueror who on the previous day still cheered the opposition' (cited in Brunkhorst 1999: 40). Owing to the coalescence of their disillusionment in this regard, their shared critique of positivism (in which Adorno followed Horkheimer's basic tenets) and their materialistically grounded critiques of philosophical idealism (Brunkhorst 1999: 36) – not to mention their close personal friendship – Adorno and Horkheimer had reached a point conducive to shared intellectual effort during their period in exile in the US. As Horkheimer later recalled of the time: 'It would be difficult to say which of the ideas originated in his [Adorno's] mind and which in my own; our philosophy is one' (Horkheimer 2004: vi).

Their collaboration – which took place initially in New York and later in southern California – ultimately culminated in one of the seminal works in twentieth century philosophy, *Dialectic of Enlightenment* (Adorno and Horkheimer 1997). Though born out of the immediate context of the rise of fascism and a rejection of the revolutionary potential of the proletariat as motor of social change, *Dialectic of Enlightenment* (which first appeared under the title *Philosophical Fragments* in 1944 and under its more commonly known title in 1947) locates these developments in a transhistorical narrative that runs right from the ancient Greeks up to the twentieth century. It is, as its original title suggests, a fragmentary work that eschews a straightforward narrative structure in favour of an essay style (as tends to be typical of much of Adorno's writing in particular (Jarvis 1998: 137)). Running through it, though, is an over-arching argument that recasts the entire history of Western philosophy, inverts the assumption of human progress through the ages and, in the process, radically challenges assumptions of earlier Critical Theory (Wyn Jones 1999: 29).

The key object of Adorno and Horkheimer's analysis is 'enlightenment'. As distinct from the common usage, the concept of 'enlightenment' has, for Adorno and Horkheimer, a very specific meaning that only partially relates to the likes of Descartes and Kant. Conventionally, in the recounting of Western political thought, enlightenment refers both to the historical period of the eighteenth century and to its concomitant advancement in knowledge and rational thought at the expense of old superstitions. Yet Adorno and Horkheimer instead seek to advance 'two theses' that seem entirely out of step with this interpretation: that 'myth is already enlightenment; and enlightenment reverts to mythology' (Adorno and Horkheimer 1997: xvi).

At the heart of Adorno and Horkheimer's account is a conception of human beings' struggle with nature. Human beings have perpetually been involved in an attempt to preserve themselves from elemental forces of nature and have, in the process, based their existence on an attempted domination of nature. The attainment of knowledge has consequently been prioritized as fundamental to self-preservation. Thus the process of 'enlightenment' is traceable even in ancient Greek and Hebrew scripts, where men battle against mythical elemental forces. 'Myth is already enlightenment' in the sense that myths are already attempts to classify and categorize, that is, they already have a 'cognitive content', as Adorno and Horkheimer attempt to illustrate in their analysis of the Odyssey (1997: 43–80).

Similarly, Adorno and Horkheimer engage in an effort of cultural criticism to show that, conversely, 'enlightenment reverts to mythology'. Modernity, which privileges technological advancement and secular rationality (features which Max Weber had identified under the rubric of disenchantment), frequently incorporates appeals to mythical and transcendental ideals. Nazi ideology, for example, combines elements of the modern (an elevation of modern technology and industrialization) with the ancient and mythological (such as appeals to a mythological Aryan past). Adorno and Horkheimer argue more generally that the purportedly value-free instruments of modernity (such as scientific knowledge and modern technology) are routinely bound up with ideological systems, and that this is in the very character of modernity despite its pretensions to the contrary. The move towards sanitized and administered societies on a grand scale simply denies and suppresses the irrational, leading to greater eruptions of violence, as is illustrated ultimately in the death camps of Nazi Germany with their industrialized forms of mass killing (Adorno 2003a). Similarly Hollywood combines modern film technology and techniques with romanticism, simply replacing the irrational with what Adorno and Horkheimer view as infantile escapism, with the effect of creating docile and passive audiences on a mass scale (Adorno and Horkheimer 1997: 120–67; Adorno 2001). Culture, which could once allow an element of individual freedom and creativity, has through the mass diffusion of film and radio become a 'Culture Industry', complete with a 'cult of celebrities (film stars) [that] has a built-in social mechanism to level down everyone who stands out in any way' (Adorno and Horkheimer 1997: 236).

Both phenomena are, for Adorno and Horkheimer, perfectly in keeping with the general trajectory of enlightenment, where reason is ultimately at the service of domination (what Adorno and Horkheimer term 'instrumental reason'). Knowledge of the natural and social worlds, and the technology and techniques developed from this, are used to control and exploit rather than emancipate, as is manifest in the system of capitalist production (Adorno and Horkheimer 1997: xv). Technology in turn encourages the tendency to treat people as means (and thus a commodity) rather than ends. This is the essence of instrumental rationality, which has become rationality's dominant form. Far from simply being a story of human progress, therefore, enlightenment is also a process of domination: an external domination of nature by human beings, an internal domination of human beings' own nature, and domination of some human beings over others. 'The fallen nature of man', Adorno and Horkheimer surmise, 'cannot be separated from social progress ... progress becomes regression' (1997: xiv–xv). This theme – that rationalization, mass production and the other frequently assumed emblems of progress actually lead to barbarism – is one that remains constant in Adorno's work (Adorno 2003a: 19).

In some senses, *Dialectic of Enlightenment* remains faithful to previously espoused elements of Critical Theory. Within this seemingly pessimistic account of human progress there is still an element of immanent critique: reason, which is seen as a tool of enlightenment, is used to critique enlightenment itself and illustrate that 'social freedom is inseparable from enlightened thought' but that enlightenment simultaneously contains the 'seed' of its own reversal (Adorno and Horkheimer: 1997: xiii). The 'critique of enlightenment' which is offered is 'intended to pave the way for a positive notion of enlightenment which will release it from entanglement in blind domination' (Adorno and Horkheimer 1997: xvi).

In other respects, though, the collaboration of Adorno with Horkheimer is in stark contrast with the latter's earlier optimism on the prospects for emancipatory societal change. This turn has been noted as particularly significant within strands of contemporary international relations theory and security studies that seek to revive and incorporate the concepts of emancipation and immanent critique (Wyn Jones 1999: 39–52; Rengger 2001: 95) as envisaged in earlier Critical Theory. This is not simply a product of Adorno's influence on Horkheimer who, as indicated previously, was already moving in a similar direction (Horkheimer 2004). Post-*Dialectic of Enlightenment*, with the memory of mass attraction to fascism in Germany still fresh, both Adorno and Horkheimer generally kept their distance from grand political projects. Adorno, on his return to Germany in the 1950s (where he became director of the re-established IfS in Frankfurt in 1957) is often seen to have been aloof from movements for social and political change of the time, distancing himself from the German student movement in which his follower Jürgen Habermas was closely involved. Adorno defended this in terms of protecting his intellectual autonomy but, as Wiggershaus notes, this stance 'did not exactly correspond to a concept of Critical Theory capable of reflecting on its social function that had been developed by Habermas and, earlier, by Horkheimer' (Wiggershaus 1986: 621).

Adorno and international relations

Adorno's lifetime was perforated by major international upheaval – two world wars, the Russian Revolution, the Wall Street Crash, and the advent of the nuclear age to name but a few – and his writings are peppered by references to such events. Yet Adorno's writings devote little time or space to accounting for these events explicitly, certainly not enough to amount to a theorization of the international that is immediately recognizable to scholars of mainstream international relations. As with his engagement with political issues more generally, Adorno's engagement with international politics is circumscribed by his desire for autonomy. Though Adorno could afford detailed examination of the astrology column of the *Los Angeles Times* (Adorno, 2001), analyses of the headline international issues of his day are comparatively spartan in detail. This is not to say that they are unimportant, or that Adorno regards them as such. On the contrary, they often play a key illustrative function in his writings. But it is precisely because they play this role that when they do occur, they tend to do so in the context of reflections so grand as to render the conventional stuff of international relations a footnote. Speaking of genocide and the use of the atomic bomb, Adorno tells us that ' … the forces against which one must act are those of the course of world history' (Adorno 2003a: 20). 'No universal history', Adorno declares in *Negative Dialectics*, 'leads from savagery to humanitarianism, but there is one leading from the slingshot to the megaton bomb' (Adorno 1973: 320). Here Adorno delivers a stipulation of the inevitability and ever-increasing destructiveness of conflict that any pessimistic realist would be proud of, but seemingly without the need to include a formal theory of state conflict, war and international relations.

A note of caution should be sounded here. The reduction of Adorno's work to the selection of key quotations, although a beast of necessity for introductory chapters of the kind offered here, risks serious damage to Adorno's carefully crafted writings in which style and positioning of text are an integral part of the argument. The previously cited quotation, for example, occurs in within the context of a discussion of Hegelian philosophy and the relationship between continuity and discontinuity (Adorno 1973: 300–358). Moreover Adorno's experience of the events of his lifetime – in particular those of fascism, war, the Holocaust, and his own exile – do play a prominent role in shaping Adorno's reflections. They are all part of what he himself termed as the 'historical dimension' of a 'damaged life' (Adorno 2005: 33).

The classic example here is Adorno's oft-cited (and arguably as often misunderstood) admonition that 'It is impossible to write poetry after Auschwitz', frequently also alternatively rendered as 'To write poetry after Auschwitz is barbaric' (Hofman 2005). Adorno's remarks here need to be situated in the broader context of his reflections on how language can ever represent the extent of human suffering (which fits within his later reflections on language, identity and non-identity). They also relate to his consideration of a further question, 'whether one can *live* after Auschwitz' (Adorno 2003b: 435, emphasis in original); that is, the question of whether or not the tendencies that had given rise to Auschwitz, such as atavistic nationalism (Adorno 2003c) and authoritarianism (Adorno *et al.* 1950), could ever be eradicated entirely.

Full understanding of Adorno's work therefore demands sustained engagement with his primary texts and an awareness of the context in which they were written, and readers are encouraged in the direction of the recommendations for further reading below. Otherwise, as Simon Jarvis puts it:

> Hastily read, Adorno can look like a pessimistic elitist who belongs to a lost age of mandarin modernism – a thinker with little illumination to offer in our own apparently very different historical circumstances ... If we lop off the bits which look difficult or obsolete – the engagement with Hegelian idealism, say – we find that even apparently unconnected aspects of Adorno's work, like his social theory or music criticism, suddenly make no sense (Jarvis 1998: 1, 3).

Bearing this in mind it would seem in one sense there is a logical opening for reference to Adorno within critical international relations. Much of the postpositivist turn in international relations theory has drawn on the Frankfurt School either directly (Linklater 1996) or as a component of critical theory more broadly understood (Smith 1996), and here there might be said to be a certain homology with Adorno's own engagement in the positivist dispute in Germany during the 1950s and 60s (Adorno 1976). However, there are few explicit linkages made here and the direction of critical International Relations theory, whilst often making reference to Adorno's contribution to Critical Theory, has for various reasons tended to skirt around Adorno rather than engage his work directly. Andrew Linklater's *Beyond Realism and Marxism: Critical Theory and International Relations* and Richard Wyn Jones' *Security, Strategy and Critical Theory* both refer to Adorno in a sympathetic but ultimately negative fashion to orient the study of international relations and security studies respectively. Linklater endorses Habermas' attempt to 'establish the basis of an alternative form of social theory' distinct from that offered by Adorno (Linklater 1990: 25). Wyn Jones looks to Horkheimer's pre-*Dialectic of Enlightenment* emphasis on emancipation and argues that 'Adorno's later work can offer no assistance to the task of lending intellectual support to the practical struggle for emancipation' (Wyn Jones 1999: 52).

Elsewhere, though, several of the concepts from Adorno's later writings have been picked up on by writers in international relations. Nicholas Rengger for example, in seeking to address the 'problem of world order' as it is addressed in critical international relations theory, invokes Adorno's concept of negative dialectic (Rengger 2001). Critical Theory, Rengger argues, has 'two modes or faces': an optimistic face, represented in the Kantian-inspired theory of Habermas and a pessimistic face exemplified primarily by Adorno's attitude towards the prospects for a critical social consciousness. If critical international relations theory is to truly advance the project of emancipation, Rengger argues, it must engage not only the 'utopian' impulse of Critical Theory (Hoffman 1987), but also its 'dark side' as emphasised in the work of Adorno (Rengger 2001: 96).

In sketching the contours of Critical Theory in international relations Rengger draws here on one of the most famous of Adorno's later concepts, that of negative dialectics. In *Negative Dialectics* (Adorno 1973), Adorno mounts a sustained and lengthy critique of identity thinking, that is, the tendency, particularly evident in Kantian idealism, to identify a particular object in terms of a universal concept through the process of categorization. In order to get away from this form of thinking, which assumes that concept and object are identical, Adorno draws once more on Hegel's idea of dialectics, but argues that it is the negative aspect of the dialectic rather than the positive that must be emphasised; where the former emphasizes unity, the latter emphasises the 'nonidentical', the 'extremity that eludes the concept'. As Adorno himself puts it:

> If negative dialectics calls for the self-reflection of thinking, the tangible implication is that if thinking is to be true – if it is to be true today, in any case – it must also be a thinking against itself. If thought is not measured by the extremity that eludes the concept, it is from the outset in the nature of the musical accompaniment with which the SS liked to drown out the screams of its victims (Adorno 1973: 365).

Adorno thus argues that concepts, language and frameworks of thought must be 'thought against' on the basis that they never completely capture that which they set out to describe and frequently relegate elements to the sphere of nonidentity. Thus, 'negative dialectics assesses the relation between concept and object, between the set of properties implied by the concept and the concept's actuality' (Held 2004: 215).

Though this all seems highly abstract, Adorno grounds his efforts in an attempt to do justice to the actuality of human suffering (and here again the reference to the SS and its victims above is indicative of the context of Adorno's writing). 'The need to lend a voice to suffering is a condition of all truth', Adorno argues (1973: 18); in other words an awareness of the corporeal actuality of human suffering should constantly drive our attention to the inadequacy of certain forms of representation to convey that suffering.

Yet, as Adorno acknowledges, concepts are all that is available for us to try and create meaning, his own included. His suggestion is that we employ 'constellations' (a term drawn from Walter Benjamin) of concepts since 'the determinable flaw in every concept makes it necessary to cite others' (Adorno 1973: 53). In this way we might hope to convey some sense of the particularity of experience, reveal specific sides of the object inaccessible to identity thinking (Held 2004: 215) and, at the same time, resist the temptation to simply reduce objects to subjective experience (which refers back to Adorno's concept of truth-content). But this also creates a hopeful allowance for 'utopian thinking' (in which Adorno draws on Ernst Bloch). Just as concepts can never entirely capture that which is, neither can they capture that which might yet come to pass; thus Adorno maintains the mutability of social relations despite his own abstraction from movements for social change.

Rengger, imitating the strategy advanced by Adorno, argues that the Habermasian character of critical international relations theory (for example, Linklater 1996) needs to engage with this 'negative' side of Critical Theory. The tendency to construe critical international relations theory as an 'emancipatory project', he argues, neglects the extent to which emancipation might itself require programmatic recommendations for the reconstitution of world order that could very well rely on instrumental reason. As noted above, Adorno has an understanding of the utopian impulse that runs against such programmatic projects, and Rengger recommends a greater role for 'Adorno-esque critique' in critical international relations theory as a counter to this tendency (Rengger 2001: 103).

Efforts in this direction have followed in the wake of criticisms of the 'discourse ethics' approach associated with Habermasian-inspired critical international relations theory which has until recently tended to dominate the employment of Frankfurt School theory in international relations. Link-later has noted that the 'critique of discourse ethics invites further discussion of background claims about human vulnerability and the capacity for suffering' and argues that 'Adorno's stress on human vulnerabilities' provides a useful starting point for an inquiry into distant suffering and cosmopolitan obligations' (Linklater 2007a: 23). Adorno observes that human beings have less difficulty in identifying the 'forms of the bad life' which must be resisted than they do in coming to agreement on the nature of the 'good life' (Adorno, cited in Linklater 2007a: 23). As Jarvis argues elsewhere, such an approach is very much in keeping with Adorno's 'utopian negativity' which 'cannot provide a blueprint for what the good life would be like, but only examines what our "damaged" life is like' (Jarvis 1998: 9). Thus Linklater can be seen to locate the basis for a 'sociology of global morals' and a notion of 'embodied cosmopolitanism' within Adorno's concern with the nature of corporeality and human suffering (Linklater 2007b; Adorno 1973: 18–19; Adorno 2005).

These recent moves indicate that the potentialities for the incorporation and application of Adorno's ideas and concepts within the study of international relations are only just beginning to be explored. More broadly it might be noted that Adorno ultimately maintains a sophisticated critical stance towards truth claims and forms of representation. Given this, his ideas might offer a bridge between critical international relations theory drawing on the Frankfurt School and the variety of post-structuralist, feminist and other critical approaches that also populate the subject. On this basis, as well as on the basis of Adorno's frequently telling insights into the nature of modern life, greater engagement between international relations theory and Adorno's work is to be encouraged.

Further reading

The touchstone for an engagement with Adorno's ideas is Adorno and Horkheimer's *Dialectic of Enlightenment* (Adorno and Horkheimer 1997) which, as outlined above, establishes several themes that recur in his later solo works. *Negative Dialectics* (Adorno 1973) is Adorno's dense but rewarding standalone treatise on epistemology. Beyond this *Minima Moralia: Reflections on a Damaged Life* (Adorno 2005) is an aphoristic work that gives fragmentary insights on a wide range of topics and owes as much to literary theory as philosophy in style; and *Aesthetic Theory* (Adorno 1984) is a posthumously published collection, intended as his magnum opus, of Adorno's reflections on artwork and aesthetics, that expands several of the points made here in this regard.

Several readers are also available that serve as useful introductions to Adorno by reprinting excerpts from his writings. Brian O'Connor (ed.) (2000) *The Adorno Reader* (Oxford: Blackwell) and Rolf Tiedemann (ed.) (2003) *Can One Live After Auschwitz? Theodor W. Adorno: A Philosophical Reader* (Stanford, CA: Stanford University Press) are particularly good in this regard, with the latter reproducing several essays that are otherwise difficult to obtain in English. Readers are encouraged toward direct use of the primary texts, but if resort to a secondary guide is needed then *Adorno: A Critical Introduction* (Jarvis 1998) is excellent and is designed to be used in conjunction with a reading of Adorno's own writings.

2 Giorgio Agamben

Nick Vaughan-Williams

Giorgio Agamben is an Italian thinker whose work does not consist of a single aim or 'big idea'. Rather, it is helpful to approach his thought as a series of overlapping fragments, which engage in a range of problems relating to language, metaphysics, aesthetics, politics and ethics. When taken as a whole, these fragments form a rich historical and philosophical mosaic that is difficult to label or classify as belonging to a particular school of thought. In recent years, especially since the publication of his work in English from the early 1990s, Agamben has had a significant impact across the humanities and social sciences and beyond. In international relations, there has been a spirited (though not uncritical) uptake of his controversial diagnosis of the nature of the relationship between politics, life and sovereign power. Increasingly, this diagnosis is taken as a starting point for many analyses of practices associated with the current 'War on Terror' unleashed by the US and its allies in the wake of the attacks of 11 September 2001. Indeed, Agamben has personally protested against the US government's response to these attacks by resigning from his position as Visiting Professor at New York University. He also refuses to travel to the US and submit to what he considers to be the 'biopolitical tattooing' of the Immigration Department. Nevertheless, the topicality of his thought belies the extent to which it is rooted in rigorous and painstakingly detailed philosophical thinking developed over the past four decades.

Intellectual biography

Agamben was born in 1942 in Rome, where he studied law and philosophy and wrote his doctoral thesis on French philosopher and Marxist activist Simone Weil. As a post-doctoral researcher, Agamben participated in Martin Heidegger's Le Thor seminars on Heraclitus and G.W.F. Hegel in 1966 and 1968. From 1974–75, he held a Fellowship at the University of London's Warburg Institute. Since then, Agamben has taught at the Universities of Verona and Marcerata in Italy, Henrich Heine University in Düsseldorf, the *Collège International de Philosophie* in Paris (where he was Director of Programmes from 1986–93), and the New School in New York. At the time of writing, he was Professor of Aesthetics in the Faculty of Arts and Design at the University of Venice. In 2006 he was awarded the *Prix Européen de L'Essai Charles Veillon*, an award for outstanding work on contemporary lifestyles and ideologies, presented at the University of Lausanne.

Agamben's impact on the Anglophone intellectual scene came relatively late in his career with the publication of a number of English translations of earlier texts in rapid succession. These texts are broadly concerned with an array of issues relating to literature, philosophy, linguistics, philology, poetics, and medieval history. In *Language and Death: The Place of Negativity* (1991) (originally published as *Il Linguaggio e la Morte: Un seminario sul luogo della negatività* in 1982), Agamben considers the relation between poetry and philosophy. This theme and questions about language and the experience of the self had been pursued in two earlier works: *Stanzas: Word and Phantasm in Western Culture* (1993) (*Stanze: La parola e il fantasma nella cultura occidentale*, 1977), which was Agamben's first major contribution to aesthetics and dedicated to Heidegger; and *Infancy and History* (1993) (*Infanzia e Storia*, 1978), a series of essays on play, history and temporality.

Some commentators identify a shift in Agamben's work towards politics and ethics marked by the publication of *The Coming Community* in 1993 (*La Communità Che Viene*, 1990) (Ek 2006). This book critiques sovereign identity politics and goes in search of alternative notions of community not based upon a unity of blood and soil but a relation of radical openness. However, positing this sort of rupture undermines significant overlaps and continuities within Agamben's thought, such as his enduring concern with human mortality and language, questions of subjectivity or 'personhood' and conditions of potentiality and being otherwise immanent within the constituted order. For example, these themes are central to Agamben's exploration of the historically contingent and politically constituted limits of the human and the animal as developed in *The Man Without Content* (1999) (*L'Uomo Senza Contenuto,* 1994), *The Open: Man and Animal* (2004) (*L'aperto: L'uomo e l'animale*, 2002) and *Remnants of Auschwitz: The Witness and the Archive* (*Quel che resta di Auschwitz*, 1999).

The latter, one in a series of texts written by Agamben known as the 'Homo Sacer' tetralogy, explores the human/animal theme in relation to the figure of the *Muselmann* in the Nazi death camps. Agamben analyses this figure, the 'drowned' or living dead 'who was giving up and was given up by his comrades', as the embodiment of the limit between man and non-man, human and in-human, and life and death (Agamben 1999: 41–86). In the camp *Muselmänner* are produced by sovereign power as subjects amenable to its sway: a form of life that is exposed to exceptional practices in its everyday existence. This form of life, which Agamben calls 'bare life' or *homo sacer*, is the paradigm for the series as a whole, which also includes: *Homo Sacer: Sovereign Power and Bare Life* (1998) (*Homo Sacer: Il potere sovrano e la nuda vita*, 1995); and *State of Exception* (2005) (*Lo Stato di Eccezione*, 2003). The next part of the 'Homo Sacer' series, *Il Regno e la*

Gloria, is yet to be published in English, but two recent texts deal with related themes: the problem of sovereignty, time and the messianic in *The Time That Remains: A Commentary on the Letter to the Romans* (2005) (*Il tempo che resta: Un commento alla Lettera ai Romani*, 2000); and the question of resistance to acts of separation upon which sovereign power rests in *Profanations* (2007) (*Profanazioni*, 2005).

Despite the delay in the arrival and reception of Agamben's work in English, the intellectual milieu in which he can be located is one that includes a number of other critical thinkers, such as Jacques Derrida, Michel Foucault, Jean-Luc Nancy, Gilles Deleuze and Félix Guattari. In the mid-1980s to mid-1990s Agamben lived and worked in Paris with some of these thinkers as well as Guy Debord, Jean-François Lyotard and a wider community of Italian radical intellectuals including Antonio Negri and Paolo Virno. More historical influences on Agamben's work include many of the canonical figures of Western political thought from Aristotle, through to Hegel and Nietzsche. However, Agamben has also been influenced heavily by earlier twentieth century thinkers: Hannah Arendt, Carl Schmitt and Walter Benjamin. Evidence of the particular importance of Benjamin is peppered throughout Agamben's work and in 1978 he became the editor of the *Complete Works of Walter Benjamin*, Italian edition, for Einaudi publishers. In addition to these philosophical influences, Agamben's work also engages, very distinctively, with a number of other genres outside the realm of formal academic literature, such as: Christian and biblical texts (especially the letters of Paul); Greek and Roman law; Italian Autonomism and Situationism; and writers such as Franz Kafka. Given the breadth and richness of Agamben's thought it is both impossible and undesirable to offer anything approximating a comprehensive survey. However, it is possible to focus on several key themes and terms around which multiple aspects of his work coalesce in order to provide a glimpse of some of the exciting and provocative directions in which it can lead.

Politics, life and sovereign power

Over the past two decades, Agamben has critiqued the dominant treatment of the relation between politics and life in political philosophy (Agamben 1998; 1999; 2005a). According to Agamben, this treatment has been shaped by the thought of Greek philosopher Aristotle. At the heart of Aristotle's conception of the state is the distinction between 'natural life' and the 'good life'. Agamben claims that this distinction reflects the way in which the Greeks had no single word for 'life'. Rather, he claims, two terms were used in its place: *zoē* (the biological fact of life) and *bios* (political or qualified life) (Agamben 1996: 151). Agamben notes that Aristotle's opposition between the biological fact of life and qualified life and his distinction between private and public spheres have had a lasting impact on the political tradition of the West. Yet, Agamben argues that these insights concerning the relationship between politics and life have largely been assumed rather than interrogated within political thought. However, for Agamben, one important exception is the work of French philosopher and historian Michel Foucault.

In *The History of Sexuality, Volume 1: The Will to Power* Foucault refers to the process by which biological life (*zoē*) has become included within the modalities of state power *(bios)* as the transition from politics to 'biopolitics'. The term biopolitics is used to describe the emergence during the seventeenth century of attempts to govern whole populations through the institutionalisation of medicine, use of vaccinations and other methods of curing and preventing disease. Foucault's argument is that, whereas for Aristotle life and politics are treated as separate, biopolitics calls into question the idea of life itself: 'modern man is an animal whose politics calls his existence as a living being into question' (quoted in Agamben 1998: 3). In other words, for Foucault, the entry of *zoē* into *bios* constitutes a fundamental shift in the relation between politics and life, where the simple fact of life is no longer excluded from political calculations and mechanisms but resides at the heart of modern politics.

Throughout his work Agamben is highly indebted to Foucault but the former makes a very different claim about the political structure of the West. He argues that 'the Foucauldian thesis will ... have to be corrected, or at least completed' because a historical shift to biopolitics has not actually taken place (Agamben 1998: 9). Rather, for Agamben '*the production of a biopolitical body is the original activity of sovereign power*' (Agamben 1998: 6). In other words, whereas Foucault reads the movement from politics to biopolitics as a historical *transformation* involving the inclusion of *zoē* in the *polis*, for Agamben the political realm is *originally biopolitical*. On Agamben's view, the West's conception of politics has always been biopolitical but this relation between politics and life has become even more visible in the context of the modern state and its sovereign practices (Agamben 1998: 6).

According to Agamben, the originally biopolitical element of politics can be detected in Aristotle's definition of the *polis* in terms of the exclusion of *zoē* from *bios*. For Agamben, the exclusion of *zoē* in this context is not entirely 'exclusive'. This is because *zoē* remains in a fundamental relation with *bios*. Indeed, *zoē* is included in *bios* through its very exclusion from it. In other words we are not dealing with a straightforward exclusion but rather an 'inclusive exclusion'. To explain what he means by inclusive exclusion Agamben introduces the notion of the 'ban', which is borrowed from French philosopher Jean-Luc Nancy (1993). If someone is banned from a community he or she continues to have a relationship with that group of people: it is precisely because of the ban that there continues to be a connection. The figure of the banned person complicates the notion of a clear separation between inclusion and exclusion: he or she who is excluded is included by virtue of their very exclusion. The idea of an inclusive exclusion is fundamental to Agamben's thought because, as we shall see, it is central to his account of the Western paradigm of sovereignty.

Agamben's approach to sovereignty is influenced by German legal and political theorist Carl Schmitt who defined the sovereign as 'he who decides on the exception' (Schmitt 2005). According to Schmitt, such a decision declares that a state of emergency exists and suspends the rule of law to allow for whatever measures are deemed to be necessary. However, Agamben also invokes Walter Benjamin's critique of Schmitt's theory of sovereignty that: 'the tradition of the oppressed teaches us that the "state of exception" in which we live is the rule' (Benjamin 2003: 392). Agamben draws on Benjamin's insight, written in a period when emergency powers were repeatedly invoked during the Weimar Republic era in Germany, in an attempt to move the notion of the exception away from the issue of emergency provisions towards a more relational and original function within the Western political paradigm (Agamben 2005a).

The diagnosis of the relation between politics, life and sovereign power put forward by Agamben brings together Nancy's concept of the ban, Schmitt's definition of sovereignty, and Benjamin's notion of the permanence of the state of the exception. For Agamben, the activity of sovereign power relies on a decision about whether certain forms of life are worthy of living. Such a decision, which is a sovereign cut or dividing practice, produces an expendable form of life that Agamben calls 'bare life'. The sovereign decision bans bare life from the legal and political institutions to which citizens normally have access. This ban renders bare life amenable to the sway of sovereign power and allows for exceptional practices such as torture, rendition or execution. Bare life is neither what the Greeks referred to as *zoē* nor *bios*. Rather, it is a form of life that is produced in a zone of indistinction between the two. On this basis, Agamben argues that it is necessary to isolate and analyse the way in which the classical distinction between *zoē* and *bios* is blurred in contemporary political life: 'Living in the state of exception that has now become the rule has ... meant this: our private body has now become indistinguishable from our body politic' (Agamben 2000: 139). Thus, elaborating on his 'correction' of the Foucauldian thesis, Agamben claims that the key feature of modern politics is not the simple inclusion of *zoē* in *bios*, but rather:

> *The decisive fact is that*, together with the process by which the exception everywhere becomes the rule, *the realm of bare life – which is originally situated at the margins of the political order – gradually begins to coincide with the political realm, and exclusion and inclusion, outside and inside, bios and zoē, right and fact, enter into a zone of irreducible indistinction* (Agamben 1998: 9, emphasis added).

Before considering the implications of this claim it is first necessary to further unpack and illustrate the main aspects of Agamben's central thesis.

Bare life

To reiterate, bare life is a form of life that is produced by sovereign power in a zone of indistinction *between zoē and bios*:

> The foundation (of the modern city from Hobbes to Rousseau) is not an event achieved once and for all but is continually operative in the civil state in the form of the sovereign decision. What is more the latter refers *immediately* to the life (and not the free will) of citizens, which thus appears as the originary political element ... *Yet this life is not simply natural reproductive life, the zoē of the Greeks, nor bios, a qualified form of life*. It is, rather, the bare life of *homo sacer* ... , a zone of indistinction and continuous transition between man and beast, nature and culture (Agamben 1998: 109, emphasis added).

In other words, bare life does not exist before or outside sovereign power relations. It is not something we are born with and can be stripped down to. Bare life is *not zoē*: any attempt at qualifying life as 'bare' or 'good' is a move away from *zoē*. Rather, bare life is something that is produced *by* sovereign power *for* sovereign power: 'bare life is a product of the machine and not something that preexists it' (Agamben 2005a: 87–88). Once the concept of bare life is untied from *zoē*, then, far from a universalistic conception of subjectivity, it can be interpreted as a form of life whose identity is always in question. What Agamben shows very helpfully is the way in which sovereign power depends upon the cultivation of this perpetual uncertainty.

Bare life is a form of life that is amenable to the sway of sovereign power because it is banned from law and politics and subject only to the whims of that power. Bare life is caught in a sort of legal and political vacuum or no-man's land: a zone of indistinction between law and non-law that is conducive to exceptional practices characteristic of sovereign power. According to Agamben, the 'locus *par excellence*' of the blurring of *zoē* and *bios* and production of bare life is the detention camp at the US Naval Base in Guantánamo Bay (Agamben 2004a: 612). Detainees held in Guantánamo are classified as 'unlawful enemy combatants' by the US government but this is not a term recognised by the UN or any other international institution. It is precisely this production of a deliberate uncertainty surrounding the status of detainees that allows for the indefinite use of exceptional measures against them. By referring to detainees as unlawful enemy combatants they are effectively 'banned' from international legal and political frameworks: citizens who commit crimes are treated as 'lawful criminals' but non-citizens defy the straightforward logic of legal/illegal. These conventional logics and frameworks, reflecting dominant notions about what form of life is eligible for protection, constitute a juridical–political culture in which it is possible for some 'humans' not to be treated as such.

Guards who stand watch over the detainees in Guantánamo confront a peculiar form of 'human' life. With no clear political or legal status, it bears no resemblance to Aristotle's conception of man in the public sphere or *bios*. Yet, neither does this life conform to what the Greeks would have called *zoē*, understood as the fact of living confined to the private sphere. Rather, the life confronted by the guards is a life that scrambles these Aristotelian co-ordinates: we no longer have any idea of the classical separation between *zoē* and *bios* in this context (Agamben 2000: 138). It is a bare life produced by the sovereign practices of the camp that is caught in a zone of indistinction between *zoē* and *bios*: a life that is mute and undifferentiated. For Agamben, such a life belongs to *homo sacer* or sacred man: a figure from Roman law whose very existence is in a state of exception defined by the sovereign. The figure of *homo sacer* is sacred in the sense that it can be killed but not sacrificed and is both constituted by and constitutive of sovereign power. Moreover, as the state of exception is less anomalous and more a permanent characteristic, according to Agamben we all potentially run the risk of becoming bare life: we are all '(virtually) *homines sacri*' (Agamben 1998: 111).

The camp

Agamben's diagnosis of the activity of sovereign power as the production of bare life in zones of indistinction between *zoē* or *bios* has important implications for the way we think about the politics of space. *Homo Sacer* ends with the provocative conclusion:

> Every attempt to rethink the political space of the West must begin with the clear awareness that we no longer know anything of the classical distinction between *zoē* and *bios*, between private life and political existence, between man as a simple living being at home in the house and man's political existence in the city (Agamben 1998: 187).

Agamben focuses on the emergence of concentration camps in the late nineteenth and early twentieth centuries, historically associated with the state of exception and martial law, in order to illustrate how the simple dichotomies between *zoē* and *bios*, private life and public existence, man as a simple living being and man's political existence in the above quotation fail to hold.

For Agamben, the space of the camp is fundamentally paradoxical. On the one hand, 'the camp is a piece of territory that is placed outside the normal juridical order' (Agamben 2000: 40). On the other hand, 'it is not simply an external space' (Agamben 2000: 40). The camp excludes what is captured inside which, as another form of inclusive exclusion, blurs the conventional spatial distinction between 'internal' and 'external'. Because law is suspended in the camp and exceptional practices become the rule Agamben argues that the camp represents: 'the most absolute biopolitical space that has ever been realised – a space in which power confronts nothing other than pure biological life without any mediation' (Agamben 2000: 41). As we have seen in the context of Guantánamo, those detained in camps 'move about in a zone of indistinction between the outside and the inside, the exception and the rule, the licit and the illicit' (Agamben 2000: 40–41).

The camp can be read as a historically contingent manifestation of the operations of sovereign power: 'the space that opens up when the state of exception starts to become the rule' (Agamben 2000: 39). However, for Agamben the camp is not understood as an anomaly or merely a historical fact (Agamben 2000: 37). Rather, he argues that the camp is 'in some sense ... the hidden matrix and *nomos* of the political space in which we live' (Agamben 2000: 37). In other words, as the spatial materialisation of the state of exception in which bare life is produced in a zone of indistinction between *zoē* and *bios*, the camp is itself a structure: 'if sovereign power is founded in the ability to decide on the state of exception, the camp is the structure in which the state of exception is permanently realised' (Agamben 2000: 40). On this basis, Agamben claims that the camp is symptomatic of the deeper workings of the juridical–political system of sovereign biopolitics. The camp reveals something fundamental to the Western paradigm born of the exception: the attempt to materialise the state of exception and create a space in which bare life and juridical rule enter into a threshold of indistinction. Hence, whilst there may be few camps such as Guantánamo, the logic upon which these places rest can be observed in territory or space conventionally defined as the 'normal' interior of the state.

Ethical–political implications

At first glance, Agamben's work seems to lead in somewhat pessimistic, even despairing, directions. Indeed, his diagnosis of the relation between politics and life, analysis of the production of bare life in zones of indistinction and prognosis that 'we are all virtually *homines sacri*' all imply a bleak picture of the possibility for contestation, change and, in short, politics. For this reason Andreas Kalyvas argues that Agamben's portrayal of the 'unstoppable march to the camp' is 'totalistic ... , and though it is concerned with politics and its eclipse, it is itself quite un-political' (Kalyvas 2005: 112). However, in an interview in 2004 Agamben replied to his critics:

> I've often been reproached for (or at least attributed with) this pessimism that I am perhaps unaware of. But I don't see it like that. There is a phrase from Marx, cited by Debord as well, that I like a lot: 'the desperate situation of society in which I live fills me with hope.' I don't see myself as pessimistic (Agamben 2004b: 123).

Central to Agamben's thinking about ethical–political praxis and resistance is his conception of the subject as an interval or remainder between what he refers to as processes of subjectification and de-subjectification. According to Agamben, the biopolitical terrain of global politics can be understood as 'a kind of de-subjectification machine: it's a machine that both scrambles all the classical identities and ... a machine that ... recodes these very same dissolved identities' (Agamben 2004b: 116). Whilst for Agamben 'there is no escape from this problem', it is nevertheless possible to think through the potential for resistance by rendering the machine inoperative on its own terms (Agamben 2004b: 116). Agamben's thought, then, does not lead to nihilism or passivity but calls for the radical invention of new practices: 'a movement on the spot, in the situation itself' (Agamben 2004b: 121).

In *The Time That Remains* Agamben gives the example of Paul's negotiation with the Jewish law that divides Jews and non-Jews. Agamben is interested in the way in which, instead of applying a universal principle to argue against this sovereign cut, Paul intervenes by taking the law on its own terms. According to Agamben, Paul does this by dividing the division itself: by introducing a further division between the Jew according to the flesh and the Jew according to the spirit. This division of the division means that, instead of a simple separation between Jews/non-Jews, there are now 'Jews who are not Jews, because there are Jews who are Jews according to the flesh, not the spirit, and [non-Jews] who are [non-Jews] according to the flesh, but not according to the spirit' (Agamben 2004b: 122). Consequently, a remainder is produced that renders the applicability and operativity of the law ineffective: a new form of subject that is neither a Jew nor a non-Jew but a 'non-non Jew' (Agamben 2005b: 51). Agamben places his hope for a kind of minority politics in this form of un-working of the system or biopolitical machine from within:

One should proceed in this way, from division to division, rather than by asking oneself: "What would be the universal communal principle that would allow us to be together?" To the contrary. It is a matter, confronted with the divisions introduced by the law, of working with what disables them through resisting, through remaining—*résister, rester,* it's the same root (Agamben 2004b: 123).

Elsewhere, Agamben links the move to render the system inoperative with notions of 'profanation', meaning to violate or transgress, and play (Agamben 2007: 73–92). He illustrates the logic of profanation through play with the example of the cat that plays with the ball of string as if it were a mouse. The game frees the mouse from being cast as prey and at the same time the predatory activity of the cat is shifted away from the chasing and killing of the mouse: 'and yet, this play stages the very same behaviours that define hunting' (Agamben 2007: 86). With this example Agamben seeks to demonstrate the profanatory potential in play as a means of creating a new use of something by deactivating an old one. The ultimate call is to subvert the given machine or apparatus according to its own logic: 'to wrest from the apparatuses – from all apparatuses – the possibility of use that they have captured' (Agamben 2007: 92).

In *Means Without End* Agamben is clear that any move to render biopolitical apparatuses inoperative must do so on the basis of his diagnosis of the relation between politics and life:

> It is by starting from this uncertain terrain and from this opaque zone of indistinction that today we must once again find the path of another politics, of another body, of another world. I would not feel up to forgoing this indistinction of public and private, of biological body and body politic, of *zoē* and *bios*, for any reason whatsoever. *It is here that I must find my space once again – here or nowhere else. Only a politics that starts from such an awareness can interest me* (Agamben 2000: 139, emphasis added).

The figure that Agamben draws upon to think through the possibility of resistance is what he calls 'whatever being' (Agamben 1993: 1996; 2000). The notion of 'whatever being' refers to being-as-such: 'the simple fact of one's own existence as possibility or potentiality' (Agamben 1993: 143). 'Whatever being' has no essence that can be separated from its attributes (Agamben 1996: 151). It constitutes a 'pure singularity' in the sense that it cannot be broken down into different parts (Agamben 1993: 67). Crucially, as far as a politics of resistance is concerned, this means that 'whatever being' lacks the features permitting the sovereign capture: 'what the state cannot tolerate in any way … is that the singularities form a community, without affirming an identity, that humans co-belong without any representable condition of belonging' (Agamben 1993: 86). The task, then, is not to mobilise resistance on the basis of universal generalised principles such as human rights. Rather, it is to explore and invent the profanatory potential that resides within remnants of forms of subjectification and de-subjectification produced by sovereign power itself. It is both impossible and imprudent to generalise too much about what this might mean in the context of resistance against the biopolitical apparatuses in the current 'War on Terror': this must be invented on a case-by-case basis, 'on the spot', so to speak.

Agamben and international relations

Agamben has made a significant impact on the discipline of international relations. Of course not all work in international relations has been uncritical of Agamben's oeuvre especially in relation to his diagnosis of the relation between politics, life and sovereign power. For example, William E. Connolly has accused Agamben of putting the problem of sovereignty to one side by transcending it altogether. According to Connolly, Agamben's approach to the problem of sovereignty is incommensurable with that problem: 'biocultural life exceeds any textbook logic because of the non-logical character of its materiality ... [it] is more messy, layered, and complex than any logical analysis can capture' (Connolly 2004: 29). On this basis, Connolly arrives at the conclusion that 'Agamben displays the hubris of academic intellectualism when he encloses political culture within a tightly defined logic' (Connolly 2004: 29).

However, Agamben's thought, whilst often challenging, offers powerful diagnostic tools for thinking about issues in contemporary world politics in new, provocative and politically engaged ways. His work has been taken up by a range of writers dealing with questions of: sovereign power, violence and resistance in the context of the 'War on Terror' (Closs Stephens and Vaughan-Williams 2008; Edkins 2000, 2007b; Edkins and Pin-Fat 2004, 2005; Edkins, Pin-Fat and Shapiro 2004; Dauphinee and Masters 2007; van Munster 2004); practices associated with security as the new paradigm of global governance (Bigo 2007); trauma, time and practices of memorialisa-tion (Edkins 2003a); the politics of global space, surveillance and borders and bordering practices in global politics (Amoore 2007; Edkins and Walker 2000; Kumar Rajaram and Grundy-Warr 2007; Vaughan-Williams 2007b, 2008; 2009), migration and patterns of global movement (Doty 2007; Kumar Rajaram and Grundy-Warr 2004); the politics of humanitarianism and human rights (Caldwell 2004; Edkins 2003b) and debates about the rule of law and sovereign exceptionalism (Connolly 2004; Neal 2006; Neocleous 2006; Prozorov 2005). Indeed, the speed and range of the uptake of Agamben's work in these and other areas has already made parts of the discipline of international relations seem increasingly inoperative.

Further reading

A good place to start for a gentle introduction to the themes of politics, life and sovereignty, bare life and the camp is Agamben's *Means Without Ends: Notes on Politics* (2000). This short book provides accessible footnotes to the primary text *Homo Sacer: Sovereign Power and Bare Life* (1998). In *State of Exception* (2005a) Agamben develops his historical and philosophical treat-ment of sovereignty in relation to the inter-war debates between Walter Benjamin and Carl Schmitt. *Remnants of Auschwitz* (1999) explores the above themes in relation to language, witness, testimony and the archive.

A useful introduction to the implications of Agamben's thought for ethical and political praxis can be found in two interviews: 'Interview with Giorgio Agamben – A Life, A Work of Art Without an Author: The State of Exception, the Administration of Disorder and Private Life' published in the *German Law Review* (2004a); and '"I am sure you are more pessimistic than I am ... " An Interview with Giorgio Agamben' in *Rethinking Marxism* (2004b). These interviews are especially useful when read alongside *The Coming Com-munity* (1993) and *The Time That Remains* (2005b). On the possibility of resistance, see the essay 'In Praise of Profanation' in *Profanations* (2007). To appreciate the philosophical underpinnings of Agamben's work readers would do well to begin with *Potentialities: Collected Essays in Philosophy* (1999). This volume contains useful texts on the messianic, the immanent tradition and the concept of potentiality that run throughout his work.

Readers are encouraged to engage directly with Agamben's texts rather than rely too heavily on secondary literature. However, three recent edited collections are helpful: Andrew Norris' *Politics, Metaphysics, and Death: Essays on Giorgio Agamben's Homo Sacer*; Matthew Calarco and Steven DeCaroli's *Sovereignty and Life: Essays on Giorgio Agamben*; and Justin Clemens, Nick Heron and Alex Murray's *The Work of Giorgio Agamben: Law, Literaure, Life*. In the context of international relations the most systematic engagement with Agamben's thought is the work of Jenny Edkins (2003a, 2003b, 2007a, 2007b) and her work with Véronique Pin-Fat (Edkins and Pin-Fat 2004, 2005). For a critical overview of Agamben's work see Catherine Mills' *The Philosophy of Agamben*.

3 Hannah Arendt

Patricia Owens

Hannah Arendt (1906–75) is one of the most important political thinkers of the twentieth-century. She is well-known for her monumental study *The Origins of Totalitarianism* (1966), her diagnosis of modern politics and society in *The Human Condition* (1958), and for coining the term 'the banality of evil' to describe a Nazi war criminal in her most controversial book, *Eichmann in Jerusalem* (1968a). Arendt did not shy away from controversy in her life-time and some of her most controversial and important ideas continue to shape political discourse. The latest surge of engagement with Arendt's writing – coinciding with the centenary of her birth in 2006 – has occurred at a time that has produced moral and political disasters very similar and in many ways related to those she addressed in the various stages of her life. As international theory has returned to the canon of political thought it is not surprising that Arendt's unique and often idiosyncratic contribution is coming to the fore. Like many others discussed in this volume, serious engagement with Arendt in international political theory is belated and welcome.

The idiosyncrasy of Arendt's writing, the difficulty of classifying her work, is important to note. The advocates of various political theories and approaches have sought to claim Arendt's legacy. As Martin Jay has pointed out, for better or for worse, Arendt's name serves as one of the many 'charismatic legitmators' of contemporary theory in the humanities and social sciences (Jay 1993: 168). Often slow to catch up with wider intellectual trends, diverse strands of international political theory have recently claimed Arendt's authority, including commentators on realism (Lang 2001; Klusmeyer 2005; Owens 2008a); the 'English School' (Williams 2002, 2005); post-structuralism (Saurette 1996); normative theory and international justice (Fine 2000; Schaap 2005; Hayden 2007); critical security studies (Booth 2007); various types of cosmopolitanism (Herzog 2004; Axtmann 2006; Owens 2008b); and post-colonialism (Owens 2007a). These efforts join an already long list of different 'Arendts' within political theory. There we find her affinities with classical republicanism (Canovan 1992); post-structuralism (Honig 1991, 1993); Critical Theory (Habermas 1983; Benhabib 1996); conservatism (Canovan, 1996); and feminism (Honig 1995).

Arendt would probably have rejected most, if not all, of this branding. She once told her students not to 'classify great thinkers' (1968b) and unlike many others, including some of those discussed in this volume, Arendt was uninterested in establishing a school of like-minded thinkers around herself. 'There are many routes to accommodation with the powers that be. The only people who will count', she wrote in 1945, 'are those who refuse to identify themselves with either an ideology or a power' (Arendt and Jaspers 1992: 23). This independence from established schools of thought has led many of her interlocutors to read into her writing what they have wanted to see, and take from her words whatever they can use. This is a special danger in the discipline of international relations which has not always resisted the temptation to compress great thinkers into its various schools of thought. In an oft-cited exchange with Hans J. Morgenthau, friend of Arendt and so-called father of international relations, he asked whether Arendt's position was 'liberal' or 'conservative'. She responded that she 'couldn't care less' because 'the real questions of this century will [not] get any kind of illumination by this sort of thing' (1979: 334). Arendt does not fit into any conventional school of thought, critical or otherwise, and this is exactly why she matters so much today (Young-Bruehl 2006).

Intellectual biography

Hannah Arendt was born into a family of middle-class secular Jews on October 14 1906 in Hanover, Germany. At 16, she began studying classics and Christian theology at the University of Berlin. At 18, she studied phenomenology at Marburg University with Martin Heidegger. And in 1925, she went to the University of Heidelberg to study with existentialist philosopher Karl Jaspers, under whose supervision she wrote her doctoral thesis on the concept of love in St. Augustine (Arendt 1995). The principle intellectual influences in these formative years include the politics and philosophy of the ancient Greeks, as well as the modern writings of Immanuel Kant (Arendt 1982), Nietzsche (Arendt 1968c), Marx (Arendt 1958, 2002) and, of course, Heidegger and Jaspers (Arendt 1994).

From the 1930s, as it became increasingly clear that anti-Semitism and Nazism were about to overwhelm life in Germany, Arendt became involved in Jewish politics. She worked for the German Zionist Organization to publicize crimes against Jews and was arrested for this work. She fled Germany for Paris without documents, becoming a stateless Jew. Political work continued, however, including rescuing Jewish children and preparing them for the exodus to Palestine. She asked herself: 'What can I specifically do as a Jew?' (1994: 12). The question was purely conditional on being attacked in these terms and the belief that it was the only appropriate, realistic basis from which to fight back (1979: 333). As she would later explain, 'you cannot say, "Excuse me, I am not a Jew; I am a human being". That is silly'. Under such circumstances of direct and immediate persecution, to defend oneself in abstract terms such as 'world citizen' would have been 'nothing but a grotesque and dangerous evasion of reality' (1968d: 18). Like Franz Fanon, Arendt's own identity as a Jew and her understanding of the principles of political resistance were shaped by a violence that was colonial in nature.

After the outbreak of the war and with the situation in France deteriorating under German occupation, Arendt was arrested again and detained as an 'enemy alien'. She escaped with her husband, Heinrich Blücher, and her mother, fleeing to the United States where she gained citizenship and where she would live for the rest of her life. She argued for the creation of a Jewish army to fight 'against Hitler as Jews, in Jewish units, under the Jewish flag' (2000: 46). Yet she expressed enormous ambivalence toward Zionist calls for the creation of an exclusively Jewish homeland. Arendt viewed all nationalism as obsolete; useful in the specific context of the nineteenth-century but in the twentieth-century it 'could no longer either guarantee the true sovereignty of the people within or establish a just relationship among different peoples beyond the national borders' (1978: 141; on Arendt's criticisms of nationalism as a bankrupt political principle see Beiner (2000)). The only viable and defensible political structure for Palestine, she argued, was a dual-state comprised of joint Arab–Jewish local councils. Without such a compromise, she presciently argued, 'the solution of the Jewish question [would] merely [produce] a new category of refugees' (Arendt 1966: 290, 1978: 239; for a discussion of Arendt's writing on refugees and statelessness see her essay 'We Refugees' in *The Jewish Writings* (2007)).

Arendt paid a price for this break with received opinion regarding Israel. This was nowhere more evident than the scandal of how one of her books, as she rightly believed, became 'the object of an organized campaign' (1968a: 283). In 1961, Arendt travelled to Jerusalem to cover for *The New Yorker* magazine the trial of Adolf Eichmann, the Nazi bureaucrat charged with directing the transportation of Jews to the death camps during World War II. The articles were expanded and published in 1963 as *Eichmann in Jerusalem: a Report on the Banality of Evil*. Arendt observed that Eichmann was an unremarkable functionary, not the sadistic monster many seemed to want him to be; 'one cannot extract any diabolical or demonic profundity from Eichmann' (1968a: 288). His evil was not radical, but banal. 'He *merely*, to put the matter colloquially, *never realized what he was doing* ... that was, in fact, the lesson one could learn in Jerusalem' (1968a: 287–88). As a result of the storm, Arendt lost many friends and her ties with the organised Jewish community were effectively severed (Aschheim 2001; Zertal 2005).

A number of things about the Eichmann book came under fire: Arendt's criticisms of the political nature of the trial; the detached tone in which she chose to write; for pointing to the fact that the Jewish Councils – the leaders not the people themselves – often cooperated with the Nazis by providing lists of names; and, of course, for not presenting Eichmann in a way many wanted him to be seen. Yet Arendt stood her ground. She faced head-on the realisation of what ordinary humans were capable of doing and believed that this must be 'the precondition of any modern political thinking' (1994: 132). While most of her critics have been forgotten, Arendt's writing on Eichmann, the Holocaust, and totalitarianism more generally have become central to our understanding of evil (Kateb 1984; Villa 1999; Bernstein 2002) and the psychology of those who commit atrocities and do not fully recognise their actions as cruel (Osiel 2001).

In addition to the Eichmann book, of course, *The Origins of Totalitarianism*, *The Human Condition*, *On Revolution*, *Between Past and Future*, *Men in Dark Times*, *Crises of the Republic*, and the posthumously published *Life of the Mind*, *The Jew as Pariah*, *Essays in Understanding*, *Lectures on Kant's Political Philosophy*, *Responsibility and Judgement*, *The Promise of Politics*, and *The Jewish Writings* all established Arendt as one of the major thinkers of her generation. Her numerous contributions to political thought afforded her a sequence of illustrious fellowships and professorships in the American Ivy League. She smoked like a chimney and at the age of sixty-nine, Hannah Arendt collapsed and died of a heart attack in her New York apartment on December 4 1975. She is buried next to her husband in the cemetery of Bard College, New York.

Totalitarianism, imperialism and the break with tradition

Hannah Arendt argued that the Second World War and especially the Holocaust revealed a rupture in the Western tradition of political thought. Everything she wrote was shaped by her conviction that the disasters of the twentieth-century had led to a break in human history of monumental proportions. Imperialism, world wars and the rise of totalitarianism had left Western moral and political traditions in tatters. Indeed, one of the most destructively dangerous elements of the Western tradition, Arendt argued, had been the effort of political philosophers to govern politics through the application of seemingly correct and rational systems of thought (Saurette 1996; Owens 2007a).

Since Plato, philosophers, engaged in the essentially passive activity of thinking in solitude, have sought to create models for political conduct often bordering on absolute standards for human behaviour. They have sought to subject political action and political opinion to the authority of philosophical reason. However, it was Arendt's conviction that no theory or philosophical framework can be 'applied' without destroying the very essence of political life. Whereas thinking is done in solitude, in a 'dialogue between me and myself' (1968c: 220), politics always encounters a plurality of opinion; political knowledge is always perspectival. There can be no unity between thought and political action (why this a problem for Habermasian-critical theory and neoconservatism see Owens 2007a: Ch.8 and 2007b). To think and to act are not the same; 'all our categories of thought and standards for judgment seem to explode in our hands the instant we try to apply them'

(Arendt 1994: 302). Arendt illustrated the danger through her study of the ideological thinking so central to the rise of totalitarianism.

Arendt argued that the novel political phenomenon of the twentieth-century was totalitarianism. The combination of ideology and terror – 'You can't say A without saying B and C and so on, down to the end of the murderous alphabet' (1966: 472) – and the deliberate effort to make human beings superfluous and destroy human spontaneity was at the heart of this distinctly new and radical form of evil. How to identify the radically new would become a central preoccupation in Arendt's writing (Baehr 2002). Yet while emphasising the horrible originality of totalitarianism, Arendt uncovered the specific configuration of large-scale historical processes, including imperialism and anti-Semitism, that 'crystallized into totalitarianism' (1994: 403). Arendt's argument about the relationship between nineteenth-century imperialism and twentieth-century totalitarianism is an important (though often forgotten) lesson for students of international history and theory. Imperial violence unleashed a dynamic of violent and racist extremism which directly contributed to the catastrophes of the First and Second World Wars.

Arendt's farsighted and prescient claim about the constitutive relationship between war in the empire and metropole makes her an important forerunner of post-colonialism in international theory. Arendt's history of the West is a global history. Her account also suggests that the conventional and broadly liberal distinctions between war and peace and between civilised fighting on the European continent and barbarous war in the colonies – so central to conventional military history and security studies – are untenable (Owens, 2007a). This makes Arendt one of the first to draw attention to the recently popular notion of 'blowback' (what she called the 'boomerang effect'), the negative and unintended consequences of imperial foreign policy (Johnson 2004; for Arendt's related diagnosis of the US defeat in Vietnam see 'Home to Roost' in *Responsibility and Judgement* (2003)). All this made Arendt suspicious of grand and ideological- or theory-driven schemes of global political transformation – an apparent specialty of Western 'political' thought.

Violence, power, and new beginnings

In most of the Western tradition of political philosophy, politics has been viewed as essentially concerned with the accumulation of power over others, of rulership. Power itself is seen as a possession, an instrument of rule that produces a hierarchical and coercive relationship between rulers and ruled. It is only a short step from here to the other dominant view in political and international thought that violence is the ultimate expression, even the essence, of power. In contrast to these classical Hobbesian and Weberian views, Arendt maintained that power and violence were not the same. In fact, they are opposites. To make sense of this we must remain attentive to the specific lexicon she developed. Arendt structured her political theory around a number of important definitions and distinctions.

Arendt defined *power* as a collective capacity that emerges between people as they act together; it belongs to the group, and disappears when the group disperses. Power only exists as a potential until it is galvanised by people acting in concert to achieve a common goal or debate their common affairs. Whereas power is an end itself, *violence* is an instrument, only a means to an end. It is the use of implements to multiply strength and command others to obey. Arendt illustrated her claims about the difference between power and violence through a number of historical examples of popular violence and non-violent action by the materially less powerful but numerically superior. Arendt's unusual distinction between power and violence can also be illustrated conceptually in terms of the justification and legitimacy of each.

Arendt was no pacifist – she wrote that pacifism was 'devoid of reality' (1966: 442) – but she disputed the view that violence could ever be legitimate, properly speaking. Justification is the political act of claiming that something is reasonable or just. This justification, which always involves political speech to a judging audience, is the most important element – the most political aspect – of any political theory of war or violence. Violence can only be justified when used to achieve concrete and short-term ends. However, power does not need to be justified with reference to any other end. It is an end in itself. What power requires is legitimacy. Legitimacy has a more precise meaning than justification. To be legitimate is to conform to existing laws or rules of the game. When people act in concert they construct these laws and rules and make and remake their own legitimacy. As Arendt put it:

> Power springs up whenever people get together and act in concert, but it derives its legitimacy from the initial getting together rather than from any action that then may follow. Legitimacy, when challenged, bases itself on an appeal to the past, while justification relates to an end that lies in the future. Violence can be justifiable, but it will never be legitimate (1972: 151).

Arendt's distinctions between power, violence, justification and legitimacy have been extended to debates about contemporary wars (Young 2002; Owens 2005a, 2007a).

Violence might be used and justified in the founding of a new political realm, but Arendt sought to end our fascination with the idea that violence was necessary for new political beginnings. We see this in her assessment of Franz Fanon. Arendt certainly had sympathy with the idea that 'decolonization is always a violent phenomenon' (Fanon 1963: 35; Cocks 2002). However, in 'On Violence', she objected to the teleological assumption that anti-colonial violence might contribute to a new more humanistic order of global freedom led by the Third World. She rejected all efforts to assimilate violence into any broader theory of historical movement, human creativity and new beginnings; the idea of violent resistance as the embodiment of historical progress. Indeed, Arendt's criticisms of Fanon can be turned against some of the more grandiose claims of Carl Schmitt. Both Schmitt and Arendt believed that the history and theory of the partisan, guerrilla insurgents and resisters to occupation, 'proves to be the key to recognizing political reality' (Schmitt 2004a: 43). But, as we will see in a moment, their conception of that reality – and the meaning of political action – is very different (Owens 2007a). Schmitt's distinction between 'friend and enemy', discussed elsewhere in this volume, reveals no deeper political meaning. It is, in fact, anti-political, representing, in Arendt's words, a 'conspicuous distain of the whole texture of reality' (1966: viii).

Arendt objected to the belief that violence could be a 'cleansing force' for the body and the bringer of 'new meanings'; that through violence the colonised could 'understand social truths' (Fanon 1963: 147). For Arendt, violence as such could not reveal any deeper truth; it is 'mute'. 'Where violence rules absolutely, as for instance in the concentration camps,' she wrote, 'everything and everybody must turn silent' (1970a: 9). Only words had the power to reveal new meanings and new knowledge. Like Marx and Fanon, as we will see, Arendt distrusted bourgeois talk and liberal political categories. But the general 'mistrust of speech' Arendt could not share; 'man, to the extent that he is a political being, is endowed with the power of speech' (1970a: 9).

Politics, plurality and the public world

Hannah Arendt assumed that there was a priority and autonomy to politics. She did not believe that the public and private sphere were entirely unrelated. But she argued that there are distinct principles and motives for political action. Unlike others such as Schmitt (1996a) who also believed in the distinctiveness of 'the political', the ultimate expression of Arendt's idea of politics is not violent conflict, a struggle to the death between enemies. It is the ability to appear before plural equals and to debate and act to build a common world. Arendt understood political action to be identical with the freedom to act with plural others to bring something new into the world. Indeed, this plurality, she argued, is 'specifically *the* condition ... of all political life' (1958: 7).

The existence of plurality, that there are many perspectives and voices that constitute the political world, is an objective fact. When plural equals come together to debate their common affairs we can say that a public realm has been created. Through speech and action this plurality of people form a 'space in-between' them which can exist 'without the intermediary of things or matter' (1958: 7). There is an important revelatory dimension to political action in Arendt's thought. Through acting and speaking in public men and women can reveal something about themselves that they would not otherwise have known. They can discover 'who' they are, a particular self that would not be possible in the absence of such constitutive action. Some have mistakenly suggested that Arendt's emphasis on speech and the public realm makes her an early thinker in the tradition of critical theory advanced by Jürgen Habermas (Habermas 1983; Benhabib 1996). However, Arendt's emphasis on contestation and disagreement, her acceptance of the contingency of all politically-relevant truth claims, is at odds with Habermas' focus on deliberative rationality and consensus-building (Canovan 1983).

When Arendt wrote about the political, public *world*, or the republic, she had something very specific in mind. The world is literally the space for politics and it is for the sake of this world, out of a concern for its continuance, those with public spirit often act. In *The Human Condition*, Arendt identified a number of modern trends contributing to the destruction of our sense of a distinctly public world. She was extremely critical of any use of Christian principles as the basis for political action, such as compassion, love, or charity. She was highly critical of efforts to make issues of 'the self' and concern for the 'life processes' of individuals the central concern of politics. The results, Arendt believed, were disastrous; 'the linkage of politics and life results in an inner contradiction that cancels and destroys what is specifically political about politics' (2005: 145). This element of Arendt's thought overlaps with the realist-republican tradition associated with Machiavelli, of politics as an artificial 'space of appearances' (Owens, 2007a, 2008a). We find that Arendt was an important forerunner of those concerned with the rise of 'biopolitics', which has recently become popular through the appropriation of the writing of Arendt and Foucault (Agamben 1998; Kinsella 2008/9; Owens 2008/9).

Arendt was a theorist of new political beginnings and the founding of new political spaces. New beginnings were always possible, she argued, given the fact of natality, the ontological root of political action. Humans 'are not born in order to die but in order to begin' (1958: 246). However, although political action can have a definite beginning it can never have a predictable end. The effort to control or predict is always overrun by the nature of political action, 'where nothing happens more frequently than the totally unexpected' (1958: 300). This is one of the reasons that she argued, *contra* Marx and others, that the most significant changes in social and political life could not be understood through the projection of continuous historical laws (for Arendt's 'theory of theory' see Luban (1983)). History is the product of events brought into being by the actions of men and women; here 'accident and infinite improbability occurs' all the time (1968c: 170).

The contingency, boundless instability and unpredictability of political action make law and territorial boundaries important. Without such conventions the world would, indeed, be little more than a Hobbesian state of nature, as neo-realist international theory suggests, or more accurately, in Arendt's words, a desert, a 'lawless, fenceless wilderness of fear and suspicion' (1966: 466). In the absence of such laws the 'space in-between' that emerges through political interaction would seem so ephemeral. Arendt's account here has been described as loosely compatible with a pluralist international society approach (Williams 2005). However, it must be remembered that Arendt never identified the 'comity of nations' or so-called 'society of European states' as embodying potentially universal and abstract norms that could be divorced from force and imperial power (Owens 2007a). Her writing was anti-nationalist and non-statist. In a 1945 essay, 'The Seeds of a Fascist International', she wrote that 'the "national state", having lost its very foundations, leads a life of a walking corpse, whose spurious existence is artificially prolonged by repeated injections of imperialist expansion' (1994: 143).

The traumas of the twentieth-century demonstrated to Arendt that 'human dignity' needed 'a new guarantee' (1966: ix). But she was extremely ambivalent about the liberal discourse of human rights (Beardsworth 2008). Indeed of all the political theories that might appropriate various elements of Arendt's thought the one least likely to do so is liberalism. 'All the so-called liberal concepts of politics,' she observed, 'simply add up private lives and personal behavior patterns and present the sum as laws of history, or economics, or politics ... they express the bourgeoisie's instinctive distrust of and its innate hostility to public affairs' (1966: 145–46). With the exception of a few passages in *Origins*, she hardly referred to human rights. Instead, she favoured the categories of action, opinions, freedom and plurality to refer to the politics in which rights would make sense (Isaac 1996). Arendt did not malign 'human rights' as such and a number of her interpreters (Cotter 2005; Birmingham 2006; Parekh 2008) have developed her writing on 'a right to have rights', 'to live in a framework where one is judged by one's actions and opinions' (1966: 296–97; see Cotter, 2005; Birmingham, 2006; Parekh, 2008). Isaac (2002) suggests that even if human rights justifications for military intervention are hypocritical, as was the case when NATO intervened in Kosovo in 1999, Arendt provides reasons for not condemning such wars on these grounds, though Owens (2007a) criticises this claim. Arendt had a distinctive response to genocide, or what she called a 'war of annihilation' (2005; Owens 2008a).

The most important rights, according to Arendt, are political rights which are wholly dependent on human conventions not any abstract inborn human dignity. The only guarantee of human dignity after the disasters of the twentieth-century was a new form of political founding, which she conceived in terms of a post-national democratic-republican model of interlinked polities (Rensmann 2007). This is a modest cosmopolitanism of inter-republic law and not a vision of global citizenship as such. In Arendt's words: 'Nobody can be a citizen of the world as he is a citizen of his country'. All things political are so by virtue of their dependence 'on plurality, diversity, and mutual limitations' (1968d: 81). The 'rights and duties' of citizenship 'must be defined and limited, not only by those of his fellow citizens, but also by the boundaries of a territory' (1968d: 81). The organisation of politics, human-made laws and conventions, is fragile and historically contingent as well as spatially bound. Everything Arendt had learned from history taught her not to seek to replace one grand scheme of global political and military transformation with another. Rather she preferred to draw attention to the continual examples of violent and non-violent political foundings, the formation of councils and small-scale republics and popular bodies not always limited by national or state frontiers.

Conclusion

Hannah Arendt's approach to theory was inspired by facts and events and not intellectual history or the history of ideas. In Arendt's mind, ideas and theories only mattered if they directly illuminated politics. Born into a generation of thinkers that, as she put it, had been 'sucked into politics as though with the force of a vacuum' (1968c: 3), Arendt was a political writer and resistance intellectual as much as a political theorist (Isaac 1992). A stateless refugee for a time, she had first-hand experience of imprisonment for political activity, occupation and struggles for liberation. She directly influenced a number of the other writers discussed in this volume including Agamben, Kristeva and Habermas. Her thought overlaps significantly with Benjamin (Arendt 1970b), Fanon, and Foucault. As indicated earlier, she was an important early forerunner of post-colonialism represented here by Fanon, Said and Spivak. Like many of these thinkers, Arendt embraced the contingency and arbitrariness of politics and viewed it as an opportunity for political renewal and democratic political founding. Perhaps for this reason we do not find in Arendt's work the despair we often encounter in the writings of Nietzsche and Adorno. In fact, she persuasively demonstrated that political action gained a new dignity after the loss of traditional sources of authority and morality that has attended the modern age; 'the abandonment' of the hierarchy of philosophy over politics 'is the abandonment of all hierarchical structures' (Arendt 1982: 29). For these and other reasons Hannah Arendt's approach to politics and to thinking remains an indispensable source for those in search of guidance not in *what* to think but *how* to think about world politics (1968c: 14).

Further reading

Arendt, Hannah (1966 [1951]) *The Origins of Totalitarianism* (new edition with added prefaces) (New York: Harcourt Brace Jovanovich). This is Arendt's first major book and endures as a major treatise on this 'novel' form of government that emerged in Europe in the middle of the twentieth-century.

Arendt, Hannah (1958) *The Human Condition* (Chicago: University of Chicago Press). In this text, Arendt explicates her reading of the activities of labour, work, and action that condition but not wholly determine the human world.

Arendt, Hannah (1968a [1963]) *Eichmann in Jerusalem: a Report on the Banality of Evil* (New York: Viking). As discussed earlier, this is certainly Arendt's most controversial and misunderstood book. Of particular interest to students of international politics is Arendt's call for a permanent international criminal court.

Canovan, Margaret, (1992) *Hannah Arendt: A Reinterpretation of Her Political Thought* (Cambridge: Cambridge University Press). This is one of the most important books in the secondary literature on Arendt. It places her writing in its proper historical context and shows how her later writing on revolution, political freedom, politics and morality were all shaped by her encounter with totalitarianism.

Lang Jr., Anthony F. and Williams, John (eds) (2005) *Hannah Arendt and International Relations: Readings across the Lines* (London: Palgrave Press). This is the first edited volume that consciously brings together the concerns of international political theory and Arendt's thought.

Owens, Patricia (2007) *Between War and Politics: International Relations and the Thought of Hannah Arendt* (Oxford: Oxford University Press). This book shows how Arendt's writing was fundamentally rooted in her understanding of war and its political significance. It assesses the full range of Arendt's historical and conceptual writing on war and introduces to international theory the distinct language she used to talk about war and the political world.

Roundtable on Hannah Arendt and Owens' *Between War and Politics: International Relations and the Thought of Hannah Arendt* (Oxford: Oxford University Press, 2007), *International Politics* Vol. 45, no. 6 (2008/9 forthcoming). The contributions are by Helen M. Kinsella ('Arendt and Analogies'), Richard Beardsworth ('Arendt and the Critique of Moralism'), Anthony Burke ('Recovering Humanity from Man: Hannah Arendt's Troubled Cosmopolitanism') and a reply by Owens ('Humanity, Sovereignty and the Camps').

Young-Bruehl, Elisabeth (1982) *Hannah Arendt: For Love of the World* (New Haven: Yale University Press). This is the award-winning definitive biography of Hannah Arendt written by one of her former students. It is a beautifully written account of not only Arendt's life but the historical and intellectual context of her most important political ideas.

4 Alain Badiou

Claudia Aradau

Alain Badiou became known to the English-speaking world particularly after the translation of his book on ethics. Following the publication of *Ethics: An Essay on the Understanding of Evil*, an upsurge in translations and exegetical work has ensued. Many of his books from the eighties and nineties have been rapidly translated into English, including the *magnum opus, Being and Event*, which sets out Badiou's theoretical framework. The sequel to *Being and Event, Logiques des mondes* [The Logic of Worlds], has been almost immediately translated into English. While translations and sophisticated analyses of his philosophical concepts have become abundant, Badiou's work has been much less interrogated for current political issues. 'Think[ing] through our actuality in the terms provided by Badiou' (Bosteels 2004: 164) is the task that international relations would need to take up too. Given the relatively recent discovery of Badiou's work in the English-speaking world, his theoretical ideas have only minimally informed questions of international politics.

Nonetheless, Badiou's theory and political engagement have always been intimately entwined. His speculative work has led to the formation of the militant organisation, *Organisation politique*, which works for direct political interventions in contemporary issues (migration, labour, 'new' wars, anti-terrorism), while the political events of May 1968 and the Chinese Cultural Revolution have left their imprint upon Badiou's theoretical development. His interventions have also attempted to dismantle the taken-for-granted opinions regarding current political events and rethink the current conjuncture from the struggle of *sans papiers* and the intervention in Kosovo to the war in Iraq or the election of Nikolas Sarkozy in France.

Badiou has defined his philosophical and political endeavour as a reconstruction of concepts and of the field of philosophy. His aim is to reconstruct concepts for a politics of radical innovation. In an interview with Bruno Bosteels, 'Can Change be Thought?' Badiou declared that his work is concerned with understanding how the new happens in particular situations:

> My unique philosophical question, I would say, is the following: can we think that there is something new in the situation, not outside the situation nor the new somewhere else, but can we really think through novelty

and treat it in the situation? The system of philosophical answers that I elaborate, whatever its complexity may be, is subordinated to that question and to no other (Badiou and Bosteels 2005: 252).

For Badiou, the question is not what happens that is important, but 'what happens that is new?' This concern with change, with the new, appears to situate Badiou in the lineage of Louis Althusser, Michel Foucault and Gilles Deleuze. For him, politics (understood as innovation, the 'new') is not the expression of reality, but a process of separation from reality (Badiou 2005). At the heart of Badiou's theoretical work there is an opposition between Being and Event, between 'what is' and what we can know on the one hand, and what can intervene within this order and change it. Through the creative conceptualisation of how the 'new' happens in a situation, Badiou offers one of the most challenging theoretical frameworks available today for under-standing transformation and resistance in politics.

Short biography and intellectual trajectory

Born in Rabat in 1937, Alain Badiou was a student of Althusser at the *École Normale Supérieure*. Like Jacques Rancière, Badiou was attracted to Althusser's philosophy to later on depart from it in an innovative philoso-phical system. His work has been influenced by the debates taking place in Marxism, structuralism, psychoanalysis and the history of science. Badiou's theoretical positions have also been shaped by the political events of May 1968, the Chinese Cultural Revolution and the fight against the colonial war in Algeria at the end of the 1950s and beginning of the 1960s. In *Ethics*, Badiou explains that his Maoist period involved a double allegiance, both to the Cultural Revolution in China, and May 1968 in France. The fidelity to these two events entails a rethinking of politics as a process of convictions, of principles and of direct organization. This fidelity emerges out of the impasses of party politics and the associational mediation between workers and intellectuals. Badiou clearly depicts the political failure of the Cultural Revolution and the need for a novel form of practicing politics:

> the Cultural Revolution, even in its very impasse, bears witness to the impossibility truly and globally to free politics from the framework of the party-state that imprisons it. It marks an irreplaceable experience of saturation, because a violent will to find a new political path, to relaunch the revolution, and to find new forms of workers' struggle under the formal conditions of socialism ended up in failure when confronted with the necessary maintenance, for reasons of public order and the refusal of war, of the general frame of the party-state (Badiou 2006c: 321).

In 1968, Badiou co-founded the *Union des communists de France marxistes-leninistes* (UCFML), a Maoist organization. Since 1985, he has been one of the leading members of *Organisation politique* together with the philosophers Sylvain Lazarus and Natasha Michel and has contributed to their bulletin *La distance politique* (renamed more recently simply *Le Journal politique*). In the wake of the failure of party politics, the *Organisation politique* represents the political invention of post-party organization that explores the possibility of political action without reliance upon party representation (liable to corruption) or mass movements (liable to fatigue) (Hallward 2002).

The fidelity to political events that has shaped Badiou's intellectual trajectory is imbricated with his fidelity to three philosophical masters: Sartre, Lacan and Althusser. From Sartre, he took the idea of subjective freedom as nothingness and followed Lacan in undertaking an analysis of the universal logic of the subject. Although critical of Althusser's theory, he thought the latter's attempt to theorise subjectivity without a subject admirable (Badiou 1998a: 67–76). Yet, those interested in placing Badiou in the context of post-1968 French philosophy will find him interviewing Michel Foucault or contributing to the *Cahiers de la psychanalyse* to which Derrida and Lacan also contributed. Badiou's theory offers answers to problems that were being debated in the context of post-1968 philosophy. One of these crises concerned the role of Marxism and the other the role of metaphysics. From Marxism, Badiou takes both the idea of revolution and the understanding that there are 'similarities between the ambitions of emancipatory politics and the working of capital', which leads him to conclude that 'we are rivals to capital' in a struggle of universalism against universalism rather than particularism against universalism (Badiou 1998b: 120). From the debates about the end of metaphysics, Badiou engages with the discreditation of truth in the hermeneutic tradition and its replacement by discourse and opinion.

Badiou has written a number of works of philosophy, from his *magnum opus, Being and Event* (and its sequel and refinement, *Logiques des mondes*, published in French in 2006); to shorter collections and essays such as *Manifesto for Philosophy, Saint Paul, Ethics*, and *Metapolitics*. Yet, his work ranges across a much larger domain: poetry, theatre, psychoanalysis, mathematics, and political theory. His intervention on Sarkozy, the newly-elected French President (2007–), *De quoi Sarkozy est-il le nom?* [The meaning of Sarkozy] has become a bestseller, with more than 20,000 copies sold in France in one year.

What is an event? Philosophical motifs

Badiou's philosophy, Hallward has argued, 'is nothing but polemical' (Hallward 2004: 1). His theoretical work explicitly distances itself from and polemicises with much of the French post-1968 philosophy. In the introduction to *Logiques des mondes,* Badiou presents his philosophical project as a polemics with what he calls 'democratic materialism', namely the conviction that there are only bodies and language (Badiou 2006b). Badiou's self-styled 'materialist dialectics' undermines this by adding the conviction that 'there are truths'. The third element, truth, is part of a philosophical triad that condenses the thought of novelty in Badiou's philosophy: event, truth and the subject. None of these elements is given, they are the result of a process that brings about change and breaks with the *status quo*.

In *Being and Event*, Badiou offers the most systematic thinking of the relationship between being and change (or what he names 'event'). Badiou's theory of the event is underpinned by his mathematical ontology. 'Mathematics as ontology' does not attempt to represent being, but to capture the processes through which being as inconsistent multiplicity becomes consistent or One. By subtracting itself from the rule and meaning of any particular language, mathematics, particularly set theory, offers a way of thinking the multiplicity of being-*qua*-being, being that is not defined by any qualities or predicates ('one is *x*'), but is self-predicating. Substituting being without substance for the being of history allows Badiou to avoid the pessimism of the Maoist position that political consciousness was coextensive with the reality of the world (Hallward 2003: 51). 'Mathematics as ontology' rejects any reconciliation or adequacy between the material world and our ideas. Through mathematics, Badiou overturns the Kantian question: 'How is pure mathematics possible?' – 'Through recourse to a transcendental subject' to 'Since pure mathematics is the ontology of being, how is the subject possible?' (Badiou 2006a: 6).

The problem to which Badiou's 'mathematical turn' offers an answer is how to think the multiplicity of being when Being is not One. Ontology, through recourse to mathematics, 'prescribes the most general rules whereby we can present as a particular thing, i.e. treat or count as *one* thing, something that, before it was thus unified or counted, was neither unified nor particular' (Hallward 2003: 5). If the One does not exist, then what exists is only an operation of the count-as-one (Badiou 2006a: 24). Ontology presents being as doubly inconsistent and unitary. Being is simple and inconsistent multiplicity. Nonetheless, to become intelligible, this multiplicity needs to be subjected to a process of becoming-one. Multiplicity must be counted-as-one, yet oneness is never a characteristic of being. The theory of mathematical sets allows Badiou to think this process of counting multiplicity as one. Sets are simply multiples which have no predefined forms. A set can incorporate a multiple in different ways which do not need to predetermine its contents.

A simple presented multiplicity is named a *situation*. Situations can range from language, society, state to the factory, urban areas or migration. There are two operations that are at work in a situation: firstly, through presentation, a situation counts the elements which belong to it and secondly, representation recounts these elements to render them as parts of the situation. The first operation involves an 'inconsistent multiplicity', while the second leads to a 'consistent multiplicity' (Bosteels 2005). Oneness is only a retroactive function that orders inconsistent multiplicity. The second operation leads to what Badiou calls the *state of the situation*. Each situation needs to be counted and transformed into a state of the situation, into consistent multiplicity. Thus, there is a difference between situations to which a multiplicity of elements *belong* and the state of the situation which *includes* particular elements. A situation is composed of the knowledge that circulates in it and assigns a place to different elements, thus including them in the consistency of one: 'The state of the situation is the operation which, within the situation, codifies its parts as sub-sets' (Badiou 2004b: 154).

The state of the situation can be conceptualised as similar to Foucault's notion of power/knowledge. Although Hallward has criticised Badiou for lacking a concept of hegemony as in Gramsci or of power as in Foucault, Badiou's definition of the 'state of the situation' can be seen in Foucauldian terms. After all, Badiou makes clear that the situation is structured by virtue of knowledge (*savoir*) and it is impossible to de-link *savoir* from the Foucauldian power/knowledge. The role of representation and of the state – which is the power of representation – is to turn simple multiplicity into the consistency of sub-parts. In *Being and Event*, both 'State' and 'state' are used to refer to the processes of counting-as-one. 'State' is capitalised following the usage of the French *État*. While the state of the situation involves a counting-as-one, the counting is not limited to social relations. Hence, State refers particularly to the political counting and representation of elements in a situation. A situation can also simply be a building, with all the elements that need to be counted to make a building functional. But the nation is also a situation to which a multiplicity of elements belong, but in which only particular categories are included. Citizens would be counted as natives, naturalised, asylum-seekers, second generation migrants etc. with particular relations being assumed among these various categories. Certain categories, however, cannot be integrated in a consistent multiplicity. Foreigners, for example, would not be counted as included in this representation of the nation.

In this context defined by set theory, Badiou's question is: how can something new emerge when the multiplicity is counted-as-one? As ontology is a situation, mathematics cannot answer this question. While mathematics can allow us to think *what is*, it is the role of philosophy to think *what happens*. The new emerges through the event, in the gap between presentation and representation. This question is probably the most unsettling political question that we are faced with: how can resistance happen, how can new political forms and subjects emerge when the world is 'counted-as-one' in various ways (for example, as globalisation, neoliberalism or 'war on terror')? Badiou's dialectics of presentation/representation, belonging/inclusion, situation/state makes explicit the operation of power which tames inconsistent multiplicity into the consistent representation of the One. Through a double count, presentation and representation, the State constitutes elements that are included in the situation and simultaneously has to deny elements that might disturb the rules of this inclusion. The role of the State is therefore one of ordering, expelling excess, and preventing inconsistency. Yet, this operation of power never completely includes all the elements that belong. Presentation is 'larger' than representation and fixing elements under the count-as-one is shown as an unstable operation that can be disrupted.

For Badiou, the event is the moment of rupturing the rules of counting-as-one and exposing the consistent multiplicity ordered by the State as inconsistent. The event does not emerge from the void, it is not a total rupture or completely new beginning. The event is connected with the elements that are excessive in the representation of a situation. They are excessive inasmuch as they cannot be included in the count-as-one and, nonetheless, they belong to the situation. Irregular migrants, for example, are represented as excessive to the count of the citizens of the nation-state. In the representational operation of power, they should not be there, as they unsettle the uniform rule of state counting based on territorial and substantive definitions of the nation. Singular elements are anomalies for the State and only exist in a process of 'internal exclusion'. While the State attempts to keep things in place, singular elements contain the potential threat of disruption.

The event qualifies as *an immanent break*: it proceeds in the situation and it surpasses the situation (Badiou 2002a: 42). Events take place in four domains: politics, love, science and art. Badiou's typical examples include the French revolution, falling in love, or a scientific discovery. The 1789 French Revolution was an event that could not be thinkable from within the structure of the *ancien régime*. The revolution ruptured the power relations that characterised the relationship between the aristocracy and the people and re-created an egalitarian relationship of rights. No matter how much knowledge we might have about the *ancien régime*, this will not allow us to understand the event of 1789. Rather, the French Revolution needs to be understood as an event that is both situated in the circumstances of the French society in the eighteenth century and supplementary to them (Badiou 2006a: 180). The French Revolution makes clear that an event is not any disruption, but a disruption that is informed by the principles of equality and universality. The French Revolution addressed everybody in that situation as a political subject and enacted the principle of equality. As the next section will show in more detail, Badiou's concept of equality is derived from the ontology of multiplicities and posits the unqualified equality of everybody with everybody else.

An event also creates a *truth* that renders the knowledge characteristic of the situation ineffective. Truth is not about interpretation, but about exposing the gaps in our understanding. Truth takes place and in so doing it convokes new subjects who will sustain it. For Badiou, truth is not the effect of a regime of power/knowledge as with Foucault, but what disrupts that regime. While knowledge is only repetition, truth is the consequence of an event that brings about the 'new' in a situation. Rather than being subordinated to power, truth disrupts power and what is given. Badiou's examples of truths range from the appearance of tragedy with Aeschylus, and of mathematical logic with Galileo, to the French Revolution. A truth can only be sparked by an event. 'Something must happen', notes Badiou, 'in order for there to be something new. Even in our personal lives, there must be an encounter, there must be something which cannot be calculated, predicted or managed, there must be a break based only on chance' (Badiou 1998b: 124). The encounter leading to two people falling in love gives rise to the truth of love – thus truth cannot be explained to an outsider, it cannot be predicted and only exists as long as the lovers remain faithful to the contingent encounter that has disrupted and redefined their lives. Truth, subject and event are part of the same process of inscribing the new into a situation and disrupting the order of things. A *subject* emerges simultaneously with an event and the process of sustaining its truth.

The opposition between Being and Event, between 'what is' and radical innovation is the basis for Badiou's critique of concepts that have been used to make sense of the world and transform it. Evil and equality are two concepts related to the emergence of the new, the event, which can clarify the potential of Badiou's system for rethinking international politics today.

Political consequences

Evil

Evil is one of the concepts that have resurfaced in the wake of 9/11. 'Our responsibility to history', President Bush told us in the wake of the September 11 2001 terrorist attacks, 'is already clear: to answer these attacks and rid the world of evil' (Bush 2001). Badiou's theory of the new refuses Evil as the starting point of a politics of protection and offers a different understanding of political action and critique of the new ideology of Evil. According to Badiou, Evil cannot be the starting point of politics, as political action commences with an event or the Good. What, then, is Evil?

Rather than simply a category of classification into Good and Evil, normal and abnormal, Evil is a modification of a truth-event. While the current invocations of Evil in the 'war on terror' close off understanding by providing a shorthand path to the understanding of the world, Badiou's concept of Evil allows us to reappraise what is at stake in these debates about Evil. The so-called 'self-evidence' of Evil in contemporary societies leads to an understanding of Good as the opposite of Evil. Whatever is not Evil, must be Good. This situation is linked with the failure of the social movements in the 1960s and the infamous 'end of history' pronounced by Francis Fukuyama at the end of the Cold War. Liberalism appeared to be the dominant ideology marking the 'end of history', because criticism of liberalism was suspended, its flaws hidden by the imaginary of worse possibilities. Badiou's diagnosis is unrelenting: Evil is used not simply as a label that divides the world into 'us' and 'them', but as a thoroughly conservative strategy that attempts to suspend critique and the transformation of liberal societies:

> Sure, they say, we may not live in a condition of perfect Goodness. But we're lucky that we don't live in a condition of Evil. Our democracy is not perfect. But it's better than the bloody dictatorships. Capitalism is

unjust. But it's not criminal like Stalinism. We let millions of Africans die of AIDS, but we don't make racist nationalist declarations like Milosevic. We kill Iraqis with our airplanes, but we don't cut their throats with machetes like they do in Rwanda, etc. (Badiou 2002b).

In light of the conservatism which Evil is summoned to sustain, Badiou argues that Evil is not the absence of Good, but the degradation of Good. Therefore, politics can no longer start from Evil, which appears to be self-evident, but needs to start from a conception of Good. 'There can be Evil', Badiou argues in *Ethics*, only 'insofar as there precedes a Good' (Badiou 2002a: 71). Good and Evil can only be thought in political situations of 'the invention and the exercise of an absolutely new and concrete reality' (Badiou 2002b).

Rather than Evil being the imperative for political action as it is in world politics today, Good should be the premise of action. Good arises with the production of universal truths through the occurrence of events, while Evil emerges through the failure of truth-processes to live up to the principles of equality and universality that give them their political content. Evil is not to be found on the side of the perceptible, of experience, but it is a form of thought. Badiou claims that it is important to think political events such as Nazism as Evil. Rather than a suspension of thought as the labelling of Evil appears to entail in current politics, Badiou offers an understanding of the political possibility of Evil.

Political interventions usually start with the naming of Evil and its isolation. The Good is supposed to follow in its turn: humanitarian disasters, genocide, terrorism, emergencies, famine are all concrete occurrences that are identified as Evil. Hence humanitarian intervention, upholding human rights and creating international courts, anti-terrorism measures and humanitarian relief missions are rendered as the Good. Badiou reverses the relationship and argues that we need to start by thinking the Good, i.e. the event in a situation. What would a political event be in the series of situations identified as Evil? Only from the position of the event can we consider what Evil is.

Simulacrum, betrayal and *disaster* are the names of Evil. Simulacrum is the Evil that results out of an event that attempts to become total and is inscribed within the confines of a community. Nazism is the example *par excellence* of the perversion of Good by inscribing it within the particularity of a community. Political events need to address everybody and be based on unqualified equality. Nazism, on the other hand, created a '*völkisch* community of the unequal and the unfree' (Adorno 2005b), in which the 'warmth' and togetherness of the community appeared as a liberation from the alienation and coldness of capitalism. Yet, by creating a community of the unequal instead of prescribing the unqualified equality of everybody with everybody, Nazism becomes a simulacrum and Evil. The simulacrum as the pseudo-event that is closed upon the particularity of community reveals the contradictions of identity politics. Identity politics can only result in pseudo-events, simulacra that limit claims and restrict the universal address of an event.

Events can never be identified with a predetermined social particularity and need to remain open.

Betrayal refers to the Evil that is the result of weakness or fatigue in subjects and is perhaps the easiest category of Evil. Subjects who need to be faithful to the 'new' that the event brings about can withdraw from participation in an event or can renounce the interpretation of situations from the vantage point of an event. Betrayal is the evil of former revolutionaries who renounce their ideals and become acquiescent to the dominant order of things.

Finally, *disaster* refers to the absolutisation of a truth-event. If simulacrum is the closure of universality upon the particularity of community, race or tradition, disaster is the 'coercive universalization' of an event (Dews 2004: 112). Just as situations have elements that are not represented, events have an element which cannot be analysed, the 'unnameable'. Events must resist the omnipotence of truths, they cannot proceed to the 'refoundation of the world' but need to happen within a world. The unnameable of politics is the community. For political events to continue as a process, the community must remain unnameable and not particularised.

Equality

Equality is another of Badiou's concepts whose reconceptualisation bears important implications for thinking politics and, perhaps even more urgently, for rethinking international politics. Equality is the principle that gives content to the new, to the event that happens. For Badiou, equality is simply the principle of belonging in a situation as all elements of a multiple belong in exactly the same way. As the 'true' principle of being-*qua*-being, equality is also the only principle of political engagement. Yet, equality is exactly the concept that is most unsettling for international political theory as well as political practice.

First, with liberalism, equality is deferred, turned into a goal to be achieved, while liberty is seen as primary. The political liberalism of equality is further undermined by economic liberalism. Only limited equality is desirable/ possible in liberalism, as inequality itself is considered to be the motor of capitalist development. The only equality that is allowed is the equality of the market. We can all enter the market and we are all exposed to the same goods in the shop windows. The equality of the market that does not exclude anybody (there is no outside to the market in neo-liberalism, everybody is potentially included) obliterates the forms of inequality that market practices of competition entail. For Badiou, the equality of the market is one of the nihilisms of the century:

> The same product is offered everywhere. Armed with this universal commercial offer, contemporary 'democracy' can forge a subject from such abstract equality: the consumer; the one who, in his or her virtuality opposite the commodity, is ostensibly identical to any other in his

or her abstract humanity as buying power. ... The principle is that anyone who is able to buy – as a matter of right – anything being sold is the equal of anyone else (Badiou 2004a: 161).

Badiou rejects this common mistrust of equality in liberalism and makes it the 'word for politics'. As the principle of belonging in the same way to a multiplicity, equality cannot be substantive and needs to remain unqualified. Equality does not presuppose a closure, does not qualify the terms it refers to and does not prescribe a territory on which to be exercised (Badiou 1992: 242).

Equality is de-linked from the social, from the idea of redistribution, solidarity or the state's solicitude towards difference, as any programmatic use would entail a closure of equality upon identity or community. *Contra* the liberal dogma, equality must not be equated with equality of status, of wages, of functions or even less with the supposedly egalitarian dynamics of contracts and reforms (Badiou 2004a: 71). It cannot be objective and it has nothing to do with the social. Any definitional and programmatic approach to equality transforms it into a dimension of State action (Badiou 2004a: 73). Thus, equality is a prescription, not 'what we want or what we project, but what we declare in the heat of the event, here and now, as what it is, and not what it should be' (Badiou 2004a). Therefore, equality cannot be defined, but only affirmed in the process of an event. When women affirm equality with men, this is not a question of how much, when and for whom. Equality is asserted as unqualified and unconditioned and the only political question is 'What can be done' in the name of this principle? (Hallward 2003: 228).

Innovative political interventions need to be faithful to the principle of unqualified equality. In discussing the situation in former Yugoslavia, Badiou argued that lasting peace requires the relinquishing of all ethnic and religious identity to the creation of a state that counts all people like one (Badiou 2006c). What is needed in the post-Yugoslav situation is actually a fidelity to the event of the constitution of Yugoslavia through the anti-fascist struggle of the Second World War. The anti-fascisct struggle was a struggle for popular liberation that did not concern 'only one people, one nation, but all the nations and peoples within the repressive monarchical order, all the people who bear the stamp of oppression, whether class, national, sexual, religious' (Pupovac 2006: 16). The intervention of the *Organisation politique* concerning the *sans papiers* is based on a similarly egalitarian prescription that applies to everybody: 'everyone who is here is from here'. In an intervention against Sarkozy's politics in France, Badiou (2007) argued that the prescription for international politics should be 'there is one world'. In the face of blatant inequalities and the assumption at the heart of both domestic and international politics that there are different worlds defined by cultural, religious and economic disparities, politics needs to follow the consequences of an assertion of the oneness of the world.

While the constitution of the international is based on the inegalitarian delimitation of inside and outside, citizens and strangers, natives and aliens,

Badiou's theory allows us to bring back unqualified equality by simply considering the international as another situation, a counted multiplicity. Prescriptions of equality are therefore *breaks* within 'what is' internally as well as internationally. They are ruptures in the inegalitarian constitution of divisions, hierarchies and forms of separation. Asserting that 'there is one world' means breaking with the all the governmental discourses that claim that some people come from a different world or that people living in Europe are still from a different world.

Egalitarian prescriptions reconstruct situations by disrupting the operation of power. They could be particularly interesting for security studies, where questions of security exclude a politics of equality. As security is a practice of creating divisions and separating categories of population, critical engagements with the securitisation of social and political problems would be well-advised to consider the implications of a politics of equality. I have argued elsewhere that 'politics out of security' can only start with the principle of unqualified equality (Aradau 2008). The situation of trafficking in women under scrutiny there could be transformed not by starting with the naming of victims and identification of Evil, but with the prescription of equality from the site of the 'internally excluded' element. The anomalous position of illegal migrant sex workers, those who are neither sex workers nor victims of trafficking according to the State's count-as-one, makes the equality of work the political prescription that interrupts the legitimation of security practices.

Conclusion

A politics of events, truth and subjects could inform research in international relations about the possibilities of political transformation. Badiou's theory of the event offers conceptual tools to assess what is new and radically innovative in global politics, and simultaneously to understand what is simply a modification of 'what is' rather than a rupture of particular situations. Claims about the changes brought about by anti-globalisation movements, cosmopolitan ideals or humanitarian principles need to be considered in light of events which establish belonging as the unqualified equality of all. I have shown how two concepts, one that describes the corruption of events (Evil) and the other that provides the very substance of events (equality) can come to be inscribed upon the thinking of international politics. These brief discussions show how questions of political novelty, of subjects and of progressive politics can be reconsidered within international relations.

Politics, in Badiou's theory and praxis, starts with clear prescriptions that are supplementary to situations by asserting the unqualified equality of everybody with everybody. If the encounter with Badiou's work can be thought of as an event, then fidelity to this event would mean thinking more and more situations in the terms offered by Badiou and proposing political prescriptions of unqualified equality against 'what is' and what is assumed as necessarily inegalitarian or different.

Further reading

Works by Badiou

Badiou, Alain (2002a) *Ethics. An Essay on the Understanding of Evil*, London: Verso. This book was intended for high-school students in France and was written, according to Badiou, in less than two weeks. While the style is highly polemical, the book undertakes to make explicit the application of Badiou's ontology to current political issues, particularly liberal interventionism in the 1990s. *Ethics* also introduces the question of Evil, which for Badiou is understood not as the opposite of Good, but as the transformation of Good.

Badiou, Alain (2004a) *Infinite Thought. Truth and the Return of Philosophy*, London: Continuum. Oliver Feltham and Justin Clemens have put together a series of essays that explore the intersection of philosophy with politics, psychoanalysis, desire, or cinema. If philosophy is 'thought under condition', therefore in relation to what happens somewhere else, philosophy also proposes 'tools and knives' for what happens to resist what is given.

Badiou, Alain (2006c) *Polemics*, trans. Steve Corcoran, London: Verso. This is a collection of essays that covers a series of interventions that Badiou made about current political issues and taken-for-granted political ideas. Essays on the 9/11 attacks, riots in the French *banlieues* or the function of democracy nowadays all form philosophical *breaks* with the knowledge and the norms of our current political situation.

Badiou, Alain (2006a) *Being and Event*, trans. Oliver Feltham, London: Continuum. Although Badiou's *magnum opus* was translated into English 20 years after its publication of French, it will not cease to surprise its new readers. Bearing similarities in intent and 'heaviness' to Heidegger's *Being and Time*, this book might appear intimidating to those not familiar with Badiou's work. However, it is the best way to clarify concepts and the details of his philosophical framework.

Secondary literature

Hallward, Peter (2004) *Badiou. Subject to Truth*, Minneapolis: University of Minnesota Press. Hallward's book is the most comprehensive introduction to Badiou's work in the Anglo-Saxon world. Hallward documents the historical context of Badiou's writing and offers clear discussions of Badiou's philosophy, pointing out questions to be asked and inconsistencies to be considered.

Aradau, Claudia (2008) *Rethinking Trafficking in Women. Politics out of Security*, Basingstoke: Palgrave Macmillan. This book reconsiders the situation of trafficking in women through Badiou's theory of the event and offers an understanding of how an innovative politics can emerge out of the site of securitisation.

5   Jean Baudrillard

François Debrix

Jean Baudrillard's thought is terrifying for many scholars of politics who wish to explore it or apply it to their work. No critical theorist in the last fifty years has been as uncompromising about the critical thought process that has to accompany any analysis of political reality as Baudrillard. Yet, as unaccommodating as his writings appear to be, Baudrillard's theoretical investigations are also some of the most open and free-rolling that one can find in contemporary theory. Baudrillard's works are invitations never to accept what is given or, rather, never to take for granted whatever reality is presented to us, observers of the global political scene. Baudrillard insists on initiating pathways of thinking that place the possibility of a challenge, or *défi*, at the high point of any critical endeavour. Truth, reality, and facts as they are imposed by meaning and representation systems must be challenged, sometimes by way of representational terror, or by unleashing the excessive energy of that which the system seeks to control in the first place.

Thus, Baudrillard's writings thrill and bore, please and upset, liberate and frighten, no doubt because they incessantly waver between reality and irony, senseless action and brilliant illusion, mobilization and indifference, transformative possibility and stark fatalism, and intellectual assurance and radical uncertainty. To some, Baudrillard is a threat to safe thinking. He is *the* postmodern 'intellectual impostor' who mobilizes words or sentences 'devoid of meaning' (Sokal and Bricmont 1998: 142). Worse yet, he is the kind of thinker who celebrates 'moral and political nihilism' (Norris 1992: 194). To others, Baudrillard has to be championed as the 'most intransigent' of the French theorists (Hegarty 2004: 1). His writing is a 'theoretical feast: an explosive moment of modernity in which the rationalist eschatology of the times is first revealed, and then subverted' (Kroker 1992: 56). Among most theorists, however, puzzlement and indecision prevail. Most of the time, whether they admit it or not, social and political thinkers do not quite know what to make of his words and ideas. As Zygmunt Bauman recognizes, 'the universe Baudrillard's vocabulary sustains is set in a different domain of experience, ... [one that] does not communicate with the realm of sociologically processed perceptions' (Bauman 1993: 23).

International relations scholars have adopted a similar posture. Since they do not know how to deal with Baudrillard, they simply ignore him. Or, when pressed, they make a passing reference to some of his concepts. Thus, when a few critical international relations theorists find the courage to study Baudrillard's work and choose to embark upon the kind of conceptual challenges Baudrillard invites us to undertake, their writings deserve to stand out. It is toward highlighting the Baudrillard-inspired critical analyses of a few contemporary international relations thinkers that this essay moves. Still, the first part of this essay clarifies Baudrillard's challenging thought and seeks to explain how it can be beneficial to students and scholars in international relations – and, beyond, to observers of the political scene – who are interested in confronting the violence of the global.

From the critique of value to the violence of the global

Jean Baudrillard was born in Reims, France in 1929. Raised in a lower middle-class family (with both peasantry and civil service/regional bureaucracy roots), Baudrillard was the first member of his family to pursue studies beyond the *baccalauréat* (French terminal high school degree). While he had hoped to join the *École Normale Supérieure* (where many French intellectuals studied), he eventually ended up studying German literature in Paris (*La Sorbonne* university), and his first job was as a German language high school teacher. Baudrillard's first publications were reviews and translations of works by Peter Weiss and Bertolt Brecht. With the help of Henri Lefebvre and Roland Barthes, Baudrillard's interests shifted towards sociological theory, and he started teaching sociology at the University of Nanterre (near Paris) in 1966. His early works, *The System of Objects* (1996a [1968]), *The Consumer Society* (1998 [1970]), and *For a Critique of the Political Economy of the Sign* (1981 [1970]), were driven by a desire to go beyond conventional Marxist theory. His initial intention was to provide sustained critical analyses of contemporary culture that would de-emphasize the conceptual importance of use-value and production and, instead, would highlight the role of representation, sign-systems, and objective signification. In *For a Critique*, Baudrillard moved away from Marxist analyses by developing a theory of signification, utility, and representation that 'combines a critique of political economy ... with one of the sign ... to fabricate a critique that can speak to a generalized political economy' (Hegarty 2004: 24). As Baudrillard explained, whereas 'the process of production and systematization of economic exchange value has been described as essential, ... [an] equally generalized process has been largely neglected: ... the transmutation of economic exchange value into sign exchange value' (Baudrillard 1981: 113). According to sociologist Mike Gane, Baudrillard's 1960's search for a political economy of sign production already demonstrated his knack for thinking beyond structures and categorizations (Gane 2000: 5). His initial intellectual endeavours were already influenced by a disposition to push critical explorations towards the excess, the radically other, or the 'accursed share' of any meaning, value, or sign system.

An important moment in Baudrillard's intellectual trajectory is the publication of his *Symbolic Exchange and Death* (1993a [1976]). In this volume, Baudrillard turns to philosopher Georges Bataille's notion of the 'accursed share' (Bataille 1991) and to anthropologist Marcel Mauss' idea of the consumption of objects as a sacrificial gift (Mauss 1990) with a view towards providing a critique of value and meaning systems in general. Baudrillard's implication is that modern society and culture have been taken over by the logic of value (from use to sign) and exchange (of goods and products, but also of meaning and knowledge). The logic of value and exchange is all about subjects: creating them, maintaining them, and sustaining them. The object is reified as that which must be possessed, accumulated, or exchanged by subjects. This system of proliferation of value and exhaustion of meaning is premised upon the erasure of the symbolic. The symbolic, for Baudrillard, is both what is excluded from value and what can return to haunt value. While the symbolic may be taken to function as a sort of vengeful reality, one that stubbornly wants to be restored, the possibilities of such a return are limited. For Baudrillard, 'the symbolic still haunts [modern social institutions] as the prospect of their own demise'. But 'this is only an obsessive memory, a demand ceaselessly repressed by the law of value' (Baudrillard 1988a: 119).

What accentuates this seemingly impossible return to the symbolic is what Baudrillard sees as the 'growing fluctuating indeterminacy' (Baudrillard 1988a: 120) of the social. Such indeterminacy is the result of everyday reality having been engulfed in structures, systems, and models of production, representation, and signification. As early as in *Symbolic Exchange*, Baudrillard refers to this total absorption and reprocessing of the reality principle in value and meaning systems as a matter of 'hyperreality' and 'simulation'. In a context of hyperreality (where simulation is the only possible horizon of appearances for both objects and subjects), the symbolic and its 'accursed share' have no choice but to manifest themselves as simulated realities. Yet, because simulation is precisely about uncertainty and indeterminacy, the challenge itself (the possibility of a return to a so-called genuine reality) may never be distinguishable from the (hyper)reality that emanates from the dominant model or code. Thus, in simulation, the condition of reversibility of the system can never be guaranteed. These considerations form the bulk of Baudrillard's analyses in a series of works (*Forget Foucault* (1987 [1977]), *Seduction* (1990a [1979]), *Simulacra and Simulation* (1983a [1981]), *Fatal Strategies* (1990b [1983]), *America* (1988b [1986]), *Cool Memories* (1990c [1987]), *The Gulf War Did Not Take Place* (1995 [1991]), or *The Illusion of the End* (1994 [1992])) for which he is perhaps best known.

In *Simulacra and Simulation*, Baudrillard develops his argument about hyperreality and the power of the simulacrum. This is the part of Baudrillard's

theory that scholars of domestic and international politics have emphasized the most, no doubt because one of Baudrillard's applications of simulation has been the practice and imagery of war and military deterrence.
Simulation is, for Baudrillard, a reflection on reality, or rather on what is
left of it once meaning, value, and sign systems, codes, models, or media
have swallowed it up. For Baudrillard, simulation emerges as an attempt (by
media and models) to recreate reality according to the codes generated by
the models and media themselves. There is, thus, a certain objective intentionality to the deployment of the simulacrum, or an attempt at imposing
another dominant reality as if it were the only one, the 'truly real' one (albeit
one for which referentiality is no longer naturally given but, instead, found
within the code or sign system itself). This is what Baudrillard expresses
in *Simulation* when, taking as a point of departure the representational
relationship between the territory and the map, he writes that 'simulation is
no longer that of a territory, a referential being or substance. It is the generation by models of a real without origin or reality: a hyperreal' (Baudrillard
1983: 2).

When meaning and value explode with the take-over of the social by sign
value, there no longer are certain criteria for what counts as reality. Simulation seeks to restore referentiality, but by way of more simulacral models, or
through a succession of *trompe l'oeil* mechanisms (*trompe l'oeil* literally
means 'fooling the eye') (Baudrillard 1990a). Instead of returning the social
to referentiality or representation, simulation propagates more hyperreality
(of signs), more undecidability (of meaning), and more uncertainty (of
value). Indeed, even when it operates as a desperate attempt at retrieving
referentiality, the 'more real than reality' simulacrum obliterates the 'reality
principle,' and any distinction between 'true' and 'false', 'real' and 'imaginary', or 'genuine' and 'fake' becomes impossible. Thus, while simulation may
be deployed strategically (as a technique that seeks to reaffirm a certain
reality), it ends up with the fateful disappearance of the real.

Baudrillard's famous treatment of the Gulf War in 1991 (Baudrillard
1995) follows this analytical logic. The Gulf War, Baudrillard argued, can
only make sense in the context of hyperreality, as a *trompe l'oeil* war. In
January 1991, a few weeks ahead of the military assault by allied powers
against Saddam Hussein's Iraq, Baudrillard claimed that the Gulf War
would not take place because, in his view, it had already taken place, perhaps
a hundred times over, by way of models, media, and military simulations
that played out all possible scenarios even before any of the events could
unfold. Once the war actually took place, Baudrillard wrote a subsequent
essay arguing that the war did *not* take place. Derided for his alleged failed
prediction (since the war, at some level, occurred) and accused of historical
revisionism by some (Norris 1992), Baudrillard nonetheless wrote that, for
most people in the Western world (*not* for the Iraqis, however), the Gulf War
did not take place in reality because it was impossible for the Western viewer
to distinguish between media signs and images of the war and an alleged

genuine representation of war violence there. For all the Western viewers knew, with all their technological arsenal, the media could have been shooting the Gulf War through a clever *mise-en-scène*, using props and actors, in some studio somewhere, or better yet, in the secret underground tunnels of the White House, for example (an ironic and humorous possibility that the popular film *Wag the Dog* – which is not about the Gulf War but about media simulation in general – evokes).

Much of Baudrillard's writing from the 1980s and early 1990s can be seen to be dominated by reflections on the effects of simulation and simulacra. Yet, as some Baudrillard chroniclers have suggested, Baudrillard's thought since the 1990s seems more interested in describing the fateful condition of a simulated social or political domain when simulation reaches a new stage. This new stage of simulation, an additional degree in the generation of the real by way of simulated sign systems, has been given different names by Baudrillard. Alternatively labelled the 'fractal', the 'virtual', the 'viral', or the 'transpolitical,' this additional stage of simulation, or what Baudrillard once called 'the successive phases of the image' (Baudrillard 1983: 11), corresponds to a 'fourth-order simulation'. At this level, the proliferation of simulated signs and codes in hyperreality is such that the condition of simulation can no longer be mobilized strategically. Models and media have lost control over simulation, a simulation that is no longer about 'masking the *absence* of a basic reality' (Baudrillard 1983: 11). Indeed, the fatal, fractal, virtual, or transpolitical fourth-order simulation is about a radical loss of referentiality. The simulacrum cannot even relate to the medium or model that generated it anymore. Instead, the fourth-order simulacrum 'bears no relation to any reality whatsoever' (Baudrillard 1983: 11), not even to the 'reality' reconstructed by simulation itself. It is 'a pure simulacrum' (Baudrillard 1983: 11–12), one whose meaning and reality effects are catapulted in all directions.

According to Baudrillard, the fourth-order simulation is transpolitical because all grounds for political activity have been removed. A 'state of utter confusion' takes hold (Gane 2000: 43), and endless circulation becomes the defining characteristic of this radicalized, viral, or virtual reality. As a result, it is not just the difference between the 'true' and the 'false' that is unascertainable anymore, but also the capacity to distinguish between various sign-generating models. Thus, the social, the economic, the sexual, or the aesthetic all collapse into each other, and they give rise to indifferent forms of the political. This transpolitical marks the irruption of a total 'indifference of combinations [of meaning, value, and signs] outside of any combinatory system or matrix' (Gane 2000: 43). Fatally, the only solution devised by the system out of this total indifference is to propagate even more circulatory flows of images and signs and to saturate the transpolitical mediascape with even more ungroundable truth-effects. This frenetic search for value, meaning, and truth through surpluses of simulated reality, through virtual reality, leads Baudrillard to chronicle many end-of-the-millennium non-events/

transcultural scenes (the year 2000, the spectre of new wars, the craving for genetic manipulation and cloning, virtual sex, pandemic fears) that become endlessly recyclable symptoms of the loss of the real and its transpolitical reconfiguration. In *Impossible Exchange* (2001 [1999]), Baudrillard concludes that what passes for the political today 'absorbs all that comes near it and converts it into its own substance', but also that the transpolitical is incapable of 'converting or reflecting itself into a superior reality that could give it some meaning' (Baudrillard 1999: 12; my translation). Thus, the transpolitical falls prey to an impossible exchange that takes the form of 'a growing undecidability of categories, discourses, strategies, and stakes' (Baudrillard 1999: 12; my translation).

In his late 1990s and early 2000s interventions, Baudrillard entertains the thought that the only thing that could break (even if only momentarily) this total proliferation of reality-effects is an unexpected, destabilizing, and perhaps violent irruption of the symbolic, of that which, once again, is posited as radically other to the real as generated by value, meaning, or sign systems. Thus, in an interesting fashion, the fourth-order transpolitical simulacrum inadvertently may bring back a critical, perhaps liberating, element. Indeed, when meaning and value systems fall prey to undecidability and indeterminacy, an 'uncertainty principle' seems to reappear. Hegarty suggests that, in the late 1990s, Baudrillard unveils a succession of concepts ('symbolic violence', 'radical illusion', 'radical thought', 'evil', or 'terror') that return his analyses to earlier concerns with symbolic exchange. Impossible exchange, in particular, is an ambiguous, uncertain, and dual principle (Hegarty 2004: 85). It is dual because, while it points to the fact that there is no longer any outside to simulation, it reveals that, at its culminating point, the logic of simulated reality is illusory. Thus, one can argue that, with the figure of impossible exchange, Baudrillard starts to mobilize an analytical challenge similar to that which Bataille's philosophy sought to introduce when it offered the notion of the 'accursed share'. Baudrillard's impossible exchange comes back to (re)introduce ambiguity, illusion, and undecidability into a system that has asserted total control over the social or the political through an alleged free flow and complete circulation of signs (and their hoped for regime of endless exchangeability).

It is also perhaps in the light of this impossible exchange that we need to make sense of Baudrillard's most recent interventions about 9/11, terrorism, and the violence of the global. While ideas such as 'radical evil' or the 'illusion of the end' are far from optimistic or even liberating outcomes, they are not nihilistic perspectives either. Recent observations by Baudrillard are fatal. But notions like impossible exchange, radical thought, or evil open up thinking to the possibility of a fleeting revenge of the symbolic, of that which is assumed by Baudrillard to be representationally violent and other to simulated reality. Finding an outside to simulated reality is something that a few international relations theorists have been concerned with too. I now turn to a brief exposition of how Baudrillardian themes find their way into some critical international relations theorists' texts.

International relations theorists take on Baudrillard

James Der Derian was one of the first international relations theorists seriously to involve Baudrillard's thought into post-Cold War analyses. To Der Derian, it was the sudden absence of a total enemy for the West – the United States, above all—after the Cold War and collapse of the Soviet Union that justified paying attention to Baudrillard's work on simulation (Der Derian 1994). The end of the Cold War had left a representational void or political gap for the West, particularly for US military diplomacy. After 1989, to mask the absence of the basic international relations/Cold War reality for the West/the United States (the loss of the absolute other), technologies and media of (computer-generated and visual) simulation were now relied upon (often by military commanders and war planners). What Der Derian calls 'the global power of simulation' would be deployed at the end of the 1980s and throughout the 1990s in a succession of actual conflicts (the Gulf War in 1990–91, the operation in Somalia in 1992–93) and fictive military-training exercises (by US forces on US military bases and in US military computer programs or gaming scenarios). As Der Derian claimed, the objective was to ensure, through simulation, '*the continuation of war by means of verisimilitude*' (Der Derian 1994: 193).

Der Derian's analyses benefited from Baudrillard's reflections on the role of the media in a context of hyperreal war. In *Antidiplomacy*, Der Derian pushes further Baudrillard's reading of the Gulf War as a conflict that 'did not take place'. Of the Gulf War, most viewers in the West mostly remembered 'the grainy, ghostly green images of the beginning and end' of it (Der Derian 1992: 180), or the infra-red images of camera-equipped bombs hitting a building, or the green dotted rays of light of an alleged Patriot missile crossing the Baghdad night sky. This (tele)visual simulation of the Gulf War reality did blur the distinction between reality and fiction, or war and gaming. As Der Derian provocatively asks: 'Was this a just war, or just a game?' (Der Derian 1992: 196). But, more importantly perhaps, Der Derian notes that, when there is no longer any way to tell the difference between war and its hyperreal renditions, all sorts of deaths and destructions become more acceptable. In this virtual context, it is the reality of war, the universe of violence and death that is international relations, that is simulated and deflected away since, as Der Derian powerfully affirms, 'a series of simulations [make] the killing more efficient, more unreal, more acceptable' (Der Derian 1994: 200).

Timothy Luke is another theorist whose work has been of salient importance for international relations thinking over the past two decades. In his work on nuclear deterrence towards the end of the Cold War (Luke 1989), Luke finds Baudrillard's initial critiques of the Marxist theory of use value helpful. Baudrillard's transposition of a political economy of goods and products into a generalized political economy of the sign allows international relations scholars to make sense of nuclear deterrence beyond explanations provided by traditional international relations theories. Just like everyday commodities exchanged and circulated throughout late modern capitalist society, nuclear warheads matter because of the endless chain of signs to which they are tied. Like commodities, nuclear weapons exist, matter, and have some 'currency' in international politics because of their sign exchange value. Thus, weapons deter, not just because of what they stand for value-wise (so much capacity for death production), but also because of what they represent as signs (Luke 1989: 221).

It is the sign value of nuclear deterrence (not its use value) that gives it meaning. It is because nuclear warheads can circulate and be exchanged *ad infinitum* in the semiotic political economy that they are so powerful (not as use exchange value, since the very point of nuclear deterrence is that weapons not be used). In other words, it is 'the symbolic economy of thermonuclear power' that allows conventional international relations (neo)realist theoretical models (about power politics, strategy, and national defense) to make sense (Luke 1989: 222). Luke's reading of nuclear deterrence as a sign system prepares him for his subsequent reflections on various aspects of international relations. What remains crucial to Luke's analyses is the notion that simulation is always at the heart of contemporary international political models. Strategies of simulation are what allow realist or even liberal frameworks to make sense and continue to propagate meaning-effects throughout global politics. Luke argues that traditional representational markers of international relations analysis seem to have disappeared as a result of a proliferation, intensification, and acceleration of 'transnational flows' (of ideas, goods, symbols, and money) (Luke 1991: 319). The consequence of such a perception regarding increased and perhaps unstoppable flows has been uncertainty and fear, particularly on the part of international relations analysts who have sought to maintain the geopolitical status quo and return international relations to the (semblance of) order of the Cold War era.

But this fear of a decentralization, disorganization, or even dissipation of traditional international relations/Cold War realities (state sovereignty above all), Luke remarks, is perhaps a ruse or an attempt to 'fool the eye' of the international relations observer too. The claim about the danger of deterritorialization operates as a *trompe l'oeil* mechanism, one that seeks to push the eye of the observer away from the constructed unreality or hyperreality and toward an allegedly more real or durable situation. Luke writes that traditional international relations theories in the post-Cold War era function as *trompe l'oeil* devices that hope to hide the fact that 'most contemporary nation-states now seem to run on "a logic of simulation, which has nothing to do with a logic of facts and an order of reasons"' (Luke 1993: 245). Similar to what happened with the sovereignty of Kuwait after Iraq invaded in 1990, the sovereignty of nation-states today is reliant upon circulating flows, immanently exchangeable signs, and proliferated vectors of economic, political, and cultural power that 'reside' as much in capital cities or presidential palaces as they do at the United Nations Security Council, at a

World Trade Organization ministerial summit, or in the administrative offices of the World Health Organization, the International Monetary Fund, or the International Atomic Energy Agency (1993: 246–47). Moreover, through the simulacrum offered by a seemingly re-empowered United Nations in the 1990s (Debrix 1999), 'all of the realist values of modern nation-states, such as autonomy, sovereignty, legitimacy, and power, are exalted' (Luke 1993: 246).

Luke's analysis reveals that it is difficult to think about international relations after the Cold War without taking into account Baudrillard's simulation. Baudrillard's reflections on simulation allow us to explain how international relations can continue to operate with the same old premises (sovereignty, power politics, anarchy, deterrence, and so forth) even when 'the fixed truths of realist terra firma implode in the code flux of hyperreal terra infirma' (Luke 1993: 256). When realists turn hyperrealists, the representational limits of international relations thinking can be transcended by way of simulation and yet preserved, since international relations' foundational concepts only have to retain a semblance of meaning, value, and reality.

Cynthia Weber is another key critical international relations theorist who has taken up the Baudrillardian challenge. Recalling some of Luke's reflections on the passage of international relations from realism/reality to hyperrealism/hyperreality, Weber's work suggests that it is sovereignty that is most dependent upon simulation as a certain strategy of the real. In *Simulating Sovereignty*, Weber suggests that, when the relationship between sovereignty and intervention is no longer antagonistic, sovereign power cannot be understood according to a logic of referential reality anymore, but rather according to a logic of simulation (Weber 1995: 31).

According to traditionally state-centric international relations interpretations, a military intervention into a state's territory is a typical violation of sovereignty. Sovereignty becomes meaningless when an invasion takes place. Weber argues that the dualistic relationship between intervention and sovereignty forms the basis of most international relations truths. But what if sovereignty is premised upon a series of discourses or a succession of signs that are made to stand in for sovereign power? Such was the configuration of sovereignty in the US military invasions of Granada and Panama in the 1980s. In these cases, multiple signs were relied upon to justify US intervention as the mark of the alleged sovereignty of both countries (and not as a negation of sovereignty, something that intervention traditionally would signify). Sovereignty became immanently exchangeable with intervention, and both stood as signs of each other. As Weber put it, 'it is no longer possible to oppose sovereignty and intervention because everyone seems to have a legitimate claim to sovereignty (the Panamanian people, General Noriega as *de facto* head of state, the Endara government, and the Bush Administration)' (1995: 121).

The consequences of this application of Baudrillard's simulation are drastic for sovereignty and the entire field of international politics. As Luke had intimated, the reliance upon Baudrillard's radical theorization of representation de-dramatizes state sovereignty (and the power states and their theorists derive from it). Sovereignty can no longer be the revered truth about the international system of states from which all sorts of claims to power, knowledge, or value emanate. Rather, as Weber provocatively argues, 'if sovereignty and intervention are everywhere, they are nowhere' (Weber 1995: 121).

The originality of Weber's turn to Baudrillard resides in the fact that she takes the analysis of simulation beyond a mere critical exploration of some important aspects or subsets of international relations analysis (war, military operational techniques, deterrence) and seeks to move it towards international relations' foundational truths. Baudrillard's writings matter to international relations scholars and students, Weber intimates, because they allow them to problematize the reality claims of dominant meaning and value systems. By launching this *défi*, Weber opens up a critical space where other radically minded theorists in turn can mobilize the explosive energy of Baudrillard's analyses. Some international relations scholars have jumped on this opportunity to release the force of Baudrillard's radical thought into contemporary reflections on the global (Debrix 1996; Hansen 1997; Reid 2007). These theorists have also sought to mobilize and expand more recent challenges introduced by Baudrillard (his reflections on the transpolitical or impossible exchange, for example). While such analytical applications remain close to Baudrillard's thought on simulation, they also intimate that Baudrillard's recent interventions cannot be easily ignored. As I suggest in the conclusion, there is still some room in critical international relations circles for a careful exploration of Baudrillard's turn-of-the-millennium challenging arguments.

The illusion of the global

In *The Transparency of Evil* (1993b [1990]) and *The Perfect Crime* (1996b [1995]), Baudrillard anticipates several issues that come back with full force after 9/11. The totality of simulation systems in transpolitical configurations is such that a virtual auto-immunization of Western societies from all sorts of anticipated risks and dangers provides a complete semblance of security (Baudrillard 1996b: 131–41). Such a simulated overprotection is also about performing a thorough cleansing of what Baudrillard calls death or evil from Western value systems at about the turn of the millennium. This ultimate desire to conquer or master death, evil, or the radically other (in a word, the symbolic) is what will doom Western transpolitical models (and their globalized extensions), Baudrillard incants. Outside these self-referential protective systems, the oppositional violence of the symbolic gains in strength. Its desire for revenge is accentuated by its evisceration from our virtual worlds.

According to Baudrillard, evil is not the grand metaphysical truth of some moral, ideological, or theological worldview. Evil, for Baudrillard, is the result of that which gets purged from the West's simulated models of global reality. Evil is opposed to good because transpolitical formulas in our global/

virtual universe are about making all reality look, feel, and be good. Evil, then, is what returns, what demands to be exchanged, and what asks to produce meaning. It is in this sense that evil is radical (and of the order of the symbolic too) because it is 'the filling up of the system by what it rejects' (Hegarty 2004: 82).

For Baudrillard, global thinking today is driven by this obsession with producing positive effects and proliferating good-affirming discourses and policies (about human rights, about poverty, about diseases, about war). Such a uniformizing thought on the global (that can be found in the writings of Francis Fukuyama or Thomas Friedman, for example) is virtual and simulated. It seeks to 'realize' a world order in which Western values are affirmed as the supposed will of all of humankind. But such a thought-process comes with a dreadful application of violence too. It is the violence of virtual models or codes that claim universalism (in its absence) and obliterate differences. As some have argued (following Baudrillard), 'what must be problematized today is not difference but its simulated and virtual erasure' (Debrix 1999: 218). Although virtual (in its manipulation of the real) and illusory (in its fateful course toward a confrontation with radical evil), the violence of the global today is still terrifying and terrorizing. It is so because global thinking postulates no limits whatsoever to the virtual reality that is supposed to make up today's reinvented universal values (globalization, human rights, democracy, or peace).

Baudrillard declares that, in the 9/11 terrorist attacks, it is actually the virtual and global West that, 'assuming God's position … , has become suicidal and declared war upon itself' (Baudrillard 2002a: 405). While this could be taken to signify that the West's own policies have caused the terrorist actions, the argument is far more complex. To appreciate the critical force of Baudrillard's thought here, one has to understand the power of simulated models as well as the oppositional reality-making systems that simulation and the symbolic come to embody in his analyses. Baudrillard's interventions on 9/11 and the War on Terror are not attempts at championing terror or terrorism (they are not about championing the violence of the global either). Rather, for Baudrillard, terrorism is but a symptom of the counter-power that inevitably returns to disseminate the singularity of the symbolic into the virtuality and uniformity of the global (and thus reveals its fatal illusion). Terrorism is not a fundamental truth or ideology. It is a symbolic principle of destabilization of the system that emerges at the very moment when the system thinks it is most complete, perfect, or total. As Baudrillard puts it: 'Terrorism invents nothing and starts nothing. Simply, it takes things to their extreme, paroxysmic level. It exacerbates a certain state of reality, a certain logic of violence and uncertainty' (Baudrillard 2002b: 36; my translation).

Thus, in the 9/11 attacks, it is not just symbolic resistance to the violence of the virtual/global that is revealed by Baudrillard. It is also the return of a radically different thought, one that seeks to reinsert the singularity of the event into political life. For Baudrillard, the event is what forces concepts away from their safe referential domains, and what 'renders useless any totalizing endeavour' (Baudrillard 2002b: 25; my translation). By seeking to reintroduce the event, Baudrillard's thought on the violence, excess, but also failure of simulation eventually reconnects with other destabilizing and deconstructive attempts by contemporary French philosophers to rethink politics through the uncertain, unpredictable, and unmasterable irruption of singularities or differences (Nancy 2000; Derrida 2005b). In the end (the end of his life too), Baudrillard asks: 'How does an event, even 9/11, keep its singularity?' (Baudrillard 2004: 143). Perhaps it is this question that students and scholars eager to challenge dominant thoughts about the global (and its violence) should ask themselves.

Further reading

The System of Objects (Jean Baudrillard, 1996a [1968], London: Verso): Baudrillard's first book. It initiates his move beyond Marxist analyses of use value and develops a semiology of objects.

Forget Foucault (Jean Baudrillard, 1987 [1977], New York: Semiotext(e)): Baudrillard criticizes Foucault's reliance on power as a system of referentiality/representation. Baudrillard suggests that the fact that power is everywhere (as Foucault implies) means that power has moved beyond representation and reality. Power has entered the era of the simulacrum.

America (Jean Baudrillard 1988b [1986], London: Verso): Baudrillard's famous journey through America's hyperreality. This volume has contributed to the popularization of his theory.

Power Inferno (Jean Baudrillard [2002b], Paris: Galilée): This volume (published in French) contains three essays written by Baudrillard in the aftermath of the 9/11 terrorist attacks ('Requiem for the Twin Towers', 'Hypotheses on Terrorism', and 'The Violence of the Global'). It contains some of his most polemical reflections on the violence of the global.

6 Simone de Beauvoir

Kimberly Hutchings

Simone de Beauvoir's life stretched across most of the twentieth century, encompassing tremendous events and changes from the impact of two world wars to post Second World War violent processes of decolonisation in Asia and Africa, the civil rights movement in the US, uprisings in Hungary and Czechoslovakia, student radicalism and the birth of second wave feminism in Europe and the USA. She was a philosopher, a feminist, a novelist, a political commentator and (sometimes) a political activist. She was also a public intellectual, part of a group of thinkers and writers who helped to develop the distinctively French phenomenological philosophy: existentialism. Jean-Paul Sartre, the leading exponent of existentialist philosophy, was Beauvoir's lover, friend and philosophical partner for fifty years, until his death in 1980. As commentators on Beauvoir have noted, her association with Sartre has often led to the dismissal of the independent value of Beauvoir's philosophical work. However, Beauvoir did make a significant contribution to traditions of critical theory, in her work on ethics and politics in *The Ethics of Ambiguity* (first published in 1947, see Beauvoir 1948) and in her groundbreaking feminist text *The Second Sex* (first published in 1949, see Beauvoir 1997).

We have an unusually detailed knowledge of Beauvoir's life. Not only did she use her personal experiences in her novels, but she was also very public about the unorthodox way she chose to live her personal life, and wrote about this extensively in her autobiographical works (Beauvoir 1959, 1965a, 1965b, 1972, Rowley 2007). Beauvoir came from a middle class family and was brought up with the stultifying expectations on girls that this implied in early twentieth century France. She challenged these expectations, however, through her brilliance as a scholar, becoming a graduate student in philosophy at the Sorbonne. During the 1930s, she developed her philosophical ideas in dialogue with Sartre, Merleau-Ponty and others, whilst also teaching philosophy and studying German phenomenology, including the work of Husserl and Heidegger. She spent most of the war in occupied Paris, during which time she studied Hegel, and published her first novel in 1943. Although Beauvoir herself played no major role in any resistance movement, it is clear from *The Ethics of Ambiguity* that the example of the French resistance during the war, for Beauvoir, posed key questions about the meaning of ethical responsibility and resistance to injustice, and the role of violence in politics. In the aftermath of the war, Beauvoir was one of the founders of the leftist journal *Les Temps Modernes*, and also aligned herself with the anti-Stalinist left in France. As an increasingly famous (notorious) public intellectual and writer, she openly opposed the French war in Algeria, and in her later years supported student radicals in 1968 and the women's movement, including campaigns against legal and political discrimination and for the legalisation of abortion. As second wave feminism took off in the 1960s, feminist scholars began to study *The Second Sex* systematically and to identify Beauvoir as a foundational feminist thinker. For some commentators, both Beauvoir and Sartre failed to live up to their own ideals as critical, committed philosophers pursuing resistance to oppression (Rowley 2007). But whether they were successful or not, there is no question that they set up a model for the meaning of being a critical theorist that continues to resonate in debates about critical theory today (Moi 2004a).

Ethics and politics

Existentialism is, above all, a philosophy of freedom. At its core is a concept of the human being or 'existent' as fundamentally defined by the gap between 'essence' and 'existence', in contrast to other sorts of beings (stones, animals) in which essence and existence coincide. Put simply, the being of a tree exactly coincides with all the attributes of 'treeness', what it *is* is equivalent to a set of finite, defining characteristics. But the being of any particular human does not coincide with any given list of attributes; human beings exist but their existence is characterised by transcendence and becoming, and they can never be equated with a finite essence except through an act of 'bad faith'. To be in bad faith is to deny one's own or others' transcendence. In *Being and Nothingness* (originally published 1943, see Sartre 1966), Sartre famously outlines examples of bad faith, where individuals seek to identify themselves entirely with some kind of essence, whether it be that of the good waiter or the desirable woman. However, although clearly sharing a lot of ground with Sartre, Beauvoir's understanding of what it means to be an 'existent' is less voluntaristic and de-materialised than Sartre's. This is evident in her early existentialist work, *The Ethics of Ambiguity*:

> From the beginning, existentialism defined itself as a philosophy of ambiguity. It was by affirming the irreducible character of ambiguity that Kierkegaard opposed himself to Hegel, and it is by ambiguity that, in our own generation, Sartre, in *Being and Nothingness*, fundamentally defined man, that being whose being is not to be; that subjectivity which realizes itself only as a presence in the world, that engaged freedom, that surging of the for-oneself which is immediately given for others (Beauvoir 1948: 9–10).

In *The Ethics of Ambiguity*, Beauvoir's purpose is to examine the implications of existentialism for ethics, and to respond to critics of existentialism who claimed that it could only result in an ethic of despair or absurdity (Beauvoir 1948:10–11). In carrying out this intention, she puts her own particular interpretation of existentialism to work using the concept of 'ambiguity' to capture the unsettled nature of the human condition. Ambiguity refers to the way in which human beings simultaneously occupy the positions of both subject (for oneself) and object (for others). Although agreeing that no human being is reducible to the ways in which they are objectified by others, Beauvoir is also critical of the argument that this means that the starting point for ethics is the unique freedom of the individual. Rather, she argues, the starting point for ethics is the recognition of ambiguity, that is, the acknowledgement of the ways in which subjectivity and objectivity are enmeshed in the situations in which ethical choices and judgments are made. The first half of Beauvoir's text is focused on classifying and evaluating the different ways in which people live out their response to the human condition. The second half of the text is focused much more concretely on exploring questions of the ethics of political action, including a specific focus on the question of whether and how the use of violence in politics might be permissible.

Beauvoir classifies different kinds of lived response to the human condition into a set of ideal types. Of these types, it is the 'serious man' who, even though he pursues the ends of justice and freedom, is nevertheless most ethically dangerous. His fundamental mistake is that he identifies himself with particular ends and values in an unquestioning and absolute way. This means that for the serious man the value of his ends are always already known to outweigh the costs inherent in the means he uses, an assumption that can easily pave the way towards tyranny. For the tyrant, the world and others are simply grist to the mill of his own desires, and the injury and death of other existents is only meaningful in terms of how well the tyrant's desires are fulfilled through that injury and death. For Beauvoir, this pure instrumentalisation of others is the defining mark of oppression. In existentialist terms, the violence of the tyrant is archetypically unjustifiable, since it is grounded on the refusal of the truth of the human condition, reducing others to a thing-like status, solely for the purposes of enhancing the tyrant's power. The problem this raises, is how does one resist the tyrant, without falling into the trap of the serious man? In order to work this out, Beauvoir explores a variety of arguments, arguments from necessity and from utility, which might be used to justify violence in resistance to oppression. However, in each case, she finds that a kind of instrumental trade-off between means and ends is involved that puts the moral justifiability of resistant violence into question.

Instrumental arguments assume a whole series of things about agency that are highly questionable. In particular they make assumptions about the relation between the agent and the world in which he/she acts and about the relation between the means and ends of action. In the case of the former, instrumental arguments assume a high level of independence and foresight in the political actor. On this account, the resistant actor is capable of detaching him/herself from his or her environment and acting upon it as an external force, predicting what the impact of that action will be. But, as Beauvoir points out, we do not know the future, our information is always partial and imperfect and our control of events is limited. Agents do not act in a vacuum, and all acts have unintended consequences (Beauvoir 1948: 115–28). Moreover, a thinking that assumes the possibility of a trade-off between present sacrifice and future freedom is also committed to the idea that one can maintain a clear distinction between the means and ends of action. Beauvoir argues that such a distinction cannot be maintained, and that in the case of political violence ends are frequently either contradicted or corrupted by means. It isn't possible, she argues, to exclude the means from the ethical meaning of the act. To exemplify this, she refers to the Cold War attitudes of both Britain and the USSR and the ways in which the means (supporting authoritarian regimes in the former case, aggrandizing Soviet power in the latter) encroach on and corrupt the ends (defending civilization and democracy and the liberation of the proletariat respectively) of these states. In the first case there is an immediate contradiction between means and ends, in the latter, the end is so mythical and distant that it has ceased to have any meaning, and the means have effectively taken over as the end (Beauvoir 1948: 124–25).

It seems from the above discussion that there can be no way out for the moral agent seeking to respond ethically to the actuality of oppression. However, the argument does not stop here; instead Beauvoir moves on to defend a conception of ethics that remains ambiguous all the way down. In the course of her discussion, Beauvoir identifies a whole range of ways in which human existence is ambiguous. All of these ambiguities ultimately refer back to the ways in which to be human is both to be and not to be subject (autonomous agency) and to be and not to be situation (identifiable with both the world and others). This suggests a different way of understanding the nature of the 'wrong' involved in oppression. Here the wrong lies not in the reduction of the other to 'thing' as such, but in the denial of the 'ambiguity' of both subject and other. Tyrants are defined not simply by the fact that they instrumentalise others but also by their identification of themselves with pure transcendence, a refusal to 'assume' their own ambiguity (Beauvoir 1948: 102). In the case of both the tyrant and the serious man, Beauvoir identifies the unethical with the subject who understands himself or herself in terms of a model of pure transcendence. In the case of the tyrant, decision-making becomes a technical rather than an ethical matter. The assumption of pure transcendence is an assumption that the world and others exist to furnish the tyrant's desires, and that the tyrant has the capacity to exert control over the world, others and therefore the future (Beauvoir 1948: 102). The serious man is different from the tyrant in that he is committed not simply to the confirmation of his own transcendence but to particular ends and values that he knows to be right. However, this moral certainty is lived in a way that mimics the tyrant's conviction as to his own transcendence, in that it legitimates the instrumentalisation of the world and others to whatever higher cause is in question. In its denial of ambiguity, the perspective of the serious man does not allow means to be put into question in relation to ends, and again reduces moral and political judgment to an essentially technical exercise.

Beauvoir's argument is that insofar as ambiguity is denied, then so is ethics (Hutchings 2007b). Her point is that once you have certainty then you move from the ground of ethics to the ground of calculation. Ethics, in contrast, is grounded in uncertainty, both at the level of who moral agents are and what moral agents know about themselves and about the outcomes of their actions. This does not mean that ethics can be evaded, however, rather, ethics becomes the ongoing struggle against the failure to affirm the ambiguous existence of both self and others (Beauvoir 1948: 157). Ethical judgment is always contextual and risky, but we have an absolute responsibility to engage in it because otherwise we deny what we are: we fall into bad faith.

Beauvoir's way of thinking about ethics is one of the threads that connects existentialist philosophy to certain themes in poststructuralist critical thought, and thereby, indirectly, to some aspects of critical international theory today. In the generation after Beauvoir, poststructuralist thinkers tended to be dismissive of existentialism as being overly individualistic and humanistic. Nevertheless, in poststructuralist writings on ethics and politics we find similar kinds of argument about the dangers inherent in the position of the serious man, and the same kind of call to accept responsibility for judgment in the absence of a knowable source of moral truth (Ashley and Walker 1990a). It's always difficult to definitively establish lines of influence between different theorists, but it is striking how themes Beauvoir identified continue to resonate in strands of normative international theory that are critical of mainstream ethics. In affirming the impossibility of identifying universal principles for action, or treating ethical issues as matters that can be resolved without remainder (and therefore outside of politics), Beauvoir is arguing along the same lines as contemporary critical international theorists who reject Kantian, utilitarian and communitarian approaches to international ethics and international political theory (Campbell 2001a, 2001b; Jabri 2001; Edkins 2000).

The Second Sex

Beauvoir is much better known as the author of *The Second Sex* than for her work on ethics, although, as we will see, there are strong continuities between them (Simons 1995, 1999). In the case of *The Second Sex* however, there can be no doubt of its direct and enduring influence on feminist thought in general and feminist international theory in particular (Grosholz 2004). It is impossible to do justice to the scale and complexity of Beauvoir's argument in *The Second Sex* within the context of this chapter. However, it is possible to draw attention to some of the key insights and claims that Beauvoir makes, how those insights and claims have been received and interpreted, and how they work through to debates in feminist international theory today. It is not an exaggeration to state that, in many ways, Beauvoir provides resources for all of the varieties of feminist thought that we find in international relations, from feminist empiricism, through feminist standpoint arguments to feminist postmodernism.

The first point to note is that *The Second Sex* is a philosophical text. Although it makes a lot of use of empirical and historical evidence and illustration, explores biological, economic and psychological theories, and draws on literary and cultural representations of sex difference, it is primarily a work of existentialism (Sandford 2006: 51–79). And, as with *The Ethics of Ambiguity*, it develops Beauvoir's particular form of existentialist philosophy, in which the concept of ambiguity, and the importance of materiality and situation is much more to the fore than notions of pure, transcendent freedom. The aim of the book is to examine the question of what it means to be a woman, or rather, the question of how 'woman' comes to be a mode of existence (Beauvoir 1997: 15). As Sandford points out, this is, for Beauvoir, inseparable from the question of how 'man' comes to be a mode of existence (Sandford 2006: 62). Historically (although not necessarily) woman is a relational concept that takes its meaning from its relation to man as both less than man (other) and radically different to man (Other) (Beauvoir 1997: 16). For Beauvoir, it is only by challenging the identification of woman as radically Other that it will become possible for woman to become other (as actual women) to man (as actual men) on equal rather than subordinated terms. In order to understand Beauvoir's argument, we have to clarify the meaning of the terms 'other' and 'Other', and in order to do this, we need to say something about the way Beauvoir is here drawing on an aspect of Hegel's philosophy in which he discusses the formation of individual self-consciousness in *The Phenomenology of Spirit*.

In his examination of the formation of individual self-consciousness, Hegel is exploring how we are able to understand and experience ourselves as subjects (Hegel 1977: 111–19). For Hegel, this is only possible if we are *recognized* as subjects, something that can only be done by another subject since, by definition, objects are not capable of doing this kind of recognizing – they are radically Other. In the *Phenomenology* he tells the story of the kinds of mistakes that subjects make in the struggle to affirm themselves as subjects. This is traced out through an allegory, in which subjects initially try to gain recognition through force, by fighting each other. But, as Hegel points out, this life and death struggle is self-defeating if the other subject is killed, since death renders him incapable of acts of recognition. The next stage, according to Hegel, is one in which instead of killing the other, subjects aim to capture the other and thus secure a long-term source of recognition in a 'serf' who is effectively forced to affirm the subjectivity of the 'Lord'. In

Hegel's story this is another mistake and the struggle for recognition goes through various iterations before it becomes clear that mutual recognition is the only answer and that this needs to be sustained by institutionalised relations of various kinds.

From the point of view of Beauvoir, trying to think through what it means to exist as woman, this Hegelian story provided a way of capturing the peculiar features of woman's subject position (Beauvoir 1997: 96–97). Right at the beginning of the text, Beauvoir points to the phenomenon that we now know as a commonplace, but that at the time had not really been thought about. In language and in social interaction, man not only occupies the position of man but also the generic position of standing in for humanity as a whole (Beauvoir 1997: 15). This means that from the start, to be identified as woman is to be identified not only as other to man but also as not equivalent to human. This position gets played out in two ways. On the one hand, woman is put in the position of the 'serf', providing a subordinated other that guarantees the recognition of man as subject. On the other hand, woman is identified as absolutely Other, outside of the human, equivalent to the objective realm of nature, or perhaps to a mystical realm of the feminine, but in either case beyond the possibility of being granted subject status at all.

Beauvoir's argument in *The Second Sex* is a sustained attempt to elucidate the meaning of woman's peculiar 'other/Other' positioning and how this has been institutionalised in a variety of ways in discourse, in economic and political life, and socially and psychologically for both women and men. It is also, however, a sustained argument against the idea that this positioning is in any way necessary, either because it reflects some enduring essence of womanliness or femininity, or because it is impossible to change (Beauvoir 1997: 295). At the heart of Beauvoir's argument is the existentialist assumption that men and women are both existents, that is to say, beings without a fixed essence. As existents 'woman' and 'man' can become fixed in their meaning only through individual and collective acts of bad faith. Materiality and situation are crucial to our existential becoming, but they do not determine it. For this reason, we need to overturn the notion of woman as 'Other' if we are to be able to tackle her subordination, since that subordination is invariably justified by a move that seeks to reduce woman to a particular essence, often by reference to biology:

> For the body, being the instrument of our grasp upon the world, the world is bound to seem a very different thing when apprehended in one manner or another. This accounts for our lengthy study of the biological facts; they are one of the keys to our understanding of woman. But I deny that they establish for her a fixed and inevitable destiny. They are insufficient for setting up a hierarchy of the sexes; they fail to explain why woman is the Other; they do not condemn her to remain in this subordinate role forever (Beauvoir 1997: 65).

The Second Sex made Beauvoir famous, though many of the immediate responses to it reflected the depth of sexism in European societies at the time (Sandford 2006: 53–54; Moi 2004a: 156). It was a generation after it was published before it came to be identified as a (if not 'the') canonic work of feminist theory. Nevertheless, the reception of Beauvoir's work within feminism has not been straightforward, moving from enthusiastic praise, to a wave of critique and, most recently, to revisionist scholarship that has argued that earlier feminist interpretations of Beauvoir, whether supportive or critical, have not done justice to the philosophical complexity of her thought (Pilardi 1995; Bauer 2004). These waves of interpretation of Beauvoir, perhaps unsurprisingly, reflect the changing concerns and priorities of feminist thinking from the 1960s through to the present day. And in examining them, we can trace the different modes of feminist thinking that have been, and continue to be, influential in the study of international relations.

In earlier phases of feminist interpretation, Beauvoir tended to be read as affirming two things: first, that there is a distinction between sex and gender; second, that women's subordination was not biologically justified: women were human in the same way as men, and should have equal status to men in all aspects of public life. Beauvoir distinguished between 'female' (a biological category) and 'woman' (an existential category). For many feminists this mapped onto the distinction that they were using between sex and gender, with sex being a biological and gender a social category. By asserting this distinction, feminists were able to argue that there was no necessary connection between biological sexual difference and social and cultural gender norms, and to campaign for equality between men and women in social life. This form of feminism inspired a range of work within the social sciences designed to highlight the unjustifiability of women's exclusion from public power, and seeking to incorporate the significance of gender (as social structure and set of normative expectations) into the analysis of how the world works. It encouraged what has become labelled 'feminist empiricism', that is to say, work that sought to include women and gender as a neglected aspect of empirical reality that needed to be taken on board if social phenomena were to be fully explained. In international relations, Cynthia Enloe's *Bananas, Beaches and Bases: Making Feminist Sense of International Politics* (1989) works in this way, exemplifying the ways in which bringing women and gender norms into focus illuminates practices of international politics from diplomacy to international trade.

Within the feminist movement the initial dominance of liberal versions of feminism, which sought to deconstruct the social reality of gender and make a world in which women were treated on the same terms as men, was challenged by the rise of a different kind of feminism. This feminism, sometimes labelled 'radical' feminism, argued that equality arguments were premised on the identification of women with men. In other words, they ultimately treated women as the same as men, without challenging men or norms of masculinity. On this account, insofar as Beauvoir was identified as an equality feminist, she became a target of critique, for being too quick to devalue what it means to be a woman, and too identified with a masculine project of transcendence and the objectification of others. In opposition to this view, radical feminism stressed the value of women's difference and argued that this should be the basis for feminist ethics and politics. This stress on women's difference led to feminist arguments in social and political theory that, rather than seeing women and gender as an aspect of empirical reality that need to be added into analysis, saw women/gender as distinctive resources for thought that provided privileged insights into the world. We can see this reflected in various forms of feminist standpoint theory in international relations. For instance J. Ann Tickner's reformulation of Morgenthau's principles of political realism in 1988, in which she argues for distinctively feminist understandings of concepts of power and agency (Tickner 1988). Or, Sarah Ruddick's argument for a distinctive feminist ethic of peace based on the practice of 'maternal thinking' (Ruddick 1990).

Feminist standpoint thinking turned away from Beauvoir, but in many ways this reflected a misreading, by both supporters and critics, of her arguments in *The Second Sex*. It is certainly the case that Beauvoir rejected essentialist accounts of 'woman' or the 'feminine', but she was insistent that woman was, at least for now, a meaningful category of existence. Existence was not a project of transcendence that reached beyond embodiment or materiality. There were distinctive aspects to being a woman that inflected and shaped living as a woman and that were not in themselves necessarily linked to subordination (Sandford 2006: 70–79):

> As a matter of fact, man, like woman, is flesh, therefore passive, the plaything of his hormones and of the species, the restless prey of his desires. And she like him, in the midst of the carnal fever, is a consenting, a voluntary gift, an activity, they live out in their several fashions the strange ambiguity of existence made body (Beauvoir 1997: 737).

What we could not know, in Beauvoir's view, was what living as a woman might mean without the constraining legacy of a subject position of Other/other, just as we could not know what it might mean to be a man without that relation to woman as Other/other. In recent re-readings of Beauvoir's work, feminist commentators have stressed the open and contextual nature of her thought and, in contrast to both liberal and radical readings, seen her as in tune with feminist arguments that have drawn attention to the complexity of both sex and gender as categories (Bauer 2001; Kruks 2001; Sandford 2006). Here we find her thought resonating with postmodernist and poststructuralist feminisms in the work of theorists such as Judith Butler, and, in the context of international relations, reflected in the growing feminist consensus that 'woman' and 'gender' do not have a uniform meaning but need to be understood contextually and as cutting across other aspects of identity (Peterson 1999).

But even if Beauvoir's understanding of sex and gender was more nuanced than had previously been supposed, there is another persuasive complaint about *The Second Sex* that is less easy to dismiss. This is that Beauvoir's argument is fundamentally Eurocentric, because Beauvoir treated the specificities of 'woman's' subject position in European (essentially French) societies as if this captured the universal truth of what it means to be a woman. However, commentators differ on whether the parochialism of Beauvoir's argument necessarily undermines the applicability of her insights into the structure of European women's oppression to the position of different women in different places and times (Moi 2004a). Much here depends on how well the idea of the other/Other position 'travels' as a way of unpacking different experiences of subordinated existence. It is perhaps worth noting that Beauvoir's existentialist feminism is closely related to Fanon's black existentialist thought. Beauvoir drew direct analogies between the position of women as other/Other and that of racially excluded groups (Beauvoir 1997: 23–24), although she argued that 'woman' had been more definitively excluded, within human history as a whole, from possibilities of mutual recognition than racialized others. Like Beauvoir, Fanon drew on the Hegelian model of the struggle for recognition to illuminate the other/Other positioning of black subjects. Like Beauvoir also, Fanon demonstrated powerfully how the other/Other identity is lived in the flesh and the psyche and the need to struggle against this at the level of the subject as well as institutionally. In this respect, Beauvoir's work is very much part of the inheritance being brought to recent critical international relations theory by postcolonial scholars (Inayatullah and Blaney 2004).

Conclusion

Beauvoir's existentialist ethics and her existentialist feminism are both grounded on an account of the fundamental ambiguity of the human condition. In contrast to Sartre, our ambiguity is not understood in terms of an absolute and irresolvable contradiction between our freedom as subjects and our objectification by others or by nature. For Beauvoir there are ways of living that are embodied, social and free. But these possibilities depend on each of us recognising the ambiguity of ourselves as well as others. Once we have done this, life becomes in many ways more difficult, ethical judgments are not clear-cut calculations, and we can no longer affirm our own subjectivity through the negation of that of others. But it is this vision of a difficult freedom that Beauvoir celebrates and that is the source of the critical power of her work in general and her analysis of the wrongs of the subordination of women in particular. Beauvoir saw it as incumbent on the critical philosopher to play his or her part in challenging oppression in both writing and in political activism. Even if she did not always live up to this ideal, there are many ways in which her life and writing can be taken as exemplary works of critique.

Further reading

There is no substitute for reading Beauvoir's own texts, although it should be
noted that there are a lot of problems with the only existing English translation of *The Second Sex* (Moi 2004b), so if you can read her in French then
do so. Margaret Simons is one of the foremost Anglophone commentators
on Beauvoir's work, and her book, *Beauvoir and The Second Sex* (1999),
includes a range of Simons' essays plus interviews with Beauvoir herself.
Stella Sandford's *How to Read Beauvoir* is an excellent introductory text on
Beauvoir's work as a whole and the collections edited by Simons and
Grosholz include essays by the most well known Beauvoir scholars. The
Cambridge Companion to Simone de Beauvoir (2003) also includes contributions from distinguished Beauvoir scholars and has a very useful and
detailed bibliography of Beauvoir's works and secondary sources. Pilardi's
essay 'Feminists Read *The Second Sex*' (1999) and Bauer's 'Must we read
Simone de Beauvoir?' (2004) are both helpful on the reception of Beauvoir's
work within feminism. Hutchings (2007b) attempts to apply Beauvoir's
ethics to feminist arguments about the justifiability of violence in politics.
Bauer (2001) and Kruks (2001) are both highly sophisticated and helpful
recent interpretations of Beauvoir as a philosopher and Kruks is particularly
useful in locating Beauvoir as an existentialist thinker in relation to Sartre,
Merleau-Ponty and Fanon.

7 Walter Benjamin

Angharad Closs Stephens

Very few theorists of international relations have engaged with the work and ideas of Walter Benjamin. This is in contrast to the great excitement for Benjamin's writings experienced in many other disciplines since the 1970s. His work has been mined for its contributions to the fields of literary criticism, social and cultural theory, philosophy, art theory and human geography. Benjamin lived and wrote in the context of some significant and particularly violent moments in global politics: these include the outbreak of the First World War in 1914; the Bolshevik's October Revolution in 1917; widespread economic depression; the inauguration of the Third Reich in 1933 and the rise of Nazi power. He experienced a 'damaged life' that was common to many of his friends and contemporaries, including Theodor Adorno, Ernst Bloch, Siegfried Kracauer, Bertolt Brecht and Georg Lukács, and which eventually forced him, like so many other of these fascinating figures, into a life in exile. What then can students of international politics learn from reading Walter Benjamin? Or, what 'illuminations' can Walter Benjamin's writings offer a study of international politics? This brief introduction to Benjamin life and life's works will explore some of the key themes in his writings, which touch on questions of history, representation and methodology. It will suggest that these broad themes are all underpinned by a persistent critique of the idea of time as progress. In concentrating on Walter Benjamin's reflections on the relationship between time and politics, we encounter some exciting avenues of thought for our studies of international relations.

Walter Benedix Schöenflies Benjamin was born on 15 July 1892 and raised in Berlin, the son of an upper middle class, affluent Jewish family. At the time of the First World War, he was active in the radical wing of the city's Youth Movement (*Jugendbewegung*) where he met his life long friend and intellectual companion, Gerhard (later Gershom) Scholem. Benjamin and Scholem found common ground in their backgrounds, in their interest in Zionism, and in their rejection of their parents' middle class materialism and assimilationist Judaism. It was the cultural and intellectual aspects of Zionism that interested both of them and not the political project. This interest continued throughout both their lives: Scholem became a scholar of Jewish thought and the Kabbalah and in 1923 fulfilled his ambition to emigrate to Palestine. Scholem never tired of working to persuade Benjamin to join him. Despite Scholem's pleas, Benjamin never acted on his half-hearted promises to join him (Scholem 2001). Although Benjamin volunteered for military service in 1914, luckily for him, he was rejected by the recruiting board. Later that year, he became devastated at the suicide of two close friends, and after that, Benjamin worked repeatedly to avoid conscription, presenting himself as a palsy victim and later, with his wife Dora's help, as suffering from sciatica. Benjamin married Dora Pollak (*née* Kellner) on 17 April 1917, following her divorce from Max Pollak, another member of the Youth Movement. She was the daughter of a well-known, Anglicist university professor, Leon Kellner, who worked as an editor and literary executor for the Zionist writings of Theodor Herzl (Scholem 2001: 27). She grew up in a Zionist environment, was well educated, and worked as an English translator. The couple had a son, Stefan, who was born on 11 April 1918.

Benjamin drew his inspiration from a diverse range of sources including German Romanticism, in particular the works of Novalis, Schlegel, and Hölderlin, Kantianism, Platonism and Jewish mysticism (Buck-Morss 1977). In these early years, he was already writing important essays, including 'On Language as Such and the Language of Mankind' (1916) and 'The Programme of the Coming Philosophy' (1918), which both engage with Kant's concept of experience. In 1919, he completed his doctoral dissertation, on 'The Concept of Art Criticism in German Romanticism', in which he compared the views of A. W. von Schlegel and J. W. van Goethe on Romantic art criticism. He began to develop his idea of 'immanent critique', which involves unfolding the layers of a work of art to reveal its 'truth content' (Gilloch 2002). This theme was developed in a critical reading of 'Goethe's *Elective Affinities*' in 1922. At this point, Benjamin was keen to acquire an academic position as lecturer in philosophy, not least in order to give him financial independence and break from a difficult relationship with his father. But the dissertation marked the beginning of the end of any academic ambition for Benjamin. In 1921, he was given the opportunity to edit his own journal, which he named *Angelus Novus* ('The New Angel' – inspired by the painting by Paul Klee) but the journal failed. In 1925, Benjamin applied for *Habilitation* (the qualification for teaching) at the University of Frankfurt, submitting a thesis on the *Trauerspiel* or German mourning-play, a particular form of seventeenth-century baroque tragic drama. Benjamin was interested in the 'allegorical' form of these plays, which presented a view of the world through fragmentation and ruination. This particular dramatic form was largely forgotten in literary circles but Benjamin sought to bring new life into it, as he would with many other themes. The examiners failed to make any sense of the convoluted thesis however, and Benjamin was asked to withdraw, ending all prospects of an academic career. For the rest of his life, Benjamin was forced to make ends meet as a freelance writer, translator and reviewer, often under dire economic circumstances and living with long periods of loneliness.

This decisive end of the possibility of an academic career marked a significant turning point for Benjamin. In 1921, his marriage to Dora began to fall apart; he became infatuated with another woman called Julia Cohn; and in 1924 he met and fell for the Latvian actress, Asja Lacis. Lacis is credited with introducing Benjamin to Bertolt Brecht in 1929 and for encouraging his interest in Communism (although he never joined the Party). Lacis never had much time for the *Trauerspiel* study, and it is during these times with Lacis that Benjamin began experimenting with his writing and how he might present his ideas. He penned urban biographies of Naples, Moscow, Marseilles and Paris. And he published a collection of fragments, aphorisms and 'thought images' under the title, *One-Way Street* (1928). This was published in the same year as the *Trauerspiel* book but represented a radically different kind of project. It is with these shorter, punchier interventions that Benjamin establishes his unique and refreshing style. Benjamin travelled extensively throughout his lifetime, but always in and across Europe. His life-long relationship with Berlin was regularly interrupted, with long visits to Switzerland, Capri, Ibiza, Nice, Svendborg in Denmark, and Paris, which from 1933 he would make his home. In 1940, as the Nazis advanced on the city, he was forced to flee. He left for the Spanish border hoping to make his way to America, but on arrival at Portbou, he and the other refugees travelling with him were told that visas would not be made available and that they would all be forced to return the following day. He committed suicide that night, on 26 September 1940, aged 48.

Reading Walter Benjamin

This introduction will concentrate on one persistent theme in Benjamin's writings: his critique of the idea of time as progress, and how this offers us a different way of thinking about politics. Benjamin attempts to rethink our ideas of time and to contest the idea that the future represents a smooth continuation of present and past. By attempting to disrupt an assumption of progress, he suggests that the future could offer something other than an extension of the same form of social and political life. Kimberly Hutchings has argued that if there is something that makes critical theory *critical* then it is a resolute openness towards the possibility of change and a desire to imagine alternative futures beyond the hegemony of the present (Hutchings 2007a). There is an important relationship between critique, time and politics: the question of how we understand the relationship between past, present and future is directly related to the challenge of imagining other political possibilities. This is what makes Benjamin interesting for critical interventions in international relations.

Benjamin's life long friend, collaborator and critic Gershom Scholem tells us that Benjamin would often ask him whether time, which must have a sequence, must also have a particular direction (Scholem 2001: 41). Questions of time form a constant theme in his writings and he presents a persistent critique of the linear and unidirectional time of progress. This is what

Benjamin famously describes as a 'homogenous, empty idea of time', a concept that was borrowed and immortalised by Benedict Anderson in his book, *Imagined Communities*. Anderson shows us that 'homogenous empty time' is crucial in enabling the idea of a nation, where we all believe we are sharing in a common past, present and future (Anderson 1991). This idea of time has been condemned for the way it presupposes a map of the future and therefore steers and limits the political possibilities available to us (Hutchings 2007a; Chatterjee 2004; Grosz 1999). In its closed and prescriptive understanding of the relationship between present and future, it presumes to already know the best form of response to the contingencies and disparities of global politics. Benjamin's writings offer an important resource for thinking about time differently. In this, they represent an attempt to think outside the traditional foundations of Western, European philosophy. Specifically, he draws on the ideas of Jewish mysticism in his attempt to work against a Kantian universal or cosmopolitan concept of history (Smith 1989: xxvi; Buck-Morss 1977; Scholem 2001).

For this reason, Benjamin would have baulked at the assumption that we could trace an unswerving trajectory of argument through his works, from the 'early ideas' to the 'developed principles'. Benjamin's works are notoriously unstraightforward: at worst they are esoteric and difficult; but for the patient reader, Benjamin gently unfurls some exciting possibilities for critical theory and challenges us to be more inventive and daring in the material we choose to study. He is irreverent, bold and ambitious in discussing an enormous range of themes, as wide-ranging as reflections on epic theatre; the task of translation; language; violence and the law; the theological and the political; photography; art; and even children's literature and stories. In the same way that Benjamin's philosophy, if he has one, cannot be coherently packaged, Benjamin's writings should not be read according to their chronological order or by selectively approaching only the so-called important essays. The way to read Benjamin is through immersion: to lose oneself in the stories, commentaries, thoughts, aphorisms, arguments, observations and metaphors. As Theodor Adorno tells us: 'Disappointment is unavoidable if one seeks results from Benjamin's philosophy; it satisfies only one who broods over it long enough to find what inheres in it' (Smith 1988: 13).

I will concentrate on two essays that are probably familiar to those reading Benjamin in English: 'The Work of Art in the Age of Mechanical Reproduction' (1935–36) and 'Theses on the Philosophy of History' (completed 1940, published posthumously in 1950). These are both available in the collection *Illuminations,* which includes an excellent introduction by Hannah Arendt (1973). These are fine places to begin exploring his writings. But in order to discover the distinctiveness and brilliance of Benjamin's approach, I will suggest that the reader must turn to *The Arcades Project.* This project was written side by side with the two essays mentioned and therefore forms an important context for them. But it also brings together Benjamin's ideas as to how we might rethink history, representation and methodology.

History and the critique of progress

The essay, 'Theses on the Philosophy of History', offers a powerful synopsis of Benjamin's approach to historical inquiry (expanded in Convolute N of *The Arcades Project*). But it also represents his great attack on the concept of progress. The essay condemns traditional 'historicism' for the way in which it tells history 'as a sequence of events like the beads of a rosary' (Benjamin 1973: 263). Benjamin argues that it takes force to organize and determine events into a straitjacketed continuum. And he claims that stories of smooth progression ultimately work in the service of the victors in society by obfuscating struggle, disagreement and resistance. Benjamin proposes that his own 'historical materialist' approach cuts across traditional historicism by 'brush[ing] history against the grain' (Benjamin 1973: 257). It does this by offering a new understanding of the relationship between past and present. Against historicism's attempt to show the past 'the way it really was' (Benjamin 1973: 255), as an authentic site that must be truthfully recovered, Benjamin adopts a methodology that seeks 'to blast open the continuum of history' (Benjamin 1973: 262). History takes place at the site of what he calls, 'now-time' (*'Jetztzeit'*). This is more than an argument that all history is written from the present or has relevance for the present. Rather, Benjamin urges that the task of the historical materialist is to conjoin 'what-has-been' and 'now-time' in a dialectical relationship, one that forces a 'flash' of new awareness. Although 'the true picture of the past flits by', the historical materialist seizes that picture from the 'homogenous empty time' of history and reveals it in a different light (Benjamin 1973: 255):

A historical materialist approaches a historical subject only where he encounters it as a monad. In this structure he recognizes the sign of a Messianic cessation of happening, or, put differently, a revolutionary chance in the fight for the oppressed past. He takes cognizance of it in order to blast a specific era out of the homogenous course of history – blasting a specific life out of the era or a specific work out of a lifework (Benjamin 1973: 263).

This moment that appears to stand outside 'homogenous empty time' is alternatively described as a 'monad', a 'flash' and in *The Arcades Project* as 'dialectics at a standstill'. It is a crucial image of Benjamin's which can be interpreted as the moment of a new understanding, insight or awareness in our readings of the past, or as a 'now of a particular recognizability' (Benjamin 1999). But as this quotation reveals, this moment might take the form of a 'Messianic' revelation, or a revolutionary political possibility.

The question of which of these possibilities most attracted Benjamin has generated intense debate among scholars of his work. What is the nature of Benjamin's 'flash' of awareness? Does it represent a political moment or a religious experience? Is Benjamin more tempted by the possibility of a

Marxist revolution or by the promise of a Jewish messianic moment? This debate has been ongoing for a long time and it is not easily resolved one way or another. But neither does it have to be resolved: Benjamin is a much more interesting figure when we read him as cultivating a different understanding of the relationship between present and future but yet as profoundly ambivalent on what this future might bring. In his personal life, Benjamin didn't believe in straightforward paths to paradise. As Hannah Arendt reminds us, Benjamin never moved to Palestine or Moscow; neither city nor trajectory ultimately offered a political solution for him. It was to Paris that he went: a city full of contradictions and multiple possibilities (Benjamin 1973).

In the 'Theses', Benjamin is fiercely critical of the way in which narratives of advancement, improvement and perfectibility have infused the social democratic movement, informing an uncritical approach to technology and a narrow idea of liberation that remains committed to a celebration of the Protestant work ethic (Buck-Morss 1977: 172): 'Nothing has corrupted the German working class so much as the notion that it was moving with the current' (Benjamin 1973: 258). Benjamin's critique of ideas of progress culminates with the image of the angel of history, which represents a lustrous but damning portrayal of modern ambitions. The angel of history has 'His face ... turned towards the past. Where we perceive a chain of events, he sees one single catastrophe which keeps piling wreckage upon wreckage and hurls it in front of his feet'. The angel would like to 'make whole what has been smashed', but he is caught in the torrent of history:

> a storm is blowing from Paradise; it has got caught in his wings with such violence that the angel can no longer close them. This storm irresistibly propels him into the future to which his back is turned, while the pile of debris before him grows skyward. This storm is what we call progress (Benjamin 1973: 257–58).

For Benjamin, there is nothing worse than the storm of 'homogenous empty time'; but there remains some hope: 'For every second of time was the strait gate through which the Messiah might enter' (Benjamin 1973: 264). The angel was based on Paul Klee's painting, *Angelus Novus* (1920) which Benjamin bought in Munich 1921 and which provided the name for his failed journal. According to Scholem, this was one of Benjamin's greatest possessions, and when he fled Paris in 1940, and had to pack all his papers and belongings into two suitcases, he cut the picture out of its frame and placed it in a case to take with him.

Representation and the 'afterlife' of the object

We might compare Benjamin's interest in the 'afterlife' of history with his interest in the 'afterlife' of the work of art, which forms the subject of another well-renowned essay, 'The Work of Art in the Age of Mechanical

Reproduction'. 'The Work of Art' has become popular among students of cultural theory, film studies and art history for its analysis of how human sense perception is organised, and how it is conditioned by different historical circumstances. The essay has also been cited as evidence of Benjamin's commitment to Marxism, given the conclusions that he draws towards the end of the essay about the role of art in politics. There is a marked contrast between the time Benjamin wrote 'The Work of Art' in 1935 and the time he came to write the 'Theses' in 1940, in that his faith in Marxism dissolves somewhat and the emphasis shifts to the theological. This was in part due to the signing of the Nazi–Soviet pact in 1939, which smashed Benjamin's hope for a Communist alternative. 'The Work of Art' is an important essay for those interested in the relationship between politics and aesthetics, and broader questions about the politics of representation. Benjamin refuses to understand the relationship between the work of art and the art critic as informed by temporal distance; the work of art is not tied to an authentic past but is, rather, constantly changing through time.

Benjamin's argument is that mechanical reproduction, witnessed in the developments of photography, film and sound recording since 1900, has destroyed the idea of the 'authentic' work of art. Comparing the way in which printing brought about a change in the availability and status of written texts, Benjamin argues that being able to reproduce a work of art in mass quantities and at immediate speed fundamentally changes the nature of the work of art by dissolving its 'aura' (or authentic identity). Whereas in eighteenth and nineteenth century bourgeois societies, it was precisely the question of the work of art's duration and its history that provided it with its beauty, this is 'liquidated' in the age of mechanical reproduction as we experience the transformation of 'the traditional value of the cultural heritage' (Benjamin 1973: 221). The contemporary world witnesses the decay of the aura as first, the work of art is taken to dramatically different social contexts and second, as art is brought closer to the 'masses'. Whereas the traditional work of art achieved its aura through its position in a 'ritual' of social, bourgeois tradition, the contemporary work of art is freed from this basis. Subsequently, art acquires a new use value, which according to Benjamin, rests in politics:

> From a photographic negative, for example, one can make any number of prints; to ask for the 'authentic' print makes no sense. But the instant the criterion of authenticity ceases to be applicable to artistic reproduction, the total function of art is reversed. Instead of being based on ritual, it begins to be based on another practice – politics (Benjamin 1973: 224).

Benjamin concludes the essay by offering the reader a stark choice between Fascism, which renders politics aesthetic in its celebration (such as in the Futurists' claim, 'War is beautiful'), or Communism, which politicises art – in mass education through cinema, for example, or through Brecht's theatre.

Adorno (Benjamin's only disciple) was apparently furious and disappointed at the distinction drawn by Benjamin in this essay between the traditional and the technical, and in the uncritical acclamation of film as a work of art that could potentially educate the masses. While the conclusions of the essay are somewhat crude and less interesting, Benjamin's destruction of the criteria of authenticity is an important one and reverberates in Heidegger, Adorno and Derrida's works. This analysis cuts to the heart of Benjamin's understanding of representation and the role of critique:

> Criticism is to be conceived not as the recovery of some original authorial intention, but as an interpretive intervention in the afterlife of the artwork. Meaning is transformed and reconfigured as the artwork is read and understood in new contexts and historical constellations (Gilloch 2002: 30).

It has also influenced poststructuralist analyses of how we might read a text. Rather than understand a work of art or literature as maintaining a steady identity through time, Benjamin is concerned with the changing meanings of a work in the course of its 'afterlife'. This is what propelled Benjamin's parallel interests in translation, interpretation and critique. He doesn't seek to recover an original meaning; as Adorno describes, he 'immersed himself in reality as in a palimpsest' (Smith 1988: 8). Similarly, in philosophical terms, he doesn't seek a return to being but as Beatrice Hanssen describes, to 'establish the becoming of phenomena in their being' (Hanssen 1998: 41).

The metropolis and methodology: Benjamin's *Arcades Project*

Benjamin's history of Paris – 'Capital of the Nineteenth Century' – forms a history, or prehistory, of modernity. Susan Buck-Morss has described it as a double text: on the one hand 'a social and cultural history of Paris in the nineteenth century' and on the other hand, a history of the origins of the present moment (Buck-Morss 1989: 47). It forms a continuation of Benjamin's attempt to bring moments of the past to 'a higher level of immediacy' through their penetration in the present, and through their concretisation in the concept of a dialectical image (Frisby 1985: 222). The work on the Arcades began as a collaborative essay with Franz Hessel after a visit to Paris in March 1926 (Gilloch 2002: 118). However, this project was to grow exponentially and pre-occupy Benjamin for the next thirteen years up until his suicide in 1940. This study cements Benjamin's reputation as a key writer on the experience of what it means to be modern – an experience that artists and writers have generally understood to be captured in the site of the city (Williams 1973; Bradbury and McFarlane 1978; Frisby 2001).

The work is famously described as Benjamin's 'unfinished' manuscript. As the Nazis advanced on Paris, and Benjamin was forced to flee to the Spanish border, he left his papers and extended archives with George Bataille, who hid them in the *Bibliothèque Nationale*. But it is also generally described as unfinishable. Its method is particularly unique, and visually, even, it looks very different from a typical academic text. *The Arcades Project* represents the closest Benjamin came to his ambition to write a book from quotations. It is formed as a collection of fragments, presenting Paris through a 'panorama of dialectical images' (Adorno in Smith 1988: 10). Benjamin tells us that he has no intention to 'say anything, merely show'. He does so by organizing his themes into alphabetically organised convolutes, which include studies of the Parisian Arcades, Fashion, Iron Construction, Haussmann's building projects, Prostitution and Gambling, Photography and the Flâneur. Each convolute subsequently divides to offer a catalogue of notes on each theme, which comprise sketched writings, selected quotations, anecdotes, stories, portraits, poetry and commentary on various books. The finished document was meant to include photographs too. It is a vast reservoir of symbols, imagery, description and analysis spanning philosophy, history, aesthetics, literature and politics. The eclectic range of themes discussed in *The Arcades Project* offers a substantial challenge to what we tend to associate as important or worthy areas of academic study. His inclination to study the margins, peripheries and silences resonates with feminist and postcolonial approaches to international relations. This search for the unanticipated and the unfamiliar is deeply political: 'not because it enacts any preconceived program of what deserves to be collected and studied and what does not, but because it refuses to accept the condition of insignificance as something natural, exposing it instead as a cultural and political construction that relies on problematic unspoken assumptions' (Richter 2007: 47).

The methodology of *The Arcades Project* challenges the concept of progress by refusing to offer a clear outline, narrative or conclusion. The closest we get to an abridged argument is the two exposés to the work, written in 1935 and 1939 respectively. These are worth reading as introductions to the project. David Frisby points out that *The Arcades Project*, as *One-Way Street* before it, represents Benjamin's attempt to explore an experience of time that is non-linear (Frisby 2001; 1985). The project captures an experience of time as fragmented, discontinuous and ephemeral – one inspired by the site of the city, and reflective of a particular idea of modern life. The metropolis forms an ideal site in which Benjamin can flesh out this alternative, discontinuous idea of time. It captures an experience of living with contingency, transiency and upheaval that is typical of the city. It also, perhaps, captures a particular understanding of global politics, as not based on a stability, order and continuity but as suffused with tension, multiplicity and difference. This concept of multiplicity informs the object that Benjamin is attempting to capture – nineteenth century Paris, but it also saturates his methodological approach. In the same way as there isn't a singular experience of life in the city to be captured, Benjamin knows that there is no such thing as a totalized or complete representation to be offered either (Frisby 1985: 6).

This concern with a particular experience of modern life, exposed in the city and formed around a non-linear idea of time, can be traced back to Baudelaire's writings on modern Paris where he tried to capture this fragmented experience of a new, modern way of life. This forms an important inspiration for Benjamin's project (Harvey 1990; Berman 1983). But Benjamin also drew on Surrealist writers, Louis Aragon's *Passage de l'Opera* and André Breton's *Nadja*. Benjamin's urban writings have been described as an example of 'micrological thinking' (Richter 2007). He seizes on particular and unexpected images of the city, such as the prostitute, the street light, the *flâneur* and the arcades, and uses them as 'thought-images' or *Denkbild* for developing a particular theme. Benjamin's favoured forms were the aphorism, the fragment, or the maxim: forms which complement an experience of the ephemeral. I expect he would have enjoyed experimenting with writing texts, blogs and e-mails. Benjamin described his methodological style as a *Denkbild* (thought-image), which Richter defines as 'a poetic form of condensed, epigrammatic writing in textual snapshots ... charged with theoretical insight' (Richter 2007: 2).

Commodification, reification and newness

The Arcades Project forms a lucid attempt to combine the historical-materialist approach with ideas drawn from Jewish Messianism. This can be gleaned in Benjamin's discussion of 'newness'. Benjamin argues that in modern life, we are obsessed with the idea of the new. The love of the new is a vital aspect of a capitalist economic system, which thrives on producing new commodities and in persuading us that we need bigger, better and grander lifestyles. Drawing on Marxist, Surrealist and Freudian categories, Benjamin claims that we treat new commodities as a 'fetish'. He argues that capitalism induces us into a dream-filled sleep from which we need to 'awaken' to a more critical sensibility. This theme of 'awakening' chimes with the idea of a 'flash' of a new understanding.

But in the same way as Benjamin rejects an idea of history underlined by the idea of progress, he refuses to understand newness solely according to the terms of evolution and advancement. He aims to frame newness in terms other than 'homogenous empty time'. To do so, he turns to the theme of fashion. Fashion captures the dialectical relationship between 'what has been' and 'now time', because fashion often revisits what has been as a source of creative inspiration. In conjoining 'what has been' and 'now time', fashion can offer a dramatic, new look. The result is comparable to the 'flash' or *'aufblitzen'* initiated by the historical-materialist approach. It presents the potential of creating something novel and unpredictable.

Benjamin's understanding of the 'new' is not offered as a straightforwardly promising concept, however. The possibility of the new is ambivalent, as is the promise of a Messianic moment or a revolutionary Communist future. Although it might embody something interesting, groundbreaking, promising, it might not necessarily represent a progressive tangent. Modernity is riddled with claims to newness, says Benjamin, but many of those claims turn out to mask more of the same. The question is, does a new intervention represent a critical interjection or not? Claims to newness can often be postulated to keep the dominant idioms of sovereign politics in place. This is the case when 'new threats' offer a reason to reaffirm discourses of national belonging and familiar practices of securitization. Similarly, under capitalism, new products and commodities serve to oxygenate a capitalist economy. We see this in fashion, where Benjamin warns that claims to newness often fail to offer much that is genuinely new:

> the history of ... dress shows surprisingly few variations. It is not much more than a regular rotation of a few quickly altering, but also quickly reinstated, nuances: the length of the train, the height of the coiffure, the shortness of the sleeves ... Even radical revolutions like the boyish haircuts fashionable today are only the 'eternal return of the same' (Benjamin 1999: 71).

The initial frenzy of interest in Benjamin's work by American and European thinkers of the New Left saw his work as irrevocably Marxist, having seized on 'The Work of Art' essay. This somewhat crude labelling of his works has been passionately countered by his friend Scholem however, a scholar of Jewish thought and the Kabbalah who has emphasised the enduring importance of Jewish mysticism for Benjamin. Theodor Adorno also tells us that the theological is an unmistakable aspect of Benjamin's writings (Smith 1988: 8). According to Buck-Morss, Adorno was the one who could see the value of both influences in Benjamin's writings and felt that Benjamin was at his best when he succeeded in weaving the two traditions together (Buck-Morss 1977). This rarely happens however. Benjamin alternates between placing his hopes in a future messianic moment and a future Marxist revolution, and leaves unresolved the question of whether these two traditions can ever be combined (Buck-Morss 1977: 141). What is distinctive and constant however is this idea of a leap 'leading out of the historical continuum into the "time of now", whether the latter is considered to be revolutionary or messianic' (Scholem quoted in Smith 1988: 85).

Further reading

In the context of current debates in international relations, students might be interested in investigating Walter Benjamin's relationship with Carl Schmitt. Benjamin admits to being indebted to Schmitt's ideas on sovereignty, but given that Schmitt was a Catholic conservative and one time member of the Nazi party, this is a complicated relationship. In interrogating Benjamin's ideas on sovereignty, law and violence, it is essential to engage with at least the second part of Jacques Derrida's 'Force of Law: The "Mystical

Foundations of Authority"' essay, in which he engages with Benjamin's 'Critique of Violence'. More recently, Samuel Weber has excoriated the finer details of this intellectual relationship in his article 'Taking Exception to Decision: Walter Benjamin and Carl Schmitt', *Diacritics,* Vol. 22, No. 3/4, Commemorating Walter Benjamin (Autumn–Winter, 1992): 5–18; it will also form part of Samuel Weber's forthcoming manuscript, *Benjamin's-abilities.*

A comprehensive selection of Walter Benjamin's writings in English translation, including previously unpublished pieces, is now available in a series of four volumes called *Walter Benjamin: Selected Writings* published by Harvard University Press (edited by Howard Eiland and Michael W. Jennings). In addition to the books and essays I mention in the text, good secondary reading materials include Caygill, Coles and Klimowski's colourful *Introducing Walter Benjamin* (1998) and Graeme Gilloch's *Walter Benjamin. Critical Constellation.* For different analyses of Benjamin's oeuvre, Susan Buck-Morss's *Dialectics of Seeing,* Howard Caygill's *Walter Benjamin The Colour of Experience,* Richard Wolin's *An Aesthetics of Redemption,* Esther Leslie's *Overpowering Conformism,* Beatrice Hanssen's *Walter Benjamin's other history: of stones, animals, human beings, and angels,* and Frederic Jameson's 'Walter Benjamin, or Nostalgia' in *Marxism and Form: Twentieth Century Dialectical Theories of Literature,* all represent important interventions in exploring the relationship between Walter Benjamin's ideas and politics. Gary Smith's two edited collections contain an excellent selection of essays, including contributions by Theodor Adorno, Gershom Scholem, Rolf Tiedemann and Jürgen Habermas.

8 Roy Bhaskar

Milja Kurki

'Science' has been a controversial notion during the twentieth century. While sciences, especially the natural sciences, have achieved great successes in enabling effective manipulation of the world around us, scientific achievements have also resulted in the development of many highly destructive inventions (e.g. nuclear weapons). The successes of science have also resulted in what some commentators consider a somewhat 'unhealthy' belief in the omnipotence of sciences in solving natural and social problems. The contestation over science has also been played out in twentieth century philosophy of science: here so-called positivist philosophers of science have defended the idea of science and the superior objectivity of systematic forms of 'scientific' inquiry, in both natural and social sciences. However, many critics have come to reject the universal appropriateness of scientific approaches – especially to the social world, where the objects of study are inherently dynamic, conscious, and unpredictable. Roy Bhaskar is a philosopher of science who is best known for having furthered our understanding of science by questioning the philosophical underpinnings of the idea of science. He has argued that both positivist 'scientists' and postpositivist 'science-sceptics' often fail to reflect adequately on the philosophical underpinnings of the idea of science – and hence come to either accept or reject the idea of social science on problematic bases. Bhaskar has, over more than three decades, sought to develop a reconstituted non-positivist conception of natural science and, premised upon it, a reconfigured idea of 'critical social science'.

Bhaskar's 'critical realist' reformulation of the aims and methods of social science has important theoretical, methodological and political consequences for the study of social sciences, international relations among them. Yet, Roy Bhaskar constitutes a somewhat curious 'critical theorist' in the context of this collection, for he is a philosopher of science, not a commentator on substantive social affairs, let alone on international politics. No direct consequences follow from his thought for the analysis of international relations. Also, his position in the critical theory lexicon is controversial because his particular brand of philosophy of science has been fiercely contested by many other 'critical theorists', in international relations and beyond. The debates between poststructuralist thinkers and Bhaskarian critical realists, for example, have been tense (Sayer 2000; Campbell 1998b; 1999a and Wight 1999). These debates have not only highlighted the inherently controversial nature of the notion of 'critical' theorising in social inquiry but also the contested role of the idea of 'science' in conceptualising the aims and methods of critical theory. Against the science-sceptic trends that have been influential in twentieth century critical theory, Bhaskar's work has sought to highlight the fact that the idea of science need not and should not be abandoned as the basis of critical social theorising: for him, science (in a non-positivist reconstituted sense) is a key aspect of 'emancipatory' critical social theory.

Context of Bhaskar's thought

Roy Bhaskar was born in 1944 to a family with Indian and English parentage. His early years are of little consequence to the discussion here, yet a short note on his experiences at university are interesting in allowing us to better understand some of the underlying motivations in his work. What is notable is that Bhaskar's entry into the study of philosophy at university was somewhat accidental and also that it was informed by a deep interest in oppressive social forces in society.

Bhaskar entered university in the 1960s to study Philosophy, Politics and Economics at Balliol College, Oxford. As a student, along with many of his 1960s contemporaries, he became deeply concerned about the problem of world poverty, and the inadequacy of modern social science, notably the science of economics, to deal with this problem. Motivated by this concern, Bhaskar eventually started work on a PhD thesis on the relevance of economic theory for underdeveloped countries. This research never got as far as he initially hoped, however, as he found himself 'distracted' by important philosophy of social science questions that he felt he should deal with prior to proceeding further into his PhD studies.

By delving into the study of philosophy of science and social science he became increasingly dissatisfied with the debates characteristic of these fields. At the time key battles in the philosophy of science were conducted between the so-called theorists of 'growth of knowledge', Popper, Lakatos, Kuhn and Feyerabend. In philosophy of social science, on the other hand, debates between the 'positivist' scientists of society and 'hermeneutic' opponents of a scientific study of social affairs were dominant. While the idea of science remained at the core of all these debates, Bhaskar was perplexed by the fact that a curiously singular discourse of science seemed to inform the debates philosophically.

The proponents of scientific inquiry in mid-twentieth century philosophy of science tended to openly draw on the long tradition of empiricist-positivist philosophy of science to justify their approach to science. Positivism is an infamously contested term but it is generally associated with the belief that 'scientific methods' can, in reference to empirical observational evidence, justify the superiority of some knowledge claims (scientific) over others (say, speculative, metaphysical or religious). Positivist philosophies of science are informed by an empiricist theory of knowledge: belief in perceptual impressions as a key way of generating and validating knowledge. For key positivists during Bhaskar's studies, such as Karl Popper (1959) and Carl Gustav Hempel (1965) for example, the best way to come to know the world was through the study of *observational regularities* in the world around us. On the basis of knowledge of general observational patterns (or laws), and equipped with a rigorous deductive logic, we could form valid and reliable scientific knowledge and make predictions through which we can exert some control over our environment, natural and social. Popper's and Hempel's positivism was premised upon a deductive and falsificationist conception of scientific logic and the progress of science (not the inductive and verificationist view of earlier 'logical' positivists), yet the key emphasis of their deductive-nomological (DN-) model of science was still on the ability to set criteria for more or less objective 'truth-approximating' knowledge. However, Thomas Kuhn's (1962) account of the history of science had posed deep challenges to this kind of perspective. Kuhn argued that, instead of working independently of their social context and seeking unbiased falsification of arguments, scientists are in fact inevitably influenced by their social context. The parameters of what is seen as 'normal science' shapes in deep ways their knowledge claims, what they study and how. Science and its superiority as a 'way of knowing' received a knock from Kuhn, then, and also simultaneously from many critical theorists of the Frankfurt School vein sceptical of the destructive outcomes of scientific knowledge during the early twentieth century (for example in the 'Marxist' Soviet Union and during the Second World War).

In the social sciences too, the idea of science was fiercely contested. The so-called interpretivist and hermeneutic scholars argued that social inquiry should not pretend to be akin to the natural sciences and should instead be focused on 'interpreting', more akin to the arts, the unique configurations of thought and meaning that agents hold. There were different strands of interpretivism: 'traditional' hermeneuticians tried to gain an understanding of the 'real meanings' that actors held, whereas more 'radical' interpretivists following Wittgenstein and poststructuralist ideas started to emphasise that we cannot claim to unearth the real meanings or reasons of actors but rather should merely study the complexity of the language games or discursive constructions that provide the context for social actors' behaviour (Bauman 1978; Hollis 1994). The interpretivists, despite the variations between them, were united in emphasising the inadequacies of the generalising, observational, predictive and 'value-neutral' conception of social science advocated by the positivists. Social inquiry, interpretivists argued, necessitates interpretive judgements and normative evaluations. Importantly, the interpretive tradition tended to be hostile to the very language of science and causation – science and causation were seen as notions fundamentally embedded within the objectivist 'instrumentally rational' social science (Horkheimer and Adorno 1972).

Substantial divisions on the idea of science characterised the study of the philosophy of science and social science as Bhaskar came to these fields. What Bhaskar noted, however, was that despite the apparent contestation, there was surprising agreement behind the scenes on the 'picture of science' adopted by the different perspectives. Little questioning of the key principles of an empiricist-positivist discourse of science were present in the debates – on the pro-science or the science-sceptic sides. Bhaskar's key contribution was, as will be seen, to dig deeper into the philosophical underpinnings of the idea of science. He reframed the idea of science – philosophically – in such a way as to take account of the challenge of the Kuhnian position, while still retaining (in a non-Popperian way) the belief that science tries to capture something about the world 'out there', in the social sciences too, despite the dynamic and linguistic nature of social objects.

In developing his distinct philosophy of science and social science, Bhaskar developed insights made initially by Rom Harré, a noted philosopher of science, and his supervisor. Harré had been developing critiques of the empiricist and the DN-model of scientific causal explanation and thus had started to make forays into what might be called a realist philosophy of science (Harré and Madden 1975). Bhaskar identified great potential in realist ideas but wanted to push their study much further than his supervisor. Bhaskar started by outlining his re-interpretation of a realist philosophy of science in *A Realist Theory of Science* (1975). He then published his influential retake on philosophy of social science, *The Possibility of Naturalism* (1998 [1979]). This was followed by *Scientific Realism and Human Emancipation* (1986), which made the argument for overcoming the fact/value distinction and the institution of 'explanatory critiques' in the social sciences. These books constituted the central arguments of his 'critical realist' answer to the philosophical problem fields in the philosophy of science and social science.

In the 1990s Bhaskar's work then moved in radically new directions, reaching beyond the classical philosophy of science territory that his thought had become relatively influential in. In 1993 and 1994 he published his key 'dialectical' works *Dialectic: the Pulse of Freedom* and *Plato etc: the Problems of Philosophy and Their Resolution*. In the new millennium, Bhaskar's work has taken its most controversial twist, with his turn to religion and 'transcendental dialectic critical realism' developed in *From East to West: The Odyssey of a Soul* (2000) and *Reflections on Meta-Reality: Transcendence, Emancipation and Everyday Life* (2002).

Bhaskar's key arguments

The distinctiveness of Bhaskar's thought lies in that, unlike many of his contemporaries, he is not ready to accept that the epistemological relativity of our knowledge (pointed to by the likes of Kuhn and Toulmin in philosophy of science and many radical interpretivists in philosophy of social science) entails the impossibility of conceiving of an independent reality of being or of a scientific approach to the study of reality. Bhaskar's philosophy is highly critical of the positivist tradition, which for him misunderstands the nature of science, but he is also critical of those positions that move to reject the idea of science altogether. Bhaskar's philosophy seeks to reconcile *ontological realism* (belief in real independently existing reality), *epistemological relativism* (the non-hierarchical pecking order of theories of knowledge) and *judgemental rationality* (the notion that we can provide 'good reasons' for why we prefer some accounts of reality to others). There are a number of different steps to his arguments. We need to here understand the core principles of: his 'transcendental realist' philosophy of science; his 'critical realist' philosophy of social science; and his conception of 'critical social science'. I will also make a brief comment on the dialectic and spiritual turns in his arguments.

Bhaskar on natural science

The first step in Bhaskar's philosophical system is his distinctive realist position on the philosophy of science. In his first book *A Realist Theory of Science* (1975) Bhaskar argued for a 'transcendental realist' position on the philosophy of natural sciences. His key argument was that empiricist-positivist accounts in philosophy of science, in prioritising empiricist epistemology (that is perceptual observation) as the basis of their view of science, have come to reduce 'reality' of the world to 'empirical reality', that which is observable. This reduction of 'what is' to 'what is perceived' is problematic, however: it has ignored the fact that the experimental practice of science actually presupposes that the objects of scientific explanation must exist not just 'perceptually' 'for us' but also ontologically ('really') on deeper unobservable levels of reality.

Bhaskar argues that positivists have failed to capture the fact that 'deep understanding' of causal powers of objects and their complex interactions is actually what natural science is 'about'. Science is not about observing laws or prediction but about *understanding* what it is about the nature of objects that generates observational laws of particular kinds. Importantly, Bhaskar argues that reality is stratified: it consists of multiple 'levels of reality', including the empirical observable reality, but also the 'actual' event-level reality and a 'deep ontological' unobservable level of reality (Bhaskar 1975: 13). Science, Bhaskar argues, studies the deeper ontological levels of reality, not just 'superficial' conjunctions of regular observations. Laws and regularities highlighted by positivists, Bhaskar points out, can only be produced 'artificially' in laboratory conditions, where the complexity of reality can be narrowed down. The ontological reality that science studies, however, consists of deep ontological 'open systems' where multiple generating mechanisms are constantly at work. It is these systems that sciences seek to understand and they do so not simply through empiricist epistemology but through an 'opportunistic' combination of epistemological perspectives, including use of the rational faculties and conventions of language available to them.

Importantly, just because the practice of science, and our everyday activities, must be underpinned by some sense of an independent and stratified reality, this does not mean that Bhaskar thinks that we can directly access it. Realism then *does not* claim 'privileged access to Truth', foundationalism or naïve objectivism, as critics often mistakenly assume (Sayer 2000: 2). For Bhaskar, our scientific accounts are but attempts, through various socially and politically engendered metaphors and analogies, to try and postulate what the (deep ontological) reality of the world consists in (by virtue of which particular event regularities may come about). Thus, scientific knowledge is 'a social product much like any other': it is socially and politically consequential and historically reflective of social and political prejudices of scientists (as many sociologists of knowledge, feminists and postcolonialists have argued). Yet, crucially, while science is a social activity, at the same time scientific 'knowledge is *of* things' (Bhaskar 1975: 21). Ontological objects of science are not *dependent* on our knowledge of them: 'if men ceased to exist sound would continue to travel and heavy bodies fall to earth' (Bhaskar 1975: 21).

But can this argument stand in the social world? Surely in the social world objects of study – social meanings, people's reasons or social structures around us – cannot be considered (ontologically or epistemologically) independent of the students of them?

Bhaskar on 'critical naturalism' in the social sciences

Bhaskar's second book *The Possibility of Naturalism* (1998 [1979]) argued that because positivists misunderstand the philosophical underpinnings of natural science, they dangerously misunderstand the nature of social sciences. Social science, Bhaskar argues, can be scientific. However, crucially, social science should not need to replicate the natural sciences in methods to be considered scientific (as the empiricist-positivists assume). This is because the *ontological* objects of study of the social sciences – ideas, beliefs, social actors, meanings, reasons, social structures and so on – are ontologically very different from the kinds of objects that the natural sciences study. The distinct nature of social objects requires that we use distinct methods and epistemological approaches to study them.

The nature of social ontology means that we must, first of all, accept that *interpretation* is fundamental to social science. Meanings and reasons held by actors need to be understood in order to understand why things happen in the social world: observation of behavioural patterns only tells us little about causal forces in the social world. Ontologically, key causal forces in the social world are *unobservable*: think of ideas, reasons, discourses and so on. This makes interpretive and inherently conceptual engagement with objects fundamental: we must grasp the nature of and relations between social objects *conceptually*. This, however, also means that it is crucial to recognise that social scientific accounts are always embedded in social and political contexts and there is no escaping *'double hermeneutic'* relations between researchers and their objects of study.

However, the double hermeneutic nature of social inquiry does not mean for Bhaskar that social sciences are not *about* something, that there are no 'real' social objects in the social world that can be studied systematically and reflexively, and that are, fundamentally, causal on our actions. We cannot assume that causalities in the social world are regular and work in universal patterns, as the positivist conception of causal analysis assumes, but this does not mean that in the social world rules, discourses, reasons and so on 'come from nowhere', unconditioned and unrestrained, and have no consequences.

Bhaskar makes a strong argument for the recognition of the reality and causality of various unobservable objects: among them most notably the idea of social structures. Human agency, he argues, exists always in the condition of being causally constrained and enabled by social structural causalities around it. Bhaskar's Transformational Model of Social Reality is deeply sceptical of individualist approaches that only accept individuals and their behaviour as a core aspect of social ontology. Bhaskar's view of social world instead leans towards a more structuralist conception of social reality, and in this sense reveals something of a Marxist root in Bhaskar's thinking (this does not, however, mean that Bhaskar's view of science is nothing but a Marxist theory of science (Brown 2007)).

A key aspect of Bhaskar's philosophy of social science is that it rejects the narrow empiricist-positivist view of science and that it thus defends the insights of various interpretivist approaches in the social sciences. Given this, one would think it logical for social theorists on the interpretive side to accept the Bhaskarian line of argument and join the effort to reclaim social science away from the positivist criteria. Yet, some important differences still remain between Bhaskar's 'critical realism' and some of the more radical versions of interpretivism: over the question of truth (can we talk of truth at all? what conceptions of truth should we work with?), the role of ontology (can ontological objects exist independently of our episteme?) and the politics of utilising scientific terminology (does reference to science entail depoliticisation?). Indeed, it is important to note that differences exist between Bhaskar's conception of critical social science and those of other twentieth century strands of critical theory. One key difference is that Bhaskar continues to maintain that not all interpretations are equally valid: we can have good ontological, evidential or epistemological reasons to prioritise some interpretations over others. Importantly, contrary to many of his contemporaries, Bhaskar on this basis maintains strongly that commitment to judgemental rationalism and to the possibility of social science constitutes a key aspect of, rather than a threat to, critical social theorising.

Bhaskar on 'critical' social science

A key aspect of Bhaskar's approach, developed initially in *The Possibility of Naturalism* (1998 [1979]) and in more detail in *Scientific Realism and Human Emancipation* (1986) is that it directly rejects the positivist separation of fact and value statements. For Bhaskar it is crucial to recognise that facts and values are mutually implicated and that this is the case in both the social and natural sciences. Bhaskar makes two claims here. First, he argues that causal/explanatory accounts are always embedded within value systems. This claim is not controversial as such but in line with most interpretivist and postpositivist understandings: all social accounts secretly carry normative leanings, in concepts and research questions themselves. However, importantly, Bhaskar goes further and argues that our scientific causal/explanatory accounts can also *direct our normative judgements*.

This is why social scientific knowledge is important for Bhaskar: scientific explanatory/causal accounts can direct us in understanding what is oppressive or delimiting about the conditions, rules, discourses or social structures that people live within. Because Bhaskar holds on to the idea that some accounts in principle can capture aspects of ontological social reality better than others (and that rational grounds can be given for theory choice), it follows that explanatory accounts can have a key role in enabling *criticism* of existing forms of oppression and in seeking transformation of social reality. Indeed, Bhaskar argues for a critical social science with emancipatory aims as its ultimate goal. Bhaskar's critical realism, as Sayer puts it, 'offers a rationale for a critical social science, one that is critical of the social practices it studies as well as of other theories' (Sayer 2000: 18). Contrary to the positivist logic, critical realists on Bhaskarian lines do not see a contradiction between explanatory and critical social science: having reclaimed the idea of causal explanation away from the positivist objectivism and value-fact distinction, they see it as self-evident that 'explanations of social practices must be critical precisely in order to be explanatory, and that the necessity of critique gives social science a potentially emancipatory character' (Sayer, 2000: 159).

These kinds of claims are of course controversial, not only for the positivists, who see the role of values and politics in the practice of social science as dangerously relativistic, but also for many twentieth century critical theorists that have moved away from the idea of truth as a normative aim and also from the notion of emancipation because of the dangers inherent in emancipatory grand narratives. Bhaskar's ideas could be seen as an attempt to reclaim a 'classical' Marx-inspired critical theory project centred around identifying real structural forms of social oppression with the aim of overcoming them. It is important to note, however, that Bhaskar does not advance Marxism, nor does he hold on to a naïve conception of emancipatory social science: he does not assume that critical social science will entail easy agreements on what constitute wrong or oppressive practices, or solutions and improvements – difficult explanatory contestations are involved, as well as important normative questions (this is elaborated well in Sayer (2000) and Patomäki (2002)). Yet, his approach emphasises that it is important to assume that we can make reasoned judgements over differential explanatory accounts of social reality and use explanatory and evidential grounds as bases for imagining 'concrete utopias' or 'possible worlds' (Patomäki, 2002).

Science, then, is not the antithesis of social critique, but rather is seen as a key facet of it.

A comment on dialectic and spiritual turns

Bhaskar is most famous for having advanced the three arguments summarised above, in other words for his 'critical realist' philosophy of science and social science. However, it should also be noted that he has recently developed radically new, if much-criticised, directions in his work. From 1993 onwards Bhaskar's thinking has taken two important turns: first a dialectic and then a spiritual turn.

'Dialectic critical realism', which Bhaskar developed in the early 1990s, was an attempt to explicitly formulate a theory of dialectics premised on a critical realist philosophy of science. I cannot claim to do full justice to this theory here. It suffices to say that his 1993 and 1994 texts developed a vision of a four-stage dialectic that drew on but also challenged in important ways modern philosophical conceptions of dialectics, notably Hegel's idea of the dialectic. The key to Bhaskar's idea of the dialectic was not only the development of an ontological aspect to dialectics, but also the idea of 'real absence' as the core of dialectics. Dialectic, for Bhaskar, signifies a process of removal (absenting) of obstacles (conceived as absence) to human flourishing. Dialectics conceived in terms of 'absenting of absences' is seen as the bedrock of criticism of oppressive social forms, and thus important for critical social science. This dialectical turn in many ways then complemented the earlier arguments Bhaskar had made on the philosophy of social science.

However, in the dialectical texts Bhaskar already highlighted some holistic failures of Western philosophy and way of life. To fully explore the failures of Western philosophy, he delved into the study of the cultural and religious underpinnings of Western philosophy. In *From East to West* (2000) Bhaskar, controversially, started to explore the idea that people could be conceived as essentially God-like. Bhaskar argued, to the dismay of many 'secular' critical realist followers, that through humans' embeddedness in oppressive social forms, they had become 'disenchanted', they had forgotten their God-like essence. Bhaskar argued for a shedding of the obstacles to our 'self-realisation' through 'unconditional love'. In his philosophy of meta-reality (2002), he further argues for critique of all forms of dualisms and dichotomies that characterise secular and religious thought in search of non-duality in self-realisation.

Bhaskar's later ideas, associated by some with New Age religiosity, have been fiercely contested by many followers of his 'classical' critical realism. Indeed, many argue that Bhaskar has turned against his earlier realist roots and hence has taken critical realism down a wrong alley during the last decade or so. Interesting debates have arisen as a result of Bhaskar's later turns, highlighting the diversity of 'critical realist' philosophical ideas, and also the paradoxical ways in which the '-ism' that Bhaskar gave rise to (critical realism) has come to challenge the legitimacy of the ideas of its founder.

Bhaskar and international relations

A number of authors have developed Bhaskarian lines of thought in their interventions in international relations, theorists such as Colin Wight (2006), Heikki Patomäki (2002, 2004, 2007), David Dessler (1989, 1991), Jonathan Joseph (2007), Jamie Morgan (2002), Touko Piiparinen (2007) and, although to a more limited extent, Alexander Wendt (1999). It is notable that these contributions have rather uniformly drawn on the 'classical' philosophy of science and social science arguments in Bhaskar's thought, ignoring by and large the later controversial turns in his thinking.

But what are the consequences of utilising Bhaskar's critical realist ideas in international relations? First, it is important to note that the fact that increasing numbers of international relations theorists are drawing on Bhaskar does not mean that his critical realism provides a distinct *theory of international relations*: constructing a new international relations theory is *not* the aim or the remit of a meta-theory of science such as critical realism. Bhaskar's ideas offer no new 'grand theory' of international relations and, indeed, critical realists in international relations tend to be sceptical of such theories (see especially Wight 2006). Three distinct 'thematic' contributions could be said to emerge from Bhaskarian interventions into international relations, however:

(1) an explicit philosophy of science justification for methodological pluralism in international relations
(2) accentuated emphasis on conditioning and social structural causes in world politics
(3) a more open recognition and engagement with the 'politics of science' in international relations.

First, Bhaskar's thought emphasises and justifies a methodologically pluralist approach to international relations. International relations, along with other social sciences, has been deeply divided over the idea of science. Both positivist and interpretivist traditions have been present and their juxtaposition has deeply influenced international relations. The debate between positivists and interpretivists was evident in the 'second debate' between traditionalists and behaviouralists in international relations (Knorr and Rosenau 1969) and can be clearly seen in international relations' so-called 'fourth debate' (Wæver 1996), which juxtaposes 'explanatory' international relations against 'understanding' international relations (Hollis and Smith 1990), or rationalist scientific international relations against reflectivist 'postpositivist' or 'postmodernist' international relations (Keohane 1988). Indeed, the core claim accepted by many in contemporary international relations follows Hollis and Smith's famous argument that there are 'two stories to be told' about world politics: scientific, looking for general causes through objective positivist scientific methods, and interpretive, looking for contingent interpreted meanings and understandings informing actors or debates (Hollis and Smith 1990).

Bhaskar's ideas question the division of the discipline into explanatory and understanding, causal and non-causal, scientific and reflectivist endeavours and, indeed, the division of international relations to 'meta-theoretical camps' has been criticised by many of those who draw on Bhaskar's ideas (Patomäki and Wight 2000; Patomäki 2002; Kurki 2006, 2008). Contra the positivist view of science, dominant among rationalist/explanatory international relations research (encapsulating many realists, liberals and some constructivists), Bhaskar's ideas provide a justification for the inclusion of interpretive approaches as a key aspect of international relations as a social science by arguing that the positivist criteria for knowledge construction are too narrow and limiting in the study of world politics, and in fact run the risk of international relations theorists missing out from their inquiries some of the most important aspects of world politics: the role of rules, such as human rights norms or balance of power, discourses, such as discourses of the war on terror or development, and social structures, such as capitalism or patriarchy. Bhaskarian ideas direct us to dismiss the overly predictive and objectivist view of science characteristic of the social scientific mainstream in international relations, for example, in the study of democratic peace (Kurki 2008). Critical realists in international relations argue that a scientific study of world political processes, such as globalisation or democratic peace, need not and should not entail the mere study of large scale regularities (e.g. law of democratic peace) but rather should take account of ontological depth (structures explaining behaviour) and contextuality (complex layers of causation). It highlights not prediction but construction of conceptual models through which the complex conditioning forces – material, discursive, and so on – can be conceived as bringing about specific kind of interactions in historical and social contexts (Patomäki 2002; Wight 2006; Kurki 2008). It also highlights the political consequentiality of the kinds of concepts (of say democracy or war) we use in our studies.

The shift towards a methodologically pluralistic international relations is important; because it invalidates the positivist attempts to hold onto a set of overly rigid criteria for theory evaluation (Nicholson 1996; King, Keohane and Verba 1994) but also because it emphasises that the positivist attempts to exclude reflectivist approaches as 'non-scientific' and hence somehow unsystematic and simplistic (Keohane 1988) is deeply problematic. Bhaskar's arguments allows us to recognise that reflectivist, supposedly non-causal and non-scientific, studies do make important knowledge claims about world politics and do so on the basis of (in most cases) well-justified ontological, epistemological, methodological *and* evidential grounds (see e.g. Campbell 1998b). If the positivist idea of science is rejected, the reflectivists need not be seen as working outside the confines of a social scientific approach.

Second, Bhaskar's ideas allow us to put more emphasis on dealing with contextual, conditioning and structural causes as important forces in international relations. Critical realists point out that the positivist view of science has a predilection for atomism and individualism (because objects of science and causes can only be observable particulars). Indeed, most 'rationalist' international relations explanations, even when terminologically structuralist, have tended to be at their root individualistic (see criticisms of Waltz posed by Wendt (1999)). Constructivists, critical theorists, historical materialists and postpositivists have been critical of individualism in international relations, calling for study of contextual forces such as rules, norms, discourses and social structures. Bhaskar's arguments would substantiate and support the arguments of these international relations theorists. Because human agents are not the only causal forces in the social world, because they are in important ways conditioned by rules, norms, and discourses, the study of conditioning causes of various kinds is fundamental to the social sciences, international relations among them.

Bhaskar's critical realism, distinctively, argues also for study of 'social structural' context. Social structures, for Bhaskar, are not mere conglomerations of actions/interests of individuals, groups, systems of input and output, or 'shared beliefs' but rather *social relations*. For critical realists, agents always exist in various social structural positions (citizen, tenant, labourer, wife), that is, in 'internal relations' with other (groups of) agents (state bureaucracy, landlord, capitalist, husband). Social structural positions (tenant/landlord, wage-labourer/capitalist, core state/peripheral state) condition and enable the actions of actors within them – materially and ideationally. Social structures are then not reducible to an individual's ideas, nor are they reducible to norms, rules, or inter-subjective understandings (see Wight's critique of the constructivist conception of structure (Wight 2006: 155–63)). It is this emphasis on the multiplicity of, but also the unintended structural nature of, social conditions that enables 'critical realism to have a cutting edge through identifying contextual constraints upon our freedoms' (Archer 1998: 203).

Third, Bhaskar's thought emphasises the importance of recognising the politically embedded nature of the assumptions we make about world politics or the methods we choose to apply in relation to that sphere. Hence, there is no apolitical study of causes of war, democratic peace, Nordic community, Russian foreign policy or democratisation. All explanations and conceptual systems in international relations are embedded within social contexts that are politically and normatively influential on the frames of reference applied to empirical study. This reinforces the claims made by other postpositivists in international relations that remind us that our analyses are politically consequential and always entail certain political and normative judgements on existing political or discursive realities.

Yet, critical realism also adds something to these claims: it has the potential to reveal that debates about science themselves are embedded in the process of social construction of world politics and that distinct political consequences follow from *whether* and *in what sense* international relations is conceived as a 'science'. Critical realism allows us to see that positivist scientists' emphasis on observable linear forms of causality, their objectivity and their tendencies towards the reproduction of methodological individualism are not short of political consequences for the study of international politics. Neither are constructivist studies of norms over material factors, or poststructuralist refusals to make judgments on 'real causes' of war or inequality, apolitical. Critical realism, too, it seems is a far from an apolitical meta-theory of science: it leans towards structural explanations, contextualised ethics and pluralism of perspectives (albeit with a commitment to rational dialogue between them). As Brown (2007) has argued, there are tendencies in Bhaskar's critical realism towards historically materialist and Marxist political leanings, although in my view these leanings do not define the scope of possible theoretical leanings it can substantiate (an important debate needs to be had about the range of theories that critical realism is compatible with). Critical realism emphasises, nevertheless, that all positions on the study of and science of international relations entail political leanings, although not specific political positions. Bhaskar's critical realism encourages us to openly recognise the 'politics of science debate' in international relations and to engage in this debate. If nothing else, then, perhaps the most important contribution that Bhaskar's writings have made is that they re-politicise and re-invigorate debates on science in the social sciences, international relations among them.

Further reading

Bhaskar, Roy (1998) *The Possibility of Naturalism: A Philosophical Critique of the Contemporary Human Sciences*, 3rd ed, London: Routledge. This is a key text to refer to in Bhaskar's writings on social sciences. See especially chapter 2.

Collier, Andrew (1994) *Critical Realism; an Introduction to Roy Bhaskar's Philosophy*, London: Verso. This book provides an excellent introduction to Bhaskar's philosophy for those seeking both a clear explication of his ideas as well as commentary on them.

Patomäki, Heikki and Colin Wight (2000) 'After Post-Positivism? The Promises of Critical Realism', *International Studies Quarterly* 44(2): 213–37. A seminal text in international relations introducing a critical realist critique of positivist and postpositivist positions.

Patomäki, Heikki (2002) *After International Relations: Critical realism and the (re)constitution of world politics*, London: Routledge. Patomäki criticises the ontological, epistemological and methodological underpinnings of 'international relations' as a field and advances an interesting set of empirical readings of world political processes drawing on the insights of Bhaskar's critical realism.

Wight, Colin (2006) *Agents, Structures and International Relations*, Cambridge: Cambridge University Press. An account of the literature on the agent-structure problem in international relations from a broadly critically realist perspective. Chapter 1 of this text is especially powerful in making a case for the study of international relations from a Bhaskar inspired critical realist viewpoint.

Forum of Scientific and Critical Realism (2007) *Millennium: Journal of International Studies* 35(2). This forum includes defences and commentaries on scientific and critical realism in international relations theory.

9 Pierre Bourdieu

Peter Jackson

The social theory of Pierre Bourdieu has been a major referent point in sociology and cultural studies since the early 1970s. Bourdieu's work has also had a significant impact on such diverse disciplines as sociology, history, criminology, law and even translation studies. At the centre of Bourdieu's sociological project is a 'theory of human practice' that marries 'subjectivist' agent-centred approaches to social theory with 'objectivist' accounts that emphasize the role of structural conditions in shaping social life. A unifying theme in all of Bourdieu's work is a critique of the cultural dynamics of domination. This critique deploys the key concepts of 'habitus', 'field', 'symbolic power' and 'symbolic violence' in considering the ways that existing social hierarchies and power relations are legitimated and reproduced by cultural representations and by practices. These representations and practices, Bourdieu argues, usually go unrecognised because of their symbolic character. But they are crucial to the process in which relations of domination are created and reproduced through the systematic imposition of categories of meaning. These categories are internalised by social actors to the extent that they secure a 'taken-for-granted' status and serve as a basis for practices. Bourdieu's focus on the inter-relationship between the material and symbolic dimensions of power in social life holds out real promise for students of international relations.

Background and intellectual development

The life and career of Pierre Bourdieu were replete with paradoxes. From a very modest lower middle-class background, Bourdieu fashioned a spectacular career and a world-wide reputation. A significant proportion of Bourdieu's most influential work is a critique of the very institution that made his career possible: the French educational system. His political project – to uncover the cultural architecture of domination within this system – was mounted from a position of undeniable dominance within the field of French academia. During the final decade of his life, after having criticised the institution of the 'public intellectual' in France for most of his career, he emerged as a major public figure of the intellectual left to criticise the dominance of neo-liberal political discourse after the Cold War.

From modest origins in south-western France, Bourdieu excelled as a student, winning a place at the prestigious *Lycée Louis-le-Grand* in Paris before going on to study philosophy at the *École normale supérieure* where his contemporaries included Michel Foucault, Jacques Derrida and Emmanuel Le Roy Ladurie. The training in philosophy Bourdieu received there was fundamental to the evolution of his social theory. The prominence of epistemological issues in both his theoretical framework and methodological strategies reflects his conception of sociology as 'fieldwork in philosophy' (Bourdieu 1990a: 3–33, 2004: 16–18). But over the course of the 1950s Bourdieu's intellectual focus evolved from philosophy to sociology via self-taught ethnography. This trajectory was, at least in part, a reaction to the dominance of Marxism and existentialism in the intellectual climate of post-1945 France (Bourdieu 2004: 21–27). Although Bourdieu was part of a generation of students that rejected this dual hegemony, his sociology is heavily influenced by both movements. It draws on both the subjectivist orientation of existentialism and the Marxist focus on structures. The result is a strikingly original approach that focuses specifically on the inter-relationship between the symbolic and the material dimensions of social life.

Bourdieu's experience in North Africa was also highly formative. After passing the *agrégation* in philosophy in 1954, he was called up to fulfil his military service as a conscript in the Algerian War of Independence. The five years Bourdieu spent in Algeria, first as a soldier in the French army and then as an assistant lecturer at the faculty of letters at the University of Algiers, exposed him to the grim realities of French colonialism and helped sharpen his sensitivity to the dynamics of domination (Bourdieu 2004: 61–86). It was also during this period that Bourdieu conducted extensive research into the Kabyle peasant society in north-eastern Algeria and in so doing laid the conceptual foundations for his 'theory of practice' (Bourdieu 1977, 2004: 49–50).

Bourdieu returned to Paris in 1960 and was appointed as teaching assistant to Raymond Aron, Professor of Sociology and Political Science at the University of Paris (Sorbonne). The relationship with Aron was an important one for Bourdieu's career. The two had much in common. Both were *normaliens* and *agrégés* in philosophy with an interest in Marx and Weber. With Aron's patronage, Bourdieu was appointed a director of studies at the *École Pratique des Hautes Études*. This post was significant in that it provided him with a base to develop his research outside the traditional career structure of the French university teaching system. From this base Bourdieu produced a remarkable body of increasingly influential work. He secured an important reputation inside France with the publication of two jointly-authored studies of worker's and peasant's culture in Algeria (Bourdieu *et al.* 1963; Bourdieu and Sayad 2000), this was followed by a co-authored critique of the class-based structure of French university education (Bourdieu and Passeron 2000), and an influential discussion of the 'craft' of sociology (Bourdieu *et al.* 1991 [1968] [English translation]). It was during the 1970s and early 1980s, however, that Bourdieu acquired a truly international profile with the appearance of *Reproduction in Education, Society and Culture* (Bourdieu and Passeron: 2000 [1970]), *Outline of a Theory of Practice* (1972 and 1977), *Distinction: A Social Critique of the Judgement of Taste* (1979 and 1984). The latter work, in particular, helped Bourdieu secure the chair in sociology at the *Collège de France* in 1982. It was from this position at the pinnacle of the French academic profession that Bourdieu produced the key works *Homo Academicus* (1984 and 1988), *The State Nobility: Elite Schools in the Field of Power* (1989 and 1996) and a number of collections of essays among the most influential of which are *In Other Words: Essays Toward a Reflexive Sociology* (1990a), *Language and Symbolic Power* (1991) and *The Fields of Cultural Production: Essays on Art and Literature* (1993). Bourdieu remained active right up to his death from cancer in 2002, at which point he had established a towering reputation both inside and outside France.

The diversity in Bourdieu's career trajectory is reflected in the many influences on his theorising. His 'science of practice' brings to bear an exceptionally wide range of intellectual approaches from Pascal's critique of Cartesian rationalism to Wittgenstein's philosophy of language. The fundamental influences on his thought were the historian and philosopher of science Gaston Bachelard and sociologists Karl Marx, Max Weber and Emile Durkheim. Bachelard's influence is manifest in the centrality of epistemological concerns to Bourdieu's theoretical approach (Bourdieu 2004: 19–20). Bachelard argued, in particular, for an historical and reflexive epistemology which subjects existing theories to constant critical scrutiny (Bachelard 1934 and 1947). Bourdieu's reading of Bachelard was fundamental in informing his focus on the role of 'pre-constructions' in shaping understandings of both social reality and social scientific enquiry (Bourdieu *et al.* 1991: 84–89 and 152–59; Swartz 1997: 30–33).

Bourdieu was profoundly influenced by Marx's insistence on class as a fundamental category of social life and on the interest-oriented character of social actions. He adapted Marx's category of 'false consciousness' to develop his theory of 'misrecognition'. Both concepts aim to demonstrate how cultural practices function to perpetuate social inequality. Crucially, however, Bourdieu does not accept the Marxist conviction that the symbolic dimensions to human existence are derivative from the material components of social life. He rejects the distinction between infrastructure and superstructure so central to Marxist analysis. Indeed, Bourdieu's key concept of the 'field' is aimed at capturing the *inter-relationship* between the material and the symbolic in human experience that is ruled out by this distinction (Swartz 1997: 40–41 and 76–94). Bourdieu's understanding of class also differs fundamentally from that of Marx. Class, for Bourdieu, can be constituted by cultural practices and representations as well as by relationships to the means of production (Bourdieu 1991: 229–48; Wacquant 2001b). This is linked to a more basic divergence: for Marx the basic human drive is that for material improvement; for Bourdieu, conversely, it is the desire for social distinction (Bourdieu 2003: 297–331 and Wacquant 2007: 263–64 and 274). All of this makes Bourdieu's approach much closer to that of Max Weber. The same is true of his conceptualisation of the social universe as an arena defined by 'endless and pitiless competition' (Wacquant 2007: 266). Weber's focus on prestige and social status, along with his reflections on the inter-relationship between symbolic practices and material interests, were developed by Bourdieu into the concepts of symbolic power and symbolic violence (Bourdieu 1987: 122–31). In this way, Bourdieu was able to expand the Marxist concept of capital to account for the fact that actors pursue cultural and symbolic as well as material forms of power and indeed will often exchange one for the other in pursuit of status and distinction (Swartz 1997: 42).

A final key influence on Bourdieu was the pioneering sociology of Émile Durkheim (Wacquant 2001b). Bourdieu's emphasis on the social origins of both schemes of perception and action owes much to Durkheim. The same is true of his emphasis on the importance of treating 'social facts' as objects of investigation (Bourdieu *et al.* 1991: 12–62). Bourdieu expanded on these themes to argue that cognitive structures are essentially internalised social structures and to develop the concept of the field as a network of objective social relations to be subjected to rigorous empirical research and analysis. Durkheim's warning about the invidious effects of 'pre-notions' in distorting social scientific enquiry reverberates strongly with Bourdieu (as it did with Bachelard) (Swartz 1997: 45–47). Also important was Durkheim's interest in social differentiation and its relationship to the division of labour within societies. This line of reasoning and investigation was central to the evolution of Bourdieu's conceptualisation of distinction. The great difference, however, is that Durkheim viewed these phenomena as a fundamentally positive trend that operates to rationalise society and to enhance its internal cohesion by limiting social conflict. For Bourdieu, however, the chief effect of the process of differentiation is to regulate conflict and to reproduce structures of social domination (Wacquant 2001b: 21–27; Swartz 1997: 48).

Bourdieu's 'constructivist structuralism'

At the core of virtually all of Bourdieu's theorising is a rejection of what he described as a series of false oppositions that have played a fundamental role in shaping enquiry in the social sciences and the humanities. 'Of all the oppositions that artificially divide social science' he insisted 'the most fundamental, and the most ruinous, is the one that is set up between subjectivism and objectivism' (Bourdieu 1990a: 135). It is this dichotomy that underpins the assumed existence of further oppositions, including that between the material and symbolic dimensions of social life and, ultimately, that between interpretation and explanation. One of the chief targets of Bourdieu's intellectual project is therefore the commonly held assumption that it is necessary to takes sides on the question of agency and structure:

If I had to describe my work in two words ... I would speak of 'constructivist structuralism' or 'structuralist constructivism' ... By structuralism, or structuralist, I mean that there exists in the social world, and not only in symbolic systems (language, myths etc.), objective structures, independent of the consciousness or the will of agents, which are capable of orienting or constraining practices and representations. By constructivism I mean that there is a social genesis to both schemes of perception, thought and action on the one hand, and social structures on the other (Bourdieu 1990a: 147).

Bourdieu's theoretical approach is in large part an attempt to illustrate how what people say and do is something other than either just a reflection of what is going on in their heads or a product of social and material structures. He therefore rejects both the subjectivist assumptions of existentialism (and post-structuralism) and the historical materialism of Marxism. One of his central arguments is that it is precisely the imposition of an artificial division between agent-centred and structure-centred approaches that functions as a central impediment to the evolution of a comprehensive theory of human practice. Bourdieu attempts to overcome this opposition by focusing on the interplay between the subjective perspectives and predispositions of social actors, their *habitus*, and the structural conditions of the particular social context in which they are acting, the *field*. It is from the interrelationship between habitus and field, he argues, that practices emerge.

'Habitus' is the concept that Bourdieu deploys to understand the cultural sources of the subjectivity of social actors. The habitus should therefore be understood as the engine of cultural action. It is, as one scholar of international relations theory has observed, 'the semi-conscious (though not innate) orientation that individuals have to the world'. This orientation 'forms a basis for practice' (Williams 2007: 25). Another way to put it would be to describe the habitus as the sum of the external social structures that are internalised by social actors to enable them to function effectively. It is constituted by conscious and unconscious learned experience on the one hand, and by the cumulative impact of practices on the other. Attitudes and inclinations are inculcated by the rhythms and habits of everyday life that are characteristic of the social and economic position occupied by the agent as well as by more formalised types of education and training. A crucial effect of both types of inculcation is the internalisation of categories of meaning. In this way hierarchies, cultural practices and codes of conduct that might otherwise seem arbitrary are 'misrecognised' (a key Bourdieusien concept) by both individuals and institutions as being both natural and legitimate. Acquired through a process of inculcation, the dispositions of the habitus become 'second nature' and generate understandings and expectations which in turn set the parameters for strategies of social action (Bourdieu 1977: 143–58, 1990b: 52–65).

The habitus is both durable and transposable. It functions at the semi-conscious level as a generating principle and organiser of practices and representations. But it can also adapt over time in response to changing external conditions in order to better enable actors to achieve their objectives. This is a crucial point: the habitus is in a continual state of evolution. It is *durable* but in no way *static*. Because it functions often at the pre-conscious level, it is 'not easily accessible to reflection and conscious transformation' (Thompson 1991: 24–25). Changes in the habitus tend therefore to be gradual and to take place when structural conditions force the actor to adapt to new circumstances. This leads to the equally important point that the habitus is a 'structuring structure' – that is to say that it also constitutes outside structures by generating strategies of action on the part of other actors that will inevitably affect external conditions (Swartz 1997: 111–13).

The habitus concept has been criticised for providing an over-determined explanation of social action stemming from an 'inescapable structural determinism' at the heart of Bourdieu's conceptual approach (Swartz 1997: 211; Jenkins 2002: 79–83). His response to this charge is that, although the habitus operates through inclinations and dispositions, it does not determine action. It is instead a 'durably installed generative principle of *regulated improvisation*' (Bourdieu 1977 [my emphasis]: 56 and 1990b: 110–19). The term 'habitus' (also used by Aristotle and by scholastic philosophers) is deployed to emphasise the actor's capacity for improvisation (Burke 2004: 56–57). Indeed, Bourdieu is at pains to stress that, not only is the habitus in a constant state of evolution, it is also capable of producing a multitude of different practices, depending on the character of the external environment (the 'field') in which it is embedded.

Two final points about the habitus should be emphasised. First, the habitus animates the action of collective social actors as well as individuals. Actors who share a similar position within a given field are likely to develop similar dispositions and thus similar practices. Bourdieu stresses that institutions inevitably develop a collective habitus in their function as social actors. This is reflected not only in internal debates on specific issues, but also in the rhythms and in the social relations that give shape to everyday working practices and social relations within a given institution. Second, the habitus plays a central role in the durability of hierarchies (Bourdieu 1998: 8–14). It is the means through which the arbitrary is comprehended as natural, legitimate and even inevitable. It determines what is imaginable and what is unimaginable for the social agent and thus what is possible and what is impossible in the everyday flow of social life. Bourdieu's habitus concept thus provides an illuminating perspective on the cultural origins of social action. The emphasis on practice as both a constituent element *and* a product of culture better captures the durability of the cultural predispositions. As Terry Eagleton observes, the concept of the habitus enables a 'matching of the subjective and the objective, what we feel spontaneously disposed to do and what our social conditions demand of us' (Eagleton 1990: 157). It is therefore a central mechanism for the reproduction of political, social and economic structures in society.

The 'field' is a second essential concept. Bourdieu's field is a 'particular social universe' that is defined by the 'stakes' ['*enjeux*'] for which social actors compete. It is among the more problematic of Bourdieu's theoretical constructs because there is a lack of clarity in nearly all of his many explanations of the concept. Matters are further complicated by the fact that Bourdieu rarely explains the field in exactly the same way twice. His most quoted description is as follows:

> In analytical terms, a field can be defined as a network, or a configuration of objective relations between positions. These positions are defined objectively in their existence and in the determinations that they impose on their occupants, agents or institutions, by their current and potential situations (*situs*) in the [wider] structure of the distribution of different currencies of power (or of capital), possession of which provides access to specific profits that are up for grabs in the field, at the same time, by their objective relations to other positions (domination, subordination, equivalents etc.). In highly differentiated societies, the social cosmos is constituted by the sum of these relatively autonomous social microcosms, spaces of objective relations which have a logic and a necessity that is specific and irreducible to those that govern other fields (Bourdieu and Wacquant 1992: 94–95).

A field is therefore a network of social relations between 'positions' that are occupied by social agents. But fields are much more than the sum of the positions of these actors. They are also defined by 'distribution of different currencies of power' and, equally importantly, by a 'logic' that is a 'specific necessity' to each field and is 'irreducible' to the logics that govern other fields. While fields are relatively autonomous, they are also constantly being shaped and re-shaped both by internal struggles and by external developments in related fields. In other formulations Bourdieu describes the field as a 'social world' that is 'constantly in the process of progressive differentiation' and also 'the sum of the structural constraints on the action of its members' (Bourdieu 1987: 134 and 86 respectively). In all of his definitions of the field, however, it is an arena of struggle where actors compete for various forms of material and symbolic power resources. A central objective is always to secure the 'distinction' which will guarantee the actor's social status and serve as a source of symbolic power which is then deployed to achieve further success (Bourdieu 1990a: 123–39). For Bourdieu, differentiation and distinction give structure to social hierarchies and provide them with legitimacy by representing them as natural. The struggle for distinction is therefore a fundamental dimension of all social life (Bourdieu and Passeron 2000: 64–68).

There is evidently a certain amorphousness to the concept of the field. This imprecision is worth accepting, however, in order to obtain the benefits that can be gained by thinking about social relations in general, and the various contexts in which politics take place, in terms of relatively distinct 'fields'. Bourdieu frequently explained the concept of a field by using the analogy of a game. The types of power that are up for grabs are the 'stakes' that give the game its character and structure and thus its distinct internal logic (Bourdieu 1990b: 80–98). This logic is animated by 'fundamental laws' that are often unwritten and even unacknowledged by participants in the game. But it nonetheless operates to regulate their behaviour by establishing the parameters of what is thinkable and what is unthinkable (Taylor 1993: 45–60; Swartz 1997: 117–36). There are rules for the game, but these rules do not dictate the actions of participants in a mechanical way. They act instead as constraints on the strategies of the various players. And they are rarely immutable. Rather, they are negotiated and re-negotiated constantly in the interplay between players and the structures of the game (Bourdieu 1990b: 80–96).

Participation in the field constitutes tacit acknowledgement of both the existence and the logic of its structures. Actors internalise the structures of the field by dint of their habitus, which constantly adjusts and develops in response to its conditions. Bourdieu describes this process as the acquisition of a 'faith in practice' that provides the 'right of entry tacitly imposed by all fields' in a process of selection and exclusion that perpetuates the conditions of the field (Bourdieu 1991: 52–63 and 80–97). Actors internalise both formal and informal structures, spoken and unspoken assumptions. For Bourdieu it is the informal and unspoken structures that constitute the most effective constraint on action because they operate at the level of the unconscious or semi-conscious. They constitute what he defines as the prevailing 'doxa': the 'silent experience of the world', that which 'goes without saying'. Bourdieu described the concept of *doxa* in opposition to that of *opinion*. To have an opinion, one must be aware of different viewpoints on a given question. In the case of doxa, conversely, one is unaware that opposing viewpoints might even exist (Bourdieu 1977: 167–68 and 1990b: 84 and 87). Doxa is thus a set of presuppositions that are cognitive as well as evaluative that condition the actor's responses to external stimuli at an almost instinctive level. At the same time, they are not subjected to scrutiny because they are not acknowledged as presuppositions. Bourdieu's conception of doxa is akin to the concept of 'unspoken assumptions' elaborated by international historian James Joll (1968 and 1992: 199–233). It goes further, however, in providing a framework with which to explore the social genesis of these assumptions. The doxa concept is also similar to the way constructivist international relations theorists understand and use 'norms' and 'normative standards' (Jepperson, Wendt and Katzenstein 1996). But again it goes further, by exhorting us to think systematically about the social and material interests at stake in these arbitrary conventions.

The other important constituent of Bourdieu's field is the 'volume' or 'distribution' of capital within the field. This is in some ways the most difficult aspect of his overall theory. At a basic level the concept has two dimensions.

First, capital constitutes the stakes over which participants in the field are in constant struggle. Second, it comprises the resources which these same participants mobilise in pursuit of their aims. Capital is thus the various currencies of power within a given field (Bourdieu, 1986: 242–44). The object is to accumulate capital and to draw upon this capital in order to secure more capital and a dominant position within the field. Capital is therefore bound up with what Bourdieu describes as the 'objective structure' of the field. But its importance is only understood by participants through the medium of their habitus. Hence this importance, and thus the fundamental logic of the field, may not always be readily apparent to observers *outside* the field.

Capital can assume many forms. It can be economic capital in terms of material possessions and financial resources. But it can also be 'cultural capital' or 'symbolic capital'. Examples of cultural capital include verbal facility, cultural awareness, acquired skills, specialised academic knowledge and educational qualifications. These attributes and qualifications provide social agents access to certain fields and can be mobilised within these fields in pursuit of agent's aims. 'Symbolic capital' is perhaps best understood as manifest in rituals of recognition and especially the accumulation of prestige. It stems from success in the acquisition and use of economic and cultural capital, but is a resource that can be mobilised in its own right in the struggle to secure and maintain distinction and dominance. Possession of symbolic capital allows dominant actors to perpetuate social hierarchies through symbolic violence. Nearly all forms of capital, like the habitus itself, are transposable and can be deployed in more than one field in pursuit of varying objectives. But they are rarely directly translatable from one field to another. A certain type of capital (most notably financial wealth) might be vital in one field but less decisive in another. The process of transposition is part of ongoing struggles between actors to alter the structure of the field in their favour (Bourdieu 1986; Swartz 1997: 73–82 and 122–29).

Similarly, strategies developed for success in one field are not automatically transferable to other games in other fields. Each field is characterised by distinct rules and norms, by the nature and volume of the capital that is up for grabs and by the positions and predispositions of the various actors. Successful action therefore requires a 'feel for the game' [a *sens du jeu*] or a 'feel for practice' [a *sens pratique*]. Such a 'feel' is a reflection of the subtle adjustment of the habitus to the objective conditions of the specific field in which the actor is operating. Successful actors, from multi-national corporations to statesmen and bureaucrats to peasants tilling their fields in North Africa, not only internalise the rules and norms of the 'game' but are also able to manipulate them and even to change them by acquiring a dominant position within the field in which they are located (Bourdieu 1990b: 54–64, 82–88 and 122–25).

A final crucial Bourdieusien concept is *symbolic violence*. Symbolic violence is best described as the imposition by *dominant* social actors of social meanings and representations of reality that are internalised by other actors as both natural and legitimate. It is particularly effective as a social practice of domination because it is not recognised as violence. Symbolic violence functions to legitimise structures of domination by representing them as natural conditions. These representations are internalised and become part of the habitus of social actors, shaping their understandings and expectations. From this premise stems the concept of *misrecognition*: a failure to identify the economic and political interests inherent in practices and resources that are represented as 'disinterested' (Bourdieu 1991: 139–40 and 209–10). 'Disinterested' practices can be represented, for example, as objective forms of knowledge, as abstract but universal moral codes, or merely as part of tradition and the natural order of things. The crucial point is that misrecognition depends upon the successful representation of self-interest as disinterest and thus on the acquisition of symbolic capital. Equally crucially, it is the possession of symbolic capital which allows actors to portray 'interested' forms of power as 'disinterested'. From this flows the ability to represent arbitrary practices of domination – such as demands for recognition and deference in return for 'public service' – as legitimate social and cultural practices that should be taken for granted (Bourdieu 1991: 51–52, 163–70 and 209–39).

To sum up, habitus, field, capital and symbolic violence are the central elements of Bourdieu's 'cultural theory of action'. In this theory, choices and strategies are the result of the interaction between the agent's habitus and the field in which the agent is acting. This interaction is an ongoing dialectical process:

> the relationship between the habitus and the field is foremost one of conditioning: the field structures the habitus which is the product of the incorporation of the immanent demands of the field ... but it is also a relationship of knowledge and of constructive cognition: the habitus contributes to the constitution of the field as a world of meaning, endowed with sense and value, worthy of the necessary investment of energy (Bourdieu and Wacquant 1992: 119).

The dynamic relationship between the habitus of the actor and the field in which action takes place is at the heart of Bourdieu's 'theory of practice'.

Any discussion of Bourdieu's social philosophy must also address the importance he attached to the principle of *reflexivity* in the work of the social scientist. Reflexivity refers to the need for the researcher to be aware of the distorting effects of her or his subjectivity. Bourdieu warned of three types of distortion in particular (Wacquant 2007: 274–75). The first is a product of the personal identity of the researcher, from their gender and class background to their nationality and ethnicity. The second arises from the researcher's location in the intellectual field in which they are operating, which is crucial determining the concepts and methods the researcher deploys as well as the potential for self-censorship arising from career interests, institutional and disciplinary attachments. Finally, Bourdieu warned of the dangers of 'scholarly bias': the temptation to 'stand back' and observe the world as if the researcher is somehow not involved in the social processes under observation (Bourdieu 1998: 127–40, 2003 73–131). To overcome these, Bourdieu exhorts the researcher to engage in constant 'epistemic reflexivity' by turning the tools of social science back on his or herself and to subject the research process itself to sustained analysis. In this way, Bourdieu argued, it is possible to 'objectivise' one's own subjectivity and thus limit the distortion that arises from the inescapable fact that knowledge construction is a social activity (Bourdieu and Wacquant 1992: 36–46).

Bourdieu and the study of international relations

Bourdieu's ideas and approach have made relatively little impact on international studies as a whole. Although his concepts have been deployed extensively in other disciplines, they are only beginning to generate interest among international relations theorists (particularly in the sub-field of security studies). And Bourdieu has been almost completely ignored by international historians (Jackson 2008). One explanation for this relative neglect may be that the discipline of international relations theory has tended to be structured around debates between various meta-theoretical positions. Within these debates comparatively little emphasis has been placed on detailed empirical investigation. Prospects for profitable engagement have not been helped by the fact that the most compatible strain of international theory, social constructivism, has until recently shown little interest in questions of power that were so central for Bourdieu (Williams 2007; Barnett and Duvall 2005).

This neglect is unfortunate because Bourdieu's social theory is intensely political in its orientation. He emphasised that culture is never 'devoid of political content' but is instead 'always an expression of it'. A theory of culture therefore 'leads naturally to a theory of politics' (Bourdieu 1990a: 35–36). Thinking about international relations in these terms offers exciting possibilities, particularly for scholars interested in the cultural dimensions to global politics. The concepts of symbolic power and symbolic violence, in the ways in which power inheres in cultural practices, offer particularly rich new perspectives on international relations. Bourdieu's understanding of political struggle as a 'struggle for the power to impose universalist claims' as 'the legitimate vision of the social world' could help open up exciting new avenues of research (Bourdieu 2003: 181 and 254–55). Bourdieu's notable foray into international politics, an essay (with Loïc Wacquant) entitled 'The Cunning of Imperial Reason', pursued this line of argument by reflecting upon the way the exportation of American culture provided a vehicle for the imposition of neo-liberal political categories and themes on global political practices and representations (Bourdieu and Wacquant 1999).

The potential of Bourdieu's theory has already been demonstrated in the limited number of works that have drawn on his ideas in the study of international relations. His notions of symbolic power and symbolic violence have been deployed, for example, in analyses of the 'fields' of domestic and international security. The result has been a series of new perspectives on the politics of threat identification as well as the role of power in the construction of diverse international regimes (Bigo 1996 and 2006; Guzzini 2000; Leander 2005 and 2007; Williams 2007; Pouliot 2008). Several scholars have also held out Bourdieu's approach as strategy for developing a more rigorous and empirically grounded constructivism in international relations theory (Wight 2006; Guzzini 2000; Leander 2002; Pouliot 2007). There are also signs that Bourdieu's theoretical synthesis of material interests and symbolic practice is beginning to influence the field of international political economy (Leander 2002 and Pop 2007).

But the rich potential of Bourdieu's conceptual framework remains largely untapped by scholars of international relations. The conceptual triad of habitus, field and capital, with the insights it offers on the anatomy and dynamics of beliefs and practices, could offer interesting new perspectives on foreign policy analysis. It could also contribute in interesting ways to debates on the role of culture in the history of international relations (Jackson 2008). The concept of symbolic capital, moreover, might provide an fascinating framework with which to consider the role of prestige in world politics. Similarly, the notion of 'misrecognition' could be deployed in an analysis of the practices of international aid and humanitarian intervention. There are, for example, exciting possibilities for synergy between Bourdieu's reflections on symbolic violence and the interesting work now being done on the role of rhetoric and framing in international politics (Jackson and Krebs 2007). Both approaches explore disguised practices of power that operate through the imposition of categories of meaning that are aimed at reproducing social relationships of domination. These and many other possible research projects remain to be developed. It is to be hoped that the literature cited above marks only the beginning of a wider engagement with Bourdieu from within the discipline of international relations.

Further reading

The best single introduction to Bourdieu's social philosophy may well be his *The Logic of Practice* (1990). To understand the evolution of his thought, *Outline of a Theory of Practice* (1977) is essential reading. On the role of language and the concepts of misrecognition, symbolic power and symbolic violence see especially his classic texts *Distinction* (1984) and *Homo Academicus* (1988) but also *Language and Symbolic Power* (1991) (which has an excellent introduction by John Thompson). For those students who can read French, *Méditations Pascaliennes* (2003 edition) provides perhaps the best overall summary of his theory of practice as well as the most comprehensive outline of his views on the role of symbolic violence in politics.

10 Judith Butler

Cristina Masters

It's not that I'm in favour of difficulty for difficulty's sake; it's that I think there is a lot in ordinary language and in received grammar that constrains our thinking – indeed, about what a person is, what a subject is, what gender is, what sexuality is, what politics can be – and that I'm not sure we're going to be able to struggle effectively against those constraints or work within them in a productive way unless we see the ways in which grammar is both producing and constraining our sense of what the world is.

—Judith Butler, *Changing the Subject*

In 1999, the journal *Philosophy and Literature* voted Judith Butler the number one bad writer of the year in response to her most cited and criticised piece of work, *Gender Trouble* (1990). Rather than dismiss her critics, Butler's response has always been one of critical engagement. In response to earlier criticisms of *Gender Trouble*, she produced a follow up text, *Bodies That Matter* (1993) (and later *Undoing Gender* (2004b)), an attempt to both clarify and rethink some of her interventions in feminism and philosophy, while simultaneously maintaining that her work must be linguistically challenging precisely because language is fundamentally implicated in subject formation. To do otherwise, she argued, would profoundly limit one to the very constraints one seeks to reject and resignify. As Sara Salih points out: 'Butler semi-humorously advises her readers to follow the example of cows and learn "the art of slow rumination" in their textual practices' (Salih 2004: 1). While criticism continues to closely follow her career, as well as a great deal of admiration and inspiration, Butler's response to her critics is particularly noteworthy as it captures the reflexive critical attitude that marks so much of her work.

In the spirit of slow rumination, what, then, is it that Judith Butler seeks to reject and resignify? What captures the critical attention of this eclectic scholar? What drives her interventions into feminism, political theory, literary theory, philosophy, and contemporary post-September 11th politics? Taking inspiration from and pushing at the boundaries of Hegelian dialectics, Foucauldian genealogy, Derridean deconstruction, and Lacanian psychoanalysis, what is at the heart of her theorising on the discursive processes of (de)sub-jectification (gendered, sexualised), ethics, violence, and the politics of mourning from *Gender Trouble* to *Precarious Life* (2004a), are two intertwined and decep-tively simple questions: *who counts as human* and *what counts as a liveable life?* Posed in a variety of ways and levelled at any number of 'political' debates ran-ging from indefinite detention in the war on terror, the ban on gays in the Amer-ican military, and the politics of censorship, to Israeli–Palestinian relations, it is to these two questions that Judith Butler continually returns.

Considering this, it is not at all surprising that critical scholars have increasingly turned to her work to think through, reformulate, trace, and chal-lenge many of the practices we are centrally concerned with in international politics: relationships of power (how it functions, how it is (re)produced and where it is (dis)located), practices of sovereignty, 'states' of exclusion, the politics of representation, questions of responsibility, and significantly, the possibility of different politics. It is interesting to note, however, that Judith Butler has gained wider popularity with scholars of international politics at the moment when her work appears to coincide with some of the field's ready made categories, for instance, sovereign power, the 'human', and the laws of war. This is especially ironic considering that as a scholar profoundly concerned with questions of intelligibility, some of her work has remained rather unin-telligible to the discipline, namely her work on gender and sexuality. Feminist theorists of international politics are among the few to take up her earlier critical insights, and her work continues to inform debates on questions of agency and the (im)possibility of feminist politics without a subject called 'woman'. And arguably it is this earlier work that perhaps provides some under-explored sites relevant to contemporary operations of sovereign power and the war on terror. One such site is whether or not the category of race can be thought through the politics of performativity and the implications therein especially concerning the production of bare life and questions of agency.

While her contributions are numerous, this chapter picks up on two sig-nificant contributions of her thinking for our thinking about 'how we think' about international politics, and even more important, for how we might undo it and do it otherwise – the politics of performativity and the politics of mourning. No doubt there is much missing. Considering, however, that Butler shares common terrain with many in this volume, chapters on critical scholars such as Michel Foucault, Emmanuel Levinas, and Jacques Derrida will undoubtedly fill in some of the gaps. And because this chapter can only be but a glimpse of her work, readers should take this as a solicitation, in particular to those who have yet to be *troubled* by Judith Butler, to critically engage her scholarship.

The spectre of sex and the politics of performativity

> To problematise subjectivity is to inquire into the forces which create abjected, excluded beings.
>
> Vivienne Jabri (1998: 611)

Hesitations around losing sight of women fundamentally reflect feminists' hesitant engagements with poststructural theories of the political. How can we speak of *woman*, when as a category she exists only as a production of technologies of gender, as an effect of power, and when we disturb her she slips out of sight? Why is it at this particular historical juncture when dominant narratives of gender are being exposed as constitutive of how we know and live in the world, and women are finally becoming the subjects of enquiry, we can no longer speak of, or as, women in any meaningful way? How is it that we now must reject identity politics when women have never been the producers of their own identity, their own subjectivity(s)? These are some of the questions that echo through the conversational spaces between a number of feminists and poststructuralists (Zalewski 1998; Jabri 2004). Suspicions hinge on the fear of exchanging one master narrative for another; one master narrative that has constituted the feminine as excluded and abject, and another that cannot speak of the feminine at all wherein the death of the subject seemingly precludes the utterance of 'I' or 'we'. As Christine Sylvester argues:

> How can we bring women into view and valorize their experiences while casting a sceptical eye on gender identities worn like birthday suits? Can we have meaningful identities and question them too, or must we choose between identity and resistance to identity? Can we theorize 'the subject as *produced* through signifying practices which precede her', while also granting personal and social significance to some of those produced practices? (Sylvester 1994: 12–13)

But as Butler argues: 'To claim that the subject is itself produced in and as a gendered matrix of relations is not to do away with the subject, but only to ask after the conditions of its emergence and operation' (Butler 1993b: 7).

While many feminists have been conscious of the dangers of representational politics, the potential of falling into the trap of essentialism, whether biological or social, the risks have appeared to be necessary when women have 'nowhere been presumed' in the terrain of (international) politics. Many have tried to circumvent these dangers by beginning from the place of social construction. The effect of such circumventions has been the separation of gender from sex, while still maintaining the two in relation: the understanding of the former as socially constituted and as such discursive, and the latter as indicative of a biological category and prediscursive.

It is in the context of this distinction that Judith Butler came to think about gender, sexuality, and the subject of feminism. Her first published book, *Subjects of Desire* (1987), explored the impact of Hegel's phenomenology on twentieth-century French philosophers. *Subjects* is interesting, however, specifically because it says nothing of what Butler is now most well-known for – queer theory and the stylisation of the body. But it was this text that brought her into contact with two thinkers who would fundamentally influence her thinking, Michel Foucault and Jacques Derrida. It is not difficult to understand why the critical attitudes of these two philosophers (genealogical and deconstructive, respectively) would have such a profound impact on her theorising, especially when one accounts for her personal familiarity with the violence of gender norms: her own coming out at the age of 16, one marked as much by joy as by violence and pain, an uncle institutionalised for his 'anatomically anomalous body', and bearing witness to the pain of gender norms experienced by many of those around her. It is rather unsurprising, then, that the separation of gender and sex in most feminist scholarship at the time would sit so uncomfortably with Butler and lead her to *trouble* the category of women as the subject of feminism. And similar to many of the critical scholars in this volume, her work is fundamentally about making sense of her own life experiences, and because of that challenging us to do otherwise.

There is a well circulated tale that quite nicely captures, I think, Butler's argument in *Gender Trouble*: a traveller stops a peasant by the roadside and asks the way to the capital. 'Well', she replies, after pondering the matter a while, 'if I were you, I wouldn't start from here.' The 'from here' is the very distinction between sex/gender where two issues are at stake: the issue of a prediscursive ontological category of sex and its relation to gender, and the debate between essentialism and constructivism, one which Butler argues misses the point of deconstruction. By sustaining biological difference while disturbing the dichotomy of gender, what remains intact, Butler argues, is the metaphysic of the binary, the naturalised opposition of sex, and as such, a compulsory and exclusionary heterosexuality. Sustaining sex as distinct from gender radically constrains who can count as human precisely because the myth of the duality persists wherein the sexed body remains as the naturalised, prediscursive scene of gendered inscriptions, thus participatory in the incarceration of identity and sexuality.

Consider this: what happens when one does not have the 'right' body, a 'properly' sexed body? When one has an anatomically anomalous body? Does one count as human? What are the possibilities for a liveable life? How can one be intelligible, and stake a claim to the realm of the human, when one literally lacks the sexed surface upon which gendered cultural inscriptions take place, where one quite literally does not have access to even the reductive realm of gender, until one chooses a sex or has one chosen for one? If one is born intersexed, for instance, how is one rendered intelligible? One's claim to intelligibility is only made possible by laying claim to a sex. But to make the claim, as Butler points out, is already to participate in gendered regimes of power. As such, while necessary, it is not sufficient to make the claim that gender is culturally produced, often in exclusionary ways for women, when the naturalised category of sex remains unproblematised. As Butler argues:

> it will be as important to think about how and to what end bodies are constructed as it will be to think about how and to what end bodies are

not constructed and, further, to ask after how bodies which fail to materialize provide the necessary 'outside,' if not the necessary support, for the bodies which, in materializing the norm, qualify as bodies that matter (Butler 1993b: 16).

The subject of feminism effects its own exclusions insofar as it participates in the heterosexist naturalisation of sex, where this distinction itself produces a realm of abjection as the sexed body haunts any attempt at resignification.

It is precisely the violent and exclusionary spectre of sex that leads Butler to 'collapse' the distinction, or in her words to reveal that 'sex has been gender all along'. Rather than sex occupying the realm of the prediscursive, sex she argues *is* the bodily effect of gender where the body materialises through regulatory gendered regimes of power/knowledge. It is *not* the surface, already present, awaiting ascription as there is no sexed doer behind the deed of gender, there is no stable or primary identity upon which gender is constituted. In denaturalising the binary of sex/gender, what becomes possible are critical readings of masculinity(s) and femininity(s) that need not coincide with a 'sexed' body. Timothy Kaufman-Osborn's reading of the torture of prisoners at Abu Ghraib by female soldiers is exemplary. His reading challenges, for instance, dominant renditions of the torture as a perversion of the feminine, where women in the military have been cast as the problem. Kaufman *troubles* this by asking: what are we bearing witness to? Is she a she who fails to be a he, or is she a he who fails to be a she? He offers a persuasive interpretation of the torture at Abu Ghraib as better understood through the production and performance of a particular militarised masculinity constituted within the cultural architecture of the US military.

This collapse is further pushed to its limits by Butler's deconstruction of constructivism (the one that misses the point of deconstruction). The constructivism she levels her critical gaze at is one that effects a *personification* of discursive constructions; one that treats the subject as both initiating and wilful. In acknowledging the power of discourse in producing subjects (instead of the subject producing discourse, i.e. essentialism), constructivism in some ways goes too far (or not far enough in deconstructive terms). It does so by constituting the relationship unilaterally, thus reducing construction to an act that is so determinative that the subject paradoxically and forcefully returns as fixed, solid, and tangible. Discourse in this sense is taken to constitute a being, an 'is', wherein one 'is' a gendered subject rather than always in the process of becoming. Take for example, Alexander Wendt's (in)famous claim that 'anarchy is what states make of it'. Grammatically, the state becomes a thing, a fixed category that can be treated as a given. This capitulates to the received grammars of international relations, and in so doing participates in producing the world as a realm of danger, constraining our ability to do otherwise.

To recover the agency lost in this kind of constructivism, and drawing on Derrida, Butler elaborates a theory of performativity:

What I propose in place of these conceptions of construction is a return to the notion of matter, not as site or surface, but as *a process of materialization that stabilizes over time to produce the effect of boundary, fixity, and surface we call matter* (Butler 1993b: 9).

Performativity is not a singular act that is temporally fixed and spatially located; it is not initiated by a subject, nor is it a theatrical performance. Rather, performativity is a *reiterative citational activity* that simultaneously 'produces' and 'destabilises' subjectivity. And it is through this process that over time, in this instance, sex/gender appear as natural. But because it must be constantly re-enacted through citational claims to the norm, what is exposed are the fissures, gaps, fractures, and instabilities of subjectivity, because the subject is always in process, always becoming. Butler's theory of performativity has informed, for instance, David Campbell's critical rereading of the state and the production of discourses of danger. Danger, he argues, rather than being an external threat to the existence of the state is its very condition of possibility as states have

no ontological status apart from the many and varied practices that constitute their reality, states are (and have to be) always in the process of becoming. For the state to end its practices of representation would be to expose its lack of prediscursive foundations; stasis would be death (Campbell 1998c: 11).

In revealing the performative nature of the state, critical scholars such as David Campbell and Cynthia Weber (1998), not only denaturalise the state, revealing it as a series of gendered discursive practices, but significantly, they open up space for subversively challenging the state. For every articulation of danger by the state in its foreign policy practices what is exposed is the very fragility and failure of its representational practices. Agency (both in reproducing the norm and challenging it), therefore, is not reduced to, or eviscerated by, the founding moment of construction, forever closed off to resistance and resignification until a 'new' discourse appears from 'out there', but rather is multiplied in time and through power relations.

Butler turns to drag to elucidate her theory of performativity and to punctuate this point. Drag, she argues, is a useful way to think about sex/gender as it exposes crucial features of the constructed nature of dominant heterosexual gender norms, namely, the 'disjuncture' between the body and the gender being performed, and thus importantly, the parodic and imitative nature of all gender identities – gender as a doing. Butler does so 'not to celebrate drag as the expression of a true and model gender, but to show that the naturalized knowledge of gender operates as a preemptive and violent circumscription of reality' (Butler 1999: xxiii). Drag is not in and of itself subversive, indeed it can reinforce (if not more so) as much as destabilise dominant gender norms. Where its subversive potential lies, however, is in the moment of uncertainty, of being unsure whether one is confronting a man or a woman; in other words, it is the moment of *not knowing*, rather than knowing, that opens up possibilities for resistance and resignification. Understanding sex as the performative material effect of heteronormative gender regimes of power potentially opens up, rather than violently fore-closing, the possibility for demanding more liveable lives. The task, as Butler (2004b) argues, is to cease legislating for all what is only liveable for some. The failure of identity, therefore, is *both* the danger and the radical possibility.

The politics of mourning

What might it mean to undergo violation, to insist upon *not* resolving grief and staunching vulnerability too quickly through a turn to violence, and to practice, as an experiment in living otherwise, non-violence in an emphatically nonreciprocal response? What would it mean, in the face of violence, to refuse to return it? (Butler 2005: 100)

Contemporary politics is predicated not only on the desire to know, but significantly the promise that we can know, definitively and resolutely. In the realm of international politics, this is signified in the American-led 'war on terror': a war that claims to know both the dangers lurking out there and the solutions to them, a war that claims to know both the perpetrators and the victims. One of the ways this has been affected is through a visual field of representation, evident in the desire of the state to 'capture' us in any number of ways: increased security at borders and airports, the compiling of biometric data, retina scans, video surveillance, photo identification, and fingerprinting. Significantly, this 'capturing' has also taken place through the media in the war on terror, the medium through which we have seemingly become intimately familiar with the *face* of war. As Butler points out, we can now claim to *know* the face of evil – Osama bin Laden, Saddam Hussein, the Taliban. We also now can claim to *know* their victims – burqa-clad women and limbless children in Afghanistan, those who died in the Twin Towers, American soldiers fighting for our freedom, and possibly all of 'us'. These are the human faces of war, both good and evil. Are these, however, humanising moments or is there also something profoundly dehumanising about them? Thinking through the Levinasian 'face', Butler (2004a: 143) asks us to consider this question. She does so to get us to think more deeply about who gets to count as human, and significantly what it means to be human.

In the former instance, it is perhaps easier to see in how putting a human face to evil, the intent is not to humanise but rather to dehumanise. We are not meant to identify with Osama bin Laden, Saddam Hussein, or the terrorists of 9/11. Indeed, they are meant to occupy a realm beyond the human, so much so that they are a threat to humanity. In the latter, however, the case of the victims, things appear to be otherwise. They are meant to put a human face to war. These are the people we are fighting for: to save, to recuperate, and to avenge. And in so doing, their humanity is (re)captured. The representations of Afghan women is particularly telling in this regard. As the reason for war, we have become intimately familiar with women in Afghanistan, we know their plight and we are willing to fight for their cause. We feel triumphant in witnessing and participating in their freedom – the shedding of burqas, of women back at work, and girls in classrooms. They have become human again. But is this the reality? Is what we are witness to, their humaness? Are they present in our representations of them? Butler (2004a: 143) asks us to consider 'what scenes of pain and grief these images cover over and derealize'. As Mary Anne Franks (2003) points out, one would think that in this war women are finally present, but paradoxically they are more absent then ever, because representations of Afghan women have reduced them to singularities that eviscerate the complexity of who they are, and importantly, who they may become. For women in Afghanistan and Iraq, the paradox is this: their very so-called freedom from totalitarian regimes, of one kind or another, has been their figural death from the realm of the political.

In contemporary practices of war, the human, Butler argues, is evacuated in the moment when we attempt to capture it through practices of representation. In other words, the Levanasian face is defaced precisely in attempts to suspend the precariousness of life: 'One would be wrong to think that the "human" is about one's ability to be transparent and thus fully intelligible. However, the human or one's access to it is precisely at the moment where representation fails, the opacity, the unknowing.' On September 11th, 2001, it was in those earliest moments that we were returned to the human, 'in its frailty and at the limits of its capacity to make sense' (Butler 2004a: 150). Because in the moment of trauma the event actually had no meaning outside of the grief, frenzy, confusion, uncertainty, and horror. Knowledge, in this instance, marked the official end of these very emotions – the end to vulnerability and the precariousness of life – through the delimitation of the event to an act of war. No longer was it about the loss of loved ones and, equally significant, the loss of those we did not know at all. 'Attack on America' had the effect of abstracting and distancing the deeply traumatic, heart-wrenching, and profoundly intimate moments of that day. The claim to *know* what happened put an end to vulnerability, uncertainty, to questioning, to contestation. As Mari Matsuda aptly points out: 'There are no questions where power resides, only declaratives' (Matsuda 2002: 476).

The incoherence we/they experienced and witnessed that day collapsed into a singular and monolithic narrative, papering over the fractures laid bare in the event through the call to a mythical and representational unity. Firefighters were transformed into the warriors on the battlefield, grieving widows as the home front, and the American administration as the Generals of War. As Jenny Edkins observes:

For Bush of course there was no trauma, just a rather unexpected military and foreign policy crisis taking him by surprise when he was out of town and coming before the administration had really found its feet. For him there was no doubting what had happened: it was a declaration of war. Terrorists had attacked America. His world had not fallen apart in unimaginable ways (Edkins 2002: 11).

The lack now captured by the hole where there once stood the phallic symbols of American power had to be reconstituted, suturing the rupture with the discourse of war. No longer was there time to waste on such things as grief. As an act of war, trauma had to be put aside; action had to replace the passivity implicit in the act of mourning. Take as exemplary:

> when firefighters' widows were interviewed on CNN, most of them gave the expected performance: tears, prayers … all except one who, without a tear, said that she does not pray for her dead husband, because she knows that prayer will not bring him back. Asked if she dreams of revenge, she calmly said that that would be a true betrayal of her husband: had he survived, he would have insisted that the worst thing to do is to succumb to the urge to retaliate (Žižek 2002: 13–14).

Within the boundaries erected through the call of war, she, however, became unhearable, a distant echo. In her refusal to return violence in the face of it, not only was her voice excised from the repetition of news clips, her disappearance from the realm of the political was exacted. The voices that did not 'fit' the developing war story, as Butler points out, quickly became relegated to the margins, with the deafening drumbeats of war slowly silencing the subversive potential of mourning.

Reading through Butler, one could argue that there is a double gesture signified in the enunciation 'Attack on America': first, the putting an end to trauma and mourning enacted the erasure of history and thus cast America into the space of exceptionality, and simultaneously constituted the attending process of rewriting a different historical narrative, one much more suitable to a call to war. By naming it as such – as exceptional – a range of other possibilities were excluded; possibilities that could have affected different politics (or perhaps affected politics itself when we consider this as a profoundly depoliticising moment). America was metaphorically unhinged from history. No other moment in American history, we were told, could compare to the event that took place that day: 'For the most part, history was only invoked to prepare America for the sacrifice and suffering that lay ahead' (Der Derian 2001: 687). But as Judith Butler argues, history should not be offered up as 'exoneration', 'explanation', or 'justification' for events such as these, but rather, history – what we can hear – can help us do differently, in other words, be and do otherwise (Butler 2004a).

While the claim to ethical violence evoked in the war on terror appears to be wrapped up in mourning and grief, Butler asks us to think about what exactly is being grieved and mourned in a call to war, in responding to violence with more violence. Is the grief and mourning for the real lives lost on September 11th? Butler's work on the melancholic subject is informative here. Drawing on Freud, Butler makes a distinction between mourning and melancholy. While mourning is a response to a real loss, melancholy is understood as the response to an imagined loss. One could argue that the official narrative of loss after the terrorist attacks was not for the real lives lost, but rather for the loss of 'heroes', the loss of an imagined sovereign power, the loss of a melancholic representation of the American self. Indeed, the trauma of the real lives lost that day had to be concealed. The 'missing persons' posters on the streets of New York after September 11th, as Jenny Edkins argues, reveal the dissonance between the real loss and the imagined loss. The posters, she argues, are

> testimony to the trauma, to the ineffectiveness of the state in safeguarding those it claims to protect, and to the lies of heroism and sacrifice. These are ordinary people who went to work and were overtaken by disaster, not heroes who sacrificed their lives for America. Just take a look at the pictures (Edkins 2007a: 36).

While the dead can be made to speak for the state, to justify and legitimise acts of war, they can also disturb the state project as they 'signal the danger that people will not forget the trauma and, not forgetting, will not be able to remember the way the state demands' (Edkins 2007a: 28). As Butler points out, the visceral photos of napalm burnt children in the Vietnam War disturbed the visual field of American identity: 'Despite their graphic effectivity, the images pointed somewhere else, beyond themselves, to a life and to a precariousness that they could not show' (Butler 2004a: 150). The 'shock, outrage, remorse, and grief' engendered by these photos led to a public demand for an end to the war. Take a look at the pictures – this is the potential subversive power of mourning; 'It is not that mourning is the goal of politics, but that without the capacity to mourn, we lose that keener sense of life we need in order to oppose violence' (Butler 2004a: xviii).

As R.B.J. Walker prosaically observed in 1997:

> Where so much recent debate about security has been predicated on the impossible dream of absolute invulnerability, a critical engagement with security would envisage it precisely as a condition of being vulnerable to the possibility of being otherwise than one has already become (Walker 1997: 78).

To choose vulnerability over security, and thus a secure identity, is difficult, but if the desire is to participate in politics that make life liveable, rather than participating in a sovereign politics premised on profoundly uninhabitable and unliveable lives, it may be the very thing we need to do to reinvoke the political. As Butler argues:

It might mean that one does not foreclose upon the primary exposure to the Other, that one does not try to transform the unwilled into the willed, but, rather, to take the very unbearability of exposure as the sign, the reminder, of a common vulnerability, a common physicality and risk (Butler 2005: 100).

For Butler ethics and responsibility is bound up in being 'awake' to the precariousness of the other, the precariousness of life, of quelling our murderous desire, the one that is at work in our desire for a transparent, knowable self. Being opaque to oneself, conceding that one can never fully give an account of oneself, our willingness to become undone in relation to others – this, Butler argues, constitutes our chance of becoming human.

Conclusion

Judith Butler continues to be a critical scholar unfaithful to disciplinary boundaries, and as such resolutely faithful to searching for those who are excluded from the realm liveability. Her array of work asks us to be different, to interrogate what is at stake in being vulnerable and open to difference. While her work rarely offers us answers to many of the critical questions she poses, the questions themselves are a call to a different kind of politics, a politics that asks after the silences, the margins, the excluded.

Further reading

Butler, Judith (2005) *Giving an Account of Oneself*, New York: Fordham University Press. Based on a series of lectures for the Department of Philosophy at the University of Amsterdam, this book explores the ethical limits of subjectivity and its attending violences through critical readings of Foucault, Hegel, Levinas, and Adorno. It reads as a challenge to ethical violence where the 'I' is placed before the Other, and instead calls for a politics predicated on the primacy of the Other.

Butler, Judith (2004a) *Precarious Life: The Powers of Mourning and Violence*, London: Verso Press. The five essays that comprise this book are in direct response to the aftermath of the terrorist attacks on September 11th, with regard both to the emergence of a hyper-security regime enacted by the American administration, and to the possibilities engendered by the vulnerabilities exposed in such an event. Collectively, the essays are a call for a public politics of critical inquiry and engagement in a context where critical inquiry is increasingly silenced for the challenges it poses to contemporary configurations of state power.

Butler, Judith (2004b) *Undoing Gender*, London: Routledge. While many have difficulty with *Gender Trouble* and *Bodies That Matter*, this text is a more accessible take on Butler's theory of performativity and its potential for undoing the strictures of heteronormative gender identity. For readers who have struggled with her earlier work, I would recommend this text as a starting point.

11 Gilles Deleuze

Robin Durie

Gilles Deleuze was a French philosopher and contemporary of such figures as Foucault, Lyotard, Lacan, Derrida and Levinas. Deleuze was born in Paris and lived there for the majority of his life. While studying at the Sorbonne, Deleuze was taught by a series of influential French philosophers, including Maurice de Gandillac, Georges Canguilhem (who was a notable influence on Foucault) and Jean Hyppolite. It was Hyppolite who did much to motivate the renaissance of Hegel studies in Paris after the war and specifically the attempt to develop a phenomenological interpretation of Hegel. Deleuze's first published work consisted in a review of Hyppolite's *Logic and Existence*, in 1954, in which he already introduces the possibility of an 'ontology of difference ... where difference is expression itself, and contradiction its merely phenomenal aspect'. Having taught at various *lycée*, Deleuze was appointed to a position at the Sorbonne in 1957. During the early 1960s, Deleuze held a position at the *Centre National de Recherche Scientifique*, before accepting a professorship at the University of Lyon in 1964. During this period, he developed a strong friendship with Michel Foucault, and it was with Foucault that, in the wake of the events of May 1968, he moved to the new Paris VIII University, at Vincennes. It was at Vincennes that Deleuze started collaborating with Félix Guattari; he also developed a friendship there with Jean-Francois Lyotard, who was appointed in the early 1970s. Deleuze stayed at Vincennes until his retirement in 1987.

In the early part of his career, he wrote a series of scholarly monographs on philosophers including Hume, Nietzsche, Kant, Bergson and Spinoza. In addition during this period he wrote books on Proust, Sacher-Masoch and Kafka. Then in 1968 and 1969 he published two works, *Difference and Repetition* and *Logic of Sense*, in which he developed his own original philosophical voice and positions (although both books drew heavily on his preceding scholarly philosophical work). Following this Deleuze entered into a notorious and frequently remarkable collaboration with the psychoanalyst Félix Guattari, which yielded two volumes under the heading of *Capitalism and Schizophrenia* – *Anti-Oedipus* in 1972 and *A Thousand Plateaus* in 1980. A final volume in their collaboration, *What is Philosophy?*, was published in

1991. The final phase of Deleuze's work on his own included works on Foucault and Leibniz, on the painter Francis Bacon, a two-volume work on cinema, and a number of collections of essays and interviews. In addition, many of Deleuze's Tuesday morning seminars, conducted while he was working at Vincennes, have been transcribed and made available on the web at 'WebDeleuze'. Finally, Deleuze staged a delightful series of short interviews for French television, in the form of an *'Abecedaire'*, in which he offered brief reflections on themes relating to his thought.

The problem of immanence

Despite his explicit rejection of the methods and theoretical positions of both phenomenology and structuralism, it is nevertheless common enough to group Deleuze along with many of his French contemporaries and characterise him as a 'philosopher of difference'. While the concept of difference does indeed feature prominently in his thought, this approach does little to help us understand either the significance or the consistency of Deleuze's thought. In order to respond adequately to these demands, we need to understand the theoretical context within which Deleuze's thinking of difference emerges. And Deleuze makes it clear that the theoretical milieu within which a philosopher creates concepts is itself determined by a philosopher's distinctive *problem*.

Let us begin, therefore, by considering the problem which determines the philosophical field of Deleuze's inquiry. Deleuze's work is determined throughout by the *problem of immanence*. More concretely, the problem of immanence itself comes to be further determined according to the particular philosopher with whom Deleuze might be engaging (e.g. Lucretius, Spinoza, Leibniz, Hume, Bergson or Foucault); or the particular field of practice with which he might be engaging (e.g. cinema or painting or music). For instance, in the case of his writing on Foucault, the problem for Deleuze becomes that of how a thinking of the outside is possible within a philosophy of immanence; in his thesis on Spinoza, the initial question concerns whether Spinoza is able to establish an immanent relation between substance and modes, or whether substance ultimately 'remains independent of' its modes; while in his work on Hume, the problem becomes one of how a mind is able to go beyond or transcend what is given in it, and become a subject with a nature and consistency. In these ways, therefore, immanence becomes determinately problematized in a number of particular theoretical fields. But how and why does immanence pose itself as a problem for Deleuze?

If Heidegger's phenomenological ontology enabled philosophy to pose once more the question of Being, then it could be argued that Deleuze was always more a thinker of *becoming* than of being. In the tenth 'Chapter' of *A Thousand Plateaus*, 'Becoming-Intense, Becoming-Animal, Becoming-Imperceptible ... ', Deleuze and Guattari make clear that neither structuralism nor evolutionism are adequate for accounting for becoming. In the former instance, this is because becoming does not reduce to a 'correspondence of relations' (Deleuze and Guattari 1988: 237) and in the latter, because becoming is not a 'filiation' (Deleuze and Guattari 1988: 238). Furthermore for Deleuze and Guattari becoming is not 'a resemblance, an imitation, or ... an identification' (Deleuze and Guattari 1988: 237). We are mistaken, they argue, if we seek to understand becoming from the perspective of the reality of what is produced by becomings – 'what is real is the becoming itself' (Deleuze and Guattari 1988: 238). For these latter reasons, it is equally important to acknowledge that theories of potentiality are also inadequate for accounting for becoming. Rather than a process derived from the principle of resemblance, becoming is, for Deleuze, first and foremost *creative*.

The history of philosophy could be said to have begun with Plato's fateful decision to accord to the Forms a transcendent status, and then to seek to explain the reality of our everyday lives by means of their more or less imperfect resemblance to, or imitation of, these transcendent Forms. Onto-logical and causal explanation by means of the principles of imitation and resemblance is typical of what Deleuze calls the *plane of transcendence*, and it is this plane of transcendence with its associated explanatory principles of imitation and resemblance which Deleuze will reject in favour of the *plane of immanence*. The nature of the difference between these two planes is set out in the 'Memories of a Plane(e) Maker' section of the tenth chapter of *A Thousand Plateaus*.

Fundamentally, the plane of transcendence is 'a hidden principle', a principle which 'makes visible what is seen and audible what is heard', that is to say, which 'causes the given to be given' but which 'itself is not given'. As a consequence, the plane of transcendence is a principle which can never itself be directly experienced but 'can only be inferred, induced or concluded from that to which it gives rise' (Deleuze and Guattari 1988: 265). In evolutionary fields the plane of transcendence would function as a plane (or plan) of development, whereas in structural fields it would function as a plane (or plan) of organisation. In either case the plane of transcendence 'always con-cerns the development of forms and the formation of subjects' (Deleuze and Guattari 1988: 265) Because it is always beyond or supplementary to that whose givenness it makes possible, and thus hidden from any of the means by which we might experience that which is given, Deleuze uses the formula ($n + 1$) to characterise the nature of the plane of transcendence. This formula – $n + 1$ – has the further advantage of indicating the geometrical sense of the plane: in mathematics, 'plane' designates a 2-dimensional manifold or surface. Typically, Euclidean geometry embeds surfaces in 3-dimensional spaces, in order to study their curvature. Thus the 3-dimensional space represents the supplementary (+1) dimension which *contains* the surface and, by implication, organises it as a figure within that space, for geometrical study.

This traditional approach to geometry was revolutionised by the work of Carl Friedrich Gauss and then later by Bernhard Riemann. This revolution was initiated by Gauss' development of a wholly new concept, namely, that a surface is a space *in itself* (it is precisely this notion of the *in itself*, pertaining to a surface *qua* space in itself, which Deleuze is seeking to capture with the philosophical concept of immanence). Thus, rather than the features of the curvature of the plane being determined by the geometry of the space within which the plane is projected, the geometry of the surface conceived as a space in itself is *intrinsic* to that surface. Riemann generalised Gauss' insights, extending them to any-spaces-whatever and thereby revolutionising the whole approach that geometry took towards space. In order to do so, Riemann introduced the notion of *n*-dimensional manifolds or *multiplicities* and this Riemannian concept of multiplicities came to occupy a central position in Deleuze's work. What is also worth highlighting is that the mathematical method which Riemann developed for analysing *n*-dimensional multiplicities was that of *differential* geometry. Differential geometry employs the techniques of differential calculus in order to study the properties of curves and surfaces from point to point. Specifically, differential geometry focuses on points of inflection and what are called 'normals to curves'. Just as Deleuze adopts the notion of the multiplicity from Riemann, in order to develop his understanding of the plane of immanence, so he will also adopt the method of differential analysis. In the cases of both multiplicities and the principle of differential analysis, his adoption of Riemannian methods was significantly filtered through his engagement with Henri Bergson. However, the method of what might be called 'local analysis' (in contrast to the universalising tendency of transcendental analysis), which is characteristic of differential geometry, is maintained throughout by Deleuze and indeed goes on to inform the explicitly political elements in his work. Specifically, this approach consists in abandoning the traditional philosophical binary of universal and particular, or one and many, and replacing it with the relation between singular and regular.

Thus just as differential geometry seeks to provide an analysis 'immanent to' the curve of singular points of inflection, and regular points normal to the curve determined by this point of singularity, so Deleuze will seek to develop a philosophical means for determining *singularities* and local fields or zones of regularity which are themselves determined by these singularities. These fields or zones can be characterised in a number of different ways, as long as we recall that there is neither structure nor genesis organising them from beyond. For instance, Deleuze and Guattari suggest that they can be characterised by 'relations of movement and rest, speed and slowness between unformed elements ... ' (Deleuze and Guattari 1988: 266). In conclusion, the differences between the planes of transcendence and immanence are summarised in the following way:

(1) forms develop and subjects form as a function of a plan(e) that can only be inferred (the plan(e) of organisation-development); (2) there are only speeds and slownesses between unformed elements, and affects between non-subjectified powers, as functions of a plane that is necessarily given

at the same time as that to which it gives rise (the plane of consistency or composition) (Deleuze and Guattari 1988: 268).

The critique of resemblance

Before considering a series of concepts with which Deleuze develops his immanent philosophy, it needs to be emphasised that while the discussion of the difference between the planes of immanence and transcendence appears to take place solely at the level of ontology, Deleuze also develops a distinctive 'epistemology' which corresponds to his immanent ontology. One leitmotif which is common to both his ontology and epistemology is the critique of resemblance. Transcendent principles are rejected by Deleuze primarily because they are never themselves given and can only ever be inferred. Resemblance, as a principle explaining the relation between transcendent principle and what is thought to be given on its basis, is rejected as such because it is a principle which lacks any real explanatory power, failing to account for *why* the given is given. Similarly, Deleuze rejects resemblance as a principle for thinking (one typical way in which philosophy has sought to explain how we think is that reasoning proceeds on the basis of recognising likenesses, from which general rules or concepts are then established or derived) because in fact resemblance offers no possibility for explaining *why* we think at all.

This 'epistemological' dimension of Deleuze's philosophy receives its fullest exposition in the third Chapter of *Difference and Repetition*, the work of original philosophy which formed the principal half of his submission for the *Doctorat D'Etat* in 1968 (alongside *The Problem of Expression in Spinoza*). Of this third Chapter and the new 'Image of Thought' which it develops, Deleuze would subsequently write that it is 'the most necessary and the most concrete' chapter of the book, serving 'to introduce subsequent books up to and including the research undertaken with Guattari' (Deleuze 1994: xvii).

This chapter involves a sustained critique of a series of figures which characterise the traditional image of thought presented by philosophy and the principles on which these figures are based, followed by a delineation of a new image of thought informed by the concepts and principles which determine the immanent philosophy which Deleuze was in the process of developing. Amongst the ways in which the image of thought is traditionally characterised by philosophy are the following:

- 'Everybody knows', by which a philosopher advances a presupposition, on the implicit assumption that nobody 'in their right mind' would fail to accept or recognise the presupposition. But such a characterisation presupposes both a common sense and a good will for thinking – as if thought 'naturally' sought for the truth, and as if this nature of thought is both common sense as well as designating a common sense for thought. But by what rights and on what grounds do we presume this common sense and nature of thinking?

- Thinking operates on the basis of recognition and resemblance – whether it be a resemblance between object and representation, particular and concept, or between representations in the faculties of the mind. By this means all modes of difference are subordinated to, and thus thought on the basis of, identity. In Kant, this characterisation of the traditional image of thought achieves its most profound formulation under the form of a *concordia* or harmony of the faculties. However, resemblance, recognition and harmony give us no account of why we think, of what *forces us to think*.

- Just as thought is assumed to possess a common sense and good nature – a will-to-truth – so error simply consists in thought's being led astray, typically as a consequence of its being interfered with by the desires and drives of the body. But the examples of the philosophers, such as mistaking Theaetetus for Theodorus or saying that 6+5 = 12, are not errors of thinking at all but rather mistakes made by children who have yet to master arithmetic, on the one hand, or a consequence of particular circumstances on the other (for instance, looking from a distance, or in poor light). Philosophy fails to consider 'genuine' error – indeed, before Nietzsche, philosophy fails to think the sense of either sense or non-sense at all.

- Finally, philosophy understands problems as modalities of solutions, such that a problem consists simply of a formulation in which certain details are not given, but whose discovery will yield a full *true* solution – indeed, the solution is in a sense already 'out there', simply waiting to be discovered. Such a characterisation has deep roots in every child's education, for instance in maths, where we learn that every given problem has a given solution which requires working out. Thinking is therefore conceived and indeed projected as working on the same basis, driven by the straightforward search for pre-determined solutions.

Each of these 'postulates' of the traditional image of thought can be seen to lie at the root of much political and international relations theory and, perhaps even more strikingly, practice: a *solution* to the Middle East 'problem' is sought; thought's common sense and good will underlie the extension into political praxis of rational choice theory and game theory; cultural difference is subordinated to universal principles in the formation of foreign policy; areas of agreement are always accorded a higher value in negotiations than principles of difference.

In contrast to this traditional image of thought and on the basis of the critique of it he developed, Deleuze advances a 'new image of thought'.

- What forces us to think? Far from recognition or resemblance forcing us to think, Deleuze argues that we are forced to think when thought encounters a certain violence – when it encounters that which cannot be thought, that which eludes the concepts with which thought normally operates. In other words, in such an encounter thought precisely *does not* recognise that with which it is confronted. On such occasions, Deleuze argues, that which is encountered 'can only be sensed' – thus, the encounter consists in an event of *sensibility* and it is in and through this sensibility that thought is awakened (Deleuze 1994: 139).

- But if this event of sensibility exceeds recognition, how is thought awakened? In what way is thought forced to think? Deleuze suggests that the event of sensibility *perplexes* thought, thereby forcing thought to *pose a problem* (Deleuze 1994: 140). Thus in contrast to the traditional image of thought and the postulate of solutions, the new image of thought requires a new postulate of problems.

With his account of problems, Deleuze's presentation of the 'new image of thought' rejoins the account of the plane of immanence which was outlined previously. The key to understanding the nature of problems, as they function in the new image of thought, lies in understanding what Deleuze means when he writes that 'problems are Ideas themselves' (Deleuze 1994: 162–210). Ideas are, as Deleuze explains in the fourth Chapter of *Difference and Repetition*, indeterminate, and it is in this indeterminacy that their problematicity resides. To understand or constitute a problem consists in determining 'the conditions under which the problem acquires a maximum of comprehension and extension ... conditions capable of communicating to a given case of solution the ideal continuity appropriate to it' (Deleuze 1994: 161). The fundamental task in maintaining the relation between the continuity of the Idea and the discontinuity of its solution, that is to say the fact that the solution differs in kind from the problem as opposed to differing merely in degree (which would be the case were the solution to the problem given in advance as it is in the postulate of the traditional image of thought), is to regain the genuine sense of both universal and singular:

> For the problem or the Idea is a concrete singularity no less than a true universal. Corresponding to the relations which constitute the universality of the problem is the distribution of singular and distinctive points which determine the conditions of the problem (Deleuze 1994: 163–211).

As we saw above, however, this is exactly the way in which Deleuze conceives of the means by which analysis functions on the plane of immanence – in opposition to the universalising tendency of analysis on the plane of transcendence.

Concepts

Having seen how the epistemology of the new image of thought converges with the ontology of the plane of immanence, we need now to turn to a series of concepts with which Deleuze seeks to determine his new immanent philosophy.

1. Multiplicities

We noted in our discussion of differential geometry that Deleuze would adopt the Riemannian notion of multiplicities. Specifically, Deleuze adopts a Bergsonian perspective on the theory of multiplicities, distinguishing between continuous heterogeneous multiplicities, and discontinuous homogeneous multiplicities (and it is worth bearing in mind that this distinction between continuous and discontinuous is already operative in the distinction we have just seen Deleuze making between the continuity of the problematic Idea and the discontinuity of its solution). In turn, this distinction will underpin the theory of difference which Deleuze develops.

At this point, the fundamental issue for Deleuze is how to think the problem as a multiplicity. The key difference between a multiplicity and a set is that sets still maintain a relation with an external or transcendent principle (or essence) which determines the elements of the set (the set of whole numbers, for instance), whereas the only determining principle of a multiplicity is that certain relations are possible between the elements of the multiplicity – whatever these elements might be – and that there are certain fundamental principles or laws which determine the form of these possible relations, these laws being the only determinate aspect of the multiplicity. The objects of the multiplicity are themselves determined solely by the relations into which they can or do enter – while remaining wholly indeterminate with respect to their own form or matter. We must therefore understand the problem as distributing the elements of the multiplicity according to the relations by which they are determined. Singular elements are then singular in relation to the distribution of ordinary or regular elements 'in the neighbourhood' and in this way owe their singularity to these elements. But equally the distribution of the continuity of regular elements is itself determined by the singular elements. A simple representation of this relation between the regular and the singular would be, as indicated above, that of the singular point at which the direction of a curve changes, and the *continua* of regular points constituting the curve on either side of the singular point. In this case singularities would represent the maxima and minima of curves.

What then is the relation between the continuity of events, the distribution of singularities which constitute the conditions of the problem, and the determined particulars that constitute the solution of the problem, from this new perspective of the problem which emerges from the critique of the postulate of solutions? Deleuze emphasises that while problems differ in kind from solutions, they nevertheless do not exist apart from their solutions. Rather, the problem 'insists and persists in the solutions'.

A problem is determined at the same time that it is solved, but its determination is not the same as its solution: the two elements differ in kind, the determination amounting to the genesis of the concomitant solution. (In this manner the distribution of singularities belongs entirely to the conditions of the problem, while their specification already refers to solutions constructed under these conditions.) The problem is at once both transcendent and immanent to its solutions. Transcendent, because it consists in a system of ideal liaisons or differential relations between genetic elements. Immanent, because these liaisons or relations are incarnated in the actual relations which do not resemble them and are defined by the field of the solution (Deleuze 1994: 163).

What this adoption of the theory of multiplicities with which to think through immanence enables, for Deleuze, is the casting aside of the traditional formulations of the one and the many, or the universal and the particular, or even of essence and accident and their replacement by a new mode of thinking the relation between the singular and the general within local distributions. In particular it allows for a differential account of the relation between both regular and singular elements within the multiplicity whereas accounts deriving from philosophies of transcendence tend to operate with principles of resemblance and recognition.

2. The virtual

The principle of resemblance or identity persists within the attempts made by philosophies of transcendence to explain change. Deleuze is, first and foremost, a thinker of becoming, and any theory of becoming entails an adequate account of change. Just as in his adoption of the theory of multiplicities and in his thinking of difference, Deleuze's theory of change owes much to his reading of Bergson.

Since Aristotle, philosophy has tended to have recourse to the principle of *potentiality* as a means for thinking change. Thus, in a process of change or becoming, an entity x becomes y precisely because x has, as a property, the *potential for becoming y*. For instance, an acorn has the potential to become an oak tree. The process of becoming or change therefore would consist in the *realisation* of this potential borne by x. But there are two fundamental problems with this theory. First, realisation entails a maintenance of identity – there is no difference between the potential acorn and the real acorn (indeed were there a difference then the theory would lose all its explanatory power). This is just the point that Kant makes in his brutal critique of ontological arguments in general. Second, as Bergson argues, the theory of potentiality actually trades on a mistaken recourse to time. The theory, Bergson argues, claims to operate from the past to the future – the oak exists potentially in the past (at the beginning of the process) and then really in the future. But in fact the theory works from the future to the past. Thus, from the existence of some entity y (e.g. an oak tree), we project back into the past its potential existence on to an entity x (the acorn). But in this projection all we are really doing is subtracting being from what exists in the present, and creating a 'potential being' by this subtraction. Potentiality ultimately lacks explanatory power both because it is a projection from the real and because it functions on the basis of its retroactive resemblance to the real – but in this way we see that the real has priority over the possible, thereby denying potentiality any power for explaining change.

Deleuze therefore rejects the notion of potentiality and in its stead introduces the notion of the virtual (also derived from Bergson). Deleuze conceives of the virtual as a multiplicity. As such, it is indeterminate. However, it can be rendered determinable and thereby given an objective consistency. In Bergson, the indeterminate multiplicity of duration is rendered determinable by memory; in Spinoza, the indeterminate multiplicity of substance is rendered determinable by attributes; and in Nietzsche, the indeterminate multiplicity of forces is rendered determinable by will-to-power. Crucially, in each of these cases the virtual multiplicities are real – but not *actual*. Thus Deleuze conceives of the process of actualisation of the virtual as a determination of what has been rendered determinable. The relation between virtual and actual is therefore a relation of difference: the virtual differs from the actual, and the process by which the virtual is actualised is a process of *differenciation*. In this way Deleuze is able to propose a new immanent means by which to think the transcendental. The transcendental no longer represents conditions of *possible* experience or being as it does in, for instance, Plato and Kant; rather, as virtual, the transcendental now accounts for the genesis of actual particular determinate existence. Just as significantly, because the virtual does not transcend the actual, the process of differenciating not only accounts for the genesis of the actual, but also affects the virtual, leading to a new determinability of the multiplicity, a novel distribution of singular and regular points (in Nietzsche, this affectivity constitutes the will-to-power precisely as *will*).

3. Difference

As the two preceding points make clear, in Deleuze's new philosophy of immanence the principle of difference replaces that of identity and resemblance, which have priority in philosophies of transcendence. In this way, Deleuze is able to think the *productivity* of difference, and on this basis the means by which novelty is generated. Again, Deleuze's thinking of difference is influenced by Bergson. From Bergson Deleuze draws a fundamental distinction between heterogeneous and homogeneous multiplicities. Significantly, this distinction stems from the difference between the two types of differential relations which subsist between the elements of continuous and discontinuous multiplicities. In discontinuous multiplicities, the relations between elements are such that a change to the multiplicity consists, in effect, in a process of division, a change in degree, such that the elements maintain their identity. It is this maintenance of identity which accounts for the homogeneity of the multiplicity. On the other hand, the relations between the elements of the continuous multiplicity are such that any change to these relations leads to a change in kind in the multiplicity and it is in this change in kind that the heterogeneity of the multiplicity consists.

Implications

What implications might this new philosophy of immanence developed by Deleuze and the new concepts with which he seeks to make sense of it have for international relations and political theory? Deleuze and Guattari adapt the distinction between continuous heterogeneous and discontinuous homogeneous multiplicities for their notion of *smooth and striated spaces*, by which they conceive of the social organisation of space. Striated spaces are discontinuous, susceptible to rigid division, with the attendant assignation of roles and locations to the people inhabiting these spaces. Centrally controlled agricultural societies, such as existed in the river valleys of China, offer clear examples of striated spaces. In smooth spaces by contrast people are free to wander *nomadically*. The nomad does not 'own' any space or land, and has no assigned place. In their wanderings, nomads encounter 'micro-environments': local distributions which may or may not offer the conditions which might enable nomads to pasture their flocks. One way or the other, guidance comes, and can only come, not from the centralised state but rather from attention to the local conditions of the micro-environment – the 'feel' of the place and of the moment. This feel is necessarily singular, rather than a universalised form or concept which the state seeks to impose.

Deleuze and Guattari go on to oppose the means by which the state wages war, by which it seeks to conserve and integrate its power, with the way in which nomadology invents new *war machines*. By war machines, Deleuze and Guattari mean modes of organisation which are innovative, as opposed to the forms of state organisation which are rigid and bureaucratic. The nomadic war machine is hostile to the rigid, organisational tendencies of the state and the striated spaces it seeks to impose. However, war is not intrinsic to it, even though the state always seeks to impose war on it. Deleuze and Guattari characterise this war waged by the state as one of *deterritorialisation*, to the extent that the nomad, and non-state societies in general, find their means of production in the earth, in the locality of the land, whereas the state seeks to move the source of social production into the body of the despotic emperor, thereby displacing territory or the earth from its organisational centrality. Empires are typically deterritorialising because they replace direct territoriality with an abstract principle of citizenship while simultaneously inventing abstract bureaucratic mechanisms for controlling movement.

However, the more a state seeks to impose rigid bureaucratic order on its society, the more it seeks to stave off change, the more it creates new possibilities for escape, because no system can ever circumscribe its elements entirely. These possibilities for escape Deleuze and Guattari call *lines of flight*. Lines of flight exist as virtual tendencies which groups or individuals actualise by actively exploring them, although such exploration always carries its own attendant dangers. Finally, this actualisation of lines of flight is one example of what Deleuze and Guattari in general characterise as *assemblages*: the set of inter-related processes which actualise virtual tendencies or multiplicities. What is of the utmost significance about assemblages is that they are not determined by some transcendent organising principle which directs the assembling. Rather, assemblages are self-organising. Indeed, the self-organising tendency of assemblages represents amongst the most striking political consequences of Deleuze's new philosophy of immanence.

Further reading

Deleuze, Gilles (1988) *Foucault*, trans. Sean Hand, Minnesota: University of Minnesota Press. A valuable work in which the political dimension of Deleuze's thought is illuminated through being cast in relief to that of Michel Foucault. Also, this book remains the best single work devoted to the thought of Foucault.

Deleuze, Gilles (1994) *Difference and Repetition*, trans. Paul Patton, London: Athlone. This is the work in which Deleuze develops his own philosophical 'system' for the first time.

Deleuze, Gilles (2004) *Desert Islands*, trans. Michael Taormina, New York: Semiotext(e). An excellent collection of articles, reviews, and interviews originally appearing between 1953 and 1974.

Deleuze, Gilles and Félix Guattari (1984) *Anti-Oedipus: Capitalism and Schizophrenia*, trans. Robert Hurley, Mark Seem and Helen Lane, London: Athlone.

Deleuze, Gilles and Félix Guattari (1988) *A Thousand Plateaus: Capitalism and Schizophrenia*, trans. Brian Massumi, London: Athlone.

Deleuze, Gilles and Félix Guattari (1994) *What is Philosophy?* trans. Graham Burchell and Hugh Tomlinson, London: Verso. This is the series of works in which Deleuze's commitment to the radical process of concept-formation achieves its most sustained register; also, the works in which the majority of the concepts which have an explicitly political import are developed.

Delanda, Manuel (2000) *A Thousand Years of Non-Linear History*, New York: Zone Books. Seeks to develop a materialist history of human societies derived from dynamical sciences, and inspired by Deleuze and Guattari.

Patton, Paul (2000) *Deleuze and the Political*, London and New York: Routledge. An excellent introduction to the political dimension of Deleuze's thought, in which the relevance of the new concepts developed by Deleuze for contemporary political science are made clear.

Protevi, John (2001) *Political Physics*, London: Athlone. Contrasts the approaches to the theme of the 'body politic' of Deleuze and Jacques Derrida.

Two helpful web-based resources are:
'WebDeleuze' available at: http://www.webdeleuze.com;
and Abecedaire' available at: http://www.langlab.wayne.edu/CStivale/D-G/ABCs.html (includes links to videos of original French TV broadcasts).

12 Jacques Derrida

Maja Zehfuss

Jacques Derrida's work has had a major impact on scholars working in the humanities and social sciences. But Derrida is famous beyond the academic world. His work has influenced artists, too, and he was involved in organising exhibitions. 'Deconstruction', a term associated with Derrida's work, has become part of our vocabulary, although it is often used in a way that is not faithful to his thought. Derrida was also active politically. The issue of teaching philosophy in schools was a concern for him throughout his life. He was involved in a group supporting dissident intellectuals in Czechoslovakia and, after participating in a secret seminar in 1981, he was imprisoned on false drug charges by the Czechoslovakian authorities. Derrida also spoke out against apartheid. When he died in 2004, he had been the protagonist of films and cartoons, and the subject of at least one rock song (Attridge and Baldwin 2004; Bennington and Derrida 1993).

Derrida was born in El-Biar, Algeria, in 1930. He was named 'Jackie', and chose to use 'Jacques' in his professional life. Algeria had been invaded and colonised by France from 1830; eventually it was made a part of France. As a Sephardic Jew Derrida was a full French citizen, unlike the vast majority of Muslim Algerians. After attending the local primary school, he moved to the *lycée* in 1941. Yet in 1942 he was expelled because he was Jewish. Anti-Semitic laws emanating from occupied France applied, although Algeria was never occupied by Germany. At this time Derrida was also subjected to physical and verbal violence. Whilst he suffered from the anti-Semitism of society, he was not comfortable at the Jewish high school either and did not attend his classes for almost a year (Bennington and Derrida 1993: 326–27). Derrida returned to his previous school in 1943, but failed the *baccalauréat* in 1947. He was dreaming of becoming a professional footballer. Nevertheless, he immersed himself in reading. After passing the *bac* in 1948, he decided to attend the *École Normale Supérieure* (ENS), the leading French institute for literature and philosophy. He left Algeria for the first time to take preparatory classes in Paris and eventually passed the entrance examination at his third attempt. At the ENS he made friends with, among others, Louis Althusser and Michel Foucault, though he later fell out with Foucault. He also met psychoanalyst Marguerite Aucoutrier, whom he married in 1957. Derrida passed his *aggrégation* in 1956, again after more than one attempt (Attridge and Baldwin 2004). After his military service, during the Algerian war, he started his first teaching post at a *lycée* in Le Mans in 1959 (Bennington and Derrida 1993: 330). In 1964 he was appointed to ENS where he remained until 1984, when he accepted a position at the *École des Hautes Études en Sciences Sociales* (Powell 2006).

Clearly, Derrida had to overcome obstacles and set-backs early in his academic career. He also struggled with ill health and depression. Yet he published three major books, *Speech and Phenomena* (1973), *Writing and Difference* (1978) and *Of Grammotology* (1998) in 1967, when he was barely in his late thirties. His work was recognised internationally and across disciplines from the 1970s. Derrida held many appointments at American universities; from 1987, he taught one semester each year at the University of California at Irvine. His appointment to a university chair in France was, however, blocked in the early 1980s (Bennington and Derrida 1993: 333). In 1992 the University of Cambridge awarded him an honorary degree, but only after a controversy over his credentials for such an honour (Derrida 1995b: 399–421). Derrida's work is, in other words, both highly influential and controversial.

It is not easy to summarise Derrida's thought. This is not merely because he published some 70 books and countless articles. People who are unfamiliar with his work sometimes balk at the words he uses, such as *différance* or undecidability. Some of them he indeed 'makes up'. Yet this is not unique to Derrida. Scholars often use terms in specific ways that depart from everyday language. Sometimes they introduce new words needed to express phenomena or relationships between them that were not previously considered important. The potential difficulty with Derrida's terms is more fundamental. As his arguments challenge the categories within which we think – that is, our language – his terms are not easily explained using that language. You have to understand the logic of his thought to appreciate *différance*, for example. Geoffrey Bennington also highlights that Derrida's work does not consist of a 'system of theses', which would be easier to summarise, but in readings of philosophical and literary texts (Bennington and Derrida 1993: 6). Often his texts perform what they say: they challenge the language used in them.

Because of what he argues Derrida considers reading extremely significant. You can tell from the care with which he approaches the texts he critiques that he loves reading. More entertainingly, his love for reading becomes clear in the film *Derrida* (Dick and Kofman 2003) during a conversation in Derrida's study. The walls are covered with books and the filmmaker asks Derrida whether he has read all of them. He smiles and says that he has read 'three or four' of them, but that he has read those very, very carefully. Derrida has certainly read more than 'three or four' books, but that he reads extremely carefully is no joke. One way of understanding his work is to focus on how he reads and why he is such a champion of reading carefully (1988). For him reading is itself an act of writing; that is, reading does not decipher the given meaning of a text but is part of creating that meaning.

So this chapter offends against the spirit of Derrida's work. You should read his texts, carefully, rather than avoid this challenge and hope that I offer a shortcut to his insights. Such a shortcut is not possible, not least because the journey is significant; it is not just a matter of where you get to in the end. Yet Derrida recognised the value of occasionally summarising his ideas. Derrida's interviews, or introductions to his work, offer useful simplifications; they should not, however, replace reading his – undoubtedly difficult – key works. What I want to do in this chapter is not to make you feel that you 'know Derrida' but to show why engaging with his texts is worth the effort. Derrida's work is difficult for the best possible reason: it makes you think. It makes you question aspects of the world that you may have taken for granted. Indeed, it makes you question the ways in which you are able to think about this world.

Deconstruction and the impossibility of presence

One widely used introduction to Derrida's thought is called *Deconstruction in a Nutshell* (Caputo 1997). This is a tease: the title recalls that during the controversy over his honorary degree from the University of Cambridge, Derrida was asked by a journalist to define deconstruction – often considered the central idea in Derrida's work – 'in a nutshell'. Derrida recounts his inability to do so and the journalist's surprise (1995b: 406). So the title draws attention to the impossibility of explaining, in a nutshell, what deconstruction is. Deconstruction unsettles the categories on which our thinking is based and that are fundamental to language. It is, therefore, difficult to express what deconstruction is within this language. Nevertheless, Derrida says: 'It is not that bad that we try to encapsulate deconstruction in a nutshell' (Derrida in Caputo 1997: 16).

To explain deconstruction, even 'in a nutshell', it is necessary to engage with what Derrida says about Western philosophy or, to put it less grandly, about how we think. Derrida argues that Western thought is structured by dichotomies, that is, by pairs of concepts that appear to be opposites of each other, such as presence/absence, identity/difference or speech/writing. You might also think of domestic/international (Ashley 1989; Edkins and Zehfuss 2005). The two terms that form a dichotomy are meant to be mutually exclusive. Something is *either* present *or* absent; it cannot be both. Derrida claims that we conceive the world in terms of such dichotomies and that this is both significant and problematic.

Significantly, the two terms within each dichotomy are not independent of each other. We need, for example, the idea of difference in order to grasp what is meant by identity. Moreover, there is a hierarchical order within each dichotomy: one term is privileged over the other. Barbara Johnson (1981: viii) points out that the 'second term in each pair is considered the negative, corrupt, undesirable version of the first'. Identity is preferred over difference, presence over absence.

Derrida (1998) is particularly interested in how Western thought in general privileges presence over absence. Derrida examines this in relation to the conceptualisation of speech as superior to writing. Speech, Derrida claims, has been seen as primary and authentic whereas writing is seen as derivative, as further removed from what is to be communicated. This is not just how philosophers have thought about it. Sometimes we find it difficult to tell how something in an e-mail is meant, for example, or we are even offended by what we think such a written communication might be saying. Often the best way to sort out this kind of uncertainty is to speak to the person concerned. Sometimes it turns out that they did not mean to say what we understood. So, you could say that speech was a better means of communication, better at transmitting the intended meaning.

We are not always able to speak to each other, however. I am writing this chapter because it is not possible for me to speak to you. If I could speak to you about Derrida's thought I could see whether you understood what I was saying and you could interrupt if my explanations were not good enough. As I write I must guess what you already know and what I need to tell you about. Again, speech seems to be the better way of communicating. Speech, however, requires speaker and addressee to be in the same place at the same time (or to use a telephone, for example, which allows them to act as though they were in the same place). This co-presence ensures that both can grasp the meaning of their communication. Perfect communication may not always happen, but it is the ideal upon which Western culture relies.

Derrida calls this 'logocentrism' (Derrida 1998: 3). This derives from the Greek word *logos*, meaning speech, logic, reason, the Word of God (Johnson 1981: ix). Derrida argues that logocentrism, which is related to the centrality of presence, is crucial. Our thinking is based on the value of presence: we 'show', 'reveal', 'make clear'. It is based on foundations, origins or some kind of 'presence' at the root of things. Derrida also calls this the 'metaphysics of presence' (Derrida 1998: 49). One important implication of this way of thinking is that representation is distinct from and inferior to presence. This is why writing is less good, something we only resort to when speech is impossible (Derrida 1988: 5). Writing represents speech, which in turn represents our thoughts; therefore writing is more removed from what is to be communicated. Crucially, for Derrida, this way of thinking cannot work. It revolves around a conception of Being built on the possibility of distinguishing clearly between presence and absence, or identity and difference, and such distinctions are impossible (Zehfuss 2002: 198).

To appreciate the impossibility of delineating presence against absence, Jonathan Culler (1983: 94) discusses the flight of an arrow. If we think of reality as presence, a paradox arises: we cannot think of the arrow's movement purely in terms of presence. At any given instant the arrow is in a particular place; it is not in motion. We can only think of the arrow as being in motion if we accept that every instant is already marked by its past and future. We know that the arrow is moving because the present is not pure: we know where the arrow has been and where it will go. So, whilst our thinking is based on conceiving presence as absolute presence, when we think about an everyday occurrence such as motion, we find that we must abandon the purity of presence. We find that the idea of presence is contaminated by its opposite, absence (Zehfuss 2002: 198–99). Expressed in Derrida's terminology, the idea of presence deconstructs. The idea of presence is shown to be impossible on the basis of the presuppositions that are necessary to it.

Relatedly, Derrida shows that speech and writing are not entirely different from each other. Rather, they are both a form of what he calls a 'system of writing in general' (Derrida 1998: 43). This argument is an example of deconstruction. 'Deconstruction' is often used to refer to a way of reading. Culler explains that to 'deconstruct a discourse is to show how it undermines the philosophy it asserts, or the hierarchical oppositions on which it relies, by identifying in the text the rhetorical operations that produce the supposed ground of argument, the key concept or premise' (Culler 1983: 86). More precisely, deconstruction addresses the dichotomies in our thought through inversion and displacement. That is, in order to critique the dichotomy speech/writing, the hierarchy has to be inverted: we must think through what it would mean to consider writing better than speech. This overturning is necessary to change how we conceive things. And we have to do this time and again because the hierarchy of binary oppositions always re-establishes itself (Derrida 1981b: 42). However, overturning the hierarchy is not enough. It doesn't change all that much. We still think in roughly the same way, just the other way around.

Let's take an example that many people have strong views about. Arguably, masculine attributes and characteristics have been valued over feminine ones. The obvious critical move – and a necessary part of a deconstructive intervention – is to subvert the hierarchy. So we might argue that the (putatively masculine) ability to rationally and objectively assess various options is not as good as the (putatively feminine) ability to take feelings into account. Doing things in a feminine way would then be better than doing them in a masculine way. But notice how this critique reproduces part of the thinking that it challenges: it accepts that 'feminine' can be distinguished from 'masculine'. This critique remains within the original system of thought. The original hierarchy remains possible and can therefore reassert itself. Thus, a second move is necessary, one that leaves behind the previous system of thought (Derrida 1981b: 42–43). Derrida calls this the displacement. A displacement would entail questioning whether 'masculine' can be thought of as separate from and opposed to 'feminine', for example. In Derrida's example of speech versus writing he argues that speech is a form of writing in general, that is, it is a system for recording and thus producing meaning. Therefore, we cannot make sense of things if we try to distinguish between speech and writing.

Derrida shows that each of the terms within a dichotomy cannot operate without their opposite. Note the difficult implications. We may *think* that presence and absence are polar opposites, mutually exclusive: something is either present *or* absent, but never both present *and* absent. But it is impossible to think this way (that is, it is impossible to think in the way that Derrida tells us we employ anyhow, that in fact we cannot escape): absence is necessary to make presence possible. Given that this challenges the structures of our thought, which is based on the centrality of presence, how can we think about this? Derrida introduces the notion of *différance* to overcome the impossible mutual exclusiveness of presence and absence. The term *différance* plays on two meanings of the French word *différer*: to differ and to defer. In one sense, *différance* refers to something being other, not identical, distinguishable. In the other sense, it means a 'temporal or temporizing mediation or a detour that suspends the accomplishment or fulfillment of "desire" or "will", and equally effects this suspension in a mode that annuls or tempers its own effect' (Derrida 1982: 8; see Zehfuss 2002: 199). You might not find this entirely clear. It is difficult to define *différance*, not least because *différance* illustrates why nothing ever simply 'is'. It is more useful to look at the effects of *différance*.

Différance produces differences, and thereby makes possible the dichotomies that are central to our thinking (Derrida 1981b: 9). To understand this it is useful to think about another conception of meaning. One might assume that a sign – 'car', for example – stands for a thing, either a meaning or a referent. The sign represents a presence in its absence. When the thing itself cannot be shown, 'we go through the detour of the sign' (Derrida 1982: 9). The sign is deferred presence. Derrida therefore argues that the possibility of the sign, although based on representing a presence, introduces the element of difference and deferral, that is, *différance*. 'Nothing ... is anywhere ever simply present or absent. There are only, everywhere, differences and traces of traces' (Derrida 1981b: 26). *Différance* therefore questions the 'authority of presence' (Derrida 1982: 10; Zehfuss 2002: 200).

This brings us back to Derrida's critique of the centrality of presence. He argues that pure presence – which would be necessary if presence were to constitute a secure foundation for our thought – is impossible. On the contrary, in Culler's words, the 'notion of presence is derived: an effect of differences' (Culler 1983: 95). Absence is not the negation of presence; instead presence is the effect of a general absence. This turns logocentric logic on its head. In Henry Staten's words: 'X is constituted by non-X' (Staten 1985: 17). He calls this the 'constitutive outside' (Staten 1985: 16): the outside is necessary for constituting any phenomenon (Zehfuss 2002: 237–38).

It is therefore important to consider what is being excluded or put aside in any analysis or representation. The silences and exclusions may tell us most about what is accepted as given or central. Deconstruction draws out the different things a text simultaneously says and the contradictions that this entails. It subverts the logic of a text by taking this logic seriously.

Deconstruction is a form of critique based on careful reading. So it is clear what deconstruction is not: a way of reading that draws out the meaning of a text. It is impossible to reproduce the author's intended meaning. Nor can a reading rely on an external referent. There is no reality beyond representation or, as Derrida famously put it: '*There is nothing outside of the text* [there is no outside-text; *il n'y a pas de hors-texte*]' (Derrida 1998: 158). This claim has created much indignation, but this reaction seems to be based on a misunderstanding. The claim is not that the 'real world' with its material effects does not exist. What Derrida calls text 'implies all the structures called "real", "economic", "historical", "socio-institutional", in short: all possible referents' (Derrida 1988: 148). That there is nothing outside of the text means that all reality is structured by differences, just as texts are, and that we have no way of referring to this 'real' except through representation and interpretations (Derrida 1988: 148; Zehfuss 2002: 239). There is no pure presence outside of the text that is then represented by signification; rather 'signified presence is always reconstituted by deferral, *nachträglich*, belatedly, *supplementarily*' (Derrida 1978: 211–12).

The idea of the supplement, which is necessary to signification, is important; it embodies the two contradictory but mutually complementary meanings of *suppléer*, to complement and to replace. A supplement is something that is added later, to enrich something that already exists, like a supplementary volume to an encyclopaedia. Such a supplement, however, never merely enriches an entity; it always threatens to replace it (Derrida 1998: 144–45). The information in the supplement supersedes what may be said in the original volumes. The same applies to the relation of the sign to what it is thought to stand for. As the 'sign is always the supplement of the thing itself' (Derrida 1998: 145), it 'takes its place' in both meanings of the term: it stands for it in its absence but also replaces it (Zehfuss 2002: 201–2). The supplement is not an essentially superfluous addition. Rather the 'presence' which it is thought to be added onto is derived from the supplement: 'Immediacy is derived' (Derrida 1998: 157). There is nothing more real than the supplement, no presence prior to the sign, the supplement. It is in this sense that there is nothing outside of the text or rather that there is no such thing as an 'outside-text', an *hors-texte*. Derrida discusses this in *Of Grammatology*, and you may wish to follow this up.

The logic of the supplement requires us to abandon forms of analysis that rely on the possibility of pure presence. We need the strategy of deconstruction. Derrida shows that our thought cannot work on the basis of its presuppositions. Derrida argues that we think in particular ways – in ways that rely on dichotomies, that privilege presence and so on – but he shows us that these dichotomies, and especially our idea of presence, do not work. His deconstructions work to subvert the text, to create a profound recontextualisation (Derrida 1988: 136), but they cannot escape the text because there is nothing outside of it. The point is not to escape the logic of logocentrism. This would be impossible, but also ineffective. Deconstruction instead uses the concepts and assumptions it subverts. Concepts can be deconstructed only by operating within them. Deconstruction is 'not a method or some tool that you apply to something from the outside ... Deconstruction is something which happens and which happens inside' (Derrida in Caputo 1997: 9). The contradictions that make a text deconstruct are already there, before anyone may engage in an activity called deconstruction. Texts deconstruct from within.

Deconstruction and decision

Clearly, deconstruction is political. It so profoundly interferes with our standard ways of conceiving the world that much of what we may have taken for granted must be reconsidered. In 'Force of Law' Derrida draws attention to the problems and contradictions involved in ideas of the law, violence and justice, using a deconstructive line of reasoning. Derrida notes that the law implies the possibility of enforcement; it is backed by force. Law is 'a force that justifies itself or is justified in applying itself' (Derrida 1992a: 5). This, though, raises the question of how to distinguish between the 'force of law' and violence which is considered unjust (Derrida 1992a: 6). Derrida draws on Walter Benjamin's text *'Zur Kritik der Gewalt'* ('Critique of Violence') to explore this. Although the German term *'Gewalt'* is often translated as 'violence', it also means 'legitimate power, justified authority' (Derrida 1992a: 6). It is impossible to clearly distinguish between these two meanings of the force of law. This becomes apparent in the founding moment of the law. Derrida asks:

> How are we to distinguish between the force of law of a legitimate power and the supposedly originary violence that must have established this authority and that could not itself have been authorized by any anterior legitimacy, so that, in this initial moment it is neither legal nor illegal – or, others would say, neither just nor unjust? (Derrida 1992a: 6)

The emergence of law and justice necessarily involves a moment of performative and interpretative force. Elsewhere Derrida discusses this in relation to the US Declaration of Independence (Derrida 2002b: 46–54). At the point of emergence, law cannot yet be an instrument of the dominant power; rather law must 'maintain a more internal, more complex relation with what one calls force, power or violence' (Derrida 1992a: 13). The disconcerting thought is that 'the operation that consists of founding, inaugurating, justifying law (*droit*), making law, would consist of a *coup de force*, of a performative and therefore interpretative violence that in itself is neither just nor unjust' (Derrida 1992a: 13). Any recourse to the law or justice is bound up with this original *coup de force*: 'since the origin of authority, the foundation or ground, the position of the law can't by definition rest on anything but themselves, they are themselves a violence without ground' (Derrida 1992a: 14).

Law and justice are linked, but they are also profoundly different. For example, when a rule is applied to a particular case, the law is accounted for, but not justice. Law is calculable. Justice, however, consists in a singular act and not in the mechanical application of rules (Derrida 1992a: 16–17). The problem of justice arises precisely when the rules do not deliver a clear or satisfying outcome, for example, when different rules are in tension with each other. Justice involves, and requires, the experience of aporia, that is, 'moments in which the decision between just and unjust is never insured by a rule' (Derrida 1992a: 16). Justice 'is an experience of the impossible' (Derrida 1992a: 16) that can only take place when a decision is made freely. A free decision must go through the aporia of the undecidable. The undecidable

> is not merely the oscillation between two significations or two contra-dictory and very determinate rules, each equally imperative ... The undecidable is not merely the oscillation or the tension between two decisions; it is the experience of that which, though heterogeneous, for-eign to the order of the calculable and the rule, is still obliged ... to give itself up to the impossible decision, while taking account of law and rules (Derrida 1992a: 24).

Crucially, the decision does not resolve the problem and go beyond the undecidable. The undecidable remains caught in every decision; this makes it impossible to call any decision fully just. Yet this does not mean that we should or indeed can dispense with justice. On the contrary, Derrida even asserts that deconstruction 'is justice' (Derrida 1992a: 15).

Jenny Edkins discusses these issues of the force of law, justice and the undecidable in relation to famine and especially Amartya Sen's claims about entitlements – that is, ownership of food – and legality. She points out that the

> process of decision cannot follow a code and is not calculable. As such it entails responsibility that cannot be evaded by an appeal to the law. This means that actions of agents of the state in forcing people to starve by protecting food stocks in shops cannot be justified by reference to law or legitimacy as Sen claims. The law itself is produced and reproduced in particular decisions. What happens cannot be legislated for in advance (Edkins 2000: 62).

Thus, decisions are significant and we need to understand more about them. When do decisions become necessary? The aporia of the undecidable arises not least when there are several contradictory demands. For example, when the imperative to uphold the legal order clashes with the imperative to feed a person who would otherwise starve, we experience a 'contradictory impera-tive'. Though contradictory, both imperatives may even derive from the same duty or rule. After all, not protecting the legal order may also endan-ger people's access to food. Derrida speaks of 'the responsibility to think, speak, and act in compliance with this double contradictory imperative' (Derrida 1992b: 79). This is difficult; for the issue arises because there is no way forward that would resolve or escape the dilemma. In a situation that calls for responsibility a decision is necessary, but anything one might do involves committing some wrong. Many difficult questions arise. David Campbell (1994) discusses the problem of responsibility and decision as a problem of international relations. In his *National Deconstruction* (1998a) he examines the Bosnian war and pursues the question of what responsibility – what he calls the 'task of outsiders' – entails.

According to Derrida, political and moral responsibility only exists where one has to go through the aporia of the undecidable (Derrida 1988: 116). Otherwise there is no decision, only a mechanical application of rules. Although this is an oversimplification, one might think of the problem of responsibility in terms of situations where different groups of people have legitimate claims that are in tension with each other. Let's assume for the moment that the intervention in Iraq was about liberating Iraqis from an oppressive regime. If that is so, then one could say the intervention involved taking responsibility for those who were freed. But it also inevitably involved not acting responsibly towards others – the combatants and Iraqi civilians killed in the process. Moreover, expending resources on this conflict might mean not being able to intervene in another, say in Darfur, and thereby failing the responsibility towards those affected by the other conflict. Yet we cannot simply ignore our responsibility. This is a constant problem: To whose call do we respond? And whom do we end up ignoring? It is not possible to act responsibly towards everyone. We do not have the capacity. In Derrida's words: 'I cannot respond to the call, the request, the obligation, or even the love of another without sacrificing the other other, the other others' (Derrida 1995a: 68). So there is a paradox at the heart of responsibility:

> As soon as I enter into a relation with the other, with the gaze, look, request, love, command, or call of the other, I know that I can respond only by sacrificing ethics, that is, by sacrificing whatever obliges me also to respond, in the same way, in the same instant, to all the others (Derrida 1995a: 68).

Acting responsibly therefore does not mean doing good rather than evil. It means negotiating a difficult situation in which no purely good way forward is possible.

This is why a decision becomes necessary: there are many demands, and it is impossible to respond to all of them. Some of them may contradict each other. The matter may be urgent (Derrida 2002b: 296). Urgency means not least that it is impossible to get all the relevant information. A choice must be made, even if all the knowledge that might be helpful is not available. Derrida points out that it is a mistake to believe that knowledge would somehow settle the matter and tell us the right way forward. We should try to know as much as possible, but knowledge is not enough. 'A decision, if there is such a thing, is never determinable in terms of knowledge' (Derrida

2002b: 229). An ethico-political decision involves a leap of faith (Derrida 2003: 118). In my *Wounds of Memory* (2007) I discuss why knowledge is not enough when we face the ethico-political question of war. It is tempting to think that, if only we had some particular knowledge (in the case of my book that is if only the Germans knew how to correctly remember the Second World War), then we would also know what to do (that is, then they would know how to use their military today). But this does not work. Situations that raise the question of responsibility are situations in which knowledge is of little help. If we *know* the best solution, the matter at issue is not one of responsibility.

This is why the rules of ethics do not alleviate this problem. On the contrary, in Derrida's view, 'far from ensuring responsibility, the generality of ethics incites irresponsibility' (Derrida 1995a: 61). Instead what Derrida calls the aporia, the experience of the impossible, is crucial. Any attempt to eliminate it, Derrida claims, eliminates responsibility itself. For responsibility to be possible, the tension which marks the aporia of the decision does, and must, remain (Derrida 1995a: 66). The application of a rule or programme is not responsible; for it 'makes of action the applied consequence, the simple application of a knowledge or know-how. It makes of ethics and politics a technology' (Derrida 1992b: 45). The aporia of the undecidable does not make responsibility impossible; depoliticisation, which turns ethical questions into technical problems awaiting technical solutions determined by pre-given rules, does (Derrida 1992b: 71–72). To bypass the aporia would be dangerous. It would merely allow us to retain a good conscience whilst being immoral.

This means that responsibility is in tension with the generality of ethics. According to Derrida,

> I can respond only to the one ... , that is, to the other, by sacrificing the other to that one. I am responsible to any one (that is to say to any other) only by failing in my responsibility to all the others, to the ethical or political generality. And I can never justify this sacrifice, I must always hold my peace about it (Derrida 1995a: 70).

He insists that just 'as no one can die in my place, no one can make a decision, what we call "a decision", in my place' (Derrida 1995a: 60). Thus, contrary to the common perception that responsibility is about public accountability and following the rules of ethics, it is, in Derrida's view, inextricably linked to silence, singularity and the aporia of decision. Responsibility is at issue in the singular act; it is not a matter of complying with an abstract rule structure. The problem of ethico-political responsibility lies precisely in 'the disparities between law, ethics, and politics, or between the unconditional idea of law (be it of men or of states) and the concrete conditions of its implementation' (Derrida 1992b: 57).

It's all to do with the decision. But, significantly, the idea of a *decision* is tricky altogether. Not only is it impossible to know whether a decision has been just or responsible or indeed whether there has been a decision at all (Derrida 1992a: 24–25) because the decision is not of the same order as knowledge; the decision that we make in response to others' demands is also not under our control. Derrida talks of a decision being 'the Other's decision in me, or through me'. That is, the decision 'exceeds my own being, my own possibility, my own potentiality' (Derrida 2006: 103). We are not somehow separate from the world that we respond to and therefore the decision can never be purely 'ours'.

So here is the problem, in a nutshell: The question of responsibility arises when there is no right way forward. Knowledge is unable to resolve this problem. We inevitably fail in our responsibility to some, and this may have serious consequences. And we are not even in control. Well, no one said thinking about politics was easy. As John Caputo says: 'Neither Derrida nor I am trying to rob you of your anxiety' (Caputo 1997: 37). This is probably true. Derrida's work certainly doesn't. But remember: nothing is ever pure. So this is all very serious and anxiety may be a good thing. Yet at least some of Derrida's work seems to be written with a smile. No one will be helped by our angst. So we might as well have some fun, whenever possible. Read Derrida's work: then you might understand what I mean.

Further reading

There is no substitute for reading Derrida's work. Reading *Of Grammatology* (1998) is crucial to understand his arguments about the impossibility of pure presence. *Writing and Difference* (1978), *Dissemination* (1981a) and *Margins of Philosophy* (1982) are also key texts for grasping deconstruction. *Limited Inc* (1988) performs a deconstruction. *Positions* (1981b) offers good summary statements about deconstruction. The shorter pieces and interviews collected in *Negotiations* (2002b) are also helpful; some directly address ethico-political questions. *Specters of Marx* (1994) and *Politics of Friendship* (1997) are probably seen as the most directly political of the books. 'Force of Law' (1992a) highlights the implications of deconstruction in the context of questions about law, violence and justice. You might also enjoy some of the shorter works or conversations, such as *Of Hospitality* (2000) and *On Cosmopolitanism and Forgiveness* (2001), though to make the most of these you have to work out deconstruction first. I recommend watching *Derrida* (Dick and Kofman 2003): some of the improvised answers are really helpful and it gives you a 'feel' for Derrida.

Culler's *On Deconstruction* (1983) provides an excellent introduction. This book is addressed to literary theorists, but ideal if you want to get to grips with the technicalities of deconstruction. Caputo's *Deconstruction in a Nutshell* (1997), which also has a long interview with Derrida, focuses more on areas that are considered political, such as justice and community. The best introduction to Derrida's thought as it relates to international politics is Edkins *Poststructuralism and International Relations* (1999). Chapter 4 is on

'Derrida and the Force of Law'; other chapters provide context and explore Foucault, Lacan and Žižek. My *Constructivism in International Relations* (Zehfuss 2002) is a Derridean critique of constructivism. It engages especially with the problematic of reality as representation. Chapter 5 introduces Derrida's thought and offers more detail on some of the themes discussed here. *Derrida: Negotiating the Legacy* (Fagan *et al.* 2007) brings together scholars from different disciplinary backgrounds; many of them engage with questions of international politics.

Richard K. Ashley's work is inspired by Derrida and uses a deconstructive line of questioning to critique traditional views of international politics (Ashley 1988, 1989). Edkins and Zehfuss (2005) provide a deconstruction of the opposition of domestic versus international. Campbell's work draws on Derrida in analysing US foreign policy in his *Writing Security* (1998c) and the break-up of the former Yugoslavia in his *National Deconstruction* (1998a). The latter is a good place to start if you want to explore what deconstruction has to offer as an analysis of international politics. Edkins' powerful engagement with famine, *Whose Hunger?* (2000), draws on arguments from 'Force of Law', especially in Chapter 3. My *Wounds of Memory* (Zehfuss 2007) examines some of the ethico-political questions raised by Derrida's thought as does Nick Vaughan-Williams' work (2005, 2007a). Campbell (1994) tackles the question of responsibility. Dan Bulley (2006) and Roxanne Lynn Doty (2006) take up Derrida's thoughts on hospitality. Larry George (2002) discusses the 'war on terrorism' as *pharmakon*, that is, as both cure and poison.

13 Frantz Fanon

Himadeep Muppidi

Reading Frantz Fanon is an exhilarating experience. His words, even in translation, speak well to the tones and aches of my social body. His sentences brace
my spine. Lost in his texts, I find myself circling and underlining, underlining
and circling one paragraph after another but reluctant to go or be anywhere
else. Captivated by their beauty, I steal his passages – copying them into my
notebooks – neatly, gently, lovingly. Taking his prescriptions, I begin to sense
and see what Fanon, I imagine, wants me to see, sense and act on decisively:
the colonial organization of international politics. Reading Fanon, you could
say, is a slightly different experience from reading *International Organization*.

If international relations is an 'American social science' then Fanon pro-
vides a particularly different 'locus of enunciation' for international politics.
This other locus speaks to and for the global majority, the 'wretched of the
Earth', who are routinely, and often rudely, summoned to knowledge of
international politics through the provincial terms (Chakrabarty 2000b) of
Europe–America–West.

> To speak means to be in a position to use a certain syntax, to grasp the
> morphology of this or that language, but it means above all to assume a
> culture, to support the weight of a civilization (Fanon 1967b: 17–18).

Fanon's distinctive contribution to international relations can be seen in
this speaking of the world from the perspective of a global majority – using its
syntax, grasping its morphology, assuming its culture – in ways that bring to
bear on colonizing imaginations the weight of multiple ways of being human.

Who was Fanon and how did he come to this postcolonial locus?

Postcolonial biography, colonial thought

Born on July 25, 1925 Fanon grew up in Fort-de-France, Martinique (Watts
1999). Early on, he was encouraged to reject his Martinican and African
heritage in favour of a colonial French one. In school, he came under the
influence of Aime Cesaire and the idea of Negritude and this led him to
resurrect and recover the anti-colonial and African heritage that he was heir

to. During the Second World War and later serving with the French army in Algeria, Fanon experienced the dislocating force of French racism and colonialism. These, in a way, brought home to him the limits of French universalism.

After obtaining a degree in psychiatry, he served at the psychiatric hospital in Blida, Algeria that was then under French colonial rule. His sympathies shifted quickly to those fighting the brutal French occupation. Fanon served with the anti-colonial FLN (*Front de Liberation Nationale*) in various capacities until he was diagnosed with leukaemia. After reluctantly agreeing to come to the U.S. for treatment, Fanon died in Washington D.C. on December 6, 1961.

As I write these two paragraphs, sketching Fanon's biography from other, recorded sources, I feel both the lightness and the heaviness of the task of representing Fanon through a story of his life. In many ways, that story was not directly connected to my reception of Fanon or my understanding of his work. Representing Fanon is an issue that merges intimately with the question of Fanon representing me and I am not sure how to un-tangle the two or even if there is any strong need or possibility of doing so.

My introduction to Fanon was through the reading of *The Wretched of the Earth* (Fanon 2004). Reading the book was like switching the audio on an arresting performance that had been muted, ignorantly, by those who had been in the room for a while. Fanon's texts not only offered me the words but a solidly built, stoutly defended, brutally concretized platform – a garrison in the midst of enemy territory, or a public platform for animals in the middle of a zookeepers' convention – from which to speak what was already implicit but never fully said.

Fanon said things that were felt but never spoken of in that fashion.

I read him, heard him saying those words and I felt those words of his coming through me, swooping up fragmented and dispersed cells, bruised tissues, flayed skin, boiling blood, jangled nerves, broken bones, tortured muscles and poisoned lungs into a forceful and singular rush, a rush that simmered to me my own integrity as a vibrant body and my fullness as a human being. At that moment, his biography did not matter. I did not wonder if he was black, white, French, Algerian, Martinican or all of the above. It did not matter because, at that moment, his voice gathered up all the details of my life and spoke them in ways that few had spoken them before. His words gave my biography a materiality that slapped me awake with my own humanness. They bled the colonizer in me even as they pumped cold air into my lungs and burnished my skin to a fiery heat.

Words

What then is in Fanon's texts that can bring such a weight so heavily, so effectively, to bear on colonial thought? Fanon's distinctive contribution to postcolonial global thought lies in his defiance, his refusal, his willingness to say 'no!'

This refusal comes through in many forms. Fanon not only names the systematic violence of the West as *colonial* but refuses – in the name of a diversely constituted humanity – to be a fragmented subject of its violent grasp. His words organize themselves (and us) as a concentrated and intense force in order to defy and return to the sender the colonizer's original violence. The intensity of this refusal, this returning of colonial violence, often gets categorized as only 'violence' but that is a problematic translation. It is problematic because the ethical force of the refusal to accept or to suffer the colonizer's violence silently is what matters here. The violence that is being returned then is not that of the colonized but the colonizer's. It is the willingness to say no to that original violence that is the deeply humanizing moment for the colonized and that's where our focus ought to be. The moment of refusal is the moment of humanity for the colonized. That that moment of refusal cannot but be experienced by the colonial *status quo* as a violence to the existing order, as a slap in the face of its continuing domination, as a refusal to accept things as they are is but to be expected.

Fanon's voice reaches us – over the decades, and now through the middle of a resurgent colonialism – because of how well he understood the nature of colonial violence and its diverse mutilations. Nowadays, it is unsettling to read almost daily accounts of soldiers from the U.S. occupation of Iraq coming back with all sorts of mental disorders and very often taking their own lives. It is unsettling because of how closely some of their accounts parallel the experiences of French colonial soldiers that Fanon writes about in his chapter on 'Colonial Violence and Mental Disorders' (Fanon 2004). Deeply cognizant of multiple ways of being human, Fanon reads the colonial West as only a deformed way of being-in-the world and rejects the endless glorification of its achievements seeing them all as eminently 'dispensable'.

It is this willingness to refuse the imaginative trophies and borders of the West, in a bold epistemic move, that allies him, in my opinion, with another major anti-colonial thinker, one often read – somewhat incorrectly – as his anti-thesis, Mahatma Gandhi. When I read Fanon, I often remember a pithy response attributed to Gandhi ['What do you think of Western civilization, Mr. Gandhi?' 'I think it would be a good idea'.]. Fanon and Gandhi speak with one voice on that issue of the West.

The nature of colonialism

Colonialism, Fanon argues, is the structured and systematic denial of the multiple human worlds of diverse peoples. To that extent, it is different from other forms of domination wherein people, even as they came under domination, remained human and were treated as humans. Colonialism, however, was different in being a 'systematized negation of the other', a 'frenzied determination to deny any attribute of humanity' to millions of people.

When encountering other ways of being human in the world, colonialism systematically and violently disordered and dislocated their social meanings, their sensibilities and their identities. In carrying through this violent disruption of the humanness and historically constituted subjectivities of other peoples, colonialism put into question the very right to existence of millions of people in this world. In the face of a power that denied them any humanity, any right to exist by virtue of being human, the colonized were repeatedly forced to ask, existentially, 'Who am I in reality?'

Encountering brutalization, instrumentalization, and extermination, the colonized confront themselves with how they are imagined by others, to ask what it is about them, their life, their world, which allows them to be denied any claims to a human status except as a promised future? What sort of international reality is it in which they could only be fit for extermination, destruction, 'thingification' or 'education'? What was wrong, limited, or missing in them – in comparison with the Whites, the Europeans – that they could be treated as another 'species' altogether, a species whose being was always already less than human? 'Who am I?' 'What is my reality?' thus became basic questions that the colonial condition forced on millions of people around the world.

But colonialism does not stop with forcing those questions on millions of humans. It also forces certain answers on them: You are nothing or only a part of Nature, unlike the European who is human and can become any thing. Humanity and human realities are those discovered, explored and re-presented by Europe. If you want to release yourself from the condition of nature, from the state of the colonized, and be liberated into the human condition – into human subjectivity and universal reality – you can only do so by transcending your nature, your natural self, your culture, and by cultivating a European subjectivity. In this respect, the cultivation and grasp of Reason – the prerogative of Greece–Rome–Europe – is what will facilitate an escape from the colonial condition into the human one:

In its narcissistic monologue the colonialist bourgeoisie, by way of its academics, had implanted in the minds of the colonized that the essential values – meaning Western values – remain eternal despite all errors attributable to man. The colonized intellectual accepted the cogency of these ideas and there in the back of his mind stood a sentinel on duty guarding the Greco-Roman pedestal. But during the struggle for liberation, when the colonized intellectual touches base again with his people, this artificial sentinel is smashed to smithereens. All the Mediterranean values, the triumph of the individual, of enlightenment and Beauty turn into pale, lifeless trinkets. All those discourses appear a jumble of dead words. Those values which seemed to ennoble the soul prove worthless because they have nothing in common with the real-life struggle in which the people are engaged (Fanon 2004: 11).

Given the trade-offs involved – in the passage from nature and nothing-ness to human subjectivity and fullness, from an illusory world into a real one, from irrationality to reason – the use of force and violence to facilitate the transformation of the colonized into the European-human appears acceptable and relatively unproblematic. It is this sort of violence – one that seemingly promotes a 'rational and progressive' end – which liberals and liberalism have long found acceptable when applied to illiberal others. As Mamdani (2004: 4) notes: 'The modern sensibility is not horrified by pervasive violence ... What horrifies our modern sensibility is violence that appears senseless, that cannot be justified by progress'.

It is the sense then that *their* violence is of a different sort – one backed by Reason – that allows modern liberals to support colonial interventions in seemingly illiberal countries in order to promote democracy, foster human rights, promote sustainable development, rescue women or many other such causes. Empire and modern liberalism not only go hand in hand (Mehta 1999) but it is this intimacy and complicity between the two that makes the indignity of colonialism invisible to the modern liberal.

Fanon's exceptionalism lies in his insightful recognition and forceful refusal of this blackmail. Central to this refusal is Fanon's richly evocative conceptualization of colonialism not as Reason but as the structuring of a specific world order – a violent structuring that must be rejected by 'all means necessary': 'colonialism is not a machine capable of thinking, a body endowed with reason. It is naked violence and only gives in when confronted with greater violence' (Fanon 2004: 23).

The colonial world, Fanon (2004: 3–4) points out, is a 'compartmentalized world', a 'Manichaean world' inhabited by 'different species'. Within this world, the colonizers and the colonized live and confront each other in mutually exclusive ways. But life, properly defined, is possible only for one of these species. Only one of them, the 'ruling species' is essential and human while 'the natives', 'the others', 'the indigenous', are understood to be 'superfluous'. What govern the relationships between the two are the institutions (the military, the police) and the languages of 'pure violence' ('rifle butts', 'napalm'). Sooner or later, the colonized understand their embeddedness in this unequal world and their structural negation within it.

This understanding, in postcolonial thought, appears frequently as an iconic moment/incident/story when the colonized, through one encounter or another with the colonizer, come to a deep and jolting awareness of their unequal and unjust containment. Such a moment is not about racism at an individual level as much as the structured denial, the structural dislocation, structural torture or structural destruction of the self within a colonial space.

With Gandhi, it is the story of being thrown out from a train in the middle of the night in South Africa and being forced to spend the night shivering in a waiting room (Gandhi 1993: 109–31). With Fanon, it is the shivers induced, in the middle of the day, by the look of a child:

> My body was given back to me sprawled out, distorted, recolored, clad in mourning in that white winter day. The Negro is an animal, the

Negro is bad, the Negro is mean, the Negro is ugly; look, a nigger, it's cold, the nigger is shivering because he is cold, the little boy is trembling because he is afraid of the nigger, the nigger is shivering with cold, that cold that goes through your bones, the handsome little boy is trembling because he thinks that the nigger is quivering with rage, the little boy throws himself into his mother's arms: 'Mama, the nigger's going to eat me up' (Fanon 1967b: 113–14).

The traumatic aspect of the story is the realization that the boundaries of the self are fixed from outside, 'over-determined from without', that the colonized self is 'the eternal victim of an essence, of an *appearance* for which he is not responsible' (Fanon 1967b: 33). A colonial space then is a space of coldness, of hostility, a space in which the colonized self is made homeless, beaten into a fixed shape or contained as an essence. It is a 'farmyard', a 'vast concentration camp', a 'bestiary', a zoo, a system of apartheid in which only the ruling species matters. International relations are akin to zoological relations where the 'inter' speaks to a relationship between the colonial European self and a colonized other in which the other is always already a lack ('The Negro is a lobotomized European', Fanon 2004: 227).

Anti-coloniality

In an influential book titled *Provincializing Europe*, Dipesh Chakrabarty (2000b) argues that postcolonial thought, in contemporary times, cannot really do away with a 'hyper-real Europe' but must see it as both 'indispensable' and 'inadequate'. Fanon's claims, unlike Chakrabarty's here, belong to a different, arguably more anti-colonial, strain within contemporary postcolonial thought. What should the postcolonials do with 'Europe' and the impoverished terms it offers for understanding the world?

Europe, Fanon asserts, was not only eminently 'dispensable' but dispensing with it was necessary in order to 'pioneer a new history' and 'new conceptions of the possibilities of being human'. Fanon argues that 'anything' is possible for postcolonial nations if they refuse to 'ape Europe' or if they stopped obsessing about 'catching up with it'. For Fanon, Europe is a problem, not the apotheosis of any virtuous principle, least of all 'civilization'.

What is the problem with Europe? Europe's greatest contribution to world history, Fanon argues, has been the systematic production of a colonial world that has resulted, among other things, in the 'slavery ... [of] four fifths of humanity' (Fanon 2004: 237) and in their merciless exploitation. Notwithstanding its loud proclamations of various universally relevant virtues, Europe has systematically denied and negated the humanity of a global majority of people.

It is in this context that Fanon wants to 'leave this Europe which never stops talking of man yet massacres him at every one of its street corners, at every corner of the world' (Fanon 2004: 235). Those who had imitated and sought to catch up with Europe had already paid a heavy price. In making this claim, Fanon points to the U.S that had, he argues, become 'a monster whose flaws, sickness and inhumanity have reached frightening proportions' (Fanon 2004: 236–37).

Was there then nothing better for postcolonial nations to do than to 'create a third Europe' (Fanon 2004: 237)? Furthermore, if the imitation and creation of Europe was the primary project for postcolonial nations, then why not, Fanon wonders, leave it to the Europeans themselves who'd do a far better job than any of the newly-independent postcolonial nations? Europe, therefore, must be dispensed with and the postcolonial must 'look elsewhere besides Europe' (Fanon 2004: 239) for models and inspiration.

The postcolonial difference

Fanon locates postcolonial difference beyond the seemingly global structures and ostensibly universal virtues presented and produced by Europe and its colonial reason. This difference is embedded within and emerges from an alternative postcolonial imaginary whose articulation requires the dislocation, fragmentation and destruction of the world of colonial reason, a world organized as a zoo. In fighting to destroy International Relations as Zoological Relations, Fanon turns realism on its head by calling for a resistance that utilizes all the means that are necessary. These means do not exclude violence but it is a colonial violence that is now shrewdly re-shaped and re-directed by the colonized: 'As soon as you and your fellow men are cut down like dogs there is no other solution but to use every means available to re-establish your weight as a human being' (Fanon 2004: 221). Recognizing the violent structuration of the world under colonialism, Fanon positions the colonized-thingified-object-animal in ways that allow it to assume responsibility for establishing its own presence in this world.

The first moment therefore is a refusal of the violence of the colonizer at multiple levels, not the least of which, as I pointed out before, is the epistemic denial of the realities of the other. Part of that fight, of the effort to reject colonial violence, lies in the denial of the 'untruths' produced about the colonized. In that regard, Fanon is clear that: 'For the colonized subject, objectivity is always directed against him' (Fanon 2004: 37). The native's fight back cannot begin therefore with a hope in either the objectivity of what passes off as knowledge under colonial conditions or even the rationality of the colonizers. Fanon's central insight here is to draw attention to the fact that 'Challenging the colonial world is not a rational confrontation of viewpoints. It is not a discourse on the universal, but the impassioned claim by the colonized that their world is fundamentally different' (Fanon 2004: 6). The primary ethic under these conditions is the ethic of 'silencing the arrogance of the colonist, breaking his spiral of violence, in a word ejecting him outright from the picture' (Fanon 2004: 9).

The anti-colonial project here gives the colonized a clear and vivid image then of what needs to be done:

To blow the colonial world to smithereens is henceforth a clear image within the grasp and imagination of every colonized subject. To dislocate the colonial world does not mean that once the borders have been eliminated there will be a right of way between the two sectors. To destroy the colonial world means nothing less than demolishing the colonist's sector, burying it deep within the earth or banishing it from the territory (Fanon 2004: 6).

But the 'blowing up of the colonial world to smithereens' cannot be an act of physical violence alone as much as a fundamental restructuring of our very way of thinking and being in the world. In this regard, the spontaneous and individual refusal and returning of the colonizer's violence, in a physical-material sense alone, is not adequate as a political project. There is no switching straight from the position of a 'colonized subject' to being 'the sovereign citizen of an independent nation' by the returning of colonial violence in only a physical sense. That is, postcoloniality cannot be the outcome of an 'unmediated physical strength' and a 'rudimentary' 'consciousness' (Fanon 2004: 88). The postcolonial project needs to move beyond nationalism to a social and economic consciousness and to move beyond limiting categories of Black-Arab/White to a new way of imagining and inhabiting the world.

This movement beyond – beyond nationalism, beyond black/white – is an aspiration common to anticolonial forces everywhere. It is this shared solidarity and common reading of the world that links the anti-colonial forces in Vietnam to those in South Africa to those in India to those in Brazil and Ecuador and Malaysia and Hawaii and so on. What is shared and imagined and produced collectively are radically anti-colonial languages and forms of social practice:

> Colonized peoples are not alone. Despite the efforts of colonialism, their frontiers remain permeable to news and rumors. They discover that violence is atmospheric, it breaks out sporadically, and here and there sweeps away the colonial regime. The success of this violence plays not only an informative role but also an operative one. The great victory of the Vietnamese people at Dien Bien Phu is no longer strictly speaking a Vietnamese one. From July 1954 onward the colonial peoples have been asking themselves: 'What must we do to achieve a Dien Bien Phu? How should we go about it?' A Dien Bien Phu was now within reach of every colonized subject (Fanon 2004: 31).

Understanding the solidaristic nature of their common struggles and the ways in which the colonized everywhere are linked to each other provides the basis of an international politics and alternative postcolonial globalities. It is for this reason that Fanon argues that the 'colonized, underdeveloped man is a political creature in the most global sense of the term' (Fanon 2004: 40).

Implications for international relations

One of the more interesting implications of teaching Fanon in international relations in the U.S. is the unease that it generates in the classroom among a variety of people: realists, liberals, pacifists. I typically spend the first few classes of 'Introduction to International Politics' teaching realism and power politics not only without encountering much resistance to the idea of violence as power but also seeing a certain romance about a world structured on that principle. I often rely on the mass vaporization of humans at Hiroshima and Nagasaki as an example to see how students respond to the issue of violence in international affairs. I find that rarely do my students pause when thinking about these deaths. The 'fact' that those vaporizations saved 'lives' or 'ended the war' quicker seems to paper over the possibilities that a demonstration of that violence might have been enough, that maybe one was okay and not two or that maybe what was at stake was not ending the war at all but the demonstration of something else. In other words, the horror of a deliberately staged mass violence neither halts the flow of reasons nor opens up the imagination, as far as I can tell, to other possibilities that might have lain in the situation.

What stands out by comparison though is the strongly negative reaction once we get to Fanon. Here I find that the prospect of violence – a violence that is nowhere in comparison to mass destruction as in Hiroshima and Nagasaki or the continuing violence of colonization – by the colonized is not only met with an instinctive aversion (almost bordering on a certain disdain that you would rely on such a 'crude' means) but also the proliferation, in classroom discussions, of the various other choices that are open to those considering this option. Many a time Fanon's recognition of decolonization as a violent process actually draws rebukes of two types:

1. That while violence might help overthrow a colonial regime, it was bound to have deleterious effects for the colonized as well and hence was better avoided; and
2. Why not the adoption of non-violent methods? Or rather, whatever happened to Gandhi?

I find this set of responses intriguing in many respects. Fanon's analysis of decolonization is a fairly nuanced analysis in which he not only reads the pathologies of colonial societies but also seeks out the limitations in the constant imitations by the postcolonial of metropolitan models (political parties, nationalism, national consciousness, national culture). He dissects these imitations systematically to show their shortcomings and also points out how they must be reconfigured in order to come closer to achieving a 'true liberation' of the colonized self.

Notwithstanding that complexity, the classroom reading of Fanon zooms very quickly to the role of violence and especially to an understanding of that violence as a 'choice of techniques' that the colonized might have and actually consider using. The focus on violence turns the question into one presenting a choice for the colonized between the figures of Gandhi and Fanon with each representing the global effectiveness of a particular technical approach to decolonization. What recedes into the background is the colonizer and his continuing violence.

Violence is read then as arising from the choice of a particular technique by the colonized rather than as a structural feature of the colonial condition. The original moment of violence and its continued structural presence is erased by a hyper-visibility of the choices of the colonized. The Gandhian moment is itself read not as a deliberate taking onto the self of the violence of the colonizer but as the disappearance of violence through the choice of the colonized, almost as if to say: why can't the colonized everywhere be so 'civilized'?

Moreover, even those realists who had been celebrating the conceptualization of power as violence now object to what they see as the romanticization of violence and point to the chapter 'Colonial War and Mental Disorders' (Fanon 2004: 181–233) as proof of its horrors. I am left wondering whether what many of them are objecting to is violence or to the fact that the violence is now being exerted by a subject of a different sort, by a subject typically at the receiving end. In other words, Fanon cannot be read or taught or engaged without reflecting on one's body and its historically produced subject position in relationship – international? global? – to others in the world.

To read Fanon is to read and understand – see – the self as it appears on one side or the other of a colonially organized world. Reading Fanon then cannot but be a reading/seeing of the coloniality or postcoloniality of one's body and its embeddedness in contemporary international relations.

Further reading

Bhabha, Homi, K. (1994) *The Location of Culture*, London and New York: Routledge. Contains classic essays reinterpreting Fanon from a contemporary postcolonial perspective.

Gibson, Nigel C. (ed.) (1999) *Rethinking Fanon: The Continuing Dialogue*, New York: Humanity Books. Essays discussing Fanon in relation to central issues in politics, feminism, culture, psychology, revolution and humanism.

Macey, David (2000) *Frantz Fanon: A Life*, London: Granta Books. Well-researched biography of Fanon.

Sartre, Jean-Paul (2001) *Colonialism and Neocolonialism*, Trans. Azzedine Haddour, Steve Brewer and Terry McWilliams, London and New York: Routledge. Essays offering a critique of French colonialism by an important and influential friend of Fanon's. Includes the well-known preface to Fanon's *Wretched of the Earth*.

Young, Robert J. C. (2001) *Postcolonialism: An Historical Introduction*, Oxford: Blackwell. An encyclopedic survey of postcolonial thought situating the work of Fanon in the context of a global history of anti-colonialism.

14 Michel Foucault

Andrew W. Neal

The work of Michel Foucault has been influential in almost every area of the humanities and social sciences. Of all the twentieth century thinkers presented in this book, the legacy of Foucault is perhaps the most intellectually promiscuous. Few thinkers can have been taken up in so many diverse fields of study and practice, from literature and philosophy to psychiatry and healthcare. Within the discipline of international relations alone, there are many diverse interpretations of his work, even among the closest of colleagues. This makes a definitive account extremely difficult, but also undesirable. Foucault has become plural, heterogeneous and dispersed. There could not be a more fitting testament to the implications of his work.

With this 'pluralization' in mind, the importance of Foucault for international relations can be considered from three angles. First, the work of Foucault disrupts some of the central concepts of the discipline, particularly its notions of power, sovereignty, structure and history. Second, in addition to this disruptive role, Foucault offers ways of thinking about forms of power and political practice that do not easily fit into traditional categories, such as governmentality and biopower. Finally, Foucault is to many an invaluable methodological resource, offering a 'toolbox' of concepts and techniques such as 'archaeology', 'genealogy', 'discourse' and 'problematization'.

Biography

> 'Anyway, my personal life is not at all interesting.'
> *Michel Foucault, an Interview with Stephen Riggins, Toronto, 1982*
> (Riggins 1983)

Foucault was born in Poitiers on 15 October 1926 into a middle-class family with a history in medical practice. His route into academia mirrored that of many of his French contemporaries; he excelled at school in academic subjects before entering the *École Normale Supèriéure* in Paris in 1946. Over the following years he studied under the eminent philosophers Maurice Merleau-Ponty, Louis Althusser and later the philosopher of science Georges Canguilhem. He qualified in philosophy, but also psychology and psychopathology in the years shortly after. In the 1950s Foucault held a post as a psychologist, followed by teaching positions in Uppsala, Hamburg and Warsaw. In 1959 he received his doctorate with a dissertation entitled *Madness and Unreason: A History of Madness in the Classical Age* (published in English as *Madness and Civilization*).

In the 1960s he held posts in Clermont-Ferrand, Tunis and finally as head of the philosophy department at a new 'experimental' university at Vincennes, Paris. This coincided with the student uprisings of 1968, which influenced Foucault's political direction and career. Having briefly joined the powerful French Communist Party in the early 1950s before leaving disillusioned, for Foucault 1968 signalled a sea-change in French intellectual life, marking the end of Marxist dominance. As he explained in an interview much later: 'The first thing that happened after 1968 was that Marxism as a dogmatic framework declined and new political, new cultural interests concerning personal life appeared' (Riggins 1983: 4).

Foucault had already had great intellectual success with his 1960s books *Madness and civilization* (1961), *The Birth of the Clinic* (1963), the towering history of ideas *The Order of Things* (1966) and the seminal work on discourse and method *The Archaeology of Knowledge* (1968). In 1969 he was elected to the highest academic institution in France, the *Collège de France* in Paris, where he was given a Chair in 'The History of Systems of Thought', a title he created himself. The recent English publication of his annual *Collège de France* lecture programmes is now nearly complete, and these have greatly enriched Foucault scholarship (Dillon and Neal 2008). In the 1970s and early 1980s he became well-known internationally, travelling widely as a visiting professor, most notably in Iran and at Berkeley. His key works from this period include perhaps his most influential book *Discipline and Punish* (1975), and the three-volume *History of Sexuality vol. 1 The Will to Knowledge* (1976); *vol. 2 The Use of Pleasure* (1984 (Foucault 1985)) and *vol. 3 The Care of the Self* (1984 (Foucault 1990)). Foucault died from an AIDS-related illness on June 25, 1984 (Alt 2008; Foucault.info 2008; The Foucault Society 2005).

Discipline and power/knowledge

When teaching Foucault in international relations, it is common to start with the idea of power. In the neorealist approach to international relations the units of the international system are power-maximizing sovereign states, agents whose behaviour and ability to act is both facilitated and constrained by a structural condition of international anarchy (Waltz 1979). In this model, power is something that is possessed and wielded. If a state has more power, it is more free to act, if it has less power, it is more constrained. Military capabilities and economic strength are often taken as measures of this kind of state power, later supplemented with neo-liberal 'soft-power' (Keohane and Nye 1977; Nye 2004).

Foucault's work on power disrupts this centred model. The common exemplar of how is the opening of his book *Discipline and Punish*, which compares two different scenes (Foucault 1999). First is the spectacle of a public execution, with a man gruesomely executed in the name of the sovereign. The executioner's blade is the symbol and expression of the sovereign's power: possessed, wielded and permanently poised as an ever present warning to obey. The second is a prison timetable taken from some 70 years later, which represents a very different mode of power. The timetable orders the daily activities of the prisoners precisely and to the minute, and includes drills, exercises, roll calls and labour in the prison workshop. This kind of power is *productive*. It aims to discipline the individual prisoners, changing them from what they were into something more useful, more ordered and more efficient. It aims to maximise the productive potential of their bodies and their faculties. It *normalizes* them according to an ideal of what a modern individual should be.

Much more than a coercive expression of sovereign power, this kind of *disciplinary power* is a *technology* of power. Its successful operation depends on a whole series of *technical knowledges* about the body and its functions, about productive ways to organise individuals, and about the correct means of training and the right types of exercise. These technical knowledges are recorded in training manuals, taught in classrooms, and organised into institutional programmes, with others trained and disciplined in their use in turn. It is a 'mechanics of power' built on a 'political anatomy' of detail (Foucault 1999: 138). Thus individuals become objects of power, the focus of a series of productive techniques and modern norms, subjected to power. They also become modern subjects, helping to perpetuate modern forms of power through their daily practices.

The prison is only one of many institutions that are central to the functioning of modern power. Foucault extends his analysis to other locations such as schools, barracks, hospitals and factories, which are linked by the operation of what Foucault calls *power/knowledge*, a society-wide (or perhaps global) network of productive power relations that depend on the operation and extension of ever-more specialised forms of knowledge. Power thereby becomes something that is not simply possessed but practiced, in every sense of the word. It is not simply a means of repression or coercion, but rather it flows throughout society in networks.

In this way power becomes *decentred* and *pluralized*. In order to function as a modern subject, every individual is disciplined and normalized through the exercise of meticulously detailed forms of power in institutions and in their relations with others. They then go on to exercise forms of power themselves in their daily lives, through their institutional, work and social relationships. Once power is considered in this way, it is very difficult to identify where it is located. Power is taken away from the Hobbesian sovereign, understood as the necessary abstraction of power to an irresistible figure towering over and above society. Instead power comes to permeate society and to both *objectify* and *subjectivate* modern subjects.

Unlike Marxist accounts of power, this is not the reproduction of productive individuals according the needs of a singular, grand system such as the market or forces of capital. Foucault's work was an implicit critique of the Marxist dominance of the post-war social sciences in France. When he spoke out against 'totalizing' theory (Foucault *et al.* 1977: 231), this is what he was referring to. Again the key move is a pluralization of the forms, techniques and locations of power, changing across time and place, not according to a grand systemic logic, but only according to requirements and opportunities that are local and particular.

Biopower

While the study of institutions is central to much of Foucault's work, the implications are more general than the institutions themselves. Foucault's focus is modern power in its plural forms, locations and practices, and the way these organise and shape human populations. Beginning in *The History of Sexuality vol. 1* (Foucault 1978) Foucault extends his study of *disciplinary power*, with its focus on the normalization of the productive individual, to *biopower*, a form of power with a focus on human life at the level of populations. It is a short step from the power/knowledge concerned with training an individual within the walls of an institution, to a power/knowledge concerned with promoting human life generally. This *biopower* is expressed, for example, in the mass public programmes that reshaped the living conditions of populations in the nineteenth century; the introduction of sanitation and public sewerage, the demolition of slums, the creation of road networks and public transportation to facilitate trade and mobility, and the highly successful programmes of mass immunisation that eradicated many mortal diseases. Similar projects exist today, with such examples as public health campaigns against smoking and drink driving, and for the promotion of exercise, healthy eating and safe sex.

Foucault offers a move from a singular and centred power that threatens death to forms of plural and decentred power that promote life. As he argues: 'Sovereignty took life and let live. And now we have the emergence of a power that … consists in making live and letting die' (Foucault 2002b: 247). While death is still an outcome of many modern practices of power, once it is considered statistically at the level of populations, policy choices about where to allocate or withhold funds often result in 'letting die' rather than directly causing to die. Examples might include the concrete numbers of lives saved by increasing funding for road safety, or not allocating more resources to tackling the AIDS pandemic.

Sovereignty and the 'archive'

The Foucauldian way of considering forms of power marks a departure with the centred way in which power is often considered in international relations, with states as the anthropomorphised agents of power. Foucault thought that the notion of sovereignty had too strong a hold on social, political and historical thought, and that too often, ways of thinking affirmed a specific kind of centred sovereignty. Instead he famously argued that: 'What we need, however, is a political philosophy that isn't erected around the problem of sovereignty ... We need to cut off the King's head: in political theory that has still to be done' (Foucault 1980: 121).

Arguably there are two ways of interpreting the move to decentre our notions of power. The first is what might be called the 'ethico-political' interpretation: that reaffirming centred forms of power through our ways of thinking and knowing closes down the possibility of resisting power and imagining alternative forms of social and political life. This is the interpretation of Foucault that inspired the earlier writings of the 'critical' turn in international relations, particularly the 'poststructuralist' thought of Richard Ashley and R.B.J. Walker exemplified in their co-edited special issue of *International Studies Quarterly* on 'Speaking the Language of Exile: Dissidence in International Studies' (Ashley and Walker 1990b).

Second is the more prosaic answer that before we can imagine alternatives we need to understand how power works in the first place. There is little in Foucault's work that could explicitly be identified as normative, and although he was certainly identified with a number of social and political causes (such as the 'Prison Information Group' and the Polish Solidarity movement), he often cultivated an image of himself as trawling through dusty archives. Indeed, much of the richness of his work comes from his weaving together of documents produced by marginal figures from history, rather than going straight for the 'greats' of Hobbes or Machiavelli (although these two do get the extensive Foucault treatment in *'Society Must Be Defended'* (Foucault 2002b) and *Security, Territory, Population* (Foucault 2007) respectively).

For Foucault, the 'archive' means much more than the library, however; delving into it is a means of 'cutting off the King's head in political theory' by insisting on the great plurality of all the things that have been said and written, most of which have been marginalised and forgotten. When history is looked at in its raw form it is a great mass of statements, documents, institutions and notions that pile up and up upon each other, interacting in curious ways. Foucault refuses to allow all this to be reduced to a grand historical narrative that affirms the sovereign presence of states or the West at the heart of world history. He complained that the 'superabundant proliferation' of 'the diversity of things said' was in general reduced to 'a sort of great, uniform text' that was taken to reveal an 'implicit, sovereign, communal "meaning"' (Foucault 2002a: 133). In response, Foucault employed what he called a method of *archaeology*, which he explained, 'is trying to operate a decentring that leaves no privilege to any centre' (Foucault 2002a: 226). Instead, 'Archaeology is a comparative analysis that is not intended to reduce the diversity of discourses' (Foucault 2002a: 54).

Discourse, archaeology and genealogy

Through his 'archaeological' analysis of the archive, Foucault can be credited, at least in part, with bringing the idea of 'discourse' into the social sciences. This has been one of the most productive legacies of the 'critical turn' in international relations, and discourse analysis is now a common methodological approach. It has become a means of gathering the things said and written on a particular subject in a particular context by a particular group of people (often political elites), in order to try to interpret what is being done politically through such statements. This kind of work often tends towards highly empiricist projects, which in some ways could be seen as being at odds with the aims of 'critical' thought, but in other ways could not be more Foucauldian.

Perhaps of more concern is when such studies focus exclusively on the statements of 'sovereign' leaders or political elites, going against the 'decentring' aims that Foucault outlined, and perhaps also against the 'dissident' ethic that is arguably central to the critical project in international relations. It is also a shame that 'discourse' has become more or less exclusively associated with speech and text, as this rather narrows the diversity that Foucault hoped the concept would convey. For example, in *The Archaeology of Knowledge* he argued that discourses are 'irreducible to language and to speech' (Foucault 2002a: 54), and his focus on the micro-practices of power/ knowledge in the institutions of modern societies bore this out (for a sustained criticism of the overly 'textual' use of Foucault see Selby (2007)).

Although Foucault never abandoned his *archaeological* method, he reshaped his approach as he became more explicitly concerned with the workings of power, supplanting *archaeology* with *genealogy*. Inspired by Nietzsche (particularly *The Genealogy of Morals* (Nietzsche 1996)), Foucault began to consider power relations as having a central role in shaping the historical 'archive'. In his famous essay 'Nietzsche, Genealogy, History', Foucault took this idea seriously by arguing that the very fabric of history consisted of relations of war, battle and 'the struggle ... forces wage against each other' (Foucault 1991: 83). As he argued: 'The successes of history belong to those who are capable of seizing [the] rules' (Foucault 1991: 86).

The idea of history as a 'struggle of forces' raises all sorts of difficult questions over the political status of social, political and historical enquiry and whether they are inherently 'partisan'. Although it is now a common critical refrain in international relations to refer to Robert Cox's famous line that that 'theory is always for someone and for some purpose' (Cox 1981: 128), it is a step further to claim that theory is a weapon in an ongoing series of wars and battles. Driven by alarm at this implication, Foucault devoted his 1975–76 series of lectures at the *Collège de France* to exploring precisely this question: 'if we have to think of power in terms of relations of force, do we therefore have to interpret it in terms of the general form of war? Can war serve as an analyzer of power relations?' (Foucault 2002b: 266). Rather than answer the question directly, Foucault returned to the 'archive', trying to trace the contours of historical discourses in which politics was considered as 'the continuation of war by other means' (Foucault 2002b: 48). So again, this is a refusal to *systematize*, and an insistence on always *historicizing* by describing discourses, techniques and practices in their particular spatial and temporal circumstances.

Historicizing and problematizing

This insistence on historicizing entails further methodological innovations. Foucault will avoid answering a research question directly or taking it out of its spatio-temporal context. Instead of trying to address particular problems through a 'problem-solving' methodology, Foucault looks at *problematizations* in history. For example, with the question of whether social, political and historical thought can be considered as weapons in an ongoing series of wars, Foucault does not try to give a definitive, reasoned, internally-valid answer, but asks how such a question became a problem historically, or rather how it was *problematized*. This marks an alternative to the binary choice offered in international relations: problem-solving theory or critical theory (Cox 1981).

An approach based on *problematizations* seeks to describe the field of relations that emerged around a problem, including: the network of people who constituted it as a problem, worked towards addressing it, and had their comments heard, taken up, discussed, rejected or modified; the kinds of language and ways of speaking used, the concepts that emerged, the techniques and methods that were developed, and the jobs, roles and types of individual that were in effect constituted and 'subjectivated' through their relationship to that problem; and the knowledges recorded, developed and passed on in response to it.

This method of *problematization* is how Foucault approached the problem of 'madness' in *Madness and Civilization* (Foucault 2001), asking how understandings of madness changed over time, from madness being considered a divine blessing to being considered an illness, and describing the techniques, institutions and forms of subjectivity that were constituted through those changing understandings. This is also how Foucault approached practices of discipline and surveillance in *Discipline and Punish*, describing the changing ways in which societal ordering came to be understood as a problem, and how diverse bodies of power/knowledge became attached to such examples as the correct means of training the soldier, the prisoner, the schoolchild and the factory worker. Similar studies include *The History of Sexuality* and *The Birth of the Clinic* (Foucault 1994).

Conclusion

In *'Society Must Be Defended'* Foucault gives us a five-step outline of his approach to questions of power that serves as a very useful summary.

First, to decentre our analysis of power, by refusing the model of power with a single centre. Instead the aim is to look at the extremities of power and the material techniques through which it intervenes in life (Foucault

2002b: 27). For students of international relations, this means consciously refusing to treat the state as a singular, acting entity on the world stage, and instead looking at the detail of diverse practices.

Second, to look at power 'externally', at the points where it is exercised and applied, not 'internally' at the level of psychology, decision, strategy or intention. This means getting away from trying to ascertain the thoughts, plans and designs of the great statesmen, whether in their words or their actions, and instead studying, empirically if need be, the sites and locations at which forms of power have their effects (Foucault 2002b: 28).

Third, not to regard power as a commodity of which one can possess more or less, or as a regime of domination between the powerful and the disempowered. Power circulates in networks, constituting individuals as both subjects and objects of power. This means not simply studying those who act, but those who are acted upon, and trying to understand the ways in which their reactions, resistances, and their practices of power in turn work to constitute wider relationships and networks (Foucault 2002b: 29).

Fourth, not to work from the top down but from the bottom up. One should begin with the mechanisms and points of application, the small details and not the big decisions (Foucault 2002b: 30).

Fifth and finally, not to begin with ideology and explore what instruments it uses, but to begin with the mechanisms and practices and explore how they get formed into ideologies and knowledges. In terms of the analysis of political ideas, this means that we should not give the ideas too much agency in themselves, but try to understand the techniques and practices that make it possible for ideas to take hold and be reproduced.

How then will we interpret Foucault's contribution to international relations? It depends what one means by international relations, as the question, or rather the problematization, is more important than the answer. While we began with a commonplace critique of neo-realism, this does not, thankfully, encompass the whole of 'international relations', especially today. A genealogy of international relations would have much to say regarding the power relations that have constituted the discipline, its disciplining practices, its techniques, its centres and its margins. It would also question why we should retrospectively reproduce international relations in the singular, even in critique, when international relations is more interesting as an increasingly undisciplined discipline, becoming plural and heterogeneous. In this sense, international relations is itself becoming more and more Foucauldian, headless, with proliferating studies on almost everything.

Further reading

Short pieces:

Foucault, Michel (1980) 'Truth and Power', in *Power/Knowledge: Selected Interviews and Other Writings 1972–1977*, Ed. Colin Gordon, New York:

Harvester Wheatsheaf, 109–33. A common way in to Foucault for students, as it contains many sharp points about the relationship of power to truth and knowledge.

Foucault, Michel (1991) 'Nietzsche, Genealogy, History', in *The Foucault Reader*, Ed. Paul Rabinow, London: Penguin, 76–100. One of Foucault's most provocative pieces, and fertile ground for those thinking about war and force.

Foucault, Michel (2002), 'Governmentality', in *The Essential Works of Michel Foucault, 1954–1984*, Ed. Paul Rabinow, London: Penguin, 201–22. Here Foucault outlines an understanding of power as the 'conduct of conduct', in contrast to the arts of the Prince found in Machiavelli. The concept of 'governmentality' has been taken up in relation to all sorts of novel modes of government such as 'global governance'.

Books

Foucault, Michel (1990) *The History of Sexuality, Vol. 1*, trans. Robert Hurley, London: Penguin. Part 5, 'Right of Death and Power over Life' is particularly interesting for students of international relations, as it introduces the notion of 'biopower' in relation to sovereign power.

Foucault, Michel (1999) *Discipline and Punish: The Birth of the Prison*, trans. Alan Sheridan, London: Penguin. For the most part meticulously historical, the key is to draw out the novelties and innovations in modern forms of power.

Foucault, Michel (2002a) *The Archaeology of Knowledge*, trans. A.M. Sheridan Smith, London: Routledge. Should be required reading for anyone thinking about discourse. Foucault problematizes discourses, questioning their boundaries and limits, in distinct contrast to treating them as discrete objects of research.

Lectures

Foucault, Michel (2002b) *"Society Must Be Defended": Lectures at the Collège de France, 1975–76*, trans. David Macey, New York: Picador. The recent translation and publication of Foucault's lectures are reinvigorating Foucault scholarship. Not only do they contain much in the way of new material, but they also reveal the evolution of Foucault's thinking, including ideas he explored but then abandoned. *"Society Must Be Defended"* is perhaps the most coherent of the lecture series, and most important for international relations. It explores the relationship of politics to war and serves as a powerful critique of modern political and strategic theory, particularly from Hobbes to Clausewitz.

Foucault, Michel (2007) *Security, Territory, Population: Lectures at the Collège de France, 1977–78*, Basingstoke: Palgrave Macmillan. One of the last of the lecture series to be published, and one of the least coherent. Nevertheless it contains much of interest to international relations, including explorations by Foucault on security as the securing of social and economic circulation, the notion of risk, and a remarkable genealogy of *raison d'état*.

Secondary reading

Dillon, Michael and Andrew Neal (eds) (2008) *Foucault on Politics, Security and War*, London: Palgrave. One of the first books to specifically engage with Foucault on questions of security and war, and to reassess Foucault in light of the recently published lectures *"Society Must Be Defended"*, *Security, Territory, Population* and *The Birth of Biopolitics*. The contributors address the war on terror, risk, biosecurity and biopolitics, AIDS, racial and ethnic conflict, and the critique of law.

Burchell, Graham, Colin Gordon, and Peter Miller (eds) (1991) *The Foucault Effect: Studies in Governmentality*, Chicago: University of Chicago Press. A key work on the concept of governmentality, including essays by Foucault and his contemporaries.

Davidson, Arnold I (1997) *Foucault and His Interlocutors*, Chicago, London: University press of Chicago. A key book in the Foucault literature, which includes contributions from Jacques Derrida, Giles Deleuze, Paul Veyne, Michel Serres and Noam Chomsky, together with responses from Foucault.

15 Sigmund Freud

Vanessa Pupavac

Sigmund Freud's psycho-analytical theories have been crucial influences on the development of post-structuralist thinking. Adorno, Fromm and Marcuse from the Frankfurt School or later thinkers like Butler, Lacan, and Žižek acknowledge their intellectual debt to Freud, although they have departed from his theories.

Freud's *Civilization and its Discontents* [1930]

Freud's *Civilization and its Discontents* outlines his view of the human condition. His dialectical model of humanity sees humanity driven by opposing forces of love and hatred, altruism and egotism, or the instincts of Eros and death (Freud 1994: 46–49). The altruistic instinct in individuals draws people together, while the destructive instinct leads people to resist (Freud 1994: 49). Freud's dialectical model of the individual encompasses the id, ego and super-ego, which broadly correspond as follows:

1. Id = instinctual self
2. Ego = developed sense of individual as self distinct from external world
3. Super-ego = internalised cultural norms or conscience.

Initially a person's ego is indistinct from the external world: the dependent infant feels oneness with world. The child's ego gradually develops through the pleasure principle, that is, we avoid pain and seek pleasure or happiness. As the child becomes more self-aware, the child identifies a father-protector figure on whom the child depends and through whom the child internalises cultural norms and develops a conscience.

The individual's dependence on a father-protector figure makes the individual fear punishment or withdrawal of love for any transgression (Freud 1994: 54). Anticipatory fear leads to instinctual renunciation. Thus the individual internalises the authority of external prohibitions. And the dread of external punishment becomes the dread of the conscience or the internal super-ego, and leads to a dynamic of personal renunciation. Individuals therefore develop their character or personality dependent on an authority figure. External authority both protects and curbs the individual, therefore the individual feels both fulfilled and deprived by external authority. Consequently the individual feels both love and hatred of external authority. Freud's concept of the Oedipus complex refers to how children both love and hate the father-protector figure. They identify with him but want to destroy him and replace him. Children love their parents because they have depended on their care. But children also hate their parents because parents cannot fulfil all their wants. Parents restrict the child's instincts and egoistic impulses and require submission to others' claims (family, community, etc.).

Tensions between the child and adults in family are repeated in tensions between the individual and society. Freud's dialectical model sees inherent tensions between the individual and society, and within the individual (between the id, ego and super-ego). The instinct of Eros draws people together against nature and is linked to the development of society and culture (Freud 1994: 49). The destructive instinct in individuals resists the merging of people and a programme of civilization (Freud 1994: 49), although it may have a creative role in attacking tradition and allowing new social relations to emerge.

People are instinctively driven to seek happiness (Freud 1994: 11), but the human condition is inevitably marked by three fundamental sources of suffering: mortality and the decay of our bodies; humanity's subordination to nature; and pain from our relations with other people (Freud 1994: 19). Individual human happiness is ultimately illusive because humans are driven by inborn opposing biological impulses, and inherent tensions exist between strategies to address sources of human suffering. There is 'no sovereign recipe', or psychological prescription to overcome the tragedy of the human condition (Freud 1994: 17). Freud is sceptical of humanity being happier under primitive conditions and believes that human progress may mitigate human suffering under nature's subordination (Freud 1994: 20–21). But civilization may undermine individual happiness because of its more developed cultural restrictions of humanity's inborn biological instincts. Freud criticises modern civilization for restricting human instincts too severely, notably civilization's restrictions on sexuality. Freud writes:

> We may expect that in the course of time changes will be carried out in our civilization so that it becomes more satisfying to our needs and no longer open to the reproaches we have made against it. But perhaps we shall also accustom ourselves to the idea that there are certain difficulties inherent in the very nature of culture which will not yield to any efforts at reform. Over and above the obligations of putting restrictions upon our instincts, which we see to be inevitable, we are imminently threatened with the dangers of a state one may call *la misere psychologique* of groups (Freud 1994: 43).

The inevitability of suffering in the human condition has tended to lower human demands for happiness, and limit human expectations to the avoidance of suffering (Freud 1994: 12). Freud is cautious about achieving human perfection, and therefore of diagnosing collective neuroses and proposing collective therapeutic solutions. Such proposals involve serious theoretical problems and political implications:

> If the evolution of civilization has such a far-reaching similarity with the development of an individual, and if the same methods are employed in both, would not the diagnosis be justified that many systems of civilization – or epochs of it – possibly even the whole of humanity – have become *neurotic* under the pressure of the civilizing trends? To analytic dissection of these neuroses, therapeutic recommendations might follow which could claim a great practical interest. I would not say that such an attempt to apply psycho-analysis to civilised society would be fanciful or doomed to fruitlessness. But it behoves us to be very careful, not to forget that after all we are dealing only with analogies, and that is dangerous, not only with men but also with concepts, to drag them out of the region where they originated and have matured. The diagnosis of collective neurosis, moreover, will be confronted by a special difficulty. In the neurosis of the individual we can use as a starting-point the contrast presented to us between the patient and his environment which we assume to be normal. No such background as this would be available for any society similarly affected; it would have to be supplied in some other way. And with regard to any therapeutic application of our knowledge, what would be the use of the most acute analysis of social neuroses, since no one possesses power to compel the community to adopt the therapy? (Freud 1994: 69–70)

Notwithstanding his caution, Freud was drawn into some political analysis.

Freud's letter to Einstein *Why War?*

In 1933 Albert Einstein invited Freud to comment on international peace. Freud's *Civilization and its Discontents*, as we have outlined, presents a dialectical, conflictual model of human nature, which stresses the tensions that underlie any achievement of personal or societal peace. The individual is the site of conflict between opposing natural instincts and social norms. Personal peace achieved by an individual is only a provisional balance of forces between the id, the ego and super-ego.

Here Freud's dialectical thinking belongs with Darwin and Marx, each in their turn mapping a conflictual account of human advancement and unsettling ideas of harmony in the individual, society and nature. Freud's psychoanalytical conflict theories are closer to Hobbes' 'war of all against all' or Clausewitzian theories of war as the continuation of politics, than peace theories' belief in the possibility of harmony, and he writes: 'Conflicts of interest between man and man are resolved, in principle, by the recourse to violence' (Freud 2000: 9).

Freud stresses that violence, not peace, is the primordial condition of humanity, against anthropological writing suggesting harmonious relations. Superior force determined whose will prevailed in early small primitive communities and still underpins modern law (Freud 2000: 9–10). The path from primitive violence to modern law is founded on the principle that the superior force of one individual can be subordinated by an alliance of weaker people, that is, the superior collective force of violence. The community develops feelings of unity and solidarity, but law still depends on the threat of violence (Freud 2000: 10).

Communities have historically found themselves in conflict with other communities – conflicts which have usually been settled by war (Freud 2000: 10). Furthermore even within communities conflicting interests will ultimately still be settled by the exercise of violence (Freud 2000: 10). The prospects for peace are distant. Anthropological discoveries of harmonious, unrestrained communities are invariably disproved on closer examination (Freud 2000: 12). It is impossible to completely suppress humanity's aggressive tendencies, although we may try to channel these instincts away from warfare and to try to strengthen the intellect to help control instinctual impulses (Freud 2000: 10). We must hope that people will find their interests in peace because modern technological warfare is so destructive of all parties' lives and does not even allow the manifestation of the old heroic warriors' honour.

Freud's political legacy

What influence did Freud's theories have on political thinking? Freud was cautious about applying psychological theories about human nature to political problems. Nevertheless the fields of political and social psychology developed to apply psychological models to political and social problems (Herman 1995). Social psychology approaches, as they developed in the interwar period, departed substantially from Freudian theories (Rieff 1961, 1966). Freud's notion of an essential antagonism between the individual and society was replaced in social psychology by a functionalist understanding taking a more benign view which saw social tensions as resolvable through professional interventions tackling alienation and improving self-understanding and interpersonal communication.

Debates over Freud's legacy have considered whether psychology has had a liberating or controlling political role. Russell Jacoby's *Social Amnesia: A Critique of Conformist Psychology from Adler to Laing* and Philip Rieff's *Triumph of the Therapeutic: Uses of Faith after Freud* put forward politically radical interpretations of Freud. Freud's theories on the role of paternal authority in developing individual conscience were taken up in the authoritarian personality thesis literature, elaborated by Adorno, Fromm and Marcuse and others, which critically analyses the role of paternal authority in facilitating fascism or prejudice. Post-Freudian counter-culture theories attacked Freudian theories for promoting conformist politics and legitimising the 'policeman in the head', as they saw the internalisation of external authority. These post-Freudian theories have influenced political theory and social policy, and have been critically analysed in their turn (Nolan 1998).

Further reading

It is well worth reading Freud's writing, rather than just relying on secondary texts. Freud is known as 'a clear and elegant writer'. To consider Freud's influence on political thinking, start with *Civilization and its Discontents* (1994) [1930] or *Why War?* (2000) [1933], both of which are summarised above.

Adam Curtis' 2002 four-part BBC documentary *Century of the Self* considers how Freud's theories and post-Freudian theories were popularised in political culture, and highlights their emancipatory promises and their oppressive practices: http://www.bbc.co.uk/bbcfour/documentaries/features/century_of_the_self.shtml

16 Antonio Gramsci

Mark Rupert

As a field of inquiry, international relations has long been dominated by a foundational vision in which politics among states was presumed to be qualitatively different from politics within them. Politics among states was thought to be characterized by the absence of sovereign authority and law, and consequently was anarchic, violence-prone, profoundly threatening, and therefore primarily concerned with the 'high politics' of interstate rivalry and national security rather than the 'low politics' of regulating economic or cultural exchange. Implicit in this view of our field was an inter-related set of stark boundaries separating the domestic from the international, the political from the cultural and economic, and state from society. Beginning in the early 1980s, these implicit boundaries and the state-centric vision of world politics were challenged by a group of scholars who deployed a conceptual vocabulary which was unfamiliar to most students of world politics, and derived from the writings of the Italian political activist and theorist Antonio Gramsci (1891–1937).

Perhaps not coincidentally, the conceptual groundwork for a Gramscian approach to international studies was laid by a scholar who came not from a background in academic international relations, but from a life of working in the International Labor Organization – Robert Cox. In a seminal series of articles, Cox expounded and drew upon Gramscian concepts to re-envision world politics in a more relational, dynamic and potentially transformative way (Cox 1981, 1983). In effect, Cox displaced states from their position of centrality in traditional international relations by re-envisioning a world politics in which different forms of state – or what Cox referred to as state/society complexes – might be historically constructed in the relational nexus between world orders and social forces (including class formations understood in relation to historical structures of production). Social forces, forms of state, and world orders were understood as integral to one another's historical construction, and these historical-structural processes were further understood to be intrinsically political, involving various kinds of socially situated actors whose collective self-understandings shaped their social identities, purposes, and horizons of political action.

At the heart of the processes continuously (re-)constructing this relational nexus were both consensual and coercive forms of power, in accordance with

Gramsci's dual vision of politics. For Gramsci, 'hegemony' was a special kind of social power relation in which dominant groups secured their positions of privilege largely (if by no means exclusively) through consensual means. That is, they elicited the consent of dominated groups by articulating a political vision, an ideology, which claimed to speak for all and which resonated with beliefs widely held in popular political culture. Under these circumstances, coercive force might recede into the background of political life, always present as a potential but not directly apparent in day-to-day political life. So, adopting this conception to the understanding of world politics, Cox (1981: 139) suggests that particular state/society complexes may be situated in relation to world order such that they are endowed with hegemonic power

> that is based on a coherent conjunction or fit between a configuration of material power, the prevalent collective image of world order (including certain norms) and a set of institutions which administer the order with a certain semblance of universality (i.e., not just as the overt instruments of a particular state's dominance).

An important implication of Cox's explicitly 'critical' approach is that world politics need no longer be narrowly identified with the behaviours of states. Rather, various forms of state as well as world orders are understood as historical products in which the agency of social forces has been condensed and concretized. Out of these constellations of historical structures, particular kinds of power relations may be produced:

> Social forces are not to be thought of as existing exclusively within states. Particular social forces may overflow state boundaries.... The world can be represented as a pattern of interacting social forces in which states play an intermediate though autonomous role between the global structure of social forces and local configurations of social forces within particular countries.... Power is seen as emerging from social processes rather than taken as given in the form of accumulated material capabilities, that is as the result of these processes. (Paraphrasing Marx, one could describe the latter, neo-realist view as the 'fetishism of power'.) (Cox 1981: 141)

Social forces such as labour are not just interest groups seeking to modify the behaviour of pre-existing states with pre-given form, but rather are actively engaged in the (re-)production of various state/society complexes, state forms and world orders. In short, social forces are integral to historical structures of state and world order, and these latter may not be adequately understood in abstraction from their historical relations with social forces. Further, hegemony should not be conflated with simple dominance, based upon a preponderance of coercive power or material resources in the hands of a given state, as had been (and continues to be) the case in much conventional international relations scholarship. Rather, hegemony represents a contested relation of social power encompassing cultural, economic and political dimensions of social life and potentially transnational in scope.

The Gramscian conceptual vocabulary highlighted by Cox was soon put to work by other scholars whose pioneering work established the usefulness and credibility of this kind of approach to the study of world politics. Enrico Augelli and Craig Murphy (1988) deployed Gramscian notions of ideological struggle, hegemony and power to understand the politics of global inequality, the challenge to the North–South structure of global privilege posed by the ideologies associated with the New International Economic Order (NIEO) movement of the 1970s, and the ways in which that challenge was undercut and global hierarchy re-established by the global debt crisis of the 1980s and the emergence of neoliberal market-based orthodoxy as a governing ideology of the global economy. In the process of establishing this neoliberal hegemony, the important role of transnational forums such as the Trilateral Commission was demonstrated in a ground-breaking study by Stephen Gill (1990). Capturing a crucial political dynamic of the late twentieth century, Gill (1995) coined the phrase 'disciplinary neoliberalism' to describe the hegemonic operation of this ideology of market fundamentalism and its associated doctrines. Major studies were published using Gramscian concepts to understand the role of industrial development and the emergence of international organization since the mid-nineteenth century (Murphy 1994), the politics of mass production in the social construction of US global hegemony in the mid-twentieth century (Rupert 1995) and the role of polyarchy (a weak form of democracy characterized by minimal popular participation and effective rule by competing elite groups) in reproducing that global hegemony in the developing world in the later twentieth century (Robinson 1996). The influence of Cox's work and of neo-Gramscian scholarship more generally has been sufficiently widespread to warrant anthologies of essays by various scholars reflecting (sometimes critically) on this school of thought (Gill 1993; Gill and Mittelman 1997; Bieler and Morton 2006). More recently, a new generation of Gramsci-inspired scholars have produced important studies of the ways in which the politics of hegemony and passive revolution (top-down reform designed to pre-empt and disable popular resistance which might otherwise be potentially democratizing or transformative) operate unevenly across multiple scales from the global to the local (Paul 2005; Bieler 2006; Morton 2007). Looking toward global politics more broadly, Gramscian concepts have been used to understand the politics of 'subaltern groups' in post-colonial contexts such as India (Arnold 2000), and have informed reflections on the politics of cultural pluralism, race and ethnicity in a globalizing world (Hall 1997). It seems reasonable to suggest, then, that Antonio Gramsci's intellectual legacy lives on in contemporary scholarship of global politics; but who was this somewhat enigmatic figure and in what context did he produce his insights on politics?

Gramsci's life: a thumbnail biography

Never a physically robust person, Antonio Gramsci's health had suffered greatly after a decade of imprisonment at the hands of Mussolini and the Italian fascists. Jailed from 1926 until just before his death in 1937, Gramsci was effectively cut off from the political ferment which had animated him for much of his life, his activity limited to the scribbling of fragmentary intellectual reflections and notes to himself – elliptical, allusive, disjointed ruminations on history, philosophy, culture and politics which must have seemed largely indecipherable to the prison censors who monitored his activity. By 1935, Gramsci's health had deteriorated to the point that he was no longer able to continue writing, and no further entries were made in his notebooks, by then numbering 29 (with several others devoted to translations of various German and Russian texts). Once a politically fearsome revolutionary activist, founder of the Italian Communist Party, member of the Italian Parliament and of the Communist International, by the time of his death the fascists may have regarded the 46-year-old Gramsci as having been successfully reduced to an historical irrelevancy by the repressive power of their state. But any such inference would have been badly mistaken. Antonio Gramsci may not have been able to stop the rise of fascism or to engender a socialist revolution in twentieth century Italy, but in the course of his struggles he left a rich intellectual and political legacy that has earned him a world-wide reputation as one of the giants of critical theory. While not uncontroversial or free of contradiction, Gramsci's brilliant activist interpretation of historical materialism – elaborated in the now famous *Prison Notebooks* – continues to offer important insights into the politics of capitalist social life, its animating tensions and possibilities, well into the twenty-first century and the era of globalization.

Raised in an impoverished family on the hardscrabble, relatively backward and provincial island of Sardinia, Gramsci was doubly marked as an outsider in the Italy of the early twentieth century. A child of peripheral poverty, he contracted a variant of tuberculosis that affected his physical development and left him a 'gobbo', a hunchback:

> Antonio Gramsci never grew to be more than four-and-three-quarters feet tall. He had two humps, one in front and the other in back, giving him a deformed appearance. His normal-sized head appeared huge and awkward on his short frame. He also walked lamely (Germino 1990: 1).

The political theorist Dante Germino argues that the profoundly painful struggles living as a Sardinian hunchback predisposed Gramsci toward a revolutionary politics of a particular quality:

> Gramsci committed himself to a kind of qualitative change in political existence – the overcoming and abolition of the distinction between

centres of prestige and peripheries of inferiority … His dedication to overcoming marginalization became the core of his theory of politics, of which a nondeterminist kind of Marxism was unquestionably a major part (Germino 1990: 14, 22).

Gramsci's early political development included exposure to Sardinian nationalist and socialist currents. After secondary school, he won a scholarship to attend university in Turin, one of the rising industrial centres of Northern Italy. There, despite chronic financial difficulties and recurrent health crises, Gramsci studied linguistics, philosophy, history, and literature. He also became increasingly engaged in politics, joining the Socialist Party (PSI). After three years of study, Gramsci left the university and devoted himself to socialist politics and journalism. His writings reflected a sustained interest in the connection between workers' cultural activity and political agency. Frustrated by the prevalence of economistic and mechanistic interpretations of Marxism grounded in a narrow reading of Marx's more economically oriented work, Gramsci was deeply impressed by the Bolsheviks' apparently effective political activism and hailed the Russian Revolution of 1917 as the 'Revolution against *Das Kapital*'.

In 1919 Gramsci became involved in publication of a journal entitled *The New Order* (*L'Ordine Nuovo*), which billed itself as a review of socialist culture. As a journalist and PSI activist, he vigorously supported the formation of workers' factory councils in the Turin industrial plants of Fiat and Brevetti. Gramsci saw the factory councils as vehicles for workers' self-determination and potentially as the nuclei of a democratic socialist society. A major industrial confrontation ensued, with employers locking workers out of the factories, and workers responding with a general strike which involved over 200,000 workers and all but shut down the city of Turin. What may have seemed a potentially revolutionary moment soon collapsed, however. There was little coordination or support from political and trade union movements outside Turin, the industrialists gained the initiative and defeated the strike piecemeal. The factory councils were supplanted by trade unions more oriented toward economic bargaining than exerting workers' control over the social apparatus of production.

While he never abandoned his conviction that grassroots self-activity was essential to meaningful political transformation, Gramsci grew increasingly skeptical of the revolutionary potential of trade unions and of the PSI. Accordingly, he participated in the founding of the Communist Party of Italy (PCI) in 1921, and became active in the Communist International (Comintern). After Mussolini and the Fascists gained control of the Italian state in 1922, the PCI was directly targeted by the fascist police and its top officials hunted down and prosecuted for subversion, conspiracy, and other alleged crimes against the state. Gramsci worked in exile in Moscow and elsewhere until he was elected to the Italian Parliament in 1924, when he returned under the protection of Parliamentary immunity and continued his work, partly in public and partly in secret, as a leader of the PCI. In 1926 the fascist security apparatus apprehended Gramsci and, parliamentary immunity notwithstanding, he began the last decade of his life as a prisoner – a prisoner, a politically committed intellectual, and a writer.

Reading Gramsci, thinking politics

Making sense of Gramsci's *Prison Notebooks* is intellectually challenging, and can seem daunting at first. But for all that seems cryptic or idiosyncratic in the *Notebooks*, it is possible to find brilliant insights into modern social life and politics scattered throughout, and to build from these a more-or-less coherent vision of historical materialism and of the kind of politics suitable to a democratizing, emancipatory project. My purpose in this section is to introduce the reader to the ways in which I have tried to make sense of Gramsci's *Notebooks*, and to invite you to begin your own process of constructive engagement with his rich, if also inchoate, intellectual legacy.

Gramsci's vision of social life was deeply indebted to Marx and to the intellectual traditions of historical materialism, as the following passage from the *Notebooks* demonstrates:

> The discovery that relations between the social and natural orders are mediated by work, by man's theoretical and practical activity, creates the first elements of an intuition of the world free from all magic and superstition. It provides a basis for the subsequent development of an historical, dialectical conception of the world, which understands movement and change ... and which conceives the contemporary world as a synthesis of the past, of all past generations, which projects itself into the future (Gramsci 1971: 34–35).

In passages such as this, Gramsci lays out a process-oriented social ontology, or theory of social reality. To paraphrase one of Marx's more justly famous statements, Gramsci was suggesting that people make their own history, but they can't just do it any way they want, as if always starting from scratch. Rather, they are historically situated social actors whose social identities, self-understandings, and capacities for action are profoundly shaped by the social relations through which they live their lives, and which they encounter as the historical legacy of the socially productive practices of preceding generations. The kinds of people we become, the ways in which we understand ourselves and our relations with the world around us, the kinds of things we typically do or are capable of doing, and the kinds of societies we live in, all are shaped by the history of our socially productive practices and the ways in which we collectively replicate, or alter, those historical practices. In this sense, human beings are both the makers and the products of this social history:

> ... one could say that each one of us changes himself, modifies himself to the extent that he changes and modifies the complex relations of

which he is the hub. In this sense the real philosopher is, and cannot be other than, the politician, the active man [*sic*] who modifies the environment, understanding by environment the *ensemble* of relations which each of us enters to take part in. If one's own individuality is the *ensemble* of these relations, to create one's personality means to acquire consciousness of them and to modify one's own personality means to modify the *ensemble* of these relations (Gramsci 1971: 352, emphasis in original).

So Gramsci was a Marxist, but importantly, a Marxist of a very peculiar sort. Whereas mechanical and deterministic interpretations of historical materialism predominated in European socialist movements of his time, Gramsci saw Marx as a dialectical theorist of purposive social action and collective self-development and, as if to underscore the identification of Marxism with social self-determination, he referred to historical materialism as the 'philosophy of praxis'. He was scathingly critical of the philosophical and political errors which underlay Bukharin's positivistic materialism (Gramsci 1971: 419–72) and of the 'economism' which abstracted economic life out of its larger social context (including political and cultural aspects) and presented the economy as an autonomous power driving social life (1971: 158–68). Gramsci explicitly rejected the belief that fundamental social change would be brought about by capitalism's economic crisis tendencies operating, almost automatically, behind the backs of human actors: 'It may be ruled out that immediate crises of themselves produce fundamental historical events; they can simply create a terrain more favourable to the dissemination of certain modes of thought, and certain ways of posing and resolving questions involving the entire subsequent development of national life [and, we might add, transnational life as well]' (1971: 184; see also 350).

In Gramsci's interpretation of Marxian materialism, human beings are who they are, and do the kinds of things that they do, by virtue of their situation in a particular historical social context. But this is not a one-way relationship of determination, and this context is not static, because human beings continually reproduce or change themselves and their world through their collective social activity (1971: 352). Nor can this be understood deterministically in terms of economic forces operating independently of human intentional activity, since humans are socially conscious beings, producers of collective meanings, for whom thinking and acting, knowing and doing, are integral aspects of the same social life-process. In this sense, 'popular beliefs ... are themselves material forces' (1971: 165). This is what Gramsci meant when, in the passage quoted above, he described 'an historical, dialectical conception of the world' (1971: 34).

In keeping with this view of human social activity, Gramsci famously maintained that practically everyone is a philosopher: 'The majority of mankind are philosophers in so far as they engage in practical activity and in their practical activity (or in their guiding lines of conduct) there is implicitly contained a conception of the world, a philosophy' (1971: 344). Meaningful progressive social change – a democratizing process in which people are increasingly able deliberately and collectively to shape their social relations, shared meanings and socially productive practices – cannot emerge (presto) from the rubble of capitalism's economic collapse like a rabbit from a magician's hat. Rather, it can only be produced through a sustained process of social self-transformation, a process which will necessarily entail political and cultural as well as economic aspects, and which will be the object of struggle among various social actors from differing social situations and animated by differing visions and political projects. For Gramsci, a crucial terrain of this profoundly political process is popular common sense.

The beliefs which animate social action are drawn from historical reservoirs of social meanings which Gramsci referred to as popular common sense. These are not necessarily coherent or complete belief systems but rather represent an accumulated assortment of various kinds of beliefs derived from mythology and folklore, religion, popularized versions of philosophical or scientific doctrines, and so forth. He described popular common sense as the result of historical processes of cultural sedimentation, the residue of a multitude of deposits, fragmentary and contradictory, open to multiple interpretations and potentially supportive of very different kinds of social visions and political projects. The resources of popular common sense could be used by dominant classes and privileged social forces to construct hegemonic belief systems that would attempt to reaffirm the *status quo* and disable alternative political projects by making fundamental social change appear to be unrealistic or unthinkable. Alternatively, counter-hegemonic social forces might find in popular common sense resources for a transformative political process, an emancipatory dialogue out of which new kinds of politics might emerge. In this way, hegemony is a double-edged sword, a locus of political struggle, in Gramsci's words a terrain of 'reciprocal siege' (1971: 239).

Gramsci's political project entailed addressing the popular common sense operative in particular times and places, making explicit the tensions and possibilities within it as well as the socio-political implications of these, in order to enable critical social analysis and transformative political practice (1971: 323–34, 419–25). 'First of all', Gramsci says of the philosophy of praxis,

> it must be a criticism of 'common sense', basing itself initially, however, on common sense in order to demonstrate that 'everyone' is a philosopher and that it is not a question of introducing from scratch a scientific form of thought into everyone's individual life, but of renovating and making 'critical' an already existing activity (1971: 330–31).

His aim was 'to construct an intellectual-moral bloc which can make politically possible the intellectual progress of the mass and not only of small intellectual groups', and thereby 'to create the conditions in which this division [between leaders and led] is no longer necessary', and in which 'the subaltern element' is 'no longer a thing [objectified, reified] but an historical person ... an agent, necessarily active and taking the initiative' (1971: 332–35, 144, 337; also 346, 349, 418). Gramsci's political project is then explicitly pedagogical, but to the extent that it is successful, this project is transformative of the teacher/student relation along with the parties embedded within that relation.

> An historical act can only be performed by 'collective man', and this presupposes the attainment of a 'cultural-social' unity through which a multiplicity of dispersed wills, with heterogeneous aims, are welded together with a single aim, on the basis of an equal and common conception of the world ... This problem can and must be related to the modern way of considering educational doctrine and practice, according to which the relationship between teacher and pupil is active and reciprocal so that every teacher is always a pupil and every pupil a teacher ... Every relationship of 'hegemony' is necessarily an educational relationship and occurs not only within a nation, between the various forces of which the nation is composed, but in the international and world-wide field, between complexes of national and continental civilizations (Gramsci 1971: 350).

The political-educational process he envisions should be distinguished from indoctrination insofar as the former entails reciprocal development and seeks to enable the student to produce new truths independent of his/her teacher and, in the process, to teach the teacher, thereby transforming their relation. The relation teacher/student (and leader/led) is then reciprocal but (in the context of capitalist modernity) initially asymmetrical: Gramsci aims at developing the reciprocity of the relation until the asymmetry approaches the vanishing point. Just as students can develop the capacity to teach their teachers, so those who were led may be enabled to participate in collective decision-making functions formerly associated with leadership (1971: 144, 350). In this sense, Gramsci's project is aimed at enabling active participation in processes of social self-determination, and aims at a profound kind of social democratization. And, please note, that this new politics, this counter-hegemonic democratizing process, need not stop at national borders. Gramsci is explicitly envisioning political processes which may be situated within particular national spaces and local conditions, but these are themselves conditioned by – and might also reshape or transform – transnational political conditions.

> What matters is that a new way of conceiving the world and man is born and that this conception is no longer reserved to the great intellectuals, to professional philosophers, but tends rather to become a popular, mass

phenomenon, with a concretely world-wide character, capable of modifying (even if the results include hybrid combinations) popular thought and mummified popular culture (Gramsci 1971: 417).

In Gramsci's political vision, the agents of this open-ended transformative process would comprise an 'historical bloc' of social forces brought together by a shared vision of a post-capitalist future rich with alternative possibilities. A necessary element of any historical bloc whose democratizing political horizons extended beyond capitalism would be the working class, non-owners of capital compelled to sell their labour in order to live and thereby socially subordinated to the capitalist wage relation. But intellectuals and political activists 'organically' related to this class or allied with it would play the crucial role of teachers/leaders, beginning to articulate a political vision grounded in the historical experiences of that class and its allies, but looking beyond the social relations of capitalism and institutional forms such as the modern state, or the patriarchal family and compulsory heterosexuality, or racialized hierarchies, toward alternative futures in which myriad possibilities for social self-determination might be realized as this historical bloc develops, negotiates new political identities, and actualizes its collective historical agency (1971: 330–43). Crucially, the goal of this process is not the permanent institutionalization of the rule of one particular, preconstituted social group or its party over all others, but the transformation of capitalist social relations and their characteristic structural separations of state/society, politics/economics, theory/practice and so on, in order to enable the devolution of implicitly class-based political rule into a more generalized social self-determination – a future for which the democratization of economic relations (the 'regulated society', 1971: 257, 263) would be a necessary condition.

Where to?

In a seminal article, Cox (1981: 128) wrote that: 'Theory is always for someone and for some purpose', suggesting that theorizing is itself an historically situated social activity, that it has social and political presuppositions as well as implications, and that the adequacy of our theories relates in part to their ability to help us reflect critically on this situatedness of scholarship, its ability to illuminate historical processes in which we are embedded and possibilities for alternative futures which we might realize through deliberate engagement with those processes. Adopting and adapting Gramscian categories, Cox showed us how we might re-envision international relations in terms of dynamic relations among social forces, forms of state, and world orders. By following his lead and crossing conventional boundaries separating the domestic from the international, the political from the cultural and economic, and state from society, we can create not just more dynamic accounts of world politics, but also in the process better understand how intellectual and practical engagement with the social relations of the present can contribute to possibilities for a more just and democratic future.

Further reading

Bieler, Andreas and Adam Morton (eds) (2006) *Images of Gramsci*, London: Routledge. Essays by theorists and international relations scholars reassessing, from a variety of perspectives, Gramsci's political theory and its relevance for contemporary global politics.

Boggs, Carl (1984) *The Two Revolutions: Gramsci and the Dilemmas of Western Marxism*, Boston: South End. Situates Gramsci's thought in relation to major intellectual and political currents of his day, especially his ambivalent relation to Leninist vanguardism.

Cox, Robert (1987) *Production, Power, and World Order*, New York: Columbia University Press. Cox's book-length exposition of a Gramscian-inspired approach to world politics.

Forgacs, David (ed.) (2000) *The Antonio Gramsci Reader: Selected Writings 1916–1935*, New York: New York University Press. Thematically organized anthology of Gramsci's most significant writings, including important selections from the *Prison Notebooks* as well as his early political journalism. Includes a glossary of key terms to aid readers new to Gramsci and his idiosyncratic vocabulary.

Jones, Steve (2006) *Antonio Gramsci*, London: Routledge. A relatively brief introductory text relating Gramsci's theory to contemporary culture and social power.

Morley, David and Kuan-Hsing Chen (eds) (1996) *Stuart Hall: Critical Dialogues in Cultural Studies*, London: Routledge. A collection of essays by and about one of the most influential contemporary practitioners of Gramscian cultural studies.

Sassoon, Anne Showstack (ed.) (1982) *Approaches to Gramsci*, London: Readers and Writers. A collection of relatively brief and accessible essays by European and British scholars designed as a 'companion' to Gramsci, includes a biographical sketch and a small but helpful 'Gramsci Dictionary'.

Sassoon, Anne Showstack (1987) *Gramsci's Politics*, Minneapolis: University of Minnesota Press. An extensive and sophisticated overview of Gramsci's political thinking.

17 Jürgen Habermas

Neta C. Crawford

Jürgen Habermas was born in Düsseldorf, Germany in 1929. Like many Germans during the 1930s and 1940s, Habermas' family was pro-Nazi, and toward the end of the Second World War, Habermas joined the Hitler Youth. After the war, Habermas became more fully aware of the brutal nature of Nazism and began his long interest in studying and promoting democracy, the thread that he himself says ties his work together. After the war, Habermas began studying philosophy and obtained a doctorate in 1954. He began studying at the Institute for Social Research in Frankfurt in 1956 under Theodor Adorno and Max Horkheimer. At the Institute for Social Research Habermas began what has been a long dialogue with Kant, Hegel, Marx and Weber, as well as with Adorno and Horkheimer and other critical theorists.

Habermas' work ranges from sociological description, through linguistics, long-range historical analysis, legal and democratic theorizing, to epistemology and morality. He has also been openly engaged in German and European politics. At risk of mangling his concerns, at the root of Habermas' work is the desire to promote radical democracy – an inclusive, participatory, informed, and deliberative democratic process. In this way, Habermas' attention to democracy and what he calls emancipatory knowledge is squarely within the broader tradition of Frankfurt School Critical Theory in which he was trained. His major books include *The Structural Transformation of the Public Sphere* (1989), *Knowledge and Human Interests* (1971), *Legitimation Crisis* (1975), the two-volume *The Theory of Communicative Action* (1984 and 1987), and *Between Facts and Norms* (1996). Habermas has also published numerous essays. Further, he has read widely in post-structuralism, American pragmatism and developmental psychology.

In addition to the sheer volume of his work, Habermas is often considered one of the most difficult to understand of the critical theorists. I will necessarily address only a few of the themes explored in his more than five-decade career. It must be admitted that the choice of theories to describe has been difficult and is somewhat arbitrary in the sense that although little of his work directly addresses problems of international relations, depending upon their knowledge interests, much of Habermas' scholarship is relevant to scholars of world politics. I focus on two related themes of Habermas' work – his early theorization of democracy and the public sphere and his later theorization of discourse ethics. The themes come together in *Between Facts and Norms* (1996). Apart from being central concerns for Habermas, these concepts have been of particular interest to scholars of international relations trying to understand the potential for non-coercive dialogue, global social movements, the functions of international institutions, and how deliberative institutions in world politics might become more democratic. Further, it is Habermas' work on argumentation and discourse ethics that has, so far, most penetrated and informed international relations theory.

Communicative action

Habermas divides social action into two main types. In strategic action, someone wants to get the other to do what they want them to do – influencing the other through the threat of sanctions or the prospect of gratification. Communicative action, on the other hand, is oriented to reaching understanding (Habermas 1979: 41, 1984 and 1987): 'I call interactions *communicative* when the participants coordinate their plans of action consensually, with the agreement reached at any point being evaluated in terms of the intersubjective recognition of validity claims' (1990a: 58). In early work Habermas also included a third type of action, symbolic or expressive action, which he describes as non-propositional symbolic expression, such as dance (Habermas 1979: 40–41, 1990b: 137). In later work, Habermas does not give expressive action the same degree of attention as communicative and strategic action.

In communicative action, the interlocutors assume that they mean the same things by particular expressions, that what they say is comprehensible to the hearer, that their propositions are true, that each is sincere and ready to take on the obligations that result from reaching consensus, and that they come to understand each other through a process of dialogue in which they listen to each other:

> Just as the Cartesian *cogito* purports to show that the self cannot be doubted or questioned but is presupposed by any act of doubting or questioning, so Habermas argues that certain ideals correlated with a way of life we ought to be striving to bring about – such as truth, sincerity, rationality, freedom, the pursuit of understanding and agreement in a context devoid of coercion – are presupposed by the exercise of language itself (Culler 1985: 134).

Communicative action is possible because interlocutors share a 'lifeworld' of background assumptions, 'a horizon of shared, unproblematic beliefs', within a context of social solidarity (Habermas 1996: 22, 1990b: 135–36). Habermas argues that practical discourses depend on content brought to them from outside. It would be utterly pointless to engage in a practical discourse without a horizon provided by the lifeworld of a specific social group and without real conflicts in a concrete situation in which the actors consider it incumbent on them to reach a consensual means of regulating some controversial social matter (Habermas 1990a: 103).

Communicative action, the search for truth between interlocutors, is the key concept of Habermas' work on law and democracy; even strategic action is presupposed by communicative action, and 'communicative action, then, depends on the use of language oriented to mutual understanding' (Habermas 1996: 18). Communication is an iterative process. When challenged, someone should be able to give a reason for their beliefs:

> participants either agree on the validity claimed for their speech acts or identify points of disagreement, which they conjointly take into consideration in the course of further interaction. Every speech act involves the raising of criticizable validity claims aimed at intersubjective recognition (Habermas 1996:18).

Habermas thus describes communicative action as rational. But, because the word rational is often equated with a rather thin view of rationality (such as rational actor theory or Western rationality), it might be less confusing to describe communicative action as depending on practical reason or 'practical discourse', with the emphasis on reason giving and argumentation (1990a: 71).

If communicative action is the key concept of Habermas' theory of law and legitimacy, communicative competence underpins the theory: communicative action (and discourse ethics) is restricted to those who possess communicative competence. Briefly, for Habermas, communicative competence is the ability of a speaker to fulfil the validity obligations of speech in communicative action: comprehensibility, truth, normative 'rightness', and truthfulness (Habermas 1979: 26–29). Comprehensibility is the minimum condition, the ability to produce grammatically correct sentences (from Chomsky's (1969) ideas of linguistic competence). The speaker should also be saying what is true in a factual sense, such as stating that gravity implies that what goes up must come down. Normative rightness is the idea that whatever normative claims the speaker makes are considered normatively valid by the community, such as 'thou shalt not kill'. Finally, the speaker must truthfully represent their beliefs and intentions:

> In contexts of communicative action, we call someone rational not only if he is able to put forward an assertion and, when criticized, to prove grounds for it by pointing to appropriate evidence, but also if he is following an established norm and is able, when criticized, to justify his

action by explicating the given situation in the light of legitimate expectations (Habermas 1984: 15).

Table 17.1 summarizes these claims and their relation to the content of speech and argument.

Habermas' articulation of the notion of communicative competence occurs relatively early in his theorization of communicative action (Habermas 1979) and he does not greatly expand on communicative competence in later work (although see Habermas 1990b: 137, 187). Rather, other characteristics of communicative competence are implied in work on moral consciousness (1990b). Although these characteristics are not developed to the same degree of specificity and analytical clarity as the initial core concepts, it is possible to specify three other characteristics that Habermas states also appear to be essential to communicative action and discourse ethics: non-violence, moral feeling (empathy) and ideal role taking.

By setting the communicatively competent subject in a discourse ethical context and insisting that only the force of the better argument convinces, Habermas strongly suggests that competent actors should be non-violent. But a promise of non-violence is not enough. To be credible, the actor should have reputation and a commitment to non-violence (Habermas 1996: 182). The ideal speech situation should approximate conditions that are 'specially immunized against repression and inequality' (1996: 228).

By moral feeling Habermas is suggesting a feeling of respect or compassion for others; moral feelings play a role in the 'constitution' of moral phenomena. Humans would not understand what was moral without such feelings: 'We would not experience certain conflicts of action as morally relevant at all unless we *felt* that the integrity of a person is threatened or violated. Feelings form the basis of our *perception* of something as moral' (Habermas 1993: 174). A lack of moral feeling is an incapacity, while those who have moral feeling are able to engage in moral reasoning:

Table 17.1 Communicative competence in Habermas

Validity Claim	Characteristic	Function	Redeemable
Comprehensibility	Understandable language	Communicate	
Truth	Verifiable propositional content	Represents facts: accurately describes the world	Reasons
Normative rightness	Normative	Establish legitimacy	Reasons
Truthfulness	Avowal	Convey sincerity and intentions	Consistent action

Someone who is blind to moral phenomena is blind to feeling. He lacks a sense, as we say, for the suffering of a vulnerable creature who has a claim to have its integrity, both personal and bodily, protected. And this sense is manifestly closely related to sympathy or compassion (Habermas 1993: 174).

Moral feelings also help us judge when someone has been harmed. Closely related to moral feeling, which Habermas clearly suggests is an emotional capacity, are a set of cognitive capacities that Habermas, drawing on G.H. Mead, calls ideal role taking; actors should be able to step out of their own perspective in order to see the world from another person's perspective:

Ideal role taking has come to signify a procedural type of justification. The cognitive operations it requires are demanding. Those operations in turn are internally linked with motives and emotional dispositions and attitudes like empathy. Where sociocultural distance is a factor, concern for the fate of one's neighbor – who more often than not is anything but close by – is a necessary emotional prerequisite for the cognitive operations expected of participants in discourse (Habermas, 1990b: 182).

Discourse ethics

Habermas has two aims in his work on communicative action and discourse ethics: to explain how intersubjective agreement, law and legitimacy are actually derived by real persons and how law gains its legitimacy (through communicative action), and to propose how decisions might become more legitimate (by the adoption of discourse ethics). His account of discourse ethics is not descriptive but prescriptive and meant as a heuristic for understanding actual deliberation. If interlocutors are not able to arrive at an agreement, they have several options. These include switching to strategic action, breaking off communication entirely, or resuming communication in a more formalized way using discourse ethical principles (Habermas 1979: 3–4, 1996: 21).

Habermas is thus presuming that social life, at a minimum, requires problem solving coordination, or more than that, requires that disagreements about what it is good to do (morality) need to be resolved in ways that are fair. Habermas, in an elaboration of Kant's Categorical Imperative, proposes that 'only those norms can claim to be valid that meet (or could meet) with the approval of all affected in their capacity *as participants in a practical discourse*' (Habermas 1990a: 66). For Habermas, 'the problems to be resolved in moral argumentation cannot be handled monologically but require a cooperative effort. By entering into a process of moral argumentation, the participants continue their communicative action in a reflexive attitude with the aim of restoring a consensus that has been disrupted' (Habermas 1990a: 67). Discourse ethics is a formal 'procedure for testing the validity of norms that are being proposed and hypothetically considered for adoption' (Habermas 1990a: 103).

In communicative action, participants eschew strategic action and come to an uncoerced understanding. One tries to convince the other through the force of the better argument. For Habermas, the key to legitimacy is rational argumentation:

> the claim that a norm lies equally in the interest of everyone has the sense of rational acceptability: all those possibly affected should be able to accept the norm on the basis of good reasons. But this can become clear only under the pragmatic conditions of rational discourses in which the only thing that counts is the compelling force of the better argument based upon the relevant information (Habermas 1996: 103).

Discourse ethics is communicative action that has become reflexive or self-conscious. The discourse ethical argument depends on presuppositions at three levels – logical and semantic rules; procedural rules for competitive argumentation; and the process of communication. At the logical and semantic level, no speaker may contradict him or herself; speakers must be consistent in their reasoning (anyone who applies a predicate to an object, must be prepared to apply that same predicate to all other objects resembling the first one in all relevant aspects); and different speakers may not use the same expression with different meanings (Habermas 1990a: 87). At the procedural level, every speaker must be sincere, asserting only what they believe and anyone who disputes a proposition or a norm must provide a reason for doing so. At the process level, discourse ethical speech must be 'immune to repression and inequality'. At this level discourse must be inclusive of every subject with the competence to speak; everyone is allowed to question any assertion, introduce assertions, and express attitudes, desires and needs. Coercion is ruled out (Habermas 1990a: 87–89). Thus, Habermas insists that discourse ethics is not a substantive project. He does not want to say what values we should hold, but rather how actors should find those values themselves and come to agreement on them.

The content of a valid agreement will be such that the general observance of the norm is accepted freely by all those who are affected by it. There is content to moral judgments, but we cannot necessarily know that content in advance of the discourse ethical dialogue. And the cognitive content represents 'more than expressions of contingent emotions, preferences, and decisions of a speaker or actor' (Habermas 1990b: 121). The legitimate substance or content of a conclusion is only agreed upon through the process of discourse ethics:

> Discourse ethics does not set up a substantive orientation. Instead, it establishes a *procedure* based on presuppositions and designed to guarantee the impartiality of the process of judging … The principle of discourse ethics prohibits singling out with philosophical authority any

specific normative contents ... as the definitive content of moral theory (Habermas 1990b: 122).

Thus, on one level, it ostensibly does not matter what gets said in a discourse ethical argument, so long as those who are participants in dialogue are competent and use discourse ethical procedures. But of course content does matter: the occasion for the argument will be motivated by the need to resolve a concrete situation and the content of the argument will be shaped by the lifeworld (Habermas 1990b: 135, 179).

Discourse ethics presumes a high level of moral consciousness or moral development:

> Reaching mutual understanding through discourse indeed guarantees that issues, reasons, and information are handled reasonably, but such understanding still depends on contexts characterized by a capacity for learning, both at the cultural and personal level. In this respect, dogmatic worldviews and rigid patterns of socialization can block a discursive mode of sociation. (Habermas 1996: 324–25)

Ideal role taking, adopting another person's perspective, is essential for discourse ethics, because otherwise we cannot know whether the norms we claim to be valid for all those who are affected by them are actually valid (justification). Empathy enables ideal role taking. Habermas is thus implicitly adding empathy of a particular sort – the ability to feel as others feel – to his view of communicative competence: 'the continued existence of this communication community ... demands of all its members an act of selfless empathy through ideal role taking' (Habermas 1993b: 154). He argues that

> at the very least, empathy – the ability to project oneself across cultural distances into alien and at first sight incomprehensible conditions of life, behavioral predispositions, and interpretive perspectives – is an emotional prerequisite for ideal role taking, which requires everyone to take the perspective of all others (Habermas 1993b: 174).

He goes on to say that:

> To view something from the moral point of view means that we do not elevate our own self-understanding and world view to the standard by which we universalize a mode of action but instead test its generalizability also from the perspective of others. It is unlikely that one would be able to perform this demanding cognitive feat without generalized compassion, sublimated into the capacity to empathize with others, that points beyond affective ties to immediate reference persons and opens our eyes to 'difference', to the uniqueness and inalienable otherness of the other (Habermas 1993b: 174–75).

The criteria for Habermasian communicative action and discourse ethics can be interpreted as too demanding, and perhaps even unrealistic. Habermas recognizes that he has articulated an ideal that is subject to the real limits of time, information, individual capacities, and the limits or indeed manipulation of institutions (Habermas 1990a: 92, 104, 1996: 325–26). Habermas has also explicitly suggested a social and political underpinning for discourse ethics when he says that discourse ethics also entails five basic categories of rights within legal communities. First, each person is 'owed a right to the greatest possible measure of *equal* liberties that are mutually compatible'. Second, rights are guaranteed to those who are members of a particular community, with the community determining membership. Third, individuals are guaranteed equal treatment; those who feel their rights have been infringed upon must be able to make a claim against the community. Fourth, citizens must have basic rights to participate in processes of opinion and will formation. Fifth, these civil rights 'imply' that there are 'basic rights to the provision of living conditions that are socially, technologically, and ecologically safeguarded, insofar as the current circumstances make this necessary if citizens are to have equal opportunities to utilize [their] civil rights' (Habermas 1996: 122–25). The fulfilment of basic rights or basic needs then becomes a precondition for full participation.

Habermas' explicit and implicit articulation of the characteristics of those who should be allowed to participate in political deliberation has a certain appeal because it seems to allow for wide participation. Yet while Habermas wants all those potentially affected by a norm to have a chance to participate, his formulation of discourse ethics nevertheless restricts participation in deliberation. Specifically, discourse takes place within communities, and those communities determine group membership (Habermas 1996: 124–25). People who are displaced, or for some reason defined as outside a community, at least in Habermas' formulation, have no right to participate in deliberation as legal persons because they are not part of a political community. But while this is an important limitation from the perspective of world politics, the restriction of deliberative participants to group members is the most obvious and least substantive limit. The notion of competence itself can lead to substantive restrictions: if we limit who can speak, we may limit what can be said. Narrow conceptions of competence – e.g. a conception of rationality that is narrowly drawn – are necessarily limiting.

The public sphere, civil society and democracy

Habermas' other major preoccupation is the setting for deliberative democracy. In his first book, *The Structural Transformation of the Public Sphere* (1989) originally published in German in 1962, Habermas begins with a distinction between public and private. The private realm is closed, and the public is open to all. Habermas develops a historical account of the development of a bourgeois public sphere in seventeenth and eighteenth century

Europe at an intermediate level between the private and public realm. The public sphere is the space (actual and abstract) for communication and opinion formation. His historical analysis traces the development of literary and political public spheres where the bourgeoisie (not the working class or the elites) could engage in discussion of, respectively, literature and art and politics.

These public spaces are sites first of all of communication, and then potentially of opinion formation. Perhaps the archetypal space for the public sphere was literary salons and coffee houses. Actors can identify social problems in the public sphere, articulate them, and connect around issues. The media perform crucial functions in the public sphere: collecting, selecting and framing information:

> As long as in the public sphere the mass media prefer, contrary to their normative self-understanding, to draw their material from powerful, well-organized information producers and as long as they prefer media strategies that lower rather than raise the discursive level of public communication, issues will tend to start in and be managed from, the center rather than follow a spontaneous course originating in the periphery (1996: 380).

For Habermas, robust public spheres depend, first, on robust private spheres and privacy and then, second, on a strong civil society. Civil society 'comprises those nongovernmental and non-economic connections and voluntary associations that anchor the communication structures of the public sphere' (Habermas 1996: 366):

> Civil society is composed of those more or less spontaneously emergent associations, organizations, and movements that, attuned to how societal problems resonate in the private life spheres, distill and transmit such reactions in amplified form to the public sphere. The core of civil society comprises a network of associations that institutionalizes problem solving discourses on questions of general interest inside the framework of organized public spheres (Habermas, 1996: 367).

In Habermas' understanding, the private sphere is the source of concerns. Civil society organizations help articulate these new issues and the public sphere is the place where the issues are communicated to a wider audience. At some points the administrative structure of governments may be forced to deal with issues raised by the public.

> In a perceived crisis situation, the *actors in civil society ... can* assume a surprisingly active and momentous role. In spite of a lesser organizational complexity and a weaker capacity for action, and despite the structural disadvantages mentioned earlier, at the critical moments of accelerated history, these actors get the chance to *reverse* the normal

circuits of communication in the political system and the public sphere (Habermas 1996: 381).

Politics and law are necessarily more circumscribed than the lifeworld. Private spheres, public spheres, and civil society are thus crucial for Habermas' conception of democracy. First, the people judge the legitimacy of the arguments made by governmental actors. And second, 'democratic procedure must be embedded in contexts it cannot itself regulate' (Habermas 1996: 305). The unconstrained, unregulated public sphere is and should be 'wild' (Habermas 1996: 307): 'Deliberative politics thus lives off the interplay between democratically institutionalized will-formation and informal opinion-formation. It cannot rely solely on the channels of procedurally regulated deliberation and decision making' (Habermas 1996: 308).

Habermas' influence in international relations

Compared to the rest of his work, Habermas has said very little directly about international relations and world politics. One exception is his critical discussion of Kant's arguments about perpetual peace (Habermas 1998). Here Habermas describes the development of a 'global public sphere' and the gradual development of human rights and international law as a 'cosmopolitan transformation of the state of nature among states into a legal order' (Habermas 1998: 149).

Habermas has also discussed nationalism, global media, and the constitution of states and the European Union. Although Habermas regularly engages his critics and interpreters, he has apparently not replied to the debate about the implications for his work for international relations theory during the mid-1990s that occurred in the German journal *Zietschrift für Internationale Beziehungen* (ZIB). In general terms, Habermas and other critical and post-structuralist theorists have been influential in the post-positivist turn in international relations theory (Diez and Steans 2005). Theorists of world politics have tended not to engage Habermas on these terms; instead, critical and constructivist international relations theorists have focused on Habermas' ideas about discourse ethics and communicative action/argumentation, hence my focus here.

Some have used Habermas' explication of communicative action and argumentation to articulate the 'logic of argumentation' as an alternative to strategic action or bargaining behavior (Alker 1996; Risse 2000). Indeed, in addition to the explication of the concept of a logic of argumentation, a rich empirical literature has developed which examines the role of argumentation in negotiation settings in world politics (Dietelhoff and Müller 2005). Dietelhoff, Müller, and other project participants deliberately investigated the role of argumentation in multilateral negotiations and report that their research 'demonstrated the importance especially of moral and ethical argumentation. However arguing could not be isolated empirically from bargaining ... arguing was ubiquitous in all negotiations. Pure bargaining was the exception' (2005: 171).

Going further, some have introduced the idea of discourse ethics to theories of world politics. Some have argued that discourse ethics offers a useful normative programme, suggesting that dialogue along discourse ethical lines is possible and desirable in an increasingly cosmopolitan world (Linklater 1998, 2005; Crawford 2002; Lynch 2002). Indeed, while offering caveats, some argue that discourse ethical dialogues have already occurred in world politics (Lynch 2000; Payne and Samhat 2004). Andrew Linklater (2005) argues that dialogic politics has the potential to open the space for including different actors in world politics.

But just as the notion of discourse ethics has been criticized in political theory, some international relations theorists find discourse ethics unsatisfactory. The criticism generally takes two forms. First, it has been argued that discourse ethics is unrealistic: it is impossible to bracket power. Second, and more fundamentally, critics charge that discourse ethics is not simply a procedural program, but carries with it a set of substantive, indeed ethnocentric, assumptions that 'privileges liberal modernity' (Hutchings 2005: 165) and, in particular, a narrow understanding of rational argumentation. Richard Shapcott offers hermeneutics as a more inclusive alternative to discourse ethics (2001). Andrew Linklater offers a defence of discourse ethics as dialogue. Specifically, Linklater suggests that Habermasian discourse ethics may be simply one articulation among several forms of dialogic interaction that could 'civilize' world politics:

The core commitments of discourse ethics – that all human beings have an equal right to belong to communication communities where they can protest against actions which may harm them, that all participants in ideal speech should enter dialogue with the conviction that no-one knows who will learn from whom, and that all should strive to reach agreements which rely as far as possible on the force of the better argument – may have been advanced in other places and in other times. We lack the evidence to say without fear of contradiction that they did not. But there is abundant evidence that the modern West is unusual in developing ethical traditions which are committed to the idea of 'non-repressive deliberation' however much political practice repeatedly clashes with that ethical ideal. This is only to suppose that the modern West may provide political actors with unusual resources for imagining and creating universal communication communities in which human beings can satisfy their needs without harming or humiliating each other. It does not follow that the West must have the last word in deciding what form this communication community should take (Linklater 2005: 147–48).

Political theorists are paying increasing attention to international politics. Specifically, some scholars working on what they call 'deliberative democracy' have sought to use Habermas' notions of a public sphere and discourse ethics to show how world politics could be more democratic and deliberative (Dryzek 2000; Bohman 2007). These authors suggest that transnational democracy is possible and argue that there is already a nascent and growing global public sphere.

Finally, some international relations scholars, perhaps most notably Hayward Alker (1996: 333), have used Habermas' discussion of emancipatory knowledge interests as a way to make peace research and international relations theory more self-conscious about both their goals and procedures. In sum, Habermas is suggesting that emancipation from systems of repression ought to be a concern of scholarship. Alker and others have thus sought to both recognize how social science is already working to shore up certain configurations of power, and how social science could be used to democratize world politics and make it more peaceful.

Further reading

One might begin a consideration of Habermas' influence on international relations as a field of inquiry by reading Ashley (1981) or more recently the overview article by Diez and Sterns (2005). For an introduction to Habermas' own thoughts on world politics, see his essay on Kant's *Perpetual Peace* (1998).

For a more general introduction to Habermas' work, I would begin with one of his later books, *Between Facts and Norms* (1996) and then work backward or forward, depending on the particular interests one brings to reading Habermas. I suggest this particular book because in it Habermas summarizes much of what is found in his earlier work on democracy and discourse ethics and then applies it to law and politics. *Between Facts and Norms* is thus synthesis and crystallization. It is not easy to follow, but is nevertheless exciting. Those who prefer to read interviews, might look at *Autonomy and Solidarity* (1986).

There are many secondary works on Habermas, including an important volume by Willliam Rehg (1994). In general, I also find translators and editors to Habermas' books to be clear and insightful. I can in particular recommend the introduction by Maeve Cook to Habermas' *On the Pragmatics of Communication* (1998) and the introduction by Thomas McCarthy to Habermas' *Communication and the Evolution of Society* (1979). One might also read the short introduction to Habermas by Finlayson (2005), who attempts to put Habermas in the context of the entire Frankfurt School and twentieth century social thought. Short introductions, including my own here, are best read alongside Habermas' own works, not as a substitute for them.

18 G.W.F. Hegel

Ritu Vij

G.W.F. Hegel, widely seen by advocates and critics alike as the inaugural thinker of modernity, is a towering figure in critical theory. Unlike Kant, for whom critique entailed an inquiry into the limits of rationality, Hegel was the first to advance a form of 'immanent critique', concerned with bringing into visibility the internal contradictions, tensions, distortions – in Hegel's term the 'negative' – of the categories of mind constitutive of knowledge. Without Hegel's systematic exposition of the movement of 'negativity' in thought and experience, much of what comprises critical thought today, including Marxist, hermeneutic, and psychoanalytic approaches to the study of modern social life, as well as postmodern and postcolonial approaches devoted to 'overcoming modernity' would, quite literally, be unthinkable. Best known as *the* theorist of freedom, espousing a purposive, if contested, notion of a progressive history that marks the movement of unitary reason or world spirit (*geist*), Hegel's contributions to the understanding of consciousness and desire as socially and inter-subjectively constituted have been pivotal to efforts to move beyond the dualism (between objective/subjective; normative/real) and empiricism that since Kant and Descartes have dominated Western philosophy and social inquiry. Hegel as a *critical* thinker of modernity, in other words, commands attention.

In considering Hegel's work, however, one must caution at the outset against the singular inaccessibility of his prose that frustrates but also rewards, abundantly and in equal measure, the sheer persistence of effort. Within disciplinary international relations although Hegel's shadow looms large, explicit discussions of his work have been limited. Centred principally on two texts, *The Phenomenology of Spirit* and *The Philosophy of Right*, scholarship in international relations has drawn attention to Hegel's putative 'realism', specifically his writings on the state and the 'international', his defence of nationalism and inter-state wars on the one hand, or conversely, liberal readings of Hegel's communitarianism that lend themselves to institutionalist perspectives in the global arena. More recently, reflecting the broad inter-disciplinary concern with the production, management, and hierarchicalizing effects of 'otherness' in global social life, Hegel's exposition of the master/slave dialectic (in *The Phenomenology of Spirit*), once seen as a

powerful and generative trans-historical theorization of the self-other problematic (by post colonial writers like Aime Cesaire and Frantz Fanon, for
instance), has been called into question. In much contemporary critical
theory, then, Hegel is cast as the central figure against which critical thought
must constantly strain to put to rest once and for all his claims about
'Absolute Knowing' and the radical denial of alterity that his speculative
idealism, it is argued, necessarily generates. In view of the rationalization of
imperialism and (European) cultural superiority that is seen to be the core, if
repressed, centre of a Hegelian cartography, the posthumously published
Philosophy of History has come into prominence in these debates. To the
extent that a critically inflected conception of the 'international' connotes,
minimally, the recognition of plurality (many states, many histories, many
life worlds), it is precisely, critics suggest, Hegel's alleged subsumption/denial
of difference that eradicates the 'international' as a valid object of inquiry in
his thought.

Of what use, then, is Hegel in contemporary critical international relations? What are the central categories in Hegel's thought that enable rather
than impede a critical global imaginary? If, as many from Foucault to Derrida remind us, we can speak to (or against) Hegel in terms that nonetheless
remain deeply Hegelian, what might the critically inclined student take from
Hegel in pursuit of an inquiry into the conditions and possibilities for imagining a more just world? While there are multiple pathways one can tread
through the Hegelian archive in response to this question, in the discussion
that follows, I can only gesture toward some of the ways in which an
engagement with Hegel's thought today may be especially timely. But first, a
brief biographical sketch.

Biographical note

Born in Stuttgart in 1770 to an upper middle-class family, and educated in
the classics, literature, and theology in Tübingen, Hegel worked as a tutor to
a wealthy Swiss family in Berne (1793–96) before moving to Frankfurt in
1797. Still a student during the fall of the Bastille in France (an event Hegel
would celebrate every year until his death), Hegel quickly moved to a Professorship at the University of Jena in 1805 where, with his friend, the philosopher Friedrich Schelling, he launched the *Critical Journal of Philosophy*.
Hegel's work during this time, simply referred to as the 'Jena Writings'
foreshadows much of the central argument of his most enduring work, *Philosophy of Right* (1821). His first major work, *Phenomenology of Spirit*
(1807), went to press just as Napoleon's armies occupied Jena. Following the
closing of the University of Jena, Hegel worked briefly as an editor of a
newspaper in Bavaria, before taking the position of headmaster at a Gymnasium (a preparatory school) in Nuremberg in1808 where he remained until
1816. His three-volume study *Science of Logic* was published during this
period in Nuremberg. The *Encyclopaedia of the Philosophical Sciences in*

Outline (1817) appeared after his move to the University of Heidelberg as Professor of Philosophy, following the defeat of Napoleon at Waterloo in 1815. In 1818, Hegel became Professor of Philosophy at the University of Berlin where he remained until his death in 1831 a few months after he was decorated by Friedrich Wilhelm III of Prussia.

Key concepts

Hegel's philosophy is grounded in a deep belief about the intrinsic need for *freedom*, understood as self-knowledge, in the development of the subject through the course of human history. Challenging Kantian notions of the radical unknowability of the world and the atomistic conception of the self-knowing subject that grounds it, Hegel's overarching purpose was to demonstrate the deeply social nature of the modern individual who could, he argued, be 'at-home-in-the-world'. This process entailed, for Hegel, a simultaneously affirmative and negative impulse: affirmative via recognition of the fundamental *interdependence* that sutured and shaped the individual to the social practices and institutions of cultural, aesthetic, economic, and political life (in the family, civil society and the state); and negative via the individual's creative and transformative capacity to shape the world (of nature, objects, and things), thereby actualizing (fashioning) a particular, specific, way of being a self. The pivotal role that ideas of relationality and interdependence play in Hegel's philosophy thus repudiate claims that 'Absolute Knowing' for Hegel implies 'absolute knowing of absolutely everything'. It is this systematic focus on the centrality of interdependence, co-constitution, or what we might simply call the *social*, as the very ground of Hegel's thought that renders his work particularly apt as a critical resource in contemporary international relations scholarship. For, any theory that takes the primacy of the social (as co-construction) as its starting point, cannot sustain a defence of either liberal authoritarianism (the notion of sovereign, autonomous, self-subsistent states or subjects), or an account of ethics (as obligation or responsibility to an/other state or subject) in global social life that is supplementary (and therefore always precarious or contingent) to an inter-national system of self-subsistent states. Thus, a Hegelian focus on relationality as the constitutive ground of difference can invigorate critical understandings of the 'human' across a range of discourses in critical international relations, including discussions of poverty, inequality, and welfare in political economy, human rights, global ethics, difference and justice. Three illustrations of this claim, speaking against the grain of critical theory's resistance to Hegelian thought, will have to suffice here.

The centrality of the 'state' in Hegel's philosophical system has rendered his work suspect in a critical international relations particularly suspicious of state-centric political imaginaries and the long history of violence associated with the exclusionary practices on which claims of state sovereignty are seen to rest. In *The Philosophy of Right* Hegel outlines a social and political philosophy, however, which sees modern social life unfolding in three primary realms (or institutions) of family, civil society and state. The family, marked by relations of love and obligation stands in sharp contrast with that of civil society, the realm of economic exchange relations where the pursuit of pure self-interest enables the realization of what Hegel calls 'subjective particularity' (individuality) (via production and consumption) that nonetheless betrays a deeply social character (via the division of labour, specialization, and the system of needs) that is the hallmark of modern (capitalist) economic life. Life within the family and civil society, however, is made possible and contained within a broader context of law and regulation via the 'administrative state' (what we would simply refer to as the 'government'). The concept of the State proper, however, as an 'ethical community', contains all three (the family, civil society and administrative state), and is best seen as an *abstract structure*, signifying primarily a *mode of relating* that enables the various forms of life contained therein (the social practices and institutions of family, civil society, and 'government'. That is, the claim about the ethicality of the State as an abstract structure is grounded, as *The Philosophy of Right* makes abundantly clear, in the *social relationality* of which it is deemed to be the highest expression. The claim that Hegel's powerful endorsement of the State (as an abstract structure or mode of relating) translates straightforwardly into an empirical defence of 'actually existing states' is thus a tenuous one, leaving open for critical uptake consideration of whether, and under what conditions, an alternative global imaginary might entail, *contra* critical repudiations of the question of the state, *re-posing* the question of the State (on Hegel's terms) in our times.

A second illustration of the timeliness of Hegel's thought in contemporary critical international relations scholarship can be made in the context of Hegel's nuanced understanding of civil society and its systemic generation of wealth and poverty. Unlike liberal readings of the virtues of the capitalist 'free-market', Hegel's conceptualization of civil society as the realm of 'universal egoism', where each pursues their own interest through exchange relations in the market offers a powerful repudiation of economistic understandings of the market. Participation in the social division of labour, and the socially constituted system of meanings and needs contained in production and consumption is, for Hegel, *intrinsic* to the realization of self and social worth. Because, however, capitalist exchange relations make livelihood dependent on exchange (labour for wages), the failure of exchange means that the market generates wealth *and* poverty, necessitating the role of the state in creating a facilitating environment for optimizing exchange relations. More pointedly, however, Hegel's deeply non-economistic conception of poverty, not as a debilitating condition of 'lack' (of income, employment, technology, or education, that has anchored, as we know all too well, a neo-colonial modernization discourse of 'development' in parts of the world most vividly seen as embodiments of 'lack'), urges the more radically critical gesture of re-posing not only what Adam Smith referred to as the 'boundary question' (between state and market), but also the more complicated question of re-thinking the 'limits' of civil society.

Finally, the 'master/slave dialectic' of *The Phenomenology of Spirit*, undoubtedly Hegel's best known contribution to a critical discourse con-cerned with the deep relationality and co-construction of self and other offers, recent critical commentary notwithstanding, one of the most powerful resources for contemporary critical international relations. For Hegel, free-dom entails the movement from various (lower) forms of consciousness (either wholly external/objective or wholly subjective/inward) to a higher stage of self-consciousness that is possible only via a dialectic of *mutual recognition*: the recognition of self afforded by an other, who is in turn duly recognized as a distinct (other) self. The power of this formulation obtains through Hegel's consideration of its phenomenological aspects in a context of servitude. In Chapter 4 'On Lordship and Bondage' in *The Phenomenol-ogy of Spirit*, Hegel traces the overturning of the feudal relationship between 'lord' and 'bondsman' as the bondsman indentured to his lord comes to a slow realization of self-worth: in transforming raw materials into objects of use for his lord via the expenditure of his energy and creative labour, the bondsman 'takes possession' of himself as independent being, whereas the 'lord' in utter dependency on the labour of the bondsman, confronts the hollow shell of his claims to (self) mastery. The necessity of one (self) to the other is made powerfully clear, all the more because Hegel's narrative of purposive history as the actualization of freedom depends on this negative duplicated self-consciousness. In the context of world history, however, it grounds a powerful vindication of anti-colonial struggles by the margin-alized, dispossessed, un-represented subjects of international relations, even as it enables a critical reading of the hollowness of claims to mastery pre-dicated on the accumulation of wealth in an increasingly unequal world. This is the case notwithstanding recent critiques (Buck-Morss 2000 and Bernasconi 1998 especially) that draw attention to the racist imagery that informs Hegel's commentary on Africa in *The Philosophy of History*, and the absence of any explicit mention of the Haitian revolution of Saint-Dominigue in 1804 in *The Philosophy of Right* (published in 1821). Tellingly, as Nesbitt (2004) points out, in *The Philosophy of Right*, Hegel abandons the feudal reference to *knechten* (bondage) and uses instead the more abstract *sklaverai* (slavery) to condemn slavery as an absolute wrong. Although he does not name it, in 1820, he could only have been referring to the Haitian revolution.

Further reading

Selected key Hegel texts

Hegel, G.W.F. (1977) *Phenomenology of Spirit*, trans. A.V. Miller, Oxford: Oxford University Press.

Hegel, G.W.F. (1976) *Hegel's Philosophy of Right*, trans. with notes T.M Knox, Oxford: Oxford University Press.
Hegel. G.W.F. (2001) *Philosophy of World History*, trans. J. Sibree, Kitchener, Ontario: Batoche Books.

Introductions to Hegel's social and political thought

Avineri, Shlomo (1972) *Hegel's Theory of the Modern State*, Cambridge: Cambridge University Press.
Kojeve, Alexandre (1969) *Introduction to the Reading of Hegel*, ed. Allan Bloom, trans. James H. Nichols, Jr., New York: Basic Books.
Plant, Raymond (1977) "Hegel and Political Economy 1 and 2", *New Left Review* 103: 79–92; and 104: 103–13.
Taylor, Charles (1975) *Hegel*, Cambridge: Cambridge University Press.

Discussions of Hegel's thought in international relations

Bernasconi, Robert (1998) 'Hegel at the Court of Ashanti', in Stuart Barnett (ed). *Hegel After Derrida*, New York: Routledge.
Brown, Chris (1992) *International Relations Theory: New Normative Approaches*, London: Harvester Wheatsheaf.
Buck-Morss, Susan (2000) " Hegel and Haiti", *Critical Inquiry*, 26 (4): 821–65.
Frost, Mervyn (1996) *Ethics in International Relations: a Constitutive Theory*, Cambridge: Cambridge University Press.
Hutchings, Kimberly (2003) *Hegel and Feminist Philosophy*, Cambridge: Polity Press.
Nesbitt, Nick (2004) 'Troping Toussaint, Reading Revolution', *Research in African Literatures* 35 (2): 18–33.
Smith, Steven B. (1983) 'Hegel's Views on War, the State, and International Relations', *The American Political Science Review*, 77 (3): 624–32.
Vij, Ritu (2009) (ed.) *Hegelian Encounters: Subjects of International Relations*, Palgrave.

19 Martin Heidegger

Louiza Odysseos

Martin Heidegger was born in Meßkirch in 1889. Under the advice of Dr. Conrad Gröber, during his years at gymnasium in Freiburg, Heidegger became interested in the Greeks but also in the thought of Franz Brentano and in particular his *On the Manifold Meaning of Being According to Aristotle* (1862). Both were to prove a great influence on him and were to lead him to engage with and eventually move beyond Edmund Husserl's phenomenology.

When Heidegger turned twenty years of age he joined the Society of Jesus at Tisis in Austria to train as a Jesuit but he was not allowed to remain there, possibly due to poor health. Entering the Albert-Ludwig University in Freiburg to study theology and prepare for the priesthood, Heidegger became exposed to Husserl's writings and began to publish his own papers and to lecture. Changing his studies to Catholic philosophy and mathematics, he devoted himself to a close and critical engagement with the work of Husserl and Wilhelm Dilthey, receiving his doctorate in 1913 for his thesis on *The Doctrine of Judgment in Psychologism* and submitting a qualifying dissertation [*Habilitationsschrift*] in 1915 under the title of *The Theory of Categories and Meaning of Duns Scotus*. Following his 1917 marriage to Elfride Petri, Heidegger entered the military but again was discharged due to poor health less than a year later. In 1919, Heidegger broke with Catholicism altogether, describing it as dogmatic. It was at this same time that Heidegger became Husserl's assistant at the University of Freiburg, where the latter had been professor of Philosophy since 1916, helping to edit his writings for *The Phenomenology of Internal Time-consciousness*. At Freiburg, Heidegger also began a longstanding association with Karl Jaspers that would be broken only with Heidegger's involvement with the Nazis in the 1930s. In 1923, with the help of neo-Kantian philosopher Paul Natorp who had been greatly impressed by the possibilities in Heidegger's 1922 essay 'Phenomenological Interpretations with Respect to Aristotle: Indication of the Hermeneutical Situation' (1992), Heidegger took up a junior position at the University of Marburg. It was during his time at Marburg that he would write his seminal *Being and Time* [*Sein und Zeit*] (1962). Rumours of his daring and brilliant lectures at Marburg, deriving from his work on the question of Being and the analysis of human existence [*Daseinanalytik*] that would form the basis of

Being and Time, spread like wildfire: Germany's philosophical circles reverberated with excitement at the prospect of a new 'hidden king of philosophy' (van Buren 1994). It was these lectures at Marburg that drew to him as students some of the most prominent thinkers of the twentieth century such as Hannah Arendt, who also became his lover, Herbert Marcuse, Hans-Georg Gadamer, Karl Löwith, Hans Jonas, and others (Wolin 2003).

Following the critical acclaim that accompanied the 1927 publication of *Being and Time*, Heidegger returned in 1928 to Freiburg to take over Husserl's chair of philosophy. Husserl himself regarded Heidegger as the only suitable successor to his professorship and the person to lead the emerging phenomenological movement, despite awareness that Heidegger's overriding concern with the question of Being increasingly differed substantially from Husserl's own focus on transcendental subjectivity and would eventually require the radicalization of phenomenology itself towards ontology and deconstruction, as is discussed below. This would be evident not only with the publication of *Being and Time* but also with the so-called 'Turn' [*Kehre*] which Heidegger's thinking underwent in the late 1920s, forming a major influence in the development of hermeneutics (most prominently associated with Gadamer, his one-time student), French phenomenology (Emmanuel Levinas) and, later, poststructuralism (Michel Foucault, Jacques Derrida, Gilles Deleuze, Jean-Luc Nancy, Philippe Lacoue-Labarthe, among others).

Even this brief account of Heidegger's life would not be complete without mention of his involvement with the National Socialists soon after Adolf Hitler's rise to power (Wolin 1991). He was elected to the rectorship of the University of Freiburg in April 1933, joining the Nazi Party a few weeks later and delivering a number of lectures offering support for Hitler and his policies, but at the same time supporting some of his Jewish students like Karl Löwith and friends like Elisabeth Blochmann. His membership of the Party would last for the entirety of the Nazi years and the Second World War, despite his resignation as rector in 1934.

Following his resignation from the position of rector, Heidegger worked on some of the major philosophical themes of his career. In 1935 he gave his famous lecture on 'The Origin of the Work of Art' and by 1938 he completed his second major book *Contributions to Philosophy* (1999b). His courses on Nietzsche contained a critical examination of power, seen to apply to National Socialist thought, and this brought Heidegger to the attention of the Gestapo, which monitored his lectures. Following Allied victory in 1945, Heidegger underwent de-nazification, being barred from teaching on the advice of his one-time associate Karl Jaspers, which lasted until 1949. His many students, most notably Marcuse who had migrated to the United States, called on Heidegger to apologize and explain his Nazi involvement but Heidegger did not, remaining perhaps committed to an ideal or philosophical national socialism (Derrida 1995c).

In post-war years, Heidegger began a friendship with Jean Beaufret who would be instrumental in making Heidegger's thought known in France and whose questions would prompt Heidegger to write his influential 'Letter on

Humanism' (1998). His work took up the question of Being again under the heading of the 'history of Being' and resulted in a series of prominent lectures, such as, *inter alia*, 'What is Called Thinking?' (1968) and 'The Question Concerning Technology' (1977b) in the late 1940s and 1950s. At this time, Heidegger resumed his friendship with Hannah Arendt, who had migrated to the US and become a prominent political thinker in her own right. Now a professor emeritus, he continued to give lectures in Germany and throughout Europe and published his multi-volume work on Nietzsche in 1961 (1991a, 1991b). In 1966 Heidegger gave an interview to *Der Spiegel*, a prominent German magazine, about his involvement with the Nazis, philosophical outlook and views of the future, which would be published only posthumously at his own request (1977c). Heidegger died on 26 May 1976 and was buried in Meßkirch.

Heidegger's concern with Being

Even those of us unfamiliar with the work of Heidegger may be aware that his lifelong project revolved around restating the question of 'Being' as *the* question of philosophy. Even in his early thought, Heidegger was concerned that the most question-worthy area of thinking had been neglected, or, more accurately, that extant answers precluded Being from presenting itself as continuously question-worthy. Indeed, he wanted to understand why and how this peculiar 'oblivion' of Being came about. His project wished precisely to interrogate the question of Being beyond its 'traditional philosophical meanings' (Sheehan 2001a: 5). For this he relied on what he called the ontological difference, which refers to a distinction between Being [*das Sein*] and beings [*das Seiende*]. This is central to Heidegger's philosophy because it is the obscuring of this distinction which leads to the forgetting or oblivion of Being in Western thought (Heidegger 1982: 318–30).

In order to refocus philosophical inquiry towards the question of Being, Heidegger suggested early on (Heidegger 1992) that the question asked by traditional ontology, namely, 'what is the being of entities or beings?' had to be preceded by a question about the *meaning* of Being, highlighting the need for reflection on the 'conditions for the possibility of having any understanding whatsoever' (Guignon 1993: 5; van Buren 1994: 38; Heidegger 1962: 25; Sheehan 2001b). In G.W. von Leibniz's words: 'why should there be any being at all and not rather nothing?' The type of inquiry Heidegger wanted to conduct into Being he called *fundamental ontology*, understood as a philosophical endeavour inseparable from the 'destruction' [*Abbau*] of ontology, which for Heidegger meant not a rejection of the ontological tradition but rather a critical re-appropriation of its positive aspects (Heidegger 1962: 6).

The reduction of Being to presence

The genesis of ontology in ancient Greece can be seen as a development facilitated in part by the linguistic existence of distinct terms for 'beings' [*ta onta*], 'to be' [*einai*] and 'the nature of beings', as expressed in the abstract noun 'being' [*ousia*]. This led the Greeks to question 'whether there is a unified meaning of *being* that accrues to all beings (in contradistinction to "what is not")'; could there be, in other words, a 'unitary concept that demarcates the realm of Being as such'? (Frede 1993: 44). On the face of it, the Greeks appeared to experience being in multiple and distinct ways: as 'an intelligible place (*Republic* 508c), an open area of truth in the sense of unconcealment (*aletheia*), light (*phos*) or radiant appearing (*phainesthai*), and emergence (*physis*)' (van Buren 1994: 31). While these apparently different metaphysical positions appeared as 'competing answers – for example, being (Parmernides), *logos* (Heraclitus), idea (Plato), category, being-in-work (Aristotle)' (van Buren 1994: 31) – they were articulated within a 'deeper unanimity' provided by a sense of Being as the *aition*, i.e. as 'a causal ground for beings', or simply as substance (van Buren 1994: 30). This emphasis on ground, substance or 'whatness' means that 'when the distinction of essence and existence arises, it is essence, whatness, which takes priority' (Stambaugh 1973: x) in Greek thought, leading it and later philosophy to privilege beings ('permanent presence', i.e. what 'factually exists') as opposed to Being ('presenc*ing*') (Stambaugh 1973: x). Interestingly, moreover, this understanding of Being as ground or substance 'was also taken to be itself a being … the highest and most honored being in the hierarchical-teleological order of the cosmos', in other words, the divine (van Buren 1994: 30–1). As such, the Greeks 'stood in an ocular relation' of seeing, gazing and wonderment to Being, replete with phenomenological possibilities yet possibilities nevertheless mediated through *logos* 'in the inclusive sense of theory, thought, and assertion' (van Buren 1994: 33).

The rise of man as subject

In thinking about substance as 'permanent presence', Heidegger became interested in a fundamental change that comes about in modernity, in which man asserts himself as this presence, as the permanent ground of all things: as *hypokeimenon* or *subjectum*. Heidegger understood 'all metaphysics' to be 'characterized by "subjectity", but in modern philosophy this is transformed into "subjectivity"' (Carr 1995: 404). In the pre-modern context of Greek philosophy there was no relation or equation of *hypokeimenon* to 'man' or human being. For the Greeks, 'subject' indicated a predicate which acted as a foundation 'which persists through … the changes that form [*morphe*] imposes on it' (Critchley 1996: 13), that is, the underlying, unchanging predicate which itself required no further foundation. This, however, as Heidegger argued, denotes 'no special relationship to man and none at all to the I' (Heidegger 1977a: 128). The creation of a relationship between man, seen as the ultimate predicate [*hypokeimenon*], and constancy, in the sense of continuous presence and certainty, must be grasped within the context of seventeenth century metaphysics and the loss of certainty resulting from the collapse of the divine ultimate foundations of the medieval order. With the advent of *modern* metaphysics, 'man' asserts himself as this final ground (Clarke 1999: 15). Man, as final foundation 'had not only to be itself one that was certain, but since every standard of measure from any other sphere was forbidden, it had at the same time to be of such a kind that through it the essence of the freedom claimed would be posited as self-certainty' (Heidegger 1977a: 148–49).

French philosopher René Descartes enabled the creation of a different, human-based, and self-sufficient kind of certainty in the seventeenth century (Heidegger 1991a: 99–100), seen best in the principle *ego cogito, ergo sum*, put forward as the essential feature of subjectivity (Heidegger 1967: 98–108, 1977a; Judovitz 1988). The distinguishing feature of metaphysics in the modern age, therefore, 'is that the metaphysical foundation is no longer claimed to reside in a form, substance, or deity outside of the human intellect but is rather found in the human being understood as subject' (Critchley 1996: 15). Descartes disregarded an *analysis* of man that would adequately account for his embeddedness *within* the world, relying instead on the idea of substance to describe the world and innerworldly entities (Heidegger 1962: 123–29). By equating the Being of the world with substance and presence, Descartes came to define human being by *distinction* to substance, as that being or entity defined by its reflective capacity, the 'I think'. In Heidegger's view, the modern conception of the subject, and therefore of man, was nevertheless infiltrated by (i.e. in opposition to) the notion of substance (Heidegger 1962: 123–31), a Cartesian legacy of the emphasis on the *cogito* to the detriment of the *sum* (Heidegger 1962: 131; McCumber 1999: 219). For Heidegger, however, grasping the subject in relation to substance was phenomenally inadequate 'as a descriptive framework for the fabric of our lives' (McCumber 1999: 206). Indeed, Heidegger wanted to challenge the reliance of the ontological tradition of philosophy on the subject, asking:

> how does man come to play the role of the one and only *subject* proper? Why is the human subject transposed into the 'I', so that subjectivity here becomes coterminous with I-ness? Is subjectivity defined through I-ness, or the reverse, I-ness through subjectivity? (Heidegger 1991: 96)

Heidegger set out to challenge the use of the modern subject, which had grounded post-Cartesian philosophy on the basis of prior presuppositions. He proposed, instead, both to abandon the equivalence of human existence to the 'I' and also to examine the structures and 'phenomenal content [*Bestand*]' of human existence obscured in post-Cartesian ontology (Heidegger 1962: 72). He therefore sought a *method* that would allow him to move beyond the theoretic construction of the modern subject and the assumptions and presuppositions that philosophy held about it, in order to access lived experience.

Phenomenology and ontology

This led Heidegger to engage with and eventually challenge Husserl's phenomenological method. Heidegger's appropriation steered phenomenology towards hermeneutics, a move that would radicalize it, moving it away from the attempt to isolate the pure ego from its perceptual objects and enable it, instead, to gain access to the *facticity* of existence, to existence *as* it shows itself (Sallis 1978: 49). Phenomenology and ontology, in this way, became explicitly intertwined because, in *hermeneutic* phenomenology, the 'perceiving subject' turns to inquire about *itself* as the perceptual object. What might life reveal itself to be, when it is not grasped by theoretical constructs that pay little attention to the facticity of life? Heidegger explored this question throughout the 1920s (Heidegger 1999a) and it is in doing so that he began interrogating 'existence' under the heading of *Dasein*, the everyday German term for existence, which literally means 'Being-there' (or, 'being the there of Being') in *Being and Time*.

Heidegger wished to tap into the implicit, non-intuitive understanding which existence has of itself (Heidegger 1962: 59) because, *'fundamental ontology*, from which almost all ontologies can take their rise, must be sought in the *existential analytic* of Dasein' (Heidegger 1962: 34). For Heidegger, 'Dasein' was the being which has some understanding of Being, although this understanding is superficial, saturated with pre-existing theories which occlude proper consideration and sanction neglect of the *question* of Being. Thus, in order to gain a better understanding of Being, Heidegger began with an investigation of the existential structures of Dasein, which, in turn, also served to call into question, to 'unwork' in other words, extant presuppositions about the modern, masterful, self-certain, reflective and sovereign subject. Heidegger began his fundamental ontology with an examination of the structures of human existence because he discerned three closely related ways in which Dasein had priority. First, Dasein is not merely present in the world: its 'presence' has the '*determinate* character of existence' and as such it exhibits ontical priority, where ontic refers to features which have to do with beings as opposed to Being. Second, Dasein has an ontological priority because Dasein's 'existence is … *determinative* for it' (Heidegger 1962: 34; emphasis added). Simply put, because Dasein is the being which asks the *question* of Being, its own existence is an issue for it. Third, 'Dasein also possesses – as constitutive for its understanding of existence – an understanding of Being of all entities of a character other than its own' (Heidegger 1962: 34). It is this understanding that Dasein has of beings which makes Dasein the being that it is. Its understanding of other entities in the world gives Dasein a priority, in that its existence is the precondition for 'all ontologies' (Heidegger 1962: 34). These priorities are revealed to be related, therefore, to *Dasein's factical being as existence*. As Jacques Taminioux clarifies:

> Heidegger at that time agrees with modern philosophy, from Descartes to Husserl, that philosophical investigation has for its ground the being

that we ourselves are. What he disagrees with is not the priority of our own being, but the ontological definition of our being (Taminiaux 1999: 235).

He proposed, therefore, that phenomenology distance itself from the post-Cartesian emphasis on the sovereign and 'worldless' subject (Øverenget 1998: 1): rather it 'ought to begin by paying attention to the intentional behaviour of man in his concrete and daily life, to the ways in which man actually comports himself to the things of the world' (Bernet 1990: 146). For this purpose, Heidegger avoided positing a theoretical account of human existence which isolates it from its world; on the contrary, he wished to show that Dasein's dealings in the world are *always already* infused with meaning, and take place within already existing and other-created intelligibility. Such availability of existing, other-determined, meaning, in turn, leads to wonderment: to the question of Being itself (Pippin 1997: 379). Dasein's paradoxical priority, in other words, lies in its capacity to ask the question of Being but at the same time to neglect it; and this led Heidegger to a phenomenological investigation of Dasein, to a uniting of phenomenology with ontology.

Methodologically, therefore, Heidegger's concern with ontology and his search for a method for ontological examination arrived at a convergence, 'a point where they are one and the same: a hermeneutics *of* facticity' (Kisiel 1993: 21; Heidegger 1999a). The genitive 'of' is a double genitive. It means that Dasein's understanding, *Verstehen*, belongs to (its) facticity; and at the same time, it means that understanding takes facticity as its object (van Buren 1994: 94). John D. Caputo argues that 'Dasein's understanding of Being is the sole condition under which both ontology and phenomenology are possible' (1978: 103). Not only is phenomenology possible solely as ontology, but '*only as phenomenology, is ontology possible*' (Heidegger 1962: 60). In other words, 'it is only under the condition that Dasein understands Being that beings can be experienced as beings (phenomenology) and that they can be understood to be (ontology)' (Caputo 1978: 103).

Moreover, Heidegger's initial attempts to refocus attention on the question of Being and on the difference between Being and beings (the 'ontological difference' which had remained 'unthought' by philosophy) entailed also the 'destruction' of traditional ontology. As Heidegger understood it, the notion of destruction, or 'deconstruction', does not *overcome* a tradition, but rather, searches for and retains its positive possibilities, which are subsequently used to transform the tradition's *problematique* and preserve it as a possible *question*. As Derrida notes: 'Heidegger recognises that economically and strategically he had to borrow the syntaxic and lexical resources of the language of metaphysics, as one must always do at the very moment that one deconstructs this language' (2002: 8). Heidegger's convergence of matter (ontology) and method (phenomenology) meant that destruction, 'a counter to the pervasive tendency of objectification' (Kisiel 1993: 117), was also rendered inseparable from phenomenology.

Existential analysis and *Being and Time*

As noted briefly above, Heidegger's search for a method with which to access lived experience and pose anew the question of Being for philosophy also led him to 'unwork' modern subjectivity (Odysseos 2007b; Pippin 1997; Critchley 1996). Specifically, Heidegger's account of Dasein as Being-in-the-world diverges substantially from previous Cartesian and post-Cartesian articulations of subjectivity. Whereas such accounts tended to posit the subject as an isolated and self-sufficient being, Heidegger's existential analytic begins, instead, from the premise that it is misleading to assume that the answer to the question 'who is Dasein?' is the (worldless, self-sufficient and masterful) 'I' (Heidegger 1991a: 85–122; Menke 1999). Heidegger's phenomenological analyses in *Being and Time* suggest, moreover, that the theoretical positing of Dasein as subject is phenomenally inadequate at the ontological level.

Importantly, avoiding the assumptions of modern subjectivity and using existential analysis to 'unwork' it enabled Heidegger to attend to existence in its facticity and reveal it in its *heteronomy*, a term which signifies the constitutive role of otherness, so that Heidegger's *magnum opus*, *Being and Time*, can be read as a *heterology*, a discourse about *to heteron*, the other. Specifically, there are four distinct, but related, elements in Heidegger's existential analysis which highlight not only the fact of the self's constitution by otherness, but also the ways in which this is manifested in the self's everyday life. First, Dasein initially and primarily [*zunächst und zumeist*] finds itself immersed in the world (understood not as nature but as a surrounding withworld). Understanding Dasein as existing primarily in the mode of 'engaged immersion' (Žižek 1999: 15) in the world helps to shift emphasis away from reflection and 'knowing' as the definitive modes of human relationality. In other words, Dasein's main relationship to other beings cannot be assumed to be one of knowing; Dasein does not initially and primarily encounter entities and the world as 'objects' of comprehension. Rather, Dasein is immersed continuously amongst things *and* other beings of its own character in a more fundamental and immediate way, allaying some of the fears about phenomenology's reliance on the knowing and perceiving subject (Levinas 1969: 45). More importantly, challenging the reflective relationship of comprehension and, therefore, of objectification, which the modern subject has towards other beings and the world, allowed Heidegger to bring to the fore the disclosive character of existence. His analyses illustrated how Dasein discloses the Being of other entities, while at the same time existing pre-reflectively and 'outside of itself' amongst the things and beings that constitute it.

Second, Dasein's dealings (or 'comportments') while immersed in daily work and other activities disclose a different conception of the *world* as such (Heidegger 1962: 18). Thinking of existence as engaged immersion enabled Heidegger to recast the 'world', not as 'nature' or a container of things, but as a web of involvements with other beings, as a background of meanings against which existence makes sense of itself *pre-reflectively*. Revealing the world as a totality of meanings, references, and relations also illuminated that this is a web which is not created by Dasein alone. Rather, Dasein's way of life, the meanings, norms and rules that help it go about its business in the world, are structured by others and are only *shared* by Dasein. This dependence that Dasein has on other-created meanings and understandings signifies that Dasein has an ontological relationship to the world.

Third, Dasein is Being-in-the-world *with others*. This means that for Dasein, existence is already coexistence. Being-there is always Being-with, to such an extent that Dasein is indistinguishable from others: existential analysis shows how Dasein is not an 'I' but the 'they' (Heidegger 1962: 25–7). Selfhood, in other words, is coexistential in its constitution, where such an understanding of 'coexistence' is not tantamount to the uniting, composition, or co-presence, of completed and autonomous subjects (Odysseos 2007b: 70–94). Finally, Dasein is fundamentally attuned to the world in which it exists and its understanding of itself and other entities is affected by this attunement. Dasein's radical attunement shows it to be a being *thrown* into its world, rather than exercising mastery and control over it; at the same time, its understanding of itself as 'possibility' indicates that Dasein is also future-oriented, that it projects itself towards the future. Taken together, the aspects of Dasein's fundamental attunement and situated understanding indicate that its world matters terribly to it; in other words, Dasein is an embedded entity better understood as *care* (Heidegger 1962: 63).

When viewed together, these analyses emerging out of Heidegger's phenomenology of everydayness contest the presuppositions of modern subjectivity and elucidate instead coexistential heteronomy of human existence (Odysseos 2007b). It is from this, Heidegger's crucial articulation and challenge to modernity's chief construct and sole foundation, that subsequent philosophy, social and international theory take their impetus to further 'unwork' the modern subject, arguably the single most important philosophical endeavour of the twentieth century. For a vast range of undertakings, from Michel Foucault's *The Order of Things* to Emmanuel Levinas' concern with the other, to international theory's attempt to speak, in the context of the end of philosophy, for an ethical, environmentally-conscious selfhood, Heidegger acts as the interlocutor (Foucault 1974; Levinas 1969; Campbell 1998; Odysseos 2003, 2007b; Seckinelgin 2006).

The question concerning technology

After the 'Turn', Heidegger began to examine the neglect of the question of Being as a particular 'sending' of Being, to be understood as if Being were, in a sense, hiding from man. He turned his attention to modernity as constituting 'the final stage in the history of the decline of the West from the great age of the Greeks to the technological nihilism of the twentieth century' (Zimmermann 1990: 3). For Heidegger, the forgetfulness of Being signals the end of philosophy, seen in its evolution into the technological 'nihilism' of metaphysics, or into a *technological* understanding of Being, by which Heidegger means knowledge produced by distinct sciences and disciplines about 'what-ness' (Heidegger 1991a; Stambaugh 1973). Modern technology, which becomes a central focus in Heidegger's later thought, has little to do with scientific processes, tools, or machines, as we are inclined to think today; rather, technology 'is a way of revealing' the world and beings within the world (Heidegger 1977b: 12). When Heidegger speaks of the planetary domination of technology, modern technology cannot be taken to mean 'a set of tools for some people's material culture – as one would speak of Roman or medieval technology – but … the phenomenal configuration of the twentieth century' (Schürmann 1987: 17).

What does it mean to suggest that technology is a way of revealing? Technology, as a human activity, has existed historically in various forms. To indicate that modern technology, while still being a form of human activity, is radically new and different, and that this tells us something important for the history of Being, Heidegger compared the modern way of revealing with that of the Greeks. For the Greeks, *technē* was a substantially different mode of revealing, a 'bringing-forth', a *poiēsis* which 'occasions' something, which brings it into unconcealment, i.e. a 'mode of *alētheuein*' (Heidegger 1977b: 13). For the modern age, however, *technē* became transformed from a 'bringing-forth' into a 'challenging' which 'sets upon' things and nature in order to regulate and order them so that their energy and use is unlocked, exposed and stored for available use (Heidegger 1977b: 13–17). Things are no longer 'objects' for a subject. Beings and nature itself are now amassed, regulated, secured and ordered as stockpiles or, in Heidegger's term, 'standing-reserve' [*Bestand*] so that they can 'stand-by … on call for a further ordering' (Heidegger 1977b: 16–17; Smith 2007: 170).

The role of 'man' or the subject also becomes reconfigured here, because, although technology in the modern age is still an activity of human beings, one cannot understand modern technology, as expounded by Heidegger, as a process in which the modern subject reigns. On the contrary, a claim is made by Being itself upon human beings 'to order the self-revealing as standing-reserve' (Heidegger 1977b: 19). This claim, made by Being *upon* modern man, is a 'destining' or 'sending' of Being (Heidegger 1977b: 24): Heidegger calls this *das Gestell*, translated as 'Enframing' or 'Set-up'. Caputo notes that 'in the world of *Gestell* Being calls to man in the form of a challenge issued to man to master the earth' (1983: 449). Humankind is not completely in control of modern technology, if it is understood in its essence, yet, there is a special place for human beings in this process of revealing, as they are called upon to execute or to bring about such ordering and regulation of entities, and to participate in this kind of revealing. Man's place in Enframing is central but ambivalent: in modernity, man 'can indeed conceive, fashion, and carry through this or that in one way or another', says Heidegger, 'but man does not have control over unconcealment' (Heidegger 1977b: 18).

Enframing, therefore, is a 'mode of world-disclosure, that Heidegger argues defines the ethos, or way of being, that characterizes the modern age' (Rayner 2001: 143) and as such it operates *through* man as the modern subject held within the grasp of modern technology, 'which is itself nothing technological' (Heidegger 1977b: 20). How has man responded to Being's challenge? Caputo suggests that:

> technological man responds to the challenge and takes up the call by means of a technical-calculative assault upon beings meant to subdue them to human purposes. The world in this epoch of *Gestell* is a storehouse of raw material, a stock-pile, which submits to the machinations and manipulations of technical man (Caputo 1983: 449–50).

The post-Cartesian, modern subject's characteristic capacity and tendency towards representational thinking and calculative knowing are not unrelated to man's aggressive appropriation of nature and his masterful relationality towards others in general (Durst 1998). It is this kind of thinking that goes on to find expression not only in production and in organisational processes, but even in the search for scientific-technical knowledge in modernity (Caputo 1983: 446). Enframing is 'the age in which man assumes the *mistaken posture* of the lord of the earth' (Caputo 1983: 455; emphasis added). The modern age of technology is the age in which modern subjectivity establishes itself as the centre of the world, in denial of the way in which it is challenged by the sending of Being. In this way, 'the subject signifies a new way of being human', a technological mode of existence, 'one that has to do with the rationalization of human capabilities through their delimitation and economization in order to master the world through representation' (Judovitz 1988: 181).

Heidegger's account of *Gestell* and of the emergence and dominance of *world-ordering* representational thought, in which entities are rendered as 'standing-reserve', also has a political significance. Eras, or epochs, are configured according to 'epochal' principles and this is not merely a determination of the phenomenal domain; rather, it involves an understanding of the political as the site of the manifestation of the epochal principle that configures a specific age (Schürmann 1987). The political becomes, then, that locus or site that 'makes public, literally exposes, the epochal principle which life otherwise obeys tacitly' (Schürmann 1987: 40), as its world-historical manifestation.

Further reading

de Beistegui, Miguel (1997) *Heidegger and the Political: Dystopias*, London: Routledge. Philosophical but accessible treatment of the political aspects of Heidegger's thought and the 'Heidegger affair'.

Farias, Victor (1989) *Heidegger and Nazism*, trans. P. Burrell and G.R. Ricci, Philadelphia: Temple University Press. Prominent initial exposition of the extent of Heidegger's involvement with the Nazis, which has itself become the subject of later critique and debate.

Heidegger, Martin (1973) *The End of Philosophy*, trans. J. Stambaugh, New York: Harper and Row. Important collection of later essays indicative of Heidegger's focus on metaphysics as history of Being, containing important pieces such as 'Overcoming Metaphysics'.

Heidegger, Martin (1985) 'The self-assertion of the German university', trans. K. Harries, *Review of Metaphysics* 38: 470–80. Heidegger's controversial address to the University of Freiburg upon his assumption of the post of Rector under the Nazis.

Heidegger, Martin (1991b) *Nietzsche*, trans. D.F. Krell, Vols 1–4, New York: Harper and Row. Important collection over four volumes of the 1936–37 lecture course, in which Heidegger critically engages with and appraises Nietzsche's break with Platonism as still caught up in a 'metaphysics of subjectivity'.

Heidegger, Martin (2000) *An Introduction to Metaphysics*, trans. G. Fried and R. Polt, New Haven: Yale University Press, and Richard Polt and Gregory Fried (eds) (2001) *A Companion to Heidegger's Introduction to Metaphysics*, New Haven: Yale University Press. Influential text of the 1935 lectures by the same name in which Heidegger interrogates the question 'Why are there beings instead of nothing?' The companion volume contains important essays on the ontological decline of the West (M.E. Zimmermann) and Heidegger's conception of politics (H. Sluga).

Hodge, Joanna (1995) *Heidegger and Ethics*, London: Routledge. Important contribution on the neglected ethical aspects of Heidegger's thought.

Mulhall, Stephen (1996) *Heidegger and Being and Time*, London: Routledge. Accessible, thematically organised and widely used introduction to Heidegger's major work.

Odysseos, Louiza (2007b) *The Subject of Coexistence: Otherness in International Relations*, Minneapolis: University of Minnesota Press. Book-length engagement with Heidegger's thought, and particularly his critique of subjectivity, critically appropriated for a reorientation of 'coexistence', 'ethics' and 'community' towards otherness in international relations.

Seckinelgin, Hakan (2006) *International Relations and the Environment: International Fisheries, Heidegger, and social method*, London: Routledge. Critical book-length engagement and use of Heidegger's thought to interrogate the philosophical basis of international relations and its understanding of the environment.

Wolin, Richard (ed.) (1991) *The Heidegger Controversy: A Critical Reader*, Cambridge: MIT Press. Critical edited collection of essays on Heidegger's involvement with the Nazis.

20 Immanuel Kant

Kimberly Hutchings

Kant spent his long working life teaching at the university in the port of Königsberg, the Prussian town in which he was born. But even though he didn't travel, he was an active participant in the philosophical debates of his time in Europe, and his ideas continue to shape and influence fields of philosophical inquiry from epistemology to the philosophy of history. From the perspective of the history of European thought in general, it is impossible to overestimate the importance of his later work, the critical philosophy published, in particular, in the texts, *Critique of Pure Reason* [1781] and *Critique of Practical Reason* [1788]. From the point of view of international relations scholars, in addition to these works, Kant's political writings, which also date from his 'critical' period, and in particular the essay *On Perpetual Peace: A Philosophical Sketch* [1795], are also very significant. Here I will highlight three areas of Kant's critical thought that have helped set the scene for later critical theorists and for contemporary international relations scholarship: knowledge, morality, and politics.

Knowledge

Eighteenth century philosophical arguments about how we justify claims to knowledge essentially fell into two categories. On the one hand, a 'rationalist' tradition argued that claims to knowledge could be securely grounded in reason, perhaps in the form of innate ideas that are inherent in humanity, or derived ultimately from God. On the other hand, an 'empiricist' tradition argued that claims to knowledge were grounded in sense-experience (what we can hear, see, touch, etc.) rather than reason.

In his *Critique of Pure Reason*, Kant famously transcended the choice between these two options by arguing that neither reason nor sense by themselves could give us knowledge about anything. Instead he argued that human knowledge was fundamentally conditioned (limited) by the categories of our understanding (which included, for instance, the concept of causation) and by our inability to experience anything outside the conditions of space and time. Thus knowledge was the product of the coming together of concepts (categories of the understanding) and spatio-temporally mediated experience. This undermined the idea that we could ever have direct knowledge of 'things in themselves' and meant that the task of philosophy essentially became the task of tracing our own limitations and being clear about what we could and could not claim about the world, a task that Kant termed 'critique'. Kant's critical theory of knowledge paved the way for later critical theory by focusing on the conditions of possibility of knowledge and experience. Later thinkers, such as Hegel and Marx, revolutionized Kant's own philosophical revolution by arguing that the conditions of possibility of knowledge and experience were not stable and trans-historical but were actually embedded in human history and society. In doing this, they raised important questions about the grounds of the critical philosopher's authority to determine which kinds of claims are legitimate and which are not. This continues to be a question that haunts critical theorists in the twentieth century.

Morality

Kant's theory of knowledge was all about acknowledging human limitation, in contrast to his moral theory, which argued for the potential of humanity to transcend our limitations. For Kant there was a clear distinction to be drawn between pure theoretical reason and pure practical reason. Our theoretical reason is limited and conditioned: we do not know things in an unmediated way, in the way that God or angels might. Morally speaking, we are also limited: we are often driven by animal passions and desires rather than by moral considerations. Nevertheless, in the case of morality, according to Kant, we *are* capable of knowing what is right. There are ways in which we can work out what our duty is, through universalising the principles on which we are planning to act and considering the implications were those principles to become universal laws (the so called 'categorical imperative'). Over and above this, however, to act morally is not simply to do the right thing, but to do the right thing for the sake of doing the right thing, rather than because it suits us.

For Kant, giving money to a beggar because you feel sorry for him is not a moral act, giving money to a beggar because charity is a universalizably good thing *is* a moral act. It is this moral capacity that human beings share that, for Kant, differentiates us from animals and makes us peculiarly worthy of respect. Perhaps the most famous implication drawn by Kant from his account of our moral capacity to know, and act on, the moral law, is his argument that human beings should never be treated merely as means but always as ends in themselves. This principle of respect for persons has been one of the inspirations for the idea of universal human rights that became so influential in the twentieth century. Kant's moral theory continues to be a crucial reference point for later critical theory and for contemporary international ethics. For some, his account of morality captures the rational and universal core of moral reasoning, which can then provide a yardstick for moral critique that operates across boundaries of culture and power. For others, however, Kant's moral theory is unable to sustain its claim to universality, is overly abstract and rationalistic, and therefore insensitive to the particularity of different experiences and ethical traditions.

Politics

Although Kant sees us as capable of acting according to the dictates of pure practical reason, he still sees human beings as fundamentally flawed and incapable of consistently transcending their baser, material appetites. For this reason, he develops a political theory, in which government and law ensure outward compliance with morality, and also provide a context in which, over time, our moral capacities can be nurtured and progress will be possible. The best political context to provide this, he argues, is a republican state, by which he means a state in which private property is institutionalised, there is a separation of powers (between legislative, executive and judiciary) and those powers are politically accountable to a citizen body of adult, male property owners. Two aspects of Kant's political theory have been of particular interest to international relations scholars: the link he makes between republican states and pacified inter-state relations and the way in which his political theory is embedded in a philosophy of history. In *Perpetual Peace: A Philosophical Sketch*, Kant outlines the necessary conditions for peaceful international relations: first, all states must be republican; second, republican states should enter into a 'pacific union' with one another in which they regulate their interactions through international law and foreswear war as a means of foreign policy; third, all states must honour a universal, cosmopolitan right of individuals to hospitality, even if those individuals are not citizens.

This condition of perpetual peace is in accordance with the requirements of morality, but Kant also argues that we can identify historical forces that are likely to bring it about. He points to 'natural' mechanisms of fear and greed that will push people towards republicanism and pacific federation regardless of morality. For instance, he argues that human conflict will eventually produce weapons so terrible that, out of fear for their survival, people will want to avoid the possibility of war; and he argues that the development of international trade will create levels of interdependence that will make war contrary to our selfish interests. Ultimately, he suggests that both our baser and our higher selves push history in the same direction of progress towards republican, market societies and pacific inter-state relations. Kant's political thought has been drawn on by liberal international relations theorists as an early statement of the contemporary theory that liberal states tend to be pacific in their relations with one another. But it has also inspired critical thinkers such as Habermas, both in terms of its vision of the republican state, and its theory of progressive historical development. In many ways, Kant set the agenda for the debate still ongoing in critical theory about the nature of the relation between morality and politics, and whether (and how) political progress is possible.

Further reading

Beiner, Ronald and Booth, William James (eds) (1993) *Kant and Political Philosophy: The Contemporary Legacy*, Newhaven & London: Yale University Press. This is a useful collection of secondary commentary on all aspects of Kant's political thought.

Caygill, Howard (1995) *A Kant Dictionary*, Oxford: Blackwell. This is an incredibly useful background text on Kant's philosophy and concepts.

Flikschuh, Katrin (2000) *Kant and Modern Political Philosophy*, Cambridge: Cambridge University Press. This is a good account of Kant's political thought and its relation to contemporary Anglo-American liberal political philosophy.

Habermas, Jürgen (2006) *The Divided West*, ed. and trans. Ciaran Cronin, Cambridge: Polity Press. Part 4 of this volume, 'The Kantian Project and the Divided West', is a good example of a contemporary critical theorist finding inspiration in Kant's philosophy.

Hurrell, Andrew (1990) 'Kant and the Kantian Paradigm in International Relations', *Review of International Studies*, 16: 183–205. A good overview of different aspects of Kant's political thought and how it can be applied in international relations.

Hutchings, Kimberly (1996) *Kant, Critique and Politics*, London: Routledge This is an exploration of Kant's concept of critique in Kant's own work and in that of later critical theorists, including Habermas, Arendt, Lyotard and Foucault.

Kant, Immanuel (1956) *Critique of Practical Reason* trans. Lewis White Beck, New York: Macmillan.

Kant, Immanuel (1983) *Critique of Pure Reason*, trans. Norman Kemp Smith, London: Macmillan.

Kant, Immanuel (1991) *Kant: political writings*, ed. Hans Reiss, trans. H. B. Nisbet, Cambridge: Cambridge University Press. This is the best collection of Kant's writings on politics, including the essay on perpetual peace.

Scruton, Roger (1982) *Kant*, Oxford: Oxford University Press. This is an accessible introduction to Kant's critical philosophy.

Williams, Howard (1983) *Kant's Political Philosophy*, Oxford: Blackwell. This is a very useful and comprehensive account of Kant's political philosophy.

Yovel, Yirmiyahu (1980) *Kant and the Philosophy of History*, Princeton NJ: Princeton University Press. This is one of the few texts to take a serious look at the role of philosophy of history in Kant's work.

21 Julia Kristeva

Vivienne Jabri

The suggestion of intimacy in relation to the political is an immediate sub-version of the conventions and orthodoxies surrounding our understanding of politics and the systems of thought that underpin this understanding. Julia Kristeva's writings, concerned as they are with the problematic of language and subjectivity, and drawing as they do from philosophy, literature, and psychoanalysis, present us with exactly such a subversion of the given order of things in political thought generally and in international relations in par-ticular. The intimacy that is suggested here makes reference to Kristeva's primary engagement with the question of subjectivity conceived not simply in terms of the subject's relationship to institutions, but subjectivity as a process in being and becoming. The disruptive element in Kristeva's thought when conceived politically is a wholesale shift away from a rationalist or even instrumental conceptualisation of politics and political participation, raising fundamental questions relating to identity, mobilisation, resistance, and the socio-political imperatives of modernity itself. If the apotheosis of modernity was/is the modern subject, then what happens to the modern project itself when its subject is no longer the rational, autonomous self of Kantian thought, but a far more troubled and complex being, always in negotiation with fragments of history, narrations un-foretold, and spaces of interaction where the subject comes face to face with her or his own strangeness?

Julia Kristeva's powerful interventions in philosophy, art criticism, and psychoanalysis combine with her more recent fictional works. Born in Bul-garia, and living and teaching in France since 1966, Kristeva's often narrational writings and interviews provide indicators of her life as an exile and a foreigner living in France and the impact of the experience of exile on her intellectual trajectory. While this trajectory suggests a shift from linguistics to a more psy-choanalytically informed philosophical engagement, Kristeva's discourse is certainly not linear in movement, but is multiple and rich in its points of refer-ence. Joining the literary journal, *Tel Quel*, and experiencing the conflicts of the Left during the 1968 period, Kristeva's early Maoist sympathies gradually gave way to a sustained critique of any totalising and totalitarian politics.

Kristeva's distinctly political project is often obscured not just by her style of writing, but by the substantial content of her engagements. She might at first glance and to the uninitiated appear somewhat removed from the concerns we have in international relations. Her most direct engagement with matters 'international' appears in a little known volume of essays, *Crisis of the European Subject* (Kristeva 2000), where she appears to deal directly with the challenges facing Europe in late modernity and specifically globalisation and its implications for Europe's self-understanding. Another earlier work, *Nations Without Nationalism* (Kristeva 1993), again deals with matters of identity, and specifically the xenophobia associated with the extremes of nationalism, delving into the possibility of nations that are cosmopolitan in ethos. However, and crucially, both these works are mere derivations from her other established books and essays upon which her reputation rests. The aim of this chapter is to reveal what we might consider to be the 'essential' Kristeva; essential not in the sense of what finally defines her work, rather essential understood in terms of how we in critical international relations have drawn on her work and seek to do so in the future in our attempts at understanding social and political life, informed by lived experience as it is manifest in the routine of daily encounters and in the face of conflict, crisis, and upheaval.

The 'poststructural turn' in international relations brought into sharp relief issues concerned with language, discourse, and subjectivity. Engagement with each of these issues challenges the confinement of politics and the political to the state and its institutions, domestic and international. The unique contribution that Kristeva brings to critical discourse is her understanding of subjectivity as the core problematic in our thinking about politics and the political. The political subject, in Julia Kristeva, emerges, somewhat controversially, not simply in the public sphere of discourse, but in the 'intimate' spaces wherein discourse is intra-subjective. This postulates a challenge to any political thinking, in that we traditionally conceive of the political as being located primarily in the public domain. The intimate then makes its imprint on the international, emerges and bursts forth, somehow interrupts the sanitised and abstracted image presented in the orthodoxies of the discipline. Engagements with Kristeva in international relations centre predominantly on her poetics as source of resistance and on her reflections on abjection and xenophobia. The 'aesthetic turn', as Roland Bleiker (1999), points out, seeks to reveal the nexus between art and politics, and specifically articulations of resistance to hegemonic discourses and exclusionary practices as these emerge in artistic practice and literary production. Kristeva's evidence base is indeed the artistic and the literary, subjectivity emergent in the text just as it is in her reading of the Western philosophical tradition, and her psychoanalytic practice. Hers is a complex intellectual trajectory that provides valuable insights into the international, insights drawn upon in critical scholarship.

Kristeva on subjectivity

The 'intimacy' of the political I refer to in the introduction points to Kristeva's conception of subjectivity in terms of the 'intimate' location of the unconscious and the imprint of the unconscious on expression and articulation. In writing of Kristeva's *The Intimate Revolt* (2002b), Cecilia Sjoholm points to its significance in political thought: 'The intimate is a sphere of singularity, irreducible to the private. The intimate revolt is in fact the only possible revolt, intimacy being that which is the most profound and the most singular in us ... ' (Sjoholm 2005: 110). Kristeva's achievement and indeed her singularity in the field of political thought is to make available to us a picture of subjectivity that is not confined to the idea that the subject is defined in relation to the outside, the external other, the discursive and institutional public domain. Rather, and in a reversal of Lacan (Sjoholm (2005: 110–12), the external, the foreign, the real, always emerge in the field of the 'intimate', the lived experience of the subject, and its articulation is a form of return to a space that is somehow prior to the symbolic outside.

In seeking what I am referring to as the essential Kristeva, it is perhaps apt to start with her own narrative, Kristeva's subjectivity, or glimpses thereof. Writing of her Bulgarian origins, 'Bulgaria, My Suffering', and how their legacy emerges in her contemporary French reality, Kristeva reveals the cosmopolitanism of the exile, even as the exile is always somehow located at the juncture of a past and a present, the here and the elsewhere. This junctural, borderline space displaces the subject while providing an exhilarating vision of the possibilities to come:

When this anxiety, which is in fact a pocket of air, a breathing hole, an amphetamine – quiets down in order to justify itself before others, I could explain to you how those men and women of whom I include myself, represent on the one hand the pulsation of the modern world surviving its famous lost values ... and on the other hand ... embody that new positivity that is forming contrary to national conformism and internationalist nihilisms (Kristeva 2000: 168).

In considering solutions to problems exemplified by Sarajevo or Chechnya, Kristeva looks to the potential of the exile condition, migrants, capable of generating

new beings of language and blood, rooted in no language or blood, diplomats of the dictionary, genetic negotiators, wandering Jews of Being who challenge authentic, and hence military, citizens of all kinds in favour of a nomadic humanity that is no longer willing to sit quietly (Kristeva 2000: 168–69).

These 'new beings' are never settled nor indeed reconciled to their condition, remaining somehow attached, if only through traces and fragments, to memories and sensibilities that also inform the present. The subject represented in Kristeva's reflections of herself is a historical and historicised subject; historical in the sense of the condition of exile and its representation in exiled writings through the ages and across cultures, and historicised in the sense that the subject is not only formed in history, but constituted as a subject in the subject's own relationship with the past. Crucial here is Kristeva's difference when compared to other poststructural thinkers; namely, this psychoanalytically informed conception of the subject, so that what we gain a handle on is not simply the Hegelian constituted subject, the subject formed in inter-subjective relations, but rather the subject whose present is always co-present with the past, fragments of recollection brought forth as the subject shifts and moves through the interstices of life.

Once we begin to acknowledge the historicity of the subject, we come to make a significant shift away from rationalist understandings of the subject or singular conceptions of identity. Rather, the subject of politics emerges as a complex being whose articulations of identity cannot be reduced to singular representations of place and time the defining moment of which might be related as much to state or culture as gender or class. The subject in Kristeva is hence always defiant of easy definition or categorisation, even as the subject shifts and negotiates her way through exactly such categorisations. There is no denial here of the significance of institutions such as the state, culture, religion, the factory, and so on. Rather, the focus is on the different modes of expression and articulation, modes that do not necessarily conform to the subject categories attributed to them. What is crucial in the Kristevan method is not how these institutions work on the subject, but rather how the subject articulates her mode of being in relation to institutions, discourses, practices, imagery, the narratives of others and self, and so on. There are no fixed identities upon which we might rely in order to somehow predict behaviour or affiliation to particular ideologies or modalities of belief.

Kristeva draws on linguistics and psychoanalysis to capture in theoretical form the complexity of the subject, even as she recognises that such capturing is always momentary, never complete. Unlike most poststructural thinkers wherein the subject is formed in language, the Kristevan subject is at once both of the discursive and the pre-discursive. Language makes its imprint on the body, just as the body makes its imprint on language. From her *Revolution in Poetic Language* (1984) to her more recent work, the subject in Kristeva is formed in two realms of language, the 'semiotic' and the 'symbolic'. Where the latter refers to the public sphere of discourse and interaction, the Law of the father, the former is 'pre-Oedipal', pre-discursive, always in the process of becoming. In Kristeva's own words,

> I looked at the primordial silences in language, the unsaid, i.e. the pre-Oedipal stages that have to do with the mother–daughter relation, this maternal imprint on the psyche and on language – what I call the 'semiotic' (distinguished from the 'symbolic' which would be the preserve of language, its signs and syntax) (Kristeva, 2002a: 22).

The 'unsaid' comes ultimately to be said, expressed and articulated, for the human being is a 'speaking subject', a 'self in language' (Kristeva 2002a: 22), but even as the subject speaks, traces of the unsaid remain, at times submerged below the surface, and at others, in literature, art, psychoanalysis, emerge in moments of creativity and confrontation with the limit, the symbolic order.

To understand Kristeva's contribution to our reflections on subjectivity demands an appreciation of this fundamental distinction she posits, drawing on Freud, between the 'semiotic' and the 'symbolic' aspects of subjective articulation. Kristeva's concern in *Revolution in Poetic Language* and elsewhere is to reveal the semiotic in language, poetry, art. The semiotic announces its creativity in relation to the symbolic; namely the existing order and its orthodoxies. As highlighted by Anne-Marie Smith

The semiotic can be seen as an articulation of the unconscious processes which fracture the common idealisation of those images and signs which secure the status quo, and guarantee the establishment. It is a constant and subversive threat to the symbolic order of things, which itself, Kristeva stresses, is no monolithic structure, but an illusion of stability (Smith 1998: 16).

Significantly in relation to the creative moment that is the semiotic, and as Anne-Marie Smith indicates: 'The semiotic, insists Kristeva, is not an extension of the language system but transversal to and coextensive with it. It is through the semiotic that we connect language as a formal system to something outside this, in the realm of the psycho-somatic, to a body and a bodily subject structuring and destructuring identity' (Smith 1998: 18).This psychoanalytically informed conception of subjectivity in Julia Kristeva then enables her to posit what might be considered to be her distinctive contribution to our understanding of subjectivity, namely the idea of the 'subject in process/on trial', an idea that immediately takes us away permanently from the confinements of rationality as the linchpin of political subjectivity and agency. The 'subject in process/on trial' is the point of departure for Kristeva as she considers, throughout her corpus, artistic creativity, revolution, nationalism and xenophobia, women's subjectivity, and the condition of exile:

The notion of the subject-in-process … assumes that we recognise, on the one hand, the unity of the subject who submits to a law – the law of communication, among others; yet who, on the other hand, does not entirely submit, cannot entirely submit, does not want to submit entirely. The subject-in-process in always in a state of contesting the law, either with the force of violence, of aggressivity, of the death drive, or with the other side of this force: pleasure and jouissance … The subject-in-process, then, gives us a vision of the human venture of innovation, of creation, of opening, of renewal (Interview in Guberman 1996: 26).

Revealingly, Kristeva's conception of the subject is not confined to the individual self, but is drawn upon in her engagements with the political, for example, the events of 1968, racism and xenophobia, European identity and globalisation. Her discourse on collectives inherently relies upon this Freudian inspired conception of the individual self, raising, for an international relations audience, questions related to how we might transpose ontological assumptions relating to the individual subject onto collectivities, such as 'Europeans' or the 'French'. However, while the orthodoxy in international relations might refer to the 'level of analysis' problem, the Kristevan subject, as we see above, should not be read as a level distinct from the social, but rather as always already imbricated with the social, with language, the symbolic, the law, order, and all manifestations of the semiotic as it emerges in the social, interactive space. Ontologically, therefore, the Kristevan subject is always at once both self and other, self and society, self and history, the historical and historicised self. There is in this sense, no essential, or biological self in Kristeva, as some feminists have argued in relation to Kristeva's conception of the 'feminine' (see for example Nancy Fraser (1992) and Judith Butler (1993a)). Rather, there is the subjectivity of woman and man differentially located in relation to the semiotic and the symbolic. There are hence no 'fixed' identities as such, but rather subjects in negotiation with past and present, the here and the elsewhere.

The stranger within

Writing in a context of increasing governmental restrictions targeted at migrants and asylum seekers, discourses that associate criminality with the migrant other, and practices that so clearly violate the rights of the individual migrant with a view to the exclusion of entire categories of population, the clear choice for the critical scholar is to somehow reveal the implicated practices and their agencies. The defining feature of international relations is the 'international' as a distinct location of politics and political subjectivity. This distinctiveness emerges from conceptions of the political in terms of borders, predominantly juridically defined and conceptualised even as they have such profound impact upon lived experience.

The international at once invokes a crossing over, a movement from the certainties of domesticity and the socio-politics of home to the unknown terrain of the strange and the foreign. The crossing of boundaries, from ancient times to Kant's reflections on the subject suggests a call for a hospitality conferred to the stranger in recognition of the stranger's loss of home, temporary or otherwise. However, the crossing of boundaries is also evocative of exclusion, displays of power, of incursion and invasion, a politics of dispossession that seeks to subsume the other in totality. Clearly within a late modern context defined primarily by the globalised nature of interaction, from the social to the economic to the political, questions relating to borders and their (dis)location come to be core to any reflection on identity, difference, the location of authority and legitimacy, as well as rights and responsibilities. Borders are hence signifiers of difference, they are symbols of identity, form geographic and juridical inscriptions, are politically contested spaces, and crucially in the present context come to be inscribed upon the bodies of subjects. Borders are hence geographic as well as corporeal and when conceived politically, borders come to be understood as the always contested terrain, even if national boundaries are long settled. For the ultimate border is the border invoked between self and other, the deserving and the undeserving, the powerful and the dispossessed.

The space of the borderline is no longer simply coterminus with the state, and certainly the 'stranger' is no longer she who belongs elsewhere. Rather, the border as a space of contest, emergency, and violence is, now in late modernity perhaps more than at any other time in history, carried corporeally by the subject targeted, so that the locations of the border with all its social, economic, political consequences are always within, on the streets and in proximate neighbourhoods. Practices of government and the panoply of securitising and exclusionary technologies of surveillance and control clearly recognise this to be the case and indeed reinforce through such practices the ever shifting location of the borderline so that it is indeed no longer at the geographic boundaries of the state but permeates society within. The dialectic is all too clear – the permeability of the geographic shifts control elsewhere, so that the corporeal comes to be the location of control.

The choice for the critical theorist is, on the one hand, to unravel, following Michel Foucault especially, practices of government geared towards the 'border' as manifest in the control and management of populations and bodies. Also in the Foucauldian vein, the critical attitude delves into the intersection between power, in all its discursive and institutional manifestations, and subjectivity. The Kristevan contribution, controversially for any Foucauldian aware of the power of the disciplines and the complicity of psychoanalysis and psychiatry generally in the production of the excluded and the marginalised, is to focus in depth on the modes of articulation generated by the subject in the face of exactly the discursive and institutional backdrop that constitutes the symbolic order. The 'speaking subject' becomes the focus of a Kristevan informed critical investigation; how the subject reflects on the world around them, on others and, crucially, on self, how such articulations might come in a remarkable heterogeneity of expressions, at times playful and creative, and at others mournful and melancholic, at times conforming to the given order of things and at others resistant and dissident. The speaking subject of a Kristevan oriented investigation may be sought in conversation, in poetry and prose, in art, in the playground and any other context wherein the subject finds voice.

Clearly there are controversies surrounding Kristeva's 'structure', the seeming confinement of the self within the remit of the semiotic and the symbolic, the pre-Oedipal, maternal, playful, the negative, and the Oedipal symbolic; a structure wherein the discursive gives way to the psychoanalytic. Any critical theorist, including the author of this chapter, would question any seemingly totalising conception of experience and practice, even when this involves a conception of language and the psyche that is, perhaps more than any other discourse of modernity, reflexive and self-analytical by definition. However, what is crucial to remember in Kristeva's conception of the subject is that she is informed by the idea of the ever-uncapturable, inaccessible element in the subject, and it is 'negativity' which she sees as the driving force behind creativity and the subject's capacity to somehow escape, to look back, to imagine the unimaginable, to articulate the 'unsaid', to see that in fearing the other, in conforming to the mass, the subject expresses a fear of the self's own abjection (for a discussion of 'negativity' in political theory generally and in Kristeva in particular see Coole (2000)). For the critical theorist to reveal all this and more is to engage with life itself in all its complexity and despite the protests of those who seek the easy and accessible, the 'policy-friendly', the bureaucratised machinery of late modernity's attempts to confine intellectual enquiry and the critical attitude.

The critical attitude in Kristeva, as must by now be evident, allows her to transpose self-transformation with societal transformation, so that the individual subject's capacity to be reconciled with difference is at once seen as the potentially transformative moment in society at large. Perhaps one of the most quoted passages from Kristeva's *oeuvre* relates this notion of self-understanding with the treatment of the other:

> Strangely the foreigner lives within us: he is the hidden face of our identity, the space that wrecks our abode, the time in which understanding and affinity founder. By recognising him within ourselves, we are spared detesting him in himself. A symptom that precisely turns 'we' into a problem, perhaps makes it impossible, the foreigner comes in when the consciousness of my difference arises, and he disappears when we all acknowledge ourselves as foreigners, unamenable to bonds and communities (Kristeva 1991: 1).

Kristeva provides a genealogical search into the notion of the 'stranger', starting in antiquity, through Christendom, into Kant's cosmopolitanism and the Romantics' self-assured sense of communal bonds, and ultimately to Freud and into our own contemporary era. In a gesture of recognition to Freud's crucial place in modernity's confrontation with itself, Kristeva states:

> After Stoic cosmopolitanism, after religious universalist integration, Freud brings us the courage to call ourselves disintegrated in order not to integrate foreigners and even less so to hunt them down, but rather to welcome them to that uncanny strangeness, which is as much theirs as it is ours (Kristeva 1991: 192).

Kristeva seems to set the condition for living with difference when she presents the ultimate challenge for contemporary life: 'How could one tolerate a foreigner if one did not know one was a stranger to oneself?' (Kristeva 1991: 182). The challenge to any critical theorist or investigator is exactly to unravel the possibility of such self-understanding and the forms in which it finds expression and articulation. The challenge is, in addition, to uncover the limits to such self-understanding in all their discursive and institutional forms, the constraints that the symbolic order imposes on self-understanding and reflection. Kristeva calls for an 'ethical course' in dealing intellectually and politically with the rise of xenophobia and racism in Europe, seeing in such discourses and practices a 'cult of origins' that generates a hate reaction against the foreigner. The trajectory of the research programme is here all too clear: 'I am convinced that, in the long run, only a thorough investigation of our remarkable relationship with both the other and strangeness within ourselves can lead people to give up hunting for the scapegoat outside their group' (Kristeva 1993: 51). This ethical course, which might indeed be conceptualised as the intellectual endeavour that is critical theory, makes possible a style of writing and a set of engagements unconfined to disciplinary limits, so that the work of art, literature, philosophy, and psychoanalysis provide the sites and sounds, as do the heterogeneity of voices and expressions in the panoply of private and public spaces wherein the intersubjective international is manifest.

It is in one of her most recent essays, 'Europe Divided: Ethics, Politics, and Religion' (Kristeva 2000), that Kristeva most blatantly comes to transpose her thoughts on the self-understanding of the subject onto a collective arena, namely Europe and transformations in European identity in the context of the technological imperative of the late capitalist order, migration, and globalisation. Here in this text Kristeva again draws on the arts, philosophy, and importantly, religion, to delve into Europe as a concept and as a distinct political space. Unsurprisingly, her starting point is to engage with what she terms 'differing conceptions of the human person and of subjectivity that are asserted and contested in this European space' (Kristeva 2000: 115). Her interest here is in conceptions of 'freedom', its formulation in the European imaginary, and specifically as it appears in the history of philosophy and religion. Placing the Kantian subject of autonomy and 'autocommencement' under the psychoanalytical lens, Kristeva points to the 'crisis' of subjectivity produced by late modern uncertainties and fragmentations. This crisis she represents in terms of 'alienation', the inability to judge, the tendency to conform to 'collective schemas', and the inability to communicate. Drawing on her practice as psychoanalyst, Kristeva describes European subjectivity as a 'shipwreck of a subjectivity incapable of autonomy and independence, because it is fundamentally incapable of representation and thought' (Kristeva 2000: 129). Then intriguingly, Kristeva juxtaposes the crisis of the (Western) European subject with her (Eastern) counterpart, the Orthodox of the East, a subject that can somehow contribute to European subjectivity:

'They' and 'we'. If we are to construct a civilisation that is not solely one of production and commercial trade, we must redefine what we understand by 'freedom'. The freedom that we have to reconstruct ... should be an autocommencement, but with the other ... The freedom of desire that is the desire for objects, knowledge and production, joined with the freedom to withdraw into intimacy and mystical participation (Kristeva 2000: 159–60).

Both elements, the universal rationalist and the spiritual come to form the mutually constitutive components of a late modern, dialogical European identity confronted as it is with what she sees as the instrumentalisation of life. Importantly, neither aspect emerges as the 'truth', but is rather a point of intersection, and through the emergent dialogue, one of a resurgent creative moment.

The 'ethical course' in Julia Kristeva emerges as narrational, transgressive and dialogical. The narrational is evident in these later writings, but it is a form of narration that is anything but linear in construction, moving as it does from one reference point to the next so that the character in Dostoyevsky is as critical to our understanding of her elaboration of subjectivity as is Bellini's Madonna, Kant's philosophy, or Hannah Arendt's engagements with the political. Just as the 'we' and the 'they' come to engage in an interplay of signifying practices, so too the textual narrations the primary object of which is to reveal the ever present possibility of the transgressive, the possibility of the moment to come. The 'speaking subject' is, as I highlight throughout, the central figure even as this figure is linguistically and textually inscribed as she engages in the social and historical spaces that at once both constrain and fascinate. 'Without negativity' Kristeva asserts in her defence of Hegel and Adorno, 'there is no longer freedom or thinking', and Hannah Arendt makes possible 'anxious thinking' as against 'calculated thinking' or the 'robotisation of humanity' (Kristeva 2002b: 114). Negativity hence points to its instantiation in what Kristeva calls the 'borderline situation', one that disrupts language and unsettles the givens of identity and social structure (for an excellent recent engagement with Kristevan 'negativity' in art see Frost 2007).

Writing in one of the most significant engagements with Kristeva's work, Cecilia Sjoholm points to the two ways in which Kristeva challenges universalising discourse and the 'sacrificial logic' that underpins it:

> The first point of criticism ... is directed against the reductive concept of identity in Western politics. The second ... is critical of the elimination of corporeality in that logic and aspires to reintroduce issues of embodiment in the political sphere (Sjoholm 2005: 60).

Where the first, as indicated in this section, assumes universality for the citizen at the expense of the 'foreigner', the second negates the impact of the corporeal on the symbolic. Kristeva's critique, as we see in this section, makes possible an engagement with the concrete and the lived.

The corporeal international

Any reflection on phenomena in the international sphere such as war and the extremes of violence, identity, conflict and exclusion, fear and trauma, as well as representations of the political that are deeply gendered, must surely engage with the corporeality of the international; that wars kill bodies, that hatred hurts, that the removal and siege of entire populations is an embodied experience in the trauma generated, in the violence perpetrated against any sense of self, that the international politics of dispossession as the defining moment of the late modern international is all too apparently felt viscerally and most intimately. Now, in late modernity, we begin to witness the interruptive, disruptive, revolt of the intimate, in all its corporeality.

Kristeva's retrieval of the corporeal in subjectivity emerges most strongly in relation firstly to what she refers as the 'abject' and secondly in relation to 'woman's time', the subjectivity of women. In critical International Relations, it is the first rather than the second that has been most engaged with, in relation to representations of the 'enemy' other as the monstrous, the abnormal (Richard Devetak (2005) and Vivienne Jabri (2006)), in relation to suicide bombers (Chan (2007) draws on Kristeva's concept of 'abjection' to write of Fanon's legacy in his reflections on resistance and the suicide bomber), and in relation to the 'hunger strike' as a form of resistance (Jenny Edkins and Véronique Pin-Fat reveal the abjection implicated in the hunger striker and asylum seeker threatened with deportation from the United Kingdom). The 'abject' is defined by Kristeva as 'something rejected from which one does not part' and what 'causes abjection' is 'what disturbs identity, system, order. What does not respect borders, positions, rules'. The abject is hence always of the subject and not exterior to the subject:

> If it be true that the abject simultaneously beseeches and pulverises the subject, one can understand that it is experienced at the peak of its strength when that subject, weary of fruitless attempts to identify with something on the outside, finds the impossible within; when it finds that the impossible constitutes its very being (Kristeva 1982: 5).

Abjection suggests rejection of all that which horrifies in the self and in other. It might be located in art, just as it is manifest in racism and xenophobia, in representations of the 'monstrous' other, in the dehumanising spaces of incarceration wherein the other is the very corporeality of rejection and denial. Just as in Kristeva's aesthetics, the abject is revealed on the canvas, the installation, or the work of literature, so too it might be said that the abjection of the other in locations such as Abu Ghraib and Guantanamo are thoroughly corporeal, violence against the body of the other aestheticised into a grotesque spectacle that variously fascinates and horrifies. The abject marks a differentiation between self and other, inside and outside, even as the subject recognises the impossibility of such differentiation.

The body, in Kristeva, is ever present in language, art, and politics. Her Freudian informed conception of the subject is determinedly corporeal, and in her elaboration of the semiotic as distinct from the symbolic, the maternal body in particular comes into view and what she refers to 'woman's time' comes to represent for Kristeva the heterogeneity of articulation as opposed to uniform and fixed notions of identity. If the body is a site of transgression, then the female body, sacrificed in the name of sovereign universality, is specifically imbued with the indeterminate and the heterogeneous. In her most deconstructive mode, and in her most controversial within feminist discourse, she calls for a 'third attitude' in feminist thought, one that rejects uniform conceptions of woman: 'the very dichotomy man/woman as an opposition between two rival entities may be understood as belonging to *metaphysics*. What can "identity", even "sexual identity", mean in a new theoretical and scientific space where the very notion of identity is challenged?' (Kristeva 1986: 209). Here in this powerful and controversial text, Kristeva rejects the patriarchal dichotomies which she sees feminist politics as having inherited, presenting instead a subject-in-process that is not confined in symbolically and hence phallocentrically defined gender, but rather as an embodied singularity with all the transgressive potential that the semiotic provides. As Stephen Chan (2007) so aptly observes in writing of Kristeva's thoughts on abjection and its overcoming, 'the movement away from annihilation towards completeness is a movement accomplished by beauty towards love and towards a certain feminine condition and a certain methodology of becoming feminine'.

The corporeal, as the sacrificed entity in the formulation of the rational subject of modernity, comes to express a presence in subversive form. The subversion, somewhat controversially, is embedded in a body politics that captures at once both horror and beauty, refuses easy categories, and engages with the innermost terrain of the subject's embodied experience.

Concluding reflections

Engaging with Kristeva as a critical theorist is always a challenge, specifically in her reliance on Freudian psychoanalysis, a discourse that can often appear totalising in its models and structures of subjectivity, even as these structures are ever open to the subject's own self-formation. While we might un-problematically draw on Kristeva in considerations of aesthetic thought and the transgressive content in art and literature, a far more difficult prospect is to extrapolate from the singular aesthetic practice to political agency and mobilisation. Similarly in relation to Kristeva's attribution of a subversive potential to pre-discursive drives that become manifest in poetic language, in the corporeality of the maternal body and so on.

Nancy Fraser, for example, is somewhat critical of what she sees as Kristeva's tendency to 'valorise transgression and innovation per se irrespective of content' (Fraser 1992: 62) and to associate transgression with aesthetic practice.

Fraser is especially critical of Kristeva's conception of subjectivity in terms of the distinction between the symbolic and the semiotic registers of language and her association of the latter with all that she sees as transgressive; the poetic, the corporeal, the feminine, the maternal, 'a sort of oppositional feminine beachhead within discursive practice' (Fraser 1992: 64). Hence, Kristeva's 'lapse into psychologism' (Fraser 1992: 64) fails to provide a basis from which we might discern how *political* agency emerges. Like Fraser, Butler is also critical of Kristeva's understanding of the transgression against the symbolic. In a powerful essay on 'The Body Politics of Julia Kristeva' (Butler 1993a), Butler questions the subversive potential that Kristeva locates in the semiotic, highlighting especially the view that the symbolic always emerges as the dominant force in the formation of the subject.

Nevertheless, and despite these very significant critiques, Kristeva's thought is of crucial significance in our engagements with subjectivity and the formation of the subject in relation to discourse and institutions. While some readers of her work might reject her reliance on Freudian psychoanalysis, others appreciate the intellectual trajectory that leads to a politics of negativity in Kristeva and how this becomes manifest in her reflections on the late modern condition and its impact for lived experience. Kristeva's ultimate contribution to critical international relations must be located in her conceptualisation of an intimate location of the political and relatedly in her retrieval of that which is sacrificed in the name of universality, difference and the corporeal.

Further reading

Kristeva, Julia (1984) *Revolution in Poetic Language*, trans. M. Waller, New York: Columbia University Press. First published in French in 1974, this is Julia Kristeva's published doctoral thesis. Its multiple references, to linguistics, art, and psychoanalysis may at first hand appear daunting in its linguistics jargon, however, this is the text that sets Kristeva's interest in poetics as resistance and is crucial to understanding her future intellectual agenda.

Kristeva, Julia (1982) *Powers of Horror: An Essay on Abjection*, New York: Columbia University Press. Irrespective of its rather complex psychoanalytic framework, a crucial text in understanding Kristeva's notion of the 'abject' and 'abjection'. Any interest in corporeal basis of hatred, fear and horror makes this essential reading.

Kristeva, Julia (1986) 'Women's Time', in Toril Moi (ed.) *The Kristeva Reader*, Oxford: Blackwell Publishers, 188–213. One of the most powerful interventions into French feminist thought, and published in English in the journal *Signs* in 1981, this essay engages with the feminist movement and provides indicators of her thought on the 'feminine', a contribution that has generated much debate in Anglophone feminism.

Kristeva, Julia (1991) *Strangers to Ourselves*, trans. Leon S. Roudiez, New York: Columbia University Press. This text must form essential reading on any course, not simply in critical theory and philosophy, but on the themes of migration, exclusion, and the politics of hatred. This is Kristeva's genealogical treatment of the figure of the 'stranger' from antiquity to the present, in literature, philosophy and the arts. This is also one of the most accessible of Kristeva's works, apart from her interviews.

Kristeva, Julia (1993) *Nations Without Nationalism*, trans. Leon S. Roudiez, New York: Columbia University Press. Reacting to increasing racism and xenophobia directed against migrants in France, this short text may be considered the 'applied' version of *Strangers to Ourselves.*

Books on Kristeva

Two excellent books that engage with the 'political' in Kristeva include Cecilia Sjoholm (2005) and the collection of essays dealing with Kristeva's crucial early works contained in Kelly Oliver (1993). An excellent introductory text on Kristeva is John Lechte and Maria Margaroni, *Julia Kristeva* (Continuum: London, 2004).

22 Emmanuel Levinas

Elizabeth Dauphinee

In recent years, the philosophical thought of Emmanuel Levinas has found its way into international relations scholarship and related fields. Levinas' unique, radical views on the ethical relation have earned his ideas of 'the Other' and 'the Face' immediate recognition among critical theorists across the social sciences. The aim of this chapter is to introduce Levinas' philosophy of ethics, and to consider some of the questions that arise when that ethics is translated into political practice. The chapter will then turn to look at some of the key international relations and related scholarship that draws on Levinasian thought, and to demonstrate how Levinas informs contemporary work in ethics and international politics.

Born in Lithuania in 1906, Levinas' intellectual and personal life was conditioned by his Jewish background – both as it informed his own cultural experience and as it was affected by the anti-Semitism of his time. He received a traditional Talmudic education and was also influenced by the great Russian novelists of the nineteenth century. As a child in 1915, he was deported in a mass expulsion of Jews from Lithuania. His family settled in Ukraine, where he experienced the anti-Semitic pogroms of the era. When the new Soviet government lifted the expulsion order in 1920, the Levinas family returned to Lithuania. Levinas left home to attend the University of Strasbourg, and later moved on to the University of Freiburg, where he studied under Husserl and Heidegger. During this time, Levinas pursued the study of phenomenology – a branch of philosophy concerned with the individual's experience of the world. When the Second World War began, Levinas served as an interpreter for the French Army. He was taken prisoner by the Germans in 1940 and spent the remainder of the war in a labour camp. His family in Lithuania perished in the Holocaust, while his wife and daughter in France were hidden in a monastery with the help of longtime friend and philosopher, Maurice Blanchot. At the war's end, Levinas taught philosophy at the *École Normale Israélite Orientale*, where he completed *Totality and Infinity*. He took up a professorship at the University of Poitiers, and then at the University of Paris, Nanterre. In 1973, he moved on to the Sorbonne, where he completed one of his most important works, *Otherwise Than Being Or Beyond Essence* (Ajzenstat 2001: 3). On his death in 1995,

Jacques Derrida announced that Levinas' work on ethics 'will have changed the course of philosophical reflection in our time' (Derrida 1999: 4).

The ethical thought of Levinas

While contemporary philosophers will be interested in the nuance of many aspects of Levinas' intellectual legacy, it is his work on ethics that has earned him the most recognition across the social sciences. The foundation of Levinasian ethics revolves around the basic claim that the Self is always infinitely responsible to the Other. This responsibility is not a choice, nor is it something we acquire through socialization or through a conscious decision to live a moral life. Responsibility is simply the condition into which we are born. It is thus not our decision, but a decision made for us by the inescapable fact of our relationship to the Other. We are called to responsibility by the Other, irrespective of what we ourselves might wish. The character of this relationship marks an important departure from the core of Western thought, because it means that we are not rational, autonomous, decision-making agents as the history of Western philosophy suggests. Rather, we are in some way dependent on the Other for our very sense of self; we are constituted in and by our relationship to the Other; we cannot be free of the Other's existence, nor of the impact of the Other on our own existence.

Our responsibility to the Other does not depend on any previous reasoning or experience, or on the details of any specific relationship. In Levinas' understanding, responsibility is not related to the particular character of our relationships with others in the world, because our actual connectedness to others – through state, community, family, and so on – implies expectation, and not ethics. Our relationships with our families and friends, for example, are made up of mutual expectations; we have (ideally) built up trust through reciprocity over time. Similarly, as members of a state, we bear rights as either citizens or legally recognized immigrants. We enjoy protection under the law, and we are reasonably well aware of our obligations to the state in return for these protections. The relationship with the Other is not based on expectations, on 'rights', or on community or familial ties; indeed, the Other is wholly unknown. For Levinas, we are responsible for those we do not know, for those who owe us nothing in terms of familial, communal, or national loyalty. Put simply, we are unconditionally responsible for the lives of Others, and this is the command that our living in the world presents us with.

Levinas' idea of responsibility stems from an awareness that our very existence always generates violence, whether we mean it to or not. As Levinas asks:

> My being-in-the-world or my 'place in the sun', my being at home, have these not also been the usurpation of spaces belonging to the other man whom I have already oppressed or starved, or driven out into a third

world; are they not acts of repulsing, excluding, exiling, stripping, killing? (Levinas 1989: 82)

What Levinas is alluding to here is the idea that our comfortable lives are always made possible by another's suffering, even when we don't intend this or are not aware of it. To take an example, let us consider an activity as seemingly innocent as fuelling one's car. One assumes this to be an innocuous undertaking. And yet we know that political conflict and war, as well as environmental degradation, follow from this unintentionally harmful activity. For Levinas, however, this condition of radical responsibility is also an *infinite* responsibility, meaning that it cannot be overcome or solved by attention to good or right living. Thus, for Levinas, one might get rid of one's car, but this does not lessen one's responsibility, because there will always be something else that injures the Other – something that we cannot anticipate or calculate. It is our *existence itself* that always causes potential injury to the Other. So immutable is the condition of this responsibility that Levinas understands it as 'a responsibility that goes beyond what I may or may not have done to the Other or whatever acts I may or may not have committed, as if I were devoted to the other man before being devoted to myself' (Levinas 1989: 83).

The point here is not to judge the Self as immoral or intentionally violent. Indeed, despite our best intentions, the Other may still be harmed. Levinas therefore refers to our obligation as a 'guiltless responsibility' (Levinas 1989: 83). This responsibility is so radical and so inescapable that Levinas even goes so far as to compare it to a hostage situation. He writes:

I am pledged to the other without any possibility of abdication. I cannot slip away from the face of the other in its nakedness ... to approach is to be the guardian of one's brother; to be the guardian of one's brother is to be his hostage (Levinas 1998: 72).

This is the rather shocking arrangement that is called forth by Levinas' notion of 'ethics as first philosophy'. And Levinas is fully aware of the shock associated with this revelation, for he describes this ethics as a 'trauma' that 'surprises ... absolutely' (Levinas 1998: 75).

In saying that 'ethics is first philosophy', Levinas means that ethics is the prior condition on which all subsequent philosophy is built. For Levinas, all ethical thought finds its source in our continuous, unconditional and infinite responsibility to (and for) the Other. This responsibility is manifested in the relationship of the face to face – in our facing of the other person. This face-to-face configuration is unique in Levinas, marking another, radical departure from classic Western philosophy. In the realm of autonomous liberal subjects, men and women are understood to relate to one another as discrete individuals in the world. The picture associated with this is of individuals standing shoulder to shoulder, facing the same direction toward the future and progress of humanity – in other words, we are all facing the same direction because we all seek the elements of what Aristotle called 'the good life'. The ethics associated with this view of the world involves maximizing benefits to oneself while minimizing harm to others in one's community. Levinas understands this view of the Self in the world to be violent in its very conception. He writes: 'Why does the other concern me? ... Am I my brother's keeper? These questions have meaning only if one has already supposed that the ego is concerned only with itself, is only a concern for itself' (Levinas 1989: 106). For Levinas, such an orientation can never provide the groundwork for a meaningful ethics. In a world characterized by the priority of the Self's ego, Others are encountered only as obstacles on the road to self-actualization, wherein 'every other would be only a limitation that invites war, domination, precaution and information' (Levinas 1989: 108). Put simply, ethics is not ethical when it is ultimately geared toward the pursuit of self-actualization.

For Levinas, the ethics evoked in facing the other, and in being faced by him or her, means that autonomous self-actualization is actually impossible. Our very being is tied indivisibly to our responsibility to the Other. This is what it means to say that we are mutually constituted subjects. We are not self-constituting, but rather constituted in relationship, and so who and what we are is always variable and subject to change. David Campbell describes Levinas' idea of 'being' as a 'radically interdependent condition' (Campbell 1998a: 173). We are continuously reminded of this interdependence by the countenance of the Other – an accusation that never goes away and from which the Self can never escape. This accusation de-subjectifies and de-centres the Self; it calls the Self into question as a moral agent and reveals that the Self's claim to autonomy is a self-delusion. No matter where or what we are, the Other always precedes us; the Other pre-exists us, and so our very existence is tied fundamentally to the Other's fate. The face to face relationship with the Other therefore confronts us with our own destitution as autonomous subjects; with our own dethronement as the sovereigns of our lives (Levinas 1998: 83).

Levinas identifies the Other as 'the naked face of the first individual to come along' (Levinas 1989: 83). He has also described the Other as the 'neighbour ... the other man ... the stranger or sojourner' (Levinas 1989: 84). He remains deliberately vague about the identity of the Other because he believes the Other to be unknowable – incalculable – outside the capacity of the Self's comprehension. Positing the Other as unknowable is crucial for Levinas' theory of ethics, because it protects the Other from being assimilated by the Self, which is necessary for the maintenance of the ethical relation. In other words, the Other, in order to remain Other, needs to be protected from the tendency of the Self to identify, classify, label, or otherwise 'know'. If we 'know' the Other, then he is no longer Other. This relates back to the fact that, for Levinas, responsibility does not rely on recognition or on pre-existing relationships. Indeed, he points out that our 'openness [to the Other] is not complete if it is on the watch for recognition. It is complete not in ... the recognition of the other, but in becoming a responsibility for him' (Levinas 1989: 108). The point here is that 'recognizing' the Other is not enough, and so this recognition does not matter. Michael Shapiro points out that an ethical encounter with the Other must allow that Other to express identity effectively from within the Other's own terms – and not from within the terms that are dictated by the Self (Shapiro 1999b: 60). This is particularly important when we consider the features of Levinasian responsibility: we do not respond to the Other of our own accord, but rather because we have been commanded to do so. One cannot give orders to oneself. One can only receive them from Others (Caputo 1993). It is for this reason that Levinas takes great care to remind us that the Other is always unknowable. It is this unknowability that protects the Other as Other, and also secures the Other's continuous claim on the Self.

As a consequence of Levinas' ambiguity concerning the identity of the Other, there is undeniably some question about what it could really mean to be responsible in practice to 'the naked face of the first individual to come along'. The answer to this question is not particularly important in the sphere of Levinasian ethical philosophy (because theoretically, Levinas' ethics works just fine), but it becomes crucial in the sphere of the political, which we now turn to discuss.

From the ethical to the political

Levinas is fully aware that his ethics runs into complications when stretched onto the socio-political world. The most obvious issue that arises is the question of to whom one can reasonably be responsible when faced with multiple and competing claims. When one is confronted with a whole host of Others making different demands, the issue of justice now raises its head, and difficult questions emerge. Who requires justice? How shall justice be determined? What criteria will be used? In the ethical world, we were faced by the unknowable Other. In the political world, we are never faced with just one Other, but always with multiple others. The original responsibility evoked by the face to face relationship with the Other is disrupted by the appearance of what Levinas calls 'the Third'. The Third is also an other, and more specifically is 'Other' to the original Other. This Third also commands our responsibility. This difficult situation – of being faced with competing Others – marks the transition to the political moment of justice which, for Levinas, is different from ethics (Levinas 2002: 157).

In the sphere of the ethical, we have seen that Levinas identifies the Other provisionally as 'the neighbour'. But how is one to respond when the neighbour to whom we are pledged is also potentially a persecutor of the Third? Levinas writes, 'the third party is other than the neighbor, but also another neighbor, and also a neighbor of the other, and not simply his fellow ... The other stands in a relationship with the third party, for whom I cannot entirely answer' (Levinas 2002: 157). This dilemma of the Third demarcates ethics and politics for Levinas, and the results are somewhat mixed. First, the entry of the Third appears to limit our original responsibility for the Other by creating a new Other to whom we are also responsible. This both limits our responsibility (to the original Other), and extends it (to the Third). Second, the entry of the Third raises the question of the Other's responsibility, as Levinas also points out that the Other is in relationship with the Third. In other words, the Other and the Third are not simply equal Others. As we are responsible to and for the Other, so is the Other responsible for the Third. So, are we responsible to the Other, or to the Third, or to some combination thereof? How do we adjudicate?

Levinas attempts to resolve the dilemma through recourse to the notion of proximity. 'Who is closest to me?' becomes an important question. Levinas' notion of proximity is the condition in which justice becomes possible. It is here that we begin to see a justification of the liberal state and its attendant functions. Levinas writes that 'justice, society, the State and its institutions ... are comprehensible out of proximity' (Levinas 2002: 159). This does not mean that the state *replaces* or otherwise annuls our ethical obligation to the Other. Indeed, the state will sometimes – perhaps even often – deliver *in*justice. But in the absence of any other mechanism through which justice might be systematically pursued, Levinas does invest the (specifically liberal) state with legitimacy as the adjudicator of competing claims. At the same time, however, we should remain aware that Levinas does not wish to elevate the state to a status it does not deserve – that is, as the final stop in the continual pursuit of justice. Furthermore, justice is not an objective adjudication of competing claims, but takes place always within this proximal setting. Levinas writes, 'justice is impossible without the one that renders it finding himself in proximity. His function is not limited to the "function of judgment", the subsuming of particular cases under a general rule. The judge is not outside the conflict' (Levinas 2002: 159). This is perhaps more plainly expressed by Dostoevsky when he writes that 'no man on earth can judge a criminal until he understands that he himself is just as guilty as the man standing before him and that he may be more responsible than anyone else for the crime' (Dostoevsky 1970: 388). It is fair to say that Levinas is wary of the state (or of any legal system) as a seat of justice, yet he continues to place significant faith in the possibilities associated with its institutions. Perhaps Levinas' thinking here is a consequence of the anti-Semitism that led to the destruction of Europe's Jews during the Second World War and his attendant belief that the juridical state of Israel could provide the only trustworthy protection for Europe's historically quintessential Other.

And yet, many scholars have argued that Levinas' faith in the state (and in the proximity that inevitably coincides with the state's borders) leads him to undermine his own ethics. In a now infamous interview in 1982, following the Israeli invasion of Lebanon and the subsequent massacres of Palestinians by Christian militias in the Sabra and Chatila refugee camps, Levinas appeared to argue that obligation could turn to enmity beyond the borders of the state. He claimed that

> the other is the neighbor, who is not necessarily kin, but who can be. And in that sense, if you're for the other, you're for the neighbor. But if your neighbor attacks another neighbor or treats him unjustly, what can you do? Then alterity takes on another character, in alterity we can find an enemy, or at least then we are faced with the problem of knowing who is right and who is wrong, who is just and who is unjust. There are people who are wrong (Levinas 1989: 294).

For many scholars, this comment seemed to solidify Levinas' commitment to the justification of state violence in certain circumstances, and particularly appeared to transform the Palestinian Other into an enemy against whom violence could be justified (Campbell 1998a; Molloy 1999; Drabinski 2000). In response to this, many Levinasian scholars – in international politics as well as other disciplines – have sought to develop a more radically responsible politics than Levinas himself imagined possible.

Levinas in international relations

International relations is no stranger to the critique of the state. Critical scholarship over at least the last two decades has increasingly identified problems with the state as the purveyor of legitimate violence. From the charge that the state operates essentially as an organized criminal gang to the claim that the identities conditioned by the state are fundamentally exclusionary and violent, international relations scholars have increasingly spotlighted the state as part of the problem rather than an agent of solutions or a purveyor of justice. Despite Levinas' own apparent shortcomings in the political sphere, scholars have sought ways to apply Levinasian ethics to an increasingly critical body of social science scholarship. Perhaps nowhere has this undertaking been so imperative as in the field of international relations, with its seemingly endless parade of conflicts, wars, socio-political, and socio-economic inequities. One of the primary themes associated with Levinasian international relations scholarship is this concrete question of obligation – when and where it arises, and what it means for the possibilities of enacting response.

Writing about the war in Bosnia, David Campbell argues that Levinasian thought is 'appealing for rethinking the question of responsibility, especially with respect to situations like the Bosnian war, because it maintains that there is no circumstance under which we could declare that it was not our concern' (Campbell 1998a: 176). In Levinas' own terms, responsibility is not a choice. It is an imperative. Campbell points out that the international community addressed the problem of Bosnia in the context of dominant presumptions about the alignment between territory and identity that was said to lie at the heart of the Bosnian war (Campbell 1998a: 165). As a result, while the violence of ethnic cleansing was clearly unacceptable from a human rights point of view, the political goals of the nationalists were understood as legitimate in the context of orthodox views of the world, which posit that nations naturally seek their own territories and armed conflict is to be expected as one of the results of this imperative. Campbell disputes this view of the world, arguing instead that a Levinasian responsibility means that ethics does not follow after the 'real world' but rather that the 'real world' as such unfolds within an ethics that is always already part of the political process. What this means is that ethics is not something that we insert into politics or into our studies of politics. Instead, ethics *conditions* political practice, whether we are willing to acknowledge it or not. This is crucially important, because ethics has traditionally been 'appended' to international relations – almost as an afterthought – and has not been seen as integral to either its study or practice. Traditional approaches presume that theories of international relations do not already have an ethical standpoint, which, of course, is not the case. What Campbell suggests is that we can change our ethical orientation in the political sphere, and thus change politics. This involves recognizing that all politics already takes an ethical position. For Campbell, responsibility in the Levinasian sense would have required the international community to stop and listen to the voices within Bosnia that were not oriented toward nationalism and/or partition, and to consider those Others who were advocating non-nationalist paradigms as potential partners in a multicultural peace process. Instead, Campbell argues, the realist investment in 'age-old hatreds', historical ethnic animosities, and nationalist violence legitimated the very conflict it seemed to want to avoid. It was the logic of realist thinking on Bosnia that undermined attempts at peace and, later, at reconciliation and refugee return (Campbell 1998a: 219–40).

As a result of the concern with responsibility, Levinasian work in international relations has also focused on how knowledge systems contribute toward unintentional violences in scholarship. For example, I have argued recently that the 'knowledge' produced by researchers about post-conflict societies involves a rapid categorization of 'good' and 'evil'. This undermines responsibility, because it suggests that the 'good' are the only group to which we are obligated (Dauphinee 2007). This is a problem that arises from the desire to classify on the basis of a presumed 'morality'. Levinas argues that exclusions emerge when we rely on scientific or accepted 'knowledge' of this type. He writes, 'the immanence of the known to the act of knowing is already the embodiment of seizure' (Levinas 1989: 76). This means that our attempt to 'know' things about the world also involves appropriating those things – making them our own in very specific, limited ways. This concern can be extended to any system of knowledge that produces relationships of violent power. Michael Shapiro, for example, argues that international relations itself constitutes an enclosed system of beliefs that undermine alternative possibilities for how we might understand and approach the world. He focuses in part on the geopolitical mapping associated with international relations, arguing that 'analyses of global violence tend to be constructed within a statecentric, geostrategic cartography, which organizes the interpretation of enmities on the basis of an individual and collective national subject and cross-boundary antagonisms' (Shapiro 1999b: 60). This boundary making produces a fundamental exclusion in its drive to secure discreet identities. Shapiro's work on the ethics of hospitality is informed in part by the question of how this exclusion works to render Others inadmissible.

Also concerned with the ethics of hospitality, Roxanne Lynn Doty has evoked Levinas' notion of responsibility in her work on Latin American migrants traversing the deserts of the US southwest. Recognizing that the moment of ethicality may well be a fleeting and incomplete one, she observes that the humanitarian placement of water stations for those attempting to cross the desert terrain are enacting a Levinasian responsibility. She points out that *Fronteras Compasivas*, the organization that erects the water stations, will never know the names, legal status, or identities of those who will rely on the life-saving water in the course of their deadly journeys. Doty describes the work of *Fronteras Compasivas* as a basic ethic of hospitality, noting that the 'practice of giving water translates theoretical radicality into a radical political practice' (Doty 2006: 66–7), something that many scholars of the Levinasian tradition are concerned with.

It is clear that Levinas' understanding of politics creates new dilemmas for responsibility in terms of the need to identify 'to whom' we are responsible. One of the challenges facing Levinasian scholarship in international relations is precisely this question of what it might mean to find ourselves infinitely obligated to Others. It seems inevitable that some selectivity will accompany any attempt to concretize Levinasian ethics. It is for this reason, of course, that Levinas himself resisted such concretization, and understood politics to be a very different realm from ethics. However, attempts have been made by subsequent scholars to explore how and when we might identify Others as in need of our responsibility. John Caputo, for example, staunchly defends the view that the Other is always a victim. He utilizes the Biblical imagery of widow, orphan, and stranger (Caputo 1993). For Caputo, obligation is directly related to the powerlessness of the victim and the degree of violence that has been perpetrated. William Connolly, however, points out that these situations 'may not pose the most difficult cases in ethics. Some of the most difficult cases arise when people suffer from injuries imposed by institutionalized identities, principles, and cultural understandings, when those who suffer are not entirely helpless but are defined as threatening, contagious, or dangerous to the self-assurance of these identities, and when the sufferers honor sources of ethics inconsonant or disturbing to these constituencies' (Connolly 1999: 129). I have argued that, because we are obligated before we know who it is we are responding to, it is possible that we will find ourselves face to face with a war criminal instead of a victim. I argued that this would not minimize our responsibility, irrespective of the discomfort we might feel at finding ourselves obligated to someone whose behaviour might repulse us (Dauphinee, 2007). Patricia Molloy has also expressed a similar view with respect to the use of the death penalty in the United States, arguing that dominant views of criminality limit empathy and undermine the possibilities for ethical response (Molloy 1999). Levinasian-inspired scholarship in the field of international relations is diversely focused in terms of subject matter, but one thing that all of these scholars share in common is an ethical concern with obligation and responsibility. It is fair to say that all of these scholars are, in their own way, pursuing the political possibilities associated with the ethics of responsibility introduced by Levinas, and that this is their primary focus.

Conclusion

The goal of this introduction to Levinas' impact in the field of international relations has not been to suggest an unproblematic theory of ethics, nor has it been to suggest a single type of ethical political practice. Indeed, theorizing the possibilities for transition from ethics to politics is perhaps one of the more challenging aspects of Levinas' unique philosophical stance, and international relations scholars pursue this challenge in unique ways. However, as Patricia Molloy points out

> although the 'passage' from ethics to politics in Levinas' thought may be a bumpy one, it does not diminish its importance in building a better international relations. It is not a matter of finding a one-size-fits-all theory of state violence, but a question of questioning the legitimacy of a state-sanctioned use of violence toward the Other/others wherever it occurs, and to ask if it is just (Molloy 1999: 233).

This sort of a task is not intended to create a universal definition of Otherness, or to standardize the form and content of responsibility. Levinas himself would most certainly object to the rigidity associated with such an undertaking, as would most scholars of international relations working in the Levinasian framework. Rather, what makes Levinas such an interesting thinker for scholars of international politics is that he disturbs our dominant understandings of who deserves what, and why. He demonstrates to us that our presumably innocent pursuit of our 'place in the sun' – enshrined by classical theory – has already banished the Other. The recognition that our existence imperils the Other is the foundation for Levinas' notion of an infinite – but guiltless – responsibility. We are responsible to the Other with no limitations and with no possibility of abdication. It is this that forms the starting point for all subsequent political thought.

The transition from ethics to politics for Levinas introduces a range of competing claims from a host of others, of which the original Other is now only one. In the realm of the political, the Other is also responsible to 'the Third' – a party which equally demands justice. This both limits and extends our responsibility, and introduces the Other's responsibility as a variable in the question of justice. While Levinas turns provisionally to the liberal state as the adjudicator of competing claims, he also recognizes the limitations of this move, and the dangers of simply implementing technical or universal solutions such as those enacted by legal institutions. What makes all of this so important for International Relations is that, first, Levinasian thought prioritizes ethics as a fundamental aspect of the political. We cannot conceive of the political as separate from the ethical. Second, Levinasian ethics causes us to rethink the way we see ourselves, stressing particularly the radical interdependence of ethical, political, and social relationships. As a consequence of this, the command to responsibility is one from which we cannot turn away because it is a part of our very constitution as human beings. This unique view of the human relationship is one that allows for a fundamental reconsideration of what international relations – as both a discipline and a practice – is meant to accomplish, for whom, and to what effect.

Further reading

Hand, Sean (ed.) (1989) *The Levinas Reader*, Oxford: Blackwell. The Reader is an abridged collection of some of Levinas' most influential and important works. Each new text is prefaced by an explanatory introduction.

Bergo, Bettina (1999) *Levinas Between Ethics and Politics*, Dordrecht: Kluwer Academic Publishers. Bergo, who translated many of Levinas' works into English, here explores and comments on the major themes of Levinas' ethical and political thought.

Campbell, David and Michael J. Shapiro (eds) *Moral Spaces: Rethinking Ethics and World Politics*, Minneapolis: University of Minnesota Press. Contains essays by various contributors that reflect on Levinas' ethics in the context of international politics.

Chanter, Tina (ed.) (2001) *Feminist Interpretations of Emmanuel Levinas*, University Park: Penn State University Press. Features a selection of essays considering the role of the feminine in Levinas – an issue that Levinas himself did not explore.

Critchley, Simon (1992) *The Ethics of Deconstruction*, Oxford: Blackwell. Analyses the complementary relationship between the ethical thought of Levinas and Derrida.

Hatley, James (2000) *Suffering Witness: The Quandary of Responsibility After the Irreparable*, Albany: SUNY Press. Considers the possibilities for Levinasian responsibility in the face of violent events that have already passed. He explores the Holocaust as a case in point.

23 Karl Marx

Milja Kurki

Karl Marx's philosophical, sociological, economic and political writings have had a deep impact on the practice of politics and international politics during the past two centuries. They have also had far-reaching influence on critical social theorising: Marx's thought has served as both the bedrock and the primary focus of theoretical challenge for most twentieth century 'critical theorists'. Yet, while the influential nature of Marx's thought is in no doubt, the precise nature of his legacy has remained contested. Various contrasting interpretations – from sympathetic 'humanist' readings to various 'deterministic' readings – have been advanced, each interpretation carrying with it important theoretical, rhetorical and political ramifications. Because of the difficult interpretational problems associated with Marx's writings, it would be impossible to provide a definitive interpretation of Marx's ideas here. The focus here, rather modestly, is on, first, giving a brief account of the context of Marx's writings before proceeding to outline some of the key concepts associated with his work. I conclude by reflecting briefly on the legacy of Marx for twentieth century critical social theory.

Life, core writings and influences

Karl Marx was born in Trier in Prussia in 1818. He studied initially at the University of Bonn and later at the *Friedrich-Willhelm Universität* in Berlin. Having completed his doctoral study on classical philosophy, he resided in Paris, Brussels, and latterly in London, his movements often dictated by the constraints levelled on his residence owing to his association with various revolutionary movements and journals. For most of his life, especially during his years spent in London, Marx lived in relative poverty and was often financially reliant on his friend and supporter Friedrich Engels, who was also, following Marx's death in 1883, responsible for editing and publishing some of his posthumous work, notably the last two volumes of *Capital*.

As with any author that wrote during a long time-span, it is difficult to pin down Marx's thought to an entirely coherent set of views: some of his arguments, and his explanatory interests, shifted significantly over the years. Marx's early works tend to be philosophical in nature and are focused on dealing with the controversies that surrounded the debate between Hegelian philosophers and the so-called 'Young Hegelians' associated with Ludwig Feuerbach (upon whose works Marx drew heavily). In his early works, such as *On the Jewish Question* (1843), *Contribution to a Critique of Hegel's Philosophy of Right* (1943), *Economic and Philosophical Manuscripts* (1944), *Theses on Feuerbach* (1845) and *German Ideology* (1846), he dealt with many of the philosophical issues that formed the cornerstone of his historically materialist conception of human nature, philosophy and reality. He set out a critique of liberal conceptions of emancipation, a critique of religion as a derivative of material exploitation, a concept of alienation and a dialectical materialist position against Hegel.

His later works, on the other hand, focused more explicitly on issues of political economy and engaged with and critiqued the writings of so-called 'classical political economists', most notably Adam Smith and David Ricardo. In these later writings, notably in the *Grundrisse* (1857), *The Preface to the Contribution to a Critique of Political Economy* (1859), *Theories of Surplus Value* (1862) and *Capital* (vol. 1 published in 1865, later volumes published posthumously in 1885 and 1894), he set out his famous interpretation of the labour theory of value and the capitalist mode of production. As Marx attempted to understand the laws and contradictions characteristic of the capitalist system, these later works took on a distinctly 'scientific' (and some say 'deterministic') tone.

Besides his contributions to philosophical, social theoretical and political economic theories, it should also be noted that Marx was also closely associated with various revolutionary movements, perhaps most notably with the International Working Men's Association (or the so-called First International). Marx and Engels' *Communist Manifesto* (1948) with its call for 'working men of all countries to unite' certainly came to play an important role in nineteenth and twentieth century socialist movements and revolutions. Indeed, it is important to note that Marx was not only a philosopher but also an active participant in the political struggles of his time. His *Theses on Feuerbach* summarises the 'practical' sentiment of his approach well: 'philosophers have only *interpreted* the world, in various ways; the point, however, is to *change* it' (Marx 1970: 30).

Key concepts

The philosophical underpinnings of Marx's social and economic theories revolved around two core ideas: a *contextual view of human nature*, and a *dialectical* and *historical materialist conception of history*. Liberal thinkers have classically taken as their starting point the notion that human beings should be conceived of as autonomous rational individuals who should be allowed to exercise their judgement free of unnecessary constraints so as to enable them to best to follow and fulfil their interests. Marx took exception with the liberal idea of human nature: for Marx, individuals must be understood not as 'abstract individuals' but as fundamentally social beings, tied to their natural and social environment. Human beings for Marx are socially and historically engendered actors that exist in multiple sets of social relations with each other that condition their actions and beliefs – although human beings are also capable of transforming their social situations (not as they please, but as conditions allow). Marx built on this idea by accepting the basic premise of Hegel's dialectical view of history, the view that history develops out of the process of negotiation of contrasting forms of consciousness. However, against Hegel, the driving forces of history for Marx were material, not 'ideational', in nature. For Marx, human beings exist in historically specific forms of material reality and it is their material social context that conditions their 'consciousness'. This, notably, does not entail that 'brute' material forces in history 'determine' our actions (in a 'when A, then B' manner), but simply that social relations are always materially embedded and that they constrain and condition our thoughts and capabilities for societal interaction and transformation. For Marx, crucially, if we analyse people in relation to their social and historical material context, we can come to discern the role of various structural forces and oppressions inherent within the modern system of capitalist economics and in the 'bourgeois democratic' governance attached to it.

The key aspects of the material context of individuals, for Marx, were the 'forces of' and 'relations of' production (the former denoting the technology and resources of production, and the latter the relations of people in production). These together constituted a *mode of production*. Marx famously argued that a shift had taken place in the mode of production underlying societal life – from a feudal system to a capitalist mode of production. He predicted a further shift towards a communist mode of production and society, arising from the contradictions inherent in the capitalist system. The key driving force of this change was the *class antagonism* existing within the capitalist mode of production. In the capitalist system, this manifested itself in the exploitation of workers (the proletariat) by capitalists. While workers earned a wage which facilitated a minimal existence, capitalists by virtue of their power position in the mode of production extracted *surplus value* from the products of the worker's labour, which they appropriated as 'profit'.

One of the key aspects of the capitalist mode of production was the specific forms of *alienation* to which it subjected the proletariat: in the capitalist mode of production workers became alienated from the products of their labour, the process of labour, their 'species-being' and their fellow workers. This alienation was supported by a system of ideology that the capitalist society propagated: through the law, the state and the semblance of democracy, the proletariat was pacified to live under a *false consciousness* which legitimised the state of their oppression and hid away the underlying economic exploitation of the proletariat. It followed that the development of *class consciousness* was necessary among the workers: it was important that they realise that their 'real interests' lay not in competing with each other for jobs but in challenging the system of capitalist exploitation. Equipped with a realisation of the 'deep running' nature of class conflict, they would come to understand that any revolutionary change would need to entail a holistic challenge to the material/productive and ideational/superstructural forces in society.

It would also be necessary to reflect on the consequences of the capitalist drive for profit on an international scale: as later Marxists (especially Lenin) argued, the profit-motive could also be seen to be a key driver of *imperialism* by capitalist states. Capitalism for Marxists is not a domestic phenomenon but a global one.

Many contentions have been made about whether Marx assumed that there would be an inevitable shift in the capitalist mode of production towards communism or whether social actors should take an active role in bringing about the end of the capitalist mode of exploitation. Marx's frequent references to the laws inherent in political economy structures seemed to imply an inexorable logic of development, although arguably the emphasis on laws (and a positivist idea of science) was a consequence of Engels' particular posthumous interpretation of Marx's work. Because of the unclear nature of Marx's view on political action, as the twentieth century unfolded so did complex debates about what constitutes legitimate proletarian political action (e.g. in Soviet and Chinese contexts) and about how change can be achieved in countries where the working classes are reluctant to take action against capitalist elites and states (e.g. Western Europe and the US). Much of twentieth century Marxist tradition and critical theory thought has focused on dealing with the tensions and unanswered questions that arose out of Marx's thinking on the logic of the capitalist system, the super-structural forces attached to it and the question of revolutionary social change. Certainly, Gramsci, the Frankfurt School and post-Marxists, such as Laclau and Mouffe, have all in their own ways sought to negotiate new interpretations of Marx's ideas for the purposes of devising emancipatory political action in their specific contexts.

Indeed, although most twentieth century critical theorists seek to go beyond Marx's categories – many of them especially expanding the analysis of ideological or cultural forms of oppression and domination – these analyses could be seen, to a significant extent, as derivatives of, although also to a significant extent as novel elaborations on, Marx's initial analysis of alienation and false consciousness within capitalist industrial society. Also, many critical theorists' emphasis on philosophy and theory as a reflection of social conditions, and on theory as closely tied to the practice of politics, also have affinities with Marx's ideas.

Of course the great confidence Marx had in the proletariat as an agent of emancipatory change, and the reductionist and deterministic aspects characteristic of his thought, have been legitimate targets of attack by later critical theorists. Marx was very much an Enlightenment figure and a believer in progressive change in society, something that is distinctly unpopular in the current era of social theory where ideas of progress, emancipation and grand political projects are in doubt. Yet, it seems fair to say that Marx still constitutes an important reference point for contemporary debates and it should not be forgotten that in dealing with world political issues such as globalisation, some theorists still consider it important to defend Marxism, especially in its 'humanist' forms. It seems then that Marx's thought is still not 'irrelevant' despite the many proclamations to that effect in the post-Cold War era: the legacy of Marx is still very much alive, and as contested as ever.

Further reading

Marx, Karl 'On the Jewish Question', various printings. An important 'early' piece by Marx, which gives a sense of the key 'critical theory' motivations evident in Marx's thinking. Notably, here Marx outlines his critique of liberal conceptions of political community and emancipation.

Marx, Karl *Communist Manifesto*. Especially chapter 1. Various printings. An excellent concise statement of the key principles and challenges posed by Marx against liberal economics and conceptions of politics.

Marx, Karl Preface to *A Contribution to a Critique of Political Economy*, various printings. A much cited and concise statement of the core principles of Marx's historical materialism.

Carver, Terrell (1991) *Cambridge Companion to Marx*. Cambridge: Cambridge University Press. An excellent set of essays on Marx, the context of his writings and their consequences.

Kellner, Douglas (1989) *Critical Theory, Marxism and Modernity*. Baltimore MD: Johns Hopkins University Press. Kellner traces the development of Marxist ideas within Frankfurt School critical theory.

24 Jean-Luc Nancy

Martin Coward

Jean-Luc Nancy's thought was referred to by Jacques Derrida as 'one of the immense philosophic works of our time' (Derrida 2005a: x). Born in 1940, Nancy graduated in philosophy in 1962 and went, after a period teaching in Colmar, to work in Strasbourg where he ultimately became Professor of Philosophy at the University of Strasbourg. Nancy's influences and interlocutors during the span of his career are many. However, several are worth noting in order to situate his work. Nancy's early philosophical work (after an association with Christian Socialism in the 1960s (James 2006: 5)) was written in collaboration with Philippe Lacoue-Labarthe. This work, which spans the period from the late 1970s to the mid 1980s, comprised critical engagements with, among others, the work of Jacques Lacan (Nancy and Lacoue-Labarthe 1992) and Jacques Derrida (Lacoue-Labarthe and Nancy 1997). Indeed, this period was characterised by a sustained engagement with deconstruction under the auspices of the Centre for Philosophical Research on the Political at the *École Normale Supérieure* in Paris. During his time as co-director of the Centre, Nancy engaged with philosophers such as Christopher Fynsk, Gayatri Chakravorty Spivak, Jean-François Lyotard and Claude Lefort (Lacoue-Labarthe and Nancy 1997). In the late 1980s, after the Centre had been dissolved, Nancy published the book for which he is probably most well known: *The Inoperative Community* (Nancy 1991). The arguments advanced in this book inspired reflections by Maurice Blanchot in his *The Unavowable Community* (Blanchot 1988). In the 1990s Nancy underwent a heart transplant and then fought against cancer. However, he maintained a regular publishing schedule, further developing his thought on community, co-existence, politics and art. His work during this later period was recently the subject of sustained reflection by Jacques Derrida in his *On Touching – Jean-Luc Nancy* (Derrida 2005a).

Nancy's published work encompasses a diverse set of concerns: philosophical commentary on, for example, Kant (Nancy 1993b), Hegel (Nancy 2002a), Heidegger and Bataille (Nancy 1991); research on the relation of the philosophical and the political (Lacoue-Labarthe and Nancy 1997); an ontology developed out of an original investigation of the nature of being-with or community (Nancy 2000); meditations on visual art (Nancy 1996) and the experience of undergoing a heart transplant (Nancy 2002b); and (more recently) reflections on war, monotheism and globalisation (Nancy 2000, 2003a, 2003b, 2007).

It is impossible in this chapter to give a comprehensive overview of this 'vast and heterogeneous' (James 2006: 1) body of work. Instead, I want to note three distinctive and yet interrelated themes in Nancy's work that should be of interest to those studying international relations: his investigation of the relationship between philosophy and politics under the auspices of the Centre for Philosophical Research on the Political; his elaboration of a co-existential ontology in the landmark books *The Inoperative Community* and *Being Singular Plural*; and his discussion of the manner in which the contemporary world is shaped by the forces of globalisation and monotheism. These themes could be said to trace a trajectory that corresponds to three historically consecutive phases in Nancy's career: a trajectory that starts with the early work under the auspices of the Centre and proceeds, via the elaboration of a mature co-existential ontology, to the recent discussions of the contemporary global condition.

Re-treating the political

In July 1980, Jean-Luc Nancy and Philippe Lacoue-Labarthe gave the opening address to a colloquium that took Derrida's essay 'The Ends of Man' (Derrida 1985: 109–36) as its 'point of departure' (James 2006: 155). The colloquium itself focused on the relationship between philosophy and politics. Later that year, supported by Althussser and Derrida, Nancy and Lacoue-Labarthe established The Centre for Philosophical Research on the Political at the *École Normale Supérieure* in Paris. The principle theme explored by Nancy and Lacoue-Labarthe during the Centre's four-year life span comprised the so-called 'withdrawal' or 'retreat' of the political.

The retreat of the political refers to the manner in which our epoch is marked by the loss of the specificity of the political (the latter conceived of as struggles over the nature, and thus regulation, of existence). Put simply, if the political is everywhere it has no specificity and, hence, its ubiquity is also a retreat. In other words, insofar as it is everywhere, politics has retreated from the idea that it has a specific place and qualities. However, this retreat of the political is not a simple withdrawal of the political into a position spatially separated from everyday life. Unlike an army's retreat from battle, the political has not left the field of social life. Rather, this retreat is a twofold dynamic. On the one hand the whole of social life becomes the arena for political power: everything is political. On the other hand, insofar as its ubiquity means it has no specificity, the nature of the political is put beyond questioning (its meaning is withdrawn from open contestation). When everything is political it becomes impossible to isolate, and thus question or contest, the specific quality of the political. The political thus becomes something assumed, unquestioned.

This retreat can be seen in the global ubiquity of political figures such as human rights. Human rights transform every aspect of our life into a political matter. There are no areas of that life to which human rights do not apply. Everything is thus political. At the heart of the idea of human rights is the figure of the human. And yet, this figure is merely assumed by the various discourses of human rights. Since human rights are everywhere, it is assumed that the human must have similar universality. As such then it is impossible to trace the (historical, geographical) specificities of the idea of the human. The idea of the human is thus put beyond question. One could say the same of the capital relation which, despite the various activities of scholars to demonstrate its specificities, remains an unquestioned assumption under the universal system of global capitalism. In both such figures we can see the retreat of the political as a simultaneous over-determination of the political by a philosophical concept (a particular idea of what is human or of the capital relation becomes that which determines the nature of social life) and, at the same time, a withdrawal of such concepts from questioning and contestation (as soon as a particular idea of humanity or relations of production and exchange are simply assumed to be the case we lose the potential to challenge them as only one philosophical concept among many).

Such a condition is referred to by Nancy and Lacoue-Labarthe as 'totalitarianism' (Lacoue-Labarthe and Nancy 1997: 126). This totalitarianism refers not to actual political regimes such as Nazism or the 'socialism' of Stalin but, rather, to the advent of societies whose fabric is determined by the universalisation of a particular philosophical idea of what it is to be human and to live together. This universalisation (whether it is consensually adopted or not) puts beyond question the idea on which society is said to be based, giving it 'the obviousness of an "it goes without saying"' (Lacoue-Labarthe and Nancy 1997: 126). That is, the specific concept on which society is predicated becomes 'common sense'. This common sense exerts a tyranny under which all forms of life must correspond to its unquestionable assumptions. It is this condition that Nancy and Lacoue-Labarthe refer to as the 'total completion of the political' (Lacoue-Labarthe and Nancy 1997: 126).

These reflections on totalitarianism lead Lacoue-Labarthe and Nancy (1997: 112) to argue that we should 're-treat' the political in a radical way: both withdraw from common schemas of political theory (which fail to question their founding assumptions) and at the same time re-trace the philosophical possibilities of politics. This re-tracing comprises a question about the social bond or the nature of being-together. Whilst this question of the nature of being-together is left largely undeveloped in the work of the Centre, it is, however, central to the texts that I will treat as the second phase of Nancy's work relevant to those who study international relations. This second phase of Nancy's work is defined by two texts: his essay (and book of the same title) *The Inoperative Community* and his more recent book *Being Singular Plural*. The (co-)ontology Nancy elaborates in these texts revolves around three concepts: community, co-existence and singularity.

Being-with: community, relationality and singularity

The Inoperative Community is a complex book that engages with a number of philosophical questions. Central to it, however, is a discussion of the nature of being-together or community. Nancy's inspiration for posing this question is dual. On the one hand the question of being-together is an urgent political question central to our era of interdependence. On the other it is one of the neglected elements of a major inspiration for Nancy's thought: Heidegger's *Being and Time*. According to Heidegger (1962: 149–68), all being is being-with. That is to say all experiences of being a self are formed in the context of always already being-with-others. Nancy draws on this observation when he notes that all understandings of being are relational (i.e. constituted in relation to others). He notes that we can see this existential priority of relationality in the paradox of being alone. Being alone is a particular mode of being with others in which those others are either ignored, denied or rejected. Being alone is thus only possible insofar as we always already exist in the context of relations with others. Being-with others, or simply being-with, thus has existential priority over other modes of being, such as being-alone (i.e. being-with others is the backdrop against which being-alone occurs).

This argument leads Nancy to note that classical understandings of 'community' (the term that most directly refers to the experience of being-with others) are flawed. Typically, community is conceived of in two ways. As Georges Van Den Abbeele (1991: xi) has noted, the *Oxford English Dictionary* proposes two etymologies for community 'the more philologically valid ... *com* + *munis* (... being bound, obligated or indebted together) and the more folk-etymological ... *com* + *unus* (... what is together as one)'. On the one hand community (*com* + *munis*) is understood in the liberal-contractarian tradition as the aggregation of pre-existent individual political subjects who become bound in their obligation to a contractual framework for reconciling differences and distributing power. In this form community is just the aggregation of individual subjects conceived ontologically as 'unencumbered and antecedently individuated ... [and thus] prior to society' (Mulhall and Swift 1996: 167).

For such an understanding, community is treated as simply the result of an empirical gathering of political subjects. It is a sort of accident that happens only because empirically we must live in the same space as each other. In other words, it is a fact of existence, but not an essential aspect of being (since the beings that make up such community are conceived of as self-contained and formed prior to society and interaction with others). This is the source of the entirety of the liberal-contractarian tradition which comprises an attempt to think about the consequences of making subjects whose essential nature is solitary share the same space (and thus the way in which we reconcile the assumed conflicts that will occur). For Nancy this understanding is back-to-front in its assumption that being-with is an empirical accident and politically problematic insofar as it assumes community is an antecedent, contingent aspect of being (almost a nuisance), not essential to it. On the other hand, community (*com* + *unus*) is understood in traditions such as nationalism and socialism to comprise the realisation of a truth of being immanent to a certain group of political subjects (e.g. the nation, the proletariat). According to this formulation community is a quality inherent to a class of subjects that requires realisation through various empirical strategies. This conception does not conceive of the elements of community as distinct however. Indeed, they are expressions of the same ontological substance and thus cannot be acknowledged as different to each other (e.g. each worker is the same as another and has no essential individual specificity). As such this community is not an instance of being-with others. To be with others there must be difference. One cannot be with that which is the same since one simply *is* (i.e. is *identical to*) that which is the same. Workers may, therefore, make up a class but they are not a community. The latter would require difference in order that we could claim it comprised an instance of being-together with others. That this is the case can also be seen in the way that nationalism memorialises death. Nationalist regimes elevate those who die for its perceived historical programme of realising its essential truth to the status of mythological heroes (Nancy 1991: 13). In doing so they make these dead others live on. In refusing to acknowledge their death, they refuse to acknowledge the ultimate relation of difference (i.e. the relation between living and dead). This is not a community of finite beings who have a relation with (or memory of) the dead, but a corporate entity that makes all elements (even the dead) into representations of the national substance. Nationalism thus pictures itself as a self-contained expression of a particular substance of being, rather than part of a community characterised by being-with others.

The problem with these understandings of community is that they assume the 'common' of this being-in-common is a 'substance uniformly laid out "under" supposed "individuals", [or] uniformly shared out among everyone like a particular ingredient' (Nancy 1991: xxxvii). Such understandings of what is common to our being-in-common thus assume 'we' share a certain substantial commonality: either we are substantially the same or all instances of a universal substance (i.e. differing states of embodiment of a certain substance). Both understandings fail to grasp community's central dynamic: being-with others (i.e. being-with difference). Moreover, such an understanding of the 'in-common' of community leads to an assumption of a substantial basis of being that simply requires a technical programme of realisation. That is, it is assumed that a certain substance is immanent to the being(s) that comprise the community and that, while this substance may be obscured or imperfectly revealed, all it requires is a technical programme to realise its potential. Nancy refers to this dynamic as 'figuration'.

Figuration refers to the manner in which a particular concept (or figure) is assumed to represent/comprise the immanent substantial basis of community.

This figure takes a number of forms (including but not limited to): individual, state, nation, and class. However, this figure is always immanent (or inherent) and thus effectively put beyond the contestation of the political arena. Rather the task is assumed to be the realisation of the substance that the figure is assumed to represent. All that fails to correspond to the decreed programme of realising this immanent substance is disavowed, elided, obscured and ultimately destroyed. Figuration is thus a disavowal of difference and, ultimately, a totalitarian philosophical determination of the political. We can see figuration in the subordination of all political life to the idea of the market or the autonomous liberal subject: figures who are assumed to represent a substance inherent to being requiring a program of empirical realisation. Despite the obvious failings of markets or the clear relationality of political life such figures continue to exercise a grip on politics under the assumption that these failings or relationalities are mere empirical imperfections of transcendental substances that can be remedied by better programs of realisation.

Figuration, however, fails to treat being-with, or relationality as an existentially prior event (or if it recognises this being-with it is only insofar as it attempts to disavow it). What happens, however, if, as Nancy suggests in *Being Singular Plural*, we treat such relationality seriously? Nancy suggests that we have to conceive of ontology as co-ontology. That is to say there is no understanding of being that is not always already being-with. All forms of subjectivity, self and identity are always conceived of in relation (even if that relation is a disavowal or negation). The existential priority of relationality prompts Nancy (2000: 21–28) to argue that the examination of what is 'between us' constitutes 'first philosophy': the most fundamental of terrains of enquiry.

For Nancy it is the relation itself that is the existentially prior moment, not the entities that are related. This is because the sense of there being an entity only arises from the relation. Self only emerges in and through differentiation from an other; identity is born in and through its relation with difference. This leads Nancy to argue that the relation is not a gap crossed between individuals, but a surface of contact at (and from) which two entities can be discerned. The relation is thus a shared border – the self marks its distinction from the other at a particular place where that self stops and its others begin. However, this border is shared – it is where self stops and where other begins. It is thus a surface of contact. This leads Nancy to note that community is not a communion with a particular substance of being – as liberals and nationalists perceive it to be – but, rather, is a communication. It is the experience of being exposed to, and thus comprehending, otherness at the borders from which our sense of being emerges. In this exposure the existential priority of being-with is communicated.

According to Nancy (2000: 9) this relational co-ontology gives rise to what he calls a 'reticulated multiplicity'. Reticulation refers to 'a division into a network or into small [spaces] with intersecting lines' (Oxford Paperback

Dictionary 1983: 564). Existence is thus constituted, according to Nancy, by the criss-crossed borders (or surfaces of contact) at which relationally defined entities emerge. Put simply, Nancy's co-existential analytic views the world as a network of relationships – a series of borders from which entities unfold – not as the realisation of a particular substance. There is no such thing as a self-contained individual identity that exists prior to any relations, no such thing as a community that exists without relation to its others. The notions of community that, through figuration, attribute a substantial basis to being-in-common try to effect an understanding of politics in which the community (or the individuals who make up community) are conceived as having a self-contained substantial basis (i.e. the possibility of existing without relation to others). And yet, Nancy notes that at a fundamental, ontological level, this is impossible. Figuration achieves the fiction of such being-without-relation only by disavowing difference. In reality, therefore, figuration can merely obscure the reticulated multiplicity, the relational being-with that is the co-existential condition.

Being-with means that all identity is constituted at the border between self and other and can never fully escape the exposure to difference that such a border implies. The sharing of surfaces of contact between self and other is both a violence (an exposure that negates the attempts of self to imagine itself as self-contained) and yet also a generative moment (the moment in which identity itself emerges out of the relation with difference). No matter how we try to deny these relations or shared surfaces of contact we can only ever cover them over, never fully disavow them. This dynamic of ontological relationality has two consequences of interest to those who study international relations.

First it means that all of the figures of community are perpetually unworked by the existential multiplicity that is ontologically prior to their existence. All the work done to realise a substantial basis for being is perpetually undone by the existential priority of relationality. A figuration can deny this relationality, but ultimately cannot hide it for ever. Community is thus *inoperative*: not broken, but unworked (Nancy 1991: 1–42). For those studying international relations this casts a new light on traditional state-centric schemas such as Kenneth Waltz's *Theory of International Politics* (Waltz 1979). At the heart of such schemas is a problem concerning co-existence and relationality: the existence of multiple entities in a supposed condition of anarchy. And yet the model of international relations developed to explain this anarchical condition rests on a dual disavowal of the insights of Nancy's co-existential analytic. On the one hand the figure of sovereignty works to realise the idea that each state has some sort of self-contained substantial basis, an autonomy, that means it can exist without relation to others. And yet, as writers such as David Campbell (1998c) have shown, sovereignty is a performative gesture that originates in relationality: it is a performance of what makes us 'us' and what makes them 'them' or the enactment of a relation of difference. On the other hand, the notion of anarchy works to similarly disavow relationality: giving the impression that nothing exists between the states of the international order. Such a concept attempts to cover over relationality with an idea of empty space. It sees the surface of contact at which a state emerges in relation to its other as a void. Nancy's co-existential analytic contests such an understanding insisting on seeing the global order as a reticulated multiplicity in which entities only emerge from the borders they share. There is no empty space, only a series of surfaces of contact at which relationality is communicated. This relationality unworks fictions and figures such as sovereignty and statehood. We must, therefore, begin to understand where the surfaces of contact are that give rise to the sense of statehood that is so central to international relations.

Second, if the reticulated multiplicity that Nancy refers to unworks all figures, can we discern alternative political structures at work? That is, if the traditional figures of political theory are bound to be unworked by relationality, how are we to discern any order at all in the world (after all, discerning order is central to studying international relations). The answer to such a question lies in tracing the outline of the reticulated multiplicity. Given that the relations, or surfaces of contact, which are the constitutive feature of the existential landscape are constantly shifting as relations are redefined (indeed all relational identity is flexible or labile), this tracing is not a simple one-off event, but rather a constant task of delineation. It thus requires a tracing out of the various networks of relationships that characterise international relations. In doing so the surfaces of contact that are constitutive of such networks will be delineated. Such a task reveals *singularities* not substances. Singularity refers to a unique set of relationships that coalesce to give rise to a discernable entity. This entity is born out of mobile relationships but stable enough that it is consistently visible. Nancy captures this idea in the concept of the *ensemble*. 'Ensemble' refers to 'the collaboration of diverse elements, and to the synchronisation of movement' (Macdonald 2003: 17–18). Ensembles are the common matter of international relations: more or less stable configurations of entities born out of relations. The state is an ensemble; global governance could be similarly described.

From the co-existential analytic to meditation on our contemporary condition

Despite the philosophical abstraction of his thought, Nancy's work has always been engaged with contemporary circumstances. His work on the retreat of the political, for example, comprised a response to the perception of the failure of the Left to offer a credible political alternative, whilst his thinking about community represents an engagement with the perceived poverty of explanations of how, in an era of interdependence and globalisation, we are to understand our being-with others. However, more recently Nancy has directly addressed two issues of contemporary concern. On the one hand he has examined the nature of globalisation and on the other has, under the rubric of a 'deconstruction of monotheism', characterised the dynamics of the post-9/11 era as a 'civil war' (Nancy 2003a). For my purposes these two themes comprise the third and final phase of Nancy's thought that is of significance for those who study international relations.

In *The Creation Of The World Or Globalisation*, Nancy examines the nature of the contemporary, globalised era. According to Nancy (2007: 54), globalisation represents the universalisation of what he refers to as a logic of 'general equivalence'. Crudely put, this refers to the globalisation of capitalism in which the commodity form represents a means of making everything equivalent to everything else. In other words commodification translates objects, subjects and events into forms where, via money, they can be rendered equivalent and, hence, exchangeable. The problem for Nancy is that such general equivalence disavows the singularity of the various different ways in which we exist. Nancy's argument rests upon the semantic difference between globalisation and the untranslatable French term '*mondialisation*'. For Nancy 'globalisation' refers to the process of the creation of a 'unitotality' (Nancy 2007: 28), or an ordering of life according to a single principle, in which difference is reduced to sameness through equivalence.

'*Mondialisation*', however, refers to the existential event of world formation. Here Nancy draws on the Heideggerian notion of 'being-in-the-world' (Heidegger 1962), arguing that being is always a process of formation of worlds. Any existence is thus a calling into existence of a world. Of course, for Nancy this world is always formed in exposure to others and thus is a relational world (or constituted in and through the relations that are its (co)existential building blocks). But it is, importantly, a singular world. My world cannot be self-contained and is always constitutively exposed to other worlds. Moreover, our worlds intersect, overlap (and are constituted in doing so) and there is nothing like the solipsism that pervades other existential accounts. But my world is nevertheless distinctively mine and, hence, singular. It is this singularity that Nancy invokes in the concept of '*Mondialisation*'. Indeed, he refers to the recognition of the singularity of world-formation as a question of 'justice' (Nancy 2007: 54). In this sense his comment could be seen to resonate with the 'One no, many yeses' (Esteva quoted in Kingsnorth 2003: 44) of the anti-globalisation movement: a phrase that indicates the need to reject the levelling dynamic of globalisation in order to preserve the multiple possibilities that it would otherwise destroy (Midnight Notes Collective 1998). Similarly, Nancy argues that a just ethos for the contemporary era will comprise a recognition and defence of the singular worlds at stake in the relentless expansion of the logic of general equivalence.

Nancy takes these themes further in his recent work on Monotheism (Nancy 2003b). Written largely after 9/11 this work grapples with the philosophical determination of the political 'unitotality' of globalisation (Nancy 2007: 28): the way in which the global is governed by a single, dominant principle and thus expressions of difference are reduced to sameness. This philosophical determination should, according to Nancy, be understood as an instance of 'ontotheology'. Ontotheology, refers to the manner in which an ontology, or theory of being, is predicated on a transcendent value (a value that is taken to be a universal essence independent of any particular empirical circumstances). In other words, the philosophical search for the ground of being (a universal truth), and the theological search for that which explains being (God as the creator) are joined into one (Inwood 1999: 149). For Nancy ontotheology and figuration coincide, with the figure being an ontotheological gesture that simultaneously attempts to name the ground of being and yet place it beyond question or to make it an assumption (an article of faith).

The ontotheological core of globalisation is, according to Nancy's later work, the monotheism associated with Christianity (Nancy 2003b). Nancy argues that this monotheism has become a universal phenomenon, spreading along with general equivalence. As such, when he reflects on the contemporary state of global order Nancy notes that there is no outside to monotheism. Monotheism and globalisation are equivalent: general equivalence and the transcendent theism that characterises religions of the book merge to provide a 'unitotality' of global proportions. This leads Nancy to claim that the war on terror must be construed as a civil war within monotheism. This notion resonates with similar understandings of contemporary political order as a form of global civil war (Hardt and Negri 2005) and thus rejects treating the war on terror as a clash of civilisations. At stake in this characterisation of globalisation and monotheism is a two-fold philosophical project. First, a return to the themes of being-with in order to demonstrate the way in which the seeming multiplicity of globalisation actually hides an unjust disavowal of singularity. Second, an ambitious attempt to trace out the philosophical traits that are at the core of the ontotheology of globalisation: namely the outlines of a deconstruction of Christianity (Nancy 2003b) that aims to demonstrate how this monotheism has philosophically determined the political in the contemporary, global era.

Conclusion: Nancy and international relations

Given the relevance of such observations for conceptualising the contemporary global condition, one would have thought that Nancy's work would be reasonably familiar to those studying international relations. However, few have engaged in a sustained manner with his thought. Those that have done so have largely concentrated on his thinking surrounding community and singularity. Michael Shapiro, for example, has drawn on Nancy's arguments concerning co-existence, and the multiplicity of voices this implies, to argue for a democratic ethos that is open to difference. Shapiro has argued that 'Nancy suggests that the singularities of subjects who find themselves in common cannot be confined within aggregated social identities'. (Shapiro 1999b: 126) This leads Shapiro (2000: 82) to argue for recognition of a 'disjointed copresence' that characterises existence and, hence, demands a 'way of constituting the political domain that resists ... closural impulses'.

Both Nick Vaughan-Williams and Fred Dallmayr address similar concerns. In his discussion of Huntington's *Clash of Civilisations* and Wallerstein's *Geopolitics and Geoculture*, Dallmayr notes that the latter's advocacy of a 'deconstruct[ion] ... without the erection of structures ... to continue the old in the guise of the new' (Dallmayr 1997: 192) resonates with Nancy's notion of an 'inoperative' community. Vaughan-Williams examines the 'ethical generality' of cosmopolitanism noting that the latter fails to address the singularities that form the constituency of any cosmopolis (Vaughan-Williams 2007a: 44). A politics premised on such singularity is thus proffered as an alternative to the stale polis/cosmopolis dichotomy that shapes much thinking regarding the possibilities of global order.

Finally, for my own part, I have argued that Nancy's co-existential analytic provides a framework within which to understand the agonistic interplay of identity and difference that is targeted by ethnic nationalism (Coward 2008). That is, ethnic nationalism abhors the originary exposure to difference that Nancy posits as an existential condition. Premised as it is on notions of autonomy and self-determination, ethnic nationalism perceives the originary relationality constitutive of (co-)existence as a form of contamination. Ethnic nationalists thus work to violently disavow the various traces of otherness that are constitutive of their identity: destroying bodies, monuments, artefacts and buildings. Ultimately, however, such campaigns are rendered void since relationality perpetually unworks all such figurations of politics (whether it be figures of ethnos, religion, nation or class). Ethnic nationalism responds to such unworking with vigorous and redoubled violence, but this does not mean that its fictions will ever become truth.

Nancy's work can thus be seen to have great potential for those studying international relations. It addresses a subject right at the heart of the discipline's subject matter: namely the problem of co-existence. All accounts of international relations in some way or another address the question of being-with others (Rosenberg 2000: 80). The problem with many of these accounts is that they reduce difference to sameness (e.g. they reduce all states to the same juridical form) and obscure the challenge of a co-existential analytic: how to construct a politics predicated not on generality and transcendent value, but rather on singularity and multiplicity. In this regard it is worth – by way of a conclusion – noting Jean-Luc Nancy's caution concerning the danger of failing to respond to such an urgent challenge:

> if we do not face up to such questions, the political will soon desert us completely, if it has not already done so. It will abandon us to political and technological economies, if it has not already done so. And this will be the end of our communities, if this has not yet come about. Being-in-common will nonetheless never cease to resist, but its resistance will belong decidedly to another world entirely. Our world, as far as

politics is concerned, will be a desert, and we will wither away without a tomb (Nancy 1991: xli).

Further reading

Heidegger, Martin (1962) *Being and Time*, trans. John Macquarie and Edward Robinson, Oxford: Blackwell. Heidegger's thought is the backdrop against which Nancy's develops. Of particular interest is Heidegger's account on pages 149–68 of the nature of *Mitsein*, or Being-with.

Hutchens, Benjamin C. (2005) *Jean-Luc Nancy and the Future of Philosophy*, Chesham: Acumen. A general introductory discussion of Nancy's work.

James, Ian (2006) *The Fragmentary Demand: An Introduction to the Philosophy of Jean-Luc Nancy*, Stanford: University of Stanford Press. The best introductory account of Nancy's thought in English. James addresses a series of thematic strands in Nancy's work including community.

Lacoue-Labarthe, Philippe and Nancy, Jean-Luc (1997) *Retreating the Political*, edited by Simon Sparks, London: Routledge. Provides English translations of Nancy and Lacoue-Labarthe's work at the Centre for Philosophical Research on the Political.

May, Todd (1997) *Reconsidering Difference: Nancy, Derrida, Levinas, and Deleuze*, Pennsylvania: University of Pennsylvania Press. Discusses the various ways in which these four thinkers, Nancy included, understand difference.

Miami Theory Collective (ed.) (1991) *Community At Loose Ends*, Minneapolis: University of Minnesota Press. A collection of essays – including one ('Of Being-in-Common') by Nancy – that address the issues of singularity and community.

Nancy, Jean-Luc (1991) *The Inoperative Community*, trans. Lisa Garbus, Peter Connor, Michael Holland and Simona Sawhney, London: University of Minnesota Press. Nancy's landmark discussion of the nature of being-in-common.

Nancy, Jean-Luc (2000) *Being Singular Plural*, trans. Robert D. Richardson and Anne E. O'Byrne, Stanford: Stanford University Press. Nancy's mature formulation of the co-existential analytic implied in his *Inoperative Community*. Includes an essay on war and sovereignty.

Sheppard, Darren, Sparks, Simon and Thomas, Colin (eds) (1997) *On Jean-Luc Nancy: The Sense of Philosophy*, London: Routledge. Collection of essays responding to, and developing upon, Nancy's work.

Smith, Jason (2002) 'Nancy's Hegel, the State, and US', in Nancy, Jean-Luc *Hegel: The Restlessness of The Negative*, trans. Jason Smith, Minneapolis: University of Minnesota Press. Smith's introduction to Nancy's *Hegel* is one of the best summaries of the nature of Nancy's thinking about the political.

25 Friedrich Nietzsche

Robin Durie

The possibility that the work of Friedrich Nietzsche could have a constructive influence on political and international relations theory was long undermined by his apparent endorsement of Aryan supremacism and anti-Semitism, alongside the explicit appropriation of his writings by admirers such as Hitler and Mussolini. However, the biographical machinations by which these gross caricatures were allowed to develop have gradually been revealed by a succession of scholars beginning with Walter Kauffman, allowing for the emergence of a 'new' Nietzsche, whose thinking has, in turn, profoundly influenced the work of writers such as Derrida, Deleuze, Foucault, Klossowski and Blanchot.

Trained in classical philology, Nietzsche was appointed to the Chair in Classical Philology at Basel, Switzerland in 1869. Increasing mental and physical ill-health led to him resigning his appointment in 1879, after which he lived off a modest pension from the Swiss government. In 1889 Nietzsche finally succumbed to the mental ill-health that had been tormenting him for the previous decade. For the final 11 years of his life, he was 'looked after' by his sister, Elisabeth Förster-Nietzsche, and she it was who set about engendering a cult of Nietzsche through the founding of a Nietzsche Archive. It was through her work – notably an edited collection of his works, a two-volume biography, and an edition of Nietzsche's working notes, published as *The Will to Power* – that Nietzsche came to be represented as a proto-Nazi, to the extent that the Führer himself attended a lavish state-sponsored funeral for Nietzsche in 1935.

But Förster-Nietzsche's work in fact consisted in a massive distortion of Nietzsche's thought. This was in part made possible by the remarkable nature of Nietzsche's style. With a few notable exceptions, Nietzsche's work was written in the form of aphorisms – often seemingly contradictory – culminating in the stunning *Thus Spoke Zarathustra*, in which Zarathustra seeks to teach a number of characters of the coming of the *Übermensch* [Overman]: the post-moral, post-theistic overcoming of humankind. But Zarathustra is consistently thwarted in his attempts, due, he believes, to the inability of his fellow-travellers to understand his teachings. He is thus led to experiment with ever-new forms of address in an attempt to enable his message to be heard and understood.

Part of the failure of these forms of address stems from what Nietzsche believed to be the dominant condition of late nineteenth century humanity: *nihilism*. Nihilism manifests itself in a social world of empty prattle, bereft of any true commitment to a possible new morality. As Deleuze has shown, nihilism consists in a profoundly *reactive* condition characterised by the tendency towards negation or 'nay-saying'. Nietzsche's critique of the decadence of European modernity is allied to his rejection of the ideals of growth and progress, and this dimension of his work in and of itself remains of fundamental importance for contemporary political and international relations theory.

To an extent, the source of this nihilism stems from 'the death of God'. In a famous series of passages in *The Gay Science*, Nietzsche depicts a madman coming into a town square proclaiming the death of God. The madman is met with scornful derision from the *bien-pensant* nihilists, not because they believe in God, but because his death is *passé*. But Nietzsche's argument is that we have yet to face up to the consequences of our supreme act of parricide – the system of morality which informs our contemporary world remains identical to that which found its provenance in Judaeo–Christian theology. Truly to confront the death of God requires us to abandon the old morality and undertake a 'revaluation of all values'. This revaluation would consist in an *overcoming* of traditional morality, in a similar way to that in which the *Übermensch* would represent an overcoming of traditional humanity.

This new morality would be, as the title of another of Nietzsche's works has it, *Beyond Good and Evil*, by which Nietzsche means not amorality but a morality which overcomes traditional moral categories such as 'good' and 'evil'. But what could the conditions be that would enable such an overcoming? First and foremost, they must consist in the possibility of calling into question the value of values. But in turn such a calling into question entails that categories such as values are not fixed or transcendental, but are instead dynamic, subject to the flow of historical forces. Furthermore it is necessary to be able to develop a means for revealing how these historical forces give rise to the valuation that values have taken on through history, in other words to the *sense* that values have accrued. This involves the creation of a new method of interpretation, which Nietzsche presents in his *Genealogy of Morality*.

The *Genealogy* is perhaps Nietzsche's most systematic work, and it is certainly the text which offers the richest resource for contemporary theorists in the disciplines of politics and international relations. In this work Nietzsche develops what amounts to a differential metaphysics of forces, showing how all bodies are the result of differential relations between forces. He demonstrates how weak bodies are able, through the simultaneous development of 'bad conscience' and guilt in strong bodies stemming from nihilistic *ressentiment* and its rendering of suffering as a virtue, to overcome strong bodies.

This differential metaphysics of forces finds its most striking formulation in Nietzsche's notion of *will-to-power*. Typically misconstrued as a body's inherent striving for power, or as an end-in-itself, in fact for Nietzsche will-to-power signifies every body's innate tendency to express its power, to seek to do – as Deleuze reminds us citing Spinoza – what it can do. Thus, what a body can do is determined both by the differential forces whose inter-relations give rise to that body and by the qualitative response expressed by that body towards this differential relation – whether affirmative or negative. It is precisely this double aspect of the body which Deleuze argues reveals the genuine nature of will-to-power.

Further reading

The following are amongst the most important Nietzsche texts for those working in the fields of international relations and political theory – they are also the works in which one finds the majority of Nietzsche's key concepts: eternal return, death of God, will-to-power, transvaluation of values, etc. In addition, the *Genealogy of Morality* is particularly important as a resource for Nietzsche's methodology.

Nietzsche, Friedrich (1974) [1882] *The Gay Science*, trans. Walter Kaufmann New York: Vintage.
Nietzsche, Friedrich (2002) [1886] *Beyond Good and Evil*, ed. Rolf-Peter Horstmann and trans. Judith Norman, Cambridge: Cambridge University Press.
Nietzsche, Friedrich (1994) [1887] *On the Genealogy of Morality*, ed. Keith Ansell-Pearson and Carol Diethe, Cambridge: Cambridge University Press.
Nietzsche, Friedrich (1978) [1891] *Thus Spake Zarathustra*, trans. Walter Kaufmann, New York: Penguin Books.
Allison, David B. (1985) (ed.) *The New Nietzsche: Contemporary Styles of Interpretation*, Cambridge, MA: The MIT Press. This is a very useful selection of 'Continental' readings of Nietzsche, including essays by Heidegger, Deleuze, Derrida, Klossowski, Kofman and Blanchot.
Deleuze, Gilles (2006) [1962] *Nietzsche and Philosophy*, trans. Hugh Tomlinson, London: Continuum. Seeks to develop a systematic reading of Nietzsche, in which genealogy is presented as the fulfilment of Kantian critique, while simultaneously being radically opposed to Hegelian dialectics. Transformed Nietzsche's reputation in France, and prompted the renaissance in French Nietzsche studies.
Foucault, Michel (1984) 'Nietzsche, Genealogy, History', in Paul Rabinow (ed.) *The Foucault Reader*, London: Penguin Books. Makes clear the nature of the influence of Nietzsche's genealogical methodology on Foucault's thinking.
Kauffman, Walter (1974) *Nietzsche: Philosopher, Psychologist, Anti-Christ*, Princeton: Princeton University Press. Amongst the best introductions to Nietzsche's life and thought, this was the work which paved the way for the rehabilitation of Nietzsche's reputation in the English-speaking world.
Klossowski, Pierre (1997) *Nietzsche and the Vicious Circle*, trans. Daniel Smith, London: Athlone. Remarkable and original, though notoriously difficult, work which seeks to establish the centrality of the thought of the eternal return for Nietzsche's work.

26 Jacques Rancière

Rens van Munster

Jacques Rancière is one of the most innovative and prolific thinkers of the current Left. Strongly inspired by the thought of Althusser, Foucault and other strands of French thought in the second half of the twentieth century, Rancière has developed an anti-foundational account of politics that is every bit as original as it is radical. Claiming that genuine emancipation involves the confirmation of equality, Rancière's main objective is to recuperate politics from the point of view of the abject. Whether he writes about political science and philosophy, cultural studies, history, pedagogy or literature, his thinking always concerns the question of how the abject might take the stage, make themselves heard and put a claim on society's members to be recognised as their equals. This relentless exploration of the ways in which a social distribution of roles, places and functions is challenged in the name of equality offers, in a time where traditional leftwing politics seems to have lost much of its critical purchase, 'one of the few consistent conceptualizations of how we are to continue to resist' (Žižek 2004b: 79).

Intellectual biography

Born in Algiers in 1940, Jacques Rancière began his academic career as a student of Louis Althusser at the prestigious *École Normale Supérieure* in Paris. He took part in Althusser's seminar on Marx, in which prominent contemporaries such as Alain Badiou, Étienne Balibar and Jacques-Alain Miller also participated. The seminar sought to retrieve in Marxism a purely scientific theory that would be unpolluted and unaffected by actually existing Marxism in the Soviet Union. To this end, Althusser developed his theory of ideology, by which he means a set of social practices – embodied in institutions and rituals – whose main function is to guarantee the reproduction of capitalist society. Because of this ideological curtain the masses are unable to recognise their real historical situation of exploitation, which they wrongly experience as one of freedom and equality. In this optic, the central task of the scientist is to reveal the workings of ideology and to assist those who could not by themselves recognise and throw off their ideological veil.

While Rancière worked solidly within the Althusserian tradition, contributing, in 1967, a chapter to the first edition of Althusser's *Lire le Capital*, he soon grew dissatisfied with his teacher's thought. In particular, the May 1968 student revolt, in which Rancière played a central role as a member of the Maoist student organisation, convinced him that Marxism only had limited theoretical and empirical relevance to social struggles that did not originate from economic class conflict. Moreover, Rancière was increasingly convinced that Althusser's theory of ideology was, in fact, a conformist theory. Dissatisfied with the strong distinction between science and ideology, he argued that the right claimed by 'enlightened' intellectuals to speak on behalf of the masses left intact the hierarchy between *bourgeoisie* and working class (Rancière 1974, 1998). Rather than emancipating the masses, structural Marxism took away their voice.

Rancière distanced himself from Althusser with his 1974 publication *La leçon d'Althusser*. This book, a veritable *coup de maître*, marked the beginning of Rancière's distinctive thought, which from then on took a more historical turn. For the next ten years, Rancière spent most of his time analysing the historical archives on worker movements in nineteenth-century France. Rather than falling into the Marxist trap of the philosopher that speaks on behalf of the poor, his historical analyses tell the stories of workers who refused to perform the social role assigned to them. Rancière recounts, chronicles and documents the multiple ways in which workers in France claimed for themselves the rights and activities originally reserved for the well-off. He shows that emancipatory acts are found not first and foremost in the worker that confronted the order from below with revolutionary pamphlets but in the workers who – by reading poetry and attending the same plays as the *bourgeoisie*, for example – crossed distinctions between labour and leisure, worker and middle-class (Rancière 1989, 1994).

These concrete struggles for emancipation in the nineteenth-century constitute the empirical background against which Rancière began to develop his conceptual framework of politics, equality and emancipation in the 1990s. Inspired by the worker movements, his thinking about politics is based upon an understanding of political struggle as an aesthetic moment. Emancipation is the result of a theatrical staging, where the excluded take the scene and transgress the boundaries between different classes:

> In order to enter into political exchange, it becomes necessary to invent the scene upon which spoken words may be audible, in which objects may be visible, and individuals themselves may be recognized. It is in this respect that we may speak of a *poetics of politics* (Rancière and Panagia 2007: 115).

Just as poetry breaks with the grammatically determined order and function of words, politics is a creative moment where the social order is rethought from the limit.

In light of his understanding of politics as a poetic appropriation, it is no surprise that Rancière's most recent writings deal with aesthetics, literature and film. The latter are seen as inextricably linked to questions of equality and (intellectual) emancipation insofar as their capability to blur the boundaries between fiction and reality can help create the conditions for disrupting existing social hierarchies. By freely circulating words and images, those not supposed to read and write are stimulated to contemplate the conditions of their existence (reality) and the possibilities for its transgression (fiction) (Rancière 2004b, 2004c, 2007).

In his own writings, Rancière also deliberately moves between science/ fiction, past/present and speaking/chronicling. His reason for doing so is as much methodological as political. From a methodological point of view, his way of writing helps retrieve and lend a voice to the deeds of those who have been relegated to the silent margins of history. But Rancière is not just interested in revising history for the sake of history. His intentions are political, using history to question and rethink the social hierarchies of our own age (Rancière 2000: 4). In other words, his aim, not unlike Foucault's genealogy, is to rediscover the voices of the past in order to make them talk to the present.

Rancière's longstanding focus on politics as a struggle, as a process of breaking down divisions and boundaries, has rightly earned him a central place among leftwing intellectuals and politicians. For example, the 2007 socialist candidate for the French Presidency, Ségolène Royal, delivered parts of his political essay, *Hatred of Democracy*, as punch lines in her election campaign. Although Rancière is probably right to argue that this was a rhetorical move more than anything else, it is nevertheless the case that his never ceasing focus on equality provides a unique starting point from which to inquire into the nature of politics and the possibility of emancipation in our age.

The presupposition of equality and the question of politics

The question of equality is at the heart of Rancière's framework. Yet, his notion of equality is unconventional and merits our attention. Rather than thinking of equality as a desired end-state or result, Rancière views equality as an activity or practice that *unmakes* social relations of oppression. Ross correctly notes that in Rancière's work, equality is 'a *pre-supposition* rather than a goal, a point of departure, a *practice* rather than a reward situated firmly in some distant future so as all to better explain its present infeasibility' (Ross 1991: 67). Although inequalities of course do exist in real life, Rancière deems it crucial to maintain the view of equality as an *a priori* assumption. The mistake made by Althusser and others, as implied by Ross, was not so much that they were anti-egalitarian (quite the opposite), but that they took *in*equality as their point of departure, constantly postponing the point of equality's realisation. For Rancière, however, equality is the *sine qua non* of every existing social order. Every social distribution and every inequality can only exist against the background of a fundamental equality. To illustrate what Rancière means by this, it is useful to invoke Rancière's (1991, 1995, 1999) example of a speech by the Roman senator Appius Claudius that took place on top of the Aventine, where plebeians, copying the proceedings of the Senate, had gathered to discuss politics and society amongst themselves. Appius Claudius, a man of noble heritage, went to the hill to explain to the plebeians that they had no business deliberating public affairs. Plebeians, he explained, were merely the stomach of the body-politic; thinking and speaking were the prerogative of the head, i.e. the senators. However, Claudius, by having to explain to the plebeians their *inequality*, actually confirmed their equality as speaking beings. In asking them to accept their lower position, he presumed the plebeians, too, were persons capable of reasoning and understanding.

Rancière's view on equality is at the core of his conception of politics: 'Politics ... is that activity which turns on equality as its principle' (Rancière 1999: ix). While political science generally operates with an understanding of politics that revolves around the organisation of power and the sets of procedures by means of which values are authoritatively located in society, Rancière instead claims that such procedures and allocations are better understood as *police*. The notion of police does not simply refer to law enforcement but, drawing upon the broader historical meaning of the term, to all practices by means of which the population is divided, classified and represented (see also Foucault 2007). Policing allocates individuals to specific classes and constructs, maintains and sediments social hierarchies and inequality.

Being opposed to the forms of accounting that policing entails, Rancière reserves the term politics for the specific and relatively rare forms of action that disrupt hierarchies and, in doing so, confirm equality:

> I propose now to reserve the term politics for an extremely determined activity antagonistic to policing: whatever breaks with the tangible configuration ... Political activity is whatever shifts a body from the place assigned to it or changes a place's destination. It makes visible what had no business being seen, and makes heard a discourse where once there was only place for noise; it makes understood as discourse what was once only heard as noise (Rancière 1999: 29–30).

Politics is characterised by a process of *subjectivation*, which refers to the situation whereby individuals create a space where equality can be verified. This requires, first and foremost, a process of dis-identification. 'Taking the stage' implies that those who are oppressed escape from the roles assigned to them and put a claim on society to be recognised as equal. For Rancière, in practice, a process of subjectivation produces inscriptions of equality and involves arguments about already existing inscriptions. While it should be stressed that politics is a creative, poetic moment rather than a physically violent one, equality is not guaranteed simply by the presence of universal inscriptions of rights. 'The "rights of man and of the citizen"', argues Rancière, 'are the rights of those who make them a reality' (Rancière 2006: 74). Rancière traces the origins of politics to the birth of democracy in ancient Greece, claiming that subjectivation (and not free elections, division of powers or any other institutional arrangement) is *the* defining feature of democracy:

> Democracy is, properly speaking, the symbolic institution of the political in the form of the power of those who are not entitled to exercise power – a rupture in the order of legitimacy and domination. Democracy is the paradoxical power of those who do not count (Rancière and Panagia 2000: 124).

What originally characterised the *demos*, Rancière suggests, is that it confronted the unequal order with a demand for equality. Contrary to what is sometimes believed, the *demos* was not made up of all free people but simply referred to the group of individuals that were no longer allowed to be enslaved but nevertheless lacked the wealth and virtue required for participation in the public sphere. However, real freedom, argued the *demos*, meant that they should be given their rightful place in the public sphere, on an equal footing with the ruling classes – even if they had no positive property (virtue or wealth) to justify their claims. Officially unqualified to take part in ruling, the *demos* could not be identified in ethnic or material terms. The only property they had was their freedom, which basically was a negative property, a negation of the existing distributions in the social order. The process of subjectivation took place when the *demos*, who could not be reduced to an existing social role or position, took the stage and represented the negative property of freedom as the common title of the political community (hence the word *demo*cracy).

Politics thus emerges when the people – the *demos*, slaves, the proletariat, women, the underclass, immigrants – declare themselves as equals by setting up a dispute between them and the ruling classes. Such a dispute is called a dissensus (as opposed to a consensus), by which Rancière means that the egalitarian polemic is a coming-together-in-conflict. Equality arises when those who have no formal right to do so appeal to the fact that already existing principles are not enacted universally. Rather than a specific form of governing, democracy thus refers to the ever-present possibility of an unpredicted subject emerging that creates a physical space (whether it is a hill, the streets, the factory or the parliament) where the claim of equality can be stated.

The disavowal of politics and consensus democracy

Rancière's interest in politics as the radical moment in which those who have no rights verify their equality is closely linked to his analysis of the ways in which the police order prevents, disavows or forecloses the democratic process of subjectivation. More specifically, he identifies three ways of denouncing democratic politics: *archipolitics, parapolitics* and *metapolitics* (Rancière 1995, 1999).

The first, archipolitics, is based on the communitarian standpoint that a community is built around a homogeneous identity (national, ethnic, cultural) with fixed borders that demarcate inside from outside and citizen from foreigner. In this view, the democratic excess simply does not exist because everybody worth counting is already accounted for. One of the most extreme versions of this position is found in the work of Carl Schmitt, who defines politics in terms of friends and enemies between whom there is no common symbolic ground. Parapolitics, second, acknowledges that social conflicts exist within society but it reduces the theoretical paradox of politics (where the logic of equality clashes with that of the police) to a practical problem of governance. Thus, some forms of liberalism are parapolitical insofar as they seek to transform conflict into a competition over offices. Finally, metapolitics denounces politics insofar as it locates the potential of subjectivation in a specific location. For example, Marxism locates politics in working class struggle only and, in doing so, denies all other struggles any political significance.

According to Rancière, parapolitics best describes the situation of Western societies in the Cold War period, when ideological conflicts between left and right were fought out between different parties competing for office. Since the end of the Cold War, however, the disavowal of politics has taken on novel forms. Contrary to those who saw in the end of the Cold War the triumph of democracy, Rancière is of the opinion that it instead marked the demise of real democratic politics. More specifically, Rancière's worries concern the rise of consensus democracy. In the post-ideological age, consensus democracy stands for the attempt to arrive at a universal consensus through the negotiation of interests between different groups and shareholders. As such, it operates on the basis that grievances in society can be addressed through a process of free deliberation and an efficient non-ideological governance of the social problems found in society. It is based on the idea that everything is and can be accounted for and that all problems can be addressed. Heralded as the Third Way by its protagonists, Rancière denounces consensus democracy as an oxymoron. His view of politics is that of a coming together in conflict (dissensus), but such a conflict is foreclosed by consensus democracy that invariably wants to remove antagonism and struggle from politics. Consensus democracy, he argues, is better understood as governance without politics or deliberation without democracy.

Two things, in particular, he finds problematic about consensus democracy. The first is its strong reliance on public opinion. Instead of being confronted with the unpredictable democratic subject that takes the stage, consensus democracy is a process of endless counting and polling of the problems and issues that are important for voters. Rather than taking account of the invisible, polling brings everything and everyone into sight. Moreover, since the solution to these problems is found in consensus, this form of 'democracy' precludes communities from developing around a dispute produced by the democratic moment of subjectivation:

> Any dispute, in this system, becomes a name of a problem. And any problem can be reduced to a simple lack ... of the means to solve it. Identifying and dealing with the lack must then be substituted for the manifestation of wrong: the objectification of problems that will have to involve state action, from the margins of choice included, the expertise called on, the parts of the social body implicated, and the partners who need to be set up for the problems to be discussed (Rancière 1999: 107).

Public opinion puts everything on display and forecloses the possibility of any democratic subject bringing forward its claim to equality. It turns all claims and disputes into addressable problems. The poetic moment of subjectivation is objectified as a problem that can be addressed within the confines of existing hierarchies. This in turn results in comprehensive networks of governance aimed at improving well-being for all kinds of groups and minorities. Yet, according to Rancière, democracy only happens when a group exists that cannot be reduced to a part of the population and its place in society (e.g. the *demos*, the proletarians) and whose demands upset the smooth functioning of economic and political systems.

The second problem is that polling leads to an exhaustive regime of rights. The identification of group-specific problems produces a culture where those groups and minorities claim the right to have their particular problems solved. Consequently, the law no longer functions as the inscription of universal rights available for emancipatory claims; rather, it becomes an instrument of governance aimed at increasing the well-being of specific groups, often through the universalisation of minority rights.

When the only political path left is to claim more rights designed for a specific minority, consensus democracy precludes minorities from making any political demands that call for the reorganisation of society as a whole. Subjects are forced to identify with the social role and position assigned to them through extensive processes of polling and rights granting. Real emancipation, however, can only happen through a process of subjectivation which ultimately is a process of dis-identification and transgression of established political forms. For Rancière, emancipation is not about getting your minority status recognised. It is not about secession but about the ability to set up a dispute that demonstrates that one is a 'joint-sharer in a common world, with the assumption, appearances to the contrary notwithstanding, that one can play the same game as the adversary' (Rancière 1995: 49).

Consensus democracy, by contrast, confirms inequality insofar as it accepts that society is made up of different groups that should not interfere with each other. It may even reinforce the image that identities are not only univocal but also incompatible and antagonistic. While its aim was to take passion and conflict out of politics, consensus democracy, paradoxically, also creates the conditions of possibility for ethnic and racial conflicts. For Rancière, this is no coincidence: when there are no political ways of negotiating otherness, the other returns in its absolute form, as the object of our hatred. Violent outbursts in the form of racism, religious fundamentalism or hooliganism and consensus democracy are thus two sides of the same coin: the suppression of real democracy.

Rancière and international relations theory

Rancière's thought provides an important intellectual reservoir for critical perspectives that are concerned with rethinking global politics from the perspective of the excluded, marginalised and oppressed. Ironically, however, Rancière himself is rather pessimistic about the possibility for a dissensual politics on the international level, even implying that his form of politics requires the presence of the state structure:

> Today, this scene [where politics confronts the police] is fractured. The responsibility of order is divided in an indecisive manner between nation-states, international institutions, and a faceless world-order: a center that is both everywhere and nowhere … The separation of these scenes makes their unification into transversal forms of subjectification close to impossible: there is no statist scene to confront (Rancière and Panagia 2007: 126).

Processes of subjectivation are always local in character. On the global level such processes are unlikely to take place, because people are too far removed from each other (Rancière 1999: 138). In such cases, as Aradau (2004: 405) has argued, emancipation evolves through more indirect strategies. These strategies establish not a direct political link with the other, but challenge practices that their states adopt towards these others. As she points out, the protests against the war on terror under the banner 'Not in Our Name' provide such an example (Aradau 2004: 405). The actions taken by the peace movement 'Ploughshares Women' provide another example of people unwilling to accept the complicity of their government in the killing of civilians elsewhere. The 'Ploughshares Women' damaged a British aircraft, which the British government had sold to Indonesia, where it would be deployed against East-Timor. As one of the spokeswomen defended herself in court: 'I am not willing for innocent civilians to be killed in my name and for this to be "justified" as providing jobs for the British people. I wish to act as a responsible member of the world community' (cited in Booth 2007: 460–61).

Although Rancière considers these indirect struggles as the main possibilities for politics on a supra-national level, several scholars have related his thought more directly to international developments, pointing out that important connections exist between the local and the international. For example, Shapiro (2002, 2005, 2006) has drawn upon Rancière's more aesthetical work to show how cultural expressions such as film, literature and photography can contest existing social divisions and open up space for imagining alternative, less exclusive arrangements of the international. Pointing out the local image of the multicultural city in the film *Pretty Dirty Things*, Shapiro (2006) contests existing geographies of the nation-state as the privileged place of belonging. While Shapiro's work strongly suggests that the international and local are interrelated, it also tends to conflate the aesthetics with politics. But even if (visual) art can assist us in thinking differently, this does not, according to Rancière, make it political. Although cultural expressions often express visions of community, 'equality is only implemented in the specific form of a particular case of dissensus' and, hence, 'literary equality is not the same as political equality' (Rancière 2004b: 53–4). Nevertheless, the relationship between the aesthetic register on the one hand and the realm of political struggle on the other remains somewhat underspecified in Rancière's work. As hinted at by Shapiro, the modes through which diverse cultural genres can be enlisted in political struggles on the international level is one aspect of Rancière's thought that could be further explored in international relations scholarship (see also Campbell and Shapiro 2007).

To date, the political aspects of Rancière's thought have been taken up most explicitly in the field of critical security studies, where Rancière's politics of equality has been posited as an alternative to processes of securitisation. Security practices exclude individuals and groups from a community, often violently. For example, whereas most states have freely given up control over the global flows of capital and goods, such states have at the same time also strengthened the control of borders when it comes to the circulation of the poor, who today move under the name of 'economic refugees', 'illegal immigrants' or '*bogus* asylum seekers'. As Rancière has defined politics mainly in metaphors of mobility and the crossing of boundaries, the securitisation of these groups – resulting in the *de facto* denial of mobility to large parts of the people of the world – constitutes one of the most significant denouncements of equality in our time. Thus, Aradau (2004, 2008) has pointed out that thinking of equality as a presumption can help to unmake the hierarchical logic security entails while, at the same time, furnishing a principle upon which a new relationality with the other can be conceived.

In a similar vein, others have shown how such forms of relationality appear not necessarily on a local level only. They have pointed out that universal rights – such as human rights and the right to free movement – are, despite the absence of the state, also inscribed on the regional or global level. In their view, Rancière's notion of rights as trophies to be taken also creates the possibility for forging new realities on an international level. For example, van Munster (2009) points out that undocumented immigrants in France, the *sans papiers*, have appropriated for themselves the European inscription of the freedom of movement. As Madjiguène Cissé, one of the spokespersons for the movement, argued: 'When these rights are under threat, it is legitimate to struggle to have them reinstated ... Freedom of movement is not something invented. It *confirms* an existing situation ... One day, "those without papers" ... requested precisely the acknowledgment of that situation' (Cissé 1997, emphasis added).

The notion that human rights and the freedom of movement are the rights of those who make something of that inscription also underlies Nyers' view on 'abject cosmopolitanism', which rethinks cosmopolitanism from the standpoint of the poor, the illegal immigrants and the cast-offs of the global order. Arguing that the immigrant is the cosmopolitan figure *per se*, he calls for a move away from an understanding of cosmopolitanism that aims at the constitution of world citizens behind the horizon of contemporary politics towards an understanding of cosmopolitanism that is located in the concrete struggles by which abject populations re-take inscriptions of equality (Nyers 2003). Drawing upon the work of Rancière, he shows that while these struggles take place on the local level, they have important implications for rethinking community on the global level. Thus, the 'No One Is Illegal' initiative and other anti-deportation campaigns are examples of abject cosmopolitanism in action insofar as they radically call into question claims to sovereignty and principles of border control. Local struggles are the concrete situations where a democratic cosmopolitanism is enacted and establishes new forms of relationality with the other. The usefulness of Rancière's views on resistance is not limited, of course, to questions of security. Questions of gender, economy and development provide areas where Rancière's work can provide important theoretical and empirical clues for analysing the disruption of social divisions.

Finally, Rancière provides an original view of the relationship between universal human rights and emancipation that could be pushed further. Rancière's view of human rights as something simultaneously present (as written inscriptions) and non-present (not enacted) points at an irresolvable *aporia* that functions as the necessary background condition for any emancipatory politics of equality (rights are out there to be taken). Unfortunately, this aporia is often not recognised. On the one hand, many liberal cosmopolitans claim that the mere extension of human rights to the global deprived as such is a sign of a more egalitarian global society. But more universal forms of belonging do not emerge through the conferral of human rights to groups deprived of it, but only through the identification with the political cause of those that resist oppressive and inhumane practices. In fact, conferring human rights upon the oppressed runs the risk of viewing the latter as passive victims to be saved, without any political voice. In these cases, as Dillon (2005) has warned, 'their' rights turn into 'our' privilege to take actions on their behalf. For example, NATO's 1999 humanitarian intervention in Kosovo was successful insofar as it contributed to the prevention of more killing, but it was much less successful in solving the political struggle over Kosovo. Contrary to what many Kosovo-Albanians hoped, Kosovo was granted not independence but the blessings of UN administration.

On the other hand, the problems involved in existing humanitarian policies do not necessarily need to imply that human rights should be abandoned as a principle. Rancière does not agree with approaches that either unmask universal rights as the hegemonic expression of Western values or as the simple cover-up for the pursuit of strategic interests. For Rancière, both sides ignore that real emancipation always unfolds through arguments and struggles about already existing rights. Human rights should not be exposed as something else – they should be verified. Rancière's view of universalism is always a 'universalism to come' (Dillon 2005), but at the same time requires the continuous confirmation of universal rights through concrete struggles.

To conclude, these examples indicate that Rancière's concepts and ideas can add to our theoretical and empirical understanding of emancipation by thinking the relation between the non-political/political, culture/politics, universal/particular and global/local in non-dichotomous terms. In particular, the focus on equality can help conceptualise the question of resistance. Whereas critical analyses of international relations have been particularly successful in decoding and destabilising hegemonic discourses, Rancière's reminder that political principles can function as the springboard for a global emancipatory politics forcefully show how the global can be reclaimed from the point of view of the abject. However, as Dillon (2005) points out, several aspects of Rancière's thought still remain underspecified: if politics is a rare event, are some forms of police more desirable than others or are all social distributions equally bad? And what form does politics take – in particular, what is the relationship between emancipation, resistance and violence? And what happens when a claim for equality is not recognised? Greater engagement between international relations and Rancière's work on such issues is to be encouraged and can provide much-needed insight into how equality can inform a progressive politics on the international level.

Further reading

Deranty, Jacques-Philippe (2003) 'Review: Jacques Rancière's Contribution to the Ethics of Recognition', *Political Theory*, 31 (1): 136–56. A concise review of Rancière's work and its relevance to political theory.

Dillon, Michael (2005) 'A Passion for the (Im)possible. Jacques Rancière, Equality, Pedagogy and Messianic', *European Journal of Political Theory*, 4 (4): 429–52. A Derridean reading of Rancière's thought that points at some problems relating to Rancière's expression of emancipation.

Hewlett, Nick (2007) *Badiou, Balibar, Rancière: Re-thinking Emancipation*, London and New York: Continuum. An extensive introduction and discussion of three former students of Althusser and their partly overlapping views on emancipation.

May, Todd (2007) 'Jacques Rancière and the Ethics of Equality', *SubStance*, 36 (2): 20–36. Todd introduces Rancière's views on equality and links it to the anarchist tradition.

Rancière, Jacques (1999) *Disagreement. Politics and Philosophy*, Minneapolis: University of Minnesota Press. His most complete and systematic outline of his framework on politics.

Rancière, Jacques (2004) *The Politics of Aesthetics*, London and New York: Continuum. An accessible introduction to his work, including a brief introduction by the translator and an essay by Slavoj Žižek.

Rancière, Jacques (2006) *Hatred of Democracy*, London and New York: Verso. A series of political essays on the subversive power of the democratic ideal.

Rancière, Jacques and Panagia, Davide (2007) 'Dissenting Words: A Conversation with Jacques Rancière', *Diacritics*, 30 (2): 113–26. An interview in which Rancière summarises some of his core ideas.

Rancière, Jacques (2001) 'Ten Theses on Politics', *Theory and Event*, 5 (3). In this condensed article, Rancière summarises his views on politics in ten statements. See also the debate published in the same journal.

Reid, Donald (1989) 'Introduction', in Jacques Rancière *The Nights of Labor. The Workers' Dream in Nineteenth-Century France*, Philadelphia: Temple University Press, xv–xxxvii. One of the better introductions to Rancière's writings up to 1989.

Ross, Kristin (1991) 'Rancière and the Practice of Equality', *Social Text*, 29: 57–71. This text critically discusses Rancière's notion of equality.

White, Hayden (1994) 'Foreword: Rancière's Revisionism', in Jacques Rancière *The names of history. On the Poetics of Knowledge*, Minneapolis: University of Minnesota Press, vii–xx. This is a useful introduction to Rancière's historical approach.

27 Richard Rorty

James Brassett

Richard Rorty falls tenuously into a volume on 'critical theorists' and inter-national relations. He doesn't meet the formal criteria of 'Critical Theory' encapsulated in the Frankfurt school project to build an Enlightenment critique of modernity, to construct a rational vision of ethical transformation (Rorty 2000). Equally, on many readings, and despite his oft-cited self-description as a 'postmodern bourgeois liberal' (Rorty 1991b), he fails to live up to the critical openness associated with poststructural theory. Indeed, Rorty himself would have been deeply skeptical of attributing any power to the word 'critical' as a formal quality of a particular type of theory or the-orist. However, principled throat clearing aside, there is much in the work and life of Richard Rorty that should be of interest for the development of critical thinking in international relations.

Rorty maintained a dialogue with key figures in critical philosophy such as Habermas and Derrida (Rorty 1998c). His written work developed an ongoing 'conversation' with an exhaustive range of critical writers including Adorno, Dewey, Foucault, Freud, Hegel, Kant, Marx, Nietzsche, Orwell, Wittgenstein, and Nabakov. Moreover, Rorty's thinking changed over his lifetime, providing good reasons for critical theorists to stop worrying about the ontological, epistemological and methodological differences between them and instead focus their energies upon what the benefits of a creative (and imaginative) engagement might look like. This change in Rorty's thinking occurred via three crucial steps:

(1) his critique of foundationalism;
(2) his use of 'conversational' method; and
(3) his celebration of sentimentality and imagination.

Combined, they mark the culmination in Rorty's thought of an approach to the world which regards knowledge as a social relation *all the way down*, and the suggestion that we should *use* such insight to support an engaged ethos of sympathetic reformism.

Each step in Rorty's thought 'can' have implications for critical thinking within international relations. For instance, in his anti-foundationalism many international relations theorists have found a productive resource to engage with human rights debates (Brown 1999) and the purported divide between cosmopolitanism and communitarianism (Cochran 1999). Also the sentimental and imaginative aspects of his thought have been deployed to flesh out the possibility (*and ambiguity*) of ethical agency in international relations (Brassett 2008a). Equally, the various criticisms of Rorty's 'inspirational liberalism' (Bernstein 2003), *which are legion*, can be good places to locate a discussion of critical theory in international relations. In a strong critique of Rorty's account of human rights, Norman Geras (1995) has raised excellent questions for how critical theorists might frame a response to atrocities like the holocaust. More sympathetically, in *Deconstruction and Pragmatism* (Mouffe 1996) we see a number of clear statements of *why* and *how* poststructural authors engage with politics and 'the political' that circumvent some of Rorty's quick and sometimes caricatured views on the political relevance of such theory.

Overall Rorty argued we should forget about finding something 'large', outside of space and time, be it 'Truth', 'God', or even a 'Method' like deconstruction, which can guide us, and instead view ourselves and our thought as finite, contingent, passing. In that sense, his central contribution to a volume on critical theorists in international relations is to remind us that theory is best understood as something *we do* for a *certain purpose*. For Rorty, it was what goes on in the spaces between 'what we do' and our own 'certain purposes' that is most important and critical theorists in international relations should guard against privileging either.

Rorty's progress: from philosophy to politics

Richard Rorty was born on October 4, 1931 in New York. He went to the University of Chicago shortly before turning 15, where he completed a master's degree in philosophy, continuing at Yale for a PhD. He taught at Princeton from 1961, then became Professor of the Humanities at the University of Virginia in 1982. In 1998 Rorty became professor emeritus of comparative literature at Stanford University. Rorty's first edited work *The Linguistic Turn* (1967) was firmly in the analytic tradition. However, he increasingly drew from the American tradition of pragmatism, particularly the writings of John Dewey. Indeed, while still within the analytic tradition, his first major work *Philosophy and the Mirror of Nature* (1979) placed John Dewey as one of the great philosophical thinkers of the twentieth century. From that point onwards Rorty engaged heavily with the tradition of continental philosophy, producing books such as *Contingency, Irony, and Solidarity* (1989), *Essays on Heidegger and Others: Philosophical Papers* (1991) and *Truth and Progress: Philosophical Papers* (1998). In the last 15 years of his life, Rorty continued to publish, including four volumes of philosophical papers, *Achieving Our Country* (1998), a political manifesto, and *Philosophy and Social Hope* (1999), a general collection. He died on June 8, 2007.

The conventional narrative of Rorty's life and career is that of a good analytical political philosopher who turned against the professional conventions of his discipline. Indeed his first major work, *Philosophy and the Mirror of Nature* (1979), is a *tour de force* critique of the conventional understanding of analytical philosophy couched in the very terminology and conventions of it. *Philosophy and the Mirror of Nature* is a root and branch attack on the epistemological assumptions of modern, Anglo-American philosophy. Rorty's prime target was the idea that there could be firm and universal foundations for philosophical enquiry. He attacks both the veracity of this idea and the special place philosophers have adopted for themselves on its back:

> Philosophy as a discipline ... sees itself as the attempt to underwrite or debunk claims to knowledge made by science, morality, art, or religion. It purports to do this on the basis of its special understanding of the nature of knowledge and of mind. Philosophy can be foundational in respect to the rest of culture because culture is the assemblage of claims to knowledge, and philosophy adjudicates such claims. It can do so because it understands the foundations of knowledge, and it finds these foundations in a study of man-as-knower, of the 'mental processes' or the 'activity of representation' which make knowledge possible (Rorty 1979: 3).

For Rorty, this view of philosophy could be seen to run through Locke who developed an understanding of 'mental processes', Descartes who worked with a notion of 'the mind' as a separate/separable entity, and finally to Kant to whom 'we owe the notion of philosophy as a tribunal of pure reason, upholding or denying the claims of the rest of culture' (Rorty 1979: 3–4). Indeed, when mixed with the scientific rigour of writers like Russell and Husserl, 'Philosophy' (with a capital 'P') 'became for the intellectuals, a substitute for religion' (Rorty 1979: 2). But, Rorty argued, in the twentieth century this self-image has become increasingly difficult to sustain. The more scientific and rigorous philosophy became 'the less it had to do with the rest of culture and the more absurd its traditional pretensions became' (Rorty 1979: 5).

Rorty attacked the tradition of analytical philosophy in withering style. For instance, his relentless grammatical questions highlight distinctions such as that between Truth (with a capital 'T') and the pragmatist view of truth as *something good in the way of belief*. In this way, he was concerned less with what truth is, than with the uses to which philosophers put the term. The effect was to humble Philosophy – or better the people who call themselves 'Philosophers' – and leave a space open for a possible dialogue with nonanalytical philosophy: the kinds of approaches that had long since been expunged by mainstream analytical philosophy. In particular, Rorty drew on the work of Wittgenstein, Heidegger and Dewey whom he described as the 'three most important philosophers of our century' (Rorty 1979: 5). And he found a common cause with them in the way each began by trying to continue the 'foundational' version of philosophy, while each ended by discarding the Kantian conception of philosophy. Crucially for Rorty,

> their later work is therapeutic rather than constructive, edifying rather than systemic, designed to make the reader question his own motives for philosophizing rather than to supply him with a new philosophical program (Rorty 1979: 5–6).

On the one hand, this thesis goes to the heart of all that is 'sacred' in modern philosophy, taking down the idols and ridiculing the dogmas. In this sense, Rorty still holds a reputation within analytical philosophy as the *enfant terrible* of his generation, someone whose work is probably best left alone as straightforward, and unconstructive, iconoclasm. On the other hand, for many outside analytical political philosophy, Rorty pointed towards a new way of 'doing philosophy'. At the end of *Philosophy and the Mirror of Nature*, he exhorted us to retain what is best in the 'conversation of mankind':

> If we see knowing not as having an essence, to be described by scientists or philosophers, but rather as a right, by current standards, to believe, then we are well on the way to seeing *conversation* as the ultimate context within which knowledge is to be understood. Our focus shifts from the relation between human beings and the objects of their inquiry to the relation between alternative standards of justification, and from there to the actual changes in those standards which make up intellectual history (Rorty 1979: 389–90).

The emphasis comes full circle to human practices. In this way, Rorty stripped away the foundations of modern philosophy by suggesting the contingency of knowledge, i.e. that there are no non-circular forms of reasoning. If we drop the relation between 'appearance' and 'reality' in favour of the relation between 'human beings' as the basis of knowledge, then we can start to view philosophical qualities like ethics, justice, reason, etc. as constructed by us and *for us*. The practical implications of such a view are twofold and have a direct bearing on the activities of critical theorists in international relations.

First, in a pragmatic sense, we should judge knowledge frameworks in terms of their outcomes as much as on their internal consistency or veracity. Despite the attractiveness of foundational critique as a critical pastime, Rorty's rendering of such critiques places the responsibility back on critical theorists. Thus, for example, while it may be somewhat dubious, from a critical standpoint, to accept separations between ideal and non-ideal theory on the part of Rawlsian and post-Rawlsian theorists of global justice, we cannot ignore the social and political impact of such thinking (Parker and Brassett

2005). Just as economists have a distinctly advantageous position in the policy making circles concerned with globalisation (for example, the International Monetary Fund, the World Trade Organization and the European Central Bank) so post-Rawlsian justice theorists like Thomas Pogge (2002) have attained a level of influence in developmental thinking which transcends the odd epistemological issue we might raise with such work.

And second, developing from this point, any divide between knowledge and reality, or between ethics and politics for that matter, is broken. This insight is of particular importance for those critical theorists within international relations engaged in debates about global ethics. Often, the international relations framing of ethical debates has been informed by a form of Realism, often supplemented by a hint of Marxism, which regards ethics as a nice idea, but only viable if the dominant interests of power concur. However, this would ignore the constitutive interdependence of ethics-politics. For Rorty, ethics is political – negotiated as a relational human construct – and politics is ethical: a process of contest that has direct ethical outcomes. Thus, for instance, while human rights may well be tied to the historical and social contingency of Western, liberal *bourgeois* society and a particular point in its emergence, this does not alter the malleability of human rights knowledge, nor the capacity of non-Western/liberal/*bourgeois* agents to author an alternative vision of human rights if they so wish (Rorty 1998b). Quintessentially, the civil rights movements who had for so long suffered at the hands of liberal theories of rights, were able to re-describe such rights as part of their ongoing struggles for recognition and security.

Overall Rorty's insights point toward an attitudinal switch. He suggested that we view philosophy as a 'voice' in the conversation of mankind – *not a subject*. This voice may well be open to problems like chance, instability, discontinuity and change. But the recognition that there is no foundation *outside space and time*, no vantage from which to judge human affairs, can itself breathe new life into critical thought. The move is an attempt at critical reconstruction. Ethics/politics is always – already relational. Dropping foundations does not mean dropping values, or the notion of progress altogether:

> it is best to think of moral progress as a matter of increasing *sensitivity*, increasing responsiveness to the needs of a larger and larger variety of people and things. Just as pragmatists see scientific progress not as the gradual attenuation of a veil of appearances which hides the intrinsic nature of reality from us, but as the increasing ability to respond to the concerns of ever larger groups of people ... so they see moral progress as a matter of being able to respond to the needs of ever more inclusive groups of people (Rorty 1999: 81).

Of course Rorty is not without his critics. In particular, controversy arises in Rorty's own particular understandings and standards of good conversation.

Many critical theorists have taken issue with the way he allowed certain issues like Truth and Method to take the full brunt of the charge of contingency, while other concepts or social facts like the state and liberalism seem to get an easier ride. Indeed, in one telling conclusion to *Philosophy and the Mirror of Nature*, he states:

> The only point of which I would insist is that philosophers' moral concern should be with continuing the conversation of the West, rather than with insisting upon a place for the traditional problems of modern philosophy within that conversation (Rorty 1979: 394).

This passage represents an intensely problematic resolution to the gamut of critical arguments made. Rorty argues that the Western voice in the conversation of mankind is (self-evidently) the best thing we have achieved and we should continue to develop it, even in light of growing doubt over its central foundations. And in many ways this is the crux of the problem. If justice is relational then how can a sense of right and wrong be retained? If there are so many problems with the discourse of modern philosophy then how can we continue to support its Western home? What of the suspicion of many cultural and poststructural theorists that it is actually Western imperialism which is at the root of many global problems? Practically speaking: if we drop the 'traditional problems' of modern philosophy, what replaces them? If it is hope – as Rorty has variously implied – then how is such hope created?

We should not understate the precariousness of Rorty's position. At the same time as he lambasted the canonical assumptions of Western philosophy, he celebrated the Western, particularly the liberal, 'voice' in the conversation of mankind. At the same time as he drew on writers like Heidegger, Gadamer, Nietzsche, and Foucault, he turned away from their sometimes anarchistic implications to assert the worth of liberal values like individualism, liberty, and justice. The position can draw attack from both sides: analytical liberal theorists charge Rorty with moral relativism and poststructuralists chide him for not following through on the implications of his argument. However, before we race to undermine Rorty's pragmatism for not meeting others' standards of what philosophy should be, we should perhaps remember that Rorty was in the business of persuasion: persuading us of the benefits of seeing things differently. Rorty's philosophical position should perhaps better be valued – *as he values others'* – on how it translates to politics and 'the political'. This can be seen most fundamentally in *Contingency, Irony and Solidarity* (1989).

Rorty's conversation: From politics to imagination

Contingency Irony and Solidarity shares a similar standing in Rorty's intellectual output with *Philosophy and the Mirror of Nature*. However, in terms of impact, *Contingency* eclipsed the latter. In part *Contingency* is a far more accessible book. Gone are the highly specialized analytic problems and into the foreground come the broad and fundamental themes and issues of human existence: the self, language, community, ethics, and above all the importance of the novel. Attached to this, it is worth stressing that Rorty's prose style became almost literary in its ability to draw ideas and characters together in order to extrapolate a summary of readings and, ultimately, a persuasive celebration of a new reading. Indeed, the four-page introduction to *Contingency* is surely one of the most remarkable and persuasive summaries of an entire book ever written. To quote at length:

> In my utopia, human solidarity would be seen not as a fact to be recognized by clearing away 'prejudice' or burrowing down to previously hidden depths but, rather, as a goal to be achieved. It is to be achieved not by inquiry but by imagination, the imaginative ability to see strange people as fellow suffers. Solidarity is not discovered by reflection but created. It is created by increasing our sensitivity to the particular details of the pain and humiliation of other, unfamiliar sorts of people. Such increased sensitivity makes it more difficult to marginalize people different from ourselves by thinking, 'They do not feel it as we would', or 'There must always be suffering, so why not let *them* suffer?'
>
> This process of coming to see other human beings as one of us rather than as 'them' is a matter of detailed description of what unfamiliar people are like and what we ourselves are like. This is a task not for theory but for genres such as ethnography, the journalist's report, the comic book, the docudrama, and especially, the novel. Fiction like that of Dickens, Olive Schreiner, or Richard Wright gives us the details about kinds of suffering being endured by people we had previously not attended. Fiction like that of Choderlos de Laclos, Henry James and Nabokov gives us the details about what sorts of cruelty we ourselves are capable of, and thereby lets us redescribe ourselves. That is why the novel, the movie, and the TV program have, gradually but steadily, replaced the sermon and the treatise as the principle means of moral change and progress.
>
> In my liberal utopia, this replacement would receive a kind of recognition which it still lacks. That recognition would be part of a general turn against theory and toward narrative. Such a turn would be emblematic of our having given up the attempt to hold all the sides of our life in a single vision, to describe them with a single vocabulary. It would amount to a recognition of ... the 'contingency of language' – the fact that there is no way to step outside of the various vocabularies we have employed and find a metavocabulary which somehow takes account of all possible vocabularies, all possible ways of judging and feeling. A historicist and nominalist culture of the sort I envisage would settle instead for narratives which connect the present with the past, on the one hand, and with utopian futures, on the other. More important, it would regard the realization of utopias as an endless process – an

endless, proliferating realization of Freedom, rather than a convergence toward an already existing Truth (Rorty 1989: xvi).

There are a number of themes and ideas emergent in this passage alone which are worthy of emphasis. First, Rorty's anti-foundationalism is avowedly moral in conception. Rather than getting caught up in fruitless and potentially imperialistic searches for the human subject, we should perhaps focus energies upon the imaginative creation of solidarity, or points of identification with the suffering of others. Second, Rorty opens the floor to new actors and genres to play a role in this creative process. He holds out the straightforward observation that a book, say Orwell's *1984*, or Nabokov's *Lolita*, can have a greater social impact, a greater moral lesson, than any amount of philosophical argument. And third, in methodological terms, Rorty placed his chips on language as the critical subject *par excellence.* It is in his understanding of language that Rorty found a way to connect up the multiple and diverse strands of philosophical critique, anti-foundationalism, sympathy towards suffering, political reformism, and celebration of imagination.

Rorty adopted an anti-essentialist position regarding language. Essentialism is the view that there is some pure essence to reality that we can grasp if only we get the correct epistemological approach. Rorty doesn't critique this image because he thinks epistemology has so far got it wrong. He simply doesn't understand what it could mean to get it 'right'. He doubts the very idea of 'Truth' as the correspondence between words and reality. For Rorty 'words' and 'sentences' are not more or less accurate representations of the essential reality of the world. Rather they are aspects of larger 'vocabularies' that have been developed to help us cope with the world. The choice between vocabularies should be motivated by a pragmatic desire to reduce cruelty and increase sensitivity to suffering.

While deeply influenced by critical and/or poststructural writers, in *Contingency Irony and Solidarity*, Rorty conceded that certain kinds of critical thinking could well pose a problem to the liberal institutions he supported. He therefore invoked a public-private split. While writers like Rawls and Habermas appear as socially useful philosophers, philosophers who can do the job of anticipating institutions that are more just and less cruel, Rorty concedes that writers like Nietszche and Derrida have been straightforwardly hostile to liberal institutions. So he argued that the latter type of thinker should be understood as 'private ironists', useful for liberalism in so far as they expand the scope of and possibilities for individual perfection. Irony doesn't need to be tied into any larger theory of society or justice, indeed it probably cannot. For Rorty, a liberal ironist meets three basic requirements:

(1) She has radical and continuing doubts about the final vocabulary she currently uses, because she has been impressed by other vocabularies, vocabularies taken as final by people or books she has encountered; (2) she realizes that argument phrased in her present vocabulary can neither

underwrite nor dissolve these doubts; (3) insofar as she philosophizes about her situation, she does not think that her vocabulary is closer to reality than others, that it is in touch with a power not herself (Rorty 1989: 73).

While these are no doubt important ethical qualities – certainly in terms of fostering a level of critical distance and reflexivity – Rorty argues that *Irony* is best regarded as a private matter. It relates best to the question of what to do with one's aloneness, of how one weaves and re-weaves the cobwebs of meaning that make up a 'self identity'. The separation is simple and straight-forwardly commonsensical (although it should be noted that the move is not necessarily congruent with the readings of Habermas and Derrida provided in the chapters of this volume). Habermas gives a good account of how to continue the shared social effort to make our institutions more just and less cruel. Derrida, who would be less useful for such projects, is more useful for retaining sensitivity towards the infinite possibilities for self-creation that may exist. It is not a question of either-or, but both-and (Rorty 1998c).

Numerous criticisms have been levied at this perceived resolution. Feminist scholars have seen it as yet another reification of public over private politics. For those like Nancy Fraser (1991) who regard the question of self-creation as a fundamentally public political issue, Rorty's view is little more than an apology for the *status quo*. In a similar vein Molly Cochran (1999) has problematized the dichotomy by arguing for a synthesis between Rorty's private irony, which she sees as a powerful imaginative tool, and Dewey's more transformative conception of the public sphere, as an arena of ethical growth for its own sake.

While sympathetic to these critiques, perhaps too much has been read into the separation? For anyone who reads Rorty as offering a 'theory' of politics then the public–private split is deeply pernicious. However, if we read Rorty as offering suggestions for alternative ways of thinking, where attention is direc-ted away from old philosophical problems in order to open new possibilities, the split is banal. This point can be elaborated in two ways.

On the one hand, Fraser may have missed the point. Rorty's notion of the private is an existential area that addresses the question of what to do with one's aloneness. It neither defines a space in the sense of a house or kitchen. Nor does it restrict the formation of public grievances around private issues. On the other hand, and following on from this point, Rorty's public–private split is not fixed. Indeed, he explicitly leaves room open for moral pro-gress to occur through the chance coincidence of a 'private fantasy with a public problem'. In one interview (1995: 62) he argued: 'I don't think private beliefs can be fenced off [from the public sphere]; they leak through, so to speak, and influence the way one behaves toward other people' (Rorty 1995: 62). And in another he categorically retorts,

> My public/private distinction wasn't an explanation of what every human life is like. I was, instead, urging that there was nothing wrong

with letting people divide their lives along the private/public line. We don't have a moral responsibility to bring the two together. *It was a negative point, not a positive recommendation about how everybody should behave* (Rorty 2002: 62–3).

In this sense, Rorty's public–private split provides a way to end, or rather ignore, the titanic struggle between, say, Habermas and Derrida by suggesting that both are useful in different ways. As Rorty conceded (but made painfully little of in his work) the thought of someone like Derrida does leak through to issues of the public realm (Bulley 2008; Edkins 2000). On the other hand, just because Habermas makes a few overleaping claims as to the universality of 'communicative rationality', and therefore might miss the importance of chance, individual creativity, and comedy, this does not mean his work is not socially useful. By 'useful' is meant providing a framework in which ethics–politics can be mediated.

Rorty's hope: irony, sympathy, and imagination

Beyond such conversational method, there is perhaps one aspect of Rorty's thought which stands out: his emphasis on hope. That is to say, once we have realized that all the apparent problems between critical theorists are not so much problems as differences of emphasis, the task is to come to terms with and foster the development of ethical diversity. Rorty provided a number of hopeful stories about how to expand sympathy via imagination. This chapter concludes by pointing to three, in particular, that should be of interest to critical scholars in international relations: irony, sympathy and imagination.

Irony

Much of Rorty's interest from *Contingency Irony and Solidarity* onwards was concerned with the possibilities to be found in irony. Within irony Rorty collected together what he regarded as some of the best critical traits across genres. This included radical doubts about the self, society, and power.

Irony also served as shorthand for a kind of novel, quintessentially *Lolita*, which engages with the capacity for harm and cruelty. Such engagements for Rorty, did not need to be 'for any purpose', in a broader social sense, they were rather of value in their own right as artistic imaginations of where existence might lead (Rorty 1989). If such irony could then be re-described by public theorists to minimize suffering in some way then so much the better for Rorty, but it does not require any further attempts to provide philosophical underpinnings for irony.

Rorty therefore regarded irony as a kind of accident, one of the best accidents in fact to have befallen liberal society, a capacity to constantly check ourselves and our own moral frameworks. Indeed, against the common analytical strategy of labelling poststructural critique as a form of anarchism, Rorty suggested that an understanding of irony in its broader sense did not require such zero-sum assessments. As he argued: 'Hostility to a particular historically conditioned and possibly transient form of solidarity is not hostility to solidarity as such' (Rorty 1989: xv). There is nothing to suggest that post-metaphysical forms of solidarity could not exist. There is nothing to suggest that solidarity cannot be 'imagined' in alternative ways.

Therefore, Rorty understood irony within a broader framework of politics as reformism. For Rorty, irony implied, or rather ensured, that our ethical goals were rendered as an infinitely ongoing project of contest and deliberation: *not a final destination*. As he suggested,

> Ironists who are inclined to philosophize see the choice between vocabularies as made neither within a neutral and universal metavocabulary nor by an attempt to fight one's way past appearances to the real, but simply by playing the new off against the old (Rorty 1989: 73).

And this act of playing the old off against the new infers a (plural), experimental process. If other vocabularies come along that match up or improve on current ones, as did feminism or environmentalism, then liberals can re-describe their own vocabulary. The combination of irony with re-description suggests a reform minded, experimental approach to achieving solidarity against suffering, a practical embodiment of, and route to achieving, sympathy in public life.

Sympathy

> The best, and probably the only, argument for putting foundationalism behind us is the one I have already suggested: it would be more efficient to do so, because it would let us concentrate our energies on manipulating sentiments, on sentimental education' (Rorty 1991a: 176).

Perhaps Rorty's key intervention on international ethics, and certainly the one which has occupied international relations scholars the most, is contained within *Human Rights, Rationality and Sentimentality* (1998b) (Brown 1999; Cochran 1996; Parker and Brassett 2005). In that paper, Rorty sets out to address the growth in importance of human rights arguments in international politics. As is now well known he argues that human rights should be seen as a *culture*. This human rights culture therefore stops short of the universalism of some human rights arguments. But in good Rortian fashion he shows how it would be best to stop the search for a universal human subject and instead to substitute the question 'What can we make of ourselves?' (Rorty 1998b: 168). As he argues:

> We pragmatists argue from the fact that the emergence of a human rights culture seems to owe nothing to increased moral knowledge, and

everything to hearing sad and sentimental stories, to the conclusion that there is probably no knowledge of the sort Plato envisaged ... In short, my doubts about the effectiveness of appeals to moral knowledge are doubts about causal efficacy, not about epistemic status (Rorty 1998b: 172).

Crucially, for Rorty, it is this possibility of weaving narratives of suffering with discourses of human rights that allows us to expand the moral community beyond our family, circle of friends, tribe, etc. (Rorty 2007).

Such a view of course holds important implications for the way in which critical theorists in international relations frame questions of global ethics. A growth of interest in narrative, such as critical cinema, for mediating some of the contentious aspects of migration or the War on Terror for instance, might provide an engaged yet self reflective form of sentimental education in essentially contested political circumstances. Equally, and drawing on this idea of education, if our focus is on the long term evolution of respect for the human capacity to suffer and a desire to alleviate such suffering, then the question of how we (critical scholars) popularize the various ethical positions we support is central (Brassett 2008b).

Imagination

Finally, it is proper to stress that Rorty was in some sense disconnected from the theoretical and practical implications of his arguments. True, he engaged in a kind of public interventionism which saw him commenting on diverse issues ranging from education through to the Cold War and terrorism. However, there is also in Rorty a certain modesty about what the role of theory and the theorist could be. He never really escaped the view of philosophy as essentially removed from public life. He referred to himself as a kind of under-labourer to great thinkers and writers. For Rorty, once the foundations are taken away, we might start to glimpse what life could be like if we focus on the benefits of critical theorists in terms of how they reduce suffering. In this sense, Rorty rejected the idea of a 'correct' interpretation of reality, or the role of the critical theorists within it, and rather substituted the idea of imagination.

Imaginative ways of continuing or changing the conversation can foster sympathy, make us understand suffering in new ways and hold out the possibility of infinite possibilities in life, as yet perhaps unimagined. For Rorty, this was all that was required:

We should remember that it is the initial Gestalt-switch, not the ensuing triumphalistic and professionalized busyness, that matters. The history of philosophy is the history of Gestalt-switches, not of the painstaking carrying-out of research programs. Such programs always trickle out into the sands eventually, but the Gestalt switchers may remain and make possible new such switches in the future. To give up on the idea that philosophy gets nearer to truth, and to interpret it as Dewey did, is to concede primacy to imagination over the argumentative intellect, and to genius over professionalism (Rorty 1998a: 11).

In this sense, it is perhaps best to leave the final word on Rorty's potential contribution on critical theory and international relations to the reader. Rorty's own talent for weaving together ideas, for showing how apparent problems are not really problems at all, and for suggesting ways to imagine ourselves at our best, is gone with him. But nevertheless his work does suggest interesting possibilities for future thinkers, if only as a demonstration of a way of doing philosophy. This chapter therefore concludes with a number of reading suggestions which might stimulate the most important faculty of Rorty's repertoire: imagination. As Rorty argued:

> To keep the conversation going is a sufficient aim of philosophy, to see wisdom as consisting in the ability to sustain a conversation, is seeing human beings as generators of new descriptions rather than beings one hopes to be able to describe accurately (Rorty 1979: 378).

Further reading

Rorty, Richard (1998b) 'Human Rights, Rationality and Sentimentality', in *Truth and Progress: Philosophical Papers Volume 3*, Cambridge: Cambridge University Press, 167–85. This is the most commonly cited piece in international relations and develops an important contribution to thinking about human rights from a pragmatic standpoint.

Rorty, Richard (1998c) 'Habermas, Derrida, and the Functions of Philosophy', in *Truth and Progress: Philosophical Papers Volume 3*, Cambridge: Cambridge University Press, 307–26. Connects up the dots between Habermas and Derrida in an original and provocative manner.

Rorty, Richard (1999) 'Trotsky and the Wild Orchids', in Rorty, Richard *Philosophy and Social Hope,* London: Penguin Books, 3–20. This autobiographical piece presents a disarmingly honest account of the factors which underpinned developments in Rorty's thinking.

For those with an interest in the broader literary concerns of Rorty, *Contingency Irony and Solidarity* contains important chapters on Orwell and Nabokov which can stand alone.

Secondary reading

Bernstein, Richard J. (2003) 'Rorty's Inspirational Liberalism', in *Richard Rorty*, eds Guignon, Charles and Hiley, David R., Cambridge: Cambridge

University Press, 124–38. Bernstein, perhaps Rorty's closest friend, provides a close critique of some of the gaps in Rorty's thinking.

Mouffe, Chantal (ed.) (1996) *Deconstruction and Pragmatism*, New York and London: Routledge. An important set of papers which draw out the tensions between Rorty and post-structuralism in a (rare) constructive tone.

Rorty, Richard (2000) *Rorty And His Critics*, Oxford: Blackwell Publishers Ltd. Dealing mainly with philosophical issues this volume brings Rorty into dialogue with some of his key contemporaries including a close and fruitful engagement with Habermas.

28 Edward Said

Latha Varadarajan

Edward Said – the late University Professor of English and Comparative
Literature at Columbia University, the music critic for the *Nation*, the man
both widely regarded (by both supporters and critics) as one of the founding
figures of the postcolonial tradition in the American academy, the outspoken
supporter of the Palestinian cause in the West – was one of the best-known
public intellectuals of the twentieth century. In a prolific career spanning
nearly four decades, Said authored more than 20 books and 125 articles and
inspired innumerable others. His influence – both during and after his lifetime – over scholarship in fields ranging from cultural studies and English
literature to anthropology and geography has itself been the subject of
scholarly scrutiny. The goal of this essay is to draw attention to a few of the
key texts and ideas associated with Said's work in light of their importance
for critical international relations scholarship.

'Beginnings'

One of the most important concepts that Edward Said expounded on in all
his writings is that of *worldliness* (Said 1983). Put simply, Said argued that
texts and their authors do not exist in a vacuum. To treat the text simply as
an inert object (that is to say for instance, a self-contained book), literature
as something divorced from the world in which it is created, or the author as
just a writer of a particular book is to miss the crucial fact that the production of the text by the author, a cultural production, is a political act that is
deeply embedded in the relations of power in any given society. To understand these relations, one needs to understand the rootedness, the socio-
political-cultural contexts that are productive of both the author and the
ideas that make up his/her text. Taking a page from Said, in order to
understand the particular intellectual and political concerns that animate his
scholarship, it is important for us to situate it in the particular 'world' in
which it emerged.

   Given his own memoirs and the extensive writings on him, much of Edward
Said's life and what he considered 'his' world are now a matter of public record.
Born in 1935 in Jerusalem (then part of British mandated Palestine), Said's

early life was marked by a distinct peripatetic tendency. His family, like many other well-off Arab families of that period, travelled frequently among the various states in the region. Although his larger extended family was based in Palestine, Said's father chose Cairo as his base of business operations. It was there that the young Said received his early education, first at an elite preparatory school and later at a school that was mainly for the children of American and British expatriates. In 1947, Said's father relocated the family to Jerusalem, but his timing was far from propitious. Within a year, the entire extended family left Jerusalem, driven away by the war. Despite the very visible trauma of the displaced Palestinians surrounding him (including his family), Said finished his schooling in Cairo and was sent to the United States for his higher education in 1951. In the next decade and a half, he moved from boarding school to Princeton and Harvard, before accepting a teaching position at Columbia in 1963. He remained a faculty member at Columbia until his death in 2003.

At one level, Said's life was one of privilege. His parents were wealthy and educated, and had embraced the cosmopolitan existence that was available to Arabs of their class in the early decades of the twentieth century. They lived in the same neighbourhoods as the European colonists and had the resources to send their children to the same schools as the British and American children. While the trauma of being forced to leave Jerusalem cannot be understated, the material reality of displacement was undoubtedly different for Said's family from what it was for millions of other Palestinians. Unlike those who had to leave behind all their possessions and faced an unknown number years in refugee camps, Said's family returned to Cairo, a city that had been a sort of home to them. And though Said would later recount being surrounded by 'the sadness and destitution of people [that he] had formerly known as ordinary middle-class people in Palestine', his return to Cairo meant slipping back – albeit with a sense of discomfort – into the life he had always known (Said 1999: 115). The patina of privilege can be seen even in Said's academic trajectory in the United States. From his undergraduate experience in Princeton, through the graduate programme at Harvard, and a teaching career in Columbia, Said never had to leave the hallowed halls of Ivy League institutions. His academic career was an exemplary success story by any standards, marked as it was by the publication of over 20 books (which have been translated into over 31 languages), memberships in associations such as the American Academy of Arts and Sciences and the Royal Society of Literature, high-ranking positions in institutions ranging from the Modern Language Association to the Council on Foreign Affairs, and the award of honorary doctorates by universities around the world.

This recounting of Said's many worldly achievements is not to present his life as one surrounded by constant adulation and institutional valorisation. This was after all a man whose support of the Palestinian cause had not just earned him the sobriquets of 'Arafat's man in New York' and 'The professor of terror', but also made him the target of death threats. Rather, it is to underscore the fact that Said's academic success was in part made possible by the very specific position he occupied – not just institutionally, but also in socio-economic terms. Said was undoubtedly aware of this and acknowledged its importance in making possible the particular paths that he had travelled in his life. However, notwithstanding this acknowledgement, in narrating the formation of his intellectual and political concerns, the crucial element that Said emphasized was the *fact of exile*.

Said's family was part of the massive exodus of Palestinians driven out of Jerusalem at the advent of the first Arab–Israeli war. In fact, it would be 45 years before Said was able to return to the land of his birth. While that added to what Said would later describe as a sense of acute alienation that he felt amongst his school-mates in Cairo's elite schools, it did not – at least at a conscious level – fundamentally alter his world-view. Sheltered to some extent from the constant reminders of that displacement during his school years in the United States, Said continued his musical training while completing his dissertation on Joseph Conrad. However, within a few years of Said's joining the Columbia faculty, Israel and the Arab states fought another war. The Six Day War of 1967 resulted in an overwhelming defeat of the Arab forces with Israel occupying the West Bank, Gaza, Golan Heights and the Sinai.

The war, which dealt a significant blow to the Palestinian hope of a return to their homeland, brought the past and the present together for Said in a way that he had not foreseen. After that moment, he was, as he said, 'no longer the same person' for the war 'seemed to embody *the* dislocation that subsumed all the other losses, the disappeared worlds of my youth, the unpolitical years of my education, the assumption of disengaged teaching at Columbia' (Said 1999: 293). Becoming cognizant of his own position as a Palestinian living in the United States, and that of Palestinians as a people without a homeland, Said moved towards a more politically conscious scholarship. In interrogating the reactions to the Arab–Israeli war in general and the Palestinian question in particular in Western media, Said started focusing on the problematic of the politics of cultural representation, and the complex interconnections between the past and the present. For, as he realized, to understand the way in which 'Arabs' were viewed in contemporary politics, one needed to understand the historically rooted political struggles that had made possible the dominant understanding of the Arab as a particular kind of political subject. To put it differently, understanding the operation of power in the contemporary world necessitated a closer look at the politics of domination and resistance over a longer period of time. Specifically, what was needed was a closer look at the colonial past.

Colonial pasts

In an article published immediately after the Arab–Israeli war, Said gave a preview of his new intellectual and political concerns by noting that the representation of the 'Arab' in the West was of a very peculiar sort (Said 1970). When talked about at all, the Arab was 'seen as a disruptor of Israel's and the West's existence'. Palestine itself was 'imagined as an empty desert ... its inhabitants inconsequential nomads possessing no stable claims to the land' (Said 1970: 5). The question of how such a representation came about formed the focus of *Orientalism*, the book that (for better or for worse) is generally viewed as the most influential of all of Said's writings. Explaining the putative subject of his analysis, Said started by pointing out that the Orient occupied a very special position in the European experience, and not just because of its supposed geographical proximity:

> The Orient is not only adjacent to Europe: it is also the place of Europe's greatest and richest and oldest colonies, the source of its civilizations and languages, its cultural contestant, and one of its deepest and most recurring images of the Other. In addition, the Orient has helped to define Europe (or the West) as its contrasting image, idea, personality, experience. Yet, none of this Orient is merely imaginative. The Orient is an integral part of European *material* civilization and culture (Said 1995: 1–2).

Acknowledging the prevalence of Orientalism as a term in academic and popular discourse, Said delineated the three main ways in which it had been understood and used. First, as an academic designation that referred to those who 'teach, write about or research the Orient'; second, as 'a style of thought based upon an ontological and epistemological distinction made between "the Orient" and, most of the time, "the Occident"'; and finally, at least since the late eighteenth century, as a 'corporate institution for dealing with the Orient'. Although Said asserts that he uses 'Orientalism' as shorthand to refer to all three, which are after all inter-related, it is the last that forms the crux of his argument. For, while the first two deal primarily with the textual production of the Orient, the last focuses on the way in which this production enables and justifies the domination of the Orient by the West. In this context, *Orientalism* can best be understood as encapsulating an analysis of the relationship between power and knowledge, and the phenomenon of Orientalism itself as a way of dealing with the orient 'by making statements about it, authorizing views of it, describing it, by teaching it, settling it, ruling over it: in short [it was the] Western style of dominating, restructuring and having authority over the orient' (Said 1995: 3).

Given this framing, Said's acknowledged indebtedness to the work of Michel Foucault should be evident even at first glance. Orientalism, as Said made very clear, was not a world-view that was restricted to a specific country, or a group of scholars in any one discipline at a certain moment of time. Rather, it was a *particular kind of discourse* that enabled not just the management of the Orient by successive generations of Europeans, but also led to it being produced as a specific kind of object in the post-Enlightenment period. The complex system of rules embodied in this discourse established the boundaries of what could be said or assumed about the 'Orient' and what could and could not be expected from its inhabitants; within this the 'orient was not (and is not) a free subject of thought and action' (Said 1995: 3). The power of this discourse lay not just in coming to know a pre-existing geographical entity (though it did have a definite geographical location for the French and the British), but actually constituting an imaginative 'Orient'. This product of what Said calls an 'imaginative geography' was not only essentially and irreconcilably different from the Occident, but had to be experienced and dealt with by the latter in very specific ways.

In explaining the emergence of this discourse, Said highlights the fact that the growth in the popularity of Orientalist study coincided with the heyday of European imperial expansionism from the early nineteenth to the early twentieth century. In other words, the production of knowledge about the Orient, far from being an innocent cultural endeavour, was very much part of a larger political project of conquest and dominance. To assert this relationship, however, is by no means to suggest that Orientalism was simply a post-facto rationalization of various imperial projects. In many ways, it actually enabled colonial projects such as Napoleon's conquest of Egypt in 1798 – a project Said describes as 'the very model of the truly scientific appropriation of one culture by another, apparently stronger one' (Said 1995: 42). What marked the French conquest of Egypt as distinct from other colonial adventures that preceded it was that Napoleon very consciously drew upon, in fact relied upon, existing Orientalist scholarship and enlisted the help of Oriental scholars to plan his Egyptian adventure. As Said puts it:

> [For] Napoleon, Egypt was a project that acquired reality in his mind, and later in his preparations for its conquest, through experiences that belong to the realm of ideas and myths culled from texts, not empirical reality. His plans for Egypt therefore became the first in a long series of European encounters with the Orient in which the Orientalist's special expertise was put directly to functional colonial use (Said 1995:80).

Drawing on the writings of Comte de Volney, whose accounts of the Islamic world were published in 1796, Napoleon made it clear to his generals that in order to conquer Egypt the French army would have to conquer the Muslims. To achieve this goal, the strategy that Napoleon adopted was a carefully calibrated one that not only focused on convincing Egyptians of the legitimacy of French occupation, but also opening up Egypt to European scrutiny. The former was necessitated in part by the size of the French Army of Occupation. Realizing that his small army could ill-afford to consistently engage in a war of attrition with the natives, Napoleon made all efforts from the very beginning of the invasion to convince the Egyptians that his army was actually fighting *for* Islam. His proclamations were translated into

Arabic, the army was constantly warned to respect Islamic sensibility, and most importantly, local imams and muftis were drafted to support the French occupation. As he left Egypt, Napoleon left strict instructions to his deputies that they were to 'always administer Egypt through the Orientalists and the religious Islamic leaders whom they could win over; any other politics was too expensive and foolish' (Said 1995: 82).

To 'open up' Egypt to European scrutiny, Napoleon enlisted the aid of numerous French scholars in fields ranging from chemistry and biology to history and archaeology who produced volumes on Egypt that emphasized not just its past greatness (through its connections to classical European civilizations like the Greeks), but also its present Barbarism and thus the need for the Napoleonic intervention at that particular juncture. The results of this endeavour were the massive 23 volumes of *Description de l'Égypte* published between 1809 and 1828:

> To restore a region from its present barbarism to classical greatness; to instruct (for its own benefit) the Orient in the ways of the West; to subordinate or underplay military power in order to aggrandize the project of glorious knowledge acquired in the process of political domination of the Orient, to formulate the Orient, to give it shape, identity, definition with full recognition of its place in memory, its importance to imperial strategy, and its 'natural' role as an appendage to Europe ...; and above all, to transmute living reality into the stuff of texts, to possess (or think that one possesses) actuality mainly because nothing in the Orient seems to resist one's power: these are the features of Orientalist projection entirely realized in the *Description de l'Égypte*, itself enabled by Napoleon's wholly Orientalist engulfment of Egypt by the instruments of Western knowledge and power (Said 1995: 86).

As Said's analysis of this event makes clear, the significance of Orientalism lies not only in its enabling specific projects, but also in making a particular world-view encompassing the Orient and the Occident (and the Oriental and the European) part of received common sense. It was to understand this process, to make sense of the meanings and implications of Orientalism in all its glory, that Said turned to the work of the Italian communist philosopher, Antonio Gramsci.

Drawing on Gramsci's writings on the analytical distinction between civil and political society, Said pointed out that the operation of culture in civil society is marked by the predominance of certain cultural forms. This predominance works not so much through brute coercion as it does through consent, producing a 'form of ... cultural leadership ... what Gramsci has identified as *hegemony*' (Said 1995: 7). The hegemony of what has been called the idea of Europe (a collective notion of a European 'us' against all non-Europeans) coupled with the hegemony of European ideas about the Orient (which in turn reaffirmed the idea of Europe and particularly

European superiority) was what gave Orientalism its power and its durability. This understanding of the cultural realm for Said could not be separated from the exercise of imperial power. But this, as far as he was concerned, did not in any way imply the denigration of culture or its relegation to a secondary status. In fact, on the contrary, emphasizing the essentially political nature of culture enabled us to see the way in which the 'internal constraints' of hegemonic systems were not merely 'unilaterally inhibiting', but actually productive for the writers and thinkers operating within them (Said 1995: 14).

This was a point that Said made much more explicitly in his later work, *Culture and Imperialism*. Focusing on canonical novels in British literature, Said argued that even when the authors themselves seemed to be unconscious of representing the empire or imperial realities, these issues constituted continuous inflections in their texts. In the essay 'Jane Austen and Empire' (which was the focus of almost all major reviews of the book), Said showed how this was true even of the novel *Mansfield Park* – one of the most beloved of Austen's novels, which ostensibly deals with the lives of the inhabitants of an English county estate (Said 1993: 80–96). Space constraints preclude a more detailed engagement with the intricacies of the novel, and therefore with Said's essay, here. But, it should be noted that Said's well crafted analysis lays out the manner in which the geographical division of the world, far from being neutral and self-evident in *Mansfield Park*, was one that was politically charged and essentially connected to the questions of colonial rule, although the latter were barely referred to in an overt manner. Through a discussion of one of the major characters, Sir Thomas Bertram, whose return from his estates in Antigua (which had not been 'doing well') marks a vital moment in the novel, Said shows the manner in which Austen synchronizes the maintenance of control, the restoration of domestic tranquillity, and the triumph of honest English values in Mansfield Park with the restoration of productivity and discipline in the colonies.

In highlighting the *worldliness* of imperial novels such as Austen's, in drawing the connections between the politics of the slave trade and the nature of domesticity in early-nineteenth century England, Said's aim was not to undermine the literary value of such work. It was rather to illustrate even more forcefully the point that he had made in *Orientalism* – the relationship between culture and empire was a mutually constitutive one. Neither could survive without the other. If nothing else, the era of French and British imperial domination proved this conclusively.

The imperial present

Said's argument about the (re)production of imperial power was not restricted to his analysis of the past. In fact, the impetus and structure of *Orientalism* made it clear that for Said imperialism was far from being a matter of dusty historical records. It was very much a constitutive feature of the contemporary international system, for despite the dissolution of the British and French Empires in the aftermath of the Second World War, the United States had proved more than willing to accept the imperial mantle. While acknowledging that 'the Orient' meant different things for Europeans and Americans – at least early on – Said's main contention was that the heritage of Orientalism continued to shape not only the American experience of Arabs and Islam, but also the contemporary political realities of the Middle East.

The final part of *Orintalism* (aptly titled 'The Latest Phase') discusses the manner in which representations of the Arab in the United States, though seemingly disjointed, had a certain political and ideological coherence. Portrayed variously as a 'camel-riding nomad', a 'caricature as the embodiment of incompetence and easy defeat', the 'Arab' took on a more menacing cast in popular discourse after the 1973 oil crisis (Said 1995: 285). A subject without a history – other than that which was given to him by the Orientalist tradition – the Arab was now also someone who through his ownership of much needed oil resources threatened the developed world. In popular culture, the roles reserved for Arabs were that of the 'slave trader, camel driver, moneychanger, colourful scoundrel … [in other words] an oversexed degenerate, capable, it is true, of cleverly devious intrigues, but essentially sadistic, treacherous, low' (Said 1995: 286–87). But such representations went beyond the stereotypes represented in Hollywood productions. Books on the Middle East replicated the virulent anti-Islamic streak of the past, laying out what were seen as the essentially *jihadist* and violent nature of the Arabs in general. Within academia, the mantle of Orientalist scholarship was passed on to the Area Studies scholars, whose work defined the field of Near Eastern and Oriental studies in the post-Second World War period. The canonical wisdom that emerged about the region drew self-consciously from the European scholarship of the preceding century to argue that Islamic (and by extension 'Middle Eastern') civilization was not only fundamentally different from 'Western civilization', but was also essentially antithetical to all the values that defined the latter. Such an argument moreover only rarely found it necessary to refer to contemporary realities in the region, choosing instead to highlight abstractions about the Orient based on classical texts. As Said pointed out, the result, notwithstanding new academic jargons, was the continued understanding of the Orient, and the Oriental, as 'something either to be feared … or to be controlled' (Said 1995: 301).

The political implications of this persistent Orientalist perspective for the people of the Middle East forms the more direct focus of the two books that, along with *Orientalism*, are generally considered to be part of a trilogy. In *The Question of Palestine* (1979), Said argued that to make sense of Zionism as a political movement, one had to contextualize it not just in the long history of anti-Semitism, but also in terms of its affiliations with other ideas and political institutions, particularly those pertaining to *accumulation* (of power, land and ideological legitimacy) and *displacement* (of people, other ideas). Doing so reveals that the political project of Zionism was one that both drew on and resonated with ideas about the Orient that were part of the prevailing common-sense in the West: the strange notion that the land meant for the new Jewish state was *an empty land* ('devoid of Arab inhabitants') that was in severe need of settlement and cultivation. It is this collaboration that according to Said has marked the encounter between Zionism and the Palestinian Arabs. Notwithstanding the genuine sufferings of the Jewish community, or for that matter the many positive aspects of the Zionist political movement, Said argued that the Palestinian Arab experience of Zionism has been strikingly similar to the experience of the colonized people of Asia and Africa in the nineteenth and twentieth centuries. Therefore, any attempt to deal with the political problems of the contemporary Middle East would have to begin with an acknowledgement of the imperial legacy of Zionism and the fact that it had, much like the colonial powers of the past, created its own victims. For Said, the critical importance of this exercise lay in the fact that without acknowledging the ways in which Zionism had reproduced the Palestinian as 'inferior' and 'subhuman' (and therefore incapable of being political actors), there could be no serious attempt to bring about a resolution to the on-going conflict in the region. An engagement with the centrality of Palestinians to the Zionist movement, coupled with an acknowledgement of them as a people with their own history was, for Said, a crucial first step in a mature political engagement between groups whose histories and political fates had become so intertwined.

The difficulties of such a task were however magnified by the prevailing common sense about Islam in general, and the Arab Muslims in particular. The media response to the OPEC oil embargo and the resultant energy crisis in Western countries had already added a new layer to existing stereotypes of Arabs – in popular representation, the figure of the rich, sinister oil sheikh joined other well-known caricatures. But, even this was overshadowed by the response to the overthrow of the Shah of Iran by the followers of Ayatollah Khomeini – an event that for Americans was indelibly linked to the Teheran hostage crisis. The depiction of this crisis, and its political fallout – in particular, the re-inscription of a particular understanding of Islam and its relation to the 'West' – became the subject of the final book of the trilogy, *Covering Islam* (1980). On November 4 1979, a group of Iranian students took over the American Embassy in Teheran and held hostage 52 American government employees. Their demand was that the US government repatriate the deposed Shah, Mohammed Reza Pahlavi, to face trial in Iran. The drama lasted for over a year during which it became the main fodder for prime-time news. As the general population watched in seemingly paralyzed horror, the popular media tried to explain the emergence of the new Islamic regime in Iran. As Said points out, most of these explanations generally tended towards sensationalist representations of a peculiar 'Persian psyche' or the rule of the 'new barbarians', who, informed by their Islamic convictions, hated the 'West' and its liberal values. Very few commentators took the trouble of situating the rise of Ayatollah Khomeini in the long history of British and American involvement in Iran, particularly in the overthrowing of the democratically elected Mossadegh government in 1953 and the installation of the brutal Pahlavi regime. They did not need to in a sense because their claims about the irrational and anti-Western nature of Islam were not made in a vacuum.

To speak of 'Islam' in the contemporary world, Said argued, was not to merely identify or describe a religion, since it served as shorthand to describe a world, a way of life that was both essentially distinct from and fundamentally opposed to the 'West'. It is therefore not surprising that Islam is generally talked about in the context of the fundamentalism, militancy, terrorism, and violence that poses a threat to the world at large, and 'Western' civilization in particular. This distinction (that makes both the 'West' and 'Islam' into monolithic entities), as Said variously argued, is produced and maintained not just by conscious action on the part of a network of academics, the foreign service, intelligence community, oil companies, multinational corporations, etc., but also by a general lack of genuine critical scholarship on the subject (Said 1995, 1993). Its ultimate effect is to reduce both 'Islam' and the 'Islamic world' to caricatures that are taken seriously only to the extent that they figure as important elements in ideas about oil, the future of Western civilization, and the fight for democracy put forth by a vast information and policy-making apparatus in the United States. At the same time, such representations, Said warned, also served to make these parts of the world more vulnerable to military interventions. In the context of the on-going occupation of Iraq, and the threat of war with Iran, these warnings take on an added weight.

Announcing the US invasion of Iraq on March 19, 2003, George W. Bush declared: 'We come to Iraq with respect for its citizens, for their great civilization and for the religious faiths they practice'. The goal of the American troops would be to 'remove a threat and restore control of that country to its own people'. Although the United States had entered the conflict 'reluctantly', its armed forces would fight *for* the Iraqi people, and leave Iraq 'as soon as their work is done'. The themes of a once great civilization that had fallen victim to tyranny, and that had degenerated to a level that required intervention from a foreign power are of course not new. In this instance, these were combined with the themes of rampant Islamic terrorisms and the proliferation of Weapons of Mass Destruction to justify the invasion. During the course of five years after 2003, as the Iraqi economy continued to be privatized, as the death toll mounted to over a million and the number of refugees to over four million, as the occupation forces continued facing resistance from a hostile population, these themes gradually gave way to other familiar ones: of people who are incapable of ruling themselves, who without the guiding hand of stern governance would fall into sectarian strife, of lands that are characterized by unruly and barbarian hordes, of tasks that are thankless but need to be taken up. In this context, learning from Said, the most important task for critical scholarship would be to pay attention to these historical continuities and interrogate the nature of the political projects they sustain to analyze and challenge the operation of imperial power. The question of what form Said claimed that challenge ought to take is one that we turn to in the final section of this chapter.

The question of resistance

At the beginning of *Orientalism*, Said laid out the many reasons why he found Foucault's work to be indispensable to understanding power in all its manifestations. But, as he argued later on, a world-view that emphasized the all-encompassing nature of power had a tendency to become fascinated solely with its operation, leaving no room for the question of resistance (Said 1983). It was on this question that, Said claimed, he and Foucault parted ways. Unlike the latter, for Said, the role played by the author was a crucial element of the production of the text, for individual writers left a 'determining imprint' even on 'the otherwise anonymous collective body of texts constituting a discursive formation like Orientalism' (Said 1995: 23). What this meant in essence was that far from being over-determined by dominant discursive structures, scholars and intellectuals had the ability to articulate specific viewpoints, exposing and challenging existing relations of power, and thus paving the way for resistance. In the specific context of Orientalism, this resistance could take the form of knowing the Orient outside of the discourse of Orientalism, and presenting this knowledge to the Orientalists (Said 1995: 336). In making this argument, Said was claiming not so much the existence of a *real* Orient that was accessible only to Orientals (he firmly believed that there was no such authentic Orient), but rather pointing to the fact that the internal consistency on which the Orientalist discourse rested was itself a political production that could and should be challenged. To understand how Said conceptualized the nature of such challenges, it is important to take a closer look at his notion of *secular criticism.*

Writing partly in response to what he saw as the main problems with literary criticism, Said argued that academia in general and intellectual knowledge in particular had become highly professionalized. The emphasis placed on disciplinary specialization and increased use of specialized jargons had meant that scholars were getting more and more disconnected, not just from their presumptive audience, but also from the world that they were supposedly writing about. Comfortable in their ivory towers, they had become devotees of the cult of professional expertise, focusing primarily on an isolated textuality, and as such had virtually ceded their ability to play an active role in changing the world. To recover that role, and to make critical scholarship more grounded and relevant, Said proposed what he called a tradition of 'secular criticism'. This was a tradition that, in contrast to 'existing theologies' of the theoretical approaches that dominated literary criticism (such as poststructuralism), encouraged both an amateur approach, and a breadth of interest (Said 1983). More importantly, this was a tradition that would be self-conscious about the connections and location of intellectual practice, its relationship to questions of ethics and justice, and most importantly to structures of power (Said 1994).

In further explicating his notion of secularism and particularly the role of a secular critic, Said made it clear that he was writing not just against the denizens of the ivory tower. He was equally opposed to those whose allegiance was to any particular political movement – any '-isms' (be it Marxism, Liberalism or Feminism) that served as labels modifying criticisms in advance. For, he argued, the 'history of thought, to say nothing of political movements is extravagantly illustrative of how the dictum "solidarity before criticism" means the end of criticism' (Said 1983: 28). The task of the secular critic would be therefore moving away from both the kind of quietism promoted by academic theorizing, and the ideologically oriented scholarship that was the product of dogmatic support for any particular cause, party or faction. In other words, the role of the critic, as Said saw it, would always be *oppositional*. Even in the 'midst of a battle' in which one supported a particular side, the emphasis had to be on keeping open the space for constant criticism. Otherwise, the seductive bog of ideology would lead to the critic getting stuck in a position of unreflective agreement, making it impossible for him/her to speak truth to power. While the position espoused by the secular critic would then be characterized by lack of certainty and ambiguities, Said welcomed this. Returning to the theme that runs through his writings, Said further argued that it was the state of *exile* that enabled secular criticism. In his particular case, the exile was also material in the sense of losing a homeland, but at a broader theoretical level, the state of exile served as a way to think about the world without being focused on or attached to any single vision. Freed from any kind of national or partisan affiliation, occupying an ambivalent relationship to culture, the state of exile allowed intellectuals to develop much needed critical faculties and thus served as the inescapable terrain from which they could challenge and disrupt the existing socio-political order.

The idea of secular criticism and the role it envisages for critical scholarship is one that has been widely celebrated in academia. As international relations scholarship develops its engagement with the life and work of Edward Said, it might be worthwhile for us to critically evaluate what exactly such scholarship would entail. To do so, it might make sense to begin with a Said-ian move: situate and analyze the worldliness of Said as an intellectual and his writings as cultural productions in socio-political contexts that go beyond that of exile or the struggle for Palestinian self-determination that Said himself highlighted. It is indeed to Said's credit that his key ideas are concerned not just with understanding the relationship between knowledge and power, but also interrogating the agency of the intellectual in perpetuating and challenging those relationships. This particular focus of his scholarship has led many scholars to remark admiringly that Said embodied Marx's ideal of the philosopher who sees his task as not just one of explaining the world, but changing it. However, it should be kept in mind that an over-riding emphasis on criticism understood as vehemently opposed to (and indeed antithetical) to political movements based on solidarity, can very easily turn the 'secular critic' into a kind of figure derided by Marx as a 'critical critic'. These distinctions, far from being a matter of mere semantics, are crucial political issues that critical scholarship needs to engage with if it is to be what Edward Said argued it ought to be – both relevant, and a locus of resistance in an imperial age.

Further reading

Said, Edward – *Orientalism* (1995); *The Question of Palestine* (1979); *Covering Islam* (1981). This trilogy lays out the main arguments made by Said about the nature of power in imperial contexts past and present. The first is a classic that was originally published in 1978, and reprinted in 1995 with an afterword by Said. The other two are more a discussion of the contemporary politics of the Middle East in general, and the Israel–Palestine issue in particular.

Said, Edward *Culture and Imperialism* (1993). This book highlights the mutually constitutive nature of cultural productions and political power by analyzing the presence of empire in classics of English literature. In the latter part of the book, Said explains the concept of exile to discuss the role of the intellectual in relation to culture and politics.

Said, Edward *The World, the Text and the Critic* (1983); *Representations of the Intellectual* (1994). The first is a key text in which Said lays out his analysis of 'worldliness', setting out the broader framework for his understanding of criticism, and the role of the critic. The second is a collection of lectures that provide a succinct version of Said's conception of the public intellectual.

For a set of essays focusing on the relevance of Edward Said to critical International Relations, see 'Forum on Edward Said and International Relations', *Millennium: Journal of International Studies*, 36 (1), December 2007: 77–145.

29 Carl Schmitt

Louiza Odysseos and Fabio Petito

To summarize Carl Schmitt's long life is to necessarily engage with and be wary of his own and his opponents' political propaganda, as little about his life and times is uncontroversial (Gottfried 1990). Schmitt was born in the provincial German Rhineland town of Plettenberg on 11 July 1888 to a Franco-German Catholic family that came from the Moselle Valley. He read law at the Universities in Berlin, Munich and Strassburg, graduating in 1915. He took up a professorship in Greifswald in 1921 and it was here that he published his *Die Diktatur* [The Dictatorship] (1994a), an influential work that was followed in theme by the seminal *Politische Theologie* [Political Theology] in 1922 (2005), when Schmitt moved to the University of Bonn. The 1920s saw Schmitt engage in the legal and political debates emerging with the various crises of the Weimar Republic and opposing legal formalism and normativism in notable works such as *Verfassungslehre* [Constitutional Theory] of 1928 (2007b). He moved academic institutions frequently, teaching at *Hochschule für Politik* in Berlin and finally moving to the University of Cologne, where he was to publish an expanded version of his 1927 pamphlet, *Der Begriff des Politischen* [The Concept of the Political], in 1932. Speaking in support of the Weimar Republic, Schmitt advocated in 1931–32 that the National Socialist German Workers (Nazi) Party be suppressed and lobbied Paul von Hindenburg, the Republic's President to imprison its leadership. He did not believe, as did other representatives of the Catholic Centre Party, with which he had been affiliated, that the Nazis could be controlled within the bounds of a coalition government.

While scholarship is right to condemn Schmitt's membership of the Nazi Party in May 1933, and his attempt to transform himself into the crown jurist of the Third Reich as well as into a *bona fide* anti-Semite in his writings, there was an element of opportunism in his doing so, as the Nazis themselves suspected. From 1935 onward, his teaching and activities were monitored and in 1936 the mouthpiece of the SS, *Das schwarze Korps*, called him to task for his Catholicism and earlier critiques of the Party's racial theories. Interned from September 1945 to May 1947, briefly by the Soviets and then by the American occupational forces, he was prohibited from returning to teaching and retreated to his hometown of Plettenberg. It is in this period of his life that he would produce important contributions in international law and politics, such as *Der Nomos der Erde im Völkerrecht des Jus Publicum Europaeum* [The Nomos of the Earth in the International Law of the Jus Publicum Europaeum] in 1950 and later *Theorie des Partisanen* [Theory of the Partisan] in 1963. He continued to travel, write and publish, with his entire corpus having what is regarded to be a 'subterranean' influence on a number of post-war thinkers such as Reinhart Koselleck, Hans Morgenthau, Hanno Kesting, and Roman Schnur, as well as prominent cultural and intellectual figures of the twentieth century such as Ernst Jünger, Walter Benjamin, Leo Strauss, Jacob Taubes, and Alexandre Kojève.

Schmitt described himself as a jurist, a scholar familiar with two areas of legal science: constitutional and international law. Both form part of public law and as such, he argued, were 'exposed to the danger from "the political"' (Schmitt 1950). For Schmitt, this 'exposure' meant that legal theory could not be dissociated from political theory in the same way that understanding international law could not be dissociated from analyses of international politics, that is, what we would call today, international theory. Schmitt's understanding of law, in fact, was radically different from the legal positivism and formalism which arguably dominated the twentieth century, with their abstract and generalising tendencies that rendered any analysis of constitutional and international law abstract and ultimately meaningless, devoid of a substantial engagement with real issues of domestic and international politics.

Schmitt's political and international thought

Schmitt's intellectual production is very large and broad in scope, spanning from legal and political thought to philosophy, theology, history and aesthetics. His writings can be grouped around three core interests: the philosophical nature of politics and sovereignty (Schmitt 1996a, 2005); the theory of the state and its forms of government (Schmitt 1996b, 1988a, 1994a); the theory and history of international law (Schmitt 2003, 2004a/2007a). Unfortunately, while Schmitt's legal and political writings during the twilight years of the Weimar Republic have had a significant and growing impact on contemporary legal and political theory in the English-speaking world, Schmitt's international thought, often referred to in continental Europe as the masterpiece of his intellectual production, had been overlooked until recently by international relations scholars (Odysseos and Petito 2007). This is partly explained by the fact that Schmitt's major works with an international focus, *The Nomos of the Earth* and *Theory of the Partisan* have only recently been made available in English (Schmitt 2003, 2004a/2007a). There is, however, a common thread linking these analyses and representing the core of Schmitt's reflection, as Carlo Galli has argued (1996), and that is the search for a legal order, domestically and internationally, capable of answering the 'tragedy of modernity', in other words, the end of the uncontested foundation for legitimacy of medieval Christian unity and the necessity to assume plurality, conflict and chaos – politics as a *pluriverse* – as ontologically given (Zarmanian 2006).

Sovereignty and 'the political'

In the early 1920s, Schmitt had put forward in *Political Theology* what is regarded as a 'decisionist' theory of sovereignty, summed up in the now increasingly familiar dictum: 'sovereign is he who decides on the exception' (Schmitt 2005: 5). Unlike theorizations of sovereignty in international relations that align this to control over population and territory and external recognition thereof, Schmitt eschewed attributing a fixed content to the notion of sovereignty. As Tracy B. Strong notes in his considered 'Foreword' to the 2005 edition, 'the nature of the sovereign ... is the making of a "genuine decision" about the exceptional case' (Schmitt 2005: xiv). Yet the exception reaffirms the rule while suspending it; or, better, it 'creates a juridical order' precisely at the moment of suspending it. Again in the words of Strong, 'the sovereign must decide both that a situation is exceptional and what to do about the exception in order to be able to create or recover a juridical order when the existing one is threatened by chaos' (Schmitt 2005: xx). This is what Giorgio Agamben calls a 'pleromatic [full] state of the law' (Agamben 2005a: 48). Unlike Hans Kelsen's attempt to rid law of its subjective elements, Schmitt firmly believed that 'all law is situational law' and that, moreover,

> the sovereign produces and guarantees the situation in its totality. He has a monopoly over this last decision [of the exceptional case]. Therein resides the essence of the state's sovereignty, which must be juristically defined correctly, not as the monopoly to coerce or to rule, but as the monopoly to decide ... The decision here parts from the legal norm, and (to formulate it paradoxically) authority proves that to produce law [to create a juridical order] it need not be based on law' (Schmitt 2005: 13, brackets indicate Strong's modification of G. Schwab's translation).

In his monograph *The Concept of the Political* (1996a), Schmitt aimed to provide a clear statement of the distinction that characterizes 'the political', a distinction that had been obscured, he believed, by the predominance of liberal thought and international practice in the years following the First World War. According to Schmitt, 'the specific political distinction to which political actions and motives can be reduced is that between friend and enemy' (Schmitt 1996a: 26). Although every distinction draws upon other distinctions to reinforce itself, the friend/enemy distinction, around which the political coalesces, may be asserted without recourse to moral, aesthetic, economic, or religious considerations. Who the enemy is can be decided solely by judging whether the other 'intends to negate his opponent's way of life and therefore must be repulsed' (Schmitt 1996a: 27).

Schmitt wished to refute the possibility of transcending war in international relations by reinstating the *position* of the political (Schmitt 1996a, 1996b), that is, by affirming an understanding of the political as related to the decision (Schmitt 1996a: 31, 2005). Schmitt reasserted the 'decision' of the political, which, he felt, had to 'rest on its own ultimate distinctions, to which all action with a specifically political meaning can be traced' (Schmitt 1996a: 26). This distinction of friend/enemy, on which the political rests, 'denotes the utmost degree of intensity of a union or separation, of an association or disassociation' (Schmitt 1996a: 26). Historical or extant political groups or collectivities, importantly, can only be *decided as* enemies if they are perceived to present an existential threat. This restricts the political to the *moment* when the political *decision* about the distinction between friend and enemy is made. The distinction between friend and enemy is decided only *in the extreme case*, that is, it is an *exception* rather than the norm (Schmitt 2005). Schmitt's reference to the public enemy – *hostis*, not *inimicus* – decided upon by the state (which *presupposes* the concept of the political) leads him to avoid any 'identitarian' (Prozorov 2007) claims about the enemy: 'An enemy exists only when, at least potentially, one fighting collectivity of people confronts a similar collectivity' (Schmitt 1996a: 28), faced with the possibility of dying and of killing. Everyday political adversaries cannot, in this conception, be 'enemies'. By allowing the political to coalesce around the decision between friend and enemy in an extreme case, Schmitt challenged the very possibility that the liberal practice of law and the establishment of international institutions could promote peace and prevent war, improving the lot of a 'universal' humanity (Odysseos 2007a). If transcendence were possible, then 'the political' is threatened (Strauss 1996: 96–101); more importantly, if decisions were not possible, juridical, political and international order could not be produced or sustained. It is Schmitt's arguments about the impossibility and, indeed, the dangers of politics which aim to get 'rid of politics' (Dyzenhaus 1998: 14), that have influenced both twentieth century political realism and also recent post-Marxist attempts to rethink social antagonism or 'agonism', in addition to, or beyond class, and within a neo-liberal political context (Mouffe 1998, 1999, 2005; Laclau 2005).

Historicising Westphalia

Schmitt wrote *The Nomos of the Earth* (2003) at a time when he believed that 'Westphalia' – this spatial, political and legal global order (the '*nomos* of the earth') embodied in the *jus publicum Europaeum* – had undergone a momentous, and for him regrettable, process of collapse, which he dates variably from the later decades of the nineteenth century to the beginning of the First World War. In its stead, Schmitt (1995) foresaw many dangers arising from the swing towards 'global pan-interventionism' by the United States of America, the effects of de-concretization and universalization of international law (that is, of 'order' without explicit spatial grounding), of diminishing pluralism in the international system, as well as the evolution of partisan warfare and terrorism.

For Schmitt, nomos is the foundational act that creates a concrete territorial order as unity of (legal) order and (spatial) orientation (*Ordnung und Ortung*) (Schmitt 2003: 67–79). The concept of nomos has very little to do with the positivist idea of 'law' as an abstract command, as a superficial literal translation might suggest. Rather, Schmitt's conception of nomos suggests that every legal order is, first and foremost, a *spatial* order constituted by an act or process of land-appropriation, for 'all law is law only in a particular location' (Schmitt 2003: 98). Spatially ordering the earth, moreover, could only occur with the emergence of 'global linear thinking', a specifically modernist approach to space, orientation and measurement (Schmitt 2003: 86–100; 1995). The *jus publicum Europaeum*, therefore, can only emerge as the first *nomos* of the earth, the first *order* of the earth, in the horizon made possible by the discovery and forcible appropriation of the 'new world'.

Ordering the earth – spatially and legally – is necessarily based on an historical event of land-appropriation; yet it is such a foundational act of force that produces rules and law, so that 'Westphalia' as a geopolitical order is also a 'community of political entities united by common rules ... considered to be mutually binding in the conduct of international affairs' (Ulmen 2003: 10). As this definition suggests, the European modern 'international society', as broadly described by the rationalist and English School traditions of international relations (Wight 1994; Linklater 2001), is one possible starting point to understand what Schmitt has in mind. Hedley Bull, in fact, defines a society of states as 'a group of states that conceive themselves to be bound by a common set of rules in their relations with one another' (Bull 1977: 13). Whereas Bull and Adam Watson understood the expansion of European international society as culminating in its universalization in the twentieth century, for Schmitt, 'Westphalia' is a global order from its very inception because its origins and very conditions of possibility lie in the epoch-making discovery of a 'new world' as a *free* space, an area regarded as open to European expansion and occupation.

Shortly after 1492, when the first maps and globes were produced, the first lines were also drawn by the appropriating European powers to divide and distribute this new global space. Schmitt illuminates how the first global lines, the Spanish–Portuguese *rayas* (Treaty of Tordesillas 1494), had a *distributive* purpose, that is, they aimed at the internal division of the new lands between two land-appropriating Christian princes within the spatial order of the *respublica Christiana* and guaranteed by the common authority of the pope as head of the Roman Catholic Church. The subsequent French–English 'amity lines', established with the Treaty of Cateau Cambrésis (1559), were based on completely different premises, embodying an *agonal* character. They set aside two distinct areas considered 'open' or 'free' spaces: on the one hand, the landmass of the 'new world', which was not recognised as belonging to the native populations, and on the other, the newly mapped and navigable seas (Schmitt 2003: 94–5). In both types of 'open space', the appropriating European powers could use force freely and ruthlessly, as these were areas 'designated for agonal tests of strength' (Schmitt 2003: 99):

> At this 'line' Europe ended and the 'New World' began. At any rate, European law, i.e., 'European public law', ended here ... Beyond the line was an 'overseas' zone in which, for want of any legal limits to war, only the law of the stronger applied (Schmitt 2003 : 93–4).

Schmitt examines explicitly how it was the need to permit and legally justify the appropriation of these lands 'beyond the line', as well as the marshalling of the seas, which led to the creation of 'Westphalia', the first European nomos with a truly *global* geopolitical character.

Schmitt, then, argues for a history of modern international politics that is inseparable, not only from the rise of scientific rationality (Schmitt 2003: 53), or even from the spread of capitalism that more commonplace narratives of modernity emphasize, but first and foremost from the processes of land appropriation of the new world by European powers. Put otherwise, Westphalia's land-appropriations and control of the navigable seas, its creation of core (European soil) and periphery ('free spaces' of the new world), are integral not only to our understanding of 'Westphalia' as a system of relations but to the very possibility of its emergence.

Highlighting in the *Nomos* both the advent of the modern European state as the vehicle of secularization and also its global geopolitical and appropriative character allowed Schmitt to trace how this interstate order was able to limit and, in this way, rationalize and 'humanize' war. By this, Schmitt meant that Westphalia had succeeded in institutionally 'bracketing' war, precisely on the basis of drawing geopolitical distinctions between European and non-European space. 'Bracketing', in the proper sense of *Hegung*, is not only a delimitation but also a 'pruning', a constant maintenance of war, much like one prunes flower borders in a garden – a politics, rather than a singular and spectacular act of law. Schmitt evaluates this occurrence as a significant legal and political achievement, for it had kept 'war at bay' (Mouffe 2007: 150) on European soil:

> Compared to the brutality of religious and factional wars, which by nature are wars of annihilation wherein the enemy is treated as a criminal and a pirate, and compared to colonial wars, which are pursued against 'wild' peoples, European 'war in form' signified the strongest possible rationalization and humanization of war (Schmitt 2003: 142).

According to Schmitt, this is the major achievement of 'Westphalia'. The interstate order which existed in Europe until 1914 had sought, through its international law, 'to prevent wars of annihilation, i.e. to the extent that war was inevitable, to bracket it' (Schmitt 2003: 246). Westphalia did not seek to end war as such – to abolish or banish it from its international relations – attempts at which have since been shown to bring about 'new, perhaps even worse types of war, such as reversions to civil war and other types of wars of annihilation' (Schmitt 2003: 246). It, rather, sought to find ways in which to gauge the opponent's strength, usually by striving for appropriation of lands in the new world or by fighting limited wars on European soil, and by recognizing the European state opponent as an enemy on equal grounds.

The development of the notion of the just and equal enemy – *justus hostis* – was the key to such an achievement. The concept evolved alongside the consolidation of the modern state because, with the predominance of this type of political entity and the weakening of the moral authority of the Church, war became 'non-discriminatory' (Schmitt 1988b), that is, divorced from substantive causes of justice: 'war came to be judged in terms of its outcome' and became a form of political relation amongst states (Schmitt 2003: 100). Any enemy that had the form of a state was a just enemy and war could be waged against it. This development avoided wars of conviction, creed and religion (that is, based on just cause [*justa causa*]) which had historically wrought destruction and allowed the denunciation and annihilation of enemies. For Schmitt, whose belief was that war was an inevitable part of world-political life, this regulation of war without substantive cause meant a 'rationalization, humanization and legalization' of war. Regarding an enemy as both a just and equal partner meant that peace could be made with that enemy: his ultimate destruction was not sought, but conflict with him was possible and regulated.

As a consequence, war became a '"war in form", *une guerre en forme*' (Schmitt 2003: 141), whereby the justice of war was no longer determined by the causes of war, but by the formal adequacy of the belligerents: they had to be *justi hostes*, bearers of the *jus belli*, that is, European sovereign states. In other words, 'war became somewhat analogous to a duel, i.e., a conflict of arms between territorially distinct *personae morales*' within the contours of the *jus publicum Europaeum* (Schmitt 2003: 141). Such wars, Schmitt suggests, were the very antithesis of disorder (Schmitt 2003: 187).

The notion of the just enemy, moreover, meant that such a system of war allowed for resistance, self-defense and balancing: given that in eliminating just cause the enemy was *a priori* just, his right to self-defense and to resistance was recognized. This also allowed for the development of the institution of neutrality for third-party states in international law. Only non-state or private war was unjust: rebels, pirates, outlaws, troublemakers, were not *justi hostes* but criminals and, as such, they could be dealt with through punitive actions in the sense of modern criminal law or 'police action'. Additionally, the *jus publicum Europaeum* allowed for the construction and maintenance of a balance (Schmitt 2003: 161), known within international relations as the 'balance of power'. This relates to the avoidance of wars of destruction, because if balance was the political and military objective, then wars could be limited to achieving it, unlike wars of just cause, which required the submission of the opponent or their forcible or normative re-socialization. Peace conferences held under the auspices of the great powers represented the legal institutionalization of the foundation of European international law, the balance of power, articulated in its two main principles: first, every important war among European states is a legitimate concern for *all* the members of the community of European states and, second, it falls upon the great powers as guarantors of European spatial ordering to recognize relevant territorial changes (Schmitt 2003: 185–212).

Post-Westphalian crises: enmity, order and war

In the last decades of the nineteenth century the *jus publicum Europaeum* entered its twilight years, which would eventually lead to its dissolution with the First World War. Schmitt identifies the end of the first *nomos* of the earth in three major processes: the evolution of the *jus publicum Europaeum* into a spaceless and generic 'International Law' and its institutionalisation in the League of Nations system (Schmitt 2003: 227–58); the transformation of the meaning of war (Schmitt 2003: 259–78 and 309–22); the new role of the United States and the emergence of the Western hemisphere as a central category of its foreign policy discourse (Schmitt 2003: 281–308; cf. 1995). Behind all these processes lay a major historical and epoch-making shift: the end of Europe as the centre of the earth. In the previous centuries, European conferences had determined the spatial ordering of the world; after the First World War, as was evident at the Paris Peace Conference, it was, for the first time, the world who would decide on the spatial ordering of Europe.

According to Schmitt, the League of Nations system failed to replace the *jus publicum Europaeum* because it was built on a highly unstable disorder, made visible first of all in the way it dealt with the issue of the limitation of war, the central purpose of any international law. Its central aim became the abolition, rather than the limitation, of war, *via* the introduction of the new concepts of discriminatory war and war as a crime. These attempts to criminalize wars of aggression, to create an international tribunal and to claim reparations for damages deriving from the legal responsibility of having waged an unjust war of aggression, all pointed to an epochal transformation in the meaning of war and enmity. They signalled, unmistakably, the end of the era of the old *nomos* of the earth. The consequences would become clear in the emergence of the new total wars of the twentieth century, wars of annihilation fought in the name of humanity, which had been, thanks to the modern means of destruction (air power), transformed into a police action against the 'disturbers' of peace, criminals and outlaws.

This transformation of war into police action, much discussed today within the context of the global war on terror, would not have been possible without the new fundamental role of the United States, which Schmitt analyzes by looking at the Western hemisphere as a central category of its foreign policy discourse. Since its formulation in the famous Monroe doctrine in 1823, the Western hemisphere represented American greater space [*Großraum*], defining the American continent as the US sphere of *special* interests. In terms of 'global linear thinking', the line of the Western hemisphere, different from a distributive *raya* and from an agonal amity line, was a defensive line around a security zone, a line of self-isolation, as well as an anti-European line based on American contempt for the old and 'corrupted' Europe. But it is during the interwar years that the originally *isolationalist* nature of the Western hemisphere gradually moved into a universalistic-humanitarian global *pan-interventionism*, which would seek to justify US intervention in all the relevant political, social, and economic issues of the earth on the basis of a return to the older views of the Just War tradition (Schmitt 1995: 445–47).

It is within this context of the demise of 'Westphalia' that Schmitt's reflections on partisan warfare should be understood. Schmitt's *Theory of the Partisan* historically traces the emergence of partisan warfare with the Spanish Civil War of 1808–13 (Schmitt 2004a: 13). Although an irregular and highly flexible and mobile fighter by the standards of regular troops, the partisan was best understood by his 'intense political commitment', usually to a 'fighting warring or politically active group' (Schmitt 2004a: 10). The intensity of the partisan's political commitment filled the caesura left open by the now undeniable end of the equivalence between the state and politics, evident in 'the state's inability to grasp the new current of political intensity' (Colombo 2007: 32). Schmitt thought that states were 'no longer able to integrate their own members and adherents so totally as a revolutionary party does its active fighters' (Schmitt 2004a: 10) and that the partisan was that new political actor 'capable of restoring "the seriousness of war" ... who sweeps away the state's grip on politics and war. The inconceivability of war among states does not promise peace but, rather, an outflow of violence that overcomes the state' (Colombo 2007: 32).

This intense commitment to a political objective is also related to the 'tellurian character of the partisan', by which Schmitt means that he is tied to a particular territory as 'the defender of house, hearth and homeland [*Haus und Herd und Heimat*]' (Schmitt 2004a: 20). For Schmitt, then, the partisan exists in an essentially 'defensive situation' that makes his political activities spatially limited, specific and concrete, rather than universal and abstract (Schmitt 2004a: 13). Just as importantly, moreover, this means that the traditional partisan still operates with an idea of limited enmity (associated with the notion of *justus hostis*), limited by its desire to *defend*, which 'preserve[s] it from the absolutism of abstract justice' (Schmitt 2004a: 13). The relinquishment of limited enmity in war was amongst the most noticeable changes once the partisan begins to identify 'with the absolute aggressiveness of a world-revolutionary or technologizing ideology' (Schmitt 2004a: 13). Indeed, Schmitt grasps the evolution from limited to absolute enmity by examining the changes to the figure of the partisan from the defensive irregular fighter of the Spanish Civil War of 1808–13 through to its theorization by Lenin and later Mao Tse-tung.

For Lenin, Schmitt argues, the absolute enemy was 'the class enemy, the *bourgeois*, the Western capitalist and his social order in every country in which they ruled' and the struggle against him, therefore, had to correspond to the enemy's own universal presence (Schmitt 2004a: 35). For a universal war against an absolute enemy no limitation remains possible. Therefore, Lenin conceived of partisan warfare as belonging 'to the realm of the methods of civil war'; what preoccupied him were 'purely tactical or strategic question[s] relating to the concrete situation', but he felt that partisan war must use any means 'legal or illegal, peaceful or violent, regular or irregular' to achieve its purpose, which was the 'communist revolution in all countries of the world; whatever serves this purpose is good and just' (Schmitt 2004a: 35).

Schmitt's mid twentieth-century reflections on the 'post-Westphalian' emerging order, and the forms of war to which its normative and geopolitical characteristics give rise, are related to his earlier question of the distinction between friend and enemy, now recast more forcefully as the question of 'unanticipated new sorts of enmity' that 'come into being' (Schmitt 2004a: 68). If we recall that central to Schmitt's definition of the political (1996a), is the *distinction* between friend and enemy and, moreover, that 'it presupposes both friend and enemy' (Schmitt 2004a: 65, 2007a: 85, n. 89), then outside the normative parameters of Westphalia, limited ('real') enmity, associated with the concept of *justus hostis*, slides into absolute enmity, in a transition from enemy to foe. This allows the 'opponents [to] mutually consign each other to the abyss of total devaluation' and make possible their physical destruction and elimination, an annihilation which becomes 'completely abstract and completely absolute' (Schmitt 2007a: 94). Annihilation is aimed at the *spectre* of an absolute enemy, who must be both produced and who must also remain elusive and abstract. It is its abstractness that allows for the enemy's total renunciation. As Jon Beasley-Murray argues, outside of the European bracketing of war,

> in this transaction of death, what is absent is an exchange or even a relation between subjects who can recognize each other: both parties, on the ground or in the air, confront an unknowable foe ... The enemy becomes abstract for both sides (Beasley-Murray 2005: 220).

Such annihilation is not necessarily aimed at a real enemy but 'serves only another, *ostensibly objective attainment of highest values*, for which no price is too high to pay. It is the renunciation of real enmity that opens the door for the work of annihilation of an absolute enmity' (Schmitt 2004a: 67, emphasis added). The spectral presence and elusiveness of the absolute enemy allows for the articulation and actualization of the 'highest values'.

The emergence of absolute designations of enmity, which can be annihilated for the 'highest values', leads to both a change in the form and scope of 'war' itself, and also to the key question of the search for a new *nomos* – order – of the earth, an issue to which Schmitt devoted some sketchy reflections in his late writings but to which he was persuaded it was too early to respond (Petito 2007). Such concerns predate and perhaps inform more recent analyses of the geopolitical specificity of the contemporary emerging global order and the unlimited scope and duration of its wars (Odysseos 2007; Reid 2004, 2006). The topicality of Schmitt's international thought is striking when we reflect on the apparently paradoxical contemporary convergence of uni-lateral-militarist and liberal-humanitarian themes in the discourse and prac-tice of the global war on terror. This immediately reminds us of Schmitt's powerful indictment, 'whoever invokes humanity wants to cheat' (Schmitt 1996a: 54), as well as of his perceptive remarks on the two-sided political nature of the concept of humanity, whereby the fight in the name of humanity implies the denial to the enemy of the very quality of being human (Schmitt 2003: 103–4; Odysseos 2007a). It was the re-emerging possibility of wars of annihilation and extermination based on a radically transformed notion of just cause which prompted Schmitt's heterodox international thought to historically recount the ambivalent achievements of 'Westphalia' in partially delimiting war among European states and to simultaneously reflect on the dangers caused by the abandonment of bracketing as a political pursuit of world-ordering.

Unfortunately Schmitt's 'international' destiny has been sealed by a mis-taken interpretation of his oft-quoted 'definition' of the political as the dis-tinction between friend and enemy, which relegates his thought, apparently beyond any doubt, to the Realist paradigm of contemporary international theorizing, presenting this as an almost perfect exemplification of the nature of international relations as power politics. For Schmitt, however, the key to any 'concept' of the political 'is not enmity *per se* but the *distinction* of friend and enemy' (Schmitt 2004a: 65, emphasis added). In other words, the poli-tical is based on the reality of difference and plurality and on the possibility of its politicization. From this it follows that the main focus of Schmitt's entire corpus, from his Weimar juridical writings to his seminal *Der Nomos der Erde*, was not enmity or conflict but rather the search for the essence of (legal) order. This is why Colombo has provocatively talked of Schmitt's 'realist institutionalism' as a constant effort to reconcile

> form and decision, effective and juridical power, in an attempt to dis-tinguish what power *always* is – the pure and simple ability to impose one's will on others – from what it *can become* through law – a 'restraining force', as Schmitt defines it, borrowing the Pauline concept of *katechon*; namely, an instance able to channel the indomitable lack of restraint of the political into juridical form (Colombo 2007: 21).

Further reading

Dyzenhaus, David (ed.) (1998) *Law as Politics: Carl Schmitt's critique of liberalism*, Durham, NC: Duke University Press. Accessible and widely-read edited collection of essays on Schmitt's engagement with liberalism.

Odysseos, Louiza and Petito, Fabio (eds) (2007) *The International Political Thought of Carl Schmitt: Terror, Liberal War and the Crisis of Global Order*, London: Routledge. A recent collection of essays engaging with the heterodox international thought of Schmitt and critically utilizing his thought for a critique of contemporary war and order.

Schmitt, Carl (1986) *Political Romanticism*, trans. G. Oakes, Cambridge: MIT Press. Schmitt's engagement and critique of the romantic movement in which he outlines the emergence of the private individual of *bourgeois* society out of the movement's drive for secularization, subjectification and privatization.

Schmitt, Carl (1993) 'The age of neutralizations and depoliticizations', trans. J. McCormick and M. Konzett, *Telos* 96: 130–42. Influential essay based on a lecture from 1939 outlining Schmitt's view of Western history as the successive search for neutral compromize and peace within the epochal central spheres of contention.

Schmitt, Carl (2005) *Political Theology: Four Chapters on the Concept of Sovereignty*, trans. G. Schwab, Chicago: University of Chicago Press. Schmitt's influential text on sovereignty, which is today extensively used in contemporary political philosophy, as in for example the work of Giorgio Agamben.

Strauss, Leo (1996) 'Notes to *The Concept of the Political*' in Schmitt (1996a). Strauss's influential and widely-read critique of Schmitt's major text.

30 Gayatri Chakravorty Spivak

Catarina Kinnvall

Gayatri Chakravorty Spivak was born in 1942 in Calcutta in Bengal. She completed her Bachelors' degree at the Presidency College of Calcutta with first-class honours in English, before moving to the United States in 1961 to take a Masters' degree at Cornell University. After a one-year fellowship at Cambridge University in England, Spivak took an instructor's position in Iowa while completing her doctoral dissertation at Cornell in 1967. Her dissertation was focused on the Irish poet W.B. Yeats (1865–1939) and was supervised by the literary critic Paul de Man (1919–83). Before arriving at Columbia in 1992, Spivak taught at several US universities. She has received numerous academic awards and has held visiting university appointments all over the world since the late 1970s. She is Director of the Center for Comparative Literature and Society and currently holds the Avalon Foundation Professorship of the Humanities at Columbia University.

Born in India to solid middle-class parents, Spivak belongs to the first generation of Indian intellectuals after independence, or what Salman Rushdie has referred to as *The Midnight Children*. She specializes in nineteenth and twentieth-century literature, Marxism, feminism, deconstruction, poststructuralism, postcolonialism and globalization and has been a member of the Subaltern Studies Group. She has sustained a critical engagement with the intellectual tradition represented by the writings of Freud, Lacan, Marx, Derrida and Foucault and has been crucial in transforming and politicizing feminist and poststructuralist critiques of psychoanalysis and Marxist thought. Her role as a postcolonial critic and feminist cannot be overestimated and it is in this capacity that her direct influence on the field of international relations has been most evident.

Major works and key ideas

Spivak became known initially for her English translation of Jacques Derrida's *Of Grammatology*. The book features an extended 'Translator's preface', that serves as an introduction both to Derrida and to Spivak herself. She has also translated and critically appraised the fiction of Mahasweta Devi: *Imaginary Maps* (1994), *Breast Stories* (1997), and *Old Women* (1999). Her books include: *In Other Worlds: Essays in Cultural Politics* (1987); *The Post-Colonial Critic: Interviews, Strategies, Dialogues* (1990); and *Outside in the Teaching Machine* (1993), a volume of essays concerned with improving higher education in a global context. This is also one of the underlying themes of what has sometimes been referred to as her *magnum opus*; *A Critique of Postcolonial Reason: Toward a History of the Vanishing Present* (1999). In this impressive book Spivak discusses the role of the migrant in multiculturalism, and identity and culture in a neo-colonial world. In *Red Thread* (2001), Spivak brings together much of her work during the last decade. In *Death of a Discipline* (2003), she maintains that we are witnessing a New Comparative Literature in the age of globalization, while in *Other Asias* (2005), she examines conflicting ideas about Asia. Apart from her many books, Gayatri Spivak is also known through interviews, lectures and numerous scholarly articles, and her long essay entitled *Can the Subaltern Speak?* (1988) has received particular attention.

Gayatri Spivak has sometimes been described as a feminist Marxist deconstructivist (MacCabe 1998), and any attempt to capture her key ideas will have to situate her work within the three fields of feminism, Marxism and deconstruction. Spivak herself has commented, however, that she rejects the idea of reconciling the three, but instead wants to preserve the discontinuities and disruptions of their discourses. She is also sceptical of any totalizing ideologies, as she sees them as being too 'deeply marked' by colonial influences (Spivak 1990: 15). Spivak's approach to her own work is often described as a journey back and forth between thinking, research, writing and teaching – what she calls the 'itinerary' of her thinking (Landry and MacLean 1996):

> If someone says that they read in an interview I gave in 1986, something that was different to what I said in, say 1976, I would simply say 'Too bad!' – and that is that! (Spivak 1990: 36–7)

This refusal to be held accountable to a vanishing present (as the subtitle to *A Critique of Postcolonial Reason* reads), is symptomatic of Spivak's refusal to be systematic in the conventional ways of Western critical thought. Instead, she intends to disturb the representational authority of Western discourse in order to grasp those fleeting moments which Western discourse is structured not to represent.

Hence giving a chronological account of Spivak's ideas does not make much sense. Instead, the topics selected in this chapter are reoccurring themes and ideas that most closely relate to international relations theory. The first set of ideas is concerned with the politics of deconstruction, the 'unlearning of our privilege as our loss' and the Native Informant. The next set speaks about Spivak as a postcolonial critic and her relationship to other postcolonial scholars. Finally, and perhaps most importantly, Spivak's thoughts on postcolonial feminism and its relationship to Marxism are discussed, especially as these relate to the subaltern woman and to subjectivity.

Politics of deconstruction: unlearning privilege and the Native Informant

There would have been no 'other worlds' for me if something new called deconstruction had not come to disrupt the diasporic space of a post-colonial academic (Spivak 1998: xxvii).

Spivak's reading and interpretation of Derrida's *Of Grammatology* in many ways spelt out her future concern with deconstructive ontology, epistemology and methodology. Like Derrida, Spivak reacts against the structuralist idea developed by Ferdinand de Saussure, and later by Roland Barthes and Claude Lévi Strauss, that language can be studied scientifically as a stable and causal representation of reality. One of the main problems with this model of language is, according to Spivak, that it has been used to represent the world as a stable object of Western knowledge. Spivak, like Derrida, is concerned with the assumed neutrality of Western thought and she argues that the development of Western philosophy, rather than being neutral, is intimately connected to the history of European imperial expansion from nineteenth century British imperialism to twentieth century US foreign policy making. The main difference between Spivak and Derrida can be found in their respective attitudes to the value of deconstruction. While Derrida has often commented on how the enterprise of deconstruction always in certain ways falls prey to its own work, Spivak sees deconstruction not as a conservative ethic, nor a radical politics, but as an intellectual ethic that enables rigorous analysis (MacCabe 1998).

Deconstruction for Spivak opens up an anti-essentialist notion of identity-as-origin as it is focused on examining the processes whereby we naturalize personal history and desire into general truth. A deconstructive strategy involves dismantling the very tradition of Western thought that has provided the justification for European colonialism and neo-colonialism. In particular, Spivak argues, we need to dismantle texts, or textuality, as general writing has provided a rhetorical structure that has served to justify imperial expansion. The notion of 'worldling' is used by Spivak to exemplify how textuality privileges and justifies colonial expansion:

As far as I understand it, the notion of textuality should be related to the notion of worldling of a world on a supposedly uninscribed territory. When I say this, I am thinking basically about the imperialist project which had to assume that the earth that it territorialized was in fact previously uninscribed (Spivak 1990: 1).

Spivak's emphasis on representation questions presumed notions of objectivity and rationality in international relations theory. By opening up the discourse to marginalized voices in society, especially in the South, Spivak also moves away from the focus on states and sovereignty. Her deconstructive strategy thus complicates traditional international relations' preoccupation with borders and territoriality as it focuses on what is outside of these borders; what is not included in the (Western) narrative:

> When a narrative is constructed, something is left out. When an end is defined, other ends are rejected, and one may not know what those ends are ... What is left out? Can we know what is left out? (Spivak 1990: 18–19)

Spivak was one of the first to articulate postcolonial theory through a deconstructive lens. She was also influential in forcing deconstruction to work outside the disciplinary boundaries of literary criticism and philosophy and in bringing deconstruction from ethics to politics and to the wider field of economic and political relations. 'Unlearning one's privilege as one's loss' thus marks the beginning of an ethical relation to the other and is, according to Landry and MacLean (1996), one of the most powerful tasks set readers by Spivak's writing and teachings. To unlearn our privileges means not only understanding the historical context in which this privileging was formed, but also working hard at gaining some knowledge of the others and attempting to speak to them in ways that make it possible for them to answer back. This is a task for everyone and there is no excuse for keeping silent, Spivak argues:

> I will have in an undergraduate class, let's say, a young, white male student, politically-correct, who will say: 'I am only a *bourgeois* white male, I can't speak' ... I say to them: 'Why not develop a certain degree of rage against the history that has written such an abject script for you that you are silenced?' (Spivak 1990: 63).

Here Spivak raises ethical concerns of representation. In this respect, she is wary of both the radical intellectuals who claim to speak on behalf of the disenfranchised and those who search for authentic voices among disenfranchised groups. Culturalism can be as problematic in terms of self-representation as in terms of representing others (Spivak 1990), a theme developed in *Can the Subaltern Speak?* and one she returns to in her later work on multiculturalism. This is also Spivak's concern when attempting to track the figure of the Native Informant:

> Soon I found that the tracking showed up a colonial subject detaching itself from the Native Informant. After 1989, I began to sense that a certain postcolonial subject had, in turn, been recoding the colonial subject and appropriating the Native Informant's position. Today, with globalization in full swing, telecommunicative informatics taps the Native Informant directly in the name of indigenous knowledge and advanced biopiracy (Spivak 1999: ix).

The question of how to represent the other entails responsibility. Here Spivak is quite clear in her ambition that responsibility depends not on one's nationality or race, but on one's position. Spivak's primary methodological goal is thus to provide textual conditions under which the Native Informant can be heard. This is also why Spivak has later replaced the 'NI' for Native Informant with the 'New Immigrant' in a financialized global economy (Sanders 2006). The ethical positioning of oneself in relation to the 'other' has thus come to represent a key concept in Spivak's work and in post-colonialism in general, thus challenging orthodox international relations approaches that have worked to privilege Eurocentric histories of othering.

The postcolonial critic

Despite Gayatri Spivak's long standing reputation within literary theory, cultural studies and sociology, it is only recently that her work has been imported into the discipline of international relations. This is mostly taking place through an increased openness to critical approaches in general as old disciplinary boundaries are breaking down and as traditional preoccupations with state-centrism are being questioned. This has become even more evident after the September 11 attacks. Not only have many international relations scholars become more aware of the intertwined fates of the West and the global South (Barkawi 2004), but they have also moved closer to matters of world politics, such as identity conflicts, transnationalism and diaspora politics. Many of these issues have existed at the heart of postcolonial studies and have not least been dealt with by Spivak in her intersectional analyses of class, race and gender on a global scale. The recent surge in globalization studies has most probably furthered the interest in postcolonial scholarship:

> Within the context of globalization, to be postcolonial seems more appropriate than to be merely metropolitan multicultural. It is a way of dealing with globalization which is after all a fairly recent phenomenon. In order to give globalization historical depth you must move it to postcoloniality (Spivak 2002: 272).

Spivak herself has become increasingly uneasy with the label 'postcolonial theorist', but it would be difficult to explain her influence on international relations theory without giving proper credit to her continued preoccupation with postcolonial scholarship and postcolonial feminist thought. Other scholars included under this umbrella are Frantz Fanon, Edward Said, Homi Bhabha and Chandra Talpade Mohanty – among others.

One of the more complex aspects of Spivak's writings is her continual attempts to relate experiences of individuals and social groups who have been historically dispossessed and exploited by European colonialism. One main concern is to show how universal categories, through what Derrida calls a *catachresis*, have been used to represent groups who are more or less internally divided, such as women, workers or the colonized. Africa, Spivak argues, constitutes such a master word, a *catachresis* or improper use of a word, as it has been imposed on a continent by a European colonial power: 'Africa is only a time-bound naming, like all proper names it is a mark with an arbitrary connection to its referent' (Spivak, quoted in Morton 2003: 122). Colonial expansion was about labelling places in such ways that they became intertwined with race-based ideas of the other; the native.

As Smith and Owens (2005) have noted, international relations has been more comfortable with class and gender than it has been with race, although race and racism have continued to shape and influence world politics in numerous ways. Spivak herself is constantly reminding us of how the academic community generally has difficulties in coming to terms with this reality (Spivak 1998). Postcolonial criticism is thus about locating knowledge as a historically created site where the process of othering takes place. Spivak's (1999) suggestion to change the title of an Essex conference in 1992 from 'Europe and Its Others' to 'Europe as an Other', documenting and theorizing the itinerary of Europe as a sovereign subject, points to an alternative 'worlding' of today's 'inter-national' relations. The aim is to show how Eurocentrism has been and continues to be the prerequisite for how we construct a vision of the other (Keyman 1997; Kinnvall 2007). The critique of Eurocentrism and universalism, on the one hand, and of the homogeneous understanding of the 'Third World' as found in some postmodernist texts, on the other, marks the strategy of postcolonial criticism and its analysis of imperialism:

> Some of the most radical criticism coming out of the West in the eighties was the result of an interested desire to conserve the subject of the West, or the West as Subject. The theory of pluralized 'subject-effects' often provided a cover for this subject of knowledge. Although the history of Europe as Subject was narrativized by the law, political economy, and the ideology of the West, this concealed Subject pretended it had 'no geopolitical determinations'. The much-publicized critique of the sovereign subject thus actually inaugurated a Subject (Spivak 1999: 248).

As a critical line of inquiry Spivak's statement can be compared to the postcolonial theorist Homi Bhabha's (1990) discussion of Edward Said's Orient. Said, Bhabha notes, fails to investigate the process in which the colonial subject is historically constructed, making Orientalist discourse appear monolithic, undifferentiated and uncontested (Bhabha, 1984: 125–33). Spivak's statement also illustrates the difficulties international relations theory has had in acknowledging the need to explore difference, and not only recognize it in forms of 'different' nation-states. In this, much conventional international relations theory continues to privilege unity over difference, presuming a sovereign, ahistorical identity. As a result, neither neo-realists, nor neo-liberals nor international relations-constructivists have felt the need to concern themselves with the 'inaccessible' discourses of postcolonialism. Instead they refer to these as marginal or alternative accounts, while in reality postcolonial scholars pose very challenging questions to international relations theorists who often remain prisoners of their own conceptions and subjectivity (McCormack, 2002: 109).

By problematizing global social relations, postcolonialists draw attention to the racist assumptions underlying much Western social scientific scholarship in its portrayal of the Third World. Current discourses on 'rogue states' can be mentioned in this regard. These states are being located exclusively in the Third World by orthodox Anglo-American international relations theorists who present them as a threat to an otherwise stable and orderly world. As Thomas and Wilkin (2004: 13) have noted,

> rarely is there an attempt to situate these states in the context of their colonial past. Equally, it is beyond reasonable debate to suggest that any of the G-8 states could themselves be rogue states in terms of their capacity for breaking of international law and using force.

Spivak's argument that the war on terrorism is part of an alibi that every imperialism has given itself must be viewed in a similar light. This, she argues, is a civilizing mission carried to the extreme:

> I am not speaking of intended rational choice. I am speaking of a cultural imaginary producing 'reason', somewhat like the repeated marching band arrangement of the 'Battle Hymn of the Republic' and the lavish use of African-Americans in the preamble to the declaration of this altogether catachrestic 'war' (Spivak 2004: 91).

'War' as *catachrestic* represents for Spivak the outcome of terror sliding into terrorism where the term 'war' names legitimate violence but also, paradoxically, peace. War and peace become interchangeable terms, even if the status of war as agent and peace as object remains. The line between agent and object starts wavering, however, when terror becomes an affect. Here Spivak discusses how the cultural imaginary affects our reasoning, as such an imaginary rests upon received binaries. For instance, when the soldier is not afraid to die s/he is brave, while when the terrorist is not afraid to die, s/he is a coward: 'The soldier kills, or is supposed to kill, designated persons. The terrorist kills, or may kill, just persons. In the space between 'terrorism' as a social movement and terror as affect, we can declare 'victory'. (Spivak 2004: 92)

Spivak is not defending suicide bombers but using this example as a warning against being stuck in received binaries – a common critique of orthodox international relations theory. Using postcolonial deconstruction to illuminate master words (as *catachrestic*) becomes a tool to challenge common interpretations of world politics, such as the war on terrorism. By focusing on the political and economic interests that are served by the economic text of globalization, and of capital, Spivak exposes how the world is represented from a particular geopolitical location of the first world to the exclusion of marginalized groups.

Postcolonial feminism and Marxist analysis: the subaltern woman

In this respect Spivak is particularly interested in the exclusion of women, especially the underprivileged woman in the global South. Spivak's feminism has been informed by French feminist thinkers, such as Luce Irigaray, Hélène Cixous and Julia Kristeva, and like them she believes that the category of feminine identity is a social construct, but one that is regulated through powerful institutions (Morton 2003). In *French Feminism in an International Frame* (Spivak 1998), Spivak explains how she became increasingly critical towards Western or French feminism and how she started to differentiate it from Third World women and international feminism. She argues that the constitution of the Western female subject differs from that of the Third World woman in terms of culture, history and social class. In her reading of the short story *Breast Giver* (1997) by Mahasweta Devi, for instance, she challenges the assumption prevalent in Western feminism that childbirth is unwaged domestic labour. She points to how the fictional character Jashoda is employed as a professional mother in an upper-class Brahmin household, which acts as a source of income for Jashoda's crippled husband. Of importance here is how the continued exploitation of Jashoda's reproductive maternal body calls into question that 'aspect of western Marxist feminism which, from the point of view of work, trivializes the theory of value and, from the point of view of mothering as work, ignores the mother as subject' (Spivak in Morton 2003: 76).

Spivak's criticism of privileged academic intellectuals who claim to speak for the disenfranchized woman in the global South has impacted on international relations feminist scholarship. The tendency by some Western feminists to make universalist claims and purport to speak for all women is viewed as a form of cultural imperialism with significant material effects. To avoid becoming proponents of such patronizing behaviour it is pertinent that we analyze the gendered effects of transnational culture and the unequal division of labour in the global economy. In this Spivak criticizes some of the French theorists, such as Julia Kristeva, for being more concerned with how other cultures challenge the authority of Western knowledge and subjectivity than about the other as a subject:

> In spite of their occasional interest in touching the other of the West, of metaphysics, of capitalism, their repeated question is obsessively self-centered: if we are not what official history and philosophy say we are, who then are we (not), how are we (not)? (Spivak 1998: 188–89)

Spivak insists that both French and Anglo-American feminism tends to privilege a focus on the self, thus not recognizing a simultaneous 'other' focus: 'not merely who am I? but who is the other woman? How am I naming her? How does she name me?' (Spivak 1998: 207). Only by paying attention to such questions can the colonized woman become a subject.

Here Spivak brings Marxism into the picture. Proceeding from Marx's ideas on the division of labour between worker and capitalist, Spivak reworks Marxist conceptions of imperialism and domination and situates women's economic exploitation in relation to the international division of labour between the Third and the First World (Sanders 2006). This division provides an ideological construction of gender that keeps the male dominant by placing women as objects of colonial historiography and as subjects of insurgency. If in the context of colonial production, the subaltern has no history and cannot speak then the subaltern female is even more deeply in shadow. Here we see a gradual emergence of the new subaltern in the New World Order, a theme that has increasingly come to preoccupy Spivak's later writings and interviews. Under post Fordism and international subcontracting, unorganized or permanently casual female labour is becoming a mainstay of world trade. As such it is supported by the poorest women in the South (Spivak 1999).

This engagement with the subaltern has also been the topic and interest of members from the Subaltern Studies Group, founded by Ranajit Guha in 1982. The term subaltern and the concept of hegemony – a concept critical to the subaltern project – were both used by Gramsci. Subaltern in Gramsci's work referred to any marginalized person or group and the works of subaltern historians were initially focused on workers and peasant movements. Subaltern historians have been particularly concerned with re-writing Indian history from below in order to contrast it with the class (and later gender) blindness of elite bourgeois national independence. One of the main contributions of the Subaltern Studies group has been to show that nationalism and colonialism were both involved in instituting a rule of capitalism in India.

In the 1990s subaltern studies became increasingly influenced by post-structuralist ideas of representation, not least due to the influence of Spivak, thus bringing it closer to ideas of postcolonialism. Spivak and Ranajit Guha co-edited *Selected Subaltern Studies* in 1988, where Spivak's essay *Deconstructing Historiography* became crucial for the direction of Subaltern Studies. The essay was particularly critical of the theoretical orientation of the subaltern project and its absence of gender questions. One of the more fundamental criticisms had to do with how the Subaltern Studies historiography operated with a gender-neutral idea of the subject that had remained uninfluenced by poststructural thinking on subjectivity (Chakrabarty 2000). It is also in this context that Spivak first used the term *strategic essentialism*, as she felt that the Subaltern Studies group was essentialist about consciousness. She has later dissociated herself from the term, mostly because she felt that it had 'been taken as an excuse for just essentialism which is an excuse for just identitarianism' (Spivak in Chakravorty *et al.* 2006: 64). Here Spivak argues that strategic essentialism can work as a context-specific strategy, but that it cannot provide long-term political solutions to end oppression and exploitation.

How to end oppression and exploitation is also at the core of her famous essay *Can the Subaltern Speak?* In this essay Spivak points to the importance of the category of woman for the representation of the modern self as a subject civilizing the uncivilized East. In doing this she combines the theoretical and political insights of deconstruction, feminism and Marxism. It was first given as a speech in the summer of 1983. The central concept of the speech had to do with resistance, that 'once a woman performs an act of resistance without an infrastructure that would make us recognize resistance, her resistance is in vain' (Spivak 1998: 62). Spivak argues that this is a social problem prevalent also in more affluent settings, since patriarchy always provides certain kinds of access to men who, through gender blindness, keep the patriarchal culture alive but unhealthy. In *Can the Subaltern Speak?* Spivak focuses on the subaltern South Asian woman and the history of sati (widow-burning) to show how the subaltern woman is constructed and controlled in paradoxical ways by both traditional patriarchal authority and by English colonialism. In the text she argues that the British colonial representation of sati excluded the voice and agency of Hindu women. Rather than supporting women's agency, British colonizers used the body of the widow as an ideological battleground for colonial power, thus justifying the systematic exploitation of territory as a civilizing mission. But the text also focuses on the Western intellectual's ability to speak on behalf of the subaltern.

The text juxtaposes the claims by French intellectuals, in this case Michel Foucault and Gilles Deleuze, to speak for the disenfranchized with the claims of a British colonialism that was set on rescuing native women from the practice of sati in nineteenth century India. In line with her criticism of Western feminism, Spivak wants to show how the benign Western intellectual, like the British colonizers and traditional Hindu patriarchal authority, may actually silence the subaltern by claiming to represent and speak for her experience. The sentence 'white men are saving brown women from brown men' (Spivak 1988) is hence as valid for radical intellectuals as it is for British colonialists who were thought to represent the widow who 'chose' to die on her husband's funeral pyre. In both cases the subaltern woman is denied a voice even when she is the object of contention. She cannot be heard by the privileged of either the First or Third Worlds. Here Spivak returns to Marx, and to a lesser extent to Derrida, in order to expose how Foucault and Deleuze both rely on a transparent model of representation in which oppressed subjects are in charge of their own destiny; 'the masses know perfectly well ... they know far better than [the intellectual] and they certainly say it very well' (Foucault in Spivak 1999: 255):

Neither Deleuze nor Foucault seem aware that the intellectual within globalizing capital, brandishing concrete experience, can help consolidate the international division of labour by making one model of 'concrete experience' *the* model. We are witnessing this in our discipline daily as we see the postcolonial *migrant* become the norm, thus occluding the native once again (Spivak 1999: 255–56).

Proceeding from Marx's distinction of *vertreten* (represent) and *darstellen* (re-represent), Spivak argues that Deleuze and Foucault conflate two meanings of representation: representation as 'speaking for' as in politics, and representation as 're-representation' as in art or philosophy. This conflation has serious implications for the oppressed groups that Deleuze and Foucault claim to speak for (workers, prison inmates, psychiatric patients in the West), as they become represented as coherent political subjects with clear political desires and interests (Morton 2003). The process of re-representation (the aesthetic) is thus subordinated to the voice of the political substitute who speaks on their behalf. This is problematic *per se*, but becomes even more so when this model is transferred to the 'Third World', Spivak argues. In particular it has worked to silence the subaltern woman.

Her main point in the essay is thus to show how the active involvement of Indian women in the independence movement has been excluded from all accounts of official history. By tracing the disappearance of the subaltern woman she is able to articulate their material and cultural histories (Morton 2003). Spivak's ethical goal is to make the subaltern heard: being heard would change her status as subaltern – she would cease to be subaltern. But this is not merely about unmediated speaking. Rather, speaking and hearing complete the speech act (Spivak in Landry and MacLean 1996: 292). Hence, it is about creating an infrastructure that makes hearing plausible, but it is also about the responsibilities of the elites. Spivak's ethical question concerns what elites must do to prevent the continued construction of the subaltern. In seeking to learn to speak to (rather than listen to or speak for) the historically muted subject of the subaltern woman, the postcolonial intellectual must systematically 'unlearn' her female privilege. This involves learning to critique postcolonial discourse:

> When I think of the masses, I think of a woman belonging to that 84% of women's work in India, which is unorganized peasant labour. Now if I could speak in such a way that such a person would actually listen to me and not dismiss me as yet another of those colonial missionaries, that would embody the project of unlearning about which I've spoken recently (Spivak 1990: 56).

Spivak's feminism thus deconstructs the division between the colonizer and the colonized to emphasize how gender is neglected in that conceptualization. Her revised version of *Can the Subaltern Speak?* (1999), also shows how this gendered subaltern is re-emerging in the New (Global) Empire, and how she (often in terms of migrant women) again becomes invisible in the shuttling between multinational capital and culturalism. Taking the subaltern seriously must hence be viewed as a fundamental challenge for a critical international relations theory concerned with issues of race, gender and postcolonial relations.

Conclusion

It is as a postcolonial feminist critic that Spivak has most persistently challenged contemporary Western thought by showing how dominant institutional and cultural discourses and practices have consistently excluded and marginalized the subaltern, especially the subaltern woman. Her focus on subaltern women's histories and her critique of the Subaltern project have radically challenged the way political identity has been conceptualized in much contemporary thought. Her emphasis on the subaltern's ability to speak has particularly problematized notions of power, resistance, knowledge, memory and history in international relations theory. By moving deconstruction as a methodology from ethics to global economic and political relations she has also been able to reconceptualize traditional Marxist concepts. And by questioning the role of elite representation she has continually used her own role as an academic to challenge the academic profession. In particular she has been able to rethink feminist thought from the perspective of non-Western women's lives and histories. These insights have been crucial for creating a global awareness of the local conditions that structure women's oppression in different parts of the world. Critical debates on globalization, nationalism, identity politics, deconstruction, postcolonialism and gender in international relations theory have thus, more or less explicitly, been informed by much of Gayatri Spivak's early ideas.

Further reading

Spivak, Gayatri Chakravorty (1976) *Of Grammatology*, Baltimore: Johns Hopkins. This book features an extended 'Translator's preface', that serves both as an introduction to Derrida and to Spivak herself.

Spivak, Gayatri Chakravorty (1987) (1998) *In Other Worlds: Essays in Cultural Politics*, New York: Methuen 1987 and Routledge 1998. This book consists of essays on Dante, Marx, Wordsworth and Mahasweta Devi. It is Spivak's most well known book and contains important ideas on feminism, Marxism, deconstruction, the subaltern and the literary text. A key text.

Spivak, Gayatri Chakravorty (1988) 'Can the Subaltern Speak?', in Cary Nelson and Lawrence Grossberg (eds) *Marxism and the Interpretation of Culture*, Urbana: University of Illinois Press. This is probably Spivak's most famous essay. Here she combines the theoretical and political insights of Marxism, feminism and deconstruction to show how the subaltern woman is constructed and controlled in paradoxical ways. A key text.

Spivak, Gayatri Chakravorty (1990) *The Post-Colonial Critic: Interviews, Strategies, Dialogues*, London: Routledge. This is a collection of twelve interviews with Spivak brought together by Sarah Harasym who wanted to make Spivak's texts more accessible to a broader readership.

Spivak, Gayatri Chakravorty (1993) *Outside in the Teaching Machine*, New York: Routledge. This is a volume of essays concerned with improving higher education in a global context. Many of the essays revise Spivak's earlier writings on French feminism and the relationship between Marxism and deconstruction. A key text.

Spivak, Gayatri Chakravorty (1999) *A Critique of Postcolonial Reason: Toward a History of the Vanishing Present*, Cambridge: Harvard University Press. This book provides a feminist perspective on deconstruction, a Marxist analysis of capital and the global division of labour, as well as a critical reading of transnational globalization and colonial/neo-colonial discourse. A key text.

Spivak, Gayatri Chakravorty (2003) *Death of a Discipline*, New York: Columbia University Press. In this book Spivak declares the death of comparative literature as we know it and sounds an urgent call for a 'new comparative literature'.

Spivak, Gayatri Chakravorty (2005) *Other Asias*, London: Wiley-Blackwells. This is a collection of essays concerned with the idea of critical regionalism and Asia as a named space, raising questions about what this space actually entails. A key text.

31 Paul Virilio

James Der Derian

Who is Paul Virilio? Born in Paris in 1932: a tall, blue-eyed Italian father; a short mother from the northern coastal region of Brittany, where he grew up. More than once he has remarked on his seaside, 'littoral' experience as a child, reflecting a future of feeling most at home on the edge: of his profession in urban architecture, of the intellectual circles of Paris, of *Le College International de Philosophie* which included along with Virilio well-known figures like Jacques Derrida and François Lyotard. From his first book to his most recent interviews, he has also emphasized that 'war was his university'. His first encounter with the speed of the war machine came at the outset of the Second World War, listening to the radio in his hometown of Nantes, hearing that the Germans had reached Orléans, and then, almost simultaneously, hearing the sound of tanks outside his window: *Blitzkrieg*. Aerial bombardments by the British and the Americans (Nantes became a major port for the German navy) also left a deep impression. Not least, he was drafted to fight in France's war with Algeria. Before taking up a career practicing and teaching urban architecture, he considered one in the art of stained-glass making. But all this rarely shows up in his official bios, which usually begin with his tenure as professor (1969), general director (1975), and president (1990) of the *Ecole Spéciale d'Architecture* in Paris; make some mention of his setting up with Claude Parent the *Architecture Principie* group and journal in 1963; and are likely to list one or more of his multiple identities: philosopher, city planner, military historian, cultural theorist, peace activist, film critic and exhibition curator.

From his 1976 exhibition (and subsequent book) on bunker archaeology to his millennial project on the integral accident, Paul Virilio's relentless inquiry into the interdependent relationships of speed and politics, technology and ecology, and war and cinema has left many a reader breathless, befuddled, and sometimes in the dust. A single Virilio sentence, full of concatenated clauses and asyndetic phrases, can collapse a century of political thought as well as dismantle a foundation of scientific absolutes. His take on the world – deterritorialized, accelerated, hyper-mediated – redefines *outlandish*. Nonetheless, when 'stuff happens', the unexpected events that defy conventional language, fit no familiar pattern, follow no recognizable conception of causality, one reaches for Virilio to illuminate the strange twists and turns of late modernity.

Virilio's work obviously resists easy summary. One is hard-pressed to find an organizing principle or a consistent theme; however, it does not take much digging to uncover an iterated warning against the contingency, vulnerability and danger of a highly technologized and densely networked life, with the attendant rise of a new military-industrial-media complex. Indeed, after 9/11, Iraq redux, and serial headlines of one more military misadventure and cascading global 'accident' after another, Virilio's works have taken on the uneasy quality of prophecy. Moving from Plato to NATO, finding high theory in daily headlines, matching intellectual alacrity with rhetorical superficiality, Virilio's hyperbolic pronouncements of the twentieth century – 'movement creates the event', 'information explodes like a bomb', 'the televised poll is now a mere pale simulation of the ancient rallying of citizens' – have become practically commonplace wisdom in the twenty-first (Virilio 1995a: 23–34).

Virilio's conceptual cosmology

Virilio's tracking of the 'virtual theatricalization of the real world', in which all politics, both high and low, form a kind of 'cathodic democracy', seems prescient (Virilio 1995a: 30–34). He seeks to reclaim an increasingly ubiquitous and invasive medium with a serious message: obsessive media vigilance of behaviour combined with political correctness have transformed democracy from an open participatory form of government into a software program for the entertainment and control of all spectators. Speed enhances this phenomenon through a global 'shrinking effect': 'With acceleration there is no more here and there, only the mental confusion of near and far, present and future, real and unreal – a mix of history, stories, and the hallucinatory utopia of communication technologies' (Virilio 1995a: 35). The coeval emergence of a mass media and an industrial army was *the* signifying moment of modernity, of a capability to war without war, producing 'a parallel information market' of propaganda, illusion, dissimulation. Technological accelerants like satellite link-ups, real-time feeds, and high-resolution video heighten the power of television to dissimulate; indeed, converging multiple media now has the power to 'substitute' realities. With the appearance of a global view comes the disappearance of the viewer-subject: in the immediacy of perception, our eyes become indistinguishable from the camera's optics, and critical consciousness goes missing.

Precariously perched at the event horizon of the integral accident, where information is sucked into a black hole of conspicuous consumption, we are unable to discern the most deleterious effects of global interconnectedness. As information flows outstrip powers of deliberation, as truth is relativized by velocity, and as crises spread like a contagion, the protective firewalls of civil society are being slowly eroded. In response, Virilio offers a remarkable array of concepts that act as *dispositifs*, investigatory instruments and prescriptive strategies that produce mental images to disturb commonsensical views of the world, to capture the highly mutable and often peculiar forms of a truth that is *out there*. Virilio is best known for his use of *speed* as a variable, *chrono-politics* as a concept, and *dromology* as a method to produce new understandings of an ever-accelerating global politics. However, in practically every book he coins new concepts which take on new heuristic as well as political value as they are reinterpreted and re-circulated by others.

Like Deleuze, Virilio construes concepts as mental images for disturbing conventional, commonsensical views of world events – but with the added visual warp of a life lived at the speed of cinema, video, light itself (see Patton 1996: 1–17). It is not, then, a criticism (nor, for that matter, an unqualified recommendation) to say that reading Virilio will probably leave one feeling mentally disturbed, usually compounded by a bad case of vertigo, since speed is not only the subject but the style of Virilio (helping to account for a dozen books in as many years). In a typical Virilio sentence, which often elongates into a full paragraph, the concepts can spew out like the detritus of a *Mir* supply-ship. Many get recycled in later books. Some, benefiting from refinement and new empirical settings, stand out like polished gems. But almost all of them provide radically different takes on the social implications of new technological forces, liberating their analysis from the customary academic dullness and expert narrowness.

Some of the concepts, often the most neologistic ones, burn brightly but briefly, flaming-out once they are lifted from Virilio's seductive rhetorical flow and subjected to the atmosphere of contemporary politics. Such might be an interpretation of one of the opening paragraphs from the last chapter of *L'Espace critique*:

> In effect, the geopolitics of nations that yesterday still presupposed the hierarchical privilege of the center over its peripheries, of the summit over the base, the 'radioconcentrism' of exchanges and horizontal communications, loses its value in the same way as does the extreme vertical densification to the benefit of an inapparent morphological configuration. The NODAL succeeds the CENTRAL in a preponderantly electronic environment, 'tele-localization' favoring the deployment of a generalized eccentricity, endless periphery, forerunner of the overtaking of the industrial urban form, but especially of the decline of the sedentary character of the metropolis to the advantage of an obligatory *interactive confinement*, a sort of inertia of human populations for which the name of *teleconcentrism* may be proposed, while waiting for that of 'homeland' to replace that of the large suburb. The secular opposition city/country is being lost while the geomorphological uniqueness of the state is dissipating (Virilio 1984: 156).

Now it is all too easy – and all too often a gambit of the hack critic – to take a complex sentence or paragraph out of context and to assert its incomprehensible character. In this paragraph Virilio is actually leading up to a very important and central claim of the book, that the *exo-colonialism* of the industrial, imperial period has become introverted – internally by the de-industrialization and pauperization of the urban centre, and externally by the rise of an intensive transnational capital and transpolitical megalopoles – into a post-industrial *endo-colonisation*: Mexico City, Shanghai, São Paulo, and the South African Homelands are presented as pointed examples. Perhaps there are simpler ways to introduce or to translate this idea. But it would probably take at least three more paragraphs and a lot of loose translation to do it.

In his first book, *The Insecurity of Territory* (*Bunker Archeologie* was published a year earlier in 1975, but it was primarily a secondary text to accompany the photography exhibition; and Virilio himself referred to *Insecurity of Territory* as his first book in an interview with the author in June 1995), Virilio introduces the concepts of *deterritorialization, nomadism,* and the *suicidal state,* which Deleuze and Guatarri pick up and brilliantly elaborate in their most significant work, *A Thousand Plateaus* (Deleuze and Guattari 1988: 345, 395–96, 520–21 n. 24, 536 n. 8, 551 n. 56). Virilio draws on Walter Benjamin's fear of an aestheticized politics, but takes it further, showing how a politics, no longer willing, no longer able to maintain representational distinctions between the real, the visual, and the virtual, *disappears into the aesthetic* (*The Aesthetics of Disappearance,* 1980). This disappearance is facilitated by the melding of military, cinematic, and techno-scientific '*logistics of perception*' (*War and Cinema,* 1984). All economies of sight and might, remnants of presence like quattrocento linear fields of perception, national-territorial politics, Cartesian subjectivity, Newtonian physics, become coordinated, and eventually subordinated by a relativist, quantum, *transpolitical* war machine (*Negative Horizon,* 1984). In political terms, this means that the geopolitics of *extensivity* and *exo-colonization* is displaced by the *chronopolitics* of *intensivity* and *endo-colonization* (*Critical Space,* 1984). In turn, episodic war gives way, through the infinite requirements and preparations of deterrence and simulations, to a permanent *pure war* (*Pure War,* 1983).

Displaying no anxiety of influence, Virilio takes Foucault's panopticon model to an extra-terrestrial level of discipline and control, offering a micro-analysis of how new technologies of oversight and organizations of control, innovated by strategic alliances of the military, industrial, and scientific communities, have made the cross-over into civilian and political sectors to create a global *administration of fear* (*Popular Defense and Ecological Struggles,* 1978). It is not so much the acuity and reach of Foucault's analysis that is extended by Virilio, as it is the *dimensionality,* showing how the control of space has been force-multiplied if not displaced by the control of pace (*Speed and Politics,* 1977). As the individual historically moves from *geocentric* (Copernican) to *egocentric* (Husserlian) to *exocentric* (Einsteinian) perspectival fields, and the species from the sedentariness of the agricultural *biosphere* to the mobility of the industrial *technosphere* to the velocity of the informational *dromosphere,* the once-progressivist identity politics of location loses out to the inertial motility of a realtime *telepresence* (*Polar Inertia,* 1990).

And long before Derrida spotted the ghost of globalization haunting post-communist Europe, Virilio was writing that Europe's future would not be decided in the various nations' foreign ministries or on the battlefield, but in the electromagnetic spectrum of informational, *cybernetic wars* of persuasion and dissuasion – that is, deterrence writ temporal and global (*Bunker Archeology,* 1975). Similarly, he presaged an ever-expanding hierarchy of contemporary virtual realities (*The Vision Machine,* 1988), where the pseudo-proximity of live news and *faux* military interventions were displacing the consumptive spectacles of Debord and the seductive simulations of Baudrillard with constant irruptive spasms of '*media-staged strategic events*' [*stratégico-médiatique*]. This was a diagnosis which Virilio applied early on to a critique of the Gulf War (*Desert Screen,* 1991), predicting a *real-time war* of short duration with high if hidden [*furtive*] intensity and costs, in contrast to most liberal intellectuals who were stunned into silence or even support by the spectacle of excess as well as seeming success of the war machine. While military strategists and think-tank courtiers were searching for a name for a new kind of warfare without war – was it netwar, cyberwar, infowar? – Virilio had already given notice of the *data coup d'etat* that had shifted the aim of battle from capturing to captivating the enemy through the *media complex* (*The Art of the Motor,* 1993). And while environmentalists try to arouse a world consciousness by warning of a possible ecological desertification of the planet, Virilio is one dimension beyond, prophesying the chronological desertification of world time, *global time,* by the negative synergy of the *integral accident* (*Open Sky,* 1995).

In short, virtuality destroys reality. On its own, perhaps not a great loss; but Virilio has his eye where others do not, on the collateral damage done to the *ethos* of reality, the highly vulnerable public space where individuals responsively interact. For Virilio, the interconnectivity of virtual systems is not ushering in a new day for democracy but a new order of *telepresence*; high-paced interconnectivity is becoming, technically and literally, a sub-stitute for the slower-paced intersubjectivity of traditional political systems. He sees the self as a kind of virtually-targeted ground-zero; once voided, concentric-circles of political fall-out spread, leaving in the vitrified rubble all responsibility for the other that forms the prior condition for truly inter-subjective, ethical, *human* relationships. This forms the *gravitas* of Virilio's body of work. In practically all of his writings it registers more as a persis-tent ethical, even spiritual pull than as a moral theory or an explicit religious sentiment (although in interviews and his teleconference at the Ars Electro-nica Symposium on Infowar in Linz, Austria (8 September 1998) Virilio has acknowledged the profound significance of Catholicism in his life). I believe it is also this deep ethical force, more so than his corrosive intellectual cri-tique, which keeps his often elliptical rhetoric and sometimes errant concepts in something resembling a coherent orbit.

It varies from reader to reader whether Virilio's concepts offer a supernova flash of illumination or a blackhole obscuring complex subjects. Not to belabour Virilio's ken for metaphors drawn from astrophysics (he once remarked that a lack of formal training in the sciences was one of Baudrillard's shortcomings), but there are in Virilio some conceptual wormholes which can take the reader to very strange and not always rewarding places. They often appear just as a rhetorical dead-end looms, and imaginative or empirical exhaustion is setting in, as Virilio tries to bolster an extravagant claim or weak concept by piling on superficial evidence, like the moment in 'The Suicidal State', where he goes from a very long, deeply political account of the persecution of *nomadism* under the German Third Reich, marked by the rounding up and killing of gypsies and bohemians, to the trivial, modern-day right of a Frenchman to park his camper anywhere he damn well pleases (Virilio 1993: 41).

At other times and different places, Virilio's wormholes can open doors of perception (think of Blake rather than Huxley) that make the trip well worth the effort. For instance, take *Polar Inertia*, one of his most difficult and philosophically dense works. Virilio returns to Germany in the 1930s, to posit the rupture between philosophy and physics as one of the reasons for technology going out of control, leading to Auschwitz and Hiroshima, and then leaps forward to identify a similar gap opening up between the power of new remote-control technologies and our ability to understand a rapidly changing environment. From this he induces an ethical imperative to rejoin current metaphysical and astrophysical thinking about everything from the beginnings of time to the end of the world as we conventionally know it. Fortunately, he has covered this ground – that is, where the ground in effect gives way to speed – in simpler ways in other works:

> In our situations of televisual experience, we are living in nothing less than the sphere of Einstein's relativity, which wasn't at all the case at the time that he wrote it since that was a world of trolley cars, and at most, the rocket. But today we live in a space of relativity and non-separability. Our image of time is an image of instantaneity and ubiquity. And there's a stunning general lack of understanding of speed, a lack of awareness of the essence of speed ... And this passage from an extensive to an intensive time will have considerable impact on all the various aspects of the conditions of our society: it leads to a radical reorganization both of our social mores and of our image of the world. This is the source of the feeling that we're faced with an epoch in many ways comparable to the Renaissance: it's an epoch in which the real world and our image of the world no longer coincide (Virilio 1991d: 139–40).

Applied Virilio

Virilio wrote that it often takes a disaster, usually of the built-in accidental sort, to reveal just how illusory our beliefs in the security systems of modernity are: the safety net often turns out to be a trap. The metaphysics of securitization go something like this: To keep us safe, we put our faith in national borders and guards, bureaucracies and experts, technologies and armies. These and other instruments of national security are empowered and legitimated by the assumption that it falls upon the sovereign state to protect us from the turbulent state of nature and anarchy that permanently lies in wait offshore and over the horizon for the unprepared and inadequately defended. But this parochial fear, posing as a realistic worldview, has taken some very hard knocks as globalization reveals its dark side. Prior to 9/11, national borders were thought necessary and sufficient to keep our enemies at bay; upon entry to Baghdad, a virtuous triumphalism and a revolution in military affairs were touted as the best means to bring peace and democracy to the Middle East; and before Hurricane Katrina, emergency preparedness and an intricate system of levees were supposed to keep New Orleans safe and dry.

The intractability of disaster, especially its unexpected, unplanned, unprecedented nature, erodes not only the very distinction of the local, national, and global, but, assisted and amplified by an unblinking global media, reveals the contingent, and highly interconnected character of life in general. Yet when it comes to dealing with natural and unnatural disasters, we continue to expect (and, in the absence of a credible alternative, understandably so) if not certainty and total safety, at least a high level of probability and competence from our national and homeland security experts

However, between the mixed metaphors and behind the metaphysical concepts of security, there lurks an uneasy recognition that no national government is up to the task of managing incidents that so rapidly cascade into global events. Indeed, they suggest that national plans and preparations for the 'big one' – a force-five hurricane, terrorist attack, pandemic disease – have become part of the problem, not the solution. Use of hyberbolic terms like 'ultra-catastrophe' and 'fall-out' to describe events like 9/11 and Katrina is telling: such events exceed not only local and national capabilities, but the capacity of conventional language itself.

An easy deflection would be to lay the blame on the respective administrations of Blair and Bush who, viewing through an inverted Wilsonian prism the world as they would wish it to be, were forced by natural and unnatural disasters to face the world as it really is – and acknowledge that not even the most sophisticated public affairs machine of dissimulations, distortions, and lies, could close this gap. Virilio reveals how all security discourse remains stuck in what Nietzsche described as the 'prisonhouse of language', in which realism serves as the supermax penitentiary for any alternative scheme seeking to escape from the event horizon created by the news hole as black hole.

Based on linear notions of causality, a correspondence theory of truth, and the materiality of power, how can realism possibly account – let alone prepare or provide remedies – for complex catastrophes, like the toppling of the World Trade Center and attack on the Pentagon by a handful of *jihadists* armed with box-cutters and a few months of flight-training? A force-five hurricane that might well have begun with the flapping of a butterfly's wings? A northeast electrical blackout that started with a falling tree limb in Ohio? A possible pandemic triggered by the mutation of an avian virus? For events of such complex, non-linear origins and with such tightly-coupled, quantum effects – how, for instance, are we to measure the immaterial power of the CNN-effect on the first Gulf War, the Al Jazeera-effect on the Iraq War, or the Nokia-effect on the London terrorist bombings? – traditional security discourse is simply – ever too simply – not up to the task.

Virilio believes the techno-cure is worse than the disease. What if worse-case scenarios, simulation training, and disaster exercises – as well as border guards, concrete barriers and earthen levees – not only prove inadequate but might well act as force-multipliers – what organizational theorists identify as 'negative synergy' and 'cascading effects' – that produce the automated bungling that transform isolated events and singular attacks into global disasters? Just as 'normal accidents' are built into new technologies – from the *Titanic* sinking to the Chernobyl meltdown to the *Challenger* – Virilio asks whether 'ultra-catastrophes' are no longer the exception but now part and parcel of densely networked systems that defy national management; in other words, 'planned disasters'.

Moreover, according to Virilio, networked information technology also affects how we interpret events, making it ever more difficult to maintain let alone discern the very distinction of intended from accidental events. According to the legal philosopher of Nazi Germany, Carl Schmitt, when the state is unable to deliver on its traditional promissory notes of safety, security and well-being through legal, democratic means, it will necessarily exercise the sovereign 'exception': declaring a state of emergency, defining friend from foe and, if necessary, eradicating the threat to the state. But what if the state, facing the global event, cannot discern the accidental from the intentional? An external attack from an internal auto-immune response? The natural as opposed to the 'planned disaster'? The enemy within from the enemy without?

The sovereign state can, as the US has increasingly done since 9/11, continue to treat catastrophic threats as issues of national rather than global security, and go it alone. However, once declared, bureaucratically installed, and repetitively gamed, national states of emergency grow recalcitrant and prone to even worse disasters. As Paul Virilio, master theorist of the war machine and the integral accident once told me: 'The full-scale accident is now the prolongation of total war by other means.'

Conclusion

For every one of Virilio's oblique concepts or extravagant theoretical claims, there are others which slice right through the sludge that is served up as political analysis or expert knowledge. By this quality alone, there is no question that he belongs in the company of Benjamin and Adorno, Debord and Baudrillard, Foucault and Deleuze, Barthes and Derrida, for taking our understanding of the discursive relationship of technology, society, and war to a higher plane of political as well as critical consciousness. He might not always match some of these thinkers in their philosophical consistency, historical knowledge, or rhetorical rigour. But as the millennium turned, he stood out from the critical crowd, as a conceptual innovator and intellectual provocateur, the one who goes to the edge and sees beyond the traditional maps of modernity. Virilio's reputation should not stand or fall by the oxyopia of his own gaze. I do believe, however, his work can be judged by the extent to which his critical concepts and insights continue to infuse and inform the debate about late modernity.

But what is one to make of his dire scan of the human condition? There is certainly more than a hint of millenarian doom to Virilio's work; but as he has made clear in more than one interview, this is not to encourage quietism but to alert the reader that the time to act is now. 'I don't believe', says Virilio, 'in the end of *the* world – I believe in the end of *a* world' (interview with Nicholas Zurbrugg, 13 January 1995). More specifically, a technologically-induced end – of the body as well as the bodypolitic – is not inevitable but increasingly possible:

> We haven't reached that point yet: what I have described is the end, or a vision of the end. What will prevail is this will to reduce the world to the point where one could possess it. All military technologies reduce the world to nothing. And since military technologies are advanced technologies, what they actually sketch today is the future of the civil realm. But this, too, is an accident (Virilio 1994c).

Other critical thinkers have provided new concepts for investigating the political and social implications of new technologies of reproduction. Yet many of them already seem out of date, stuck in place and, to use a word Virilio favours, *folklorique*, when compared to the restless yet, in all its time*full*ness, strangely rustless conceit of Virilio, that the proliferation of high-speed, realtime, cinematic, global, computer networked – in a word – *virtual* systems of how we see, has forever changed how we know, the other. In an essay which originally appeared in *Le Monde Diplomatique*, Virilio maps the social consequences:

> What lies ahead is a disturbance in the perception of what reality is; it is a shock, a mental concussion. And this outcome ought to interest us. Why? Because never has any progress in a technique been achieved without addressing its specific negative aspects. The specific negative aspect of these information superhighways is precisely this loss of orientation regarding alterity (the other), this disturbance in the relationship with the other and with the world. It is obvious that this loss of

orientation, this non-situation, is going to usher in a deep crisis which will affect society and hence, democracy (Virilio 1995b).

And in an interview he warns, when distance and distinctions between mental and visual images collapse, multiple, intensive, coterminous substitutions of reality begin to *war with another*:

> From now on everything passes through the image. The image has priority over the thing, the object, and sometimes even the physically-present being. Just as real time, instantaneousness, had priority over space. Therefore the image is invasive and ubiquitous. Its role is not to be in the domain of art, the military domain or the technical domain, it is to be everywhere, to be reality ... I believe that there is a war of images ... And I can tell you my feelings in another way: winning today, whether it's a market or a fight, is merely not losing sight of yourself (Virilio 1988: 4–7).

At the end of a long lunch together at *La Coupole* in Paris, Virilio put this all much more succinctly, in the aphoristic style he favours for interviews: 'Interactivity is to real space what radioactivity is to the atmosphere'. Before I could get my head around the thought – I was stuck trying to imagine the virtual equivalent of thyroid cancer – he tempered one hyperbolic statement by another, declaiming: 'I am in love with technology!' Since I knew from the difficulty in arranging the interview that this was a man without e-mail, fax, or even an answering machine, I asked him to explain the apparent contradiction. It's just that he wasn't about to make it easy for the intellectual love of his life. Another aphorism followed: like Jacob, he wrestled with the angel of technology not to prove his disbelief, but to prove his *freedom* to believe. Sound cosmological advice, I believe, for all in search of a meaningful life in a world full of global insecurity and radical contingency.

Further reading

Life is too short to read *all* of Virilio. My *Virilio Reader* (Blackwell, 1998) provides a core sample drawn from 'classic' works, like *Bunker Archaelogy, Speed and Politics, Negative Horizon, War and Cinema, Polar Inertia, The Vision Machine, The Art of the Motor* and *Desert Screen*. A great pleasure is to experience Virilio at his spoken best: he is a master of the interview genre – corrosive, analytical and prophetic, all at once and *tres vitement* – beginning with his unparalleled exchange with Sylvere Lotringer, *Pure War* (Semiotext(e), 1983) through *Virilio Live* (Sage, 2001). His fascination with technologically-induced disasters hits an apogee in *The Original Accident* (Polity, 2007); not for the faint of heart. His influence on others is as wide as it is deep, on international relations thinkers like David Campbell, Ron Deibert, Ian Douglas, Timothy Luke, R.B.J. Walker, Cynthia Weber, among others; but also among philosophers (Deleuze and Guattari); critical theorists (Hardt and Negri); political theorists (William E. Connolly and Michael Shapiro); cultural theorists (like John Armitage, Doug Kellner, and Mark Poster); new media theorists (like Alex Galloway, Eugene Thacker, and Mackenzie Wark); and, not so strangely, military strategists in the U.S., French, and Israeli militaries, to name a few.

32 Slavoj Žižek

Diane Rubenstein

Slavoj Žižek is a Lacanian Marxist philosopher from Slovenia who put all of these improbable terms together on the theoretical map with his ground-breaking *The Sublime Object of Ideology* (1989). This book announced three ambitious aims: to introduce Lacanian fundamental concepts while presenting Lacan as an Enlightenment (and not as a post-structuralist) figure; to return to and reposition Hegel as a theorist of difference; and last, to contribute to a theory of ideology by reading canonical Marxist concepts (such as commodity fetishism) in the context of Lacanian ones (such as *surplus enjoyment*) that have an oblique or little relation to them. It was Žižek's provocative wager that these three goals were interrelated: 'the only way to "save Hegel" is through Lacan and this Lacanian reading of Hegel … opens up a new approach to ideology, allowing us to grasp contemporary ideological phenomena' (Žižek 1989: 7). Žižek's ascendancy on the theoretical scene in the late 1980s and early 1990s could not have been a more untimely reminder (against those such as Francis Fukuyama) that the post-Cold War era was not a post ideological one. Indeed, the impact of his work has left little of the political or cultural field unanalyzed – whether it is a question of the films of Hitchcock or Spielberg, resurgent ethnic nationalism, human rights or multicultural tolerance.

Žižek's influence has been especially pronounced in contrast to other Lacanian theorists due to his engagement with both popular culture and contemporary politics. This has made psychoanalytic concepts more accessible to a broader community of readers. Yet there are many challenges in presenting his work. Unlike many of the other authors in this volume such as Levinas, Žižek does not present his arguments in a systematic or progressive way (as would a traditional philosopher or formal theorist) but as a reiterative process. A thesis is re-presented in different discursive contexts that highlight other aspects of it. As Ernesto Laclau states, texts reach 'points of interruption rather than conclusion, thus inviting the reader to continue for him or herself the discursive proliferation in which the author has been engaged' (Žižek 1989: xii). The open-endedness of his writing does not lead to the easy refinement of concepts. Nor is conceptual cogency facilitated by the sheer enormity of how much Žižek publishes. Rex Butler comments on the outpouring of material: in 2000, three books; in 2001, four; in 2002, four books. 'One of the paradoxes of this is that it seems that as his work becomes more and more explicitly anti-capitalist, it is also becoming more commodified' (Butler 2005: 12). Moreover his archive is vast and arduous, drawing on contemporary and classical thinkers such as Giorgio Agamben, Louis Althusser, Alain Badiou, Judith Butler, Gilles Deleuze, Jacques Derrida, René Descartes, Martin Heidegger, Immanuel Kant, Søren Kierkegaard, Blaise Pascal, Saint Paul, Jacques Rancière, and F.W.J. Schelling. The final difficulty resides in the blurring of the boundaries between Žižek as a critic of popular culture and as a pop-cultural phenomenon (Dean 2006: xv). For Žižek is a celebrity icon, subject of a 2005 documentary, home to a myspace page (see the URL http://profile.myspace.com/index.cfm?fuseaction = user. viewprofile&friendid = 16287877), so omnipresent as to warrant a regular column in the *Chronicle of Higher Education* called 'Žižek Watch' by Scott McLee.

Žižek is an out-sized and excessive *persona* and, not surprisingly, his critical contributions, (such as the *Real, object a, master signifier*) have all circled around notions of excess as constitutive of subjectivity and the symbolic order. While Žižek's importance for the social sciences has been in the theory of ideology, his use of Lacanian psychoanalysis offers significant reframings of debates central to international relations concerning sovereignty, racism and ethnic violence, human rights and humanitarian intervention.

Short biography

Slavoj Žižek was born in 1949 in Ljubljana (the capital of the former Yugoslav republic of Slovenia) as the only child of professional parents. In an interview with Christopher Hanlon, Žižek mused about why it was Ljubljana (and not Zagreb or Belgrade) that should have become the robust centre of Lacanianism. Slovenia was a microcosm of the entire philosophical scene from analytic philosophy to Heideggerianism to the Critical Theory of the Frankfurt School. There was neither a psychoanalytic orthodoxy nor a state philosophy of dialectical materialism (Hanlon 2001: 3).

Žižek's early intellectual formation was also shaped by his time spent as an adolescent at the state-sponsored *Cinematheque* that showed Hollywood and European art films. Žižek saw one or two films a day, five days a week. Žižek's love for Western art forms paralleled his aversion for right wing nationalist Slovenian poetry and cinema. As a student at the University, he submitted a four-hundred-page thesis 'The Theoretical and Practical Relevance of French Structuralism', a survey of the work of Lacan, Derrida, and Kristeva, which was not passed until he added a supplement with a more Marxist critique. Yet, even this revised thesis did not obtain Žižek a normal teaching job. In 1977, he worked for the Central Committee of the League of Slovene Communists, until he received his present job in 1979 at the Institute for Sociology. As this was not a humanities field, Žižek's work was therefore oriented towards a conceptual understanding of nationalism in the context of Slovenian national identity. In 1981, he spent a year in Paris attending the seminar of Jacques Alain Miller, a student of Althusser and Lacan's heir and disciple as well as son-in-law. After Miller helped him obtain a teaching fellowship in Paris, he wrote a second thesis (*Le plus sublime des hystériques-Hegel passe*) which contained in abbreviated form – and in reverse order – his first two books: *The Sublime Object of Ideology* and *For They Know Not What They Do: Enjoyment as a Political Factor*. He also went into analysis with Miller.

In the eighties, Žižek was involved in opposition movements (Committee for the Protection of Human Rights) and played an important role in the creation of the Liberal Democratic Party, which grew out of the student movement. This was a moderate centre left party in opposition to both the right wing nationalists and the communists and affiliated with feminist and ecological issues (Butler 2005; Mead 2003; Boynton 1998). In 1990, Žižek came in fifth for the four-member collective Slovenian presidency. Astra Taylor's (2005) documentary contains some entertaining footage of the presidential debate. There are two features common to both Žižek's political engagement as well as his thought. The first is the matter of continual revision and self-contradiction. Cultural Minister Josef Skok indicated that this was the reason that Žižek did not play a larger political role. The second concerns the grounds for his ambivalence about Slovenian independence. He was quite critical of it theoretically, but embraced it for its political expediency. This paradoxical formulation – something that is good in practice but not in theory – is a position he maintains relative to populism (that of Hugo Chavez, for example) in his most recent *In Defense of Lost Causes* (Žižek 2008: 264–65)

Žižek has taught as a visiting professor and lectured widely throughout the world. He is presently the International Director of the Birkbeck Institute of the Humanities at the University of London and senior researcher at the Institute of Slovenia, the University of Ljubljana.

Politicizing psychoanalysis

Žižek's inventive fusion of Marxism and Lacanian psychoanalysis did have two important precedents: Louis Althusser's essay 'Ideology and Ideological State Apparatuses' (1971) and Ernesto Laclau and Chantal Mouffe's *Hegemony and Socialist Strategy* (1985). Žižek built upon the Althusserian concept of 'interpellation' as well as Laclau and Mouffe's 'antagonism' to rethink the relations between subjectivity, identification and collective life. Žižek's revision of Althusser utilizes the Lacanian ideas concerning *fantasy* (sometimes spelled *phantasy* to distinguish Lacanian usage) and different types of identification (symbolic versus imaginary) while the critique of Laclau and Mouffe develops Lacan's concepts of the Real and *object a*.

The Sublime Object's account of ideological fantasy begins with a counterintuitive reading of Marx's famous sentence on commodity fetishism: 'They do not know it but they are doing it'. Rather than seeing a problem of insufficient knowledge that needs to be remedied, Žižek reads this sentence otherwise: it is not our knowing that is uninformed, it is rather our doing that is uninformed by our knowing. We are fetishists, Žižek states, not cognitively, but in practice. He gives the standard Marxist example of how, when we use money we 'forget' that it is not a natural embodiment of wealth, but a piece of paper backed by social conventions. Thus what is overlooked is not reality but the *illusion* that structures this very reality. Greater knowledge will not necessarily ameliorate this situation in which people 'know' but 'act' as if they did not know. (The psychoanalytic term referring to this pattern, characteristic of fetishism, is called *disavowal*.) Žižek designates as ideological fantasy this double illusion 'overlooking the illusion which is structuring our real, effective relation to reality' (Žižek 1989: 32–3).

Fantasy is not unconscious, an illusion, subjective delusion, error, or counterfactual belief opposed to real material interests (as in 'false consciousness' arguments). It is, rather, 'objective' in that it subtends reality. When Žižek argues for the objective status of ideology (or belief) he is taking Lacan's side against that of Freud. For Freud, we awaken from a dream to reality. For both Žižek and Lacan, we construct a dream to continue sleeping, to avoid trauma or to elude the Real of our desire. Indeed, Žižek will repeatedly state the pedagogical usefulness of fantasy: 'Fantasy teaches us how to desire' (Žižek 1989: 118, 1997: 7, 2006a: 40, 2006b: 47). Fantasy works like a Kantian transcendental schema (or a more prosaic object like an aircraft safety instruction card); it mediates between a symbolic structure and the positivity of an object we encounter in reality. The aircraft safety card instructs us what to do in an emergency at the same time as, for Žižek, it 'gentrifies' catastrophe (Žižek 1997: 3).

Fantasy allows certain objects to stand in for an object of desire in a formal symbolic structure. Žižek – who is diabetic – will give the example of a piece of strawberry cake he wants to eat. But the question of fantasy as illustrative of desire is not a simple empirical question. It is not that Žižek wants to eat the piece of cake that he cannot get in reality (due to either dessert scarcity or functional reasons such as diet maintenance). Rather there is a more fundamental question of identification at stake here: 'How do I know that I want strawberry cake?' (Žižek 2006b: 47, 1997: 7). For if fantasy is linked to desire, it is not the subject's personal proclivities that are at issue as much as an intensely social one, concerning others, especially socially important Others. It is not a question of what I want but what Žižek will designate as '*Che Vuoi*': 'What do the others want from me?' Or, 'what am I for the Other?' If we return to Žižek's strawberry cake example, it is not an arbitrary selection, but one related by Freud's daughter Anna. Her recollected fantasy of cake eating was one of pleasing her parents by taking on the role of a child enjoying a cake given by an indulgent parent. The desire that fantasy stages is the Other's desire, which makes it a deeply inter-subjective process, an attempt to answer the question 'What does society – the big Other – want from me?'

Žižek situates the process of *identification* in relation to this question of the Other's desire. Identifications are of two types: *imaginary* or *symbolic*. The imaginary identification corresponds to 'a first, instinctive conception ... in which we identify with the image of the Other' (Butler 2005: 53). For Žižek, it is 'identification with the image in which we appear to be likeable to ourselves, with the image repeating "what we would like to be"' and is allied with Freud's ideal ego (*Idealich*). Symbolic identifications are identifications 'with the very place *from where* we are being observed, *from where* we look at ourselves so that we appear to ourselves likeable, worthy of love' (Žižek 1989: 105). Another way that Žižek frames this is by saying that imaginary identifications are about resemblance where symbolic ones are about what is 'inimitable, the point that eludes resemblance' (Žižek 1989: 109). One could illustrate this opposition by the example of the injunction to love thy neighbour. An appeal based on imaginary identification would be based on the extent to which the neighbour is 'like' or 'resembles' (or is otherwise intelligible) to me. This neighbour might eat food or have other cultural habits that I could understand. One based on symbolic identification would figure the neighbour as an abstract bearer of rights, a universal citizen. Žižek's critique of multiculturalism recognizes unacknowledged identifications at play in paradigms of liberal tolerance (Žižek 2001: 240, 2002: 64–7, 2003: 152–57).

Two further points should be noted. Identifications are never 'spontaneous', even and especially imaginary ones that appear 'instinctive' or intuitive. Žižek gives the example of Kurt Waldheims's election in the 1986 Austrian presidential campaign. Rather than a feature to be downplayed, it was Waldheim's 'traumatic' past that was the trait of identification. Right wing ideologies have proved adept at proffering weakness, guilt or other failed characteristics as points of identification. Jacqueline Rose has made an analogous argument to that of Žižek concerning Margaret Thatcher's appeal, which was not despite, but because of features normally seen as aversive:

> What if Thatcher was re-elected not despite the repugnance that many feel for her image, but also in some sense because of it? What if that force of identity for which she is castigated somewhere also operates as a type of pull? (Rose 1993: 46)

Žižek's second point is that imaginary identifications (the question of a model image or of playing a role) are embedded within a prior structuring gaze: '*for whom* is the subject enacting this role. Which *gaze* is considered when the subject identifies with a certain image?' (Žižek 1989: 106). In other words, it is the symbolic identification (or gaze) that will determine what image comes to be seen as idealized.

For Žižek, humanitarian interventions such as that in Bosnia were predicated on these questions of gaze and identification:

> The traumatic element is thus the gaze of the helpless other – child, animal – who does not know why something so horrifying and senseless is happening to him: not the gaze of a hero willingly sacrificing himself for some Cause, but the gaze of a perplexed victim. And in Sarajevo we are dealing with the same bewildered gaze ... This gaze makes us all guilty (Žižek, 1994: 211).

But Žižek goes on to say that compassion for the victim is a way to avoid the ethical pressures of that insistent gaze:

> The examples of 'compassion with the suffering in Bosnia' that abound in our media illustrate perfectly Lacan's thesis on the 'reflexive' nature of desire: desire is always desire for a desire. That is to say, what these examples display above all is that compassion is the way to *maintain the proper distance* towards a neighbor in trouble ... In other words, our compassion, insofar as it is 'sincere', presupposes that *in it, we perceive ourselves in the form we find likeable*: the victim is presented so that we see ourselves in the position from which we stare at her ... (Žižek 1994: 211).

But one must also understand that place ('the proper distance') from which we have staged this 'imaginary' pose of compassion and humanitarian assistance. The (symbolic) fantasy space of 'the Balkans' is that of the West's Other 'a place of savage ethnic conflicts where nothing is forgotten and nothing learned, where old traumas are replayed again and again ... ' Far from being the Other of Europe, ex-Yugoslavia was, rather, Europe itself in its Otherness, the screen on to which Europe projected its own repressed reverse (Žižek 1994: 212). This reversal of look and gaze, image and screen (that Žižek adapts from Lacan's *Seminar XI*) reorients debates concerning ethnic nationalism and the limits/obligations of humanitarian intervention. 'The principle obstacle to peace ... is not "archaic ethnic passions" but the very innocent gaze of Europe fascinated by the spectacle of these passions' (Žižek 1994: 212).

Žižek's political resolutions involve shifts in identification, something he calls 'traversing the fantasy' which is based upon the final stage of a Lacanian analysis. Here the subject more fully identifies with (or enacts) his symbolic mandate. This dissolves the original imaginary identification (a model is no longer used to imitate) and the contents of this original imaginary identification/ideal ego are radically changed (retroactively) as a result of the act of assuming the symbolic identification. It is important to remember (as with the prior case of ideological fantasy) that traversing the fantasy does not mean that one is abandoning it or adopting a more pragmatic viewpoint. Rather, it means that one is even more profoundly claimed by it, in Richard

Boothby's words, 'in the sense of having been brought into an even more intimate relation with that real core of the phantasy that transcends imaging' (Žižek 2002: 18). Žižek gives the example of a rock group (*The Top List of the Surrealists*) that played in Sarajevo during the Bosnian war whose songs mobilized all the racist clichés about 'stupid Bosnians'. Žižek contends that it was precisely this 'direct confrontation with obscene racist fantasies' through an enactment or assumed (i.e. playful) identification that was far more productive in mobilizing solidarity during this difficult time of war and deprivation than a factual rebuttal of racism (or some other well-intended attempt at alternative dispute mediation) based on the premise that these images 'do not represent people as they "really are"' (Žižek 2002: 18–19). Needless to say, the type of practice associated with 'traversing the fantasy' involves a wholly different politics from that we habitually associate with hate speech protocols.

Žižek's revision of Althusserian interpellation could not be more potentially useful for studying international relations. In Althusser's famous account of ideological interpellation or hailing, an individual becomes a subject when he answers a (policeman's) call. The political subject is assimilated to the order of law and language through this work of hailing (interpellation) which is based on a prior moment of misrecognition (what Lacan designated as the 'mirror stage', where a chronologically false image of corporeal integrity and mastery is offered in the mirror or mirroring gaze of the supportive caregiver; this is the Subject that the subject comes to identify with). Althusser's theory is derived from an earlier period of Lacan's teaching, centred on the Symbolic Order (relations of language and kinship). Žižek's account of identification is located in Lacan's later period of the Real and the *object a*. The shift in Lacan's thinking can be seen in relation to trauma. In the fifties, 'the traumatic event is defined as an imaginary entity which had not yet been fully symbolized …; but in the seventies trauma is *real*–it is a hard core resisting symbolization' (Žižek 1989: 162). Trauma (as with fantasy) is not necessarily factual nor an empirical occurrence. What is important is that it produces displacements or repetitions (i.e. structural effects). It plays the role of a necessary presupposition such as the myth of the primal parricide in Freud's *Totem and Taboo*.

Žižek, relying on the Real, sees the working of ideology in an unconscious way as a 'traumatic, senseless call'. Where Althusser speaks of it as a symbolic process–as 'an ideological experience of Meaning and Truth', for Žižek, there is always a leftover, a 'stain of traumatic irrationality and senselessness sticking to it'. But this leftover (this part that will be designated as *object a*, which will also function as the object-cause of enjoyment) is not an obstacle to ideological identification. It acts paradoxically: 'far from hindering full submission of the object to the ideological command, is the very condition of it' (Žižek 1989: 43). As it has been Žižek's turn to the Lacanian Real that distinguishes his work from earlier theorists who have also attempted 'some friendly amendments' to Althusser's theory of ideology, a few remarks are in order (Biesecker 1998: 225). Although the Real does not exist (in the sense of 'really existing', taking place in reality) it does have a set of properties, and produces a series of effects in the symbolic reality of subjects. Similarly, the *object a* is defined as a 'pure void which functions as the object-cause of desire'. An excellent example of the *object a* was the Millennium Bug: a 'glitch' or defect which is allocated a positive cause (Žižek 2001: 254–56). These properties make it the province of jokes. Žižek recounts the following: 'Is this the place where the Duke of Wellington spoke his famous words? Yes, this is the place, but he never spoke those words'. *Those never spoken words* are the Lacanian real (Žižek 1989: 163). Put somewhat differently, the real is a radical negativity that never appears but 'must none the less be presupposed if we want to account for the present state of things' (Žižek 1989: 162). The Real is a deeply paradoxical entity as it lacks nothing and is precisely that lack around which the symbolic order is structured. For Lacan, God is Real. Enjoyment (*jouissance*), one of the terms that is most fundamental to Žižek's understandings of the political, of racism, ethnic conflict and nationalism is embedded in the Real: 'the Real *par excellence* is *jouissance*: *jouissance* does not exist, it is impossible but it produces a number of traumatic effects' (Žižek 1989: 164).

Both concepts – the Real and the *object a* – are causes which work by what Althusser designated as 'structural' or 'effective' causality: a 'presence' is situated in the effects it produces. Moreover, here the effects are present in a distorted, displaced way. Both Lacan and Žižek define the Real (paradoxically) as impossible and urge us to grasp this impossibility through its effects. Žižek notes that it was Laclau and Mouffe who first traced out this conceptual development in their notion of *antagonism* as a central limit, or impossible kernel which in itself is nothing; but which must be constructed retroactively, from a series of its effects: 'as the traumatic point which escapes them, it prevents a closure of the social field' (Žižek 1989: 163–64). In such a manner, Žižek invites us to reconsider 'class struggle' – not as a final signifier giving closure to a socio-symbolic field but as pure negativity or traumatic limit that prevents totalization of this field.

Žižek and international relations

It may seem ironic that some of the potentially most useful concepts for international relations are these very terms (the Real, *object a*, *jouissance*) designated as 'chimerical' ones that exceed symbolization but can be signified through inconsistencies, holes, slippages, or tracked through missed encounters, repetitions or shadow plays. Yet it has been in relation to these Lacanian ideas that Žižek has offered incisive readings of the resurgence of ethnic nationalisms, the passionate attachment to fundamentalisms of the right and of western liberal democracies. Indeed, it was Jacques Lacan who predicted the rise of racism in the Western European nations in the sixties and Žižek extended this analysis to the formerly socialist states of Eastern and Central Europe. Žižek reframes 'nationalism' in relation to the Real as either the 'nation Thing' or 'the ethnic Thing' – 'Thing' refers to the German *Das Ding*, a 'traumatic real object fixing our desire'. The Thing is literally riveting, the stuff of horror films; it could be the hockey mask worn by Jason Voorhees from *Friday the 13th* or Jack Nicholson's psychotic grin in either *The Shining* or as the Joker in *Batman*. Or it produces 'awe', like the Greek vase that is also organized around a central void (discussed by Heidegger as an example of a 'sacred Thing at its dawn') (Žižek 2003: 147). The question is why does this object – in this case the ethnic Thing – fascinate us? This question opens onto democratic subjectivity.

Žižek and Lacan presuppose a different subject of liberal democracy, which alters their conception of nationalism and the stakes of identification. For them, the subject of liberal democracy is a Cartesian, abstract subject, that is, an empty, 'inhuman' point or abstraction, devoid of any particular contents. Žižek constructs a homology between this subject (of the *Cogito* as a point of self-reference and radical doubt) and the 'zero state' of preambles found in democratic proclamations 'all people *without regard to* (race sex, religion, wealthy, social status)'. He notes the act of 'violent abstraction' at work in the language of 'without regard to'. This produces, in both Lacan and Žižek's views, a subject deprived of any support for a *positive substantial* identity. Indeed, it is precisely this lack of identity that gives the concept of identification such importance and resonance in liberal democratic societies (as well as in psychoanalytic theory); 'the subject attempts to fill out its constitutive lack … by identifying with some master signifier guaranteeing its place in the symbolic network' (Žižek 1991b: 163). Democracy is thus not made to measure for a humanist vision or a communitarian social order, as it is a formal assemblage of abstract individuals. It is the attempt to fill out this barren structure with a more humane content that will lead to totalitarian temptations.

But the problem with the subject of democracy as a pure singularity (unsupported by and emptied of all positive content) is not where some neoconservative critics see it. It is not that this subject 'bowls alone' or, more generally, that abstraction would dissolve all social ties. As we have seen with other aspects of Žižek's (and Lacan's) thought, abstraction can never totally succeed; there will always be a remainder, what Žižek calls a 'pathological' stain or 'leftover'. As with other concepts in Žižek's arsenal, this remainder has a certain *a priori* status: 'it is the positive condition of the democratic break' (i.e. the dissolving of the particular contents that constitutes the democratic subject) and 'its very support' (Žižek 1991b: 165). This leftover is none other than 'nationalism': 'the production of the subject of democracy is possible only through allegiance to some national Cause'. For Žižek, nationalism, recast as Freudian Cause or Thing, is a privileged type of materialized enjoyment (*jouissance*): it is not just *a* way, rather, *the* way that enjoyment erupts into the social field.

This reframing of nationalism around the constitution of the democratic subject has been an incredibly productive vantage point for Žižek to look at not just events in Bosnia and ethnic nationalisms in Eastern Europe, but to evaluate attempts at European integration and their setbacks (such as the 2005 'No' vote on the European Constitution, consideration of Turkey as an EU member – see Žižek 2008: 266; 269–73), debates on secularism and *laïcité* in liberal democratic societies whether concerning the wearing of the headscarf (Žižek 2005: 115), female circumcision or issues attendant on immigration. For Žižek, a nation organizes itself through its collective practices of enjoyment. What is at stake in ethnic conflict is possession of 'the nation Thing'. This can occur by someone enjoying differently (having access to other forms of enjoyment – other foods, customs, smells, that threaten ours) or otherwise threatening our enjoyment (by taking our jobs, not behaving 'patriotically' and otherwise ruining 'our way of life'.) Yet there is a paradox concerning enjoyment of this national Thing: it is imagined as being simultaneously inaccessible to the Other (i.e. their habits are 'foreign' to me) and threatened by them. Perhaps a bit more counter-intuitively, Žižek sees multicultural or hegemonic liberal democratic tolerance as the flip side of ethnic racism. 'The other is welcomed insofar as its presence is not intrusive, insofar as it is not really the other. Tolerance coincides with its opposite' (Žižek 2005: 120). He illustrates this delightfully with the example of the dinosaur song in Spielberg's *The Land Before Time* that concludes with a refrain praising all the differences it takes to make a world. Žižek reads this as a 'collaboration-in-differences' ideology at its purest that disavows the vertical antagonism (i.e. power differential between carnivore dinosaurs and herbivores; large and small ones 'devouring each other') replacing it with a horizontal one of complementary differences (Žižek 2002: 64–5). But one of the lessons of Lacan and Žižek is that there is no 'peaceful coexistence' between fantasies.

Žižek has himself effectively deployed Lacanian psychoanalysis to address most of the pressing security and rights issues in the post 9/11 world, whether it pertains to the use of torture, the issue of free speech (and Danish cartoons), ecological catastrophes and their mediatization. Yet his work has not been generally taken up in the larger literature in international relations with the exception of Jenny Edkins' chapter on his contribution to ideology (1999: 107–23) and her work on famine and on trauma and memory (Edkins 2000, 2003a); or Renata Salecl (1994). Salecl extends Žižek's analysis of the Bosnian War and considers larger implications of fantasy and the social symptom in relation to issues of women in post-socialism; distributive justice (Eastern Europe's failure to accept liberal democracy as endemic to liberal democracy's project); a former USSR serial killer as a failed case of interpellation; and the fraught relation between sexual difference and feminism in the discourse of human rights. More recent work (1998) continues the focus on hate speech and human rights, feminine *jouissance* and a Romanian case study. Jacqueline Rose's work also posits fantasy as deeply implicated in and structuring of power relations, whether in the analysis of perverse leader identifications such as Thatcher, or in affects attendant to World Wars (1993) and the Truth and Reconciliation Hearings in South Africa (2003).

While one might offer some criticisms of Žižek's work, I believe that the absence of any 'Žižekian' school in international relations could be traced to larger resistances to psychoanalysis in the social sciences more generally. A criticism of Žižek's work that might be worth considering is the degree to which he has over-generalized the notion of the social symptom. A related problem is that notwithstanding the concepts of 'impossibility' and the Real, there is not one example from the staggering array of socio-cultural or political examples that does not (relatively effortlessly) yield to his conceptual arsenal. This would appear to work against the ethic of a psychoanalytic tradition in which knowledge does not inhere in the master, but is part of an on-going process of transferences and resistances in which the unconscious plays its part.

However, I think that Žižek's work (and psychoanalysis) will play an increasingly important role in international relations in the field of ethics and human rights. Žižek has recently offered a cogent restatement of his criticisms of the de-politicizing effects of human rights as they are framed as attached to suffering victims who cannot be seen as political agents. He questions the type of politicization human rights projects such as humanitarian interventions (for famine relief or to alleviate genocide) provoke against the powers they stand opposed to: 'Do they stand for a different formulation of justice, or do they stand in opposition to collective justice projects?' (Žižek 2005: 126). For preventing suffering may function as an implicit prohibition of larger projects of socio-political transformation.

One of Žižek's most provocative claims is that psychoanalysis is the privileged discourse for ethics in that it is the only one that does not rely upon the mechanism of disavowal. Moreover, it presents what standard ethical treatments exclude: a consideration of the 'uncanniness', 'monstrosity', or 'foreignness' of the neighbour. As such it offers a counterpoint to the traditional humanist philosophical underpinnings of most human rights discourses. Yet neither Freud nor Lacan were simple advocates of human rights. Lacan proposed the neologism 'humanhysterianism' (*humanitairerie*) in the context of a description of racism as an anxiety ridden defence against the proximity of the Other's enjoyment (*jouissance*) (Lacan 1990: 33). Freud too was deeply mistrustful of national identifications (Žižek 2006b: 256). The psychoanalytic ethical tradition (represented by Freud, Lacan and Žižek) differs considerably from the Levinasian deferential respect for an unknowable or unfathomable Otherness. It resists what Žižek calls 'the ethical domestication of the neighbour'. Indeed, Žižek would claim that it is only psychoanalysis that fully addresses the neighbour in all his 'humanity' which would include his 'disavowed inhumanity'. What is most disruptive to this view of ethics is the suspicion that there might be something about the neighbour that is incompatible with universality: 'Every ethics that remains humanist in the name of avoiding the inhuman core of being human disavows the abyssal dimension of the neighbour. "Man", "human person" is a mask that conceals the pure subjectivity of the neighbour' (Žižek 2008: 16).

We are far from the ideas seen in both Derrida and Levinas of an 'infinite debt' to an abyssal Otherness. Rather, Žižek and Lacan's ethical posture is more neatly resumed by Butler and Stephens as 'correlative to the suspension of the big Other' (Butler and Stephens 2005: 373). We have already noted this at work in the end point of 'traversing the fantasy'. If we return to the conception of fantasy (as construction), we see that it is one way to face 'the enigma of the Other'. As we can never know what the Other wants from us, fantasy fills in the void or covers over the gap. For Žižek, it gives us an answer to this ultimately unanswerable question:

> It enables us to evade the unbearable deadlock in which the other wants something from us but we are at the same time incapable of translating the desire of the Other into a positive interpellation, into a mandate with which to identify (Žižek 1989: 114–15).

Fantasy is a double and paradoxical entity: it supplies the contours of our desire (it acts as a frame), but it also acts as a defence which helps us confront the 'unbearable enigma' or over-proximity of the Other's particular way of enjoying.

A way of attacking the hold that fantasy has on us (the basis of social or hegemonic power and the point of ideology critique) is to experience the lack of the Other (and not that of the subject himself). Žižek contends that Lacan's most radical insight is not that the subject is split or divided (or barred) but that the symbolic order itself (the big Other) is also (Žižek 1989: 122). One of Lacan's more gnomic utterances is that 'there is no Other of the Other'. This has been interpreted to say that there is no final guarantee of the symbolic order. Or, that there is a lack in the big Other; the big Other does not have it all as it too is structured around an impossible kernel or antagonism. This lack in the Other is a structural necessity for the symbolic order's functioning yet it offers a way out. If the Other were not split (or barred or fractured) there would be little recourse for the subject but 'total alienation': a 'subjection without remainder'. A lack in the Other means that there is some non-integratable *object a* (or surplus/remainder). The subject now can avoid alienation. There is another path (a 'de-alienation') open that Lacan calls 'separation'; the subject is not separated from the object by language, rather '*the object is separated from the Other itself*, that the Other itself "hasn't got it"' … that is to say is in itself blocked, desiring; that there is also a desire of the Other' (Žižek 1989: 122). It is the Other's lack that gives the subject 'a breathing space'. He can now allow himself to identify his own lack with the lack in the Other. This horizon of ethics holds great promise for the political. For Žižek, it leads to the formulation of an ethics based on Pauline love (love as the giving of what one does not have), as well as an affirming of revolutionary utopian practices, of attachments through 'belief in the founding dream rather than the enjoyment of founding violence' (Dean 2006: 177).

Further reading

Any serious engagement with Žižek's work would begin with either of his first works, *The Sublime Object of Ideology* (1989) or *For They Know Not What They Do: Enjoyment as a Political Factor* (1991a, second edition 2002). Žižek provides cogent and entertaining presentations of the ideas of Lacanian psychoanalysis in *Looking Awry: An Introduction to Jacques through Popular Culture* (1991b), *Enjoy Your Symptom! Jacques Lacan in Hollywood and Out* (1992), as well as in *How to Read Jacques Lacan* (2006b).

Readers who are interested in Žižek's responses to contemporary politics in the post 9/11 world can choose between either of his two short collections of essays: *Welcome to the Desert of the Real* (2002) or *Iraq: The Borrowed Kettle* (2004). A fuller critique of both liberal democracy and different fundamentalisms is elaborated in *Did Anybody Say Totalitarianism?* (2001) and *In Defense of Lost Causes* (2008).

Žižek's greatest philosophical contribution is to be found in three of his books: *Tarrying with the Negative: Kant, Hegel and the Critique of Ideology* (1993), *The Ticklish Subject: The Absent Centre of Political Ontologies* (1999) and *The Parallax View* (2006a). Žižek sees this latter work as the supplement – 'The Ticklish *Object*' to his 1999 *opus*.

Students in search of excellent secondary volumes on Žižek can consult Jodi Dean, *Žižek's Politics* (2006) or Rex Butler's *Slavoj Žižek: Live Theory* (2005). Rex Butler and Scott Stephens' edited volume of Žižek's writings *Slavoj Žižek: Interrogating the Real* (2005) provides a superbly edited selection as well as an informative glossary of terms.

Lastly, Astra Taylor's documentary *Žižek!* (2005) presents interviews, selections from his writings, and footage of Žižek lecturing and philosophizing in a plethora of venues, including his bed!

Bibliography

Adorno, Theodor W. (1973) *Negative Dialectics,* London: Routledge & Keegan Paul.
—— (1976) *The Positivist Dispute in German Sociology,* London: Heinemann.
—— (1984) *Aesthetic Theory* London: Routledge.
—— (1999) *The Complete Correspondence, 1928–1940. Theodor W. Adorno and Walter Benjamin,* (ed.) Henri Lonitz and trans. Nicholas Walker, Cambridge: Polity Press.
—— (2001) *The Stars Down to Earth and Other Essays on the Irrational in Culture,* London: Routledge, 2001.
—— (2003a) 'Education after Auschwitz', in Rolf Tiedemann (ed.) *Can One Live After Auschwitz? Theodor W. Adorno: A Philosophical Reader,* Stanford, CA: Stanford University Press.
—— (2003b) 'Metaphysics and Materialism', in Rolf Tiedemann (ed.) *Can One Live After Auschwitz? Theodor W. Adorno: A Philosophical Reader,* Stanford, CA: Stanford University Press.
—— (2003c) 'The Meaning of Working Through the Past', in Rolf Tiedemann (ed.) *Can One Live After Auschwitz? Theodor W. Adorno: A Philosophical Reader,* Stanford, CA: Stanford University Press.
—— (2005a) *Minima Moralia: Reflections on a Damaged Life,* London: Verso.
—— (2005b) *Critical Models. Interventions and catchwords,* trans. Henry W. Pickford, New York: Columbia University Press.
—— (2007) *Philosophy of Modern Music,* London: Continuum.
—— and Max Horkheimer (1997) *Dialectic of Enlightenment,* London: Verso.
—— *et al.* (1950) *The Authoritarian Personality,* New York: Harper.
Agamben, Giorgio (1993) *The Coming Community,* trans. M. Hardt, Minneapolis: University of Minnesota Press.
—— (1996) 'Form-of-Life', in Paolo Virno and Michael Hardt (eds) *Radical Thought in Italy: A Potential Politics,* Minneapolis: University of Minnesota Press.
—— (1998) *Homo Sacer: Sovereign Power and Bare Life,* trans. Daniel Heller-Roazen, Stanford: Stanford University Press.
—— (1999) *Remnants of Auschwitz: the Witness and the Archive,* New York: Zone Books.
—— (2000) *Means Without Ends: Notes on Politics,* trans. V. Binetti and C. Casarino, Minnesota: University of Minneapolis Press.
—— (2004a) 'Interview with Giorgio Agamben – A Life, A Work of Art Without an Author: The State of Exception, the Administration of Disorder and Private Life', *German Law Review,* 5 (5): 609–14.
—— (2004b) ''I am sure you are more pessimistic than I am … ' An Interview with Giorgio Agamben', *Rethinking Marxism,* 16 (2): 115–24.

—— (2005a) *State of Exception*, trans. Kevin Attell, Chicago: University of Chicago Press.

—— (2005b) *The Time That Remains: A Commentary on the Letter to the Romans*, trans. P. Dailey, Stanford: Stanford University Press.

—— (2007) *Profanations*, trans. J. Fort, New York: Zone Books.

Ajzenstat, Oona (2001) *Driven Back to the Text: The Premodern Sources of Levinas' Postmodernism*, Pittsburgh: Duquesne University Press.

Alker, Hayward R. (1996) *Rediscoveries and Reformulations: Humanistic Methodologies for International Studies*, Cambridge: Cambridge University Press.

Allison, David B. (1985) (ed.) *The New Nietzsche: Contemporary Styles of Interpretation*, Cambridge, MA: The MIT Press.

Alt, Casey (2008) *A Very Non-Foucauldian History of Michel Foucault*. http://www.stanford.edu/dept/HPS/BirthOfTheClinic/biohome.htm (accessed 15 April 2008).

Althusser, Louis (1971) 'Ideology and Ideological State Apparatus', in *Lenin and Philosophy and Other Essays*, trans. Ben Brewster, New York: Monthly Review Press.

Amoore, Louise (2007) 'Vigilant Visualities: The Watchful Politics of the War on Terror', *Security Dialogue*, 38 (2): 215–32.

Anderson, Benedict R.O.G. (1991) *Imagined communities: reflections on the origin and spread of nationalism*, London: Verso.

Antonio, Robert J. (1981) 'Immanent critique as the core of critical theory: its origins and development in Hegel, Marx and contemporary thought', *British Journal of Sociology*, 32 (3): 300–45.

Aradau, Claudia (2004) 'Security and the Democratic Scene: Desecuritization and Emancipation', *Journal of International Relations and Development*, 7 (4): 388–413.

—— (2008) *Rethinking Trafficking in Women. Politics out of Security*, Basingstoke: Palgrave Macmillan.

Archer, Margaret (1998) 'Introduction: realism in the social sciences', in Margaret Archer *et al.* (eds) *Critical Realism: Essential Readings,* London: New York, 189–205.

Arendt, Hannah (1958) *The Human Condition*, Chicago: University of Chicago Press.

—— (1966) *The Origins of Totalitarianism*, New York: Harcourt Brace Jovanovich.

—— (1968a) *Eichmann in Jerusalem: a Report on the Banality of Evil*, New York: Viking.

—— (1968b) 'Power and Violence', Lecture delivered at Bard College, New York. http://www.bard.edu/arendtcollection/digitalproject.htm.

—— (1968c) *Between Past and Future: Eight Exercises in Political Thought*, New York: Viking.

—— (1968d) *Men in Dark Times*, New York: Harcourt, Brace, and World.

—— (1970a [1963]) *On Revolution*, New York: Viking.

—— (1970b) 'Introduction: Walter Benjamin: 1892–1940' in Walter Benjamin, *Illuminations*, trans. Harry Kohn, edited by Hannah Arendt, London: Jonathan Cape, 1–55.

—— (1972) *Crises of the Republic*, New York: Harcourt Brace Jovanovich.

—— (1978) *The Jew as Pariah: Jewish Identity and Politics in the Modern Age*, edited and introduction by Ron H. Feldman, New York: Grove Press.

—— (1979) 'On Hannah Arendt', in Melvyn Hill (ed.) *Hannah Arendt: The Recovery of the Public World*, New York: St. Martin's Press, 301–39.

—— (1982) *Lectures on Kant's Political Philosophy*, edited and with an interpretive essay by Ronald Beiner, Chicago: University of Chicago Press.

—— (1994) *Essays in Understanding, 1930–1954*, New York: Harcourt Brace.

—— (1995) *Love and Saint Augustine*, edited by Joanna Vecchiarelli Scott and Judith Chelius Stark, Chicago: University of Chicago Press.

—— (2000 [1941]) 'The Jewish Army – the Beginning of a Jewish Politics?' in *The Portable Hannah Arendt*, edited by Peter Baehr, London: Penguin, 46–8.

—— (2002) 'Karl Marx and the Tradition of Western Political Thought', *Social Research* 69 (1): 273–319.

—— (2003) *Responsibility and Judgement*, edited and with an introduction by Jerome Kohn, New York: Schocken.

—— (2005) *The Promise of Politics*, edited and with an introduction by Jerome Kohn, New York: Schocken.

—— (2007) *The Jewish Writings*, edited by Jerome Kohn and Ron H. Feldman, New York: Schocken.

—— and Jaspers, Karl (1992) *Correspondence, 1926–1969*, edited by Lotte Kohler and Hans Saner, trans. by Robert and Rita Kimber, New York: Harcourt Brace Jovanovich.

Arnold, David (2000) 'Gramsci and Peasant Subalternity in India', in *Mapping Subaltern Studies and the Postcolonial*, edited by V. Chaturvedi, London: Verso, 24–49.

Aschheim, Steven E. (ed.) (2001) *Hannah Arendt in Jerusalem*, Berkeley, CA: University of California Press.

Ashley, Richard K. (1981) 'Political Realism and Human Interests', *International Studies Quarterly*, 25: 204–36.

—— (1988) 'Untying the Sovereign State: A Double Reading of the Anarchy Problematique', *Millennium: Journal of International Studies*, 17 (2): 227–62.

—— (1989) 'Living on Border Lines: Man, Poststructuralism, and War', in James Der Derian and Michael J. Shapiro (eds) *International/Intertextual Relations: Postmodern Readings of World Politics*, Lexington, MA: Lexington Books.

Ashley, Richard K. and Walker, R.B.J. (1990a) 'Reading Dissidence/Writing the Discipline: crisis and the question of sovereignty in international studies', *International Studies Quarterly*, 34: 367–416.

—— (1990b) 'Speaking the Language of Exile: Dissidence in International Studies', *International Studies Quarterly*, 34 (3): 259–68.

Attridge, Derek and Baldwin, Thomas (2004) 'Jacques Derrida', *Guardian*, 11/10/04.

Augelli, Enrico and Murphy, Craig (1988) *America's Quest for Supremacy and the Third World*, London: Pinter.

Avineri, Shlomo (1972) *Hegel's Theory of the Modern State*, Cambridge: Cambridge University Press.

Axtmann, Roland (2006) 'Globality, Plurality and Freedom: the Arendtian Perspective', *Review of International Studies* 32 (1): 93–117.

Bachelard, Gaston (1934) *Le nouvel esprit scientifique*, Paris: Presses Universitaires de France.

—— (1947): *La formation de l'esprit scientifique: contribution à une psychoanalyse de la connaissance objective*, Paris: J. Vrin.

Badiou, Alain (1992) *Conditions*, Paris: Editions du Seuil.

—— (1998a) *Abrégé de métapolitique*, Paris: Editions du Seuil.

—— (1998b) 'Politics and Philosophy. Interview with Peter Hallward', *Angelaki* 3 (3): 113–33.

—— (2002a) *Ethics. An Essay on the Understanding of Evil*, London: Verso.

—— (2002b) 'On Evil: An Interview with Alain Badiou' *Cabinet* 5 (5). http://cabinet magazine.org/issues/5/alainbadiou.php (accessed 21 August 2003).

—— (2004a) *Infinite Thought. Truth and the Return of Philosophy*, trans. Oliver Feltham and Justin Clemens, London: Continuum.

—— (2004b) *Theoretical Writings*, trans. Ray Brassier and Alberto Toscano, London: Continuum.

—— (2005) *Politics: A Non-Expressive Dialectics*, Lecture at the Birkbeck Institute for Humanities, 26 November. Transcribed by Robin Mackay. Urbanomic London. http://blog.urbanomic.com/sphaleotas/archives/badiou-politics.pdf (accessed 20 December 2007).

—— (2006a) *Being and Event*, trans. Oliver Feltham. London: Continuum.

—— (2006b) *Logique des mondes*, Paris: Seuil.

—— (2006c) *Polemics*, trans. Steve Corcoran, London: Verso.

—— (2007) *De quoi Sarkozy est-il le nom?* Paris: Lignes.

—— and Bosteels, (Bruno 2005) 'Can Change Be Thought? A Dialogue with Alain Badiou', in Gabriel Riera (ed.) *Alain Badiou. Philosophy and Its Conditions*, New York: State University of New York, 244–60.

Baehr, Peter (2002) 'Identifying the Unprecedented: Hannah Arendt, Totalitarianism, and the Critique of Sociology', *American Sociological Review* 67 (6): 804–31.

Balakrishnan, Gopal (2000) *The Enemy: an intellectual portrait of Carl Schmitt*, London: Verso.

Barkawi, Tarak (2004) 'Globalization, Culture, and War: On the Popular Mediation of "Small Wars"', *Cultural Critique*, 58: 115–47.

Barnett, Michael and Duvall, Raymond (2005) *Power in Global Governance*, Cambridge: Cambridge University Press.

Bataille, Georges (1991) *The Accursed Share*, New York: Zone Books.

Baudrillard, Jean (1981) *For a Critique of the Political Economy of the Sign*, St Louis: Telos Press.

—— (1983) *Simulacra and Simulation*, published as *Simulations*, New York: Semiotext(e).

—— (1987) *Forget Foucault*, New York: Semiotext(e).

—— (1988a) 'Symbolic Exchange and Death', in Mark Poster (ed.) *Jean Baudrillard: Selected Writings*, Stanford: Stanford University Press, 119–48.

—— (1988b) *America*, London: Verso.

—— (1990a) *Seduction*, London: Macmillan.

—— (1990b) *Fatal Strategies*, New York: Semiotext(e).

—— (1990c) *Cool Memories*, London: Verso.

—— (1992) *L'Illusion de la fin, ou la grève des événements*, Paris: Galilée.

—— (1993a) *Symbolic Exchange and Death*, London: Sage.

—— (1993b) *The Transparency of Evil*, London: Verso.

—— (1995) *The Gulf War Did Not Take Place*, Bloomington: Indiana University Press.

—— (1996a) *The System of Objects*, London: Verso.

—— (1996b) *The Perfect Crime*, London: Verso.

—— (1998) *The Consumer Society*, London: Sage.

—— (1999) *L'Échange impossible*, Paris: Galilée.

—— (2002a) 'L'Esprit du Terrorisme' [The Spirit of Terrorism], in Stanley Hauerwas and Frank Lentricchia (eds), *Dissent from the Homeland: Essays after September 11*, Durham: Duke University Press.

—— (2002b) *Power Inferno*, Paris: Galilée.

—— (2004) 'Interview with Jean Baudrillard', in Paul Hegarty (ed.), *Jean Baudrillard: Live Theory*, London: Continuum, 134–49.

Bauer, Nancy (2001) *Simone de Beauvoir: philosophy and feminism*, New York: Columbia University Press.

358   Bibliography

—— (2004) 'Must We Read Simone de Beauvoir?', in Emily Grosholz (ed.) *The Legacy of Simone de Beauvoir*, Oxford: Clarendon Press, 115–35.

Bauman, Zygmunt (1978) *Hermeneutics and Social Science: Approaches to Understanding*, London: Hutchinson

—— (1993) 'The Sweet Scent of Decomposition', in Chris Rojek and Brian Turner (eds), *Forget Baudrillard?* London: Routledge, 22–46.

Beardsworth, Richard (2008) 'Arendt and the Critique of Moralism', *International Politics* 45 (4) (July), pp. 506–513.

Beasley-Murray, Jon (2005) 'The common enemy: tyrants and pirates', *South Atlantic Quarterly*, 104: 217–25.

Beauvoir, Simone de (1948) *The Ethics of Ambiguity*, trans. B. Frechtman, New York: Philosophical Library.

—— (1959) *Memoirs of a Dutiful Daughter*, trans. James Kirkup, London: André Deutsch.

—— (1965a) *The Prime of Life*, trans. P. Green, London: André Deutsch.

—— (1965b) *Force of Circumstance*, trans. R. Howard, London: André Deutsch.

—— (1972) *All Said and Done*, trans. Patrick O'Brian, London: André Deutsch.

—— (1997) *The Second Sex*, trans. H. M Parshley, London: Vintage Books.

Beiner, Ronald (2000) 'Arendt and Nationalism', in Dana Villa (ed.) *The Cambridge Companion to Hannah Arendt*, Cambridge: Cambridge University Press, 44–62.

Beiner, Ronald and Booth, William James (eds) (1993) *Kant and Political Philosophy: the contemporary legacy*, Newhaven and London: Yale University Press.

Benhabib, Seyla (1996) *The Reluctant Modernism of Hannah Arendt*, Thousand Oaks, CA: Sage Publications.

—— (2004) *The Rights of Others*, Cambridge: Cambridge University Press.

Benjamin, Andrew (ed.) (1989) *The Problems of modernity: Adorno and Benjamin*, London, Routledge.

Benjamin, Walter (1973) *Illuminations*, (ed.) Hannah Arendt and trans. Harry Zohn, London: Fontana.

—— (1978) *Reflections: essays, aphorisms, autobiographical writings*, (ed.) Peter Demetz and trans. Edmund Jephcott, New York: Schocken Books.

—— (1979) *One-Way Street, and other writings*, trans. Edmund Jephcott and Kingsley Shorter, London: NLB.

—— (1999) *The arcades project*, Cambridge, Mass. and London: Belknap Press.

—— (2003) 'On the Concept of History', in Howard Eiland and Michael Jennings (eds) *Walter Benjamin: Selected Writings, Volume 4, 1938–1940*, Cambridge, MA and London: The Bellknap Press of Harvard University Press.

Bennington, Geoffrey and Jacques Derrida (1993) *Jacques Derrida*, trans. Geoffrey Bennington, Chicago: University of Chicago Press.

Berman, Marshall (1983) *All That Is Solid Melts Into Air*, London and New York: Verso.

Bernasconi, Robert (1998) 'Hegel at the Court of Ashanti', in Stuart Barnett (ed.), *Hegel After Derrida*, New York: Routledge.

Bernet, Rudolf (1990) 'Husserl and Heidegger on intentionality and being', *Journal of the British Society for Phenomenology* 21 (2): 136–52.

Bernstein, Richard (2002) 'Arendt: Radical Evil and the Banality of Evil', in *Radical Evil: a Philosophical Interrogation*, Cambridge: Polity.

—— (2003) 'Rorty's Inspirational Liberalism', in *Richard Rorty*, ed. Guignon, Charles and Hiley, David R., Cambridge: Cambridge University Press, 124–38.

Bhabha, Homi (ed.) (1990) *Nation and Narration*, London and New York: Routledge.

—— (1984) 'Of Mimicry and Man: The Ambivalence of Colonial Discourse', *October* 28: 125–33.
Bhaskar, Roy (1975) *A Realist Theory of Science*, 2nd ed., Brighton: Harvester Press.
—— (1986) *Scientific Realism and Human Emancipation*, London: Verso.
—— (1989) *Reclaiming Reality: A Critical Introduction to Contemporary Philosophy*, London: Verso.
—— (1991) *Philosophy and the Idea of Freedom*, Oxford: B. Blackwell.
—— (1993) *Dialectic: The Pulse of Freedom*, London: Verso.
—— (1994) *Plato Etc.: The Problems of Philosophy and Their Resolution*, London: Verso.
—— (1998 [1979]) *The Possibility of Naturalism: A Philosophical Critique of the Contemporary Human Sciences*, 3rd ed., London: Routledge.
—— (2000) *From East to West: The Odyssey of a Soul*, London: Routledge.
—— (2002) *Reflections on Meta-Reality: Transcendence, Emancipation and Everyday Life*, London: Sage.
Bieler, Andeas (2006) *The Struggle for a Social Europe*, Manchester: Manchester University Press.
Bieler, Andreas and Adam Morton (eds) (2006) *Images of Gramsci*, London: Routledge.
Biesecker, Barbara A. (1998) 'Rhetorical Studies and the "new" Psychoanalysis: What's the Real Problem? On Framing the Problem of the Real' *Quarterly Journal of Speech*, 84: 222–59.
Bigo, Didier (1996) *Polices en réseaux: l'expérience européenne*, Paris: Presses de Sciences Po.
—— (2006) 'Globalized (in)security: the field and the ban-opticon', in Didier Bigo and Anastassia Tsoukala (eds) *Illiberal Practices of Liberal Regimes: the (in)security games*, Paris: L'Harmattan, 5–49.
—— (2007) 'Detention of Foreigners, States of Exception, and the Social Practices of Control of the Banopticon', in Prem Kumar Rajaram and Carl Grundy-Warr (eds) *Borderscapes: Hidden Geographies and Politics at Territory's Edge*, Minnesota: University of Minnesota Press, 3–34.
Birmingham, Peg (2006) *Hannah Arendt and Human Rights: The Predicament of Common Responsibility*, Bloomington, Indiana University Press.
Blanchot, Maurice (1988) *The Unavowable Community*, Barrytown: Station Hill Press.
Bleiker, Roland (1999) '"Give It the Shade", Paul Celan and the Politics of Apolitical Poetry', *Political Studies*, 48: 661–76.
Bohman, James (2007) *Democracy Across Borders: From Demos to Demoi*. Cambridge: MIT Press.
Booth, Ken (2007) *Theory of World Security*, Cambridge: Cambridge University Press.
Bosteels, Bruno (2004) 'On the Subject of the Dialectic', in Peter Hallward (ed.) *Think Again. Alain Badiou and the Future of Philosophy*, London: Continuum, 150–64.
—— (2005) 'Post-maoism: Badiou and politics' *positions* 13 (3): 575–634.
Bourdieu, Pierre (1977) *Outline of a Theory of Practice*, Cambridge: Cambridge University Press [(1972) *Esquisse d'une théorie de la pratique, précédé de trois études d'ethnologie kabyle*, Berne: Librairie Droz].
—— (1984) *Distinction: a social critique of the judgement of taste*, Cambridge Mass.: Harvard University Press.
—— (1986) 'The Forms of Capital', in John.G. Richardson (ed.) *Handbook of Theory and Research for the Sociology of Education*, Westport: Greenwood Press, 241–58.

—— (1987) 'Legitimation and structured interests in Weber's sociology of religion', in Scott Lash and Sam Whimster (eds) *Max Weber, Rationality and Irrationality*, Boston: Allen and Unwin, 119–36.

—— (1988) *Homo Academicus*, Cambridge: Polity Press [(1984) *Homo Academicus*, Paris: Éditions de Minuit].

—— (1990a) *In Other Words: essays toward a reflexive sociology*, Stanford: Stanford University Press [(1987) *Choses dites*, Paris: Éditions de Minuit].

—— (1990b) *The Logic of Practice*, Stanford: Stanford University Press [(1980) *Le sens pratique*, Paris, Éditions de Minuit].

—— (1991) *Language and Symbolic Power*, Cambridge: Polity Press.

—— (1996) *The State Nobility: elite schools in the field of power*, Cambridge: Polity Press [(1989) *La Noblesse d'état. Grandes écoles et esprit de corps*, Paris: Éditions de Minuit].

—— (1998) *Practical Reason*, Stanford: Stanford University Press [(1994) *Raisons pratiques. Sur la théorie de l'action*, Paris: Seuil].

—— (2003) *Méditations Pascaliennes*, 2nd ed., Paris: Seuil.

—— (2004) *Esquisse pour une auto-analyse*, Paris: Raisons d'agir.

—— Chamboredon, Jean-Claude and Passeron, Jean-Claude (1991) *The Craft of Sociology: Epistemological Preliminaries*, New York: Verlag Walter de Gruyter & Co.

—— Darbel, Alain, Rivet, Jean-Paul and Seibel, Claude (1963) *Travail et travailleurs en Algérie*, Paris: Mouton.

——, and Passeron, Jean-Claude (2000) *Reproduction in Education, Culture and Society*, 2nd ed., London: Sage.

—— and Sayad, Abdelmalek (1964) *Le déracinement, la crise de l'agriculture traditionelle en Algérie*, Paris: Éditions de Minuit.

—— and Wacquant, Loïc (1992) *An Invitation to Reflexive Sociology*, Chicago: University of Chicago Press.

—— (1999) 'The Cunning of Imperialist Reason', *Theory, Culture and Society*, 16 (1): 41–58.

Boynton, Robert S. (1998) "Enjoy Your Žižek!" *Lingua Franca* 7.

Bradbury, Malcolm and McFarlane, James. W. (1978) *Modernism, 1890–1930*, Hassocks: Harvester Press.

Brassett, James (2008a) 'A Pragmatic Approach to the Tobin Tax Campaign: The Politics of Sentimental Education', in *European Journal of International Relations*, forthcoming.

—— (2008b) 'Cosmopolitanism vs. Terrorism? Discourses of Ethical Possibility Before and After 7/7', *Millennium: Journal of International Studies*, 36 (2): 311–37.

Brodersen, Momme, (1996) *Walter Benjamin: a biography*, London: Verso.

Brown, Chris (1992) *International Relations Theory: New Normative Approaches*, London: Harvester Wheatsheaf.

—— (1999) 'Universal Human Rights: A Critique', in *Human Rights in Global Perspective*, eds Tim Dunne and Nicholas J. Wheeler, Cambridge: Cambridge University Press, 103–27.

—— (2007) 'Situating Critical Realism', *Millennium Journal of International Studies*, 35 (2): 409–16.

Brunkhorst, Hauke (1999) *Adorno and Critical Theory*, Cardiff: University of Wales Press.

Buck-Morss, Susan (1977) *The origin of negative dialectics: Theodor W. Adorno, Walter Benjamin, and the Frankfurt Institute*, Hassocks: Harvester Press.

—— (1989) *The dialectics of seeing: Walter Benjamin and the Arcades project*, Cambridge, Mass. and London: MIT Press.

—— (2000)' Hegel and Haiti', *Critical Inquiry*, 26 (4): 821–65.
Bull, Hedley (1977) *The Anarchical Society: a study of order in world politics*, London: Macmillan.
—— (1995) 'Society and Anarchy in International Relations', in James Der Derian (ed.) *International Theory: Critical Investigations*, Basingstoke: Macmillan.
—— and Watson, Adam (eds) (1984) *The Expansion of International Society*, New York: Oxford University Press.
Bulley, Dan (2006) 'Negotiating Ethics: Campbell, Ontopology and Hospitality', *Review of International Studies* 32 (4): 645–63.
—— (2008) 'Foreign Terror? London Bombings, Resistance, and the Failing State', *British Journal of Politics and International Relations*, 10 (3) (August), pp. 379–394.
Burke, Anthony (2008) 'Recovering Humanity from Man: Hannah Arendt's Troubled Cosmopolitanism', *International Politics* 45, (4) (July), pp. 514–521.
Burke, Peter (2004) *What is Cultural History?* Cambridge: Polity.
Bush, George (2001) *Prayer Service Remarks at the Washington National Cathedral*. http://www.opm.gov/guidance/09-14-01gwb.htm (accessed 20 December 2007).
—— (2003) 'Address to the Nation', March 19. http://www.whitehouse.gov/news/releases/2003/03/20030319-17.html (accessed 20 May 2008).
Butler, Judith (1990, 1999) *Gender Trouble: Feminism and the Subversion of Identity*, London: Routledge.
—— (1993a) 'The Body Politics of Julia Kristeva', in Kelly Oliver (ed.) *Ethics, Politics and Difference in Julia Kristeva's Writing*, New York and London: Routledge.
—— (1993b) *Bodies That Matter: On the Discursive Limits of 'Sex'*, London: Routledge.
—— (2004a) *Precarious Life: The Powers of Mourning and Violence*, London: Verso Press.
—— (2004b) *Undoing Gender*, London: Routledge.
—— (2005) *Giving an Account of Oneself*, New York: Fordham University Press.
Butler, Rex (2005) *Slavoj Žižek: Live Theory*, London: Continuum.
—— and Stephens, Scott (2005) *Interrogating the Real: Slavoj Žižek*, London: Continuum.
Calarco, Matthew and DeCaroli, Steven (eds) (2007) *Sovereignty and Life: Essays on Giorgio Agamben*, Stanford: Stanford University Press.
Caldwell, Anne (2004) 'Bio-Sovereignty and the Emergence of Humanity', *Theory and Event*, 7 (2).
Campbell, David (1994) 'The Deterritorialization of Responsibility: Levinas, Derrida, and Ethics after the End of Philosophy', *Alternatives*, 19: 455–84.
—— (1998a) *National Deconstruction: Violence, Identity, and Justice in Bosnia*, Minneapolis: University of Minnesota Press.
—— (1998b) 'MetaBosnia: Narratives of the Bosnian War', *Review of International Studies* 24 (2): 261–82.
—— (1998c) *Writing Security: United States Foreign Policy and the Politics of Identity*, 2nd ed., Minneapolis: University of Minnesota Press.
—— (1999a) 'Contra Wight: The Errors of Premature Writing', *Review of International Studies*, 25 (1): 317–22.
—— (1999b) 'The Deterritorialization of Responsibility: Levinas, Derrida, and Ethics After the End of Philosophy', in David Campbell and Michael J. Shapiro (eds) *Moral Spaces: Rethinking Ethics and World Politics*, Minneapolis: University of Minnesota Press.
—— (2001a) 'Justice and International Order: the case of Bosnia and Kosovo', in Jean-Marc Coicaud and Daniel Warner (eds) *Ethics and International Affairs*, Tokyo, New York and Paris: United Nations University Press, 103–27.

—— (2001b) 'Why Fight? Humanitarianism, Principles and Poststructuralism', in Hakan Seckinelgin and Hideaki Shinoda (eds) *Ethics and International Relations*, Basingstoke: Palgrave, 132–60.

—— and Shapiro, Michael J. (eds) (2007) 'Special Issue on Securitization, Militarization and Visual Culture in the World of Post-9/11', *Security Dialogue*, 38 (2).

Canovan, Margaret (1983) 'A Case of Distorted Communication: A Note on Habermas and Arendt', *Political Theory* 11(1): 105–16.

—— (1992) *Hannah Arendt: A Reinterpretation of Her Political Thought*, Cambridge: Cambridge University Press.

—— (1996) 'Hannah Arendt as a Conservative Thinker', in Larry May and Jerome Kohn (eds) *Hannah Arendt: Twenty Years Later*, Cambridge, MA: MIT Press, 11–32.

Caputo, John D. (1978) 'The Question of Being and Transcendental Phenomenology: Reflections on Heidegger's Relationship to Husserl', in John Sallis (ed.), *Radical Phenomenology: essays in honor of Martin Heidegger*, Atlantic Highlands, NJ: Humanities Press, 84–105.

—— (1983) 'Heidegger's god and the lord of history', *New Scholasticism* 57 (4): 439–64.

—— (1993) *Against Ethics*, Indianapolis: University of Indiana Press.

—— (ed.) (1997) *Deconstruction in a Nutshell: A Conversation with Jacques Derrida*, New York: Fordham University Press.

Card, Claudia (ed.) (2003) *The Cambridge Companion to Simone de Beauvoir*, Cambridge: Cambridge University Press.

Carr, David (1995) 'The question of the subject: Heidegger and the transcendental tradition', *Human Studies* 17 (4): 403–18.

Carr, Edward Hallett (1981) *The Twenty Years' Crisis 1919–1939: an introduction to the study of international relations*, 2nd edn, Basingstoke: Macmillan.

Carver, Terrell (1991) *Cambridge Companion to Marx*. Cambridge: Cambridge University Press.

Caygill, Howard (1995) *A Kant Dictionary*, Oxford: Blackwell.

—— (1998) *Walter Benjamin: the colour of experience*, London: Routledge.

——, Coles, Alex and Appignanesi, Richard (1998) *Introducing Walter Benjamin*, Duxford: Icon.

Chakrabarty, Dipesh (2000a) 'Subaltern Studies and Postcolonial Historiography', *Nepantla: Views from South*, 1 (1): 9–32.

—— (2000b) *Provincializing Europe: Postcolonial Thought and Historical Difference*, New Jersey: Princeton University Press.

Chakravorty, Swapan, Milevska, Suzana, and Barlow, Tani, E. (2006) *Conversations with Gayatri Chakravorty Spivak*, Oxford: Seagulls Books.

Chan, Stephen (2007) 'Fanon: The Octogenarian of International Revenge and the Suicide Bomber of Today', *Cooperation and Conflict*, 42 (2): 151–68.

Chatterjee, Partha (2004) *The politics of the governed: reflections on popular politics in most of the world*, New York and Chichester: Columbia University Press.

Chomsky, Noam (1969) *Aspects of the Theory of Syntax* Cambridge, Mass.: MIT Press.

Cissé, Madjiguène (1997) *The Sans-Papiers: The New Movement of Asylum Seekers and Immigrants without Papers in France: A Woman Draws the First Lesson*, London: Crossroads.

Clarke, Paul B. (1999) *Autonomy Unbound*, Aldershot: Ashgate.

Clemens, Justin, Nick Heron and Alex Murray (eds) (2008) *The work of Giorgio Agamben: Law, Literature, Life*, Edinburgh: Edinburgh University Press.

Closs Stephens, Angharad and Nick Vaughan-Williams (eds) (2008) *Terrorism and the Politics of Response*, London and New York: Routledge.

Cochran, Molly (1996) 'Is There a Role for the Liberal Ironist in IR Theory?', *Millennium: Journal of International Studies*, 25, (1): 29–52.

—— (1999) *Normative Theory and International Relations*, Cambridge: Cambridge University Press.

Cocks, Joan (2002) 'Imperialism, Self-Determination, and Violence: Rosa Luxembourg, Hannah Arendt, and Franz Fanon', in *Passion and Paradox: Intellectuals Confront the National Question*, Princeton, NJ: Princeton University Press, 45–70.

Colombo, Alessandro (2007) 'The "realist institutionalism" of Carl Schmitt' in Louiza Odysseos and Fabio Petito (eds) *The International Political Thought of Carl Schmitt: terror, liberal war and the crisis of global order*, London: Routledge.

Connolly, William E. (1999) 'Suffering, Justice, and the Politics of Becoming', in David Campbell and Michael J. Shapiro (eds) *Moral Spaces: Rethinking Ethics and World Politics*, Minneapolis: University of Minnesota Press.

Connolly, William (2004) 'The Complexity of Sovereignty', in Jenny Edkins, Véronique Pin-Fat and Michael J. Shapiro (eds) *Sovereign Lives: Power in World Politics*, London and New York: Routledge, 23–41.

Cook, Maeve (1998) 'Introduction', in Jürgen Habermas *On the Pragmatics of Communication*, Cambridge, MA: MIT Press, 1–19.

Coole, Diana (2000) *Negativity and Politics*, New York and London: Routledge.

Cotter, Bridget (2005) 'Hannah Arendt and "the Right to Have Rights"' in Anthony F. Lang Jr. and John Williams (eds) *Hannah Arendt and International Relations: Readings Across the Lines*. London: Palgrave Press, 95–112.

Coward, Martin (2008) *Urbicide: The Politics of Urban Destruction*, London: Routledge.

Cox, Robert W (1981) 'Social Forces, States and World Orders', *Millennium: Journal of International Studies* 10 (2): 126–55.

—— (1983) 'Gramsci, Hegemony, and International Relations', *Millennium: Journal of International Studies* 12: 162–75.

Crawford, Neta (2002) *Argument and Change in World Politics: Ethics, Decolonization, and Humanitarian Intervention*, Cambridge: Cambridge University Press.

Critchley, Simon (1996) 'Prolegomena to any post-deconstructive subjectivity', in Simon Critchley and Peter Dews (eds) *Deconstructive Subjectivities*, Albany: State University of New York Press, 13–45.

Culler, Jonathan (1983) *On Deconstruction: Theory and Criticism after Structuralism*, London: Routledge.

—— (1985) 'Communicative Competence and Normative Force', *New German Critique*, 35: 133–44.

Dallmayr, Fred (1997) 'An "Inoperative" Global Community? Reflections on Nancy', in Sheppard, Darren, Sparks, Simon and Thomas, Colin (eds) *On Jean-Luc Nancy: The Sense of Philosophy*, London: Routledge.

—— (2001) 'Conversation Across Boundaries: Political Theory and Global Diversity', *Millennium: Journal of International Studies*, 30: 331–47.

Dauphinee, Elizabeth (2007) *The Ethics of Researching War: Looking for Bosnia*, Manchester: Manchester University Press.

Dauphinee, Elizabeth and Masters, Cristina (eds) (2007) *The Logics of Biopower and the War on Terror: Living, Dying, Surviving*, Basingstoke and New York: Palgrave Macmillan.

Dean, Jodi (2006) *Žižek's Politics*, New York: Routledge.

Debrix, François (1996) 'Deploying Vision, Simulating Action: The United Nations and its Visualization Strategies in a New World Order', *Alternatives: Global, Local, Political*, 21 (1): 67–92.

—— (1999) *Re-Envisioning Peacekeeping: The United Nations and the Mobilization of Ideology*, Minneapolis: University of Minnesota Press.

Delanda, Manuel (2000) *A Thousand Years of Non-Linear History*, New York: Zone Books.

Deleuze, Gilles (1988) *Foucault*, trans. Sean Hand, Minnesota: University of Minnesota Press.

—— (1990) [1969] *The Logic of Sense*, New York: Columbia University Press.

—— (1994) [1968] *Difference and Repetition*, trans. Paul Patton, London: Athlone.

—— (2004) *Desert Islands*, trans. Michael Taormina, New York: Semiotext(e).

—— (2006) [1962] *Nietzsche and Philosophy*, trans. Hugh Tomlinson, London: Continuum.

—— and Félix Guattari (1984) [1972] *Anti-Oedipus: Capitalism and Schizophrenia*, trans. Robert Hurley, Mark Seem and Helen Lane, London: Athlone.

—— (1988) [1980] *A Thousand Plateaus: Capitalism and Schizophrenia*, trans. Brian Massumi, London: Athlone.

—— (1994) [1991] *What is Philosophy?* trans. Graham Burchell and Hugh Tomlinson, London: Verso.

Der Derian, James (1992) *Antidiplomacy: Spies, Terror, Speed, and War*, Oxford: Blackwell.

—— (1994) 'Simulation: The Highest Stage of Capitalism?', in Douglas Kellner (ed.) *Baudrillard: A Critical Reader*, Oxford: Blackwell, 189–207.

—— (1998) *The Virilio Reader*, Oxford: Blackwell.

—— (2001) 'Global Events, National Security, and Virtual Theory', *Millennium: Journal of International Studies*, 30 (3): 669–90.

Derrida, Jacques (1973) *Speech and Phenomena and Other Essays on Husserl's Theory of Signs*, Evanston, IL: Northwestern University Press.

—— (1978) *Writing and Difference*, trans. Alan Bass, London: Routledge.

—— (1981a) *Dissemination*, trans. Barbara Johnson, London: The Athlone Press.

—— (1981b) *Positions*, trans. Alan Bass, London: Athlone Press.

—— (1982) *Margins of Philosophy*, trans. Alan Bass, Chicago: The University of Chicago Press.

—— (1985) *Margins of Philosophy*, trans. Alan Bass, Chicago: University of Chicago Press

—— (1988) *Limited Inc*, Evanston, IL: Northwestern University Press.

—— (1992a) 'Force of Law: The "Mystical Foundation of Authority"', trans. Mary Quaintance, in David Gray Carlson, Drucilla Cornell and Michel Rosenfeld (eds) *Deconstruction and the Possibility of Justice*, New York: Routledge.

—— (1992b) *The Other Heading: Reflections on Today's Europe*, trans. Pascale-Anne Brault and Michael B. Naas, Bloomington: Indiana University Press.

—— (1994) *Specters of Marx: The State of Debt, the Work of Mourning, and the New International*, trans. Peggy Kamuf, New York: Routledge.

—— (1995a) *The Gift of Death*, trans. David Wills, Chicago: University of Chicago Press.

—— (1995b) *Points … Interviews, 1974–1994*, ed. Elisabeth Weber, trans. Peggy Kamuf and others, Stanford: Stanford University Press.

—— (1995c) 'Heidegger, philosopher's hell', in *Points ... : Interviews, 1974–1994*, Stanford: Stanford University Press.

—— (1997) *Politics of Friendship*, trans. George Collins, London: Verso.

—— (1998) *Of Grammatology*, trans. Gayatri Chakravorty Spivak, corrected ed., Baltimore: The Johns Hopkins University Press.

—— (1999) *Adieu to Emmanuel Levinas*, trans Pascale-Anne Brault and Michael Naas, Stanford: Stanford University Press.

—— (2000) *Of Hospitality: Anne Dufourmantelle Invites Jacques Derrida to Respond*, Stanford: Stanford University Press.

—— (2001) *On Cosmopolitanism and Forgiveness*, trans. Mark Dooley and Michael Hughes, London: Routledge.

—— (2002a) 'Force of Law: The "Mystical Foundations of Authority"', in Andijar, Gil (ed.) *Jacques Derrida: Acts of Religion*, London and New York: Routledge.

—— (2002b) *Negotiations: Interventions and Interviews 1971–2001*, ed. and trans. Elizabeth Rottenberg. Stanford, CA: Stanford University Press.

—— (2002c) *Positions*, trans. A. Bass, 2nd English ed., London: Continuum.

—— (2003) 'Autoimmunity: Real and Symbolic Suicides', in Giovanna Borradori, *Philosophy in a Time of Terror: Dialogues with Jürgen Habermas and Jacques Derrida*, Chicago, IL: University of Chicago Press.

—— (2005a) *On Touching – Jean-Luc Nancy*, trans. Christine Irizarry, Stanford: University of Stanford Press.

—— (2005b) *Rogues: Two Essays on Reason*, Stanford: Stanford University Press.

—— (2006) *Deconstruction Engaged: The Sydney Seminars*, ed. Paul Patton and Terry Smith, Sydney: Power Publications.

Dessler, David (1989) 'What's at Stake in the Agency and Structure Debate?', *International Organization*, 43 (3): 441–74.

—— (1991) 'Beyond Correlations: Towards a Causal Theory of War', *International Studies Quarterly*, 35 (3): 337–55.

Devetak, Richard (2005) 'The Gothic Scene of International Relations: ghosts, monsters, terror and the sublime after September 11', *Review of International Studies*, 31: 621–43.

Dews, Peter (2004) 'States of Grace: The Excess of the Demand in Badiou's Ethics of Truths', in Peter Hallward (ed.) *Think Again. Alain Badiou and the Future of Philosophy*, London: Continuum, 106–19.

Dick, Kirby and Kofman, Amy Ziering (2003) *Derrida*, Jane Doe Films.

Dietelhoff, Nicole and Müller, Harald, (2005) 'Theoretical Paradise – Empirically Lost? Arguing with Habermas', *Review of International Studies*, 31: 167–79.

Diez, Thomas and Stearns, Jill (2005) 'A Useful Dialogue? Habermas and International Relations', *Review of International Studies* 31: 127–40.

Dillon, Michael (2005) 'A Passion for the (Im)possible. Jacques Rancière, Equality, Pedagogy and the Messianic', *European Journal of Political Theory*, 4 (4): 429–52.

Dillon, Michael and Neal, Andrew (eds) (2008) *Foucault on Politics, Security and War*, London: Palgrave.

Dostoevsky, Fyodor (1970) *The Brothers Karamazov*, New York: Bantam Books.

Doty, Roxanne Lynn (2006) 'Fronteras Compasivas and the Ethics of Unconditional Hospitality', *Millennium: Journal of International Studies*, 35 (1): 53–74.

—— (2007) 'States of Exception on the Mexico–U.S. Border: Security, "Decisions" and Civilian Border Patrols', *International Political Sociology*, 1 (1): 113–37.

Drabinski, John (2000) 'The Possibility of an Ethical Politics: From Peace to Liturgy', *Philosophy and Social Criticism* 26 (4): 49–73.

Dryzek, John (2000) *Deliberative Democracy and Beyond: Liberals, Critics, Contestations*, Oxford: Oxford University Press.

Durst, David C. (1998) 'Heidegger on the Problem of Metaphysics and Violence', *Heidegger Studies* 14: 93–110.

Dussel, Enrique (1998) 'Beyond Eurocentrism: The world system and the limits of modernity' in Fredric Jameson and Masao Miyoshi (eds) *The Cultures of Globalization*, Durham, NC: Duke University Press.

Dyzenhaus, David (1998) 'Introduction: why Carl Schmitt?' in David Dyzenhaus (ed.) *Law as Politics: Carl Schmitt's critique of liberalism*, Durham, NC: Duke University Press.

Eagleton, Terry (1981) *Walter Benjamin, or, Towards a revolutionary criticism*, London: NLB.

—— (1990) *Ideology*, London: Verso.

Edkins, Jenny (1999) *Poststructuralism and International Relations: Bringing the Political Back In*, Boulder, CO: Lynne Rienner.

—— (2000) *Whose Hunger: Concepts of Famine, Practices of Aid*. Minneapolis; University of Minnesota Press.

—— (2002) 'War Stories, War Silences – September 11 and the Timing of Memory', paper presented at the International Studies Association Annual Convention, New Orleans.

—— (2003a) *Trauma and the Memory of Politics*. Cambridge: Cambridge University Press.

—— (2003b) 'Humanitarianism, humanity, human', *Journal of Human Rights*, 2 (2): 253–58.

—— (2007a) 'Missing Persons: Manhattan September 2001' in Elizabeth Dauphinee and Cristina Masters (eds) *The Logics of Biopower and the War on Terror: Living, Dying, Surviving*, Basingstoke and New York: Palgrave Macmillan, pp. 25–42.

—— (2007b) 'Whatever politics', in Calarco, Matthew and Steven DeCaroli (eds) *Sovereignty and Life: Essays on Giorgio Agamben*, Stanford: Stanford University Press.

——and Zehfuss, Maja (2005) 'Generalising the International', *Review of International Studies* 31 (3): 451–72.

—— and Walker, R.B.J. (eds) (2000) 'Zones of Indistinction: Territories, Bodies, Politics', Special Issue, *Alternatives: Global, Local, Political*, 25 (1).

—— and Pin-Fat, Véronique (2004) 'Introduction: Life, Power, Resistance' in Jenny Edkins, Véronique Pin-Fat and Michael J. Shapiro (eds) *Sovereign Lives: Power in Global Politics*, London and New York: Routledge, 1–23.

—— (2005) 'Through the wire: Relations of power and relations of violence', *Millennium: Journal of International Studies*, 34 (1): 1–25.

——, Pin-Fat, Véronique and Shapiro, Michael J. (eds) (2004) *Sovereign Lives: Power in World Politics*, London and New York: Routledge.

Ek, Richard (2006) 'Giorgio Agamben and the Spatialities of the Camp', *Geografiska Annaler*, 88 (B) (4): 363–86.

Elliot, Anthony (2004) *Social Theory since Freud: Self and Society after Freud*, London and New York: Routledge.

Enloe, Cynthia (1989) *Bananas, Beaches and Bases: making feminist sense of international politics*, London: Pandora.

Fagan, Madeleine, Glorieux, Ludovic, Hasimbegovic, Indira and Suetsugu, Marie (eds) (2007) *Derrida: Negotiating the Legacy*, Edinburgh: Edinburgh University Press.

Fanon, Frantz (1963) *The Wretched of the Earth*, New York: Grove Press.
—— (1967a) *A Dying Colonialism*, trans. Haakon Chevalier with an Introduction by Adolfo Gilly, New York: Grove Weidenfeld.
—— (1967b) *Black Skin, White Masks*, trans. Charles Lam Markmann, New York: Grove Weidenfeld.
—— (2004) *The Wretched of the Earth*, trans. Richard Philcox with commentary by Jean-Paul Sartre and Homi K. Bhabha, New York: Grove Press.
Ferris, David S. (ed.) (2004) *The Cambridge Companion to Walter Benjamin*, Cambridge: Cambridge University Press.
Fine, Robert (2000) 'Crimes against Humanity: Hannah Arendt and the Nuremburg Debates', *European Journal of Social Theory* 3 (3): 293–311.
Finlayson, James Gordon (2005) *Habermas: A Very Short Introduction*, Oxford: Oxford University Press.
Flikschuh, Katrin (2000) *Kant and Modern Political Philosophy*, Cambridge: Cambridge University Press.
Foucault, Michel (1974) *The Order of Things: archaeology of the human sciences*, London: Tavistock.
—— (1978) *The History of Sexuality, the Will to Knowledge*, trans. by Robert Hurley, Vol. 1, New York: Random House.
—— (1980) 'Truth and Power', in *Power/Knowledge: Selected Interviews and Other Writings 1972–1977*, ed. Colin Gordon, New York: Harvester Wheatsheaf, 109–33.
—— (1984) 'Nietzsche, Genealogy, History', in Paul Rabinow (ed.) *The Foucault Reader*, London: Penguin Books.
—— (1985) *The History of Sexuality: The Use of Pleasure*, Vol. 2, London: Penguin.
—— (1990) *The History of Sexuality: The Care of the Self*, trans. Robert Hurley, Vol. 3, London: Penguin.
—— (1991) 'Nietzsche, Genealogy, History', in *The Foucault Reader*, ed. Paul Rabinow, London: Penguin, 76–100.
—— (1994) *The Birth of the Clinic: An Archaeology of the Medical Perception*, New York: Vintage.
—— (1999) *Discipline and Punish: The Birth of the Prison*, trans. by Alan Sheridan, London: Penguin.
—— (2001) *Madness and Civilization: A History of Insanity in the Age of Reason*, trans. Richard Howard, London: Routledge.
—— (2002a) *The Archaeology of Knowledge*, trans. by A.M. Sheridan Smith, London: Routledge.
—— (2002b) *'Society Must Be Defended': Lectures at the Collège de France, 1975–76*, trans. David Macey, New York: Picador.
—— (2007) *Security, Territory, Population: Lectures at the Collège de France, 1977–78*, Basingstoke: Palgrave Macmillan.
——, and Colin Gordon (1980) *Power/Knowledge: Selected Interviews and Other Writings, 1972/1977*, Brighton: Harvester Press.
——, Bouchard, Donald Fernand, and Simon, Sherry (1977) *Language, Counter-Memory, Practice: Selected Essays and Interviews*, Oxford: Blackwell.
Foucault.info. (2008) *Biography*, http://foucault.info/foucault/biography.html, (accessed 14 April 2008).
Franks, Mary Anne (2003) 'Obscene Undersides: Women and Evil Between the Taliban and the United States', *Hypatia* 18 (1): 135–56.

Fraser, Nancy (1991) 'From Irony to Prophecy to Politics: A Response to Richard Rorty', *Michigan Quarterly Review* 30 (2): 259–66

—— (1992) 'The Uses and Abuses of French Discourse Theories for Feminist Politics', *Theory Culture & Society*, 9: 51–71.

Frede, Dorothea (1993) 'The question of being: Heidegger's project', in Charles Guignon (ed.) *The Cambridge Companion to Heidegger*, Cambridge: Cambridge University Press, 42–69.

Freud, Sigmund (1959) [1922] *Group Psychology and the Analysis of the Ego*, London: Hogarth.

—— (1994) [1930] *Civilization and its Discontents*, New York: Dover Publications.

—— (2000) [1933] 'Why War?', in David Barash (ed.) *Approaches to Peace: A Reader in Peace Studies*, Oxford: Oxford University Press.

Frisby, David (1985) *Fragments of modernity: theories of modernity in the work of Simmel, Kracauer and Benjamin*, Cambridge: Polity.

—— (2001) *Cityscapes of modernity: critical explorations*, Cambridge: Polity.

Fromm, Erich (1941) *Escape from Freedom*, New York: Holt, Rinehart and Winston.

Frost, Lola (2007) Unpublished PhD thesis, Department of Fine Art, Goldsmiths College, University of London.

Frost, Mervyn (1996) *Ethics in International Relations: a Constitutive Theory*, Cambridge: Cambridge University Press.

Galli, Carlo (1996) *Genealogia della politica: Carl Schmitt e la crisi del pensiero politico moderno*, Bologna: Il Mulino.

Gandhi, Mohandas Karamchand (1993) *An Autobiography: My Experiments with Truth*, Boston: Beacon Press.

Gane, Mike (2000) *Jean Baudrillard: In Radical Uncertainty*, London: Pluto Press.

George, Larry N. (2002), 'The Pharmacotic War on Terrorism: Cure or Poison for the US Body Politic?', *Theory, Culture & Society* 19 (4): 161–86.

Geras, Norman (1995) *Solidarity in the Conversation of Humankind: The Ungroundable Liberalism of Richard Rorty*, London: Verso.

Germino, Dante (1990) *Antonio Gramsci: Architect of a New Politics*, Baton Rouge: Louisiana State University Press.

Gill, Stephen (1990) *American Hegemony and the Trilateral Commission*, Cambridge: Cambridge University Press.

—— (1993) *Gramsci, Historical Materialism, and International Relations*, Cambridge: Cambridge University Press.

—— (1995) 'Globalization, Market Civilization, and Disciplinary Neoliberalism', *Millennium: Journal of International Studies* 24: 399–423.

—— and Mittelman, James (1997) *Innovation and Transformation in International Studies*, Cambridge: Cambridge University Press.

Gilloch, Graeme (2002) *Walter Benjamin: critical constellations*, Cambridge: Polity Press in association with Blackwell Publishers Ltd.

Gottfried, Paul (1990) *Carl Schmitt: politics and theory*, Westport, CT: Greenwood Press.

Gramsci, Antonio (1971) *Selections from the Prison Notebooks*, New York: International Publishers.

Grosholz, Emily R. (ed.) (2004) *The Legacy of Simone de Beauvoir*, Oxford: Clarendon Press.

Grosz, Elizabeth A. (1999) Becoming ... An Introduction, in Grosz, Elizabeth. A. (ed.) *Becomings: explorations in time, memory and futures*, Ithaca: Cornell University Press.

Guberman, Ross, M. (1996) 'A Conversation with Julia Kristeva', Interview conducted by Ina Lipkowitz and Andrea Losselle, New York: Columbia University Press.

Guignon, Charles (1993) 'Introduction', in Charles Guignon (ed.) *The Cambridge Companion to Heidegger*, Cambridge: Cambridge University Press.

Guzzini, Stefano (2000) 'A Reconstruction of Constructivism in International Relations', *European Journal of International Relations*, 6 (2): 147–82.

Haacke, Jürgen (2005) 'The Frankfurt School and International Relations: On the Centrality of Recognition', *Review of International Studies,* 31:181–94.

Habermas, Jürgen (1971) *Knowledge and Human Interests*, Boston: Beacon Press.

—— (1979) 'What is Universal Pragmatics?', in Jürgen Habermas *Communication and the Evolution of Society*, Boston: Beacon Press, 1–68.

—— (1983) 'Hannah Arendt: On the Concept of Power', *Philosophical–Political Profiles*, London: Heinemann, 171–87.

—— (1984/1987) *The Theory of Communicative Action*, vols 1 and 2, Boston: Beacon Press.

—— (1986) *Autonomy and Solidarity: Interviews*, edited and introduced by Peter Dews, London: Verso.

—— (1990a) 'Discourse Ethics: Notes on a Program of Philosophical Justification,', in *Moral Consciousness and Communicative Action*, Cambridge: MIT Press, 43–115.

—— (1990b) 'Moral Consciousness and Communicative Action', in *Moral Consciousness and Communicative Action*, Cambridge: MIT Press, pp. 116–94.

—— (1993a), *Justification and Application: Remarks on Discourse Ethics*, Cambridge: MIT Press.

—— (1993b) 'Morality, Society, and Ethics: An Interview with Torben Hviid Nielsen', in Jürgen Habermas, *Justification and Application: Remarks on Discourse Ethics*, Cambridge: MIT Press.

—— (1996) *Between Facts and Norms: Contributions to a Discourse Theory of Law and Democracy*, Cambridge, MA: MIT Press.

—— (1998), 'Kant's Idea of Perpetual Peace: At Two Hundred Years' Historical Remove', in Jürgen Habermas *The Inclusion of the Other: Studies in Political Theory*, Cambridge: MIT Press.

—— (2006) *The Divided West*, ed. and trans. Ciaran Cronin, Cambridge: Polity Press.

—— and Derrida, Jacques (2003) *Philosophy in a Time of Terror: dialogues with Jürgen Habermas and Jacques Derrida*, Chicago: University of Chicago Press.

Hall, Stuart (1997) 'Old and New Identities, Old and New Ethnicities', in *Culture, Globalization and the World-System*, edited by A. King, Minneapolis: University of Minnesota Press, 41–68.

Hallward, Peter (2002) 'Badiou's Politics: Equality and Justice', *Culture Machine* 4. http://culturemachine.tees.ac.uk/Cmach/Backissues/j004/Articles/hallward.htm (accessed 30 June 2007).

—— (2003) *Alain Badiou: Subject to Truth*, Minnesota: Minnesota University Press.

—— (2004) 'Introduction: "Consequences of Abstraction"', in Peter Hallward (ed.) *Think Again. Alain Badiou and the future of philosophy*, London: Continuum (1–20).

Hanlon, Christopher (2001) 'Psychoanalysis and the Post-Political: An Interview with Slavoj Žižek' *New Literary History*, 32: 1–21.

Hansen, Lene (1997) 'A Case for Seduction?' *Cooperation and Conflict*, 32 (4): 369–97.

Hanssen, Beatrice (1998) *Walter Benjamin's other history: of stones, animals, human beings, and angels*, Berkeley and London: University of California Press.

Hardt, Michael and Negri, Antonio (2005) *Multitude: War and Democracy in the Age of Empire*, London: Penguin.

Harré, Rom and Madden, Edward H. (1975) *Causal Powers: A Theory of Natural Necessity*, Oxford: Blackwell.

Harvey, David (1990) *The Conditions of Postmodernity: An inquiry into the origins of cultural change*, Cambridge, MA: Blackwell.

—— (2003) *Paris, capital of modernity*, New York and London: Routledge.

Hayden, Patrick (2007) 'Superfluous Humanity: An Arendtian Perspective on the Political Evil of Global Poverty', *Millennium: Journal of International Studies* 35 (2): 279–300.

Hegarty, Paul (2004) *Jean Baudrillard: Live Theory*, London: Continuum.

Hegde, Radha, S. and Shome, Raka (2002) 'Postcolonial Scholarship – Productions and Directions: An interview with Gayatri Chakravorty Spivak', *Communication Theory*, 12 (3): 271–86.

Hegel, G.W.F. (1976) *Hegel's Philosophy of Right*, trans. with notes T.M Knox, Oxford: Oxford University Press.

—— (1977) *Phenomenology of Spirit*, trans. A.V. Miller, Oxford: Oxford University Press.

—— (2001) *Philosophy of World History*, trans. J. Sibree, Kitchener, Ontario: Batoche Books.

Heidegger, Martin (1962) *Being and Time*, trans. John Macquarie and Edward Robinson, Oxford: Blackwell.

—— (1967) *What is a Thing?* trans. W.B. Barton, Jr. and V. Deutsch, Chicago: Henry Regnery.

—— (1968) *What is Called Thinking?* trans. J.G. Gray, New York: Harper and Row.

—— (1977a) 'The age of the world picture', trans. W. Lovitt, in *The Question Concerning Technology and Other Essays*, New York: Harper and Row, 115–54.

—— (1977b) 'The question concerning technology', trans. W. Lovitt, in *The Question Concerning Technology and Other Essays*, New York: Harper and Row, 3–35.

—— (1977c) 'Only a god can save us now: an interview with Martin Heidegger', *Graduate Faculty Philosophy Journal* 6(1): 5–27.

—— (1982) *The Basic Problems of Phenomenology*, trans. A. Hofstadter, revised ed., Bloomington: Indiana University Press.

—— (1991a) *Nietzsche*, trans. D.F. Krell, Vol. IV: Nihilism, New York: Harper and Row.

—— (1991b) *Nietzsche*, trans. David F. Krell, Vols 1–4, New York: harper and Row.

—— (1992) 'Phenomenological interpretations with respect to Aristotle: indication of the hermeneutical situation', *Man and World* 25: 355–93.

—— (1998) 'Letter on humanism', trans. F.A. Capuzzi, in William McNeill (ed.), *Pathways*, Cambridge: Cambridge University Press, 239–76.

—— (1999a) *Ontology: the hermeneutics of facticity*, trans. J. van Buren, Bloomington: Indiana University Press.

—— (1999b) *Contributions to Philosophy (From Enowning)*, trans. P. Emad and K. Maly, Bloomington: Indiana University Press.

Held, David (2004) *Critical Theory: Horkheimer to Habermas*, Cambridge: Polity Press.

Hempel, Carl G. (ed.) (1965) *Aspects of Scientific Explanation and Other Essays in the Philosophy of Science*, London: Macmillan/Free Press.

Herman, Ellen (1995) *The Romance of American Psychology: Political Culture in an Age of Experts*, Berkeley: California University Press.

Herzog, Annabel (2004) 'Political Itineraries and Anarchic Cosmopolitanism in the Thought of Hannah Arendt', *Inquiry* 47: 20–41.

Hobsbawn, Eric (1994) *Age of Extremes: the short twentieth century 1914–1991*, London: Abacus.

Hoffman, Mark (1987) 'Critical Theory and the Inter-Paradigm Debate', *Millennium: Journal of International Studies*, 16 (2): 231–49.

Hofman, Klaus (2005) 'Poetry after Auschwitz – Adorno's Dictum', *German Life and Letters*, 58 (2): 182–94.

Hollis, Martin (1994) *The Philosophy of Social Science: An Introduction*, Cambridge: Cambridge University Press.

Hollis, Martin and Smith, Steve (1990) *Explaining and Understanding International Relations*, Oxford: Clarendon Press.

Honig, Bonnie (1991) 'Declarations of Independence: Arendt and Derrida on the Problem of Founding a Republic', *American Political Science Review* 85 (1): 97–114.

—— (1993) 'The Politics of Agonism: A Critical Response to "Beyond Good and Evil: Arendt, Nietzsche, and the Aestheticization of Political Action" by Dana R. Villa', *Political Theory* 21 (3): 528–33.

—— (ed.) (1995) *Feminist Interpretations of Hannah Arendt*, Pennsylvania: Pennsylvania State University Press.

Hoogvelt, Ankie (2001) *Globalization and the Postcolonial World*, 2nd edn, Basingstoke: Palgrave.

Horkheimer, Max (1972) 'Traditional and Critical Theory' in *Critical Theory: Selected Essays*, New York: Seabury Press. Jarvis, Simon (1998) *Adorno: A Critical Introduction*, Cambridge: Polity Press.

—— (2004) *Eclipse of Reason*, London: Continuum.

Horkheimer, Max and Adorno. Theodor (1972) *Dialectic of Enlightenment*, trans. John Cumming, Seabury, New York: Continuum.

Hull, Isabel V. (2005) *Absolute Destruction: Military Culture and the Practices of War in Imperial Germany*, Ithaca: Cornell University Press.

Hurrell, Andrew (1990) 'Kant and the Kantian Paradigm in International Relations', *Review of International Studies*, 16: 183–205.

Hutchings, Kimberly (1996) *Kant, Critique and Politics*, London: Routledge.

—— (2003) *Hegel and Feminist Philosophy*, Cambridge: Polity Press.

—— (2005) 'Speaking and Hearing: Habermasian Discourse Ethics, Feminism and IR', *Review of International Studies*, 31:155–65.

—— (2007a) 'Time and Critique in International Relations theory', *Review of International Studies Special Issue*, 33: 71–90.

—— (2007b) 'Simone de Beauvoir and the Ambiguous Ethics of Political Violence', *Hypatia: Journal of Feminist Philosophy*, 22 (3): 111–32.

Hyppolite, Jean (1997) [1954] *Logic and Existence*, New York: State University of New York Press.

Ijsseling, Samuel (1982) 'Heidegger and the Destruction of Ontology', *Man and World*, 15: 3–16.

Inayatullah, Naeem and Blaney, David (2004) *International Relations and the Problem of Difference*, London: Routledge.

Inwood, Michael (1999) *A Heidegger Dictionary*, Oxford: Blackwell.

Isaac, Jeffrey C. (1996) 'A New Guarantee on Earth: Hannah Arendt on Human Dignity and the Politics of Human Rights', *American Political Science Review* 90 (1): 61–73.

—— (2002) 'Hannah Arendt on Human Rights and the Limits of Exposure, or Why Noam Chomsky is Wrong about the Meaning of Kosovo', *Social Research* 69 (2): 263–95.

—— (2002) *Arendt, Camus, and Modern Rebellion*, New Haven: Yale University Press.

Jabri, Vivienne (1998) 'Restyling the Subject of Responsibility in International Relations', *Millennium: Journal of International Studies*, 27 (3): 591–611.

—— (2001) 'Restyling the Subject of Responsibility in International Relations', in Hakan Seckinelgin and Hideaki Shinoda (eds) *Ethics and International Relations*, Basingstoke: Palgrave, 161–84.

—— (2004) 'Feminist Ethics and Hegemonic Global Politics', *Alternatives* 29: 265–84.

—— (2006) 'Shock and Awe: Power and the Resistance of Art', *Millennium: Journal of International Studies*, 34 (3): 819–39.

Jackson, Patrick.T. and Krebs, Ronald R. (2007) 'Twisting Tongues and Twisting Arms: the power of political rhetoric', *European Journal of International Relations*, 13 (1): 35–66.

Jackson, Peter (2008) 'Pierre Bourdieu, the "Cultural Turn" and the practice of international history', *Review of International Studies*, 34 (1): 155–81.

Jacoby, Russell (1977) *Social Amnesia: A Critique of Conformist Psychology from Adler to Laing*, Hassocks: Harvester Press.

James, Ian (2006) *The Fragmentary Demand: An Introduction to the Philosophy of Jean-Luc Nancy*, Stanford: University of Stanford Press.

Jameson, Fredric (1971) 'Walter Benjamin, or Nostalgia', in *Marxism and Form: Twentieth Century Dialectical Theories of Literature*, Princeton: Princeton University Press.

Jarvis, Simon (1998) *Adorno: A Critical Introduction*, Cambridge: Polity Press.

Jay, Martin (1993) 'Name-Dropping or Dropping Name? Modes of Legitimation in the Humanities', *Force Field: Between Intellectual History and Cultural Critique*, New York: Routledge.

—— (1996a) *The Dialectical Imagination: A History of the Frankfurt School and the Institute of Social Research, 1923–1950*, Berkeley: University of California Press.

—— (1996b) 'Urban Flights: The Institute of Social Research between Frankfurt and New York', in David M. Rasmussen (ed.) *The Handbook of Critical Theory*, Oxford: Blackwell.

Jenkins, Richard (2002) *Pierre Bourdieu*, 2nd ed., London: Routledge.

Jepperson, Ronald, Wendt, Alexander and Katzenstein, Peter (1996) 'Norms, Identity and Culture in National Security', in Peter Katzenstein (ed.) *The Culture of National Security*, New York: Columbia University Press, 33–75.

Johnson, Barbara (1981) 'Translator's Introduction', in Jacques Derrida, *Dissemination*, trans. Barbara Johnson, Chicago: University of Chicago Press.

Johnson, Chalmers (2004) *Blowback: The Costs and Consequences of American Empire*, 2nd edn, New York: Owl Books.

Joll, James (1968) '1914: the unspoken assumptions. An Inaugural Lecture', London: London School of Economics.

—— (1992) *The Origins of the First World War*, 2nd ed., London: Longman.

Joseph, Jonathan (2007) 'Philosophy in International Relations: a Scientific Realist Approach', *Millennium: Journal of International Studies*, 35 (2): 345–59.

Judovitz, Dalia (1988) *Subjectivity and Representation in Descartes: the origins of modernity*, Cambridge: Cambridge University Press.

Kalyvas, Andreas (2005) 'The Sovereign Weaver: Beyond the Camp', in: Andrew Norris (ed.), *Politics, Metaphysics, and Death: Essays on Giorgio Agamben's Homo Sacer*, Durham and London: Duke University Press.

Kant, Immanuel (1956) *Critique of Practical Reason* trans. Lewis White Beck, New York: Macmillan.

—— (1983) *Critique of Pure Reason*, trans. Norman Kemp Smith, London: Macmillan.

—— (1991) *Kant: political writings*, ed. Hans Reiss, trans. H. B. Nisbet, Cambridge: Cambridge University Press.

Kateb, George (1984) *Hannah Arendt: Politics, Conscience, Evil*, Totowa, NJ: Rowman and Allanheld.

Kauffman, Walter (1974) *Nietzsche: Philosopher, Psychologist, Anti-Christ*, Princeton: Princeton University Press.

Kaufman-Osborn, Timothy (2008) 'Gender Trouble at Abu Ghraib?', in Terrell Carver and Samuel A. Chambers (eds) *Judith Butler's Precarious Politics: Critical Encounters*, London: Routledge, 204–20.

Kearney, Richard (1994) *Modern Movements in European Philosophy*, Manchester: Manchester University Press.

Kellner, Douglas *Critical Theory, Marxism and Modernity*. Baltimore MD: Johns Hopkins University Press, 1989.

Keohane, Robert Owen (1988) 'International Institutions: Two Approaches', *International Studies Quarterly*, 32: 379–96.

——, and Nye, Joseph S., (1977) *Power and Interdependence: World Politics in Transition*, New York: Little Brown.

Keyman, Fuat (1997) *Globalization, State, Identity/Difference: Toward a Critical Social Theory of International Relations*, New Jersey: Humanities Press.

King, Gary., Keohane, Robert O. and Verba. Sidney (1994) *Designing Social Inquiry; Scientific Inference in Qualitative Research*, Princeton: Princeton University Press.

Kingsnorth, Paul (2003) *One No, Many Yeses: A Journey to the Heart of the Global Resistance Movement*. London: Free Press.

Kinnvall, Catarina (2007) 'Civilizations, Neo-Gandhianism and the Hindu Self', in Martin Hall and Patrick Jackson, *Civilizational Identity: The production and Reproduction of 'Civilizations' in International Relations*, New York: Palgrave.

Kinsella, Helen M. (2008) 'Arendt and Analogies' *International Politics* 45(4), (July), pp. 437–505.

Kisiel, Theodore (1993) *The Genesis of Heidegger's Being and Time*, Berkeley: University of California Press.

Klossowski, Pierre (1997) *Nietzsche and the Vicious Circle*, trans. Daniel Smith, London: Athlone.

Klusmeyer, Douglas (2005) 'Hannah Arendt's Critical *Realism*: Power, Justice, and Responsibility', in Anthony F. Lang Jr. and John Williams (eds) *Hannah Arendt and International Relations: Readings Across the Lines*, London: Palgrave, 113–78.

Knorr, Klaus and Rosenau. James N. (eds) (1969) *Contending Approaches to International Politics*, Princeton: Princeton University Press.

Kojeve, Alexandre (1969) *Introduction to the Reading of Hegel*, ed. Allan Bloom, trans. James H. Nichols, Jr., New York: Basic Books.

Kristeva, Julia (1982) *Powers of Horror: An Essay on Abjection*, New York: Columbia University Press.
—— (1984) *Revolution in Poetic Language*, trans. M. Waller, New York: Columbia University Press.
—— (1986) 'Women's Time', in Toril Moi (ed.) *The Kristeva Reader*, Oxford: Blackwell Publishers, 188–213.
—— (1991) *Strangers to Ourselves*, trans. Leon S. Roudiez, New York: Columbia University Press.
—— (1993) *Nations Without Nationalism*, trans. Leon S. Roudiez, New York: Columbia University Press.
—— (2000) *Crisis of the European Subject*, trans. Susan Fairfield, New York: Other Press.
—— (2002a) 'Revolt, She Said, an Interview by Philippe Petit', trans. Brian O'Keeffe and edited by Sylvere Lotringer, Los Angeles, CA: Semiotext(e).
—— (2002b) *The Intimate Revolt*, trans. Jeanine Herman, New York: Columbia University Press.
Kroker, Arthur (1992) *The Possessed Individual: Technology and the French Postmodern*, New York: St. Martin's Press.
Kruks, Sonia (2001) *Retrieving Experience: subjectivity and recognition in feminist politics*, Ithaca NY: Cornell University Press.
Kuhn, Thomas (1962) *The Structure of Scientific Revolutions*, Chicago: University of Chicago Press.
Kumar Rajaram, Prem and Grundy-Warr, Carl (2004) 'The Irregular Migrant as Homo Sacer: Migration and Detention in Australia, Malaysia and Thailand', *International Migration*, 42 (1): 33–64.
—— (eds) (2007) *Borderscapes: Hidden Geographies and Politics and Territory's Edge*, Minneapolis and London: University of Minnesota Press.
Kurki, Milja (2006) 'Causes of a divided discipline: rethinking the concept of cause in International Relations theory', *Review of International Studies*, 32 (2): 189–216.
—— (2007) 'Critical Realism and Causal Analysis in International Relations theory', *Millennium: Journal of International Studies*, 35 (2): 361–78.
—— (2008) *Causation in International Relations: Reclaiming Causal Analysis*, Cambridge: Cambridge University Press.
Lacan, Jacques (1990) *Television: A Challenge to the Psychoanalytic Establishment*, trans. Jeffrey Mehlman, New York: Norton.
—— (1992) *The Seminar of Jacques Lacan, Book VII: The Ethics of Psychoanalysis, 1959–1960*, (ed.) Jacques-Alain Miller, trans. Dennis Porter, New York: Norton.
—— (1998) *The Seminar of Jacques Lacan, Book XI: The Four Fundamental Concepts of Psychoanalysis*, ed. Jacques-Alain Miller, trans. Alan Sheridan, New York: Norton.
Laclau, Ernesto (2005) 'On real and absolute enemies', *CR: The New Centennial Review*, 5: 1–12.
—— and Chantal Mouffe (1985) *Hegemony and Socialist Strategy: Towards a Radical Democratic Politics*, trans. Winston Moore and Paul Cammack, London: Verso.
Lacoue-Labarthe, Philippe and Nancy, Jean-Luc (1997) *Retreating the Political*, edited by Simon Sparks, London: Routledge.
Landry, Donna and MacLean, Gerald (1996). *The Spivak Reader: Selected Works of Gayatri Chakravorty Spivak*, London: Routledge.
Lang Jr., Anthony F. (2001) *Agency and Ethics: The Politics of Military Intervention*, New York: State University of New York Press.

——, Anthony F. and John Williams (eds) (2005) *Hannah Arendt and International Relations: Readings Across the Lines*, London: Palgrave Press.

Lausten, Carsten and Diken, Bulent (2002), 'Zones of Indistinction: Security, Terror, and Bare Life', *Space and Culture*, 5 (3): 290–307.

Leander, Anna (2002) 'Do we really need reflexivity in IPE? Bourdieu's two reasons for answering affirmatively (contribution to a colloquium on Pierre Bourdieu)', *Review of International Political Economy*, 9 (4): 601–9.

—— (2005) 'The Power to Construct International Security: On the Significance of Private Military Companies', *Millennium: Journal of International Studies* 33 (3): 803–26.

—— (2007) 'Thinking Tools: Analyzing Symbolic Power and Violence', in Audie Klotz and Deepa Prakash (eds) *Qualitative Methods in International Relations*, London: Palgrave.

Levinas, Emmanuel (1969) *Totality and Infinity: an essay on exteriority*, trans. A. Lingis, The Hague: Martinus Nijhof.

—— (1989) *The Levinas Reader*, Sean Hand (ed.) Oxford: Blackwell.

—— (1998) *Of God Who Comes to Mind*, trans. Bettina Bergo, Stanford: Stanford University Press.

—— (2002) *Otherwise Than Being or Beyond Essence*, trans. Alphonso Lingis, Pittsburgh: Duquesne University Press.

Linklater, Andrew (1990) *Beyond Realism and Marxism: Critical Theory and International Relations*, Basingstoke: Macmillan.

—— (1996) 'The achievements of critical theory', in Steve Smith, Ken Booth and Marysia Zalewski (eds) *International Theory: Positivism and Beyond*, Cambridge: Cambridge University Press.

—— (1998) *The Transformation of Political Community: Ethical Foundations of the Post-Westphalian Era*, Columbia, SC: University of South Carolina Press.

—— (2001) 'Rationalism', in Scott Burchill, Richard Devetak, Andrew Linklater, Matthew Paterson, Christin Reus-Smit and Jacqui True, *Theories of International Relations*, New York: Palgrave.

—— (2005) 'Dialogic Politics and the Civilizing Process', *Review of International Studies*, 31: 131–54.

—— (2007a) 'Distant Suffering and Cosmopolitan Obligations', *International Politics*, 44 (1): 19–36.

—— (2007b) 'Towards a sociology of global morals with an "emancipatory intent"', *Review of International Studies* 33: 135–50.

Luban, David (1983) 'Explaining Dark Times: Hannah Arendt's Theory of Theory', *Social Research* 50 (1): 215–48.

Luke, Timothy W. (1989) 'What's Wrong with Deterrence? A Semiotic Interpretation of National Security Policy', in James Der Derian and Michael J. Shapiro (eds) *International/Intertextual Relations: Postmodern Readings of World Politics*, New York: Lexington Books, 207–29.

—— (1991) 'The Discipline of Security Studies and the Codes of Containment: Learning from Kuwait', *Alternatives: Global, Local, Political*, 16 (3): 315–44.

—— (1993) 'Discourses of Disintegration, Texts of Transformation: Re-Reading Realism in the New World Order', *Alternatives: Global, Local, Political*, 18 (2): 229–58.

Lynch, Marc (2000) 'The Dialogue of Civilizations and International Public Spheres', *Millennium: Journal of International Studies*, 29: 307–30.

—— (2002) 'Why Engage? China and the Logic of Communicative Engagement', *European Journal of International Relations*, 8: 187–230.

MacCabe, Colin (1998) 'Foreword', in Gayatri Chakravorty Spivak, *Spivak: In Other Worlds*, New York: Routledge.

Macdonald, Amanda (2003) 'Working up, working out, working through: translator's notes on the dimensions of Jean-Luc Nancy's thought', *Postcolonial Studies*, 6 (1): 11–21.

Mamdani, Mahmood (2004) *Good Muslim, Bad Muslim: America, the Cold War, and the Roots of Terror*, New York: Three Leaves.

Marcuse, Herbert (1991) *One Dimensional Man: Studies in the ideology of advanced industrial society*, London: Routledge, second edition.

Marx, Karl (1970) 'Theses on Feuerbach', in *Marx and Engels: selected works*, London: Lawrence and Wishart.

—— 'On the Jewish Question', various printings.

—— *Communist Manifesto*. various printings.

Marx, Karl Preface to *A Contribution to a Critique of Political Economy*, various printings.

Matsuda, Mari (2002) 'Among the mourners who mourn, why should I among them be?', *Signs: Journal of Women in Culture and Society* 28 (1): 475–77.

Mauss, Marcel (1990) *The Gift: The Form and Reason for Exchange in Archaic Societies*, New York: Norton.

Mbembe, Achille (2003) 'Necropolitics', *Public Culture*, 15: 11–40.

McCormack, Brian (2002) 'Postcolonialism in an Age of Globalization: Opening International Relations Theory to Identities in Movement', *Alternatives: Global, Local, Political*, 27 (1): 99–116.

McCumber, John (1999) *Metaphysics and Oppression: Heidegger's challenge to western philosophy*, Bloomington: Indiana University Press.

Mead, Rebecca (2003) 'The Marx Brother: How a Philosopher From Slovenia Became an International Star' *The New Yorker, May 5*.

Mehta, Uday (1999) *Liberalism and Empire: A Study in Nineteenth Century British Liberal Thought*, Chicago: University of Chicago Press.

Menke, Christoph (1999) 'Modernity and subjectivity: from an aesthetic point of view', *Graduate Faculty Philosophy Journal*, 21 (2): 217–32.

Midnight Notes Collective (1998) Midnight Notes 12: One No, Many Yeses. http://www.midnightnotes.org/oneno.html (Accessed 10 April 2008).

Mills, Catherine (2008) *The Philosophy of Agamben*, Stocksfield: Acumen.

Moi, Toril (2004a) 'Meaning What We Say: the "politics of theory" and the responsibility of intellectuals', in Emily Grosholz (ed.) *The Legacy of Simone de Beauvoir*, Oxford: Clarendon Press, 139–60.

—— (2004b) 'While We Wait: notes on the English translation of *The Second Sex*', in Emily Grosholz (ed.) *The Legacy of Simone de Beauvoir*, Oxford: Clarendon Press, 37–68.

Molloy, Patricia. (1999) 'Face to Face with the Dead Man: Ethical Responsibility, State-Sanctioned Killing, and Empathetic Impossibility', in David Campbell and Michael J. Shapiro (eds) *Moral Spaces: Rethinking Ethics and World Politics*, Minneapolis: University of Minnesota Press.

Morgan, Jamie (2002) 'Philosophical Realism in International Relations Theory: Kratochwil's Constructivist Challenge to Wendt', *Journal of Critical Realism*, 1 (1): 95–118.

Morton, Adam (2007) *Unravelling Gramsci*, London: Pluto.

Morton, Stephen (2003) *Gayatri Chakravorty Spivak*, London: Routledge.

—— (2007) *Gayatri Spivak: Ethics, Subalternity and the Critique of Postcolonial Reason*, Cambridge: Polity.

Mouffe, Chantal (ed.) (1996) *Deconstruction and Pragmatism*, New York and London: Routledge.

—— (1998) 'Carl Schmitt and the paradox of liberal democracy', in David Dyzenhaus (ed.) *Law as Politics: Carl Schmitt's critique of liberalism*, Durham, NC: Duke University Press.

—— (ed.) (1999) *The Challenge of Carl Schmitt*, London: Verso.

—— (2005) *On the Political*, London: Routledge.

—— (2007) 'Carl Schmitt's warning on the dangers of a unipolar world', in Odysseos, Louiza and Petito, Fabio (eds) *The International Political Thought of Carl Schmitt: terror, liberal war and the crisis of global order*, London: Routledge.

Mulhall, Stephen and Swift, Adam (1996) *Liberals and Communitarians*, Second Edition, Oxford: Blackwell.

Müller, Jan-Werner (2003) *A Dangerous Mind: Carl Schmitt in post-war European thought*, New Haven, CT.: Yale University Press.

—— (2006) '"An irregularity that cannot be regulated": Carl Schmitt's theory of the partisan and the "war on terror"', paper presented at the 'Jurisprudence and the War on Terrorism' conference at Columbia Law School, 22nd April.

Murphy, Craig (1994) International Organization and Industrial Change. Oxford: Oxford University Press).

Nancy, Jean-Luc (1991) *The Inoperative Community*, trans. Lisa Garbus, Peter Connor, Michael Holland and Simona Sawhney, London: University of Minnesota Press.

—— (1993a) 'Abandoned Being', in *The Birth to Presence*, trans. Brian Holmes, Stanford: Stanford University Press.

—— (1993b) *The Experience of Freedom*, trans. Bridget McDonald, Stanford: University of Stanford Press.

—— (1996) *The Muses*, trans. Peggy Kamuf, Stanford: University of Stanford Press.

—— (2000) *Being Singular Plural*, trans. Robert D. Richardson and Anne E. O'Byrne, Stanford: Stanford University Press.

—— (2002a) *Hegel: The Restlessness of The Negative*, trans. Jason Smith, Minneapolis: University of Minnesota Press.

—— (2002b) 'L'Intrus', *The New Centennial Review*, 2 (3): 1–14.

—— (2003a) 'The Confronted Community', *Postcolonial Studies*, 6 (1): 23–36

—— (2003b) 'Deconstruction of Monotheism', *Postcolonial Studies* 6 (1): 37–46

—— (2007) *The Creation of the World or Globalisation*, trans. François Raffoul and David Pettigrew, Albany: SUNY Press.

—— and Lacoue-Labarthe, Philippe (1992) *The Title of the Letter: A Reading of Lacan*, Albany: SUNY Press.

Neal, Andrew (2006) 'Foucault in Guantanamo: Towards an Archaeology of the Exception', *Security Dialogue*, 37 (1): 31–46.

Neocleous, Mark (2006) 'The Problem with Normality: Taking Exception to "Permanent Emergency"', *Alternatives: Global, Local, Political*, 31: 191–293.

Nesbitt, Nick (2004) 'Troping Toussaint, Reading Revolution', *Research in African Literatures* 35 (2): 18–33.

Neumann, Volker (2001) 'Introduction to section on Carl Schmitt' in Arthur Jacobson and Bernard Schlink (eds) *Weimar: a jurisprudence of crisis*, Berkeley, CA: University of California Press.

Nicholson, Michael (1996) *Causes and Consequences in International Relations; a Conceptual Study*, London: Pinter.

Nietzsche, Friedrich (1974) [1882] *The Gay Science*, trans. Walter Kaufmann. New York: Vintage.

—— (1978) [1891] *Thus Spake Zarathustra*, trans. Walter Kaufmann, New York: Penguin Books.

—— (1994) [1887] *On the Genealogy of Morality*, ed. Keith Ansell-Pearson and Carol Diethe, Cambridge: Cambridge University Press.

—— (2002) [1886] *Beyond Good and Evil*, ed. Rolf-Peter Horstmann and trans. Judith Norman, Cambridge: Cambridge University Press.

Nietzsche, Friedrich Wilhelm (1996) *On the Genealogy of Morals: A Polemic: By Way of Clarification and Supplement to My Last Book Beyond Good and Evil*, Oxford: Oxford University Press.

Nolan, James (1998) *The Therapeutic State*, New York: New York University.

Nolte, Ernst (1987) *Der Europäische Bürgerkrieg 1917–1945: Nationalsozialismus und Bolschewismus*, Frankfurt: Propyläen.

Norris, Andrew (2005) 'Giorgio Agamben and the Politics of the Living Dead', in Andrew Norris (ed.), *Politics, Metaphysics, and Death: Essays on Giorgio Agamben's Homo Sacer*, Durham and London: Duke University Press.

Norris, Christopher (1992) *Uncritical Theory: Postmodernism, Intellectuals, and the Gulf War*, London: Lawrence and Wishart.

Nye, Joseph S. (2004) *Soft Power: The Means to Success in World Politics*, New York: Public Affairs and Oxford : Oxford Publicity Partnership.

Nyers, Peter (2003) 'Abject Cosmopolitanism: The Politics of Protection in the Anti-Deportation Movement', *Third World Quarterly*, 24 (6): 1069–93.

Odysseos, Louiza (2003) 'On the Way to Global Ethics? Cosmopolitanism, "Ethical" Selfhood and Otherness', *European Journal of Political Theory* 2 (2): 183–207.

—— (2007a) 'Crossing the Line? Carl Schmitt on the "Spaceless Universalism" of Cosmopolitanism and the War on Terror' in Louiza Odysseos and Fabio Petito (eds) *The International Political Thought of Carl Schmitt: terror, liberal war and the crisis of global order*, London: Routledge.

—— (2007b) *The Subject of Coexistence: otherness in international relations*, Minneapolis: University of Minnesota Press.

—— and Petito, Fabio (eds) (2007) *The International Political Thought of Carl Schmitt: terror, liberal war and the crisis of global order*, London: Routledge.

Osiel, Mark J. (2001) *Mass Atrocity, Ordinary Evil, and Hannah Arendt: Criminal Consciousness in Argentina's Dirty War*, New Haven: Yale University Press.

Øverenget, Einar (1998) *Seeing the Self: Heidegger on Subjectivity*, Dordrecht: Kluwer Academic Publishers.

Owens, Patricia (2005a) 'Hannah Arendt: A Biographical and Political Introduction', in Anthony F. Lang Jr. and John Williams (eds) *Hannah Arendt and International Relations: Reading across the Lines*, London: Palgrave Press, 27–40.

—— (2005b) 'Hannah Arendt, Violence, and the Inescapable Fact of Humanity', in Anthony. F. Lang Jr. and John Williams (eds) *Hannah Arendt and International Relations: Reading across the Lines*, London: Palgrave Press, 41–65.

—— (2007a) *Between War and Politics: International Relations and the Thought of Hannah Arendt*, Oxford: Oxford University Press.

—— (2007b) 'Beyond Strauss, Lies, and the War in Iraq: Hannah Arendt's Critique of Neoconservativism', *Review of International Studies* 33 (2): 265–83.

—— (2008a) 'The Ethic of Reality in Hannah Arendt', in Duncan Bell (ed.) *Political Thought and International Relations: Variations on a Realist Theme*, Oxford: Oxford University Press.

—— (2008b) 'Humanity, Sovereignty and the Camps' *International Politics* 45 (6): pp. 522–530.

Oxford Paperback Dictionary (1983) *Oxford Paperback Dictionary*, Second Edition, Oxford: Oxford University Press.

Parekh, Serena (2004) 'A Meaningful Place in the World: Hannah Arendt on the Nature of Human Rights', *Journal of Human Rights* 3 (1): 41–53.

—— (2008) *Hannah Arendt and the Challenge of Modernity: A Phenomenology of Human Rights*, London: Routledge.

Parker, Owen and Brassett, James (2005) 'Contingent Borders, Ambiguous Ethics: Migrants in (International) Political Theory', *International Studies, Quarterly* 49 (2): 233–53.

Patomäki, Heikki (2002) *After International Relations: Critical realism and the (re) constitution of world politics*, London: Routledge.

—— (2004) *Possible World: Democratic Transformation of Global Institutions*, London: Zed Books.

—— (2007) *The Political Economy of Global Security: War, Future Crises and Changes in Global Governance*, London: Routledge.

—— and Wight, Colin (2000) 'After Post-Positivism? The Promises of Critical Realism' *International Studies Quarterly*, 44 (2): 213–37.

Patton, Paul (1996) 'Introduction', in *Deleuze: A Critical Reader*, Oxford: Blackwell.

—— (2000) *Deleuze and the Political*, London and New York: Routledge.

Paul, Darel (2005) *Rescaling International Political Economy*, London: Routledge.

Payne, Rodger A. and Samhat, Nayef H. (2004) *Democratizing Global Politics: Discourse Norms, International Regimes, and Political Community*, Albany: State University of New York.

Peterson, V. Spike (1999) 'Political Identities/Nationalism and Heterosexism', *International Feminist Journal of Politics*, 1 (1): 34–65.

Petito, Fabio (2007) 'Against World Unity: Carl Schmitt and the western-centric and liberal global order' in Louiza Odysseos and Fabio Petito (eds) *The International Political Thought of Carl Schmitt: terror, liberal war and the crisis of global order*, London: Routledge.

Piiparinen, Touko (2007) 'Rescuing Thousands, Abandoning a Million: What Might an Emancipatory Intervention Have Looked Like in Rwanda?' *International Relations*, 21 (1): 47–66.

Pilardi, Jo-Ann (1995) 'Feminists Read *The Second Sex*', in Margaret A. Simons (ed.) *Feminist Interpretations of Simone de Beauvoir*, Pennsylvania: Pennsylvania State University Press, 29–43.

Pippin, Robert B. (1997) *Idealism as Modernism: Hegelian variations*, Cambridge: Cambridge University Press.

Plant, Raymond (1977) 'Hegel and Political Economy 1 and 2', *New Left Review* 103: 79–92; and 104: 103–13.

Pogge, Thomas (2002) *World Poverty and Human Rights: cosmopolitan responsibilities and reforms*, Cambridge: Polity.

Pop, Liliana (2007) 'Time and crisis: framing success and failure in Romania's post-communist transformations', *Review of International Studies*, 33: 395–413.

Popper, Karl (1959) *The Logic of Scientific Discovery*, London: Hutchinson.

Pouliot, Vincent (2007) 'Sobjectivism': Toward a Constructivist Methodology', *International Studies Quarterly*, 51 (2): 359–84.

—— (2008) 'The Logic of Practicality: A Theory of Practice of Security Communities', forthcoming in *International Organization* (Spring).

Powell, Jason (2006) *Jacques Derrida: A Biography*, London: Continuum.

Protevi, John (2001) *Political Physics*, London: Athlone.

Prozorov, Sergei (2005) 'X/Xs: Towards a General Theory of the Exception', *Alternatives: Global, Local, Political*, 30 (1): 81–112.

—— (2006) 'Liberal enmity: the figure of the foe in the political ontology of liberalism', *Millennium: Journal of International Studies*, 35: 75–99.

—— (2007) 'The Ethos of Insecure Life: reading Carl Schmitt's existential decisionism as a Foucauldian ethics', in Odysseos, Louiza and Petito, Fabio (eds) *The International Political Thought of Carl Schmitt: terror, liberal war and the crisis of global order*, London: Routledge.

Pupovac, Ozren (2006) 'Project Yugoslavia: The Dialectics of the Revolution', *Prelom* 8. http://www.prelomkolektiv.org/pdf/prelom08.pdf (accessed 25 January 2008).

Rajaram, Prem (2002) 'Theodor Adorno's Aesthetic Understanding: An Ethical Method for International Relations', *Alternatives*, 27 (3): 351–72.

Rancière, Jacques (1974) *La leçon d'Althusser*, Paris: Gallimard.

—— (1989) *The Nights of Labor. The Workers' Dream in Nineteenth-Century France*, Philadelphia: Temple University Press.

—— (1991) *The Ignorant Schoolmaster. Five Lessons in Intellectual Emancipation*, Stanford: Stanford University Press.

—— (1994) *The Names of History. On the Poetics of Knowledge*, Minneapolis: University of Minnesota Press.

—— (1995) *On the Shores of Politics*, London and New York: Verso.

—— (1998) 'Althusser', in Simon Critchley and William Ralph Schroeder (eds) *A Companion to Continental Philosophy*, Oxford: Blackwell, 530–48.

—— (1999) *Disagreement. Politics and Philosophy*, Minneapolis: University of Minnesota Press.

—— (2000) 'Literature, Politics, Aesthetics: Approaches to Democratic Disagreement', *SubStance*, 92: 3–24.

—— (2004a) *The Philosopher and His Poor*, Durham: Duke University Press.

—— (2004b) *The Politics of Aesthetics*, London and New York: Continuum.

—— (2004c) *The Flesh of Words. The Politics of Writing*, Stanford: Stanford University Press.

—— (2004d) 'Who Is the Subject of the Rights of Man?' *South Atlantic Quarterly*, 103(2/3): 297–310.

—— (2006) *Hatred of Democracy*, London and New York: Verso.

—— (2007) *The Future of the Image*, London and New York: Verso.

—— and Panagia, Davide (2000) 'Dissenting Words: A Conversation with Jacques Rancière', *Diacritics*, 30 (2): 113–26.

Rayner, Timothy (2001) 'Biopower and Technology: Foucault and Heidegger's way of thinking', *Contretemps* 2: 142–56.

Rehg, William (1994) *Insight and Solidarity: The Discourse Ethics of Jürgen Habermas*, Berkeley: University of California Press.

Reid, Julian (2004) 'War, liberalism, and modernity: the biopolitical provocations of "Empire"', *Cambridge Review of International Affairs*, 17: 63–79.

—— (2006) *The Biopolitics of the War on Terror: life struggles, liberal modernity, and the defence of logistical societies*, Manchester: Manchester University Press.

—— (2007) *The Biopolitics of the War on Terror: Life Struggles, Liberal Modernity, and the Defence of Logistical Societies*, Manchester: Manchester University Press.

Rengger, Nicholas (2001) 'Negative Dialectic? The Two Modes of Critical Theory in World Politics', in Richard Wyn Jones (ed.) *Critical Theory and World Politics*, Boulder, CO: Lynne Rienner.

Rensmann, Lars (2007) 'Revisiting the Origins of Euro-Republicanism: Hannah Arendt and the Normative Foundations of Post-National Democracy in Europe'. Paper presented at the American Political Science Association Annual Convention, Chicago, USA, September.

Richter, Gerhard (2007) *Thought-Images. Frankfurt School Writers' Reflections from Damaged Life*, Stanford: Stanford University Press.

—— (ed.) (2002) *Benjamin's ghosts: interventions in contemporary literary and cultural theory*, Stanford: Stanford University Press and Cambridge: Cambridge University Press.

Rieff, Philip (1961) *Freud: The Mind of the Moralist*, New York: Doubleday Anchor.

—— (1966) *The Triumph of the Therapeutic: Uses of Faith After Freud*, New York: Harper and Row.

Riggins, Stephen H. (1983) 'Michel Foucault: An Interview', *Ethos*, 1 (2): 4–9.

Risse, Thomas (2000) 'Let's Argue! Communicative Action in World Politics', *International Organization*, 54: 1–39.

Robinson, William (1996) *Promoting Polyarchy*, Cambridge: Cambridge University Press.

Rorty, Richard (1979) *Philosophy and the Mirror of Nature*, Oxford: Blackwell.

—— (1989) *Contingency, Irony and Solidarity*, Cambridge: Cambridge University Press.

—— (1991a) *Objectivity, Relativism and Truth: Philosophical Papers, Volume One*, Cambridge: Cambridge University Press.

—— (1991b) 'Postmodernist Bourgeois Liberalism', *Objectivity, Relativism and Truth: Philosophical Papers, Volume One*, Cambridge: Cambridge University Press, 197–202.

—— (1995) 'Richard Rorty: Toward a Post-Metaphysical Culture', Interview by Michael O'Shea, *The Harvard Review of Philosophy*, Spring: 58–66.

—— (1998a) 'Introduction', in *Truth and Progress: Philosophical Papers Volume 3*, Cambridge: Cambridge University Press, 1–18.

—— (1998b) 'Human Rights, Rationality and Sentimentality', in *Truth and Progress: Philosophical Papers, Volume 3*, Cambridge: Cambridge University Press, 167–85.

—— (1998c) 'Habermas, Derrida, and the Functions of Philosophy', in *Truth and Progress: Philosophical Papers Volume 3*, Cambridge: Cambridge University Press, 307–26.

—— (1999) *Philosophy and Social Hope*, London: Penguin Books.

—— (2000) 'Universality and Truth', in *Rorty And His Critics*, Oxford: Blackwell Publishers Ltd, 1–30.

—— (2002) *Against Bosses, Against Oligarchs: A Conversation with Richard Rorty*. An Interview with Derek Nystrom and Ken Puckett. Chicago, Prickly Paradigm Press.

—— (2007) 'Justice as a Larger Loyalty', in *Philosophy as Cultural Politics: Philosophical Papers Volume 4*, Cambridge: Cambridge University Press, 42–48.

Rose, Jacqueline (1993) *Why War?* Oxford: Blackwell.

—— (2003) *On Not Being Able to Sleep: Psychoanalysis and the Modern World*, Princeton, N.J.: Princeton University Press.

Rosenberg, Justin (2000), *The Follies of Globalisation Theory: Polemical Essays*, London: Verso.

Ross, Kristin (1991) 'Rancière and the Practice of Equality', *Social Text*, 29: 57–71.

Rowley, Hazel (2007) *Tête-à-Tête: The Lives and Loves of Simone de Beauvoir and Jean-Paul Sartre*, London: Vintage Books.

Ruddick, Sara (1990) *Maternal Thinking: towards a politics of peace*, London: The Women's Press.

Rupert, Mark (1995) *Producing Hegemony*, Cambridge: Cambridge University Press.

Said, Edward (1970) 'The Arab Portrayed', in Ibrahim Abu-Lughod (ed.), *The Arab–Israeli Confrontation of June 1967: An Arab Perspective*, Evanston, IL: Northwestern University Press.

—— (1978) *Orientalism*, New York: Panthenon.

—— (1979) *The Question of Palestine*, New York: Vintage.

—— (1981) *Covering Islam*, New York: Vintage.

—— (1983) *The World, the Text and the Critic*, Cambridge, MA: Harvard University Press.

—— (1993) *Culture and Imperialism*, London: Chatto and Windus.

—— (1994) *Representations of the Intellectual*, London: Vintage.

—— (1995) *Orientalism*, London and New York: Penguin.

—— (1999) *Out of Place: A Memoir*, New York: Knopf.

Salecl, Renata (1994) *Spoils of Freedom*, New York: Routledge.

—— (2003) *(Per) versions of Love and Hate*, London: Verso.

Salih, Sara with Judith Butler (2004) *The Judith Butler Reader*, Oxford: Blackwell Publishing.

Sallis, John (1978) 'The origins of Heidegger's thought', in John Sallis (ed.) *Radical Phenomenology: essays in honor of Martin Heidegger*, Atlantic Highlands, N.J.: Humanities Press.

Sanders, Mark (2006) *Gayatri Chakravorty Spivak: Live Theory*, London: Continuum.

Sandford, Stella (2006) *How to Read Beauvoir*, London: Granta Books.

Sartre, Jean-Paul (1966) *Being and Nothingness: a phenomenological essay on ontology*, trans. Hazel Barnes, New York: Washington Square Press.

Saurette, Paul (1996) '"I Mistrust All Systematizers and Avoid Them": Nietzche, Arendt and the Crisis of the Will to Order in International Relations Theory', *Millennium: Journal of International Studies* 25 (1): 1–28.

Savage, Mike (2000) 'Walter Benjamin's urban thought: a critical analysis', in Mike Crang and Nigel J. Thrift (eds) *Thinking space*, London: Routledge.

Sayer, Andrew (2000) *Realism and Social Science*, London: Sage.

Schaap, Andrew (2005) 'Forgiveness, Reconciliation and Transitional Justice', in Anthony F. Lang Jr. and John Williams (eds) *Hannah Arendt and International Relations: Readings Across the Lines*, London: Palgrave Press, 67–93.

Scheuerman, William E. (1999) *Carl Schmitt: the end of law*, Lanham, MD: Rowman and Littlefield.

Schmitt, Carl (1950) *Ex captivitate salus*, Köln: Greven.

—— (1988a) *Crisis of Parliamentary Democracy*, trans. E. Kennedy, Cambridge: The MIT Press.

—— (1988b) *Die Wendung zum diskriminierenden Kriegsbegriff*, Berlin: Duncker & Humblot.

—— (1994a) *Die Diktatur*, Berlin: Duncker und Humblot.

—— (1994b) *Positionen und Begriffe im Kampf mit Weimar-Genf-Versailles 1923–1939*, Berlin: Duncker and Humblot.

—— (1995) 'Die letzte globale Linie', in *Staat, Großraum, Nomos: Arbeiten aus den Jahren 1916 – 1969*, ed. G. Maschke, Berlin: Duncker & Humblot.

—— (1996a) *The Concept of the Political*, trans. G. Schwab, Chicago: University of Chicago Press.

—— (1996b) *The Leviathan in the State Theory of Thomas Hobbes: Meaning and Failure of a Political Symbol*, trans. G. Schwab and E. Hilfstein, Westport, CT: Greenwood Press.

—— (1996c) *The Tyranny of Values*, trans. S. Draghici, Corvallis, OR: Plutarch Press.

—— (2003) *The Nomos of the Earth in the International Law of the Jus Publicum Europaeum*, trans. G. L. Ulmen, New York: Telos Press.

—— (2004a) *Theory of the Partisan: a Commentary/Remark on the Concept of the Political*, trans. A.C. Goodson, East Lansing, MI: Michigan State University Press.

—— (2004b) *On the Three Types of Juristic Thought*, trans. J.W. Bendersky, Westport, CT: Praeger.

—— (2005) *Political Theology: Four Chapters on the Concept of Sovereignty*, trans. G. Schwab, 3rd edition, Chicago and London: the University of Chicago Press.

—— (2007a) *Theory of the Partisan: Intermediary Commentary on the Concept of the Political*, trans. G.L. Ulmen, New York: Telos Press.

—— (2007b) *Constitutional Theory*, trans. J. Seitzer, Duke University Press.

Scholem, Gershom G. (2001) *Walter Benjamin: the story of a friendship,* trans. Harry Zohn, New York: New York Review Books.

Schürmann, Reiner (1987) *Heidegger on Being and Acting: from principles to anarchy*, trans. C.-M. Gros and R. Schürmann, Bloomington: Indiana University Press.

Scruton, Roger (1982) *Kant*, Oxford: Oxford University Press.

Seckinelgin, Hakan (2006) *International Relations and the Environment: international fisheries, Heidegger, and social method*, London: Routledge.

Selby, Jan (2007) 'Engaging Foucault: Discourse, Liberal Governance and the Limits of Foucauldian IR', *International Relations*, 21 (3): 324–45.

Shapcott, Richard (2001) *Justice, Community and Dialogue in International Relations*, Cambridge: Cambridge University Press.

Shapiro, Michael J. (1999a) 'Globalization and the Politics of Discourse', *Social Text*, 17 (3): 111–29.

—— (1999b) 'The Ethics of Encounter: Unreading, Unmapping the Imperium', in David Campbell and Michael J. Shapiro (eds) *Moral Spaces: Rethinking Ethics and World Politics*, Minneapolis: University of Minnesota Press.

—— (2000) 'National Times and Other Times: Re-Thinking Citizenship', *Cultural Studies*, 14 (1): 79–98.

—— (2002) 'Social Science, Geophilosophy and Inequality', *International Studies Review*, 4 (2): 25–42.

—— (2005) 'The Discursive Spaces of Global Politics', *Journal of Environmental Policy & Planning*, 7 (3): 227–38.

—— (2006) 'The Sublime Today: Re-partitioning the Global Sensible', *Millennium: Journal of International Studies*, 34 (3): 657–81.

Sheehan, Thomas (2001a) '*Kehre* and *Ereignis*: a prolegomenon to *Introduction to Metaphysics*', in Richard Polt and Gregory Fried (eds), *A Companion to Heidegger's Introduction to Metaphysics*, New Haven: Yale University Press.

—— (2001b) 'A paradigm shift in Heidegger research', *Continental Philosophy Review* 34: 183–202.

Simons, Margaret A. (1999) *Beauvoir and The Second Sex: feminism, race and the origins of existentialism*, Lanham: Rowman and Littlefield.

Simons, Margaret A. (ed.) 1995) *Feminist Interpretations of Simone de Beauvoir*, Pennsylvania: Pennsylvania State University Press.

Sjoholm, Cecilia (2005) *Kristeva and the Political*, London and New York: Routledge.

Smith, Anne-Marie (1998) *Julia Kristeva: Speaking the Unspeakable*, London: Pluto Press.

Smith, Gary (ed.) (1988) *On Walter Benjamin: critical essays and recollections*, Cambridge, Mass.: London, MIT.

—— (1989) *Benjamin: philosophy, aesthetics, history*, Chicago: University of Chicago Press.

Smith, Gregory B. (2007) *Martin Heidegger: paths taken, paths opened*, Lanham, MD: Rowman & Littlefield.

Smith, Steve (1996) 'Positivism and Beyond', in Steve Smith, Ken Booth and Marysia Zalewski (eds) *International Theory: Positivism and Beyond*, Cambridge: Cambridge University Press.

Smith, Steve and Owens, Patricia (2005) 'Alternative Approaches to International Theory', in John Baylis and Steve Smith, *The Globalization of World Politics: An Introduction to International Relations*, Oxford: Oxford University Press.

Smith, Steven B. (1983) 'Hegel's Views on War, the State, and International Relations', *The American Political Science Review*, 77 (3): 624–32.

Soguk, Nevzat (2006) 'Splinters of Hegemony: Ontopoetical Visions in International Relations', *Alternatives*, 31: 377–404.

Sokal, Alan and Bricmont, Jean (1998) *Intellectual Impostures*, London: Profile Publishing.

Spivak, Gayatri Chakravorty (1987) *In Other Worlds: Essays in Cultural Politics*, New York: Methuen.

—— (1990) *The Post-Colonial Critic: Interviews, Strategies, Dialogues*, London: Routledge.

—— (1998) *In Other Worlds: Essays in Cultural Politics*, New York: Routledge.

—— (1999) *A Critique of Postcolonial Reason: Toward a history of the vanishing present*, Cambridge: Harvard University Press.

—— (2001) *Red Thread*, Cambridge: Harvard University Press.

—— (2002) in Radha S. Hegde and Raka Shome, 'Postcolonial Scholarship – Productions and Directions: An interview with Gayatri Chakravorty Spivak', *Communication Theory*, 12 (3): 271–86.

—— (2003) *Death of a Discipline*, New York: Columbia University Press.

—— (2004) 'Terror: A Speech After 9/11', *Boundary*, 31 (2): 82–111.

—— (2005) *Other Asias*, London: Wiley-Blackwell.

Stambaugh, Joan (1973) 'Introduction' in Martin Heidegger, *The End of Philosophy*, trans. Joan Stambaugh, New York: Harper and Row.

Staten, Henry (1985) *Wittgenstein and Derrida*, Oxford: Basil Blackwell.

Swartz, David (1997) *Culture & Power: the sociology of Pierre Bourdieu*, London: University of Chicago Press.

Sylvester, Christine (1994) *Feminist Theory and International Relations in a Postmodern Era*, London: Cambridge University Press.

Taminiaux, Jacques (1999) 'Heidegger on Values', in James Risser (ed.), *Heidegger Toward the Turn: essays on the work of the 1930s*, Albany: State University of New York Press, 225–39.

Taubes, Jakob (1987) *Ad Carl Schmitt: gegenstrebige Fügung*, Berlin: Merve Verlag Berlin.

Taylor, Charles (1993) 'To Follow a Rule … ', in Edward LiPuma, Moishe Postone and Craig Calhoun (eds) *Bourdieu: critical perspectives*, Chicago: University of Chicago Press, 45–60.

—— (1975) *Hegel*, Cambridge: Cambridge University Press.

The Foucault Society (2005) *Biography of Michel Foucault*, http://www.foucaultsociety.org/resources/michel_foucault.asp, (accessed 15 April 2008).

Thomas, Caroline and Wilkin, Peter (2004) 'Still Waiting after all these Years: The Third World' on the Periphery of International Relations', *British Journal of Politics and International Relations*, 6: 241–58.

Thompson, John B. (1991) 'Preface', to *Language and Symbolic Power*, Cambridge: Polity.

Tickner, J. Ann (1988) 'Hans Morgenthau's Principles of Political Realism: a feminist reformulation', *Millennium: Journal of International Studies*, 17 (3): 429–40.

Treaty of Versailles (1919) *Documents of the Treaty of Versailles*. http://www.worldcourts.com/pcij/eng/documents/1919.06.28_versailles_treaty.htm (accessed 4 April 2008).

Ulmen, Gary L. (1987) 'Return of the Foe', *Telos* 72: 187–93.

—— (2003) 'Translator's introduction', in Schmitt, Carl (2003) *The Nomos of the Earth in the International Law of the Jus Publicum Europaeum*, trans. G.L. Ulmen, New York: Telos Press.

van Buren, John (1994) *The Young Heidegger: rumor of the hidden king*, Bloomington: Indiana University Press.

Van Den Abbeele, Georges (1991) 'Introduction', in Miami Theory Collective (eds) *Community at Loose Ends*, Minneapolis, University of Minnesota Press.

van Munster, Rens (2004) 'The War on Terrorism: When the Exception Becomes the Rule', *International Journal of Semiotics of Law*, 17: 141–53.

—— (2009) *Immigration, Security and the Politics of Risk in the EU*, London: Palgrave, forthcoming.

Vaughan-Williams, Nick (2005) 'Protesting Against Citizenship', *Citizenship Studies*, 9 (2): 167–79.

—— (2007a) 'Beyond a Cosmopolitan Ideal: the Politics of Singularity', *International Politics*, 44 (1): 107–24.

—— (2007b) 'The Shooting of Jean Charles de Menezes: New Border Politics?' *Alternatives: Global, Local, Political*, 32 (2): 177–95.

—— (2008) 'Borders, territory, law', *International Political Sociology*, 4 (2): 322–338.

—— (2009) *Border Politics : the Limits of Sovereign Power*, Edinburgh: Edinburgh University Press.

Vij, Ritu (2009) (ed.) *Hegelian Encounters: Subjects of International Relations*, Palgrave. Forthcoming.

Villa, Dana (1999) *Politics, Philosophy, Terror: Essays on the Thought of Hannah Arendt*, Princeton, NJ: Princeton University Press.

Virilio, Paul (1984) *L'éspace critique*, Paris: Christian Bourgois.

—— (1986 [1977]) *Speed & Politics: An Essay on Dromology*, New York: Semiotext(e).

—— (1988) 'Interview with Paul Virilio', in *Block 14* (Autumn).

—— (1989 [1984]) *War and Cinema: The Logistics of Perception*, London and New York: Verso.

—— (1990 [1978]) *Popular Defense & Ecological Struggles*, New York: Semiotext(e).

—— (1991a [1980]) *The Aesthetics of Disappearance*, New York: Semiotext(e).

—— (1991b [1984]) *The Lost Dimension*, New York: Semiotext(e).

—— (1991c) *L'écran du désert: chroniques de guerre*, Paris: Galilée.

—— (1991d) 'Interview', in *Art and Philosophy*, Milan: Giancarlo Politi Editore.

—— (1993) 'L'état suicidaire', in *L'insécurité du territoire*, Paris: Galilée.

—— (1994a [1975]) *Bunker Archeology*, Princeton: Princeton Architectural Press.

—— (1994b [1988]) *The Vision Machine*, Bloomington and London: Indiana University Press and British Film Institute.

—— (1994c) 'Cyberwar, God and Television', interview with Louise Wilson, *ctheory* (21 October).

—— (1995a [1993]) *The Art of the Motor*, Minneapolis: University of Minnesota Press.

—— (1995b) 'Speed and Information: Cyberspace Alarm!', trans. Patrice Riemens, *ctheory* (27 September).

—— (1997 [1995]) *Open Sky*, London: Verso.

—— (1999 [1990]) *Polar Inertia*, London: Sage.

—— (2005 [1984]) *Negative Horizon: An Essay in Dromoscopy*, London: Continuum.

—— and Lotringer, Sylvère (1997 [1983]) *Pure War*, Revised Edition. New York: Semiotext(e).

Wacquant, Loïc (2001a) 'Further notes on Bourdieu's "Marxism"', *International Journal of Contemporary Sociology*, 38 (1): 103–9.

—— (2001b) 'Durkheim and Bourdieu: the common plinth and its cracks', *International Journal of Contemporary Sociology*, 38 (1): 12–27.

—— (2007) 'Pierre Bourdieu', in Rob Stones (ed.) *Key Sociological Thinkers*, 2nd edition, London: Palgrave, 2007, 261–77.

Wæver, Ole (1996) 'The Rise and Fall of the Interparadigm Debate', in Steve Smith, Ken Booth and Marysia Zalewski (eds) *International Theory; Positivism and Beyond*, Cambridge: Cambridge University Press, 149–85.

Walker, R.B.J. (1997) 'The Subject of Security', in Keith Krause and Michael C. Williams (eds) *Critical Security Studies*, Minneapolis: University of Minnesota Press, 61–81.

Waltz, Kenneth Neal (1979) *Theory of International Politics*, Reading, Mass. and London: Addison-Wesley.

Watts, Richard (1999), 'Frantz Fanon', in Kwame Anthony Appiah and Henry Louis Gates, Jr. (eds) *Africana: The Encyclopedia of the African and African American Experience*, New York: Basic Civitas Books.

Weber, Cynthia (1995) *Simulating Sovereignty: Intervention, the State and Symbolic Exchange*, Cambridge: Cambridge University Press.

—— (1998) 'Performative States', *Millennium: Journal of International Studies*, 27 (1): 77–95.

Wendt, Alexander (1999) *Social Theory of International Politics*, New York: Cambridge University Press.

Wiggershaus, Rolf (1994 [1986]) *The Frankfurt School: Its History, Theories and Significance*, Cambridge: Polity Press.

Wight, Colin (1999) 'MetaCampbell: The Epistemological Problematics of Perspectivism', *Review of International Studies* 25 (1): 311–16.

—— (2006) *Agents, Structures and International Relations: Politics as Ontology*, Cambridge: Cambridge University Press.

Wight, Martin (1994) *International Theory: the three traditions*, London: Leicester University Press.

Williams, Howard (1983) *Kant's Political Philosophy*, Oxford: Blackwell.

Williams, John (2002) 'Territorial Borders, Toleration and the English School', *Review of International Studies* 28 (4): 737–58.

—— (2005) 'Hannah Arendt and the International Space In-Between?', in Anthony F. Lang Jr. and John Williams (eds) *Hannah Arendt and International Relations: Readings Across the Lines*, London: Palgrave Press, 199–220.

Williams, Michael C. (2007) *Culture and Security: symbolic power and the transformation of the international security order*, London: Routledge.

Williams, Raymond (1973) *The country and the city*, London: Hogarth,

Wolin, Richard (1994) *Walter Benjamin: an aesthetic of redemption*, Berkeley: London, University of California Press.

—— (2003) *Heidegger's Children: Hannah Arendt, Karl Lowith, Hans Jonas, and Herbert Marcuse*, Princeton: Princeton University Press.

—— (ed.) (1991) *The Heidegger Controversy: a critical reader*, Cambridge: MIT Press.

Wyn Jones, Richard (1999) *Security, Strategy and Critical Theory*, Boulder, Co.: Lynne Rienner.

Young, Iris Marion (2002) 'Power, Violence, and Legitimacy: A Reading of Hannah Arendt in an Age of Police Brutality and Humanitarian Intervention', in Martha Minnow (ed.) *Breaking the Cycle of Hatred: Memory, Law, and Repair*, Princeton: Princeton University Press, 260–87.

Young-Bruehl, Elisabeth (1982) *Hannah Arendt: For Love of the World*, New Haven: Yale University Press.

—— (2006) *Why Arendt Matters*, New Haven: Yale University Press.

Yovel, Yirmiyahu (1980) *Kant and the Philosophy of History*, Princeton NJ: Princeton University Press.

Zalewski, Marysia (1998) 'Where is Woman in International Relations? "To Return as a Woman and Be Heard"', *Millennium: Journal of International Studies*, 27 (4): 847–67.

Zarmanian, Thalin (2006) 'Carl Schmitt and the problem of legal order: from domestic to international', *Leiden Journal of International Law*, 19: 41–67.

Zehfuss, Maja (2002) *Constructivism in International Relations: The Politics of Reality*, Cambridge: Cambridge University Press.

—— (2007) *Wounds of Memory: Politics of War in Germany*, Cambridge: Cambridge University Press.

Zertal, Idith (2005) '*Between Love of the World* and *Love of Israel*' in *Israel's Holocaust and the Politics of Nationhood*, trans. Chaya Galai, Cambridge: Cambridge University Press.

Zimmerman, Michael E. (1990) *Heidegger's Confrontation with Modernity: technology, politics, art*, Bloomington: Indiana University Press.

Žižek, Slavoj (1988) *Le Plus Sublime des Hystériques – Hegel Passe*, Paris: Hors Ligne.

—— (1989) *The Sublime Object of Ideology*, London: Verso.

—— (1991a) *For They Know Not What They Do: Enjoyment as a Political Factor*, London: Verso.

—— (1991b) *Looking Awry: An Introduction to Jacques Lacan Through Popular Culture*, Cambridge, MA: MIT Press.

—— (1992) *Enjoy Your Symptom: Jacques Lacan in Hollywood and Out*, New York: Routledge.

—— (1993) *Tarrying with the Negative: Kant, Hegel, and the Critique of Ideology,* Durham, NY: Duke University Press.

—— (1994) *The Metastases of Enjoyment: Six Essays on Women and Causality,* London: Verso.

—— (1997) *The Plague of Fantasies,* London: Verso.

—— (1999) *The Ticklish Subject: The Absent Centre of Political Ontology,* London: Verso.

—— (2001) *Did Somebody Say Totalitarianism? Five Interventions on the (Mis)use of a Notion,* London: Verso.

—— (2002) *Welcome to the Desert of the Real,* London: Verso.

—— (2003) *The Puppet and the Dwarf: The Perverse Core of Christianity,* Cambridge, MA: MIT Press.

—— (2004a) *Iraq: The Borrowed Kettle,* London: Verso.

—— (2004b) 'The Lesson of Rancière', in Jacques Rancière *The Politics of Aesthetics,* London and New York: Continuum, 69–79.

—— (2005) 'Against Human Rights', *New Left Review,* 34: 115–31.

—— (2006a) *The Parallax View,* Cambridge, MA: MIT Press.

—— (2006b) *How to Read Lacan,* New York: Norton.

—— (2008) *In Defence of Lost Causes,* London: Verso.

Index

A Contribution to a Critique of Political Economy (Marx) 250
A Critique of Postcolonial Reason: Toward a history of the vanishing present (Spivak) 318, 329
A Kant Dictionary (Caygill) 220
'A Passion for the (Im)possible. Jacques Rancière, Equality Pedagogy and Messianic' (Dillon) 276
A Thousand Plateaus: Capitalism and Schizophrenia (Deleuze and Guattari) 3, 125, 126–7, 136, 333
A Thousand Years of Non-Linear History (Delanda) 136
abjection 231
abortion 67
absence 140–2
Absolute Knowing 212, 213
Abu Ghraib prison 118, 231
accursed share, the 56
Adorno, Theodor 7–18, 40, 77, 80, 84, 87, 88, 171, 174, 187, 230, 278
Adorno: A Critical Introduction (Jarvis) 18
Adorno Reader, The (O'Connor ed.) 18
Aesthetic Theory (Adorno) 18
Aesthetics of Disappearance, The (Virilio) 333
Afghanistan 121
After International Relations: Critical realism and the (re)constitution of world politics (Patomäki) 101
'After Post-Positivism The Promises of Critical Realism' (Patomäki, and Wight) 101
Agamben, Giorgio 19–30, 40, 307, 342
'The age of neutralizations and depoliticizations' (Schmitt) 316
Agents, Structures and International Relations (Wight) 101

Algerian War of Independence 43, 67, 103, 137, 138, 151
alienation 247–8, 352
Alker, Hayward 198
Allison, David B. 265
Althusser, Louis 43, 44, 137, 161, 252, 266–7, 268, 342, 343, 347–8
ambiguity 68, 69, 70, 71, 279
America (Baudrillard) 65
An Aesthetics of Redemption (Wolin) 88
An Introduction to Metaphysics (Heidegger) 210
Anderson, Benedict 80
Angelus Novus (journal) 78
Angelus Novus (Klee) 82
antagonism 348, 352
anti-coloniality 155–6
Antidiplomacy (Der Derian) 60
anti-foundationalism 278–9, 285, 288–9
antinomies 10
Anti-Oedipus: Capitalism and Schizophrenia (Deleuze and Guattari) 125, 136
anti-Semitism 7, 32–3, 35, 137, 235, 240, 263, 305
Antonio Gramsci (Jones) 185
Antonio Gramsci Reader: Selected Writings 1916–35 (Forgacs ed) 185
Appius Claudius 269
Approaches to Gramsci (Sassoon) 185
Arab, the: experience of Zionism 300; representations of 299, 300–2
Arab-Israeli Wars 294
Aradau, Claudia 52, 273
Arcades Project, The (Benjamin) 80, 81, 84–6
archaeology 165, 166
Archaeology of Knowledge, The (Foucault) 162, 166, 169

archipolitics 271
Architecture Principie group 330
archive, the 164–5
Arendt, Hannah 21, 31–41, 80, 82, 200, 201
Aristotle 21, 21–2, 133, 238
Armitage, John 340
Aron, Raymond 103
art 10, 78, 83–4
Art of the Motor, The (Virilio) 334, 339
Ashley, Richard K. 149, 165, 198
assemblages 136
astrology 14
Aucoutrier, Marguerite 137
Augelli, Enrico 178
Augustine, St. 32
Auschwitz 15
Austen, Jane 298
authority figures 171–2
Autonomism 21
Autonomy and Solidarity (Habermas) 198

Bachelard, Gaston 104
bad faith 67
Badiou, Alain 42–53, 266, 342
Badiou, Balibar, Rancière: Re-thinking Emancipation (Hewlett) 276
Badiou. Subject to Truth (Hallward) 52
balance of power 311–2
Balibar, Étienne 266
ban, the 22–3
banality of evil, the 31, 33–4
Bananas, Beaches and Bases: making feminist sense of international politics (Enloe) 73
bare life 20–1, 23, 24–5
Barthes, Roland 319
Bataille, Georges 56, 84–5
Baudrillard, Jean 54–65
Bauer, Nancy 76
Bauman, Zygmunt 54
Beasley-Murray, Jon 314
Beaufret, Jean 200–1
Beauvoir, Simone de 66–76
Beauvoir and the Second Sex (Simons) 76
becoming 126–7, 133–4
Beiner, Ronald 220
Being 43, 45, 48, 199–210, 238
Being and Event (Badiou) 42, 44, 45, 46, 52
Being and Nothingness (Sartre) 67

Being and Time (Heidegger) 199–200, 204, 206–7, 254, 262
Being Singular Plural (Nancy) 252, 253, 256, 262
beings 201–2, 208
belief systems 183
Benjamin, Walter 8, 11, 17, 21, 23, 29, 40, 77–88, 144, 306, 333
Benjamin'sabilities (S. Weber) 88
Bennington, Geoffrey 138
Bergo, Bettina 245
Bergson, Henri 128, 133–4
Bernstein, Richard J. 290
betrayal 50
Between Facts and Norms (Habermas) 187, 188, 198
Between Past and Future (Arendt) 34
Between War and Politics: International Relations and the Thought of Hannah Arendt (Owens) 41
Between War and Politics: International Relations and the Thought of Hannah Arendt (Roundtable on) 41
Beyond Good and Evil (Nietzsche) 264, 265
Beyond Realism and Marxism: Critical Theory and International Relations (Linklater) 15
Bhabha, Homi, K. 159, 321, 322
Bhaskar, Roy 89–101
Bible, the 21
Bieler, Andreas 185
biopolitical tattooing 19
biopower 164
bios 22, 23, 24–5
birth of the clinic, The (Foucault) 162, 167
Blanchot, Maurice 263
Bleiker, Roland 222
Bloch, Ernst 7, 8, 17, 77
blowback 35
Blücher, Heinrich 33
bodies, sexed 117–8
Bodies That Matter (Butler) 114, 124
body, the 232
'The Body Politics of Julia Kristeva' (Butler) 233
Boggs, Carl 185
Booth, William James 220
Boothby, Richard 346–7
borders 226–7
Bosnia 241–2, 346–7, 350
Bosteels, Bruno 42–3
boundaries 226–7

Bourdieu, Pierre 102–13
Breast Giver (Devi) 317, 324
Brecht, Bertolt 77, 79
Brentano, Franz 199
Brown, Chris 101
Buck-Morss, Susan 84, 87, 88
Bull, Hedley 309
Bulley, Dan 149
Bunker Archeologie (Virilio) 333, 334, 339
Burchell, Graham 170
Bush, George W. 301
Butler, Judith 114–24, 171, 233, 342, 352
Butler, Rex 341–2, 353

Calarco, Matthew 30
Cambridge Companion to Marx (Carver ed) 250
Cambridge Companion to Simone de Beauvoir 76
camp, the 25–6
Campbell, David 119, 146, 149, 238, 241–2, 245, 257, 339
'Can Change be Thought' (Badiou) 42–3
Can One Live After Auschwitz Theodor W. Adorno: A Philosophical Reader (Tiedemann ed.) 18
Can the Subaltern Speak (Spivak) 318, 320, 326–8, 328
Canguilhem, Georges 125, 161
Canovan, Margaret 40–1
Capital (Marx) 246
capital, Bourdieu on 109–10, 111, 113
capitalism 87, 182, 214, 246, 247–50
Caputo, John 139, 148, 205, 208–9, 243
Carver, Terrell 250
catachresis 321–2
Categorical Imperative, the 191
categorisation 5
causality 95
Caygill, Howard 88, 220
Century of the Self (TV series) 173–4
Chakrabarty, Dipesh 155
Chan, Stephen 232
change 43; Badiou on 45–8; Deleuze on 133–4; Gramsci on 183–5; Kristeva on 228
Chanter, Tina 245
charismatic legitmators 31
charity 218
Chavez, Hugo 343
Chechnya 223

Chen, Kuan-Hsing 185
Chinese Cultural Revolution 42, 43
Christianity 21, 260
chronopolitics of intensivity 333
Cissé, Madjiguène 275
citizenship: Badiou on 46; rights and duties 39–40
civil rights 194, 282
civil society 24, 195–6, 214–5
civilization, Freud on 172
Civilization and its Discontents (Freud) 171–3, 175
Cixous, Hélene 324
Clash of Civilisations (Huntington) 261
class 104, 185, 247–50, 267, 314, 348
Cochran, Molly 286
coercive universalization 50
coexistence 207
Cold War, the 60, 60–1, 69, 271, 289
collective action 36
collective man 183
Collier, Andrew 101
Colombo, Alessandro 315
colonialism 150–60, 295–300, 318, 319, 322, 325, 326, 333
Colonialism and Neocolonialism (Sartre) 159
Columbia University 10
Coming Community, The (Agamben) 20, 29
communication 189, 192
Communication and the Evolution of Society (Habermas) 198
communicative action 188–91, 191–2, 194, 196–7
communicative competence 189–90, *190*
Communism 79
Communist Manifesto (Marx and Engels) 246, 250
Communist Party of Italy (PCI) 180–1
communitarianism 279
community: biopolitical element 28; conceptions of 254–5; Nancy on 254–8; and openness 20; relationality 254–8; Rorty on 284
Community At Loose Ends (Miami Theory Collective) 262
comprehensibility 189
concentration camps 25–6, 37
Concept of the Political, The (Schmitt) 305
conflict, increasing destructiveness of 14
Connolly, William E. 28–9, 340
consensus democracy 270–3

conservatism 49
constellations 17
constructivism 118–9
Constructivism in International Relations (Zehfuss) 149
constructivist structuralism 105–13
Consumer Society, The (Baudrillard) 55
Contingency Irony and Solidarity (Rorty) 283–7, 287–8, 290
continuity and discontinuity 14
Contributions to Philosophy (Heidegger) 200
conversation 282–3
Cook, Maeve 198
corporeal international, the 231–2
cosmopolitanism 39, 279
counter-culture theories 174–5
Covering Islam (Said) 304
Cox, Robert 166, 176–8, 185
Creation Of The World Or Globalisation, The (Nancy) 259
Crises of the Republic (Arendt) 34
Crisis of the European Subject (Kristeva) 222
Critchley, Simon 245
critical naturalism 94–5
critical realism 89–90, 95, 98–101; dialectic 95–7
Critical Realism; an Introduction to Roy Bhaskar's Philosophy (Collier) 101
critical security studies 31
critical social science 89–90, 95–7
Critical Space (Virilio) 333
critical theory 9–11, 15–6, 17, 31
Critical Theory, Marxism and Modernity (Kellner) 250
criticism 84
Critique of Practical Reason (Kant) 217, 220
Critique of Pure Reason (Kant) 217, 220
'Critique of Violence' (Benjamin) 88
Culler, Jonathan 140–1, 148
cultural capital 110
cultural sedimentation 183
cultural theory 83
culture 12–3
Culture and Imperialism (Said) 298, 304
Culture Industry 12–3
'The Cunning of Imperial Reason' (Bourdieu and Wacquant) 112
Czechoslovakia, secret seminar, 1981 137

Dallmayr, Fred 261
danger 119
Darfur 146
Dasein 204–5, 206–7
Davidson, Arnold I. 170
de Beistegui, Miguel 209
De quoi Sarkozy est-il le nom [What does Sarkozy stand for] (Badiou) 44
Dean, Jodi 353
Death of a Discipline (Spivak) 318, 329
death penalty 244
Debord, Guy 21
DeCaroli, Steven 30
decision 144–8
decolonization 158, 299
Deconstructing Historiography (Spivak) 325
deconstruction 137–49, 205, 317, 318, 319–21
Deconstruction and Pragmatism (Mouffe) 279, 291
Deconstruction in a Nutshell (Caputo) 139
Deibert, Ron 339
Delanda, Manuel 136
Deleuze, Gilles 21, 43, 125–36, 200, 263, 264, 265, 326–7, 332, 333, 340, 342
Deleuze and the Political (Patton) 136
deliberative democracy 197–8
democracy 187, 189, 194, 196, 197–8, 270, 270–3, 349
democratic materialism 44–5
demos, the 270
Deranty, Jacques-Philippe 276
Derian, James Der 60, 339
Derrida (film) 138–9, 148
Derrida, Jacques 21, 44, 84, 87–8, 103, 115, 117, 125, 137–49, 200, 205, 212, 251, 252, 263, 278, 285, 286, 287, 317, 319, 321, 326, 330, 342, 352
Derrida: Negotiating the Legacy (Fagan et al.) 149
Descartes, Rene 12, 203, 211, 280, 342
Desert Islands (Deleuze) 136
Desert Screen (Virilio) 334, 339
desire 344–5
Dessler, David 98
de-subjectification 27
deterrence 60–1
deterritorialization 135, 333
Devi, Mahasweta 317, 324
Dewey, John 278, 279, 280–1, 286, 290

Dialectic of Enlightenment (Adorno and Horkheimer) 11–4, 18
Dialectic: the Pulse of Freedom and Plato etc: the Problems of Philosophy and Their Resolution (Bhaskar) 92
dialectics 16; Bhaskar on 92, 97; critical realism 97; of history 247; materialist 44–5
Dialectics of Seeing (Buck-Morss) 88
dichotomies 139–42
Did Anybody Say Totalitarianism (Žižek) 353
Dien Bien Phu, battle of 157
Diez, Thomas 198
différance 138, 142
difference 126, 134
Difference and Repetition (Deleuze) 125, 129, 131, 136
differential geometry 128
differential metaphysics 264–5
differentiation 108
dignity 39
Dillon, Michael 169–70, 275, 276
Dilthey, Wilhelm 199
Disagreement. Politics and Philosophy (Rancière) 276
disasters 50, 335–7
Discipline and Punish (Foucault) 162, 163, 167, 169
discourse 118, 166–7
discourse ethics 17, 190, 191–4, 197–8
discursive constructions, personification of 118
disenchantment 12
dislocation 294
displacement 299–300
Dissemination (Derrida) 148
'Dissenting Words: A Conversation with Jacques Rancière' (Rancière and Panagia) 276
distinction 108
Distinction (Bourdieu) 113
Distinction: a social critique of the judgement of taste (Bourdieu) 104
Divided West, The (Habermas) 220
domination, and reason 13
Doty, Roxanne Lynn 149, 243
Douglas, Ian 339
doxa 109
drag 119–20
Durkheim, Emil 104, 105
Dyzenhaus, David 315

Eagleton, Terry 107
Eclipse of Reason (Horkheimer) 11
Edkins, Jenny 30, 121–2, 145, 148–9, 149, 350
education 106
Egypt, French conquest of 296–7
Eichmann, Adolf 33–4
Eichmann in Jerusalem (Arendt) 31, 33–4, 40
Eiland, Howard 88
Einstein, Albert 173–4
Elective Affinities (Goethe) 78
emancipation 13, 15, 268, 272, 273, 275–6
emancipatory knowledge 187
emancipatory project, critical theory as 17
embodied cosmopolitanism 17
empathy 193
empires 135
Encyclopaedia of the Philosophical Sciences in Outline (Hegel) 212–3
End of Philosophy, The (Heidegger) 210
endo-colonisation 333
Enframing 208–9
Engels, Friedrich 246, 248
English School, the 31, 309
Enjoy Your Symptom! Jacques Lacan in Hollywood and Out (Žižek) 353
enjoyment 348, 350
enlightenment, Adorno and Horkheimer's analysis of 11–4
Enloe, Cynthia 73
enmity, definitions of 314–5
epistemological relativism 93
equality 50–2, 194, 268, 268–70, 272–3
Eros 171, 172
errors, genuine 130
escapism 12
Essays in Understanding (Arendt) 34
essentialism 116
ethics 67–70, 75, 115, 124, 147, 229–30, 235–45, 282, 284, 289, 352; discourse 17, 190, 191–4, 197–8
Ethics: An Essay on the Understanding of Evil (Badiou) 42, 43, 52
Ethics of Ambiguity, The (Beauvoir) 66, 66–7, 67–70, 71
Ethics of Deconstruction, The (Critchley) 245
ethnography 103
eurocentrism 322
Europe, Fanon on 155–6

'Europe Divided: Ethics, Politics, and Religion' (Kristeva) 229–30
Event 43, 44–8
evil: banality of 31, 33–4; Badiou on 48–50; Baudrillard on 63–4; Levinas and 242; Nietzsche on 264
evolutionism 126–7
exclusion 22–3, 115
exile, fact of 294, 303
existentialism 66, 67–70, 71, 72, 75, 103, 106, 206–7
exo-colonialism 333
expressive action 188

face to face, the 237–9
facts 95–6
false consciousness 247
family, the 214
Fanon, Frantz 33, 36–7, 40, 75, 150–60, 231, 321
fantasy 343–8, 350, 352
Farias, Victor 209–10
femininity 118, 141
feminism 31, 67, 70–5, 73–4, 75, 114–24, 226, 232, 286, 317, 318, 324–8
Feminist Interpretations of Emmanuel Levinas (Chanter) 245
'Feminists Read *The Second Sex*' (Pilardi) 76
Feuerbach, Ludwig 246
field, the 102, 104, 106, 108–10, 111, 113, 128
Fields of Cultural Production: essays on art and literature, The (Bourdieu) 104
figuration 255–7, 260
film studies 83, 274
Finlayson, James Gordon 198
First World War 77
Flikschuh, Katrin 220
fluctuating indeterminacy 56
For a Critique of the Political Economy of the Sign (Baudrillard) 55
For They Know Not What They Do Enjoyment as a Political Factor (Žižek) 343, 353
'Force of Law: The "Mystical Foundations of Authority"' (Derrida) 87–8
Forgacs, David 185
Forget Foucault (Baudrillard) 65
Förster-Nietzsche, Elisabeth 263
Forum of Scientific and Critical Realism 101
Foucault (Deleuze) 136

Foucault, Michel 21, 22, 38, 40, 43, 44, 103, 115, 117, 125, 126, 137, 149, 161–70, 200, 212, 227, 263, 266, 278, 283, 295, 302, 317, 326–7, 333
Foucault and His Interlocutors (Davidson) 170
Foucault Effect: Studies in Governmentality (Burchell, Gordon, and Miller) 170
Foucault on Politics, Security and War (Dillon and Neal eds) 169–70
foundationalism 288–9
Fragmentary Demand: An Introduction to the Philosophy of Jean-Luc Nancy (James) 262
Frankfurt School, the 8–9, 15, 17, 187, 248, 278
Franks, Mary Anne 121
Frantz Fanon: A Life (Macey) 159
Fraser, Nancy 232–3, 286
freedom: and enlightenment 13; existentialism and 67, 75; Hegel on 211, 213, 215; Kristeva on 229–30; subjective 44
French Feminism in an International Frame (Spivak) 324
French Revolution, the 47
Freud, Sigmund 9, 123, 171–5, 225, 228, 278, 317, 344, 351
Friedman, Thomas 64
friend/enemy distinction 307–8, 315
Frisby, David 85
From East to West: The Odyssey of the Soul (Bhaskar) 92, 97
Fromm, Eric 8, 171, 174
Fukuyama, Francis 48, 64, 341
fundamental laws 109
Fynsk, Christopher 251

Gadamer, Hans-Georg 200, 283
Galli, Carlo 306
Galloway, Alex 340
Gandhi, Mahatma 152, 154
Gandillac, Maurice de 125
Gane, Mike 55
Gauss, Carl Friedrich 127–8
Gay Science, The (Nietzsche) 264, 265
gender 73, 74–5, 114–24, 328
Gender Trouble (Butler) 114, 115, 117, 124
genealogy 166–7, 168
Genealogy of Morals, The (Nietzsche) 166
genocide 14, 39, 242, 351

geometry 127–9
George, Larry 149
Geras, Norman 279
German idealism 7–8, 8
German Law Review 29
German Romanticism 78
German Zionist Organization 32
Germino, Dante 179–80
Gestell 208–9
Gibson, Nigel C. 159
Gill, Stephen 178
Gilloch, Graeme 88
Giving and Account of Oneself (Butler) 124
global public sphere 196
globalization 46, 63–5, 178, 226, 258–60, 317, 318, 321, 331, 334, 336
Goethe, J. W. van 78
good 48–9, 242, 264
Gordon, Colin 170
'Governmentality' (Foucault) 169
Gramsci, Antonio 46, 176–86, 248, 297, 325
Gramsci's Politics (Sassoon) 185
Granada 62
Greek law 21
Guantánamo Bay 24–5, 26, 231
Guattari, Félix 21, 125, 126–7, 128–9, 135–6, 333, 340
Guha, Ranajit 325
guiltless responsibility 237
Gulf War, First 57–8, 60, 61, 334

'Habermas, Derrida, and the Functions of Philosophy' (Rorty) 290
Habermas, Jürgen 14, 15, 16, 38, 40, 88, 187–98, 278, 285, 286, 287
habitus 102, 106–7, 110, 111, 113
Hallward, Peter 44, 46, 52
Hand, Sean 245
Hannah Arendt: A Reinterpretation of Her Political Thought (Canovan) 40–1
Hannah Arendt and International Relations: Readings across the Lines (Lang and Williams, eds.) 41
Hannah Arendt: For Love of the World (Young-Bruehl) 41
Hanssen, Beatrice 84, 88
Hardt, Michael 340
Harré, Rom 92
Hatley, James 245
Hatred of Democracy (Rancière) 268, 276
Hegarty, Paul 59

Hegel, G.W.F. 7, 9, 10, 16, 21, 66, 71–2, 116–7, 187, 211–6, 218, 230, 247, 278, 341
hegemony 177–8, 297–8, 352
Hegemony and Socialist Strategy (Laclau and Mouffe) 343
Heidegger, Martin 19, 20, 32, 66, 84, 126, 199–210, 235, 254, 262, 280–1, 283, 342
Heidegger and Being and Time (Mulhall) 210
Heidegger and Ethics (Hodge) 210
Heidegger and Nazism, (Farias) 209–10
Heidegger and the Political: dystopias (de Beistegui) 209
Heidegger Controversy: a critical reader, The (Wolin) 210
Hempel, Carl Gustav 91
hermeneutics 200
Herzl, Theodor 78
Hessel, Franz 84
Hewlett, Nick 276
high politics 176
Hindenburg, Paul von 305
historical materialism 106, 182, 246, 246–50
historicizing 167
history: Arendt on 38; Benjamin's critique of 79–88; dialectic of 247; Foucault on 165, 166, 167; Gramsci on 181–2; Hegel on 211; Rancière and 268
History of Sexuality (Foucault) 22, 162, 164, 167, 169
Hitler, Adolf 11
Hobbes, Thomas 165
Hodge, Joanna 210
Hollis, Martin 98–9
Hollywood 12
Holocaust, the 34, 235, 335
Homo Academicus (Bourdieu) 104, 113
homo sacer 20–1, 25
Homo Sacer: Sovereign Power and Bare Life (Agamben) 20, 29
Homo Sacer tetralogy (Agamben) 20–1
Horkheimer, Max 8, 9–11, 18, 187
hospitality 243
How to Read Beauvoir (Sandford) 76
How to Read Jacques Lacan (Žižek) 353
Human Condition, The (Arendt) 31, 34, 38, 40
human rights 39–40, 49, 253, 274–6, 279, 288–9, 351

Human Rights, Rationality and Sentimentality (Rorty) 288–9, 290
human/animal 20–1
humanitarian interventions 49, 346, 351
humanity, Freud's model 171–3
hunger strikes 231
Hurrell, Andrew 220
Husserl, Edmund 199, 200, 204, 235, 280
Hutchens, Benjamin C. 262
Hutchings, Kimberly 76, 79, 220
hyperreality 56
Hyppolite, Jean 125

idealism 16
ideas, Deleuze on 131
Identifications 345–7
identity: Deleuze on 130, 133; Kristeva on 222, 226, 232; Levinas on 238–9; Rorty on 286; sexual 232; sovereign 20–1; Spivak on 319; thought as basis for 130; and women 115–20
identity politics 49–50
ideology 35, 168, 303, 318, 341, 343–4, 347–8
'Ideology and Ideological State Apparatuses' (Althusser) 343
Il Regno e la Gloria (Agamben) 20–1
Illuminations (Benjamin) 80
Images of Gramsci (Bieler and Morton eds) 185
imagination 283–7, 287, 289–90
imaginative geography 296
Imagined Communities (Anderson) 80
immanence 126–9
immanent critique 13, 78, 211
imperialism 35, 248, 295–300
Impossible Exchange (Baudrillard) 59
In Defense of Lost Causes (Žižek) 343, 353
In Other Words: essays toward a reflexive sociology (Bourdieu) 104
In Other Worlds: Essays in Cultural Politics (Spivak) 318, 328
indistinction, zones of 24–5, 26
individual, the: Freud's model 171–3; Marx on 246–50; Nancy on 255
individualism 100
Infancy and History (Agamben) 20
Infinite Thought. Truth and the Return of Philosophy (Badiou) 52
information, Virilio on 331–5
Infowar 334
injustice 67

Inoperative Community, The (Nancy) 251, 253, 254–8, 262
Insecurity of Territory, The (Virilio) 333
inspirational liberalism 279
Institut für Sozialforschung (Institute of Social Research, or IfS), Frankfurt 8–10, 187
institutions, Kristeva on 224
instrumental arguments 68–9
instrumental rationality 13
insurgency 37
internal/external distinctions 25–6
International Atomic Energy Agency 62
international justice 31
International Labor Organization 176
International Monetary Fund 62
International Political Thought of Carl Schmitt: terror, liberal war and the crisis of global order, Thei (Odysseos and Petito eds) 316
international politics, definition of 5
International Relations and the Environment: international fisheries, Heidegger, and social method (Seckinelgin) 210
international system, expansion of European 308–12
interpellation 347–8
interpretivists 91, 98–9
intimacy 221–34
Intimate Revolt (Kristeva) 223
Introducing Walter Benjamin (Caygill, Coles and Klimowski) 88
Iran 300–1
Iraq 42, 121, 146, 152, 353; First Gulf War 57–8, 60, 61, 334; invasion of, 2003 301–2
Iraq: The Borrowed Kettle (Žižek) 353
Irigaray, Luce 324
irony 285–6, 287–8
Isaac, Jeffrey C. 39
Islam and the Islamic world 299, 300–2
Israel 240–1
Italy 179

Jacoby, Russell 174
'Jacques Rancière and the Ethics of Equality' (May) 276
James, Ian 262
Jarvis, Simon 15, 17, 18
Jaspers, Karl 32, 199, 200
Jay, Martin 31
jazz 7

Jean-Luc Nancy and the Future of Philosophy (Hutchens) 262
Jennings, Michael W. 88
Jew as Pariah, The (Arendt) 34
Jewish law 27
Jewish mysticism 78, 80, 86, 87
Jewish Writings, The (Arendt) 33, 34
Johnson, Barbara 139-40
Joll, James 109
Jonas, Hans 200
Jones, Steve 185
Joseph, Jonathan 98
judgemental rationality 93
Julia Kristeva (Lechte and Margaroni) 234
Jünger, Ernst 306
just enemy, the 311-2
justice 144-8, 240, 281-2
justification 36

Kafka, Franz 21
Kalyvas, Andreas 26
Kant (Scruton) 220
Kant, Critique and Politics (Hutchings) 220
Kant, Immanuel 7, 10, 12, 16, 32, 78, 130, 133, 134, 187, 191, 196, 198, 211, 217-20, 228, 278, 280, 342
Kant and Modern Political Philosophy (Flikschuh) 220
Kant and Political Philosophy: the contemporary legacy (Beiner and Booth) 220
'Kant and the Kantian Paradigm in International Relations' (Hurrell) 220
Kant and the Philosophy of History (Yovel) 220
Kant: political writings (Reiss ed) 220
Kantianism 78
Kant's Political Philosophy (Williams) 220
Kauffman, Walter 263, 265
Kaufman-Osborn, Timothy 118
Kellner, Douglas 250, 340
Kellner, Prof Leon 78
Kelsen, Hans 307
Kesting, Hanno 306
Kierkegaard, Søren 342
Kircheimer, Otto 8
Klee, Paul 82
Klossowski, Pierre 263, 265
knowledge: and enlightenment 12; Kant on 217-8; and power 163; Rorty on 278, 281-2; scientific 94; virtue of (*savoir*) 46

Knowledge and Human Interests (Habermas) 187
Kojève, Alexandre 306
Koselleck, Reinhart 306
Kosovo 39, 42, 275-6
Kracauer, Siegfried 7, 77
Kristeva, Julia 40, 221-34, 324
Kruks, Sonia 76
Kuhn, Thomas 90, 91
Kuwait 61

La distance politique 44
La leçon d'Althusser (Rancière) 267
labour, division of 105, 325
Lacan, Jacques 44, 125, 149, 171, 223, 317, 341, 342, 344, 347-8, 348-9, 350, 351, 352, 353
Lacis, Asja 79
Laclau, Ernesto 248, 341, 343
Lacoue-Labarthe, Philippe 200, 251, 252-3, 262
Lang, Anthony F. Jr. 41
language: Kristeva on 221, 224-5, 228; and philosophy 20; Rorty on 284, 285; Spivak on 319; and suffering 15
Language and Death: the Place of Negativity (Agamben) 20
Language and Symbolic Power (Bourdieu) 104, 113
Late Marxism 8
law: Derrida on 144-8; fundamental laws 109; Greek 21; Habermas and 189, 191, 196; Jewish 27; Roman 21; Schmitt on 307
Law as Politics: Carl Schmitt's critique of liberalism (Dyzenhaus ed) 315
Lazarus, Sylvain 44
Le Journal politique 44
Le Roy Ladurie, Emmanuel 103
League of Nations, the 312
Lebanon 240-1
Lechte, John 234
Lectures on Kant's Political Philosophy (Arendt) 34
legal order 306-15
legitimacy 36, 102, 191, 196, 306-7
Legitimation Crisis (Habermas) 187
Leibniz, G.W. von 201
Lenin, V.I. 313-4
Les Temps Modernes 67
Leslie, Esther 88
L'Espace critique (Virilio) 332
'Letter on Humanism' (Heidegger) 200-1

Lévi Strauss, Claude 319
Levinas, Emmanuel 115, 125, 200, 235–
  45, 236, 341, 351, 352
Levinas Between Ethics and Politics
  (Bergo) 245
Levinas Reader, The (Hand ed) 245
liberalism 39, 48–9, 50–1, 154, 285–6
liberty 194
life, biopolitical element 21–3, 28
Life of the Mind (Arendt) 34
Limited Inc (Derrida) 148
lines of flight 135–6
Linguistic Turn, The (Rorty) 279
linguistics 224–5
Linklater, Andrew 15, 17, 197
Location of Culture, The (Bhabha) 159
Locke, John 280
Logic and Existence (Deleuze) 125
Logic of Practice (Bourdieu) 113
Logic of Sense (Deleuze) 125
Logiques des mondes [The Logic of
  Worlds] (Badiou) 42, 44
logocentrism 140
*Looking Awry: An Introduction to
  Jacques Looking Awry: An
  Introduction to Jacques through
  Popular Culture* (Žižek) 353
Los Angeles Times, astrology column 14
Lotringer, Sylvere 339
low politics 176
Lowenthal, Leo 8
Löwith, Karl 200
Lukács, Georg 7, 8, 9, 77
Luke, Timothy 60–2, 339
Lyotard, Jean-François 21, 125, 251,
  330

McCarthy, Thomas 198
Macey, David 159
Machiavelli, N. 165
McLee, Scott 342
Madness and Civilization (Foucault)
  162, 167
man, as subject, Heidegger on 202–3,
  208
Man Without Content, The (Agamben)
  20
*Manifesto for Philosophy, Saint Paul,
  Ethics* (Badiou) 44
Mao Tse-Tung 313
Maoism 43–4, 45, 221
Marcuse, Herbert 8, 171, 174, 200
Margaroni, Maria 234
Margins of Philosophy (Derrida) 148

market, the, equality of 50–1
Marx, Karl 7, 10, 37, 104, 181, 187,
  218, 246–50, 278, 303–4, 317, 326–7
Marxism 8, 43, 44, 55, 83, 103, 104,
  106, 162, 164, 180, 267, 271, 282,
  317, 318, 324–8, 344
masculinity 118, 141
master/slave dialectic 215
materialist dialectics 44–5
maternal thinking 74
mathematics 45, 46
Matsuda, Mari 121
Mauss, Marcel 56
May 1968, riots 42, 43
May, Todd 262, 276
Mead, G.H. 191
Means Without End (Agamben) 28, 29
media simulation 57–8, 60
Méditations Pascaliennes (Bourdieu)
  113
memory 134
Men in Dark Times (Arendt) 34
Merleau-Ponty, Maurice 66, 161
metaphysics 44, 202–3, 264–5, 336
Metapolitics (Badiou) 44
meta-reality 97
methodological pluralism 98, 98–9
Miami Theory Collective 262
Michel, Natasha 44
migrants 226–30, 243, 318
military intervention 62
*Millennium: Journal of International
  Studies* 101, 304
Miller, Jacques-Alain 266, 343
Miller, Peter 170
*Minima Moralia: Reflections on a
  Damaged Life* (Adorno) 18
misrecognition 111
modernity 12, 87, 202, 207–9, 221, 306
Mohanty, Chandra Talpade 321
Molloy, Patricia 244
monad 81
mondialisation 259–60
monotheism 259–60
Monroe doctrine 313
*Moral Spaces: Rethinking Ethics and
  World Politics* (Campbell and
  Shapiro eds) 245
morality 17, 190–3, 218–9, 219, 264–5
Morgan, Jamie 98
Morgenthau, Hans J. 32, 74, 306
Morley, David 185
Morton, Adam 185
Mouffe, Chantal 248, 279, 291, 343

mourning, politics of 115, 120–4
Mulhall, Stephen 210
multiplicities 45–6, 128, 132–3, 134,
   135–6, 256–7, 258, 260–1
Murphy, Craig 178
Muselmänner 20
'Must we read Simone de Beauvoir'
   (Bauer) 76
mythology 12

Nabakov, Vladimir 278, 285
Nancy, Jean-Luc 21, 22, 200, 251–62
'Nancy's Hegel, the State, and US'
   (Smith) 262
National Deconstruction (Campbell) 149
nationalism 33, 222, 225–6, 255, 261,
   349–50
Nations Without Nationalism (Kristeva)
   222, 234
Natorp, Paul 199
nature, and enlightenment 12
Nazism 12, 49, 77, 187, 305
Neal, Andrew 169–70
negative dialectics 16
Negative Dialectics (Adorno) 14, 16, 18
Negative Horizon (Virilio) 333, 339
negativity 211, 228, 230
Negotiations (Derrida) 148
Negri, Antonio 21, 340
neo-colonialism 318
neo-liberalism 50, 178
networks 108
Neumann, Franz 8
new, the 43
New Age religiosity 97
New International Economic Order
   (NIEO) 178
New Left, the 87
*New Nietzsche: Contemporary Styles of
Interpretation* (Allison ed) 265
newness 86–7
Nietzsche (Heidegger) 210
Nietzsche, Friedrich 9, 21, 32, 40, 134,
   166, 263–5, 278, 283, 285, 336
'Nietzsche, Genealogy, History'
   (Foucault) 166, 169, 265
Nietzsche and Philosophy (Deleuze) 265
Nietzsche and the Vicious Circle
   (Klossowski) 265
*Nietzsche: Philosopher, Psychologist,
Anti-Christ* (Kauffman) 265
nihilism 264
nomadism 333, 335
nomads 135

nomos 308–12
Nomos of the Earth, The (Schmitt) 306,
   308
normative rightness 189
normative theory 31
Norris, Andrew 30
'Notes to *The Concept of the Political*'
   (Strauss) 316
nuclear weapons 14, 60–1, 158
Nyers, Peter 275

O' Connor, Brian 18
objectivism 102
obligations 17
occupation, resisters to 37
Odysseos, Louiza 210, 316
Oedipus complex 172, 227–8
Of Grammatology (Spivak) 328
Of Grammotology (Derrida) 138, 143,
   148, 317, 319
Of Hospitality (Derrida) 148
Oliver, Kelly 234
On Cosmopolitanism and Forgiveness
   (Derrida) 148
On Deconstruction (Caputo) 148
On Deconstruction (Culler) 148
*On Jean-Luc Nancy: The Sense of
Philosophy* (Sheppard, Sparks and
Thomas eds) 262
*On Perpetual Peace: a philosophical
sketch* (Kant) 217, 219
On Revolution (Arendt) 34
On the Genealogy of Morality
   (Nietzsche) 264, 265
'On the Jewish Question' (Marx) 250
*On the Manifold Meaning of Being
According to Aristotle* (Brentano) 199
On the Pragmatics of Communication
   (Habermas) 198
On Touching – Jean-Luc Nancy
   (Derrida) 251
'On Violence' (Arendt) 36–7
One-Way Street (Benjamin) 79
ontological realism 93
ontology 45, 46, 94, 95, 201, 204–5, 256
ontotheology 259–60
Open: Man and Animal, The
   (Agamben) 20
opinion 109
oppression 68, 96
order of things, The (Foucault) 162
Organisation politique 42, 44, 51
Orientalism 295–300, 302, 322
Orientalism (Said) 295–300, 302, 304

'The Origin of the Work of Art'
(Heidegger) 200
Original Accident, The (Virilio) 339
Origins of Totalitarianism, The (Arendt)
31, 34, 39, 40
Orwell, George 278, 285
Osama bin Laden 120
Other, the 206, 244–5, 352; Levinas on
236–41, 242; women as 70–5; Žižek
on 345, 346
Other Asias (Spivak) 318, 329
*Otherwise Than Being Or Beyond
Essence* (Levinas) 235
Outline of a Theory of Practice
(Bourdieu) 104, 113
Outside in the Teaching Machine
(Spivak) 318, 329
Overpowering Conformism (Leslie) 88
Owens, Patricia 39, 41

pacifism 36
Palestine 292, 292–4, 294, 300, 303
Panagia, Davide 276
Panama 62
Parallax View, The (Žižek) 353
parapolitics 271
Parent, Claude 330
Paris 84–6
participation, Habermas and 194
partisan warfare 313–4
Pascal, Blaise 104, 342
Patomäki, Heikki 98, 101
patriarchal authority 326
Patton, Paul 136
Paul, St 27, 342
peace 219
perception, sense of 83–4, 105
Perfect Crime, The (Baudrillard) 63
performativity 118–20
Petito, Fabio 316
phantasy 343–8, 350, 352
'Phenomenological Interpretations
with Respect to Aristotle: Indication
of the Hermeneutical Situation'
(Heidegger) 199
phenomenology 126–36, 200, 204–5
*Phenomenology of Internal Time-
consciousness, The* (Husserl) 199
Phenomenology of Spirit, The (Hegel)
71–2, 211, 212, 215
philosophy: and poetry 20; Rorty's
attack on 280–3
Philosophy and Literature (journal) 114
Philosophy and Social Hope (Rorty) 279

Philosophy and the Mirror of Nature
(Rorty) 279, 280–1
Philosophy of History, The (Hegel) 212,
215
Philosophy of Right, The (Hegel) 211,
212, 213–4, 215
Piiparinen, Touko 98
Pilardi, Jo-Ann 76
Pin-Fat, Véronique 30
Plato 34, 127, 134
Platonism 78
Ploughshares Women 273
plurality 37–8
poetic appropriation 267–8
poetry 15, 20
Pogge, Thomas 282
Polar Inertia (Virilio) 335, 339
Polemics (Badiou) 52
police 269
political, the re-treatment of the 252–3
political, the, Schmitt on 307–8, 314,
315
political action: contingency of 38–9;
Organisation politique and 44
Political Physics (Protevi) 136
political realism 74
political rights 39–40
Political Romanticism (Schmitt) 316
Political Theology (Schmitt) 305, 307,
316
political-educational process 183–5
politics: Arendt on 37–40; biopolitical
element 21–3, 28; Kant on 219;
Rancière and 268–73, 274; Schmitt
on 306–7; state-centric 176–7
*Politics, Metaphysics, and Death:
Essays on Giorgio Agamben's Homo
Sacer* (Norris) 30
Politics of Aesthetics, The (Rancièr) 276
Politics of Friendship (Derrida) 148
Pollock, Freidrich 8
Popper, Karl 90, 91
popular common sense 183
*Popular Defense and Ecological
Struggles* (Virilio) 333
Positions (Derrida) 148
positivism 11, 90–1, 93, 95–6, 98–9
Possibility of Naturalism (Bhaskar) 92,
94, 95, 101
post Fordism 325
*Post-Colonial Critic: Interviews,
Strategies, Dialogues, The* (Spivak)
318, 329
postcolonial difference 156–7

postcolonialism 31, 154–5, 155–6, 156–7, 292–304, 317, 318, 320, 321–8
Postcolonialism: An Historical Introduction (Young) 159
Poster, Mark 340
post-Marxists 248
postmodernism 74
postpositivism 96, 100–1
poststructuralism 31, 70, 74, 84, 116, 187, 200, 222, 317
Poststructuralism and International Relations (Edkins) 148–9
Potentialities: Collected Essays in Philosophy 30
potentiality 133–4
power: Arendt on 35–7; biopower 164; Bourdieu on 108; Butler on 115, 118; Derrida on 144–8; disciplinary 163; ethico-political 165; Foucault on 162–5, 167–8; hegemonic 177–8; and knowledge 163; legitimacy 36; productive 163; Said on 302–4
Power Inferno (Baudrillard) 65
Powers of Horror: An Essay on Abjection (Kristeva) 233
practice, science of 104
practice, theory of 111
praxis 183
Precarious Life: The Powers of Mourning and Violence (Butler) 115, 124
pre-constructions 104
pre-notions 105
presence 140–2, 201–2
prestige 105
Prison Notebooks (Gramsci) 179, 181–5
private sphere, the 194, 196
privilege, unlearning 319–21
Prix Européen de L'Essai Charles Veillon 20
problematization 167, 168
problems: Deleuze on 131, 132–3; solving 191
Production, Power, and World Order (Cox) 185
production, relations of 104, 247–9
profanation 27–8
Profanations (Agamben) 21, 29
progress, Benjamin's critique of 79–88
Promise of Politics, The (Arendt) 34
Protevi, John 136
Provincializing Europe (Chakrabarty) 155
proximity 240

psychoanalysis 7, 43, 171–5, 224–5, 227, 233, 317, 343–8, 350–2
public service 111
public sphere, the 38, 194–5, 196, 197–8
public/private distinction, Rorty's 286–7
pure transcendence 69–70
Pure War (Virilio) 333, 339

Question of Palestine, The (Said) 299–300, 304

racism 226, 229, 350
radical innovation 42–3
Rancière, Jacques 43, 266–77, 342
'Rancière and the Practice of Equality' (Ross) 276
rational argumentation: 192
rationality 189, 287; instrumental 13
Real, the 347–8, 351
realism 31, 282
Realist Theory of Science (Bhaskar) 92, 93
reality 93–4, 95, 334, 344–8
reason 13, 154, 217–9
recognition, struggle for 71–2
Reconsidering Difference: Nancy, Derrida, Levinas, and Deleuze (May) 262
Red Thread (Spivak) 318
Reflections on Meta-Reality: Transcendence Emancipation and Everyday Life (Bhaskar) 92
reflexivity 111–2
regulated improvisation 107
Rehg, William 198
Reid, Donald 276
Reiss, Hans 220
reiterative citational activity 119
relationality 254–8, 274–5
Remains: A Time That Remains: A Commentary on the Letter to the Romans, The (Agamben) 21
Remnants of Auschwitz: The Witness and the Archive (Agamben) 20, 29
Rengger, Nicholas 16, 17
representation 115, 319–21, 327
Representations of the Intellectual (Said) 304
Reproduction: in education society and culture (Bourdieu and Passeron) 103–4
republicanism 31, 38, 219
re-representation 327
researchers, Bourdieu on 111–2

resemblance 127, 129–31, 133
resistance 28, 67, 68, 231, 275, 302–4
responsibility 115, 145–8, 236–7, 238–9,
  239, 241–4, 245
Responsibility and Judgement (Arendt)
  34
*Rethinking Fanon: The Continuing
  Dialogue* (Gibson) 159
Rethinking Marxism 29
*Rethinking Trafficking in Women.
  Politics out of Security* (Aradau) 52
reticulated multiplicity 256–7, 258
Retreating the Political (Lacoue-
  Labarthe and Nancy) 262
revealing 208
'Review: Jacques Rancière's
  Contribution to the Ethics of
  Recognition' (Deranty) 276
Revolution in Poetic Language
  (Kristeva) 224–5, 233
rhizomatic reading 3
rhizome, the 3
Ricardo, David 246
Richter, Gerhard 86
Rieff, Philip 174
Riemann, Bernhard 127–8
rogue states 323
role taking 190–1, 193
Roman law 21
Rorty, Richard 278–91
Rorty And His Critics (Rorty) 291
'Rorty's Inspirational Liberalism'
  (Bernstein) 290
Rose, Jacqueline 345, 350
Ross, Kristin 276
Royal, Ségolène 268
Ruddick, Sarah 74
Russell, Bertrand 280
Russian Revolution 77, 180

Saddam Hussein 120
Said, Edward 40, 292–304, 321, 322
Salecl, Renata 350
Salih, Sarah 114–24
Sandford, Stella 71, 76
Sarajevo 223, 347
Sarkozy, Nikolas 42, 44, 51
Sartre, Jean-Paul 44, 66, 67, 159
Sassoon, Anne Showstack 185
Saussure, Ferdinand de 319
Schelling, Friedrich 212, 342
Schlegel, A. W. von 78
Schmitt, Carl 21, 23, 29, 37, 87, 271,
  305–16, 337

Schnur, Roman 306
Scholem, Gerhard (later Gershom) 77–
  8, 79, 87, 88
science: Bhaskar on 89–101; empiricist-
  positivist tradition 90–1; history of
  43; politics of 98, 100–1;
  transcendental realist 93–4; universal
  appropriateness 89
Science of Logic (Hegel) 212
*Scientific Realism and Human
  Emancipation* (Bhaskar) 92, 95–6
Scruton, Roger 220
Seckinelgin, Hakan 210
Second Sex, The (Beauvoir) 66, 67, 70–
  5, 76
Second World War 11, 32–3, 34, 66–7,
  79, 84–5, 151, 187, 235, 240, 305, 330
secular criticism 302–4
securitisation 274, 336
Security, Strategy and Critical Theory
  (Wyn Jones) 15
Security, Territory, Population
  (Foucault) 165, 169

'The Seeds of a Fascist International'
  (Arendt) 39
Selected Subaltern Studies (Spivak and
  Guha eds) 325
self, the: boundaries of 155; Kristeva on
  226; Levinas on 236, 237, 238–9;
  Nancy on 256; Rorty on 284, 286
'The self-assertion of the German
  university' (Heidegger) 210
self-understanding 229–30
semiotic, the 224–5, 233
Sen, Amartya 145
September 11 2001 terrorist attacks 19,
  48, 59, 64–5, 121–3, 321, 336–7
serious man, the 68, 69–70
sex and sexuality 70–5; Butler on 115–
  20; Freud on 172
Shapcott, Richard 197
Shapiro, Michael 242–3, 245, 260–1,
  274, 340
Sheppard, Darren 262
Simons, Margaret 76
Simulacra and Simulation (Baudrillard)
  56–7
simulacrum 49–50, 56–9
Simulating Sovereignty (C. Weber) 62–3
simulation 56–9, 60, 62, 62–3
singularities 28, 128, 132, 147, 258, 349
Situationism 21
situations 45–6

Sjoholm, Cecilia 223, 230, 234
Skok, Josef 343
Slavoj Žižek: Interrogating the Real (R.
  Butler and Stephens eds) 353
Slavoj Žižek: Live Theory (R. Butler)
  353
Smith, Adam 215, 246
Smith, Anne-Marie 225
Smith, Gary 88
Smith, James 262
Smith, Steve 98–9, 322
*Social amnesia: a critique of conformist
  psychology from Adler to Laing*
  (Jacoby) 174
social forces 177–8
social hierarchies 102, 106, 107
social psychology 174–5
social relations 100, 108–10
social science 91–2; Bhaskar on 94–7;
  critical 89–90, 95–7; critical
  naturalism 94–5
social structural context 99–100
Society Must Be Defended (Foucault)
  165, 167, 169
soft-power 162
sovereignty: biopolitical element 21–3,
  28–9; Butler on 115; decentralization
  of 61–2; decisionist theory of 307–8;
  Foucault on 164–5; and identity 20–
  1; production of bare life 24–5;
  Schmitt on 23, 307–8; and simulation
  62–3; Spivak on 319–20
*Sovereignty and Life: Essays on Giorgio
  Agamben* (Calarco and DeCaroli) 30
space 127–9; Arendt on 38; colonial
  155; politics of 25–6; public 194–5;
  smooth and striated 135
Spanish Civil War 11
Spanish Civil War (1808–13) 313
Sparks, Simon 262
speaking subject, the 227, 230
'Speaking the Language of Exile:
  Dissidence in International Studies'
  (Ashley and Walker) 165
Spectres of Marx (Derrida) 148
speech, Derrida on 140, 141
Speech and Phenomena (Derrida) 138
speed, Virilio's concept of 331–2, 333–4
Speed and Politics (Virilio) 333, 339
Spivak, Gayatri Chakravorty 40, 251,
  317–29
Stalinism 8, 67
*Stanzas: Word and Phantasm in
  Western Culture* (Agamben) 20

state, the 21; Arendt on 39; Badiou on
  46–7; and disasters 337; and gender
  119; Hegel on 213–4; Levinas on 236,
  240–1, 245; Schmitt on 308; Spivak
  on 319–20
*State Nobility: elite schools in the field
  of power, The* (Bourdieu) 104
state of exception 23, 26
State of Exception (Agamben) 20, 29
state of nature 38–9
state/society complexes 176–8
status 105, 108
Stephens, Scott 352, 353
stranger, the 226–30
Strangers to Ourselves (Kristeva) 233
strategic action 188, 189
strategic essentialism 325–6
Strauss, Leo 306, 316
Strong, Tracy B. 307
*Structural Transformation of the Public
  Sphere, The* (Habermas) 187
structuralism 43, 126, 126–7;
  constructivist 105–13
*Stuart Hall: Critical Dialogues in
  Cultural Studies* (Morley and Chen
  eds) 185
subaltern studies 325–8
*Subject of Coexistence: otherness in
  international relations, The*
  (Odysseos) 210
subjectification 27
subjectivation 269–70, 273
subjective freedom 44
subjectivitism 102
subjectivity 44, 106–7, 207, 221, 222–6,
  231
Subjects of Desire (Butler) 116
Sublime Object of Ideology, The (Žižek)
  341, 343, 343–4, 353
suffering 15, 16, 172–3, 237, 289
*Suffering Witness: The Quandary of
  Responsibility After the Irreparable*
  (Hatley) 245
suicidal state 333, 335
suicide bombers 231, 323–4
supplement, the 143–4
Sylvester, Christine 116
symbolic capital 110, 111, 113
Symbolic Exchange and Death
  (Baudrillard) 56
symbolic power 102, 105, 113
symbolic violence 102, 105, 110–1, 113
symbolism 56, 102, 113, 224–5, 345
sympathetic reformism 278

sympathy 287, 288–9
System of Objects, The (Baudrillard)
  55, 65
'Taking Exception to Decision: Walter
  Benjamin and Carl Schmitt' (S.
  Weber) 88
Taminioux, Jacques 204–5
*Tarrying with the Negative: Kant,
  Hegel and the Critique of Ideology*
  (Žižek) 353
Taubes, Jacob 306
Taylor, Astra 343, 353
technology, Heidegger on 207–9
'Ten Theses on Politics' (Rancière) 276
terror, and totalitarianism 35
terrorism and terrorists 19, 48, 59, 64–5,
  120–4, 289, 321, 323–4, 336–7
texts, Derrida on 143
Thacker, Eugene 340
Thatcher. Margaret 345
'The Ends of Man' (Derrida) 252
Theory of Communicative Action, The
  (Habermas) 187
Theory of International Politics (Waltz)
  257
Theory of the Partisan (Schmitt) 306,
  313–4
'Theses on the Philosophy of History'
  (Benjamin) 80, 81–2
Third, the 239–40
Third Reich 77, 335
Third Way, the 271
Thomas, Caroline 323
Thomas, Colin 262
thought: Deleuze on 129–31; Heidegger
  on 209; and political action 34–5;
  representational 209; responsibility to
  think 145–6
thought-images 86
Thus Spoke Zarathustra (Nietzsche)
  263–4, 265
*Ticklish Subject: The Absent Centre of
  Political Ontologies, The* (Žižek) 353
Tickner, J. Ann 74
Tiedemann, Rolf 18, 88
time, as progress 79–88
Time That Remains, The (Agamben) 27
torture 118
totalitarianism 11–4, 34–5, 253
Totality and Infinity (Levinas) 235
trade unions 180
Traditional Theory 9
training 106
transcendence 127, 133, 134

Transformational Model of Social
  Reality 95
transnational democracy 198
transnational flows, acceleration of 61
Transparency of Evil, The (Baudrillard)
  63
transpolitical simulacrum 58–9
*Triumph of the Therapeutic: Uses of
  Faith after Freud* (Rieff) 174
'Trotsky and the Wild Orchids' (Rorty)
  290
truth 44–5, 47–8
Truth 280, 283
'Truth and Power' (Foucault) 168–9
*Truth and Progress: Philosophical
  Papers* (Rorty) 279
truth content 78
Turn, the 200
*Two Revolutions: Gramsci and the
  Dilemmas of Western Marxism, The*
  (Boggs) 185
tyrants 68, 69–70

ultra-catastrophes 337
Unavowable Community, The (Nancy)
  251
uncertainty 70
Undoing Gender (Butler) 114, 124
*Union des communists de France
  marxistesleninistes* (UCFML) 43
United nations 61–2
United States of America: death
  penalty 244; Declaration of
  Independence 144; Fanon on 156;
  hegemony 178; invasion of Iraq 301;
  military interventions 62; Monroe
  doctrine 313; representations of the
  Arab 299; Schmitt on 308, 312, 312–3
universalism 322
urgency 146
utopian negativity 17
utopianism 16, 17

value, Baudrillard's critique of 56
values 95–6
Van Den Abbeele, George 254
van Munster, Rens 275–5
Vaughan-Williams, Nick 149, 261
Vietnam War 35, 123
violence: Arendt on 36–7; Beauvoir on
  69; Butler on 115, 120–4; colonial
  151–2, 152–3, 154, 156–7, 158–9;
  ethical 122–3; Freud on 173–4;
  Kristeva on 231–2; Levinas on 236–7,

240–1, 241–4; and the politics of
mourning 115, 120–4; state 240–1,
241–4; symbolic 102, 105, 110–1, 113
Virilio, Paul 330–40
Virilio Live (Sage) 339
Virilio Reader (Derian) 339
Virno, Paolo 21
virtual, the 133–4
virtuality 334
Vision Machine, The (Virilio) 334, 339

Wacquant, Loïc 112
Wag the Dog (film) 58
Waldheim, Kurt 345
Walker, R.B.J. 123, 165, 339
Walter Benjamin, Critical Constellation
(Gilloch) 88
'Walter Benjamin, or Nostalgia'
(Jameson) 88
Walter Benjamin: Selected Writings
(Eiland and Jennings eds) 88
*Walter Benjamin The Colour of
Experience* (Caygill) 88
*Walter Benjamin's other history: of
stones, animals, human beings, and
angels* (Hanssen) 88
Waltz, Kenneth 257
war: of annihilation 314, 315;
cybernetic 334; Deleuze and Guattari
on 135; Derrida on 147; Foucault on
166–7; Freud on 173–4; Kristeva on
231–2; partisan 313–4; Schmitt on
307–8, 310–2, 312–5; Spivak on 323;
universal 314; Virilio on 333, 334
War and Cinema (Virilio) 333, 339
war crimes 33–4
war machines 135
War on Terror 19, 28, 29, 46, 64, 120–4,
260, 289, 323–4
Wark, Mackenzie 340
Watson, Adam 309
WebDeleuze 126, 136
Weber, Cynthia 62–3, 119, 339
Weber, Max 7, 9, 12, 104, 104–5, 187
Weber, Samuel 88
Weimar Republic, the 23, 305, 306
Welcome to the Desert of the Real
(Žižek) 353
Wendt, Alexander 98
Western Marxism 8

Westphalia, Schmitt's historicising of
308–12
What is Philosophy (Deleuze and
Guattari) 125, 136
White, Hayden 276
Whose Hunger (Edkin) 149
Why War (Freud) 173–4, 175
Wiggershaus, Rolf 14
Wight, Colin 98, 101
Will to Power, The (Nietzsche) 263
Williams, Howard 220
Williams, John 41
Wittgenstein, Ludwig 104, 278, 280–1
Wolin, Richard 88, 210
women: Afghan 121; Badiou on 51;
Beauvoir on 70–5; and identity
115–20; as the Other 70–5; and the
politics of mourning 120–4; subaltern
studies 325–8
'Women's Time' (Kristeva) 233
'The Work of Art in the Age of
Mechanical Reproduction'
(Benjamin) 80, 82–4
World, the Text and the Critic, The
(Said) 304
World Health Organisation 62
World Trade Organization 61–2
worldliness 292
Wounds of Memory (Zehfuss) 147,
149
Wretched of the Earth, The (Fanon) 151
writing, Derrida on 141
Writing and Difference (Derrida) 138,
148
Writing Security (Campbell) 149
Wyn Jones, Richard 15

Young, Robert J. C. 159
Young Hegelians 246
Young-Bruehl, Elisabeth 41
Yovel, Yirmiyahu 220
Yugoslavia 51, 149, 346

Zionism 33, 77–8, 299–300
Žižek! (Taylor) 353
Žižek, Slavoj 149, 171, 341–52
Žižek's Politics (Dean) 353
zoē 22, 23, 24–5
zones of regularity 128–9
Zurbrugg, Nicholas 338

Lightning Source UK Ltd.
Milton Keynes UK
UKOW06f1111200915
258923UK00005B/123/P